Communication Yearbook 30

CHRISTINA S. BECK
EDITOR

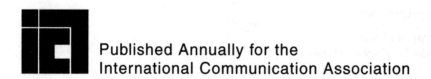

Published Annually for the
International Communication Association

LEA LAWRENCE ERLBAUM ASSOCIATES, PUBLISHERS
2006 Mahwah, New Jersey   London

Senior Acquisitions Editor: Linda Bathgate
Editorial Assistant: Karin Wittig-Bates
Cover Design: Kathryn Houghtaling-Lacey
Cover logo design: Sam Luna
Full-Service Compositor: MidAtlantic Books and Journals, Inc.

This book was typeset in 10/12 pt. Times Roman, Italic, Bold, and Bold Italic.

Lawrence Erlbaum Associates, Inc., Publishers
10 Industrial Avenue
Mahwah, New Jersey 07430
www.erlbaum.com

Library of Congress :

ISSN: 0147-4642
ISBN: 0-8058-6015-0 (case)

Books published by Lawrence Erlbaum Associates are printed on
acid-free paper, and their bindings are chosen for strength and durability.

Printed in the United States of America
10 9 8 7 6 5 4 3 2 1

Editorial Assistant: Jennifer Scott

CONTENTS

THE INTERNATIONAL COMMUNICATION ASSOCIATION

The International Communication Association (ICA) was formed in 1950, bringing together academics and other professionals whose interests focus on human communication. The Association maintains an active membership of more than 4,000 individuals, of whom some two-thirds are teaching and conducting research in colleges, universities, and schools around the world. Other members are in government, law, medicine, and other professions. The wide professional and geographic distribution of the membership provides the basic strength of ICA. The Association is a meeting ground for sharing research and useful dialogue about communication interests.

Through its divisions and interest groups, publications, annual conferences, and relations with other associations around the world, ICA promotes the systemic study of communication theories, processes, and skills. In addition to *Communication Yearbook*, the Association publishes the *Journal of Communication, Human Communication Research, Communication Theory, Journal of Computer-Mediated Communication, A Guide to Publishing in Scholarly Communication Journals*, and the *ICA Newsletter*.

For additional information about ICA and its activities, visit online at www.icahdq.org or contact Michael L. Haley, Executive Director, International Communication Association, 1730 Rhode Island Ave. NW, Suite 300, Washington, DC 20036 USA; phone (202) 530-9855; fax (202) 530-9851; email ica@icahdq.org.

Editors of the *Communication Yearbook* series:

Volumes 1 and 2, Brent D. Ruben
Volumes 3 and 4, Dan Nimmo
Volumes 5 and 6, Michael Burgoon
Volumes 7 and 8, Robert N. Bostrom
Volumes 9 and 10, Margaret L. McLaughlin
Volumes 11, 12, 13, and 14, James A. Anderson
Volumes 15, 16, and 17, Stanley A. Deetz
Volumes 18, 19, and 20, Brant R. Burleson
Volumes 21, 22, and 23, Michael E. Roloff
Volumes 24, 25, and 26, William B. Gudykunst
Volumes 27, 28, and 29, Pamela J. Kalbfleisch
Volume 30, Christina S. Beck

Mass Communication
Holli A. Semetko, *Emory University*

Organizational Communication
Steven R. Corman, *Arizona State University*

Intercultural/Development Communication
Min-Sun Kim, *University of Hawai'i at Mānoa*

Political Communication
Gianpietro Mazzoleni, *University of Milan*

Instructional/Developmental Communication
Lynda Lee McCroskey, *California State University–Long Beach*

Health Communication
John C. Lammers, *University of Illinois at Urbana-Champaign*

Philosophy of Communication
Christina Slade, *Macquarie University*

Communication and Technology
Joseph B. Walther, *Cornell University*

Popular Communication
Debra L. Merskin, *University of Oregon*

Public Relations
Hochang Shin, *Sogang University*

Feminist Scholarship
Marian J. Meyers, *Georgia State University*

Communication Law & Policy
Matt Jackson, *Pennsylvania State University*

Language and Social Interaction
François Cooren, *University of Montreal*

Visual Studies
Michael Griffin, *Macalester College*

Special Interest Group Chairs

Gay, Lesbian, Bisexual, and Transgender Studies
David J. Phillips, *University of Texas at Austin*
Katherine Sender, *University of Pennsylvania*

Intergroup Communication
Hiroshi Ota, *Aichi Shukotoku University*
Bernadette Maria Watson, *University of Queensland*

Journalism Studies
Thomas Hanitzsch, *Technical University of Ilmenau*

Ethnicity and Race in Communication
Isabel Molina, *University of Illinois at Urbana-Champaign*

Game Studies
James H. Watt, *Rensselaer Polytechnic Institute*

Guest Reviewer List

Kathy Adams	California State University at Fresno
Ty Adams	University of Louisiana, Lafayette
Roger Aden	Ohio University
Scott Althaus	University of Illinois at Urbana-Champaign
Austin Babrow	Purdue University
Glenda Balas	University of New Mexico
Kevin G. Barnhurst	University of Illinois at Chicago
Linda-Renee Bloch	Bar-Ilan University
Robert Bostrom	University of Kentucky
Harry Bouwman	Delft University of Technology
Josh Boyd	Purdue University
Maria Brann	West Virginia University
Bernadette Calafell	Syracuse University
Joseph N. Cappella	University of Pennsylvania
Teodora Carabas	Towson University
Lori Charron	Concordia University
Lynn Cooper	Wheaton College
Stephanie J. Coopman	San José State University
Fernando Delgado	Minnesota State University, Mankato
James Price Dillard	Penn State University
Kathryn Dindia	University of Wisconsin–Milwaukee
Lynda Dee Dixon	Bowling Green State University
Julie Duck	University of Queensland
Athena du Pre	University of West Florida
Sandra Faulkner	Syracuse University
Jim Fetzer	University of Minnesota Duluth
Cindy Gallois	University of Queensland
Kathleen M. Galvin	Northwestern University
Robert Gobetz	University of Indianapolis
Alberto Gonzalez	Bowling Green State University
Michael Griffin	Macalester College
Barrie Gunter	University of Leicester
Claudia Hale	Ohio University
Teresa Harrison	University at Albany
Lynn Harter	Ohio University
Jake Harwood	University of Arizona
Andrea Hollingshead	University of Southern California
Jeroen Jansz	University of Amsterdam
Tricia S. Jones	Temple University
Krishna Kandath	University of New Mexico
Louis H. Kauffman	University of Illinois at Chicago
Michael Kent	Montclair State University
Joann Keyton	University of Kansas
Susan L. Kline	Ohio State University
Elly A. Konijn	Free University of Amsterdam
Marwan Kraidy	American University
Timothy Kuhn	University of Colorado

Wendy Leeds-Hurwitz	University of Wisconsin–Parkside
Dan Linz	University of California–Santa Barbara
Judith N. Martin	Arizona State University
Robert McPhee	Arizona State University
Mary Meares	Washington State University
Caryn Medved	Ohio University
Michaela D. E. Meyer	Christopher Newport University
Susan Ohmer	University of Notre Dame
Michael J. Papa	Central Michigan University
Zhongdang Pan	University of Wisconsin–Madison
Hee Sun Park	Michigan State University
Jill Purdy	University of Washington, Tacoma
Karen Riggs	Ohio University
Rajiv N. Rimal	Johns Hopkins University
Jeffrey Robinson	Rutgers University
Elesha Ruminski	College of Mount St. Joseph
Kevin O. Sauter	University of St. Thomas
David Seibold	University of California–Santa Barbara
Holger Schramm	Universitat Zurich
Timothy Sellnow	North Dakota State University
Holli A. Semetko	Emory University
Hochang Shin	Sogang University
Michelle Shumate	North Dakota State University
L. J. Shrum	University of Texas at San Antonio
Sandi Smith	Michigan State University
J. Michael Sproule	Saint Louis University
Jeffrey St. John	Ohio University
Maureen Taylor	Rutgers University
Candice Thomas-Maddox	Ohio University–Lancaster
Karen Tracy	University of Colorado
Sarah J. Tracy	Arizona State University
Lidwien van de Wijngaert	Universiteit Utrecht
Bas van den Putte	University of Amsterdam
Jan A. G. M. van Dijk	University of Twente
Gabriel Vasquez	Purdue University
Kim Walsh-Childers	University of Florida
Bernadette Watson	University of Queensland
Richard West	University of Southern Maine
Robert Westerfelhaus	College of Charleston
Ronald F. White	College of Mount St. Joseph
Richard Wiseman	California State University, Fullerton
Andrew Wood	San José State University
Terri Kelley Wray	James Madison University
Gust A. Yep	San Francisco State University

EDITOR'S INTRODUCTION

A s I prepared my application for this editorial position, I decided to review the history of *Communication Yearbook* by revisiting earlier volumes and, in particular, the introductions that were written by the 11 previous editors. Although each editor embraced a distinct vision for this publication, all produced volumes that captured critical moments in the communication discipline and encouraged our scholarly community to progress in its collective understanding of various empirical and theoretical issues.

Communication Yearbook 30 continues the tradition of publishing rich, state-of-the-discipline literature reviews, a mission of this publication since *Communication Yearbook 19*. As I crafted the call for this first volume under my editorship, I chose to "cast my net wide" by electing not to focus on a specific "theme" per se. Instead, I sought submissions that demonstrated the most potential to enhance our knowledge about a communication concept or concern as well as to expand our awareness about the possible implications of that literature for others in the discipline. I challenged authors to articulate the ways in which their respective reviews could impact (and be informed by) other areas of communication research.

I encouraged such reflections to spark conversations about the ways in which bodies of literature can complement and enrich other works in our discipline. How can a given area of research contribute to larger discussions in our discipline? How can it serve as an important piece of a broader puzzle in our society? Indeed, the myriad complexities of contemporary life (e.g., globalization, technological advances, tensions between roles and allegiances, even natural disasters) raise the stakes (and challenges) of communication for everyday interactants. Perhaps more than ever before, rigid situational definitions and personal/professional/relational identities crumble as previously distinct boundaries blur. Although individual studies provide useful perspectives on difficult relational, health, social, organizational, cultural, and political issues, space and time preclude authors from discussing all dimensions. Yet, collectively, our discipline can generate more integrative and holistic responses. To do so, however, we need to seek each other's work with an eye toward such synthesis and collaboration. Thus, as part of each chapter in this volume, I urged authors to consider intersections with and contributions to other areas of research within the broader communication discipline.

Another common (yet incidental) thread weaves through these chapters in *Communication Yearbook 30*. To some extent, each takes up the issues of legitimacy, viability, and labeling. What counts as a "persuasive message" or an "appropriate topic shift"? How can/should organizations and/or their representatives legitimately participate in public discourse? How can individuals viably accomplish the dueling (often concurrent yet competing) roles of employee and parent? Can parents be "serious" candidates for promotion amid the demands and rewards of family life? What counts as "collaboration," "bullying," or "forgiveness"? What language should a "real" Hawaiian speak? What should be treated as an "acceptable" depiction of a Latina/o? Why does an "older adult" watch television?

In many instances, our scholarly fascination with labeling, legitimacy, and viability extends to popular culture as well. As I worked on the final stages of this volume, I must confess to indulging myself with a few "guilty pleasures"— watching television shows such as *Commander in Chief*, *The West Wing*, *Desperate Housewives*, and *Boston Legal*. (Okay, all work and no play . . .). Each week, these shows wrestle with related concerns: Can a woman or Latino be taken seriously as a "legitimate" president? What counts as "viable" enactment of roles such as "house husband," "stay-at-home dad," or "first lady/gentleman/person"? How should such labels be "accurately" constructed and by which stakeholders? Can a mother be taken as a "serious" employee? How do messages or topics work to position a president, staff member, attorney, or client as "effective," "loyal," "sympathetic," or "ethical"?

As the following chapters reveal, our research cannot produce monolithic responses to such questions that fit all circumstances, cultures, and people. In light of the chaos of our current world, fragmented identities and cultures, and clashes between dominant ideologies and marginalized groups, our discipline cannot (and, indeed, should not) advance singular recommendations about what makes a message, a person, a group, an organization, or a culture "legitimate" or "viable." Simple prescriptions for successfully enacting a role or handling a situation elude us. However, our research can (and should) reveal considerations, complications, and constraints that propel us toward more robust understandings of the implications of communication for our ongoing societal struggles with legitimacy, viability, and labeling in a diverse and multidimensional world. In their respective reviews of literature, the chapters in this volume share thoughtful and critical examinations of previous investigations, and in so doing, they offer intriguing snapshots of the state of the field in those areas without undermining the complexities of communication for interactants in this era.

CHAPTER INTRODUCTIONS

The book begins with an emphasis on messages, one of the most central concerns of communication scholars. Indeed, choices about message content and structure pervade everyday talk, formal and informal presentations, mediated campaigns, and interpersonal and public persuasive efforts. In this opening chapter, Daniel J. O'Keefe and Jakob D. Jensen concentrate on two particular types of messages with a compelling meta-analysis of the relative persuasiveness of gain-framed and loss-framed messages. This chapter provides a valuable examination of data and claims regarding these types of messages, and scholars in the areas of persuasion, health communication, and political communication should be especially interested in its conclusions.

In chapter 2, the volume moves to a discussion of conversational topic. As Nicholas A. Palomares, James J. Bradac, and Kathy Kellermann observe, the issue of topic reaches across traditional "divisions" in our discipline, molding the tenor and content of interpersonal conversations, health care interviews, political debates, talk shows, etc. The authors explore four central perspectives of conversational topic, and they conclude by detailing the implications of this body of research for scholars with interests in various contexts of social interaction and public and mediated discourse.

Chapter 3 shifts our attention to the organizational context. Rebecca J. Meisenbach and Jill J. McMillan trace the historical development of organizational rhetoric research. As they highlight in this chapter, issues in contemporary organizational rhetoric encompass crisis communication, maintenance communication, power and voice, and corporate social responsibility. Especially in light of public and private responses to recent natural disasters and corporate scandals, this chapter features rich, timely insights for scholars in the areas of organizational communication, rhetoric, health communication, political communication, crisis communication, and international communication.

In chapter 4, Annis G. Golden, Erika L. Kirby, and Jane Jorgenson explore ever-blurring boundaries between work and family. They identify theoretical, empirical, and practical intersections between research on work (primarily by organizational communication scholars) and family (primarily by family communication scholars), urging conversations between these two sub-areas in the communication discipline. In fact, near the end of their chapter, the authors express their respective personal struggles with perceived disciplinary boundaries and professional identities. Given this volume's emphasis on dialogue across our discipline, I believe that the authors' candid commentaries hold immense value, particularly for discourse on professional positioning and programs of research.

The call by Golden, Kirby, and Jorgenson for collaboration leads nicely into Laurie Lewis's chapter on this important topic. As Lewis details in her chapter, collaboration constitutes a popular construct, yet it remains elusive in terms of operationalization. In this review, Lewis notes definitional and methodological themes in prior investigations, and she builds on earlier work by advancing a model of collaboration. She closes by illuminating the potential value of collaboration research for communication scholars in interpersonal, organizational, health, political, intercultural, and international contexts.

However, as Maili Pörhölä, Sanna Karhunen, and Sini Rainivaara elaborate in their chapter on bullying, interactants can (and sometimes do) employ communication to ostracize and hurt others rather than to connect with them. Drawing from research across the globe, these authors describe the pervasive problem of bullying in school and work environments. Pörhölä et al. convincingly situate bullying as a communication concern, detailing types of bullying as well as typical responses. Moreover, they specify communication theories from varied research traditions that could prove useful for scholars and practitioners as work continues on resolving this difficult social and interactional problem.

From the rather dark discussion of bullying, we turn to the more positive communicative accomplishment of forgiveness. Douglas Kelley and Vincent Waldron review interdisciplinary approaches to defining and examining forgiveness. However, as in the chapter by Pörhölä et al., Kelley and Waldron persuasively argue for a communication orientation to the study of forgiveness. As abundant conflicts plague relationships between countries, communities, coworkers, family members, friends, etc., the enactment of forgiveness offers ripe opportunities for investigations by communication scholars.

In our increasingly global society, one such clash involves the threat that dominant groups raise in terms of linguistic and cultural viability and legitimacy. Grounding their analysis theoretically in the ethnolinguistic vitality framework, Mikaela L. Marlow and Howard Giles explain the difficulties that indigenous groups face in preserving traditional languages, practices, and identities in light of dominant group influences. Featuring the example of Hawaiian language revitalization efforts, Marlow and Giles emphasize the need for scholars in our discipline to explore the significance of language and cultural disputes and resolutions from interpersonal, organizational, political, mediated, and cross-cultural communication perspectives.

Even in efforts to acknowledge diversity, however, stakeholders encounter challenges in classifying and characterizing individuals from nondominant groups. In his chapter, Esteban del Río artfully articulates the complexities of representation and identity for Latina/os. Referring to the "Latina/o problematic," del Río explains that a single category or representation fails to capture the rich diversity of individuals within this population of citizens. Through this study of representation and identity for Latina/os, del Río underscores critical problems with labeling individuals of a particular race, group, or culture as a singular "type."

Margot van der Goot, Johannes W. J. Beentjes, and Martine van Selm continue this conversation in their review of research on older adults and their television viewing patterns. Drawing on life-span research as a theoretical foundation, van der Goot, Beentjes, and van Selm synthesize and critique scholarly investigations into the reasons for and uses of television viewing among older adults. As our global population ages, this work fosters stronger understanding about the role of television in the lives of older adults, especially in relation to their concurrent emphasis on (and participation in) interpersonal, intergenerational, health, organizational, political, and religious communication.

SUMMARY OF PROCESS

I received 64 submissions to *Communication Yearbook 30*, and I selected 11 proposals to be developed into chapters for this volume, based on feedback from a blind, peer-review process. Unfortunately, scheduling conflicts prevented one of the authors from completing her work in time for publication, and she elected to withdraw her chapter. Each chapter in *Communication Yearbook 30* received feedback during at least two rounds of peer reviews.

This volume features work from researchers in the United States, the Netherlands, and Finland. Combined with an international pool of reviewers, *Communication Yearbook 30* benefited from a global effort of diverse scholars across a wide range of divisions in the International Communication Association.

GRATEFUL ACKNOWLEDGMENTS

As I have confessed on many occasions during the two years since my appointment, my work on *Communication Yearbook* has truly taught me just how much I don't know. Although it would be impossible to know everything about all aspects of our discipline (hence, a powerful reason for a publication such as *Communication Yearbook*), the incredible array of submissions pushed me well beyond the boundaries of my own areas of research and "expertise."

Thus, I requested and received enormous assistance from members of my editorial board as well as additional reviewers for this volume. Nearly 120 individuals provided invaluable input on submissions, and 27 individuals contributed additional comments on the selected chapters throughout the revision process. I really cannot applaud all of these participants in the process enough. I relied on reviewers as I made difficult selection decisions, and I valued their expertise and candid analyses of submissions. They supplied alternative perspectives, additional sources, and insightful critique and encouragement, and I know that each chapter in this volume profited greatly from their expert counsel.

Throughout this past year, I have depended on my editorial assistant, Jennifer Scott, for her efficiency, wisdom, good humor, tact, discretion, and addiction to e-mail. Now nicknamed "Nancy Drew" for her ability to track down potential reviewers or elusive pieces of information for authors, Jennifer became more than my right hand. I count her as an invaluable colleague in my editorial adventures. I know that I speak on behalf of many authors in this volume as I thank her for her willingness to go above and beyond the call of duty in finding sources, suggesting possible revised chapter titles, and communicating with grace and professionalism.

I also thank Michaela D. E. Meyer for helping me with background research as I began my journey with *Communication Yearbook 30* as well as

Stephanie Young for her assistance with final details on this volume. Furthermore, I appreciate the support of my colleagues in the School of Communication Studies at Ohio University and the assistance and encouragement of Karin Wittig Bates and Linda Bathgate at Lawrence Erlbaum Associates. Finally, I am forever grateful to the kind and generous expression of confidence from the Publications Committee of the International Communication Association. I truly cherish this editorial opportunity, and I thank them for granting me the chance to do this work.

On a quick personal note, I cannot close without affectionately acknowledging the sacrifices and support of my husband, Roger C. Aden, and our children, Brittany Nicole, Chelsea Meagan, and Emmy Grace. I appreciate their respective patience and indulgence as I blurred my own professional and personal boundaries on occasion by cluttering the dinner table and living room with stacks of *CY* files. I thank them for inspiring me to embrace all of the diverse roles that I play at home, in our community, and at work and, as such, to celebrate the complexities and joy of juggling identities and commitments. I dedicate this volume to each of them.

Dr. Christina S. Beck
Editor

Communication
Yearbook
30

CHAPTER CONTENTS

1 The Advantages of Compliance or the Disadvantages of Noncompliance? A Meta-Analytic Review of the Relative Persuasive Effectiveness of Gain-Framed and Loss-Framed Messages

DANIEL J. O'KEEFE
Northwestern University

JAKOB D. JENSEN
University of Illinois at Urbana-Champaign

A meta-analytic review of the relative persuasiveness of gain- and loss-framed messages (based on 165 effect sizes, N = 50,780) finds that loss-framed appeals are not generally more persuasive than gain-framed appeals. For encouraging disease prevention behaviors, gain-framed appeals are more persuasive than loss-framed appeals; for encouraging disease detection behaviors, gain- and loss-framed appeals do not differ significantly in persuasiveness. The relative persuasiveness of differently framed appeals seems little influenced by (a) whether the gain-framed appeals emphasize the attainment of desirable states or the avoidance of undesirable states or (b) whether the loss-framed appeals emphasize the attainment of undesirable states or the avoidance of desirable states.

In a great many circumstances, persuaders have a choice about how to cast their discussion of the consequences of the policy or course of action that they recommend. On the one hand, the persuader can emphasize the desirable aspects of following his or her recommended course of action—the

Correspondence: Daniel J. O'Keefe, Department of Communication Studies, Frances Searle Building, Northwestern University, 2240 N. Campus Drive, Evanston, IL 60208-3545; email: d-okeefe@northwestern.edu

Communication Yearbook 30, pp. 1–43

gains associated with compliance, the advantages of adopting the communicator's proposal, and so on. On the other hand, the persuader can underscore the undesirable aspects of not following the recommended policy—the disadvantages of failing to adopt the suggested course of action, the losses or undesirable outcomes associated with noncompliance, and so forth. That is, a message's contents can be framed in two basic ways: a positive ("gain") frame that emphasizes the advantages of compliance or a negative ("loss") frame that emphasizes the disadvantages of noncompliance.

Of course, a given message might contain both kinds of appeals. But, at least sometimes, one of these broad possibilities might enjoy some persuasive advantage over the other. This article provides a meta-analytic review of the research evidence bearing on the question of the relative persuasiveness of gain-framed and loss-framed appeals.

As a clarification: The phrase *message framing* (and affiliated terms) has been used to capture a diverse lot of message variations. Our interest concerns specifically what is commonly called "gain-loss" persuasive message framing, the difference between appeals emphasizing the desirable consequences of compliance and appeals emphasizing the undesirable consequences of noncompliance. This contrast differs from variations in the framing of news stories (e.g., Gamson, 1992; Gamson & Modigliani, 1989; Iyengar, 1991); for instance, a story about a Ku Klux Klan rally might be framed as an issue of free speech or as a disruption of public order (Nelson, Clawson, & Oxley, 1997). Our focal contrast also differs from the contrast between outcomes phrased in terms of desirable effects and those phrased in parallel terms of undesirable effects; for example, a medical procedure can be described as having either a 90% survival rate or a 10% mortality rate (see, e.g., Levin, Schnittjer, & Thee, 1988). For some reviews of these and other kinds of "framing" research, see Druckman (2001); Elliott and Hayward (1998); Levin, Schneider, and Gaeth (1998); Mintz and Redd (2003); Moxey, O'Connell, McGettigan, and Henry (2003); and Wicks (2005).

BACKGROUND: POSITIVE-NEGATIVE ASYMMETRIES AND DECISION FRAMING

One reason for suspecting some difference in persuasiveness between gain-framed and loss-framed messages is provided by research indicating asymmetries between positive and negative information, such that negative information is more powerful than positive information. One such asymmetry is that negative information generally has a disproportionate impact on decisions compared with otherwise equivalent positive information (Rozin & Royzman, 2001). Another is that negative stimuli are preferentially detected; that is, negative stimuli are detected at lower levels of input or exposure than are positive stimuli (Dijksterhuis & Aarts, 2003). A third is that negative events evoke stronger and more rapid reactions (of various sorts) than do positive events (Taylor, 1991). Taken together, these findings indicate that negative information is more potent than positive information—which suggests that loss-framed messages might be more persuasive than gain-framed messages.

Another reason for expecting different effects from gain- and loss-framed messages comes from research findings concerning (what can be called) decision framing. In these studies, participants indicate a preference between two decision options. One of the options (the less risky one) is described as having certain outcomes; the other (more risky) option is described as having equivalent probabilistic outcomes. For instance, in Tversky and Kahneman's (1981) classic research circumstance, participants were asked to imagine that the United States is preparing for the outbreak of a disease that is expected to kill 600 people if nothing is done, with two alternative courses of action proposed. If option A (the less risky option) is chosen, 200 people will be saved; if option B (the riskier choice) is selected, there is a one-third chance that 600 will be saved and a two-thirds chance that no one will be saved.

The general research question in this area of work is what influences the choice between more risky and less risky options. One factor that has been extensively studied is the "framing" of the options, that is, whether the description of the options emphasizes the gains or the losses associated with each. In the previous paragraph, the outcomes were expressed in terms of lives saved, but equivalent outcomes could be expressed in terms of deaths: If option C is chosen, 400 people will die, and if option D is chosen, there is a one-third probability that nobody will die and a two-thirds probability that 600 people will die.

In Tversky and Kahneman's (1981) research, faced with the choice between option A and option B, participants strongly preferred the less risky option A—but given the substantively identical choice between option C and option D, participants strongly preferred the more risky option D. That is, participants were more likely to prefer a risky (vs. less risky) option when it was presented in a way that emphasized avoiding possible losses than when it was presented in a way that emphasized obtaining possible gains. An extensive body of research has sought to identify limits to this effect, factors that influence the size of the effect, and so forth (e.g., Bless, Betsch, & Franzen, 1998; Levin & Chapman, 1993; Li, 1998; for some review discussions, see Kuhberger, Schulte-Mecklenbeck, & Perner, 1999; McGettigan, Sly, O'Connell, Hill, & Henry, 1999). But for present purposes, the relevant points are that otherwise equivalent gains and losses appear to not always be psychologically equivalent and that losses appear to have some motivating power that equivalent gains do not.

For two reasons, however, decision framing research does not speak directly to the question of the effects of different ways of framing persuasive messages. One is that the format of decision framing research does not involve the presentation of any persuasive message. Participants choose between two decision alternatives; they receive no arguments or appeals supporting a particular choice, and nothing in the experimental materials advocates a particular alternative. The other reason is that the outcome variable of interest in decision framing research is characteristically not persuasion but rather the likelihood of choosing a relatively risky option. Students of persuasion will want to know how alternative appeals influence the acceptance of an advocated view or action, quite apart from the action's riskiness.

Although research on positive-negative asymmetries and decision framing does not directly address questions of persuasive message effects, these findings naturally give rise to a hypothesis concerning persuasive messages, namely, that appeals emphasizing potential losses will be more persuasive than appeals emphasizing potential gains. Given that people are more willing to take a risk to avoid (or minimize) losses than to obtain gains, and given that negative information seems more powerful than parallel positive information, one might expect that, broadly speaking, it will be more persuasive to focus on potential losses from noncompliance than on potential gains from compliance.

GAIN-LOSS MESSAGE FRAMING RESEARCH: PREVIOUS REVIEWS AND POSSIBLE MODERATORS

Previous Reviews

A great deal of research has been directed specifically at exploring the possibility that gain-framed and loss-framed messages might be differentially persuasive. The extant review discussions of this research have not been comprehensive. Wilson, Purdon, and Wallston (1988) discussed eight research reports. Kuhberger's (1998) meta-analysis examined 13 "message compliance" studies, and the outcome variable of interest was not persuasiveness, but rather inclination toward risky options. Edwards, Elwyn, Covey, Matthews, and Pill (2001) reviewed seven studies, reflecting their interest in clinical settings and consequent narrow inclusion criteria. Salovey, Schneider, and Apanovitch (2002) focused on 12 experiments associated with Salovey's research program and briefly discussed about another dozen research reports. The current review is based on 165 cases (effect sizes), which suggests that previous reviews have been remarkably selective in their coverage of the literature.

Moreover, earlier reviews have not always carefully screened the studies discussed. For example, in discussing the relative effectiveness of gain- and loss-framed messages, Salovey et al. (2002, p. 393) cited publications by Kalichman and Coley (1995); Marteau (1989); McNeil, Pauker, Sox, and Tversky (1982); Treiber (1986); and Wilson, Kaplan, and Schneiderman (1987). But none of these studies contrasted gain-framed and loss-framed persuasive messages. Kalichman and Coley compared a loss-framed message against one with unframed information; Marteau and McNeil et al. compared preferences for medical procedures expressed in terms of the probability of living or the probability of dying; Treiber compared a gain-framed appeal against a combined gain-and-loss-framed appeal; Wilson et al. presented participants with differently described decision options, not persuasive messages.

Even so, previous reviews do suggest two broad research questions meriting examination. First, is there an overall difference in persuasiveness between gain-framed and loss-framed messages? Research on decision framing and positive-negative asymmetries might lead one to anticipate that loss-framed messages will generally be more persuasive than gain-framed messages.

Second, what factors moderate the relative effectiveness of gain- and loss-framed appeals? Even if one type of framing enjoys some general persuasive advantage, it may also be the case that the size (or direction) of that difference changes, depending on other factors. A very large number of such factors have been suggested, though the available research evidence seems modest for most. For example, only limited evidence concerns such suggested moderators as mood (Keller, Lipkus, & Rimer, 2003) and ambivalence (Broemer, 2002). But two particular possible moderating factors deserve some special attention.

Possible Moderators

Disease detection vs. disease prevention behaviors. Perhaps the most well-known proposed moderating factor, at least in the realm of health behavior, is whether the advocated action is a disease detection behavior (such as a skin cancer examination) or a disease prevention behavior (such as using sunscreen). Several studies have seemed to suggest that loss-framed messages will be more persuasive than gain-framed messages for detection behaviors, whereas gain-framed messages will be more persuasive than loss-framed messages for prevention behaviors (for discussion, see Rothman & Salovey, 1997; Salovey et al., 2002).

Such differential persuasiveness of gain- and loss-framed appeals has been seen to be predicted and explained by prospect theory (Kahneman & Tversky, 1979) and specifically by the finding that "choices involving gains are often risk averse and choices involving losses are often risk taking" (Tversky & Kahneman, 1981, p. 453). That is, as indicated by the results of decision framing research, persons are more likely to undertake risky (uncertain) behaviors when potential losses are salient but prefer risk-averse choices when gains are prominent. This principle is taken to explain the differential persuasiveness of gain- and loss-framed appeals by virtue of differences in the uncertainty associated with detection and prevention behaviors. Specifically, "the perceived uncertainty or risk (e.g., of finding an abnormality) associated with detection behaviors leads us to predict that loss-framed messages should be more persuasive in promoting them. However, prevention behaviors might not be perceived as risky at all," which implies that "gain-framed messages may be more likely to facilitate performing prevention behaviors" (Salovey et al., 2002, p. 394).

Desirable or undesirable kernel states. A second possible moderator is the specific phrasing of the gain- and loss-framed appeals. As noted by various commentators (e.g., Dillard & Marshall, 2003; Rothman & Salovey, 1997; Wilson et al., 1988), gain- and loss-framed appeals can each take two forms, with the resulting four possibilities represented in a 2×2 array in which the contrasts are (a) whether the outcome described is a desirable or an undesirable one and (b) whether the outcome is described as one that is attained (acquired, achieved, made more likely) or avoided (averted, not realized, made less likely). That is, a gain-framed appeal might take the form "If you perform the advocated action, desirable outcome X will be obtained," or the form "If you perform the advocated action, undesirable outcome Y will be avoided." A loss-framed appeal might take the form "If you do not perform the advocated action, desirable outcome X will be avoided," or the form "If you do not perform the advocated action, undesirable outcome Y will be obtained."

It is not yet clear whether these variations influence the relative effectiveness of gain- and loss-framed messages. The review of Devos-Comby and Salovey (2002) suggested that "empirical work has not generally shown differences between the two ways of operationalizing loss or gain" (p. 292) but cited only two studies.

However, coding messages for this moderator encounters a potential difficulty. Although the 2×2 array described above (desirable vs. undesirable outcome, attained vs. avoided outcome) is a useful abstract representation of possible gain-loss message variations, it does not always map easily onto concrete appeals. Consider, for example, an appeal such as "If you take your hypertension medication, you will reduce the risk of heart disease." This appeal plainly focuses on the desirable consequences of compliance (i.e., is gain-framed), but it might be interpreted as suggesting either (a) compliance will produce a desirable outcome (the desirable outcome of reducing the risk of heart disease) or (b) compliance will avert—reduce the likelihood of—an undesirable outcome (the undesirable outcome of heart disease). Obviously, having some systematic way of handling such cases will be crucial to unraveling message framing variations.

Our analysis sorts out such cases by focusing on the message's explicit linguistic representation of the kernel state of the consequence under discussion. The kernel state is the basic, root state mentioned in the message's description of the consequence. For instance, in the case of "If you take your hypertension medication, you will reduce the risk of heart disease," the kernel state is "heart disease," which is plainly an undesirable state. Thus, we treat that appeal as one that emphasizes the desirable consequences of compliance by discussing an undesirable kernel state ("heart disease") that will be avoided. By comparison, "If you take your hypertension medication, you will increase your chances of having a healthy heart" is an appeal describing a desirable kernel state ("healthy heart") that will be attained by compliance. Similarly, complex appeals such as "if you don't follow this recommended diet, you'll fail to do what you can to reduce the risk of heart disease" and "if you don't follow this recommended diet, you'll fail to do what you can to have a healthy heart" can be seen to be loss-framed appeals (i.e., appeals focused on the consequences of noncompliance) with, respectively, undesirable ("heart disease") and desirable ("healthy heart") kernel states.

This approach permits examination of the possibility that any difference in the relative persuasiveness of gain- and loss-framed appeals might depend on whether the appeals refer to desirable or undesirable kernel states. In particular, any differences in persuasiveness between gain-framed and loss-framed appeals might be accentuated when the gain-framed appeal has desirable kernel states (e.g., "healthy skin"), when the loss-framed appeal has undesirable kernel states (e.g., "skin cancer"), or when both circumstances obtain; conversely, any such differences might be minimized if the gain-framed appeal has undesirable kernel states, if the loss-framed appeal has desirable kernel states, or if both conditions obtain.[1]

METHOD

Identification of Relevant Investigations

Literature search. Relevant research reports were located through personal knowledge of the literature, examination of previous reviews and textbooks, and inspection of reference lists in previously located reports. In addition, articles were identified through computerized database searches (through at least May 2005) of ABI-INFORM, CINAHL (Cumulative Index of Nursing and Allied Health Literature), Current Contents, Dissertation Abstracts, EBSCO, ERIC (Educational Resources Information Center), Linguistics and Language Behavior Abstracts, MEDLINE, PsycINFO, and PsycINFO-

Historic, with the use of various appropriate combinations of terms such as *framing, framed, frame, appeal, message, persuasion, persuasive, gain, positive, positively, benefit, loss, negative, negatively, threat,* and *valence.*

Inclusion criteria. The studies selected had to meet three criteria. First, the study had to compare gain-framed and loss-framed persuasive messages. A gain-framed message emphasizes the desirable consequences of compliance with the advocated view; a loss-framed message emphasizes the undesirable consequences of noncompliance. Excluded by this criterion were studies that compared a gain-framed appeal with a combined gain-and-loss frame (Treiber, 1986; Wilson, Wallston, & King, 1990), studies that compared one framing form with unframed information (Abood, Coster, Mullis, & Black, 2002; Kalichman & Coley, 1995), studies that confounded a gain-loss framing manipulation with other manipulations (e.g., Gonzales, Aronson, & Costanzo, 1988), and studies of decision framing, that is, studies in which participants chose between differently described alternatives without any particular alternative being advocated (e.g., Fagley & Miller, 1997; Levin & Chapman, 1993; Paese, Bieser, & Tubbs, 1993; Quattrone & Tversky, 1988; Smith & Levin, 1996; Tversky & Kahneman, 1981).

In general, this criterion was applied so as to exclude imperfect realizations of the message contrast of interest. For example, for greater comparability, we excluded studies in which something like a gain-loss framing variation was accomplished through visual materials. Isen and Noonberg (1979) and Pancer, Deforest, Rogers, and Schmirler (1979) varied charitable appeals by having accompanying pictures depict either a needy child or a child who had received assistance (see also Cunningham, Steinberg, & Grev, 1980, Experiment 2; Gore et al., 1998).[2] Similarly, we excluded manipulations that did not straightforwardly involve descriptions of the consequences of performing or not performing the recommended action. For instance, Blanton, Stuart, and VandenEijnden (2001) contrasted a "negatively framed communication that emphasized the undesirable attributes of people who made unhealthy decisions" and a "positively framed communication that emphasized the desirable attributes of people who made healthy decisions" (p. 848; similarly, see Blanton, VandenEijnden, et al., 2001; Stuart & Blanton, 2003). For examples of various other (excluded) imperfect realizations, see Cameron and Leventhal (1995); Christophersen and Gyulay (1981); Gibson (1962); Gierl, Helm, and Satzinger (2000); Hart (1972); Kirscht, Haefner, and Eveland (1975); Krishnamurthy, Carter, and Blair (2001); Lehmann (1970); Melvin (1995); Orth, Oppenheim, and Firbasova (2005); and Van Den Heuvel (1982).

Second, the advantages and disadvantages discussed in the messages—the outcomes of following or not following the communicator's views—had to be outcomes that were not under the control of the communicator. Studies of the use of promises and threats (as when a parent promises a child rewards for good behavior or threatens punishment for misbehavior) were excluded by this criterion, as were any studies in which the outcomes were under the communicator's control, regardless of whether the message variation was labeled as a difference between promises and threats (e.g., Kishor & Godfrey, 1999; Perry, Bussey, & Freiberg, 1981; Weimann, 1982).[3]

Third, appropriate quantitative data relevant to persuasive effects (e.g., attitude change, intention, or behavior) had to be available; where it was not provided in the report, we made efforts to obtain information from authors. Excluded by this criterion were studies of effects on other outcome variables, including judgments of expected persuasiveness (Montazeri & McEwen, 1997; Ohme, 2001) and perceived vulnerability (e.g., Meyer & Delhomme, 2000), and studies for which appropriate quantitative information could not be obtained (e.g., Burroughs, 1997; Devos-Comby, McCarthy, Ferris, & Salovey, 2002; Giles, 2002; Gnepa, 2001; Horgen & Brownell, 2002; Mann, Sherman, & Updegraff, 2004; Martin & Marshall, 1999; Martinez, 1999; McCroskey & Wright, 1971; Merrill, 2003; Miller et al., 1999; Rothman, Salovey, Antone, Keough, & Martin, 1993; Salmon, Loken, & Finnegan, 1985; Umphrey, 2001; Wegener, Petty, & Klein, 1994; Yalch & Dempsey, 1978).[4]

Outcome Variable and Effect Size Measure

Outcome variable. The outcome variable was persuasion, as assessed through attitude change, postcommunication agreement, behavioral intention, behavior, and the like. When multiple indices of persuasion (e.g., assessments of attitude and of intention) were available, we averaged the effects to yield a single summary. Most studies reported only immediate (short-term) effects; where both immediate and delayed effect size information was available (e.g., Jones, Sinclair, & Courneya, 2003), only immediate effects were included, to maximize comparability across studies.

Effect size measure. Every comparison between a gain-framed message and its loss-framed counterpart was summarized using r as the effect size measure. Differences indicating greater persuasion with gain-framed messages were given a positive sign.

When correlations were averaged (e.g., across several indices of persuasive effect), we computed the average with the r-to-z-to-r transformation procedure, weighted by n. Wherever possible, multiple-factor designs were analyzed by reconstitution of the analysis, such that individual-difference factors (but not, e.g., other experimental manipulations) were put back into the error term (following the suggestion of Johnson, 1989).[5]

Moderating Factors

Message topic. Cases were classified by message topic, and six broad topical categories were distinguished: disease detection behaviors (e.g., skin cancer examinations), disease prevention behaviors (e.g., minimizing sun exposure), other health-related behaviors (e.g., acquiring hearing aids), sociopolitical subjects (public policy matters such as needle exchange programs), advertising of consumer products and services (e.g., ads for life insurance or detergent), and other (i.e., otherwise unclassified, e.g., taxpayer compliance or recycling participation).[6]

Kernel state phrasing. The kernel states in each appeal were identified; as discussed above, a kernel state is the basic, root state mentioned in the message's description of the consequence under discussion. We coded each appeal as containing exclusively desirable kernel states (e.g., "healthy heart," "attractive skin"), exclusively undesirable kernel states (e.g., "heart disease," "skin cancer"), a combination of desirable and undesirable kernel states, or as indeterminate with respect to kernel-state phrasing (as when insufficient detail was available about the messages).

Unit of Analysis

The unit of analysis was the message pair, that is, the pair composed of a gain-framed message and its loss-framed counterpart. We recorded a measure of effect size for each distinguishable message pair found in the body of studies. Usually, a given message pair was used only in a single investigation, so only one effect size estimate was associated with the pair. But some message pairs were used in more than one study, with the result that several effect size estimates could be associated with that message pair. These multiple estimates were averaged to yield a single summary estimate before inclusion in the analysis. Such accumulation occurred in the following cases. Data from Broemer (2002, Study 1) and Broemer (2004, Study 1) were combined and reported as Broemer (2004) Study 1 combined; data from Experiment 1 and Experiment 2 by Keller et al. (2003) were combined and reported as Keller et al. (2003); data from Experiments 1, 4A, and 5 by A. Lee and Aaker (2004) were combined and reported as A. Lee and Aaker (2004) grape juice promotion and grape juice prevention; data from Meyerowitz and Chaiken (1987) and Lalor (1990) were combined and reported as Meyerowitz and Chaiken (1987) combined; data from Shiv (1996), Shiv, Britton, and Payne (2004), and Shiv, Edell, and Payne (1997) were combined and reported as Shiv airline on-time, airline on-time and amenities, and detergent.

Whenever a study included more than one message pair and reported data separately for each pair, each pair was treated as providing a separate effect size estimate (e.g., Knapp, 1989; van Assema, Martens, Ruiter, & Brug, 2001). Some studies included more than one message pair but did not report results in ways that permitted the computation of separate effect sizes for each pair (e.g., Bower & Taylor, 2003; Gardner & Wilhelm, 1987; Hessling, 1996; Steward, Schneider, Pizarro, & Salovey, 2003); we computed a single effect size in such cases, with the consequence that the present analysis underrepresents the amount of message-to-message effect variability in these data.

In some cases, the same primary data served as the basis for multiple reports (e.g., both a dissertation and a subsequent publication). When a given investigation was reported in more than one outlet, it was treated as a single study and analyzed accordingly. The same research was reported (in whole or in part) by Allen (1969), Dembroski (1969), Evans, Rozelle, Lasater, Dembroski, and Allen (1970), Lasater (1969), and Rozelle, Evans, Lasater, Dembroski, and Allen (1973), recorded under Evans et al. (1970); Berger and Smith (1997) and Smith and Berger (1996), recorded under the former; Berger and Smith (1998), Smith (1996), Smith and Berger (1998), and Smith and Wortzel (1997), recorded under Smith (1996); Finney (2001) and Finney and Iannotti (2002), recorded under the former; Hasseldine (1997) and Hasseldine and Hite (2003), recorded under the former; Knapp (1989) and Knapp (1991), recorded under the former; Lalor (1990) and Lalor and Hailey (1990), with, as noted above, results reported under Meyerowitz and Chaiken (1987) combined; Lawatsch (1987) and Lawatsch (1990), recorded under the former; Levin, Gaeth, Evangelista, Albaum, and Schreiber (1999) and Levin, Gaeth, Evangelista, Albaum, and Schreiber (2001), recorded under the latter; Looker (1983) and Looker and Shannon (1984), recorded under the former; Mundorf et al. (2000) and Schneider, Salovey, Pallonen, et al. (2001), recorded under the latter; Robberson (1985) and Robberson and Rogers (1988), recorded under the former; Shiv (1996) and Shiv et al. (1997), recorded under Shiv airline on time and Shiv detergent.

Meta-Analytic Procedures

The individual correlations (effect sizes) were initially transformed to Fisher's zs; the zs were analyzed with random-effects procedures (Borenstein & Rothstein, 1999; Hedges & Vevea, 1998; Shadish & Haddock, 1994), with results then transformed back to *r*. A random-effects analysis was used in preference to a fixed-effects analysis because of an interest in generalizing across messages (for some discussion, see Erez, Bloom, & Wells, 1996; Hedges & Vevea, 1998; Jackson, 1992, p. 123; National Research Council, 1992; Raudenbush, 1994; Shadish & Haddock, 1994).

RESULTS

As a preliminary observation, it should be underscored that the present review has a rather broader evidentiary base than previous reviews. For example, some studies included here apparently have never been cited in any previous review discussion of persuasive message framing effects (e.g., Looker & Shannon, 1984; Ramirez, 1977).

Overall Effects

Effect sizes were available for 165 cases, with a total of 50,780 participants.[7] Details for each included case are contained in Table 1–1. Across all 165 cases, the random-effects weighted mean correlation was .016. The limits of the 95% confidence interval for this mean were −.004 and .035, indicating no significant persuasive advantage for one framing form over the other ($p = .11$). This analysis, however, included one case with a very large sample size (Berger & Smith, 1997; $N = 18,144$); this single study contributed approximately 36% of the total *N*. A reanalysis excluding this case yielded a mean *r* of .016 ($k = 164$), which was also not significantly different from zero ($p = .13$); the 95% confidence interval limits were −.005 and .038.

Moderating Factors

Table 1–2 provides a summary of the results concerning the effects of the main moderating variables considered individually.

Disease prevention vs. disease detection. For messages advocating disease prevention behaviors, gain-framed messages enjoyed a significant persuasive advantage over loss-framed messages (mean *r* = .046). For messages advocating disease detection behaviors, gain- and loss-framed messages did not significantly differ (mean *r* = −.027).

Phrasing of kernel states in gain-framed appeals. As indicated in Table 1–2, gain- and loss-framed appeals did not dependably differ in persuasiveness

TABLE 1–1
Cases Analyzed

Study	r	N	Codings[a]
Al-Jarboa (1996)	−.078	120	5/3/3
Apanovitch, McCarthy, & Salovey (2003)	.064	425	1/3/3
Arora (1998) library	.088	141	5/3/3
Arora (1998) resort	.095	141	5/1/2
Arora (2000)	−.157	210	1/3/1
Arora & Arora (2004)	.088	267	2/2/4
Banks et al. (1995)	−.011	133	1/3/1
Benz Scott (2000) immediate	−.067	194	2/3/3
Benz Scott (2000) future	.011	193	2/3/3
Berger & Smith (1997)	.016	18,144	6/1/1
Block (1993) self-exam	−.222	57	1/2/1
Block (1993) sun exposure	.174	58	2/2/1
Block & Keller (1995) Study 1	−.077	94	3/2/1
Bono Santos & Rodriguez Torronteras (1991)	.067	86	2/1/1
Bower & Taylor (2003)	−.206	208	3/3/1
Brenes (1999)	.016	142	1/4/4
Broemer (2002) Study 2	−.079	120	2/3/3
Broemer (2002) Study 3	−.036	80	2/2/1
Broemer (2004) Study 1 combined	−.104	140	2/2/1
Broemer (2004) Study 2	.167	60	1/3/3
Broemer (2004) Study 3	.196	144	2/2/1
Brondino (1997)	.040	98	2/3/1
Brug, Ruiter, & van Assema (2003) Study 2	.039	149	2/4/4
Brug et al. (2003) Study 3	−.061	92	2/4/4
Cesario, Grant, & Higgins (2004) prevention	−.169	53	2/3/3
Cesario et al. (2004) promotion	.115	53	2/1/2
C. Chang (2002)	.168	160	5/1/2
C.-T. Chang (2003) mouth rinse	.302	51	2/4/4
C.-T. Chang (2003) disclosing gum	−.043	52	1/4/4
C.-T. Chang (2003) rinse tablets	.620	49	2/4/4
C.-T. Chang (2003) disclosing strips	.698	50	1/4/4
Chebat, Limoges, & Gelinas-Chebat (1998) ATMs	.290	56	5/4/3
Chebat et al. (1998) student loans	−.102	56	5/4/3
Cothran, Schneider, & Salovey (1998)	−.085	218	1/4/4
Cox & Cox (2001) anecdotal	−.306	55	1/3/3
Cox & Cox (2001) statistical	.046	55	1/2/1
Davis (1995)	.108	218	6/3/3
Detweiler, Bedell, Salovey, Pronin, & Rothman (1999)	.115	217	2/3/3
Dibble (1998)	.032	283	6/3/1
Evans et al. (1970)	.239	234	2/1/1

(continued)

TABLE 1–1 (*Continued*)

Study	r	N	Codings[a]
Ferguson, Bibby, Leaviss, & Weyman (2003) Study 4	.295	65	2/3/3
Ferguson et al. (2003) Study 5 noise	.009	188	2/3/3
Ferguson et al. (2003) Study 5 handling	.000	263	2/3/3
Ferguson et al. (2003) Study 6 consequences	−.161	49	2/3/3
Ferguson et al. (2003) Study 6 solutions	−.066	49	2/3/3
Finney (2001)	−.044	628	1/2/1
Fischer & Nabi (2001) sunscreen	−.191	79	2/3/1
Fischer & Nabi (2001) skin exam	.144	87	1/3/1
Ganzach & Karsahi (1995) check	−.318	117	5/3/3
Ganzach & Karsahi (1995) cash	−.161	123	5/3/3
Ganzach, Weber, & Ben-Or (1997) Study 2	−.230	144	5/3/3
Ganzach et al. (1997) Study 3	−.150	175	5/1/1
Gardner & Wilhelm (1987)	.167	203	5/4/4
Gintner, Rectanus, Achord, & Parker (1987)	.051	177	1/4/4
Grantham & Irani (2004)	.101	274	6/4/4
Greenlee (1997)	.107	134	2/3/3
Hashimoto (2002)	−.013	166	2/2/1
Hasseldine (1997) legal sanctions	.023	196	6/2/1
Hasseldine (1997) conscience	.000	201	6/3/3
Hessling (1996)	.121	273	2/2/3
Hoffner & Ye (2004)	.000	154	2/1/1
Homer & Yoon (1992)	.034	239	2/1/3
Hsiao (2002) exercise prevention	.546	49	2/3/3
Hsiao (2002) exercise detection	−.378	51	2/3/3
Hsiao (2002) testing prevention	−.300	46	1/3/3
Hsiao (2002) testing detection	.308	46	1/3/3
Jayanti (2001)	.007	69	2/4/4
Jones et al. (2003)	.048	192	2/3/3
Keller et al. (2003)	−.024	162	1/3/3
Knapp (1989) health	.046	38	2/3/1
Knapp (1989) social	−.084	40	2/1/1
Lauver & Rubin (1990)	−.060	116	1/1/2
Lawatsch (1987)	.071	72	2/1/3
A. Lee & Aaker (2004) grape juice promotion	.188	204	5/1/2
A. Lee & Aaker (2004) grape juice prevention	−.199	173	5/2/1
A. Lee & Aaker (2004) Experiment 2 promotion	.055	85	2/1/2
A. Lee & Aaker (2004) Experiment 2 prevention	−.173	78	2/3/3
A. Lee & Aaker (2004) Experiment 3 high risk	−.312	45	2/3/3
A. Lee & Aaker (2004) Experiment 3 low risk	.382	36	2/3/3
C. Lee, Brown, & Blood (2000) self-exam	−.106	137	1/1/2
C. Lee et al. (2000) sunscreen/clothing	.119	132	2/2/1

(*continued*)

TABLE 1–1 (*Continued*)

Study	r	N	Codings[a]
Lemieux, Hale, & Mongeau (1994) vivid high fear	.039	51	2/4/4
Lemieux et al. (1994) pallid high fear	.132	50	2/4/4
Lemieux et al. (1994) vivid low fear	.070	50	2/4/4
Lemieux et al. (1994) pallid low fear	.019	50	2/4/4
Lerman et al. (1992)	−.011	203	1/4/4
Levin et al. (2001)	−.127	224	2/2/1
Levin, Gaeth, Schreiber, & Lauriola (2002)	.021	102	2/2/1
Littlejohn (1997) Experiment 1	−.019	240	6/3/3
Littlejohn (1997) Experiment 2	.010	388	6/1/3
Looker (1983)	.006	227	2/1/1
Lord (1994)	−.003	120	6/3/3
Lowenherz (1991)	.006	83	2/4/4
Maheswaran & Meyers-Levy (1990)	.023	98	1/3/3
Martin & Lawson (1998)	−.049	177	6/1/1
McArdle (1972)	−.080	80	3/1/1
McCall & Ginis (2004)	.311	29	2/3/3
McCaul, Johnson, & Rothman (2002)	−.012	6,522	2/2/1
McKee et al. (2004)	.067	271	2/3/3
Meyerowitz & Chaiken (1987) combined	−.219	91	1/3/3
Meyers-Levy & Maheswaran (2004)	.270	147	2/3/3
Millar & Millar (2000)	.079	277	2/3/3
Mitchell (2001)	−.010	125	3/4/4
Myers et al. (1991)	−.035	2,201	1/4/4
Oshikawa (1965) Abel	−.117	123	5/1/3
Oshikawa (1965) Baker	.141	119	5/1/3
Pedley (1986)	−.309	20	2/3/3
Phelan (2003)	.000	60	1/4/4
Powell & Miller (1967)	−.208	126	6/1/1
Radecki (1997)	−.012	385	6/4/4
Ramirez (1977)	.030	116	2/4/4
Reese (1997)	.168	40	3/3/1
Richardson et al. (2004)	−.233	382	2/4/4
Rivers et al. (2005) detection	−.016	238	3/4/4
Rivers et al. (2005) prevention	.000	242	3/4/4
Robberson (1985) health	−.190	24	2/3/3
Robberson (1985) self-esteem	.537	24	2/1/3
Robertson & Welbourne (2000) positive scenario	−.024	80	2/4/4
Robertson & Welbourne (2000) negative scenario	.001	80	2/4/4
Rothman, Martino, Bedell, Detweiler, & Salovey (1999) Experiment 1 detection	−.349	40	1/3/3
Rothman et al. (1999) Experiment 1 prevention	.052	40	2/3/3

(*continued*)

TABLE 1–1 (Continued)

Study	r	N	Codings[a]
Rothman et al. (1999) Experiment 2 detection	−.305	60	1/2/1
Rothman et al. (1999) Experiment 2 prevention	.182	60	2/2/1
Ruiter, Kok, Verplanken, & van Eersel (2003)	−.099	110	1/4/4
Schmitt (2004)	−.055	150	1/4/4
Schneider, Salovey, Apanovitch, et al. (2001) multicultural	−.138	264	1/4/4
Schneider, Salovey, Apanovitch, et al. (2001) targeted	.047	264	1/4/4
Schneider, Salovey, Pallonen, et al. (2001)	.186	437	2/4/3
Sen, Gurhan-Canli, & Morwitz (2000)	.208	147	6/4/4
Shannon & Rowan (1987)	.031	138	2/4/4
Sheer (1995) threat-L	.093	205	2/3/2
Sheer (1995) threat-S	.178	205	2/3/2
Shiv airline on-time	.089	161	5/3/1
Shiv airline on-time and amenities	−.066	310	5/3/1
Shiv detergent	−.117	380	5/1/1
Simmering (1993) nonsocial	−.030	78	2/3/1
Simmering (1993) social	.027	77	2/1/3
Smith (1996)	.050	390	5/1/1
Smith & Petty (1996) Experiment 1 strong	−.185	32	6/4/4
Smith & Petty (1996) Experiment 1 weak	.356	28	6/4/4
Steward (2002) Study 1 education	−.083	91	4/3/3
Steward (2002) Study 1 exchange	−.163	89	4/3/3
Steward (2002) Study 2	−.064	244	4/1/3
Steward et al. (2003)	.013	853	2/3/3
Thorsteinson & Highhouse (2003) Experiment 1	.587	69	6/1/2
Thorsteinson & Highhouse (2003) Experiment 2	.453	100	6/4/4
Thorsteinson, Highhouse, & Fay (1999) Experiment 1	.025	94	6/1/2
Turner (2004)	.021	246	3/4/4
Tykocinski, Higgins, & Chaiken (1994)	.029	39	3/4/4
Umphrey (2003)	.085	128	1/3/3
van Assema et al. (2001) low-fat	.035	75	2/3/1
van Assema et al. (2001) fruit & vegetable	.068	66	2/3/1
Vasilias (1999)	−.007	270	2/3/1
Wenburg (1969)	.013	532	6/3/1
Wheatley & Oshikawa (1970)	−.022	154	5/1/3
Wilkin (2004) condom	.150	118	2/4/4
Wilkin (2004) Pap	−.039	118	3/4/4
Williams, Clarke, & Borland (2001)	−.089	307	1/4/4
Yalch & MacLachlan (1977)	.098	184	5/1/1
Yates (1982) solar-isolated	−.056	58	5/1/1

(continued)

TABLE 1–1 (*Continued*)

Study	r	N	Codings[a]
Yates (1982) solar-integrated	.159	57	5/1/1
Yates (1982) insulation-isolated	−.141	30	5/1/1
Yates (1982) insulation-integrated	−.193	26	5/1/1
Ying (2001) concrete	−.021	140	1/3/3
Ying (2001) abstract	.069	140	1/3/3

[a]The coding judgments, in order, are topic category (1 = disease detection, 2 = disease prevention, 3 = other health, 4 = sociopolitical, 5 = consumer advertising, 6 = other); gain kernel-state language (1 = desirable states, 2 = undesirable states, 3 = both desirable and undesirable states, 4 = indeterminate); and loss kernel-state language (1 = undesirable states, 2 = desirable states, 3 = both desirable and undesirable states, 4 = indeterminate).

TABLE 1–2
Summary of Results

	k	N	Mean r	95% CI	Q(df)
All cases	165	50,780	.016	−.004, .035	465.7 (164)**
Topic of advocacy					
Health					
Disease prevention	74	16,255	.046	.015, .078	193.1(73)**
Disease detection	34	7,112	−.027	−.072, .018	89.6(33)**
Other	10	1,430	−.038	−.092, .016	9.4(9)
Sociopolitical	3	424	−.089	−.183, .007	.6(2)
Consumer advertising	25	3,805	−.013	−.074, .049	77.0 (24)**
Other topics	19	21,754	.060	.006, .114	71.2(18)**
Gain kernel language					
Desirable	36	23,277	.022	−.018, .063	98.7(35)**
Undesirable	19	9,431	−.006	−.055, .042	39.6(18)*
Both desirable and undesirable	65	9,540	−.002	−.036, .033	156.2(64)**
Indeterminate	45	8,532	.052	.005, .098	166.5(44)**
Loss kernel language					
Undesirable	49	31,917	−.012	−.039, .014	92.8(48)**
Desirable	12	1,679	.098	−.009, .202	48.0(11)**
Both desirable and undesirable	61	8,934	.007	−.031, .044	164.7(60)**
Indeterminate	43	8,250	.046	−.001, .092	149.1(42)**

*p < .01. ** p < .001.

when the gain-framed appeal was phrased in terms of desirable kernel states (mean $r = .022$), undesirable kernel states (mean $r = -.006$), or a combination of desirable and undesirable kernel states (mean $r = -.002$). The 95% confidence intervals for these three means overlap substantially; these data contain no indication that the relative persuasiveness of gain- and loss-framed appeals varies as a consequence of the phrasing of the kernel states in gain-framed appeals.

Phrasing of kernel states in loss-framed appeals. As indicated in Table 1–2, gain- and loss-framed appeals did not dependably differ in persuasiveness when the loss-framed appeal was phrased in terms of undesirable kernel states (mean $r = -.012$), desirable kernel states (mean $r = .098$), or a combination of desirable and undesirable kernel states (mean $r = .007$). The 95% confidence intervals for these three means overlap substantially; these data contain no indication that the relative persuasiveness of gain- and loss-framed appeals varies as a consequence of the phrasing of the kernel states in loss-framed appeals.

Gain-framed and loss-framed kernel states considered jointly. As depicted in Table 1–3, in the 17 cases in which the gain-framed appeal referred to desirable kernel states and the loss-framed appeal referred to undesirable kernel states, gain- and loss-framed appeals did not significantly differ in persuasiveness (mean $r = -.007$). No study examined appeals in which the gain-framed appeal referred to undesirable kernel states and the loss-framed appeal referred to desirable kernel states.

DISCUSSION

Overall Effects

Gain-framed and loss-framed appeals do not generally differ in persuasiveness. Despite the apparent psychological nonequivalence of gains and losses (as indicated by decision framing research) and despite various asymmetries between positive and negative information and events (e.g., the preferential detection of negative stimuli), loss-framed appeals are not in general more persuasive than gain-framed appeals. In fact, no subset of cases analyzed here displayed a significant advantage for loss-framed appeals over gain-framed appeals.

This result may illustrate the dangers of relying on generalizations about psychological states and processes as a basis for principles of persuasive message design. Good evidence indicates that negative information commonly has a greater impact on decisions than positive information does, that negative

TABLE 1–3
Joint Gain and Loss Kernel Phrasing

Gain kernel phrasing	Loss kernel phrasing			
	Desirable	*Undesirable*	*Combination*	*Indeterminate*
Desirable				
Mean *r*	.091	−.007	.020	
95% CI	−.042, .221	−.059, .045	−.053, .093	
k	10	17	9	0
N	1,269	20,568	1,440	
Q(df)	45.7(9)***	36.6(16)**	13.2(8)	
Undesirable				
Mean *r*		−.025		
95% CI		−.076, .026		
k	0	17	1	1
N		8,891		
Q(df)		31.9(16)*		
Combination				
Mean *r*	.136	−.008	−.010	
95% CI	.039, .230	−.057, .041	−.054, .034	
k	2	15	48	0
N	410	2,458	6,672	
Q(df)	.8(1)	18.1(14)	129.8(47)***	
Indeterminate				
Mean *r*			.139	.045
95% CI			−.062, .329	−.003, .092
k	0	0	3	42
N			549	7,983
Q(df)			5.0(2)	147.2(41)***

$*p < .05.$ $**p < .01.$ $*** p < .001.$

stimuli are preferentially detected, that negative events evoke stronger psychological reactions than do positive events, and so forth. It stands to reason that loss-framed appeals would, in general, have more persuasive impact than gain-framed appeals, but they do not. (An equally natural supposition might be that negative political campaign advertising would be significantly more persuasive than positive advertising, but it is not. See Allen & Burrell, 2002; Lau, Sigelman, Heldman, & Babbitt, 1999.) Translating psychological generalizations into corresponding principles of communication may be more challenging than commonly supposed.

In considering how to explain these results, we wish to draw attention to a little-emphasized aspect of the contrast between gain-framed and loss-framed appeals. The feature most commonly emphasized in distinguishing these two appeal types is the valence of the outcome discussed—positive outcomes ("gains") in gain-framed appeals, negative outcomes ("losses") in loss-framed appeals. But another element distinguishes these two appeal types; gain-framed appeals focus on the consequences of *compliance*, whereas loss-framed appeals focus on the consequences of *noncompliance*. (It is important to not be misled by the common labeling of these appeal types. Instead of being called *gain-framed* and *loss-framed* appeals, these might with equal appropriateness have been termed *compliance-focused* and *noncompliance-focused* appeals.)

A number of research findings offer some indirect support for supposing that focusing the audience's attention on action (compliance, the desired behavior) might enhance persuasion. For instance, imagining the hypothetical performance of a behavior can increase behavioral intentions and the likelihood of subsequent behavioral performance (e.g., Gregory, Cialdini, & Carpenter, 1982; Sherman & Anderson, 1987). Engaging in behavioral self-prediction (that is, predicting whether one will engage in a behavior) can make subsequent behavioral performance more likely (the "self-prophesy" effect; see, e.g., Spangenberg & Greenwald, 1999; Spangenberg, Sprott, Grohmann, & Smith, 2003). Persuasive messages that provide a more specific description of the advocated action have been found to be more effective than those providing a general description or no description at all (for reviews, see O'Keefe, 1997, 2002). Having people specify when and where they would perform a given behavior has been found to make people more likely (compared with a no-treatment control group with equivalently positive intentions) to perform the behavior (the effect of "implementation intention" interventions; e.g., Gollwitzer & Brandstatter, 1997; Sheeran & Orbell, 2000; Sheeran & Silverman, 2003).

In short, a variety of evidence suggests that focusing the audience's attention on the desired behavior may enhance persuasion. Hence, rather than focusing people's attention on what will happen if they keep doing what they're doing, it might be more persuasive to instead focus their attention on what will happen if they change their behavior; that is, compliance-focused appeals could have some persuasive advantage over noncompliance-focused appeals, just because of their subtly greater focus on the advocated action. However, any such advantage could presumably be easily neutralized by whatever persuasive advantage was conferred on noncompliance-focused appeals by virtue of the fact that those appeal draw attention to undesirable outcomes (with all of the impact attendant to negative states). On balance, then, one might expect rather little difference in general between gain-framed and loss-framed appeals—which is precisely the result obtained here.

Obviously, the contrast between gain- and loss-framed appeals necessarily confounds (a) a contrast between a focus on the consequences of compliance and a focus on the consequences of noncompliance and (b) a contrast between discussion of desirable consequences and discussion of undesirable consequences. This confounding occurs because the relevant communicative function is persuasion. Persuasive appeals naturally take two broad forms, either "compliance produces desirable outcomes" or "noncompliance produces undesirable outcomes." As a general rule, a persuader will not assert "compliance produces undesirable outcomes" or "noncompliance produces desirable outcomes." But this means that it is impossible to disentangle the two different potential contributions to any observed gain-loss persuasive message framing effects—the contribution of having the message being compliance-focused or noncompliance-focused and the contribution of having the message discuss desirable or undesirable outcomes.

Moderating Factors

Phrasing of kernel states. It seems plausible to suppose that any differences in persuasiveness between gain-framed and loss-framed appeals might be accentuated when the gain-framed appeal has desirable kernel states (e.g., "healthy skin"), when the loss-framed appeal has undesirable kernel states (e.g., "skin cancer"), or when both circumstances obtain; similar reasoning underlies the supposition that any such differences might be minimized if the gain-framed appeal has undesirable kernel states, if the loss-framed appeal has desirable kernel states, or if both conditions obtain. But these variations in the phrasing of appeals make no detectable difference in the relative effectiveness of gain- and loss-framed messages.

For two reasons, however, the research evidence on this matter is not as extensive as one might like. First, many research reports did not provide sufficiently detailed descriptions of the appeals, thus preventing coding of this moderator. Second, not all possible combinations of gain- and loss-appeal kernel phrasing are well represented in the literature. Still, the research evidence to date gives little reason to suspect that the phrasing of kernel states makes much difference in the relative persuasiveness of gain- and loss-framed appeals.

Disease prevention vs. disease detection. As hypothesized by various commentators (e.g., Salovey et al., 2002), when the message advocated a disease prevention behavior, gain-framed appeals were significantly more persuasive than loss-framed appeals. For disease prevention behaviors, then, these results offer a straightforward practical implication concerning the design of effective persuasive messages, namely, gain-framed appeals should be preferred over loss-framed appeals. The observed mean effect size ($r = .046$) is not large in absolute terms, but it is characteristic of the effect magnitudes commonly observed in persuasion effects research.[8]

Contrary to expectation, when the message advocated a disease detection behavior, gain- and loss-framed appeals did not significantly differ in persuasiveness. This result casts doubt on the need for the explanatory mechanism most often invoked to explain putative gain-loss message framing differences, namely, differences in the riskiness of detection and prevention behaviors. As discussed above, the suggestion has been that the uncertainty (riskiness) of detection behaviors makes loss-framed messages more persuasive, whereas the lack of risk associated with prevention behaviors makes gain-framed appeals more persuasive (e.g., Salovey et al., 2002). But this explanation is offered to account for a phenomenon that turns out not to be genuine: disease detection behaviors are not more successfully influenced by loss-framed appeals than by gain-framed appeals.

To be sure, the effects of gain-loss message framing variations appear not to be parallel for disease prevention behaviors and for disease detection behaviors. But understanding this nonparallelism requires a perspective broader than just these two topics of advocacy. In general, gain-framed and loss-framed appeals do not significantly differ in persuasiveness—not for disease detection behaviors, other health-related topics, sociopolitical questions, or consumer advertising. Only for disease prevention behaviors and "other" topics (a motley collection encompassing such topics as recycling participation, taxpayer compliance, job advertising, and college course selection) does any dependable difference in persuasiveness appear.[9] Thus, the relevant question is not "why are the results different for disease prevention behaviors and disease detection behaviors?" but rather "why are the results for disease prevention behaviors different from almost everything else?"

Two broad possibilities suggest themselves. Something may be distinctive about the realm of disease prevention that makes gain-framed appeals on this subject especially successful, or something may be distinctive about how the gain-loss appeal variation has been realized in disease-prevention studies that yields the observed effects.

The distinctiveness of disease prevention behaviors. If the observed effect is to be explained as a consequence of something distinctive about disease prevention behaviors, the key task obviously becomes the identification of that distinctive feature. As previously discussed, one suggestion has been that disease prevention behaviors are relatively low-risk behaviors and hence (following prospect-theory reasoning) are likely to be more successfully influenced through gain-framed appeals than loss-framed appeals.

This explanation is unlikely to be very satisfactory. Although it has become common to describe disease prevention behaviors as relatively less risky (especially in contrast to putatively more risky disease detection behaviors), it is not plain that this characterization is well grounded. One potential source of confusion here is the word "risk" and its variants (e.g., "risky"). Colloquially, something that is "risky" is dangerous. In that colloquial sense, it might make sense to think of prevention behaviors as relatively not risky (it's hard to see how eating more fruits and vegetables might be dangerous) and to think of detection behaviors as relatively risky (a danger-filled outcome is possible, namely, discovering an abnormal condition).

But prospect theory's sense of "risk" refers to uncertainty about outcomes, regardless of the dangerousness or valence of the events; a decision option is "risky" when its outcomes are uncertain, even if the outcomes are desirable ones (Kahneman & Tversky, 1979). Understood in this way, disease detection behaviors and disease prevention behaviors might be seen as not differentially "risky," that is, not especially different with respect to the certainty of their consequences. People might easily think many disease prevention behaviors are "risky," that is, uncertain ("If I exercise regularly, I might or might not still have a heart attack"), and the perceived uncertainty associated with such behaviors may not differ from that associated with disease detection behaviors ("If I have a mammogram, it might or might not show that I have breast cancer"). In any event, an assumption that disease prevention behavior outcomes are relatively certain (low-risk) and disease detection behavior outcomes are relatively uncertain (high-risk) is problematic.

Hence, appealing to the putatively low-risk character of prevention behaviors is not a satisfactory basis for explaining the observed persuasive advantage of gain-framed appeals over loss-framed appeals in that domain. Indeed, no suitable differentiating factor seems to be on the horizon. However, the present results do place some constraints on any explanation of this sort. Notice that gain- and loss-framed appeals do not differ significantly in persuasiveness in (for example) consumer advertising messages. The implication of this result is that any putatively distinctive feature of disease prevention behaviors (that is, any such feature that is appealed to as a basis for explaining why gain-framed appeals are more successful in that domain than are loss-framed appeals) must presumably be one that distinguishes such behaviors both from disease detection behaviors and from consumer behaviors.

The distinctiveness of experimental realizations. A second possible account of why gain-framed appeals are more persuasive than loss-framed appeals in the realm of disease prevention is that something is distinctive about the experimental realizations of gain-loss appeal variations in disease-prevention studies. For example, it might have been the case that, in disease-prevention studies, the phrasing of the kernel states was such as to maximize the comparative effectiveness of gain-framed appeals. But, as indicated earlier, no particular way of phrasing the kernel states makes much difference in the relative persuasiveness of gain- and loss-framed appeals.

Unfortunately, the brevity of the usual message descriptions in research reports constrains exploration of many such possibilities. For example, messages might vary in the strength or "dose" of the framing manipulation. Imagine, for instance, one study in which the messages in the gain-loss message pair had identical contents for 90% of the message (that is, the framing variations consisted of 10% of the message) and another study in which only 40% of the contents overlapped (that is, the framing variations consisted of 60% of the message). It might be that such dosing variations systematically influence the appearance of differences in the relative persuasiveness of gain- and loss-framed appeals, but without fuller access to message contents, no post hoc examination of such hypotheses is possible.

Caveats and Limitations

As with any literature review, the conclusions here are necessarily constrained by the state of the research literature. For instance, one might have liked to have known whether any differential persuasiveness of gain- and loss-framed appeals is attenuated in a circumstance in which the gain-framed appeal referred to undesirable kernel states and the loss-framed appeal referred to desirable kernel states, but we found no studies that exemplified such a comparison. And, as with any review, different findings might have emerged if different analytic decisions had been made. For instance, imperfect experimental realizations of the message contrast could have been included, or different sorts of outcomes might have been distinguished. Of course, nothing forecloses the pursuit of such analytic possibilities in the future.

It might be noticed that, because message texts were unavailable, a number of cases could not be coded for the phrasing of kernel states (or for various other potential moderators, such as the "dose" of the framing manipulation). If one supposes that the particulars of the concrete realizations of abstract message types might have some systematic influence on observed effects, it will be important that the research community have access to the messages. The common publication practice has been to provide brief descriptions of the message manipulations, descriptions sufficient to provide assurance that the desired message contrast was indeed realized. We believe that, in the long run, providing more extensive descriptions (ideally, access to complete messages) will better serve the research community's ends.

Even acknowledging these limitations, however, it seems apparent that the persuasive effects of gain- and loss-framed appeals are rather more complex than commonly supposed. For instance, although previous reviews have commonly asserted that gain- and loss-framed appeals differ in persuasiveness for messages advocating disease detection behaviors, our more extensive examination of the existing research literature failed to find confirming evidence.

And these results plainly speak to broader substantive, theoretical, and methodological questions than simply (for example) the design of health communications. As a substantive illustration, the surprising lack of overall difference in persuasiveness between gain- and loss-framed appeals suggests that even in as-yet sparsely researched areas, such as sociopolitical advocacy, loss-framed appeals ought not be expected to enjoy a substantial advantage. Theoretically, these findings illustrate the gap between an understanding of psychological states and processes and a grasp of principles of communication and message design; many areas of communication research seem to have been shaped by psychological generalizations, whereas our findings suggest that translating psychological principles into principles of communication can be problematic. Finally, results such as these offer a cautionary methodological note of broad relevance: selective or piecemeal literature reviews can too easily endorse appealing but misleading conclusions. General claims about messages want correspondingly general evidence—evidence of precisely the sort that broad, systematic research reviews can provide.

ACKNOWLEDGMENTS

Thanks to Lisa Benz Scott, Gretchen Brenes, Chingching Chang, Debbie Chang, Jean-Charles Chebat, Dee Lisa Cothran, Lisa Evans, Eamonn Ferguson, Susan Grantham, Roland Helm, Cynthia Hoffner, Amy Latimer, Deanna Lawatsch, Angela Lee, Brett Martin, Norman Mundorf, Robin Nabi, Kathleen Phelan, Sherri Robertson, Rob Ruiter, Peter Salovey, Todd Thorsteinson, Monique Turner, Patricia van Assema, Holley Wilkin, and Richard Yalch for supplying primary-research information and to the Information Resource Retrieval Center at the University of Illinois at Urbana-Champaign Library for their cheerful assistance.

NOTES

1. In experimental realizations of gain-loss message framing variations, an interest in experimental control can make some confounding inevitable. If messages are matched with respect to either the attained-avoided contrast or the desirable-undesirable kernel state contrast, then the gain-loss message variation will be confounded with the other contrast. That is, if both messages are phrased in terms of avoided states (e.g., "compliance reduces the chances of skin cancer" and "noncompliance reduces the chances of healthy skin"), then the gain-loss contrast will be confounded with the desirable-undesirable kernel state contrast because the gain-framed appeal will have an undesirable kernel state ("skin cancer") and the loss-framed appeal will have a desirable kernel state ("healthy skin"); if appeals are matched with respect to the valence of the kernel states (e.g., "compliance reduces the chances of skin cancer" and "noncompliance increases the chances of skin cancer"), then the gain-loss contrast will be confounded with the attained-avoided contrast.

2. Without taking sides on the question of the argumentative status of nonlinguistic entities (see, e.g., Birdsell & Groarke, 1996; Blair, 1996, 2004; Fleming, 1996), we note that, at a minimum, visual materials are not exemplary instances of arguments (see O'Keefe, 1982, pp. 14–15).

3. Promises, like gain-framed messages, emphasize some desirable outcome of compliance; threats, like loss-framed messages, emphasize some undesirable outcome of noncompliance. But, conventionally understood, the outcomes invoked in promises and threats are ones under the control of the influencing agent (and so, for example, the effectiveness of promises and threats may turn in large part on the receiver's beliefs about such things as the communicator's willingness to carry out the pledged future act). This aspect of promises and threats makes those message forms sufficiently distinctive that they are put aside here.

4. A reader wondered whether the inability to include these insufficient-information cases makes for a conservative picture of overall effects. Any discussion of this question is necessarily speculative, but two considerations suggest that our reported results are unlikely to differ much from what might have been obtained had information been available about these cases. First, these cases commonly either had smaller samples (e.g., $N = 52$ for Burroughs, 1997; $N = 63$ for Mann et al., 2004) or had statistically nonsignificant overall differences between framing conditions (e.g., Giles, 2002; Gnepa, 2001; Horgen & Brownell, 2002; Martin & Marshall, 1999; Martinez, 1999; Miller et al., 1999; Wegener et al., 1994), even with larger samples (e.g., for Devos-Comby et al., 2002, N was approximately 500; for McCroskey & Wright, 1971, $N = 176$; for Merrill, 2003, $N = 165$). That is, generally speaking, the effect sizes in these studies either must have been relatively small or were based on small samples; the implication is that the mean effects we report here are unlikely to have been dramatically larger if we had been able to include these cases (i.e., our estimates are not notably conservative). Second, the number of analyzed cases (165) is relatively large compared with the number of unavailable cases. Taken together, these two considerations suggest that the unavailability of information about these cases is likely to have had little effect on the general picture presented here.

5. We did not adjust effect sizes for unreliability, range restriction, or other such factors. We share Rosenthal's (1991, p. 25) view that "the proper goal of a meta-analysis . . . is to teach us better what *is*, not what might some day be in the best of all possible worlds when all our independent and dependent variables are perfectly measured, perfectly valid, perfectly continuous, and perfectly unrestricted in range."

6. As noted by Salovey and Wegener (2003, p. 61), some health-related behaviors might plausibly be described as either (or both) a disease-detection behavior and a disease-prevention behavior. For example, Pap tests and colonoscopies provide both early detection of cancer and prevention of cancer (by virtue of the opportunity for identification and removal of precancerous

abnormalities). In such cases, persuaders might invoke either appeals emphasizing the disease-detection aspects of the advocated action or appeals underscoring the disease-prevention aspects. One potentially useful way of analyzing such "dual-function" behaviors would be to distinguish cases based on whether the appeals used to underwrite the recommended action stressed detection or prevention. But because so few studies of such dual-function behaviors are available, we classified such behaviors as "other health-related behaviors."

7. These are, overwhelmingly, independent effect sizes. As described earlier, if a study contained multiple relevant outcomes (dependent variables), effect sizes were initially computed separately for each outcome and then averaged to yield a summary estimate of persuasive effect for that study. Thus, each of the 165 effect sizes is based on a distinct human sample (with the exception of the two effects associated with Sheer's (1995) within-subjects design) and on a distinct manipulation (message pair).

8. As examples from other meta-analytic reviews (with effects expressed as the absolute value of an n-weighted mean r, computed with the r-z-r transformation procedure, using the individual effect sizes reported in each meta-analysis): The mean effect on request compliance of the door-in-the-face strategy is .08 (O'Keefe & Hale, 1998) and that of the foot-in-the-door strategy is .11 (Dillard, Hunter, & Burgoon, 1984). The mean persuasive effect associated with variations in language intensity is .02 (Hamilton & Hunter, 1998) and that of rhetorical questions is .05 (Gayle, Preiss, & Allen, 1998). The mean difference in persuasive effects between one-sided messages and refutational two-sided messages is .07 and that between one-sided messages and non-refutational two-sided messages is .03 (O'Keefe, 1999).

9. The significant effect for "other" topics becomes just barely nonsignificant if the single study with a very large sample (Berger & Smith, 1997) is excluded: mean $r = .071$ ($k = 18$), $p = .051$; the 95% confidence interval limits were $-.000$ ($-.0002$) and .142.

REFERENCES

References marked with an asterisk indicate studies included in the meta-analysis.

Abood, D. A., Coster, D. C., Mullis, A. K., & Black, D. R. (2002). Evaluation of a "loss-framed" minimal intervention to increase mammography utilization among medically un- and under-insured women. *Cancer Detection and Prevention, 26,* 394–400.

*Al-Jarboa, F. A. (1996). An investigation of the effects of mood, type and level of involvement characterizing consumer products and message framing on advertising effectiveness (Doctoral dissertation, University of Illinois at Urbana-Champaign, 1996). *Dissertation Abstracts International, 57* (1997), 3585A (UMI No. AAG-9702437).

*Allen, B. P., Jr. (1969). The relationships among the effects of persuasive appeals, toothbrushing behavior, attitude toward dental hygiene, intention to behave, and reported behavior (Doctoral dissertation, University of Houston, 1969). *Dissertation Abstracts International, 30* (1969), 397–398B (UMI No. AAT-6911991).

Allen, M., & Burrell, N. (2002). The negativity effect in political advertising: A meta-analysis. In J. P. Dillard & M. Pfau (Eds.), *The persuasion handbook: Developments in theory and practice* (pp. 83–96). Thousand Oaks, CA: Sage.

*Apanovitch, A. M., McCarthy, D., & Salovey, P. (2003). Using message framing to motivate HIV testing among low-income, ethnic minority women. *Health Psychology, 22,* 60–67.

*Arora, R. (1998). The effect of message framing and involvement on attitude and intention. *Journal of Customer Service in Marketing and Management, 4*(2), 1–16.

*Arora, R. (2000). Message framing and credibility: Application in dental services. *Health Marketing Quarterly, 18*(1/2), 29–44.

*Arora, R., & Arora, A. (2004). The impact of message framing and credibility finding for nutritional guidelines. *Services Marketing Quarterly, 26*(1), 35–53.

*Banks, S. M., Salovey, P., Greener, S., Rothman, A. J., Moyer, A., Beauvais, J., et al. (1995). The effects of message framing on mammography utilization. *Health Psychology, 14,* 178–184.

*Benz Scott, L. A. (2000). Design and evaluation of effective persuasive heart disease prevention messages targeting young adult women (Doctoral dissertation, Johns Hopkins University, 2000). *Dissertation Abstracts International, 61* (2000), 1350B (University Microfilms no. AAT-9964055).

*Berger, P. D., & Smith, G. E. (1997). The effect of direct mail framing strategies and segmentation variables on university fundraising performance. *Journal of Direct Marketing, 11*(1), 30–43.

*Berger, P. D., & Smith, G. E. (1998). The impact of prospect theory based framing tactics on advertising effectiveness. *Omega: International Journal of Management Science, 26,* 593–609.

Birdsell, D. S., & Groarke, L. (1996). Toward a theory of visual argument. *Argumentation and Advocacy, 33,* 1–10.

Blair, J. A. (1996). The possibility and actuality of visual argument. *Argumentation and Advocacy, 33,* 23–39.

Blair, J. A. (2004). The rhetoric of visual arguments. In C. A. Hill & M. Helmers (Eds.), *Defining visual rhetorics* (pp. 41–61). Mahwah, NJ: Lawrence Erlbaum Associates.

Blanton, H., Stuart, A. E., & VandenEijnden, R. J. J. M. (2001). An introduction to deviance-regulation theory: The effect of behavioral norms on message framing. *Personality and Social Psychology Bulletin, 27,* 848–858.

Blanton, H., VandenEijnden, R. J. J. M., Buunk, B. P., Gibbons, F. X., Gerrard, M., & Bakker, A. (2001). Accentuate the negative: Social images in the prediction and promotion of condom use. *Journal of Applied Social Psychology, 31,* 274–295.

Bless, H., Betsch, T., & Franzen, A. (1998). Framing the framing effect: The impact of context cues on solutions to the "Asian disease" problem. *European Journal of Social Psychology, 28,* 287–291.

*Block, L. G. (1993). The effects of perceived efficacy, message framing and vividness on the persuasiveness of a fear appeal (Doctoral dissertation, Columbia University, 1993). *Dissertation Abstracts International, 54* (1994), 2652A (UMI No. AAC-9333731).

*Block, L. G., & Keller, P. A. (1995). When to accentuate the negative: The effects of perceived efficacy and message framing on intentions to perform a health-related behavior. *Journal of Marketing Research, 32,* 192–203.

*Bono Santos, E., & Rodriguez Torronteras, A. (1991). Dos sistemas de persuasion para la deshabituacion tabaquica: Un ensayo controlado [Two systems of persuasion to quit smoking: A controlled trial]. *Atencion Primaria, 8*(1), 12–16.

Borenstein, M., & Rothstein, H. (1999). *Comprehensive meta-analysis: A computer program for research synthesis.* Englewood, NJ: Biostat.

*Bower, A. B., & Taylor, V. A. (2003). Increasing intention to comply with pharmaceutical product instructions: An exploratory study investigating the roles of frame and plain language. *Journal of Health Communication, 8*, 145–156.

*Brenes, G. A. (1999, August). *The effects of message framing on mammography compliance.* Paper presented at the annual meeting of the American Psychological Association, Boston, MA.

*Broemer, P. (2002). Relative effectiveness of differently framed health messages: The influence of ambivalence. *European Journal of Social Psychology, 32*, 685–703.

*Broemer, P. (2004). Ease of imagination moderates reactions to differently framed health messages. *European Journal of Social Psychology, 34*, 103–119.

*Brondino, M. J. (1997). Message framing effects on risky decision making in the context of AIDS prevention programming (Doctoral dissertation, University of South Carolina, 1997). *Dissertation Abstracts International, 58* (1998), 6277B (UMI No. ADG-9815485).

*Brug, J., Ruiter, J. A., & van Assema, P. (2003). The (ir)relevance of framing nutrition education messages. *Nutrition and Health, 17*, 9–20.

Burroughs, T. E. (1997). The effect of message framing on perceptions of risk, perceptions of control and health behavior decisions (Doctoral dissertation, Washington University, 1997). *Dissertation Abstracts International, 58* (1998), 5187B (UMI No. ADG-9807741).

Cameron, L. D., & Leventhal, H. (1995). Vulnerability beliefs, symptom experiences, and the processing of health threat information: A self-regulatory perspective. *Journal of Applied Social Psychology, 25*, 1859–1883.

*Cesario, J., Grant, H., & Higgins, E. T. (2004). Regulatory fit and persuasion: Transfer from "feeling right." *Journal of Personality and Social Psychology, 86*, 388–404.

*Chang, C. (2002, July). *Effectiveness of ad framing for consumption products.* Paper presented at the annual meeting of the International Communication Association, Seoul, South Korea.

*Chang, C.-T. (2003, June). *The influences of message framing, perceived product innovativeness, and health involvement on advertising effectiveness of healthcare products.* Paper presented at the meeting of the European Association for Consumer Research, Dublin, Ireland.

*Chebat, J.-C., Limoges, F., & Gelinas-Chebat, C. (1998). Limits of the effects of advertising framing: The moderating effects of prior knowledge and involvement. *Advances in Consumer Research, 25*, 324–333.

Christophersen, E. R., & Gyulay, J.-E. (1981). Parental compliance with car seat usage: A positive approach with long-term follow-up. *Journal of Pediatric Psychology, 6*, 301–312.

*Cothran, D. L., Schneider, T., & Salovey, P. (1998, July). *The effects of message framing and involvement on mammography use in low income women.* Paper presented at the Yale Summer Fellows' Conference, New Haven, CT.

*Cox, D. S., & Cox, A. D. (2001). Communicating the consequences of early detection: The role of evidence and framing. *Journal of Marketing, 65*(3), 91–103.

Cunningham, M. R., Steinberg, J., & Grev, R. (1980). Wanting to and having to help: Separate motivations for positive mood and guilt-induced helping. *Journal of Personality and Social Psychology, 38*, 181–192.

*Davis, J. J. (1995). The effects of message framing on response to environmental communications. *Journalism and Mass Communication Quarterly, 72*, 285–299.

*Dembroski, T. M. (1969). Locus of control and the effectiveness of persuasive communications: Changing dental health practices as measured by a chemical agent (Doctoral dissertation, University of Houston, 1969). *Dissertation Abstracts International, 30* (1969), 2614A (UMI No. AAT-6921750).

*Detweiler, J. B., Bedell, B. T., Salovey, P., Pronin, E., & Rothman, A. J. (1999). Message framing and sunscreen use: Gain-framed messages motivate beach-goers. *Health Psychology, 18*, 189–196.

Devos-Comby, L., McCarthy, D., Ferris, H., & Salovey, P. (2002, April). *Integrated theory of reasoned action predicts later condom use among low-income inner-city women.* Paper presented at Center for Interdisciplinary Research on AIDS Science Day, New Haven, CT.

Devos-Comby, L., & Salovey, P. (2002). Applying persuasion strategies to alter HIV-relevant thoughts and behavior. *Review of General Psychology, 6*, 287–304.

*Dibble, L. E. (1998). An exploration of the effects of self-guide matching and self-discrepancy matching on the processing of persuasive messages: Does matching increase or decrease thoughtful processing? (Doctoral dissertation, Ohio State University, 1998). *Dissertation Abstracts International, 59* (1999), 5617B (UMI No. ADG-9911181).

Dijksterhuis, A., & Aarts, H. (2003). On wildebeests and humans: The preferential detection of negative stimuli. *Psychological Science, 14*, 14–18.

Dillard, J. P., Hunter, J. E., & Burgoon, M. (1984). Sequential-request strategies: Meta-analysis of foot-in-the-door and door-in-the-face. *Human Communication Research, 10*, 461–488.

Dillard, J. P., & Marshall, L. J. (2003). Persuasion as a social skill. In J. O. Greene & B. R. Burleson (Eds.), *Handbook of communication and social interaction skills* (pp. 479–513). Mahwah, NJ: Lawrence Erlbaum Associates.

Druckman, J. N. (2001). The implications of framing effects for citizen competence. *Political Behavior, 23*, 225–256.

Edwards, A., Elwyn, G., Covey, J., Matthews, E., & Pill, R. (2001). Presenting risk information: A review of the effects of "framing" and other manipulations on patient outcomes. *Journal of Health Communication, 6*, 61–82.

Elliott, C. S., & Hayward, D. M. (1998). The expanding definition of framing and its particular impact on economic experimentation. *Journal of Socio-Economics, 27*, 229–243.

Erez, A., Bloom, M. C., & Wells, M. T. (1996). Using random rather than fixed effects models in meta-analysis: Implications for situational specificity and validity generalization. *Personnel Psychology, 49*, 275–306.

*Evans, R. I., Rozelle, R. M., Lasater, T. M., Dembroski, T. M., & Allen, B. P. (1970). Fear arousal, persuasion, and actual versus implied behavioral change: New perspective utilizing a real-life dental hygiene program. *Journal of Personality and Social Psychology, 16*, 220–227.

Fagley, N. S., & Miller, P. M. (1997). Framing effects and arenas of choice: Your money or your life? *Organizational Behavior and Human Decision Processes, 71*, 355–373.

*Ferguson, E., Bibby, P. A., Leaviss, J., & Weyman, A. (2003). *Effective design of workplace risk communications*. Norwich, England: Health and Safety Executive.

*Finney, L. J. (2001). Health beliefs, message framing and mammography screening compliance: Measurement development and theory testing (Doctoral dissertation, Miami University, 2001). *Dissertation Abstracts International, 62* (2001), 1641B (UMI No. AAT-3009844).

*Finney, L. J., & Iannotti, R. J. (2002). Message framing and mammography screening: A theory-driven intervention. *Behavioral Medicine, 28*, 5–14.

*Fischer, J. C., & Nabi, R. (2001, May). *Priming frames: Can framing effects extend beyond message topic?* Paper presented at the annual meeting of the International Communication Association, Washington, DC.

Fleming, D. (1996). Can pictures be arguments? *Argumentation and Advocacy, 33*, 11–22.

Gamson, W. A. (1992). *Talking politics*. New York: Cambridge University Press.

Gamson, W. A., & Modigliani, A. (1989). Media discourse and public opinion on nuclear power: A constructionist approach. *American Journal of Sociology, 95*, 1–37.

*Ganzach, Y., & Karsahi, N. (1995). Message framing and buying behavior: A field experiment. *Journal of Business Research, 32*, 11–17.

*Ganzach, Y., Weber, Y., & Ben-Or, P. (1997). Message framing and buying behavior: On the difference between artificial and natural environment. *Journal of Business Research, 40*, 91–95.

*Gardner, M. P., & Wilhelm, F. O., Jr. (1987). Consumer responses to ads with positive vs. negative appeals: Some mediating effects of context-induced mood and congruency between context and ad. *Current Issues and Research in Advertising, 10*, 81–98.

Gayle, B. N., Preiss, R. W., & Allen, M. (1998). Another look at the use of rhetorical questions. In M. Allen & R. W. Preiss (Eds.), *Persuasion: Advances through meta-analysis* (pp. 189–201). Cresskill, NJ: Hampton Press.

Gibson, J. W. (1962). Direct and indirect attitude scale measurements of positive and negative argumentative communications (Doctoral dissertation, Ohio State University, 1962). *Dissertation Abstracts, 23* (1963), 3023 (UMI No. AAT-6300050).

Gierl, H., Helm, R., & Satzinger, M. (2000). Die wirkung positiver und negativer aussagen in der werbung vor dem hintergrund des message framing [The effect of positive and negative statements in the advertisement against the background of message framing]. *Zeitschrift für betriebswirtschaftliche Forschung, 52*, 234–256.

Giles, M. E. (2002). *The effects of message framing on osteoporosis preventive behaviors: The role of optimism*. Unpublished master's thesis, Saint Joseph's University, Philadelphia, PA.

*Gintner, G. G., Rectanus, E. F., Achord, K., & Parker, B. (1987). Parental history of hypertension and screening attendance: Effects of wellness appeal versus threat appeal. *Health Psychology, 6*, 431–444.

Gnepa, T. J. (2001). Persuading small manufacturing companies to become active exporters: The effect of message framing and focus on behavioral intentions. *Journal of Global Marketing, 14*(4), 49–66.

Gollwitzer, P. M., & Brandstatter, V. (1997). Implementation intentions and effective goal pursuit. *Journal of Personality and Social Psychology, 73*, 186–199.

Gonzales, M. H., Aronson, E., & Costanzo, M. A. (1988). Using social cognition and persuasion to promote energy conservation: A quasi-experiment. *Journal of Applied Social Psychology, 18*, 1049–1066.

Gore, P., Madhavan, S., Curry, D., McClurg, G., Castiglia, M., Rosenbluth, S. A., et al. (1998). Persuasive messages: Development of persuasive messages may help increase mothers' compliance of their children's immunization schedule. *Marketing Health Services, 18*(4), 32–43.

*Grantham, S., & Irani, T. (2004, August). *An ounce of prevention: The role of critical thinking and message frames in addressing low-involvement environmental risks*. Paper presented at the annual conference of the Association for Education in Journalism and Mass Communication, Toronto, Canada.

*Greenlee, T. B. (1997). Alternative communication strategies to influence risky behavior: Addressing the AIDS pandemic (Doctoral dissertation, University of Rhode Island, 1997). *Dissertation Abstracts International, 58* (1998), 3218B (UMI No. ADG-9805233).

Gregory, W. L., Cialdini, R. B., & Carpenter, K. M. (1982). Self-relevant scenarios as mediators of likelihood estimates and compliance: Does imagining make it so? *Journal of Personality and Social Psychology, 43*, 89–99.

Hamilton, M. A., & Hunter, J. E. (1998). The effect of language intensity on receiver evaluations of message, source, and topic. In M. Allen & R. W. Preiss (Eds.), *Persuasion: Advances through meta-analysis* (pp. 99–138). Cresskill, NJ: Hampton Press.

Hart, E. J. (1972). The effects of contrasting messages on cancer control: Behavior of females in lower socioeconomic conditions. *Journal of School Health, 42*, 262–264.

*Hashimoto, S. (2002). *The effect of message framing on college women's folic acid intake attitudes, intentions, and behavior*. Unpublished master's thesis, University of Cincinnati, OH.

*Hasseldine, D. J. (1997). The effect of framing persuasive communications on taxpayer compliance (Doctoral dissertation, Indiana University, 1997). *Dissertation Abstracts International, 58* (1997), 968A (UMI No. AAG-9727934).

*Hasseldine, J., & Hite, P. A. (2003). Framing, gender and tax compliance. *Journal of Economic Psychology, 24*, 517–533.

Hedges, L.V., & Vevea, J.L. (1998). Fixed- and random-effects models in meta-analysis. *Psychological Methods, 3*, 486–504.

*Hessling, R. M. (1996). *Message framing and health: The interaction of personal relevance and perceived severity.* Unpublished master's thesis, Iowa State University, Ames.

*Hoffner, C. A., & Ye, J. (2004, May). *News about sunscreen and skin cancer: The role of framing and social comparison.* Paper presented at the annual meeting of the International Communication Association, New Orleans, LA.

*Homer, P. M., & Yoon, S.-G. (1992). Message framing and the interrelationships among ad-based feelings, affect, and cognition. *Journal of Advertising, 21*(1), 19–33.

Horgen, K. B., & Brownell, K. D. (2002). Comparison of price change and health message interventions in promoting healthy food choices. *Health Psychology, 21*, 505–512.

*Hsiao, E. T. Y. (2002). Using message framing to promote regular physical activity in college-age women and men (Doctoral dissertation, Ohio State University, 2002). *Dissertation Abstracts International, 63* (2003), 3461B (UMI No. AAT-3059265).

Isen, A. M., & Noonberg, A. (1979). The effect of photographs of the handicapped on donation to charity: When a thousand words may be too much. *Journal of Applied Social Psychology, 9*, 426–431.

Iyengar, S. (1991). *Is anyone responsible? How television frames political issues.* Chicago: University of Chicago Press.

Jackson, S. (1992). *Message effects research: Principles of design and analysis.* New York: Guilford Press.

*Jayanti, R. (2001, June). *Are negative frames more persuasive than positive frames for senior citizens? An exploratory investigation of age differences in framing effects.* Paper presented at the meeting of the European Association for Consumer Research, Berlin, Germany.

Johnson, B. T. (1989). *DSTAT: Software for the meta-analytic review of research literatures.* Hillsdale, NJ: Lawrence Erlbaum Associates.

*Jones, L. W., Sinclair, R. C., & Courneya, K. S. (2003). The effects of source credibility and message framing on exercise intentions, behaviors, and attitudes: An integration of the elaboration likelihood model and prospect theory. *Journal of Applied Social Psychology, 33*, 179–196.

Kahneman, D., & Tversky, A. (1979). Prospect theory: An analysis of decision under risk. *Econometrica, 47*, 263–291.

Kalichman, S. C., & Coley, B. (1995). Context framing to enhance HIV-antibody-testing messages targeted to African American women. *Health Psychology, 14*, 247–254.

*Keller, P. A., Lipkus, I. M., & Rimer, B. K. (2003). Affect, framing, and persuasion. *Journal of Marketing Research, 40*, 54–64.

Kirscht, J. P., Haefner, D. P., & Eveland, J. D. (1975). Public response to various written appeals to participate in health screening. *Public Health Reports, 90*, 539–543.

Kishor, N., & Godfrey, M. (1999). The effect of information framing on academic task completion. *Educational Psychology, 19*, 91–101.

*Knapp, L. G. (1989). The effects of type of value appealed to and valence of appeal on children's intentions and toothbrushing behavior (Doctoral dissertation, University of Alabama, 1989). *Dissertation Abstracts International, 51* (1990), 3114B (UMI No. AAT–9022265).

*Knapp, L. G. (1991). Effects of type of value appealed to and valence of appeal on children's dental health behavior. *Journal of Pediatric Psychology, 16*, 675–686.

Krishnamurthy, P., Carter, P., & Blair, E. (2001). Attribute framing and goal framing effects in health decisions. *Organizational Behavior and Human Decision Processes, 85*, 382–399.

Kuhberger, A. (1998). The influence of framing on risky decisions: A meta-analysis. *Organizational Behavior and Human Decision Processes, 75*, 23–55.

Kuhberger, A., Schulte-Mecklenbeck, M., & Perner, J. (1999). The effects of framing, reflection, probability, and payoff on risk preference in choice tasks. *Organizational Behavior and Human Decision Processes, 78*, 204–231.

*Lalor, K. M. (1990). *The effects of message framing and feelings of susceptibility to breast cancer on reported frequency of breast self-examination.* Unpublished master's thesis, University of Southern Mississippi, Hattiesburg.

*Lalor, K. M., & Hailey, B. J. (1990). The effects of message framing and feelings of susceptibility to breast cancer on reported frequency of breast self-examination. *International Quarterly of Community Health Education, 10*, 183–192.

*Lasater, T. M. (1969). An examination of the relationships among dogmatism, cognitive and behavioral changes and persuasive communications within the context of a dental health program (Doctoral dissertation, University of Houston, 1969). *Dissertation Abstracts International, 30* (1969), 2618A (UMI No. AAT-6921759).

Lau, R. R., Sigelman, L., Heldman, C., & Babbitt, P. (1999). The effects of negative political advertisements: A meta-analytic assessment. *American Political Science Review, 93*, 851–875.

*Lauver, D., & Rubin, M. (1990). Message framing, dispositional optimism, and follow-up for abnormal Papanicolaou tests. *Research in Nursing and Health, 13*, 199–207.

*Lawatsch, D. E. (1987). A comparison of the effect of two teaching strategies on nutrition knowledge, attitudes and food behavior of preschool children (Master's thesis, Montclair State College, 1987). *Master's Abstracts International, 26* (1988), 291 (UMI No. AAG-1331737).

*Lawatsch, D. E. (1990). A comparison of two teaching strategies on nutrition knowledge, attitudes and food behavior of preschool children. *Journal of Nutrition Education, 22*, 117–123.

*Lee, A. Y., & Aaker, J. L. (2004). Bringing the frame into focus: The influence of regulatory fit on processing fluency and persuasion. *Journal of Personality and Social Psychology, 86*, 205–218.

*Lee, C. K.-C., Brown, R., & Blood, D. (2000). The effects of efficacy, cognitive processing and message framing on persuasion. *Australasian Marketing Journal, 8*(2), 5–17.

Lehmann, S. (1970). Personality and compliance: A study of anxiety and self-esteem in opinion and behavior change. *Journal of Personality and Social Psychology, 15*, 76–86.

*Lemieux, R., Hale, J. L., & Mongeau, P. A. (1994, November). *Reducing risk behaviors related to sun exposure: The effects of fear appeals, vividness, and message framing.* Paper presented at the annual meeting of the Speech Communication Association, New Orleans, LA.

*Lerman, C., Ross, E., Boyce, A., Gorchov, P. M., McLaughlin, R., Rimer, B., et al. (1992). The impact of mailing psychoeducational materials to women with abnormal mammograms. *American Journal of Public Health, 82*, 729–730.

Levin, I. P., & Chapman, D. P. (1993). Risky decision making and allocation of resources for leukemia and AIDS programs. *Health Psychology, 12*, 110–117.

*Levin, I. P., Gaeth, G. J., Evangelista, F., Albaum, G., & Schreiber, J. (1999, December). *How positive and negative frames influence the decisions of persons in different cultures.* Paper presented at the Seventh Cross-Cultural Consumer and Business Studies Research Conference, Cancun, Mexico.

*Levin, I. P., Gaeth, G. J., Evangelista, F., Albaum, G., & Schreiber, J. (2001). How positive and negative frames influence the decisions of persons in the United States and Australia. *Asia Pacific Journal of Marketing and Logistics, 13*(2), 64–71.

*Levin, I. P., Gaeth, G. J., Schreiber, J., & Lauriola, M. (2002). A new look at framing effects: Distribution of effect sizes, individual differences, and independence of types of effects. *Organizational Behavior and Human Decision Processes, 88*, 411–429.

Levin, I. P., Schneider, S. L., & Gaeth, G. J. (1998). All frames are not created equal: A typology and critical analysis of framing effects. *Organizational Behavior and Human Decision Processes, 76*, 149–188.

Levin, I. P., Schnittjer, S. K., & Thee, S. L. (1988). Information framing effects in social and personal decisions. *Journal of Experimental Social Psychology, 24*, 520–529.

Li, S. (1998). Can the conditions governing the framing effect be determined? *Journal of Economic Psychology, 19*, 133–153.

*Littlejohn, C. R. (1997). Measuring the effects of message framing on the behavior of recycling in a residential recycling program (Doctoral dissertation, Florida State University, 1997). *Dissertation Abstracts International, 58* (1997), 623A (UMI No. ADG-9726466).

*Looker, A. C. (1983). A comparison of two persuasive strategies in changing the nutrition knowledge, attitudes, and behavior of adults (Doctoral dissertation, Pennsylvania State University, 1983). *Dissertation Abstracts International, 44* (1983), 117B (UMI No. AAG-8312649).

*Looker, A., & Shannon, B. (1984). Threat vs. benefit appeals: Effectiveness in adult nutrition education. *Journal of Nutrition Education, 16*, 173–176.

*Lord, K. R. (1994). Motivating recycling behavior: A quasiexperimental investigation of message and source strategies. *Psychology and Marketing, 11*, 341–358.

*Lowenherz, J. L. (1991). Effects of safe sex persuasive communications varying explicitness and fear versus health promotion videos (Doctoral dissertation,

Hofstra University, 1991). *Dissertation Abstracts International, 52* (1992), 3892B (UMI No. AAG-9134596).

*Maheswaran, D., & Meyers-Levy, J. (1990). The influence of message framing and issue involvement. *Journal of Marketing Research, 27*, 361–371.

Mann, T., Sherman, D., & Updegraff, J. (2004). Dispositional motivations and message framing: A test of the congruency hypothesis in college students. *Health Psychology, 23*, 330–334.

Marteau, T. M. (1989). Framing of information: Its influence upon decisions of doctors and patients. *British Journal of Social Psychology, 28*, 89–94.

*Martin, B., & Lawson, R. (1998). Mood and framing effects in advertising. *Australasian Marketing Journal, 6*(1), 35–50.

Martin, B., & Marshall, R. (1999). The interaction of message framing and felt involvement in the context of cell phone commercials. *European Journal of Marketing, 33*, 206–218.

Martinez, T. S. (1999). Message framing and college students' HIV-preventive behavior (Doctoral dissertation, University of Connecticut, 1999). *Dissertation Abstracts International, 60* (2000), 4303B (UMI No. AAT-9942585).

*McArdle, J. A. (1972). Positive and negative communications and subsequent attitude and behavior change in alcoholics (Doctoral dissertation, University of Illinois at Urbana-Champaign, 1972). *Dissertation Abstracts International, 34* (1973), 877B (UMI No. AAT-7317317).

*McCall, L. A., & Ginis, K. A. M. (2004). The effects of message framing on exercise adherence and health beliefs among patients in a cardiac rehabilitation program. *Journal of Applied Biobehavioral Research, 9*, 122–135.

*McCaul, K. D., Johnson, R. J., & Rothman, A. J. (2002). The effects of framing and action instructions on whether older adults obtain flu shots. *Health Psychology, 21*, 624–628.

McCroskey, J. C., & Wright, D. W. (1971). A comparison of the effects of punishment-oriented and reward-oriented messages in persuasive communication. *Journal of Communication, 21*, 83–93.

McGettigan, P., Sly, K., O'Connell, D., Hill, S., & Henry, D. (1999). The effects of information framing on the practices of physicians. *Journal of General Internal Medicine, 14*, 633–642.

*McKee, S. A., O'Malley, S., Steward, W. T., Neveu, S., Land, M., & Salovey, P. (2004). How to word effective messages about smoking and oral health: Emphasize the benefits of quitting. *Journal of Dental Education, 68*, 569–573.

McNeil, B. J., Pauker, S. G., Sox, H. C., Jr., & Tversky, A. (1982). On the elicitation of preferences for alternative therapies. *New England Journal of Medicine, 306*, 1259–1262.

Melvin, J. D. (1995). Effects of knowledge of diabetes and positive and negative instructional films on denial and mood of type I and type II diabetics (Doctoral dissertation, Auburn University, 1995). *Dissertation Abstracts International, 56* (1995), 1733B (UMI No. AAC-9525364).

Merrill, J. T. (2003). Message framing and behavioral intention for seat belt use: A consequence approach to health communication (Master's thesis, Utah State University, 2003). *Master's Abstracts International, 42* (2004), 32 (UMI No. AAT-1415139).

Meyer, T., & Delhomme, P. (2000). Quand chacun pense être moins expose que les autres aux risques mais plus receptif aux messages de prevention pour la santé [When each person thinks he is less exposed to risks than others, but more receptive to health prevention messages]. *Santé Publique, 12*, 133–147.

*Meyerowitz, B. E., & Chaiken, S. (1987). The effect of message framing on breast self-examination attitudes, intentions, and behavior. *Journal of Personality and Social Psychology, 52*, 500–510.

*Meyers-Levy, J., & Maheswaran, D. (2004). Exploring message framing outcomes when systematic, heuristic, or both types of processing occur. *Journal of Consumer Psychology, 14*, 159–167.

*Millar, M. G., & Millar, K. U. (2000). Promoting safe driving behaviors: The influence of message framing and issue involvement. *Journal of Applied Social Psychology, 30*, 853–866.

Miller, S. M., Buzaglo, J. S., Simms, S. L., Green, V., Bales, C., Mangan, C. E., et al. (1999). Monitoring styles in women at risk for cervical cancer: Implications for the framing of health-relevant messages. *Annals of Behavioral Medicine, 21*, 27–34.

Mintz, A., & Redd, S. B. (2003). Framing effects in international relations. *Synthese, 135*, 193–213.

*Mitchell, M. M. (2001). Risk, threat, and information seeking about genital herpes: The effects of mood and message framing. *Communication Studies, 52*, 141–152.

Montazeri, A., & McEwen, J. (1997). Effective communication: Perception of two anti-smoking advertisements. *Patient Education and Counseling, 30*, 29–35.

Moxey, A., O'Connell, D., McGettigan, P., & Henry, D. (2003). Describing treatment effects to patients: How they are expressed makes a difference. *Journal of General Internal Medicine, 18*, 948–959.

*Mundorf, N. H., Schneider, T. R., Salovey, P., Pallonen, U., Smith, N. F., & Steward, W. T. (2000, November). *Message framing and smoking cessation*. Paper presented at the annual meeting of the National Communication Association, Seattle, WA.

*Myers, R. E., Ross, E. A., Wolf, T. A., Balshem, A., Jepson, C., & Millner, L. (1991). Behavioral interventions to increase adherence in colorectal cancer screening. *Medical Care, 29*, 1039–1050.

National Research Council. (1992). *Combining information: Statistical issues and opportunities for research*. Washington, DC: National Academy Press.

Nelson, T. E., Clawson, R. A., & Oxley, Z. M. (1997). Media framing of a civil liberties conflict and its effect on tolerance. *American Political Science Review, 91*, 567–583.

Ohme, R. K. (2001). Social influence in media: Culture and antismoking advertising. In W. Wosinska, R. B. Cialdini, D. W. Barrett, & J. Reykowski (Eds.), *The practice of social influence in multiple cultures* (pp. 309–324). Mahwah, NJ: Lawrence Erlbaum Associates.

O'Keefe, D. J. (1982). The concepts of argument and arguing. In J. R. Cox & C. A. Willard (Eds.), *Advances in argumentation theory and research* (pp. 3–23). Carbondale: Southern Illinois University Press.

O'Keefe, D. J. (1997). Standpoint explicitness and persuasive effect: A meta-analytic review of the effects of varying conclusion articulation in persuasive messages. *Argumentation and Advocacy 34*, 1–12.

O'Keefe, D. J. (1999). How to handle opposing arguments in persuasive messages: A meta-analytic review of the effects of one-sided and two-sided messages. In M. E. Roloff (Ed.), *Communication yearbook 22* (pp. 209–249). Thousand Oaks, CA: Sage.

O'Keefe, D. J. (2002). The persuasive effects of variation in standpoint articulation. In F. H. van Eemeren (Ed.), *Advances in pragma-dialectics* (pp. 65–82). Amsterdam: Sic Sat.

O'Keefe, D. J., & Hale, S. L. (1998). The door-in-the-face influence strategy: A random-effects meta-analytic review. In M. E. Roloff (Ed.), *Communication yearbook 21* (pp. 1–33). Thousand Oaks, CA: Sage.

Orth, U. R., Oppenheim, P. P., & Firbasova, Z. (2005). Measuring message framing effects across Europe. *Journal of Targeting, Measurement, and Analysis for Marketing, 13*, 313–326.

*Oshikawa, S. (1965). An experimental study of the comparative effectiveness of positive and negative appeals in written life insurance advertisements (Doctoral dissertation, University of Washington, 1965). *Dissertation Abstracts, 26* (1966), 4310 (UMI No. AAT-6515401).

Paese, P. W., Bieser, M., & Tubbs, M. E. (1993). Framing effects and choice shifts in group decision making. *Organizational Behavior and Human Decision Processes, 56*, 149–165.

Pancer, S. M., Deforest, C. D., Rogers, I. K., & Schmirler, D. M. (1979). The use of displays in soliciting charitable donations. *Social Behavior and Personality, 7*, 33–37.

*Pedley, M. J. (1986). *The effects of message framing on smoking cessation among pulmonary patients.* Unpublished master's thesis, Vanderbilt University, Nashville, TN.

Perry, D. G., Bussey, K., & Freiberg, K. (1981). Impact of adults' appeals for sharing on the development of altruistic dispositions in children. *Journal of Experimental Child Psychology, 32*, 127–138.

*Phelan, K. (2003, May). *Effects of gain-loss message framing and knowledge of breast cancer on breast self-examinations amongst college women.* Paper presented at the Psi Chi Midwestern Regional Convention, Chicago, IL.

*Powell, F. A., & Miller, G. R. (1967). Social approval and disapproval cues in anxiety-arousing communications. *Speech Monographs, 34*, 152–159.

Quattrone, G. A., & Tversky, A. (1988). Contrasting rational and psychological analyses of political choice. *American Political Science Review, 82*, 719–736.

*Radecki, C. M. (1997). Communicating wishes regarding posthumous organ donation: A test of cognitive, affective and social mechanisms of persuasion (Doctoral dissertation, State University of New York at Albany, 1997). *Dissertation Abstracts International, 58* (1998), 3969B (UMI No. AAT-9802412).

*Ramirez, A. (1977). Social influence and ethnicity of the communicator. *Journal of Social Psychology, 102*, 209–213.

Raudenbush, S. W. (1994). Random effects models. In H. Cooper & L. V. Hedges (Eds.), *The handbook of research synthesis* (pp. 301–321). New York: Russell Sage Foundation.

*Reese, J. (1997). *The effects of message framing and intervention approach on self-perception of hearing handicap and hearing aid use in elderly veterans.* Unpublished master's thesis, University of South Florida, Tampa.

*Richardson, J. L., Milam, J., McCutchan, A., Stoyanoff, S., Bolan, R., Weiss, J., et al. (2004). Effect of brief safer-sex counseling by medical providers to HIV-1 seropositive patients: A multi-clinic assessment. *AIDS, 18,* 1179–1186.

*Rivers, S. E., Salovey, P., Pizarro, D. A., Pizarro, J., & Schneider, T. R. (2005). Message framing and Pap test utilization among women attending a community health clinic. *Journal of Health Psychology, 10,* 65–77.

*Robberson, M. R. (1985). Effects of positive and negative appeals to health and self-esteem on intentions to exercise (Doctoral dissertation, University of Alabama, 1985). *Dissertation Abstracts International, 46* (1986), 4455B (UMI No. AAT-8600771).

*Robberson, M. R., & Rogers, R. W. (1988). Beyond fear appeals: Negative and positive persuasive appeals to health and self-esteem. *Journal of Applied Social Psychology, 18,* 277–287.

*Robertson, S., & Welbourne, J. (2000, August). *Developing effective messages to reduce workplace violence.* Poster presented at the National Institute for Occupational Safety and Health Science Day, Morgantown, WV.

Rosenthal, R. (1991). *Meta-analytic procedures for social research* (rev. ed.). Beverly Hills, CA: Sage.

*Rothman, A. J., Martino, S. C., Bedell, B. T., Detweiler, J. B., & Salovey, P. (1999). The systematic influence of gain- and loss-framed messages on interest in and use of different types of health behavior. *Personality and Social Psychology Bulletin, 25,* 1355–1369.

Rothman, A. J., & Salovey, P. (1997). Shaping perceptions to motivate healthy behavior: The role of message framing. *Psychological Bulletin, 121,* 3–19.

Rothman, A. J., Salovey, P., Antone, C., Keough, K., & Martin, C. D. (1993). The influence of message framing on intentions to perform health behaviors. *Journal of Experimental Social Psychology, 29,* 408–433.

*Rozelle, R. M., Evans, R. I., Lasater, T. M., Dembroski, T. M., & Allen, B. P. (1973). Need for approval as related to the effects of persuasive communications on actual, reported, and intended behavior change: A viable predictor? *Psychological Reports, 33,* 719–725.

Rozin, P., & Royzman, E. B. (2001). Negativity bias, negativity dominance, and contagion. *Personality and Social Psychology Review, 5,* 296–320.

*Ruiter, R. A. C., Kok, G., Verplanken, B., & van Eersel, G. (2003). Strengthening the persuasive impact of fear appeals: The role of action framing. *Journal of Social Psychology, 143,* 397–400.

Salmon, C. T., Loken, B., & Finnegan, J., Jr. (1985). Direct mail in a cardiovascular health campaign: Use and effectiveness. *Evaluation and the Health Professions, 8,* 438–452.

Salovey, P., Schneider, T. R., & Apanovitch, A. M. (2002). Message framing in the prevention and early detection of illness. In J. P. Dillard & M. Pfau (Eds.), *The persuasion handbook: Developments in theory and practice* (pp. 391–406). Thousand Oaks, CA: Sage.

Salovey, P., & Wegener, D. T. (2003). Communicating about health: Message framing, persuasion, and health behavior. In J. Suls & K. Wallston (Eds.), *Social psychology foundations of health and illness* (pp. 54–81). Oxford, England: Blackwell.

*Schmitt, S. K. (2004). The effects of message framing on women's goal and implementation intentions to obtain a blood cholesterol screening test (Doctoral dissertation, Walden University, 2004). *Dissertation Abstracts International, 65* (2004), 482B (UMI No. AAT-3119877).

*Schneider, T. R., Salovey, P., Apanovitch, A. M., Pizarro, J., McCarthy, D., Zullo, J., et al. (2001). The effects of message framing and ethnic targeting on mammography use among low-income women. *Health Psychology, 20,* 256–266.

*Schneider, T. R., Salovey, P., Pallonen, U., Mundorf, N., Smith, N. F., & Steward, W. T. (2001). Visual and auditory message framing effects on tobacco smoking. *Journal of Applied Social Psychology, 31,* 667–682.

*Sen, S., Gurhan-Canli, Z., & Morwitz, V. (2000). *Withholding consumption: A social dilemma perspective on consumer boycotts.* Unpublished manuscript, Temple University, Philadelphia, PA.

Shadish, W. R., & Haddock, C. K. (1994). Combining estimates of effect size. In H. Cooper & L. V. Hedges (Eds.), *Handbook of research synthesis* (pp. 261–281). New York: Russell Sage Foundation.

*Shannon, B., & Rowan, M. L. (1987). Threat vs. benefit appeals for motivating adults to participate in a weight-control class. *Journal of the American Dietetic Association, 87,* 1612–1614.

*Sheer, V. C. (1995). Sensation seeking predispositions and susceptibility to a sexual partner's appeals for condom use. *Journal of Applied Communication Research, 23,* 212–229.

Sheeran, P., & Orbell, S. (2000). Using implementation intentions to increase attendance for cervical cancer screening. *Health Psychology, 19,* 283–289.

Sheeran, P., & Silverman, M. (2003). Evaluation of three interventions to promote workplace health and safety: Evidence for the utility of implementation intentions. *Social Science and Medicine, 56,* 2153–2163.

Sherman, R. T., & Anderson, C. A. (1987). Decreasing premature termination from psychotherapy. *Journal of Social and Clinical Psychology, 5,* 298–312.

*Shiv, B. (1996). The effects of negative versus positive advertising on brand attitudes and choice in a constructive world (Doctoral dissertation, Duke University, 1996). *Dissertation Abstracts International, 57* (1996), 1742A (UMI No. DA-9626392).

*Shiv, B., Britton, J. A. E., & Payne, J. W. (2004). Does elaboration increase or decrease the effectiveness of negatively versus positively framed messages? *Journal of Consumer Research, 31,* 199–208.

*Shiv, B., Edell, J. A., & Payne, J. W. (1997). Factors affecting the impact of negatively and positively framed ad messages. *Journal of Consumer Research, 24,* 285–294.

*Simmering, M. J. (1993). Effects of social and non-social messages regarding weight on women's weight loss intentions as a function of self-presentational style (Doctoral dissertation, Columbia University, 1993). *Dissertation Abstracts International, 54* (1993), 4447B (UMI No. AAI-9333865).

*Smith, G. E. (1996). Framing in advertising and the moderating impact of consumer education. *Journal of Advertising Research, 36*(5), 49–64.

*Smith, G. E., & Berger, P. D. (1996). The impact of direct marketing appeals on charitable marketing effectiveness. *Journal of the Academy of Marketing Science, 24*, 219–231.

*Smith, G. E., & Berger, P. D. (1998). Different message-framing for different direct response marketing goals: Choice versus attitude formation. *Journal of Interactive Marketing, 12*(2), 33–48.

*Smith, G. E., & Wortzel, L. H. (1997). Prior knowledge and the effect of suggested frames of reference in advertising. *Psychology and Marketing, 14*, 121–143.

Smith, S. M., & Levin, I. P. (1996). Need for cognition and choice framing effects. *Journal of Behavioral Decision Making, 9*, 283–290.

*Smith, S. M., & Petty, R. E. (1996). Message framing and persuasion: A message processing analysis. *Personality and Social Psychology Bulletin, 22*, 257–268.

Spangenberg, E. R., & Greenwald, A. G. (1999). Social influence by requesting self-prophesy. *Journal of Consumer Psychology, 8*, 61–69.

Spangenberg, E. R., Sprott, D. E., Grohmann, B., & Smith, R. J. (2003). Mass-communicated prediction requests: Practical application and a cognitive dissonance explanation for self-prophesy. *Journal of Marketing, 67*(3), 47–62.

*Steward, W. T. (2002). Framing messages to maximize support for public policies: Effects of perceived outcome and attitude toward affected group (Doctoral dissertation, Yale University, 2002). *Dissertation Abstracts International, 63* (2002), 1612B (UMI No. AAT-3046231).

*Steward, W. T., Schneider, T. R., Pizarro, J. & Salovey, P. (2003). Need for cognition moderates responses to framed smoking-cessation messages. *Journal of Applied Social Psychology, 33*, 2439–2464.

Stuart, A. E., & Blanton, H. (2003). The effects of message framing on behavioral prevalence assumptions. *European Journal of Social Psychology, 33*, 93–102.

Taylor, S. E. (1991). Asymmetrical effects of positive and negative events: The mobilization-minimization hypothesis. *Psychological Bulletin, 110*, 67–85.

*Thorsteinson, T. J., & Highhouse, S. (2003). Effects of goal framing in job advertisements on organizational attractiveness. *Journal of Applied Social Psychology, 33*, 2393–2412.

*Thorsteinson, T. J., Highhouse, S., & Fay, T. (1999, August). *Effects of message framing in job advertisements on organizational attractiveness.* Paper presented at the conference of the Academy of Management, Chicago, IL.

Treiber, F. A. (1986). A comparison of the positive and negative consequences approaches upon car restraint usage. *Journal of Pediatric Psychology, 11*, 15–24.

*Turner, M. M. (2004, May). *Mood congruence or mood repair? The effect of message framing, mood, and message quality on information seeking regarding genital herpes.* Paper presented at the annual meeting of the International Communication Association, New Orleans, LA.

Tversky, A., & Kahneman, D. (1981). The framing of decisions and the psychology of choice. *Science, 211*, 453–458.

*Tykocinski, O., Higgins, E. T., & Chaiken, S. (1994). Message framing, self-discrepancies, and yielding to persuasive messages: The motivational significance of psychological situations. *Personality and Social Psychology Bulletin, 20*, 107–115.

Umphrey, L. R. (2001). The effects of message framing and message processing on cognitive and behavioral outcomes: An examination of breast self-examination messages (Doctoral dissertation, University of Arizona, 2001). *Dissertation Abstracts International, 62* (2001), 2681B (UMI No. AAT-3016500).

*Umphrey, L. R. (2003). The effects of message framing and message processing on testicular self-examination attitudes and perceived susceptibility. *Communication Research Reports, 20*, 97–105.

*van Assema, P., Martens, M., Ruiter, R., & Brug, J. (2001). Framing of nutrition education messages in persuading consumers of the advantages of a healthy diet. *Journal of Human Nutrition and Dietetics, 14*, 435–442.

Van Den Heuvel, K. (1982). *Teaching strategies in preschool nutrition education.* Unpublished master's thesis, Pennsylvania State University, University Park.

*Vasilias, J. G. (1999). Investigating the effects of message content, source and mode of presentation on AIDS related attitudes and intentions (Doctoral dissertation, Loyola University of Chicago, 1999). *Dissertation Abstracts International, 60* (1999), 877B (UMI No. AAT-9917809).

Wegener, D. T., Petty, R. E., & Klein, D. J. (1994). Effects of mood on high elaboration attitude change: The mediating role of likelihood judgments. *European Journal of Social Psychology, 24*, 25–43.

Weimann, G. (1982). Dealing with bureaucracy: The effectiveness of different persuasive appeals. *Social Psychology Quarterly, 45*, 136–144.

*Wenburg, J. R. (1969). The relationships among audience adaptation, source credibility, and types of message cues (Doctoral dissertation, Michigan State University, 1969). *Dissertation Abstracts International, 30* (1970), 5555A (UMI No. AAC-7009656).

*Wheatley, J. J., & Oshikawa, S. (1970). The relationship between anxiety and positive and negative advertising appeals. *Journal of Marketing Research, 7*, 85–89.

Wicks, R. H. (2005). Message framing and constructing meaning: An emerging paradigm in mass communication research. In P. J. Kalbfleisch (Ed.), *Communication yearbook 29* (pp. 333–361). Mahwah, NJ: Lawrence Erlbaum Associates.

*Wilkin, H. A. (2004, November). *Mixed messages: Implications of combining detection and prevention messages for HPV and cervical cancer.* Paper presented at the annual meeting of the National Communication Association, Chicago, IL.

*Williams, T., Clarke, V., & Borland, R. (2001). Effects of message framing on breast-cancer-related beliefs and behaviors: The role of mediating factors. *Journal of Applied Social Psychology, 31*, 925–950.

Wilson, D. K., Kaplan, R. M., & Schneiderman, L. J. (1987). Framing of decisions and selections of alternatives in health care. *Social Behavior, 2*, 51–59.

Wilson, D. K., Purdon, S. E., & Wallston, K. A. (1988). Compliance to health recommendations: A theoretical overview of message framing. *Health Education Research: Theory and Practice, 3*, 161–171.

Wilson, D. K., Wallston, K. A., & King, J. E. (1990). Effects of contract framing, motivation to quit, and self-efficacy on smoking reduction. *Journal of Applied Psychology, 20*, 531–547.

Yalch, R. F., & Dempsey, M. C. (1978). Selling a city: An experimental study of the communication effects of message tone. *Advances in Consumer Research, 5*, 5–11.

*Yalch, R. F., & MacLachlan, D. (1977). *Persuasive effects of varying an appeal's tone, supporting evidence, and source credibility.* Unpublished paper, University of Washington, Seattle.

*Yates, S. M. (1982). Using prospect theory to create persuasive communications about solar water heaters and insulation (Doctoral dissertation, University of California at Santa Cruz, 1982). *Dissertation Abstracts International, 44* (1983), 2019B (UMI No. AAI-8323465).

*Ying, J. (2001). *The effects of persuasive message strategies on melanoma detection information.* Unpublished master's thesis, University of Auckland, Auckland, New Zealand.

CHAPTER CONTENTS

2 Conversational Topic along a Continuum of Perspectives: Conceptual Issues

NICHOLAS A. PALOMARES
University of California, Davis

JAMES J. BRADAC
University of California, Santa Barbara

KATHY KELLERMANN
Trial Behavior Consulting, Inc., Los Angeles

The literature regarding conversational topic is vast. Conversational topic, however, has various conceptualizations. For example, some studies examine topic changes, whereas others examine the broad subjects about which people talk. Four different perspectives (i.e., topic as a noun phrase, topic as a bounded unit, topic as a perception of language users, and topic as a subject matter of talk), focusing on different conceptions of topic for ostensibly different purposes, emerge across the literature, and, as a result, grasping the literature as a whole is difficult. This chapter highlights each perspective by pointing to the questions already answered and others remaining to be answered. In doing so, within each perspective, we review relevant research, offer critiques and suggestions for future research, and discuss conceptual issues. Spanning the four different perspectives, several general points elucidate commonalities throughout the conversational topic literature. We therefore present our own conceptualization of conversational topic following from our explication of the conceptual issues (such as topical abstractness, globality-locality, prototypicality, and focus) that emerge in light of the four perspectives. Finally, we draw conclusions based on our explication of conversational topic for various areas within the communication discipline.

Topic is one of the most fundamental concepts in the empirical examination of human communication. Topic as a communication concept, in other words, permeates and has utility for a wide variety of areas

---

Correspondence: Nicholas A. Palomares, Department of Communication, One Shields Avenue, University of California, Davis, CA 95616; email: napalomares@ucdavis.edu

Communication Yearbook 30, pp. 45–97

within the communication discipline. Media researchers, for example, focus on the topic (or content[1]) of media messages and how topic determines, in part, the type and extent of media effects. Specifically, agenda-setting research suggests that media sources influence the topics about which individuals are concerned; that is, the topics that the media address affect the topics about which the public thinks and discusses (Dearing & Rogers, 1996). Media research that focuses on television also finds the concept of topic fundamentally important. Extensive content analyses of violence (Wilson et al., 1997) and sex (Farrar, Kunkel, Biely, Eyal, & Donnerstein, 2003) on television focus on the topics of media messages. Farrar et al., for example, examined television's portrayal of sexual topics on primetime programming, including specific topics on sex as well as topics relating to the risks and responsibilities associated with sexual behaviors. Furthermore, media effects research demonstrates that the impact of media on certain outcomes, such as sexual socialization, depends on the specific sexual topics (e.g., talk about risks and responsibility) of television messages (Donnerstein & Smith, 2001; Greenberg & Hofschire, 2000; Malamuth & Impett, 2001).

Work in other areas of human communication also reveals the significance of topic as a core communication concept. For example, the phenomenon of groupthink demonstrates that a group suffering from groupthink self-censors and contains mindguards who squelch adverse opinions and unwanted information on certain topics; restricting talk on certain topics, in other words, contributes to poor decision making (Janis, 1982, 1989; Janis & Mann, 1977). Furthermore, topic is essential to consider when one is delivering a public speech; significant portions of many textbooks on public speaking are devoted to how to select and narrow the topic of a speech (e.g., S. A. Beebe & S. J. Beebe, 2005; McKerrow, Gronbeck, Ehninger, & Monroe, 2002; O'Hair & Stewart, 1998). Topic pervades the field of communication; its investigation is fundamental to the study of human communication and spans several divisions within the field.

Perhaps topic's most significant contribution to the study of communication is in the broad area of interpersonal communication and social interaction, spanning various contexts (Cappella, 1994; Ellis, 1992; McLaughlin, 1984; Ng & Bradac, 1993; Nofsinger, 1990). Topics provide a way to advance, maintain, or disengage personal, family, and work-based relationships (Afifi & Guerrero, 2000; Dailey & Palomares, 2004; Kellermann & Palomares, 2004). Individuals attend to topics and construct their interactions accordingly (G. Brown & Yule, 1983; Button & Casey, 1984; Tracy, 1985). People use topics strategically as a means of control and power by expressing their topical dominance over others in health (Erickson & Rittenberg, 1987) and close relational contexts (Folger & Sillars, 1980). Topics offer a means for friends to enact and embrace their gender identity (Cameron, 1998). Individuals accommodate others via topics (Chen & Cegala, 1994). Individuals use topics as basic building blocks in their cognitive representations of conversation (Kellermann, 1995). The use of topics varies cross-culturally, pointing to topic as a source of intercultural miscommunication (Chen & Cegala, 1994; Hinkel, 1994; Scollon & Wong-Scollon, 1991). In fact, topic-free social interaction *may* be impossible to accomplish; even ritual interaction has an implicit point. Because of topic's significance across various contexts (e.g., health, family, work, intercultural, etc.) in social interaction and interpersonal communication, the current chapter focuses on the role of topic in conversation; that is, we limit our discussion to the concept of *conversational topic* and its role in the broad area of social interaction and interpersonal communication.[2]

Despite the weight that conversational topic has for the study of social interaction and interpersonal communication, a unified, precise definition of the concept remains elusive. As G. Brown and Yule (1983) stated, "the basis for the identification of 'topic' is rarely made explicit. In fact, 'topic' could be described as the most frequently used, unexplained, term in the analysis of discourse" (p. 70). Their observation, made more than two decades ago, still rings true today. Across the literature, conversational topic is defined inconsistently from various conceptual perspectives. As a result, the extant knowledge generated across each perspective is diverse and hard to grasp as a whole. Absent from the literature is an analysis of research on conversational topic that elucidates the various perspectives and the knowledge claims afforded within each perspective. Such an analysis would provocatively highlight the questions on conversational topic already answered and others remaining to be answered. To address this void in the conversational topic literature, we present an analysis of relevant research on conversational topic. Our overarching goal is to bring some meaningful order to the vast number of investigations on conversational topic. Our strategy is to explicate and analyze conversational topic across the literature by highlighting four different perspectives from which examinations of conversational topic have been approached.

CONCEPTUALIZING CONVERSATIONAL TOPIC

Our evaluation of the literature on conversational topic revealed various ways of conceptualizing the concept. There are various continua along which these conceptualizations of conversational topic fall (e.g., psychological-textual, structure-content, etc.). We find merit in each continuum and draw upon all continua in our explication of conversation topic; yet we primarily employ a single continuum (i.e., level of abstraction) for our discussion because, as we subsequently argue, the level of abstraction continuum provides the most parsimonious means of classifying the literature on conversational topic.

The Level of Abstraction Continuum for
Conversational Topic and Its Four Perspectives

Along a continuum of the level of abstraction, four different conceptual perspectives of topic emerge. These perspectives constitute research traditions (Laudan, 1977), in which "objects" are examined from different standpoints. ("Object" is especially apt here because a synonym is "point," which is one of the synonyms for "topic.") The four perspectives vary with regard to their level of abstraction or "size." The first and "smallest" perspective literally views topic as a noun phrase. Bypassing the difficulty with defining topic, the second notion treats topic as a bounded unit, concentrating on a topic's surrounding shifting devices. The third conception (i.e., topic as a perception of language users) focuses on individuals' understanding of topic. This third perspective highlights individuals' abilities to identify, segment, and make judgments about topics, and it situates topics accordingly. Finally, the most abstract perspective holds topic to be the subject matter of talk. This notion is not concerned with the segmentation of topics in conversations, but rather, it treats topics as large categorical entities about which individuals converse.

We refer to the four perspectives ranging in their levels of abstraction as separate categories; yet, important to remember is that the four perspectives fall along a continuum. In other words, fuzzy boundaries exist between the four perspectives, which are not mutually exclusive. The use of one perspective does not preclude the use of another. Rather, research on topic potentially can demonstrate slippage and overlap between perspectives, and we find this opportunity theoretically and methodologically advantageous. (We extend our discussion of this potential in greater detail toward the end of this chapter.) Thus, the four perspectives, falling along a level-of-abstraction continuum, demonstrate a useful and heuristic means of categorizing the conversational topic literature.

In fact, our most basic purpose in this chapter is to critically illuminate the relationships and differences among perspectives and thus inform a large and diverse group of scholars. We aim to demonstrate how research from one perspective can inform the other perspectives by analyzing the perspectives and suggesting avenues for future inquiry on conversational topic. We believe that our comments and suggestions can stimulate novel research and theory construction within and across the four perspectives. In addition, we draw from the four perspectives as a whole to generate a unified, precise conceptualization of conversational topic. In other words, we rely on the four perspectives and their similarities and differences in our explication to suggest a novel conceptualization for conversational topic. We develop a conceptualization of conversational topic that flows directly from our explication of the conceptual issues that surface within and across the four perspectives. In doing so, we bring some unity to the literature and encourage continued interest in investigating those central questions awaiting answers within and across perspectives.

Other Continua for Conversational Topic

As previously mentioned, various continua cut across the conversational topic literature. As such, we could have organized the work on conversational topic along other continua besides the level of abstraction. For example, Goutsos (1997) noted that studies on topic could focus on how people structure topics relative to what people talk about. Studies on topic fluctuate from an emphasis on the form, organization, and construction of topical talk to an emphasis on the substance and content of topical talk (i.e., a structure-content continuum). Bifurcating this distinction, a structural emphasis treats topic as action-based, whereas emphasis on content treats topic as semantic-based. That is, topics are actions interlocutors perform (structure) or subjects in speech (content). Our inspection of the literature also suggests a possible continuum based on the source of emergence for topics (i.e., a psychological focus compared with a textual focus; e.g., van Dijk, 1977, 1980). In other words, topics vary with regard to the extent to which they emanate from people's mental processes or discourse (i.e., a psychological-textual continuum). Polarizing this continuum, topics are a part of one's cognitions or part of speech (or texts) separate from one's cognitions. Another continuum is based on the method of inquiry (cf., Bradac, 1999; Tracy, 1993). The core distinction of this continuum is between quantitative and qualitative methods (e.g., experimental versus conversation analytic methods).

We find these additional continua notable, yet, as categorization frameworks, restricting. The structure-content continuum, for example, is useful for categorizing research examining how people change topics, but it poses limited utility for categorizing research on how topics can facilitate power and control, since both the structure (e.g., Ainsworth-Vaughn, 1992; Erickson & Rittenberg, 1987) *and* the content (e.g., Palmer, 1989) of topics can influence power. On the other hand, the psychological-textual continuum can handle research on topical power and control well because these concepts constitute psychological factors; however, this continuum leaves research on changing topics difficult to categorize because a focus on the person who changes the topic is more psychological, but a focus on the specific linguistic indicators of topic changes is more textual. The qualitative-quantitative methods distinction also is restrictive, given that research on most, if not all, aspects of conversational topic can be examined with different methods (Bradac, 1999).

We considered alternative continua as the categorization scheme for this discussion, ultimately concluding that a topic's level of abstraction was the most parsimonious because it provided an optimal means to capture the vast amount of literature on conversational topic. We do not consider the level of abstraction to be flawless; still, it affords the most advantageous categorization system relative to other potential continua. Nevertheless, even though we employ the level of abstraction to organize our discussion, we do not ignore other continua and the issues they raise. In fact, whenever appropriate throughout our discussion, we highlight points suggested by other continua to demonstrate their significance in the literature. Furthermore, in our closing section, we discuss how the intersections of various continua that traverse the conversational topic literature can stimulate novel and meaningful research.

However, first, we discuss each of the four perspectives in turn along the continuum of level of abstraction. Within each perspective, we review and critique the research on conversational topic, and we discuss conceptual issues that emerge in light of research within that orientation. Our chapter, thus, devotes four major sections to the four perspectives on topic, with each section partitioned into three subsections: definition and summary of research, critiques and suggestions for future research, and conceptual issues. We trust that this format is not unacceptably procrustean and that it will facilitate useful comparisons. In a section toward the end of this chapter, we offer general comments on the topic literature within and across the various continua, our own conceptualization of conversational topic emerging from our assessment of the literature, and a brief discussion of how our explication of conversational topic carries several implications for various areas within the field of communication.

TOPIC AS A NOUN PHRASE

Definition and Summary

This perspective on conversational topic treats topic at a micro level, literally as a noun phrase. Take the following example of two friends standing in front of speaker A's new car:

A: The tires are great. Nice color, too.

B: Anyway, did you get an extended warranty?

A: No. But, I only paid 27,000 dollars and the mileage is great.

According to the topic-as-a-noun-phrase perspective, this short exchange contains seven topics (i.e., noun phrases): (the) tires; nice color; you; (an) extended warranty; I; 27,000 dollars; and (the) mileage. This perspective derives from the grammatical sense of the word (i.e., sentential or sentence topic; see Reinhart, 1981, for a review). Hockett (1958) claimed that sentences contain a topic and a comment, wherein comments offer new information on the topic of each sentence. Therefore, at least in English, topics are usually subjects, whereas comments are usually predicates. For current purposes, conversational topic is literally a noun alone or that which is embedded in a noun phrase but not the topic-comment structure as reviewed elsewhere (Reinhart, 1981; Schlobinski & Schütze-Coburn, 1992). For example, Chen wrote, "Topic, being the basic information unit of discourse . . . , is defined as a noun phrase that refers to a concrete or an abstract entity. . . ." (1996, p. 3). Similar to Schank's (1977) view of topic as pairs of sentences, this notion of topic extends primarily from Prince's (1981) taxonomy of given-new information, which "makes distinctions between five categories of topics, based on the cognitive availability, or familiarity, of the referent with respect to its location (contextual or textual) or logical connection to other topics" (Chen, p. 5). This distinction allows for an examination of the topic's familiarity to interlocutors, its degree of explicitness. Topic consists of a noun phrase referring to any entity (i.e., object, event, person, state, idea, etc.) and the interlocutors' cognitive awareness of the referent.

The limited amount of research that treats conversational topic as a noun phrase focuses mainly on topic management and has demonstrated the importance of relational and individual difference variables. In a series of studies, Chen and associates examined topic management in relation to intercultural communication. In the first study, Chen and Cegala (1994) discovered that more explicit topic development occurred (i.e., noun phrases were made explicit) for mixed native and nonnative speaker (MNNS) dyads, and, therefore, accommodation took place. Furthermore, they found partial support for the claim that Americans in MNNS dyads used more explicit and less implicit topic shifts than Americans in native speaker (NS) dyads, which again indicated accommodation. Thus, lending partial support for communication accommodation theory (Giles, Mulac, Bradac, & Johnson, 1987), Chen and Cegala concluded that "MNNS dyads make a greater effort than NS dyads to accommodate by using topic-management strategies that render information explicitly available" (p. 407). Furthermore, according to Chen's (1995) research, compared with respondents with low interactional involvement, respondents with high interactional involvement empathized more with others and adapted their topic selection to their listeners in intercultural interactions. Examining interactional involvement and topic selection in intercultural and intracultural dyads, this study concluded that interactional involvement was linked to topic selection relative to relational qualities of the interaction (e.g., intercultural versus intracultural). Chen (1996) also examined cognitive complexity, situational influence, and topic selection in intracultural and intercultural interactions. Although this study did not find statistically significant differences in topic selection between individuals high and low in cognitive complexity, significant results emerged when intercultural and intracultural interactions were considered. Specifically, communicators with high cognitive complexity employed fewer situationally evoked topics than communicators who scored low in cognitive complexity during intercultural interactions.

Finally, this body of research highlights differences between social classes in topic management. A study of adolescent discussion groups revealed that some syntactic differences attributable to social class result from different conversational styles (Hemphill, 1989). By referencing previously mentioned topics (i.e., using cross-speaker anaphora), working-class speakers used more cooperative topic management strategies than did middle-class speakers. Research from the perspective of topic as a noun phrase thus suggests how topic management can vary as a function of relational and individual difference variables.

Critique and Future Research

The first critique of literature from this perspective concerns the micro nature of conversational topic. Conceptualizing topic as a noun phrase allows strong operationalization, clear replication, and accurate comparison of results across studies. However, this conceptualization raises some important questions regarding its face validity. Is conversational topic in some sense larger than a noun phrase? Is it possible for individuals to talk about a specific topic but never mention it by name? In the example above, does that conversation about a new car include seven topics (i.e., the seven noun phrases) or simply one (i.e., a new car)? If the latter, how can we know that the topic is a new car if a corresponding noun phrase is not uttered? Thus, conceptualizing topic at a concrete level of abstraction, such as the noun phrase, is problematic because slippage may occur between researchers' technical definition and speakers' intuitive sense of what the topic is. Furthermore, such a micro conception of topic muddies discernment of how and when interlocutors change topics. As in the above example, is each noun phrase a different topic or a reinstantiation of the same topic? What is conceptually and methodologically lost by limiting topic to nominal forms? Future research could attempt to justify the use of the perspective of topic as a noun phrase, perhaps by replicating existing findings by the other three topical perspectives.

A strength of this perspective lies in its explanatory and predictive nature. Most of the topic literature is descriptive in nature. Descriptive research can be usefully heuristic. However, advancing theory with predictions and explanations has additional utility. The literature of the perspective of topic as a noun phrase is theoretical in terms of explanation and prediction, and it does not focus solely on description. For example, research from this orientation has established the importance of relational and individual difference effects in topic management. Future research should continue to examine the antecedents for and consequences of the use of different types of topics (e.g., high versus low familiarity). No *necessary* connection exists between the perspective of topic as a noun phrase and theoretical motivation; it should be useful for the other perspectives to adopt a theoretical focus increasingly, particularly the perspective of topic as a bounded unit.

Conceptual Issues: Noun Phrase versus Topical Focus

We can think of many counterexamples that fail to support the claim that topics are nominal forms or are located solely in noun phrases. Consider the sentence "People shop on a daily basis." "Shop" and "daily" are both stressed in the act of utterance; the former is a verb and the latter, an adverb. Moreover, in many imaginable contexts, these stressed words carry most of the information, as evidenced by rewriting the sentence as "People shop daily." In all but unusual contexts, interactants understand that shoppers are people, so the first word provides little information. However, given "people," many options emerge: People walk, talk, eat, breathe, swim, and so forth, so the word "shop" eliminates these alternatives, reduces uncertainty, and, therefore, provides key information (Babrow, 1992). "Shop" also presents many options: People can shop frantically, furtively, frivolously, and faithfully, or they can shop in malls, grocery stores, their homes, and farmers' markets; again, by eliminating alternatives, "daily" clarifies "shop." A part of the topic of the sentence is clearly "shop," a verb. Some would suggest that the adverb "daily" is a comment on the topic (Hockett, 1958), but this word is highly informative, so by the criterion of informativeness, no basis exists for distinguishing between "shop" and "daily" as candidates for topic. Moreover, one can imagine the topic "shop daily" being extended, as in: "Yes, this is possible only in developed countries, where there is considerable wealth." Many examples of topical verbals can be offered, such as the discourse unit "Could you open something? It's stuffy. Open something?" and the exchange "What did you do?" "I lied." However, something of an illusion occurs in the distinction made between nominal and verbal forms in reference to topic because verbal forms can be nominalized (and vice versa): "People shop daily" becomes "Shopping is done daily." Thus, the existence of topics is not necessarily limited to noun phrases.

Other cases merit consideration. Compare the sentences "John kissed Mary" and "John admired Mary." First, note that each word in each sentence carries information, about agents, patients, or actions. Second, verbs in the two sentences differ; "kiss" is a descriptive action verb, and "admire" is an experiencer state verb. Third, in these cases, the verbs produce different attributions about causality, despite the fact that the sentences are structurally identical: John is the cause of kissing, but Mary is the cause of admiration. That these verbally induced differences in causal attribution participate in a general pattern has prompted considerable investigation and some debate (Corrigan, 2001; Rudolph & Forsterling, 1997). Notably, particular linguistic differences stress a certain *focus* of attention on varying causal agents and, more generally, on different features of the sentences.

Research from other literatures also underscores the importance of individuals' emphasis on certain linguistic aspects relative to others. Many linguistic devices function to direct a hearer's or reader's attention; that is, these devices control or influence the orientation. One of the *linguistic masking devices* of Ng and Bradac's (1993) is labeled *permutation*, which refers to the ordering and re-ordering of words within a sentence for the purpose of controlling attributional prominence. For example, in the sentence "John kissed Mary," "John" is more prominent than in the sentence, "Mary was kissed by John" (Turnbull, 1994). Ng and Bradac hypothesized that attributional prominence increases assignment of responsibility to the entity made positionally prominent. So, in the first sentence, "John" has a high probability of being seen as the causal agent as a result of both permutation and verb type. Turnbull referred more generally to "thematic structure," which denotes any linguistic devices used to convey attributional prominence in a narrative (compare Halliday, 1970). Turnbull suggested that, "compared to nonthematic information, thematic information receives more [cognitive] processing, is more integrated and organized, and, therefore, more accessible [cognitively]" (pp. 134–135). Furthermore, his research offers support for a "thematic structure effect": "judgments of responsibility of thematic as compared to nonthematic targets are more accessible and extreme" (p. 135).

Critical linguists and others also demonstrate the importance of one's focus during comprehension. They have noted that adjectives denoting socially marked categories (e.g., African American, young) should be and typically are adjacent to the noun that they modify in order to maintain or enhance stylistic acceptability (Thomas & Wareing, 1999). For example, "the hasty young man" is better formed than "the young hasty man," and "the hasty African American man" is better than "the African American hasty man." The general principle seems to be: Place important, marked, cognitively salient adjectives adjacent to the words modified. Comparing "the young black man" with "the black young man" suggests that ethnicity is more salient cognitively in this society than is age (Bradac, 2000). "Adjectival adjacency" signals prominence or focus.

Rather than conceptualizing topic as a noun phrase, we think that conceptualizing topic as the *object of focus* is more accurate and useful. Actions (i.e., verbs) can be this object as well as people and things (e.g., nouns). Not infrequently, the object of focus can be a compound of elements, as in "You lied." The focus can expand and contract during a segment of conversation. Many linguistic devices and strategies may establish the object of focus, as highlighted above. Often these strategies co-occur with interactional devices such as "grabbing the floor." So, someone may say as she interrupts her colleague to grab the floor: "The real problem is that you are *distorting* the facts," to which the colleague may respond: "I am not distorting."

TOPIC AS A BOUNDED UNIT

Definition and Summary

The line of research viewing topic as a bounded unit concentrates on the communicative devices that signal the shifting, transitioning, or changing of topics in conversations. This perspective recognizes the difficulty of segmenting topics accurately and consistently in a sense that is larger than the noun phrase or utterance. In fact, some of this research openly acknowledges "that a shift or a shade defines a new topic" (Crow, 1983, p. 155). Furthermore, most of this research holds "that studies of topicality in conversation must not merely pay attention to 'content' but must address matters of 'structure' as well" (Maynard, 1980, p. 284; i.e., the structure-content continuum). When compared with the view of topic as a noun phrase, this perspective would not claim that every noun phrase in a conversation constitutes a topic, but that topics exist between certain segments of a conversation linguistically or paralinguistically signaled by topic-shifting devices. Interactants indicate changes in topical talk by various structures. To refer to the "new car" example above, topics would not change until signaled as such. Therefore (assuming no paralinguistic indicators), three topics (i.e., "the car's aesthetic appeal," "the car's warranty," and "the car's specifications") would be separated by the use of the two discourse markers, "anyway" and "but." Stated differently, this approach comprises a "black-hole" conception of topic: you cannot easily see black holes, but you can infer their existence from forces that they exert. Similarly, researchers from this perspective emphasize the examination of topics via the forces they exert, just as an astrophysicist would investigate a black hole through an analysis of its influence on other objects.

Much of this research is typological by nature; it focuses on beginnings and endings of topics and how conversationalists change topics. One of the first typologies of topic shifts (Maynard, 1980) has its roots in the model of turn-taking developed by Sacks, Schegloff, & Jefferson (1974). As Maynard argued, the basic premise of this classic conversation analytic study is that topics change because of failed speaker transitions. In other words, the turn-taking system provides ways to change topics. Various indicators of topic changes include silences, token responses (e.g., "um"), the ending of a story, "[t]he absence of recipient talk at a transition relevance place" (p. 270; i.e., absent solicits), refocusing, disagreements, and combinations thereof. Maynard provided many illustrative examples from actual conversations, to which readers are referred for more details. According to Maynard, when the turn-taking system "falters" (e.g., no response from a speaker is made), a new topic can be introduced.

Another typology of topic-shifting strategies centers on the beginning of a topic and its relationship to the prior utterance (i.e., coherence or lack thereof). Crow's (1983) typology of topic shifts stems from a corpus of couples' conversations. His categories of topic shifts emphasize the nature of the shift in terms of its relationship to the previous topic. After acknowledging various maintenance devices, which advance topics (see Reichman, 1978), Crow described four types of topic shifts: coherent shift, renewal, noncoherent shift, and insert. A coherent shift includes topic initiation, which involves an attempt to bring up a new topic after speakers close a previous topic, and topic shading, which introduces a new topic by explicitly relating the topic to the current topic. A renewal, or "shift back to an earlier topic after one or more other topics or topic-shifting attempts have intervened" (p. 144), marks the second category of shifts. Third, noncoherent shifts are abrupt shifts unrelated to the current topic. Inserts constitute the last type of shift, resembling noncoherent shifts in terms of abruptness; however, speakers do not advance them. Using this typology of topic shifts in an examination of couples' conversations, Crow found that "the longer the couple has been together the more topic shifts they perform in their conversations" (p. 153). Thus, this typology offers a coding scheme to identify and describe the relational nature of topic shifts, and it illustrates how these shifts occur, and, consequently, section topics in conversations.

In a series of articles, Button and Casey (1984, 1985, 1988/1989) described the mechanisms for generating new topics in conversations via topic-initial elicitors. Within a conversation analytic framework, these studies examined various conversations and detailed diverse ways in which topics can be initiated. Speakers introduce new topics in such a way that they flow from (i.e., they are related to) the previous topic and "are disjunct or segmented from prior topics" (Button & Casey, 1988/1989, p. 62). Again, the general argument is that topics are bounded within diverse indicators that speakers use to initiate topics.

Howe (1991), realizing that much of the topic-changing literature concentrates on topic beginnings, examined topic closings or endings. In her discussion of topic change in conversations, Howe concluded that topic closings are marked by the use of summary assessments, acknowledgment tokens, repetitions, laughter, and pauses. The last three indicators are self-descriptive,

whereas the first two are characterized by specific content or words, or intonation pattern. Furthermore, these topic-ending devices occur before a new
topic begins and can function together to end a topic.

Most of the research viewing topic as a bounded unit is descriptive/typo-
logical in nature. Further examples include a study by Jefferson (1993) that
illustrated how minimal responses, recipient assessments, and recipient com-
mentary signal topic shifts, as well as research by Drew and Holt (1995, 1998)
that demonstrated how figures of speech (e.g., "take it with a pinch of salt")
"occur regularly in topic-transition sequences, and specifically in the turn
where a topic is summarized, thereby initiating the closing of a topic" (1998,
p. 495). A significant amount of other research focuses on an assortment of
indicators (e.g., intonation, emotions) that signal a topic change.[3] Additional
research has examined topic-shifting indicators in languages other than English, such as Greek (Bakker, 1993) and Korean (Song, 1996). In addition to
this descriptive research, which importantly demonstrates that speakers
change topics via highly specialized linguistic and paralinguistic devices,
another body of research uses comparative analyses.

In a comparison of American and Japanese business conversations,
Yamada (1990) showed how cultural differences in the nature of topic-shifting
strategies could possibly lead to stereotype confirmation and miscommunication. Using a conversation analytic framework to study intercultural interactions, Yamada found that "American participants used formulaic talk to
close explicitly and shift topics, whereas the Japanese participants did not
explicitly close topics, but used silence to shift topics instead" (pp. 249–250).
Following a discussion of the different strategies, Yamada argued that stereotypes (e.g., "Americans get the last word" and "Japanese are evasive") may
be reinforced and miscommunication could occur if these different strategies
are used in intercultural interactions. Thus, this study, along with another contrasting Chinese, Korean, Japanese, and American topic introduction patterns
(Scollon & Wong-Scollon, 1991), makes valuable contributions to the topic
literature by pointing to cultural differences in the use of topic-shifting
devices, the introduction of topics, and the interpretation of these differences,
all of which have important consequences.

Additional comparative studies suggest differences in the use of topic-
shifting devices relating to power. Utilizing and adding to Maynard's (1980)
typology, Ainsworth-Vaughn (1992) closely examined 12 physician-patient
encounters. This study, concerned with power differentials, illustrated how
two main types of topic transitions (i.e., reciprocal and unilateral) varied in
conversational dominance. Female physicians employed more reciprocal topic
transitions, which evenly allocate power, whereas male physicians used more
unilateral transitions, which allocated more power to the speaker. A similar
study (Erickson & Rittenberg, 1987) detailed how foreign doctors, who were

accustomed to power asymmetries in physician-patient relationships, prevented patients from bringing up certain topics (e.g., stories that help explain a medical condition) by controlling the topic through devices, such as close-ended questioning and interruptions. Using a comparison technique, these studies underscored the importance of considering group membership and power differentials during the study of conversational topic.

Other studies compared topic-shifting techniques of men and women. First, West and Garcia (1988) revealed that men initiated twice as many topics as women did overall. Furthermore, they determined that no sex differences existed in topic changes when such changes were collaborative (i.e., both interlocutors wished to change the topic) or after an exhausted topic (i.e., no additional talk on the current topic occurred). However, men initiated all unilateral topic changes. Men unilaterally changed topics "in the course of women's turns-in-progress . . . in the midst of ongoing topic development . . . [and] in ways that curtailed such development" (p. 568). Second, using strangers in dyads, McLaughlin et al. (1985) conducted an experiment in which one of the two interactants was instructed to insert a predesignated brag. Among other findings, their study suggested that females used more reciprocal questions and topical control strategies than men, although these results approached statistical significance. Importantly, these studies affirm the importance of examining topic across groups, particularly men and women.

The latter half of the studies in this section advance descriptions of the former half by showing how different factors relate to the use of topic-shifting strategies or devices, which are central to this perspective. Other examples include studies comparing topic-shifting devices between normal individuals and individuals with dementia of the Alzheimer type (Garcia & Joanette, 1997) and acquainted and unacquainted peers (Maynard & Zimmerman, 1984). Again, these studies point to differences in how speakers use topic-shifting strategies.

Critique and Future Research

A strong aspect of this literature is the classification and categorization of topic-transition indicators, which stem from the use of rich, illuminating examples (from the qualitative side of the method continuum). Many linguistic and paralinguistic topic-shifting devices/strategies have been described within this perspective. Furthermore, some of the research using this perspective goes beyond typological studies by comparing the topical use of different groups of people, which is beneficial because comparisons are fundamental to the creation of knowledge (Bradac, 2001; Campbell & Stanley, 1963).

On the other hand, research of this descriptive nature is limiting. For example, most of the studies from the perspective of the topic as a bounded unit, even those studying unique situations such as focus-group discussions (Myers, 1998) and political interviews (Nofsinger, 1988/1989), do not offer comparisons. With this limitation in mind, future research could involve comparative studies that utilize the extant typologies of topic-shifting indicators to examine how these devices can illuminate differences in other factors such as gender, power, intergroup relations, relational intimacy, situation, politeness, etc. More specifically, the following research questions could be addressed: At what level of explicitness do men and women use topic-shifting devices, and what are the antecedents for and consequences of any sex differences? Do particular types of situations yield more explicit topic shifts than do others (say, formal versus informal); if so, why? Does the non-normative use of shifting devices affect impressions of the communicative competence of topic shifters? More broadly, do people view others differently, depending on type of shifting device used? Finally, what mechanisms explain the effects of intimacy and culture on topic shifts?

Although important, studies that compare the uses of shifting devices do not necessarily advance theory. In fact, most of the studies that offer comparisons do not provide theoretical explanations for the observed differences. Thus, the application of current communication theories to the literature on topic as a bounded unit could prove meaningful. For example, employing communication accommodation theory (Giles et al., 1987), future research could examine how convergence and divergence manifest in topic-shifting devices (e.g., perhaps interactants who use divergent dialects in order to reinforce their different group identities are relatively more likely to use topic shifts as a means of control). Applying conversational constraint theory (Kellermann & Park, 2001) to topics in order to explore the appropriateness and efficiency of various topic-shifting tactics and other factors could shed light on the use of these devices and help to advance the theory. No doubt, this perspective includes other potentially valuable and relevant theoretical applications as well.

Finally, an implicit assumption drawn from this literature is that virtually *all* topics are bounded or contain borders that signal the transition between topics; that is, speakers indicate topic shifts in some manner. G. Brown & Yule (1983) argued: "This type of approach to the analysis of discourse is based on the principle that, if we can identify the boundaries of units—where one unit ends and another begins—then we need not have a priori specifications for the content of such units" (p. 95). They contended: "[S]peakers often do not provide such explicit guidelines to help . . . select chunks of discourse for study" (p. 69). Therefore, when using this perspective, scholars must be cognizant of possible difficulties in identifying topic shifts. Quantitatively inclined scholars will likely want to check the reliability of their own or others' coding of topic shifts and indicators. Perhaps more importantly, future research could investigate the accuracy of this assumption in relation to other factors. Topic shifts might not be signaled in certain situations (e.g., those demanding great urgency to change a topic, such as an emergency) compared with other (non-urgent) situations. The level of explicitness of topic-shifting devices may change because of urgency, formality, and other situational dimensions. Such a research agenda will make meaningful contributions to the literature.

Conceptual Issues: Topical Boundaries and Points of View

The bounded-unit perspective and other traditional conceptions of topic, such as topic/comment and global/local, suggest that topics are discrete entities with clear boundaries. This conception is handy for analytic purposes; it allows the investigation of topic maintenance and change, for example. This orientation seems reasonable, to the extent that interactants, indeed, perceive topics categorically in the way that they orient to phonemes of a language. Certainly, some pairs of interactants will immediately agree on "basketball" when asked, "What were you talking about?" (Lin, Harwood, & Bonnesen, 2002). In other cases, however, one interactant may say "basketball" and the other "Shaquille O'Neal," and this reference may indicate more than loose representation. One interactant may have focused on O'Neal, whereas the other may not have even known who O'Neal is. The permeability of topical boundaries makes coordination possible in the following hypothetical example.

A: The playoffs are starting on Saturday.

B: Yeah, the Heat again. They've got Shaq. He can do anything. Just overpowers everyone.

A: I think Sacramento. I grew up there, so maybe I'm biased. The whole team is aggressive.

B: Yeah, like Shaq. He's a fighter. I love his slam-dunk.

A: In the West, it's going to be the Suns, I think, as good as they are. Maybe the Spurs.

B: The Spurs have two very good players, but neither is as good as Shaq. I mean, when it's the Spurs versus the Heat, it's Shaq all the way.

In this example, speaker A may view the topic as talking about "basketball," whereas speaker B may say the topic is "Shaquille O'Neal." Despite this misalignment in the speakers' topical points of view, the conversation is coordinated. Coordination is facilitated by the topical boundaries, which are permeable (i.e., not rigid); this lack of rigidity can endure (i.e., withstand) misalignment. Specific to the example, coordination between speakers A and B occurs because their different viewpoints (on what the topic is) are unproblematic, as the fluidity or permeability of the topical boundaries allows slippage between "O'Neal" and "basketball."

Bradac (2002) supported this argument when briefly conceptualizing *message*:

> The notion of coherence suggests that messages are perceived as units; they are bundles of significance. But the boundaries of these bundles shift or even change drastically as message recipients change perspectives and purposes. For example, a film constitutes a message for many casual viewers, and global judgments of this message are made: "*The Negotiator* was really good." On the other hand, for film students analyzing a film closely, particular scenes will constitute messages, even short scenes: "That visual transition is excellent—it establishes appropriate expectations." A film analyst's significant scene may not even be noticed by the casual viewer. Messages are meaningful units, the boundaries of which vary across occasions, purposes, and recipients. . . . (p. 49)

Topics are not "bundles of significance" (i.e., messages), but they are constituted in these bundles. On the other hand, like messages, a topic may be construed differently by different conversational participants with dissimilar goals, motives, and interests, as in the basketball example. Despite differences in speakers' topic construals, coordination typically occurs. This conversational accomplishment is provocative and interesting. Likely, for whatever reasons, interactants typically assume that remarks are relevant (Grice, 1975). Furthermore, differences in topical orientation will not usually be noticed and will not disrupt the flow of conversation, even when they become clear post facto when the interactants are asked, "What was the topic?" In a sense, they may perpetuate the illusion of topical agreement and adherence. This situation may be a subtle form of miscommunication that does not lead to negative outcomes (Coupland, Giles, & Wiemann, 1991). It reflects the pervasiveness of the assumptions of interactional cooperation and individual coherence (Kellermann & Sleight, 1989); the former assumption (in some form) may even be made by apes (Goody, 1995). We have no idea how frequently this type of subtle misalignment may occur. This hypothesis could be used to probe, perhaps illuminate, various aspects of conversation (e.g., miscommunication, coordination, and coherence), and it could be tested against interactants' perceptions, possibly after they view a videotape of a candidate conversation.

This conceptualization treats topic as a multilayered phenomenon, with slippage between and among the layers. Interactants collaborate to sustain a conversation, even when they have different goals and interests and, therefore, different perspectives and at least somewhat different points of view on what the topic *is*.

TOPIC AS A PERCEPTION OF LANGUAGE USERS

Definition and Summary

The individual language user is central to the third perspective. This perspective on topic extends from the idea that individuals, as users of the language, are equipped to make judgments about topics, just as they are about sentence grammaticality and acceptability (Bradac, Martin, Elliott, & Tardy, 1981). This perspective is based on the assumption that "the analyst is often forced to depend on intuitive notions about where one part of a conversation ends and another begins" (G. Brown & Yule, 1983, p. 69), as well as other judgments about topics such as coherence. This perspective differs from the previous two by focusing not on the language *used*, but on the language *user* (who may be a respondent, a coder, or a researcher) to make judgments about topics, regarding segmentation, coherence, and other factors (i.e., the psychological side of the psychological-textual continuum). Referring to the "new car" example again, this perspective concentrates on the perceptions of language users, who may categorize the exchange as talk about one topic (i.e., "speaker A's new car"). Various models of topic (e.g., G. Brown & Yule, 1983; Goodenough & Weiner, 1978; Goutsos, 1997; Keenan & Schieffelin, 1976; Mentis, 1991, 1994; Svennevig, 1999; van Dijk, 1977, 1980) exist within this perspective. In the following, research supporting the current perspective is discussed. Work within this perspective is then reviewed.

Over a series of studies, Tracy and colleagues (Planalp & Tracy, 1980; Tracy, 1982, 1983, 1984a, 1984b; Tracy & Moran, 1983; see Tracy, 1985, for a review) examined topical coherence, which is a part of successful topic management. The study by Planalp and Tracy demonstrated that naïve subjects can reliably identify topic changes in conversations, and it supported the basic assumption that individual language users can make decisions about topics. Across all of their studies, Tracy and associates concluded that individuals have a global perception of topic rather than a micro or local sense of topic.

Much of Tracy's research is based on the hierarchical structure of conversations termed issue-event (see Reichman, 1978), in which "an issue is an abstract principle, a generalization, what we typically think of as the main point . . . [and] the event is an episode, a concrete example of the more abstract issue" (Tracy, 1985, pp. 40–41). The issue focuses on a global topic, and the event (i.e., local topic) is a specific advancement of the global topic. Using this idea and concerned with coherent topic maintenance, Tracy (1982) found that people tend to identify the issue as the topic. Tracy (1983) also discovered that issue extensions (i.e., a subsequent remark on the global topic) were viewed as more competent than event extensions (i.e., a subsequent remark on the local topic). Thus, support exists for the contention that certain advancements of topics (i.e., those that extend a macro topic rather than a micro topic) are preferred over others. Subsequent studies (Tracy, 1984a, 1984b; Tracy & Moran, 1983) showed that individuals responded to utterance pairs either maintaining a global topic or relating a new topic to a global topic rather than to a local topic. Investigations from other lines of research (Palmer & Badzinski, 1986; Cegala et al., 1989) revealed that people were able to agree on the shifting and segmentation of specific topics in conversations at the global level. Thus, support abounds for the current perspective on conversational topic, namely, that individuals as users of the language can make judgments about topics. Furthermore, this research affirms that communicators prefer to maintain topic continuity or conversational coherence at a global level, which is an issue discussed and examined by others as well (e.g., Bublitz, 1989; Bublitz, Lenk, & Ventola, 1997; Craig & Tracy, 1983; Orletti, 1989; Tannen, 1990a, 1990b).

Another group of investigations indicated how individuals actively and strategically orient toward topic. In a discussion of topic progression, Bergmann (1990) contended that speakers are concerned with the context or present situation, a notion that he dubbed "local sensitivity." This paper argued that individuals employ the environment or current situation (via talking about it) to influence the progression of topics. Similarly, Foppa (1990) reasoned that language users behave intentionally, and, therefore, an examination of topic must be concerned with individual intentions. Specifically, "any deviation from or violation of the principle of neutral coherence may be taken as an indication of the existence of certain strategic, interactive or 'what for' intentions on the part of the violator" (p. 198). Öhlschlegel and Piontkowski (1997) drew on this concern in a study of topic progression and social categorization. They found that individuals violated neutral coherence toward the outgroup members when intergroup categorization was highly salient. This study demonstrates that individuals strategically used topic progression when building and maintaining intergroup and intragroup relationships. Furthermore, Folger and Sillars (1980) found that interactants perceived topic changes as dominant, and Palmer (1989) concluded that the more a speaker directed a conversation away from the current topic, the more the speaker was perceived to be dominating the conversation. Overall, these studies highlight how interactants actively utilize topic strategically, which has significant consequences for social dominance and power.

Another body of research, viewing topic as a perception of language users, takes a developmental slant on conversational topic. This research can be partitioned into two major areas. First, the development of topic management strategies in children has been explored. Not surprisingly, the general finding of this research is that children learn topic management skills as they develop. A number of studies detail the specifics of this developmental trend.[4] Some noteworthy findings include the following: the number of topic changes in children's conversations decreases with age (e.g., Brinton & Willbrand, 1980); mothers assist children in learning topic management skills (e.g., Wanska & Bedrosian, 1985), and children initially talk about the here and now but acquire the ability to talk about the past, future, and fantasy over time (e.g., Marvin, 1994; Moerk, 1975). The second area, dealing with developmental issues, emphasizes mental disabilities that result in topic-based speech pathologies.[5] This research generally compares typical individuals with mentally disabled individuals to shed light on the learning of topic-management skills and to determine ways of providing effective therapy in order to improve these skills. These two areas of research significantly contribute to the literature by directing attention to the processes by which users of the language gain knowledge of and utilize topic.

Overall, research from this perspective highlights the language user. That is, this perspective examines language users' understanding of topic and conceptualizes topic accordingly.

Critique and Future Research

Notably, this research has established that naïve individuals have a common general understanding of topic, which includes a global view of topics, when topic changes occur, how to maintain coherence, etc. In fact, some of the models even lay out a representation of how individuals use and understand topic. This emphasis on the language user is distinct from any other perspective in that the others (for the most part) ignore issues centering on the language user. Hence, this perspective concentrates largely on the psychological side of the psychological-textual continuum, relative to research in other perspectives. Despite the psychological focus, many of the assumptions of this research depend heavily on researchers' notions of topic and not on how individuals *actually* understand "topic" in everyday discourse. Researchers' assumptions are implicitly conveyed in items on researcher-designed measures, for example. Thus, future research could elucidate individuals' intuitive notion of topic more so from the language user's viewpoint relative to the researcher's point of view. A goal of this kind of research might be to formulate a "lay theory" of topic, based on data reflecting naïve respondents' implicit knowledge. Lay theories describe the concepts and structures that people use to understand a particular phenomenon, such as electricity (D. Gentner & D. R. Gentner, 1983), intelligence (Sternberg, Conway, Ketron, & Bernstein, 1981), and loneliness (Lunt, 1991). Various methods can be used to construct lay theories, but a common approach initially uses open-ended questions about the phenomenon of interest and then, on the basis of these responses, creates more structured tasks that yield data amenable to multidimensional scaling, for example (Cole & Bradac, 1996). Using such a procedure, researchers may examine what people believe about the nature of topics, the basis for segmenting topics, and so forth.

Furthermore, a portion of the research within this user-perception perspective explores how individuals strategically use topic. Although an important step, much more can be learned within this realm. Do individuals use topic manipulation for purposes other than achieving conversational dominance, and, if so, how (see Kellermann & Palomares, 2004)? For example, how do individuals use topic for communicative goals, such as compliance gaining, relational escalation (and de-escalation), information seeking, comforting, etc.? How does topical use vary as a function of one's communicative goal(s)? Does the strategic use of topics facilitate the achievement of certain goals more than it does for others, and, if so, how, why, and what characteristics inherent to the goals explain this phenomenon? Examining the various ways in which individuals utilize topic with various goals would be advantageous. Not coincidentally, this observation leads to the next section.

Conceptual Issues: Global versus Local Topics

A few more things can be said about the communicative uses of topical globality. The global-local distinction is clear to speakers in everyday contexts, as suggested above. In 2002, a friend of one of the authors was talking about Al Gore's presidential viability and then began to comment at some length about his shaved beard. At some point, she realized that she had been talking about his beard for quite a while (too long, by her judgment) and signaled a shift back to the global topic, saying "Anyway. . . ." This kind of lay understanding of the global-local distinction is codified in the phrase "going off on a tangent." Many stock expressions indicate speakers' primary orientation to global topics: "Getting back to the point . . . ," "We're getting off track," "What's that got to do with anything?", "Stick to the point," and so on. Protracted deviations from globality violate a pragmatic rule—specifically, Grice's (1975) relevance maxim. Indeed, adherence to the global issue is what Grice appears to mean by "relevance."

Globality and locality of topics can be used by speakers in performing perlocutionary acts. An often used device of comedy writers is having one character talk about global topic A, often sexual, and a second character talk about global topic B, normally innocuous, in a situation where neither character realizes that two different topics are being discussed. The result is that local things said regarding global topic B take on a double meaning, and one of these meanings is unintended by and unknown to the speaker discoursing about B, who often appears foolish—a situation of *double entendre*. In real life, two speakers may initially raise different global topics, but typically, confusion will soon arise and will be dispelled quickly as the speakers coordinate their local efforts. A person who pursues global topic B, while others are talking about global topic A, may be labeled stereotypically as senile or "crazy" if the behavior is perceived as unintentional or may be judged to be "clowning around" if the behavior appears intentional—the "madness or badness" attributional syndrome (Watzlawick, Beavin, & Jackson, 1967). The stereotypical attribution of senility or absentmindedness also may be produced by a speaker's frequent and lengthy extensions of local topics without regard to the global topic (Ruscher & Hurley, 2000).

In some situations, a speaker may be asked a local topical question about global topic A and may be reluctant to address this local topic. A paradigm case constitutes a press conference where a reporter asks the secretary of defense or presidential press secretary a question about a military operation that is in progress. Here, the speaker has five options: to remain silent, to state that he or she will not answer the question, to answer the question directly and truthfully, to give a direct answer which is a lie, or to evade the question.

The first option (i.e., silence) will not satisfy most questioners. Some politicians frequently use the second option (i.e., refusal). This option can be used by a speaker with legitimate authority who has the *right* not to answer; accordingly, it may produce or reinforce an impression of power (Ng & Bradac, 1993). Answering the question truthfully, the third option, may be disadvantageous; if there is no disadvantage attached, the speaker has no reason not to be truthful. The fourth option (lying) may be risky if the question is posed unambiguously and the truth is likely to surface. Evasion, the final option, may be a good choice if some conditions are met. Evasion occurs when a speaker is asked a question about local topic A, subsumed by global topic Z, and s/he responds with an utterance that corresponds to a different local topic B *yet maintains* the global topic Z. To be effective, an evasive utterance must *not* be perceived by hearers as irrelevant to local topic A or global topic Z, and, furthermore, it must be a defensible response when the truth surfaces subsequently. Both of these requirements may be met in various ways, such as through the use of strategic ambiguity (Eisenberg, 1998, 2001); one plausible but topically irrelevant meaning can be favored by the speaker presentationally, and later the speaker can claim to have intended the second meaning, which corresponds more closely to the surfacing truth. This move has been labeled "devious evasion" (Bradac, Friedman, & Giles, 1986; Ng & Bradac, 1993). Speakers accomplish devious evasion in a number of ways, including responding to a local topical question, "Will we win the war?" about a global "war" topic with a diversionary local topical response that maintains the global topic "the war": "We've made several substantial incursions. I won't map them out for you for obvious reasons, but I can tell you that we are moving in a northern province and the terrain there is very challenging, as you know." In this case, the local topic in the question, "winning the war," was diverted by maintaining the global topic "the war" through statements about other local topics (e.g., "strategic war movements," "war terrain"). From our perspective, this kind of response occurs frequently in military briefings and political interviews (compare Galazinski, 2000).

This globality-locality tactic also may be used to delay the development of an uncomfortable topic in a friendship context. Research on equivocal communication (Bavelas, Black, Chovil, & Mullett, 1990a, 1990b) holds that certain communicative contexts create a conflict situation wherein people face telling either a hurtful truth or a punishable lie. Because people are averse to both of these options, communicators do not alter *what* is said (i.e., the truthfulness of their response), but rather "*how* it is said, that is, whether it is clear or equivocal" (Bavelas et al., 1990b, p. 137). We offer a different explanation for the phenomena examined by Bavelas and colleagues based on the current conceptualization of conversational topic; that is, "equivocal" messages are *not* alterations of clarity—they deviate from the local topic, while maintaining the global topic. In other words, when faced with telling a hurtful truth or a punishable lie, communicators do not necessarily respond equivocally (i.e., ambiguously); people simply change local topics while maintaining the global topic. An increase in response clarity is not *always* the solution.

An actual example taken from research by Bavelas and associates (1990b) best illustrates the topical globality-locality explanation for utterances in conflict (i.e., avoidance-avoidance) communicative situations. When participants who hated a particular theatrical play were asked, "How did you like the performance?" by someone who had a vested interest in the play, which created a situation "where both true and false messages were problematic" (p. 155), participants responded by uttering statements such as, "You'll probably go to a better showing that I did" (p. 157). An utterance of this kind is *not* necessarily ambiguous or unclear (i.e., equivocal); rather, the message *is* clear and unambiguous (i.e., not equivocal), while maintaining honesty. Alternatively, based on our conceptualization of topic, the response extends from a new local topic (i.e., "going to a different showing of the play") while maintaining the global topic (i.e., "the play/performance") *and* ignoring the local topic (i.e., "enjoyment of the play/performance"), both of which were invoked in the question (i.e., "How did you like the performance?"). That is, the person answering the question advances a different local topic, while sustaining the global topic, yet sidestepping the local topic and avoiding telling a hurtful truth or a punishable lie. Research on news interviews also supports this explanation (e.g., Heritage & Greatbatch, 1991; Nofsinger, 1988/1989). Despite a news interviewer's question on a specific local topic, an interviewee can choose to advance a different local topic while maintaining the global topic. According to Nofsinger, discussion of the global topic is maintained, while the interviewer and interviewee vie over what the local topic(s) should be.

TOPIC AS A SUBJECT MATTER OF TALK

Definition and Summary

The perspective that views topic as a subject matter of talk maintains that people's talk can be sorted into various categories. This perspective assumes that people talk about certain things or subjects, and it does not focus on accurately and reliably segmenting topics in specific conversations, as some other perspectives do. This view does not center on how people maintain conversational coherence, how people change topics, or how topic management occurs. This perspective on conversational topic is primarily concerned with topic as the content, subject matter, issues, foci, or ideas on which individuals converse (i.e., the content side of the structure-content continuum). Stated differently, this perspective values classifying the topics that people discuss (and do not discuss), the antecedents for and consequences of talking (and not talking) about certain topics, how these broad topics occur in conversations, and similar issues.

Relating this perspective to the "new car" example, this view of topic would not be concerned with a speaker using a topic-shifting device to change the topic from talking about "the car's warranty" to talking about "the car's specification." Furthermore, this perspective would not include the emergence of seven or three topics or how people change the topic to maintain coherence. Rather, scholars holding this view would claim that no topic change occurred in the conversation and that "cars" or, more abstractly, "transportation," not "the tires," "the car's warranty," or "speaker A's new car" count as topics. Thus, the perspective of topic as a subject matter of talk treats a topic as a relatively large categorical entity about which people talk (and do not talk).

In a program of research (for a review, see Kellermann, 1995) examining what strangers talk about during initial interactions, Kellermann and associates (Kellermann, 1991; Kellermann, Broetzmann, Lim, & Kitao, 1989; Kellermann & Lim, 1989, 1990) argued that conversational behavior is both routine and flexible. They contended that interactants cognitively represent topics as scenes in memory; conversational partners organize topics (or scenes) within a larger cognitive structure called a conversation memory organization packet (MOP). Within a conversation MOP, speakers cognitively organize conversational behavior such that a set of prescriptions emerges for how conversations flow. Pertinent to the topic literature, Kellermann et al. (1989) found that a conversation MOP exists for initial interactions. Therefore, Kellermann (1995) asserted: "Individual scenes (topics) are weakly ordered, but . . . groups of scenes (topics) are strongly ordered. In other words, at any particular point in time, multiple scenes (topics) are likely, although the nature of the scenes that are appropriate at different points in time in the conversation varies" (p. 188). Thus, topics occur regularly and in a loosely ordered pattern during interaction between strangers, as influenced by the initial interaction MOP. Furthermore, Kellermann (1995) asserted that a universal scene exists for any given topic, such that talk on most topics (e.g., hometowns, religion, etc.) follows a similar pattern: (a) get facts, (b) discuss facts, (c) evaluate, (d) explain, (e) discuss goals/intentions, and (f) discuss enabling conditions for goals/intentions. That is, talk on any given topic follows the same loosely ordered pattern. This line of research has shown that cognitive frameworks or MOPs loosely determine when and what to talk about with strangers and how to talk about any specific topic.

Another line of research within this perspective deals with taboo topics or topic avoidance (i.e., topics that are not to be discussed) in close relationships. One of the first examinations of topic avoidance (Baxter & Wilmot, 1985) found that 97% of participants avoided talking about at least one topic (i.e., the relationship's current/future status, extra-relationship activities, relationship norms, prior relationships, conflict-inducing topics, and negative information) with their relational partners. Further research has confirmed and advanced these findings (e.g., Guerrero & Afifi, 1995a, 1995b). Moreover, related research has examined the reasons for and the consequences of avoiding topics in close relationships.[6] Roloff and Johnson (2001) also pursued the antecedents for and consequences of reintroducing taboo topics, finding, among other results, that "topics can be reintroduced when the original conditions leading to their banishment are no longer relevant" (p. 46), and yet other research has investigated the consequences of employing various topic avoidance strategies in different relational types (Dailey & Palomares, 2004). Additional studies investigated disclosures (i.e., revealing information on specific topics) in close relationships (e.g., Aries & Johnson, 1983; Baxter & Widenmann, 1993; Petronio & Martin, 1986). For example, Petronio and Martin probed gender differences in the anticipation of positive and negative ramifications of disclosures on four different topics (i.e., parental, achievement, sexual, and global) and discovered that men expected more negative ramification for disclosures on achievement than women. In general, these investigations point to the importance of examining what topics are not discussed and the ramifications of not talking (and talking) about taboo or sensitive topics.

Research within the perspective of topic as subject matter of talk has reached the overall conclusion that men and women tend to talk about different things. Specifically, this body of literature pursues what men and women converse about when talking with others (usually friends). In a review and meta-analysis of the gender topic literature from 1922 to 1990 (i.e., Bischoping, 1993; Carlson, Cook, & Stromberg, 1936; Kipers, 1987; Landis, 1927; Landis & Burtt, 1924; Meil, 1984, as cited in Bischoping, 1993; Moore, 1922; Sleeper, 1930, as cited in Bischoping, 1993; Stoke & West, 1930; Watson, Breed, & Posman, 1948), which included her 1990 replication of Moore's 1922 study, Bischoping concluded that women and men, consistently, but to varying degrees, have talked about different topics since the 1920s. Women discuss the opposite sex and appearances more than men do, whereas men converse about work and money more than women do. The following two investigations, although similar to the previous set in their interests, used different techniques. First, Haas and Sherman (1982) asked male and female respondents about the frequency of various topics they discuss with diverse types of individuals. Again, this study revealed gender differences. Women's talk focused more on family, relationship problems, men, health, pregnancy and menstruation, food, things they have read, movies, television, clothing, and rape than men's talk. Men, on the other hand, talked more about women, sex, money, news, sports, hunting, and fishing than women. Martin's (1997) investigation of conversations with same-sex and cross-sex friends found similar results. In this study, participants were asked to identify conversations taking place between male friends, female friends, or cross-sex friends and to indicate what features of the conversation influenced their conclusions. Martin discovered that respondents were better than expected by chance at accurately distinguishing the conversations, with the topic of talk as the most common indicator of dyadic sex composition. Specifically, men most frequently discussed sports, women, fighting, and other topics, while women talked most about relationships, men, clothing/changing clothes, and other topics. Consistency across these and other studies[7] suggests that differences between men and women exist in topical talk.

Along similar lines, researchers have examined disparities in topical talk among various cultures. Haviland (1977) cataloged topics of casual conversations among Zinacantan Indians in southern Mexico. The majority of the topics pertained to social matters, whereas less frequent topics included sexual activities, divorce, child support, drunkenness, kin disputes, violence, murder, quarreling, and nicknames as well as nonsocial topics such as work, wealth, and religion. Hinkel (1994) examined topical appropriateness in cross-cultural conversations. Comparison of judgments of topical appropriateness of Chinese, Japanese, Korean, Indonesian, Arabic, and American speakers highlighted cultural differences. Specifically, the topics of age, money, life in the United States, recreation, weather, travel, self, and residence were perceived to be inappropriate to discuss by non-Americans. These studies point to cultural differences in what people talk about and what they perceive as appropriate to discuss.

Critique and Future Research

Taken as a whole, these analyses within the perspective of topic as a subject matter of talk exhibit various important features. First, topics relate to each other, such that during informal initial interactions, discussion of specific topics at particular moments in conversations is not erratic. Certain topics are more likely to appear than others, and these topics surface in a loosely organized fashion. Future research could expand on this notion by examining the interconnectedness or relatedness of various topics in an attempt to understand the ways in which conversations typically progress. Studies could take a network analysis (Monge & Contractor, 2003; Wasserman & Faust, 1994) standpoint on topics to examine topical networks. In conversations, are transitions between more related topics, such as sports and weather, more common than transitions between less related topics, such as sports and religion? Do speakers judge changes from one topic to another as more appropriate or acceptable than other topic changes (see Parker, 1980)? What topics constitute the most central nodes in topical networks of various relational types, and why (see Jefferson, 1984)? How does the relational type of a dyadic conversation influence topical networks? Answering these and other questions would shed light on the ways in which conversations flow from certain topics to others in foreseeable ways via topical networks. A final suggestion combines the bounded-unit perspective to the subject-matter perspective: Do interactants signal topic changes more explicitly between relatively unrelated topics (e.g., changing from travel to persons known in common to personal faults) than changes between more related topics (e.g., changing topics from education to long-term goals/intentions to occupation)? Answering these and other related questions could be useful for understanding how conversation is concomitantly dynamic, flexible, and predictable (see Kellermann, 1995).

Second, research within this perspective has shown that speakers do not discuss all topics equally. The motives for people not talking about certain topics and how to bring such topics back on the table in intimate relationships have been studied and shown to be important. Future research could investigate these findings further by examining the topics that interactants avoid in different types of relationships (e.g., brother-sister, grandchild-grandparent, employee-employer, student-instructor, etc.). The consequences of and antecedents for such variation also could be explored. The reverse also could be studied: what topics are *most* likely to be discussed in various types of relationships? Do people talk about different things, depending on their conversational partner; do such distinctions lead to variance in relationship development and decline (see Kellermann & Palomares, 2004; Lin et al., 2002)? Investigating topic avoidance strategies and their effectiveness in various relationships as well as the impact of topic avoidance strategies on relational development will shed more light on the dynamics of topic avoidance (see Dailey & Palomares, 2004).

Finally, this literature demonstrates variations between men and women in their topical use. Although this is important, more can be explored. For example, why do gender-based topical differences exist, and what role does gender identity play (Cameron, 1998)? Are some topics considered more appropriate for one gender than for the other, and why? Do men and women avoid different topics and for what reason(s)? Why and how does talk on certain topics, relative to others, increase the extent to which gender is salient for individuals (e.g., Palomares, 2004; Postmes & Spears, 2002)? What consequences emerge when people converse on certain topics in mixed-sex compared with same-sex interactions, and why? Future research could also investigate interaction effects with sex, intimacy of relationship, formality of situation, relational goals, etc.

A few problems also exist within this perspective. First, this "largest" view is perhaps the most experimental (i.e., nonqualitative). Thus, despite significant contributions, an overriding concern with the literature using this macro notion of topic stems from its generalization of specific conversations into broad propositions and claims. Should research about such an idiosyncratic phenomenon (i.e., conversation) be unconcerned with its various idiosyncrasies? More specifically, what theoretically meaningful information is gained and lost in the process of topical abstraction? Although important to note, this discussion is more appropriate for metatheoretical deliberations (see, for example, Berger, 1977; Bradac, 1999; Bradac & Giles, 2004; Cushman, 1977; Delia, 1977; Monge, 1977). A second problem involves finding appropriate labels for topics, which reflects a deeper problem of deciding what level of abstraction to use for the categorization of topics (see Kellermann & Palomares, 2004). Comparisons between studies will be impossible if one researcher's "social activity" topic includes conversations at work, whereas the same category for another researcher does not. If a researcher conducts a cluster analysis or some related technique to group specific topics into higher order constructs (as do Kellermann & Palomares, 2004, and Lin et al., 2002), it becomes important for other researchers attempting a replication to define the constructs with reference to the same topics or to have a good reason for not doing so. An indefinitely large number of topics can emerge, depending on topical categorization. For example, concerning talk about Sophia's pet cockatiel, should the topic be labeled as a very concrete topic, such as a pet cockatiel named Freddy whom Sophia loves, or as something progressively more abstract, such as Freddy the cockatiel, cockatiels, birds, pets, animals, creatures, or things that make people happy? What level of abstraction, in other words, is most appropriate for the labeling of a particular topic? Finding labels for topics is a considerable problem that must be addressed accordingly. Kellermann and Palomares, in their examination of participants' recollections of 500 conversations from various relational types (e.g., parent-child, co-workers, doctor-patient), generated a list of 90 topics (based primarily on participant-generated topical labels at a midlevel of abstraction) that could be utilized in future research. Third, this perspective does not easily allow for an examination of topic management (as it privileges content over structure) because it overlooks the action-based processes surrounding topics. Despite some underlying concerns, this perspective adds much to the literature by examining the *substance* of conversation—the "what" of interpersonal communication—which may be what most people mean by "topic" in the everyday lexicon.

Conceptual Issues: Topical Abstractness, Categories, and Fuzzy Sets

The preceding discussion indicates that researchers working within the subject-matter perspective have operated at a high level of abstraction compared with, say, researchers within the bounded-unit perspective. Yet, the former investigators, at least, have not discussed the implications of this fact. Abstractness is not an easy concept, but it has largely been taken for granted in research on conversational topic. Notably, the level of abstraction is relative, such that compared with "bird," "chicken" is concrete, but compared with "free-range hen," "chicken" is abstract. So, "chicken" cannot be categorized simply in terms of an absolute level of abstractness;[8] it depends on the particular conversation, the surrounding verbal context. Even apart from the relativistic effect of verbal context, a given concept participates in a hierarchy of related concepts with an indefinitely large number of members: animal/two-legged animal, with feathers/fur, male/female, large-beaked/small-beaked, dirty/clean, and so forth. Also, although quantitative techniques exist for grouping empirically derived topics into higher-order units (e.g., cluster analysis), the attributes that characterize and differentiate the units must be specified through the use of other statistical techniques, such as multidimensional scaling. Thus, the abstractness concept as usually conceived is problematic—a dimension with an unknowable number of unstable levels, with intervals of varying sizes.

Despite these problems, abstractness has been a useful variable in some areas of research, such as research on "intergroup linguistic bias." Semin and

Fiedler's linguistic category model (1988; Arcuri, Maass, & Portelli, 1993; Cole & Leets, 1998; Maass, Salvi, Arcuri, & Semin, 1989) distinguishes among descriptive action verbs ("He hit John"), interpretative action verbs ("He hurt John"), state verbs ("He hates John"), and adjectives ("He is hurtful"). As one moves from descriptive action verbs through adjectives, the state of affairs depicted becomes more abstract and less bound to a particular time and place. So, abstractness here varies inversely with the extent of temporal and spatial connection. People are more likely to use abstract forms when speaking about negative behaviors of outgroup members and to use concrete forms when speaking about positive outgroup behaviors. The converse is true for discourse about ingroup behaviors (Cole & Leets, 1998; Maass, et al., 1989). In short, interactants tend to indicate the fleeting nature of negative ingroup behavior and the enduring quality of positive ingroup behavior, while suggesting the fleeting character of positive outgroup behavior and the enduring aspect of negative outgroup behavior.

Nominal forms can also participate in the process described by the linguistic category model. Ng and Bradac (1993) offer the concept of *linguistic masking devices*, three of which pertain here: truncation, nominalization, and generalization. Regarding truncation, a speaker may use agent deletion: "Jim hit John" versus "John was hit." The latter utterance is more abstract because of its relative inclusiveness: Anyone may have hit John. From another perspective, it omits potentially important details. Similarly, by the transformation of adverbial phrases into noun phrases, significant information can be deleted: "I will hit John" versus "Hitting will occur." Generalization resembles categorical abstraction as discussed above: "People are aggressive toward John" versus "I am likely to hit John." The language variable *verbal immediacy* is also pertinent here (Bradac, Bowers, & Courtright, 1979; Wiener & Mehrabian, 1967); the utterance "I really like your hat" is less immediate than "I really like you." In this case, the more immediate utterance also is more abstract, as a result of its nonselectivity—"you" includes many unspecified attributes, not just a hat.

Verbal immediacy, linguistic masking devices, and the linguistic category model assume that abstraction can be operationalized with reference to *specific* linguistic criteria and within *specific* domains (e.g., times and places; Bradac et al., 1979; Ng & Bradac, 1993; Semin & Fiedler, 1988). Perhaps topical abstraction can be examined along these lines rather than the line of a simple hierarchy of categories, discussed above, which differentiates categories without reference to specific criteria. Importantly, these three areas of language research suggest that abstractness can be manipulated by speakers to produce effects (although often speakers remain unaware of their use of high or low immediacy, state verbs, nominalization, and so forth). If the topic is "our romance," for example, one partner could say, "I really like you," and the other could respond, "I really like my times with you too." This response could be an attempt to achieve a relational de-escalation or nonadvancement goal on the part of the second speaker. Thus, topical abstractness can be conceptualized as the extent to which a label for a topic is removed from the immediate situational and contextual utterance (i.e., the distance a topical label is from an utterance). Arguably, the topical label "our romance" is less removed from the statement "I really like you" than from the statement "I really like my times with you too." On the other hand, the topical label "our times together" is more removed from the first statement than the second. Topical abstractness is conversationally specific; a topical label for one conversation may be more or less abstract relative to another conversation.

In a discussion of topical abstractness, the notion of "category" arises because speakers invoke a hierarchy of discrete classes, the members of which are increasingly inclusive as one ascends the structure. This kind of hierarchy works very well in taxonomic sciences such as botany or zoology, where clear criteria for categorical membership are specified, but in everyday life, the classification of objects is much less tidy. There is evidence that people typically do not think categorically; instead, they spontaneously, naïvely, and variously group objects (that are commonsensically related) into fuzzy sets on the basis of prototypicality (Aitchison, 1994).

A fuzzy set has indefinite boundaries, organized according to degree of prototypicality, with prototypical members at the center and other members dispersed increasingly toward the periphery as prototypicality decreases. Despite between-person variability, some cultural consensus exists on prototypicality (Rosch, 1978), such that for many Americans, apples and bananas are at the center of the set containing fruits, whereas mangoes are less central, as are guavas, and kiwi fruit; breadfruit, tomatoes, and cucumbers typically would be highly peripheralized. Increasing prototypicality should be associated with an increasing number of consensual responses to the question, "What is the first fruit that comes to mind?"; decreasing recognition time (i.e., decreasing response latency) in a word-recognition task; higher likelihood of nodal activation in a semantic network; and so forth.

Modeling "topic" from our theoretical standpoint of prototypicality, rather than categorical classification, might be stimulating and useful. Communicators may view conversational remarks in terms of their *degree* of adherence to the global topic and the *extent* to which topically local remarks advance global topical progress. Indeed, this orientation seems likely. Some remarks may adhere closely to the prototypical topic, say the opening of the baseball season: "I'm not sure of the exact date, but it's early in April" or "I wonder if there will be a lot of homers again this year." Some may seem coherent, but relatively peripheral: "Yeah, this time of year always makes me think of spring flowers." Others may be highly peripheral: "I always like hotdogs." Still others may fall outside the set: "What time do you have?" or

"Cute baby." Situational contingencies explain some remarks that fall outside the set; these remarks may be seen as introducing appropriate side issues and, we hypothesize, often will be less noticeable and will be perceived as less deviant than highly peripheral remarks within the set. Generally, as peripherality increases, remarks may be recognized as increasingly deviant, and if these remarks are made frequently by the same speaker across situations, hearer attributions of speaker communicative incompetence may occur. Tolerance for and noticeability of peripherality may vary with hearers and situations. Courtroom trials and charged negotiations likely require a narrow latitude of acceptance for peripherality.

Remarks close to the prototypical topic will be transparent, that is, they will not be noticed by an interaction partner; the necessity to explicitly signal such prototypical topic changes will be minimal. At some point, as remarks deviate from the prototype, they will become noticeable or opaque (i.e., explicitly signaled); they will be taken as a sign of deviance. This kind of pattern, where interactants may not notice behavior close to a model or norm but negatively evaluate large normative departures, is a familiar one in other domains of communication, such as linguistic complexity (Bradac, Desmond, & Murdock, 1977) and the negativity effect (Kellermann, 1989). We expect, however, that remarks far from prototypicality will be more or less explicitly signaled, depending on the constraints (e.g., appropriateness and efficiency) that guide changes in topic (Kellermann & Park, 2001).

COMMENTS AND CAVEATS

Recognizing (with optimism nevertheless) that most "formal attempts to identify topics are doomed to failure" (G. Brown & Yule, 1983, p. 68), the preceding discussion focused on an explication of conversational topic viewed along a continuum of perspectives (based on the level of abstraction). In this section, we detail comparisons across the four perspectives, examine the intersections among the various continua that cut across the literature, synthesize the conceptual issues that we discussed throughout the chapter to suggest our own conceptualization of conversational topic, and, finally, draw on our explication of conversational topic to inform a wider range of research about implications for the empirical examination of human communication.

Cross-Perspective Comparisons

Each perspective on conversational topic has merit; each poses unique advantages and disadvantages, some of which already have been discussed. The goals and purposes of future researchers should determine the perspective taken, not any inherent superiority of one perspective over another. As mentioned at the outset of this chapter, the four perspectives are not intended to represent mutually exclusive categories. Rather, fuzzy boundaries exist between perspectives, and research does not necessarily reside solely within one perspective at any particular point along the level of abstraction continuum. In other words, a study could approach conversational topic from multiple perspectives. We find this multiperspective approach conceptually and methodologically profitable. Rather than confining research to a single perspective, future research might usefully bridge or combine perspectives on conversational topic, which might yield more powerful tests of hypotheses through conceptual and methodological triangulation. Such triangulation could be used advantageously in attempts to replicate previous findings.

Indeed, some research already discussed in this chapter utilizes two or more perspectives to varying degrees. For example, Kellermann's (1995) work on the conversation MOP arguably could embrace the language-user perspective as well as the subject-matter perspective. Research within the bounded-unit perspective (i.e., Boden & Bielby, 1986; de Beaugrande, 1992) explores how topic changes occur through talk on the subject-matter topics of historical life events and emotion. These examples and others highlight one perspective while concomitantly drawing on another. Fusions of multiple perspectives typically occur at an implicit level. Future research can benefit from an explicit, thoughtful integration of perspectives because results that transcend the idiosyncrasies necessarily confounded with any single perspective are *ipso facto* more robust than perspective-bound results and because integration could produce arresting hybrids.

Each perspective imposes distinct modes of concept operationalization in research, which engenders distinct issues and problems. Each perspective has special strengths and weaknesses, so in empirical research, multiple conceptualizations and operationalizations used within and across studies to test a given hypothesis or to explore a conversational pattern are highly desirable. We have already suggested several cross-perspective blends. For example, how do language users perceive different types of topic-shifting devices? Are topical transitions between related subject matters signaled less directly than transitions between unrelated subject matters? Do language users consider noun phrases topics, or are noun phrases too specific? Using multiple perspectives in examinations of conversational topic will cast a brighter light on the concept, as each perspective targets particular types of questions (cf., Bradac, 1999; Tracy, 1993).

Cross-Continuum Intersections

Just as cross-perspective hybrids engender utility for the understanding of topic, so do the intersections among the various continua. We relied heavily on the level of abstraction continuum for our synthesis of the conversational topic literature; yet, the other continua (e.g., structure-content) maintain significance. In particular, intersections between the various continua provide novel and interesting ways of exploring aspects of conversational topic and related phenomena.

Special insights, for instance, surface at the intersection of the level of abstraction and the structure-content continua. Research focusing on language users' perceptions has demonstrated topic's significance across the structure-content continuum; users of the language attend to both the content *and* structure of topics. Conversationalists assert power via *how* they construct topical talk (e.g., Folger & Sillars, 1980), as well as *what* they choose to talk about (e.g., Erickson & Rittenberg, 1987). Although arguably less apparent, examining topic within the noun-phrase, bounded-unit, and user-perception perspectives can reveal topic's integral role in the structure (i.e., management) and content (i.e., substance) of conversation. For example, the subject-matter perspective, characterized by an abstract, molar approach to topic, has largely ignored details of discourse structure and processes; yet we have suggested how this perspective could be used to probe topical structure and management in novel and exciting ways (e.g., *how* do interactants switch and chain abstract subject-matters unobtrusively to gain control and exert influence?). At the intersection of the abstraction and structure-content continua, links between the molecular bounded-unit perspective and the molar subject-matter perspective also emerge in productive, harmonious ways; the occurrence of certain topic-shifting devices may depend on the content of what is being said. These illustrations reveal the utility of considering the intersection of the structure-content and the level of abstraction continua; at any given level of abstraction, topic can be examined with regard to content *and* structure.

Other continua cut across the level of abstraction continuum. For example, research with a qualitative focus has shown that conversational topic can be used strategically at various levels of abstraction; simultaneously, research with a quantitative focus has accomplished the same. That is, the intersection of the quantitative-qualitative continuum with the abstraction continuum has illuminated novel pieces of the puzzle. Notably, to an extent, methodological emphasis and level of abstraction have been confounded. The "micro" noun-phrase perspective and the "macro" subject-matter perspective have been associated mainly with a quantitative social scientific method, whereas the "middle range" bounded-unit perspective has been associated with a qualitative conversation analytic method. Uniquely, the language-user perspective has drawn from both types of methods. This confounding has not been driven by conceptual factors, but rather, it has been based on convenience (e.g., ease of operationalization), on accident, and perhaps on the special (and limiting) training of the researchers. As we suggested above, future work should be goal driven, based on meaningful research questions and hypotheses, rather than on reflexively (i.e., instinctively) chosen methods. Furthermore, the full spectrum of the intersection of these two continua warrants investigation.

Our discussion of the various cross-continuum intersections is not exhaustive. Other intersections are possible between the level of abstraction continuum and other continua. Moreover, the level of abstraction continuum need not be included in cross-continuum intersections; for example, research could be approached at the intersection of the structure-content and psychological-textual continua. We find examining topic at the crossroads of the various continua advantageous.

An Emerging Conceptualization

We have implied our own conceptualization of conversational topic throughout the chapter, which serves as an alternative to the conceptualizations inherent in the four perspectives, yet capitalizes on many of the conceptual issues emerging within and across the four perspectives. Summarizing across our explication of topic, a conversational topic is the interactive object of focus, whether viewed by interaction participants or researchers, which can be abstracted at different levels and advanced globally or locally to varying degrees of prototypicality and overlap, across interactants and observers with unique points of view as a result of dissimilar goals, attitudes, and interests. This definition is spawned from the conceptual issues that emerged across the perspectives discussed throughout the chapter. We drew from the diverse literature on conversational topic, which approaches the concept from various perspectives, to present a novel conceptualization for conversational topic.

This definition is a relatively fluid and dynamic conceptualization, which suggests new research questions. Most obviously, can researchers and lay respondents identify shifts in the object of focus—established by permutation, verb type, adjectival adjacency, and other prominence-controlling linguistic features? How do these objects differ from or relate to topics identified as noun phrases and subject matters, particularly? What demonstrable advantages do we gain in viewing topic as a shifting object of focus—say, advantages in predicting relationship type from topic (as do Kellermann & Palomares, 2004, from a subject-matter perspective)? If large-scale topic shifts are, indeed, linguistically signaled (Ainsworth-Vaughn, 1992; Maynard, 1980), are the relatively subtle and ductile topical gradations suggested by our conceptualization indicated similarly or differently? Lay respondents perceive global to local shifts (and vice versa) conceived as dichotomous variables (Tracy, 1985); if globality and localization are viewed as continuous variables (e.g., as members of a fuzzy set), do interactants perceive finer gradations? Are other types of topical gradations perceived? If the dynamic and fluid gradations suggested by our conceptualization are signaled and if lay respondents actually perceive these gradations, do they have interactional and evaluative consequences? If the answer to some concrete version of these sequential questions is "yes," our conceptualization may well merit further development.

Implications

At the start of our discussion, we maintained the significance of topic as a broad communication concept; we argued that topic is fundamental to empirical examinations of human communication because it spans many divisions in the field. We end our discussion by briefly considering some potential ways in which the research, issues, perspectives, and conceptualization offered on *conversational topic* have implications for various subdisciplines in the field of communication.

Implications for social interaction across interpersonal contexts. Conversational topic is important to social interaction and interpersonal communication across several communicative contexts. A major aspect of conversational topic involves its facilitation of power for interlocutors. Talking and not talking on particular topics provide individuals with ways to maintain, gain, subvert, and negate power in a wide range of communicative contexts. For example, in professional settings, talking about specialized topics in ways that lead to attributions of high intelligence and expertise could generate power for a speaker. Also, compared with using a relatively indirect and polite topic avoidance strategy (e.g., displaying physical affection or complimenting), a child who frequenty uses a direct and rude strategy (e.g., threatening or being offensive) to avoid a topic abruptly when talking with a parent in a familial interaction likely will impact their relative levels of power (cf. Dailey & Palomares, 2004). In health contexts, studies that we reviewed (e.g., Ainsworth-Vaughn, 1992; Erickson & Rittenberg, 1987) revealed how medical doctors demonstrate power over patients by controlling the topic and directing the conversation. In political contexts (e.g., debates), perhaps power is asserted through topical talk in both the structure and content of topics. In fact, research has demonstrated that presidential candidates, over the latter half of the twentieth century, who talked about policy topics more than personal character topics relative to their opponents were more likely to win elections (W. L. Benoit, 2003). In a wide range of communicative contexts, topic plays a key role in power relations among conversationalists.

Conversational topic also affects various communicative contexts in that communicators' cognitive representations of their interactions with others rely on topics. Kellermann's (1995) conversation MOP work, which established that people use topics as basic building blocks in their cognitive representations of initial interactions with strangers, focused on a restricted form of interaction; yet topics likely play a role in the cognitive representations of other forms of interaction. Individuals process, store, recall, and report conversations at a topical level rather than at an utterance level (Brinton & Fujiki, 1989; Daly, Bell, Glenn, & Lawrence, 1985; Housel, 1985; Koriat, Goldsmith, & Pansky, 2000; Stafford, Waldron, & Infield, 1989). In fact, even after a significant delay, people can remember the content of their conversations at relatively high levels of accuracy when recalling at a topical level, but not at an utterance level (P. J. Benoit & W. L. Benoit, 1988, 1994; W. L. Benoit & P. J. Benoit, 1990; Hjelmquist, 1984; Hjelmquist & Gidlund, 1985; Murphy & Shapiro, 1994). We expect that people maintain topical level information as scenes in MOPs that organize topical talk in their interactions with others across various communicative contexts (cf. Kellermann & Palomares, 2004). These cognitive structures, in other words, facilitate the structure and content of topics in conversation so that people can perform interaction routines, fulfill communicative functions, and achieve their goals. The cognitive representation of topics in MOPs, for example, corresponds to actual topical talk when people get to know each other during an initial interaction (Kellermann, 1995). Conceivably, the cognitive organization of topics also corresponds to the progression of topics in other contexts, such as when people seek help from doctors in health contexts or comfort a friend or family member. These topically based cognitive representations may even determine the topics people talk about and when and how they talk about them in various communicative contexts.

Implications for other areas of communication. Not only can the issues we presented on conversational topic inform work within the area of interpersonal communication and social interaction, but these issues could be transported into other areas of communication to inform the broader concept of topic. Public speaking might consider the potential for misalignment of the speaker's point of view on what the topic is relative to the audience's point of view. The global-local topic distinction might provide novel insights for the delivery of a speech. For example, do the judgments that an audience makes regarding a speaker or the effectiveness of a speech depend on the extent to which local topical advancements are peripheral (i.e., deviant from the topical prototype)? Media research using content analysis could explicitly contemplate the level of abstraction that is most appropriate for topic. A content analysis with a specific interest in sex, for example, may wish to distinguish between various sexual topics at a relatively concrete level of abstraction (e.g., Farrar et al., 2003). Other content analyses of the media, on the other hand, might be concerned with topics that require a higher level of abstraction. Zhao and Gantz's (2003) content analysis of fictional television programs, for example, used a relatively abstract topical distinction of work versus social topics, as that level was most appropriate for their research purposes. A consideration and justification of the level at which topics are abstracted will benefit content analysis research. Media effects research also may find utility in issues such as the topical prototypicality of media messages. Perhaps media effects are greater when messages are more prototypical as opposed to peripheral. Moreover, the extent of a particular media effect might depend on the media consumer's point of view on the topic of a media message. Research on group decision making could take into account the various sifting devices used to gain control and power in a group, as well as whether group members value certain statements on a particular issue, depending on the topical prototypicality of the statements. Group leaders, for example, could be more effective when their topical advancements are closer to the topical prototype relative to peripheral topical progressions. In their use of the broader concept of topic, these and other areas within the communication field may profit from a consideration of the conceptual issues pertaining to conversational topic.

Pragmatic implications across communicative contexts. The conceptual issues surrounding conversational topic have practical implications for communicators. The relationship between topic and power suggests pragmatic ways in which speakers can use topics to acquire power, particularly when they do not readily have access to such power. Patients in health contexts, for example, can be more actively involved in their health care once they become aware of the ways in which doctors may control the topic, thereby implicitly exerting power over patients. By recognizing the ways in which doctors direct conversations to particular topics, patients can refocus the conversation onto topics about which they are most concerned. Students in pedagogical contexts could profit as well. Students might receive higher accolades from instructors when their comments are topically prototypical as opposed to peripheral. Perhaps teaching effectiveness depends on whether the topical points of view of students and instructors overlap; as topical overlap increases, so does teaching effectiveness. Additional pragmatic implications emerge when conversational topic is considered.

CONCLUSION

Throughout the literature, scholars have approached conceptual discussions of conversational topic with both negative and positive sentiments. Ellis (1992), for example, stated that "it is probably impossible to be precise about the nature of topicality, or to assume that we can formally specify the relationship between texts and topics, but the concept still has strong explanatory value" (p. 119). Our primary purpose of this chapter was to demonstrate that, although conceptual integration is an arduous task, conversational topic is not immune to it. That is, we intended to bring some meaningful order to the relevant literature in our explication and analysis of conversational topic by highlighting four different perspectives from which scholars examine this area. We hope that our comments and suggestions stimulate novel research and theory construction across the four perspectives on conversational topic and other areas in the field of communication that draw on the broader concept of topic.

ACKNOWLEDGMENTS

A prior version of this chapter was presented at the International Communication Association Conference in Seoul, South Korea, July 2002. Keren Eyal deserves gratitude for her comments on a portion of the chapter.

NOTES

1. Media research typically uses the term *content* to refer to what media messages are about (i.e., the content of media messages). A synonym of *content*, however, is *topic*; both terms broadly refer to what a message (i.e., communication) is about. Thus, media research does not always explicitly refer to topic; yet researchers implicitly use the term *topic* when referring to the content of media messages. That is, media researchers' explicit focus on the content of media messages implies a focus on the topic of these messages (i.e., what messages are about).

2. Henceforth, the terms *conversational topic* and *topic* are used interchangeably unless otherwise specified.

3. These indicators include redundancies (Marlin & Barron, 1972); intonation patterns (G. Brown & Yule, 1983; Holdgrafer & Campbell, 1986; Schaffer, 1984); returns to a prior topic (Sirois & Dorval, 1988); shared historical life events, time periods, and social experiences (Boden & Bielby, 1986); emotions (de Beaugrande, 1992); topic initiation in Usenet newsgroups (Gruber, 1995), and topic asides or side sequences (Grimes, 1982).

4. See Bedrosian (1985), Bloom, Rocissano, & Hood (1976), Brinton & Fujiki (1984), Brinton & Willbrand (1980), Dawson (1937), Flannagan, Baker-Ward, & Graham (1995), Foster (1981, 1986), French, Lucariello, Seidman, & Nelson (1985), Garvey (1977, 1984), Kavanaugh, Whittington, & Cerbone (1983), Keenan and Schieffelin (1976), Kertoy & Vetter (1995), Lucariello (1990), Marvin (1994), Marvin, Beukelman, Brockhaus, & Kast (1994), McShane (1990), Moerk (1975), Mulcahy (1973), Raffaelli & Duckett (1989), Schober-Peterson & Johnson (1989), Wanska & Bedrosian (1985, 1986), and Wanska, Bedrosian, & Pohlman (1986).

5. See Adams & Bishop (1989), Bedrosian (1993), Bedrosian & Willis (1987), Brinton & Fujiki (1989, 1993), Brinton, Fujiki, & Powell (1997), Fey (1986), Fox, Sohlberg, & Fried-Oken (2001), Kuder & Bryen (1993), Mentis (1991, 1994), Mentis, Briggs-Whittaker, & Gramigna (1995), and Ridley, Radford, & Mahon (2002).

6. See Afifi & Burgoon (1998), Afifi & Guerrero (1998, 2000), Baxter & Wilmot (1985), Caughlin & Afifi (2004), Caughlin & Golish (2002), Dailey & Palomares (2004), Golish (2000),

Golish & Caughlin (2002), Goodwin & Lee (1994), Guerrero & Afifi (1995a, 1995b), Roloff & Ifert (1998, 2000), Sargent (2002), Vangelisti (1994), and Vangelisti & Caughlin (1997).

7. See Chambliss & Feeny (1992), Clark (1998), Dunbar, Duncan, & Marriott (1997), Haas (1979), Klein (1971), Komarovsky (1967), Langer (1970a, 1970b), Levin & Arluke (1985), Samter, Burleson, Kunkel, & Werking (1994), and Stuart, Vanderhoof, & Beukelman (1993).

8. R. Brown (1978) refers to the basic object level to indicate a degree of abstraction where the object in question is at the highest level it can be while still being visualizable. A "fruit" cannot be visualized, whereas a "banana" can be. This level may be a kind of absolute anchor point. As one departs from this point, going upward, abstraction increases ("organic thing"); with downward departure, abstraction decreases ("brown banana"). Perhaps a rigorous way to quantify abstraction would be to score a concept at the basic object level 0 and give one point for each particularizing attribute: brown banana = 1, fuzzy brown banana = 2, limp fuzzy brown banana = 3, and so forth; the higher the score, the less abstract the object. However, this metric works only for downward departures from the basic object level—if banana = 0, what is the score of "organic thing"? Is it -2 or -10? Moreover, even for downward scoring, things become absurd in the realm of actual sentences. How does one score "The duck who swam in the deep pond ate fat worms"? The depth of the pond and the size of the worms have some connection to the duck, but not the same kind of connection as swimming and eating.

REFERENCES

Adams, C., & Bishop, D. V. M. (1989). Conversational characteristics of children with semantic-pragmatic disorders. I. Exchange structure, turn taking, repairs and cohesion. *British Journal of Disorders of Communication, 24*, 211–239.

Afifi, W. A., & Burgoon, J. K. (1998). "We never talk about that:" A comparison of cross-sex friendships and dating relationships on uncertainty and topic avoidance. *Personal Relationships, 5*, 255–272.

Afifi, W. A., & Guerrero, L. K. (1998). Some things are better left unsaid. II. Topic avoidance in friendships. *Communication Quarterly, 46*, 231–249.

Afifi, W. A., & Guerrero, L. K. (2000). Motivations underlying topic avoidance in close relationships. In S. Petronio (Ed.), *Balancing the secrets of private disclosures* (pp. 165–179). Mahwah, NJ: Lawrence Erlbaum Associates.

Ainsworth-Vaughn, N. (1992). Topic-transitions in physician-patient interviews: Power, gender, and discourse change. *Language in Society, 21*, 409–426.

Aitchison, J. (1994). *Words in the mind: An introduction to the mental lexicon* (2nd ed.). Oxford, England: Blackwell.

Arcuri, L., Maass, A., & Portelli, G. (1993). Linguistic intergroup bias and implicit attributions. *British Journal of Social Psychology, 32*, 277–285.

Aries, E., & Johnson, F. (1983). Close friendship in adulthood: Conversational content between same-sex friends. *Sex Roles, 9*, 1183–1195.

Babrow, A. S. (1992). Communication and problematic integration: Understanding diverging probability and value, ambiguity, ambivalence, and impossibility. *Communication Theory, 2*, 95–130.

Bakker, E. J. (1993). Boundaries, topics, and the structure of discourse: An investigation of the ancient Greek particle Dé. *Studies in Language, 17*, 275–311.

Bavelas, J. B., Black, A., Chovil, N., & Mullett, J. (1990a). *Equivocal communication.* Thousand Oaks, CA: Sage.

Bavelas, J. B., Black, A., Chovil, N., & Mullett, J. (1990b). Truths, lies, and equivocations: The effects of conflicting goals on discourse. *Journal of Language and Social Psychology, 9,* 135–161.

Baxter, L., & Wilmot, W. W. (1985). Taboo topics in close relationships. *Journal of Social and Personal Relationships, 2,* 253–296.

Baxter, L. A., & Widenmann, S. (1993). Revealing and not revealing the status of romantic relationships to social networks. *Journal of Social and Personal Relationships, 10,* 321–337.

Bedrosian, J. L. (1985). An approch to developing conversational competence. In D. N. Ripich & F. M. Spinelli (Eds.), *Social discourse problems* (pp. 231–255). San Diego, CA: College Hill.

Bedrosian, J. L. (1993). Making minds meet: Assessment of conversational topic in adults with mild to moderate mental retardation. *Topics in Language Disorders, 13,* 36–46.

Bedrosian, J. L., & Willis, T. L. (1987). Effects of treatment on topic performance of a school-age child. *Language, Speech, and Hearing Services in Schools, 18,* 158–167.

Beebe, S. A., & Beebe, S. J. (2005). *Public speaking handbook.* Boston: Allyn & Bacon.

Benoit, P. J., & Benoit, W. L. (1988). Conversational memory employing cued and free recall. *Central States Speech Journal, 39,* 18–27.

Benoit, P. J., & Benoit, W. L. (1994). Anticipated future interaction and conversational memory using participants and observers. *Communication Quarterly, 42,* 274–287.

Benoit, W. L. (2003). Topic of presidential campaign discourse and election outcome. *Western Journal of Communication, 67,* 97–112.

Benoit, W. L., & Benoit, P. J. (1990). Memory for conversational behavior. *The Southern Communication Journal, 56,* 24–34.

Berger, C. R. (1977). The covering law perspective as a theoretical basis for the study of human communication. *Communication Quarterly, 25,* 7–18.

Bergmann, J. R. (1990). On the local sensitivity of conversation. In I. Marková & K. Foppa (Eds.), *The dynamics of dialogue* (pp. 201–226). New York: Harvester Wheatsheaf.

Bischoping, K. (1993). Gender differences in conversation topics, 1922–1990. *Sex Roles, 28,* 1–18.

Bloom, L., Rocissano, L., & Hood, L. (1976). Adult-child discourse: Developmental interaction between information processing and linguistic knowledge. *Cognitive Psychology, 8,* 521–552.

Boden, D., & Bielby, D. D. (1986). The way it was: Topical organization in elderly conversation. *Language and Communication, 6,* 73–89.

Bradac, J. J. (1999). Language-sub(1 . . . n) and social interaction-sub(1 . . . n): Nature abhors uniformity. *Research on Language and Social Interaction, 32,* 11–20.

Bradac, J. J. (2000). Much ado about power, and rightly so! *Journal of Language and Social Psychology, 19,* 499–507.

Bradac, J. J. (2001). Theory comparison: Uncertainty reduction, problematic integration, uncertainty management, and other curious constructs. *Journal of Communication, 51*, 456–476.

Bradac, J. J. (2002). Extending the domain of speech evaluation: Message judgments. In P. Glenn, C. LeBaron, & J. Mandelbaum (Eds.), *Studies in language and social interaction: In honor of Robert Hopper* (pp. 45–56). Mahwah, NJ: Lawrence Erlbaum Associates.

Bradac, J. J., Bowers, J. W., & Courtright, J. A. (1979). Three language variables in communication research: Intensity, immediacy, and diversity. *Human Communication Research, 5*, 257–269.

Bradac, J. J., Desmond, R. J., & Murdock, J. I. (1977). Diversity and density: Lexically determined evaluative and informational consequences of linguistic complexity. *Communication Monographs, 44*, 273–283.

Bradac, J. J., Friedman, E., & Giles, H. (1986). A social approach to propositional communication: Speakers lie to hearers. In G. McGregor (Ed.), *Language for hearers* (pp. 127–152). Oxford, England: Pergamon.

Bradac, J. J., & Giles, H. (2004). Language and social psychology: Conceptual niceties, complexities, curiosities, monstrosities, and how it all works. In K. Fitch & R. A. Sanders (Eds.), *Handbook of language and social interaction* (pp. 201–230). Mahwah, NJ: Lawrence Erlbaum Associates.

Bradac, J. J., Martin, L. W., Elliot, N. D., & Tardy, C. H. (1981). On the neglected side of linguistic science: Multivariate studies of sentence judgment. *Linguistics, 18*, 967–995.

Brinton, B., & Fujiki, M. (1984). Development of topic manipulation skills in discourse. *Journal of Speech and Hearing Research, 27*, 350–358.

Brinton, B., & Fujiki, M. (1989). *Conversational management with language-impaired children: Pragmatic assessment and intervention.* Rockville, MD: Aspen.

Brinton, B., & Fujiki, M. (1993). Communication skills and community integration in adults with mild to moderate retardation. *Topics in Language Disorders, 13*, 9–19.

Brinton, B., Fujiki, M., & Powell, J. M. (1997). The ability of children with language impairment to manipulate topic in a structures task. *Language, Speech, and Hearing Services in Schools, 28*, 3–11.

Brinton, B., & Willbrand, M. L. (1980). Pragmatic and syntactic aspects of topic change in child-child discourse. In R. S. Haller (Ed.), *Papers from the 1979 Mid-America Linguistic Conference* (pp. 52–61). Lincoln: University of Nebraska–Lincoln.

Brown, G., & Yule, G. (1983). *Discourse analysis.* Cambridge, England: Cambridge University Press.

Brown, R. (1978). A new paradigm of reference. In G. A. Miller & E. Lenneberg (Eds.), *Psychology and biology of language and thought: Essays in honor of Eric Lenneberg* (pp. 151–166). New York: Academic.

Bublitz, W. (1989). Topical coherence in spoken discourse. *Studia Anglica Posnaniensia, 22*, 31–51.

Bublitz, W., Lenk, U., & Ventola, E. (Eds.). (1997). *Coherence in spoken and written discourse.* Philadelphia: John Benjamins.

Button, G., & Casey, N. (1984). Generating topic: The use of topic initial elicitors. In J. M. Atkinson & J. Heritage (Eds.), *Structures of social action: Studies in conversation analysis* (pp. 167–190). Cambridge, England: Cambridge University Press.

Button, G., & Casey, N. (1985). Topic nomination and topic pursuit. *Human Studies, 8,* 3–55.

Button, G., & Casey, N. (1988/1989). Topic initiation: Business-at-hand. *Research on Language and Social Interaction, 22,* 61–92.

Cameron, D. (1998). Performing gender identity: Young men's talk and the construction of heterosexual masculinity. In J. Coates (Ed.), *Language and gender: A reader* (pp. 270–284). Oxford, England: Blackwell.

Campbell, D. T., & Stanley, J. C. (1963). *Experimental and quasi-experimental designs for research.* Chicago: Rand McNally.

Cappella, J. N. (1994). The management of conversational interaction in adults and infants. In M. L. Knapp & G. R. Miller (Eds.), *Handbook of interpersonal communication* (2nd ed.) (pp. 380–418). Thousand Oaks, CA: Sage.

Carlson, J. S., Cook, S. W., & Stromberg, E. L. (1936). Sex differences in conversation. *Journal of Applied Psychology, 20,* 727–735.

Caughlin, J., & Afifi, T. D. (2004). When is topic avoidance unsatisfying? Examining moderators of the association between avoidance and dissatisfaction. *Human Communication Research, 30,* 479–513.

Caughlin, J. P., & Golish, T. D. (2002). An analysis of the association between topic avoidance and dissatisfaction: Comparing perceptual and interpersonal explanations. *Communication Monographs, 69,* 275–295.

Cegala, D. J., Dewhurst, M., Galanes, G. J., Burggraf, C., Thorpe, J. M., Keyton, J., et al. (1989). A study of participants' judgments of topic change during conversation: Global versus local definitions. *Communication Reports, 2,* 62–71.

Chambliss, C. A., & Feeny, N. (1992). Effects of sex of subject, sex of interrupter, and topics of conversation on the perceptions of interruptions. *Perceptual and Motor Skills, 75,* 1235–1241.

Chen, L. (1995). Interaction involvement and patterns of topical talk: A comparison of intercultural and intracultural dyads. *International Journal of Intercultural Relations, 19,* 463–482.

Chen, L. (1996). Cognitive complexity, situational influences, and topic selection in intracultural and intercultural dyadic interactions. *Communication Reports, 9,* 1–12.

Chen, L., & Cegala, D. (1994). Topic management, shared knowledge, and accommodation: A study of communication adaptability. *Research on Language and Social Interaction, 27,* 389–417.

Clark, R. A. (1998). A comparison of topics and objectives in a cross section of young men's and women's everyday conversations. In D. J. Canary & K. Dindia (Eds.), *Sex differences and similarities in communication: Critical essays and empirical investigations of sex and gender in interaction* (pp. 303–319). Mahwah, NJ: Lawrence Erlbaum Associates.

Cole, T., & Bradac, J. J. (1996). A lay theory of relational satisfaction with best friends. *Journal of Social & Personal Relationships, 13,* 57–83.

Cole, T., & Leets, L. (1998). Linguistic masking devices and intergroup behavior: Further evidence of an intergroup linguistic bias. *Journal of Language and Social Psychology, 17,* 348–371.

Corrigan, R. (2001). Implicit causality in language: Event participants and their interactions. *Journal of Language and Social Psychology, 20,* 285–320.

Coupland, N., Giles, H., & Wiemann, J. M. (Eds.). (1991). *"Miscommunication" and problematic talk.* Thousand Oaks, CA: Sage.

Craig, R. T., & Tracy, K. (Eds.). (1983). *Conversational coherence.* Beverly Hills, CA: Sage.

Crow, B. K. (1983). Topic shifts in couples' conversations. In R. T. Craig & K. Tracy (Eds.), *Conversational coherence* (pp. 136–156). Beverly Hills, CA: Sage.

Cushman, D. P. (1977). The rules perspective as a theoretical basis for the study of human communication. *Communication Quarterly, 25,* 30–45.

Dailey, R. M., & Palomares, N. A. (2004). Strategic topic avoidance: An investigation of topic avoidance frequency, strategies used, and relational correlates. *Communication Monographs, 71,* 471–496.

Daly, J. A., Bell, R. A., Glenn, P. J., & Lawrence, S. (1985). Conceptualizing conversational complexity. *Human Communication Research, 12,* 30–53.

Dearing, J. W., & Rogers, E. M. (1996). *Agenda-setting.* Thousand Oaks, CA: Sage.

Dawson, M. A. (1937). Children's preferences for conversational topics. *The Elementary School Journal, 37,* 429–437.

de Beaugrande, R. (1992). Topicality and emotion in the economy and agenda of discourse. *Linguistics, 30,* 243–265.

Delia, J. G. (1977). Alternative perspective for the study of human communication: Critique and response. *Communication Quarterly, 25,* 46–62.

Donnerstein, E., & Smith, S. (2001). Sex in the media. In D. G. Singer & J. L. Singer (Eds.), *Handbook of children and the media* (pp. 289–307). Thousand Oaks, CA: Sage.

Drew, P., & Holt, E. (1995). Idiomatic expressions and their role in the organization of topic transition in conversation. In M. Everaert, E. van der Linden, A. Schenk, & R. Schreuder (Eds.), *Idioms: Structural and psychological perspectives* (pp. 117–132). Hillsdale, NJ: Lawrence Erlbaum Associates.

Drew, P., & Holt, E. (1998). Figures of speech: Figurative expressions and the management of topic transition in conversation. *Language in Society, 27,* 495–522.

Dunbar, R. I., Duncan, N. D. C., & Marriott, A. (1997). Human conversational behavior. *Human Nature, 8,* 231–246.

Eisenberg, E. M. (1998). Flirting with meaning. *Journal of Language and Social Psychology, 17,* 97–108.

Eisenberg, E. M. (2001). Building a mystery: Toward a new theory of communication and identity. *Journal of Communication, 51,* 534–552.

Ellis, D. G. (1992). *From language to communication.* Hillsdale, NJ: Lawrence Erlbaum Associates.

Erickson, F., & Rittenberg, W. (1987). Topic control and person control: A thorny problem for foreign physicians in interaction with American patients. *Discourse Processes, 10,* 401–415.

Farrar, K., Kunkel, D., Biely, E., Eyal, K., & Donnerstein, E. (2003). Sexual messages during prime-time programming. *Sexuality and Culture, 7*, 7–37.

Fey, M. E. (1986). *Language interventions with young children.* San Diego, CA: College Hill.

Flannagan, D., Baker-Ward, L., & Graham, L. (1995). Talk about preschool: Patterns of topic discussion and elaboration related to gender and ethnicity. *Sex Roles, 32*, 1–15.

Folger, J. P., & Sillars, A. L. (1980). Relational coding and perceptions of dominance. In B. W. Morse & L. A. Phelps (Eds.), *Interpersonal communication: A relational perspective* (pp. 322–333). Minneapolis, MN: Burgess.

Foppa, K. (1990). Topic progression and intention. In I. Marková & K. Foppa (Eds.), *The dynamics of dialogue* (pp. 178–200). New York: Harvester Wheatsheaf.

Foster, S. (1981). The emergence of topic type in children under 2;6: A chicken and egg problem. *Papers and Reports on Child Language Development, 20*, 52–60.

Foster, S. H. (1986). Learning discourse topic management in the preschool years. *Journal of Child Language, 13*, 231–250.

Fox, L. E., Sohlberg, M. M., & Fried-Oken, M. (2001). Effects of conversational topic choice on outcomes of augmentative communication intervention for adults with aphasia. *Aphasiology, 15*, 171–200.

French, L., Lucariello, J., Seidman, S., & Nelson, K. (1985). The influence of discourse content and context on preschoolers' use of langauge. In L. Galda & A. Pellegrini (Eds.), *Play language and stories* (pp. 1–28). Norwood, NJ: Ablex.

Galazinski, D. (2000). *The language of deception: A discourse analytical study.* Thousand Oaks, CA: Sage.

Garcia, L., & Joanette, Y. (1997). Analysis of conversational topic shifts: A multiple case study. *Brain and Language, 58*, 92.

Garvey, C. (1977). The contingent query: A dependent act in conversation. In M. Lewis & L. A. Rosenblum (Eds.), *Interaction, conversation and the development of language* (pp. 63–93). New York: John Wiley & Sons.

Garvey, C. (1984). *Children's talk.* Cambridge, MA: Harvard University Press.

Gentner, D., & Gentner, D. R. (1983). Flowing waters or teeming crowds: Mental models of electricity. In D. Gentner & A. L. Stevens (Eds.), *Mental models* (pp. 99–129). Hillsdale, NJ: Lawrence Erlbaum Associates.

Giles, H., Mulac, A., Bradac, J. J., & Johnson, P. (1987). Speech accommodation theory: The first decade and beyond. In M. L. McLaughlin (Ed.), *Communication yearbook 10* (pp. 13–48). Beverly Hills, CA: Sage.

Golish, T. D. (2000). Is openness always better? Exploring the role of topic avoidance, satisfaction, and parenting styles of stepparents. *Communication Quarterly, 48*, 137–158.

Golish, T. D., & Caughlin, J. P. (2002). "I'd rather not talk about it": Adolescents' and young adults' use of topic avoidance in stepfamilies. *Journal of Applied Communication Research, 30*, 78–106.

Goodenough, D. R., & Weiner, S. L. (1978). The role of conversational passing moves in the management of topical transitions. *Discourse Process, 1*, 395–404.

Goodwin, R., & Lee, I. (1994). Taboo topics among Chinese and English friends: A cross-cultural comparison. *Journal of Cross-Cultural Psychology, 25*, 325–338.

Goody, E. N. (1995). *Social intelligence and interaction*. Cambridge, England: Cambridge University Press.

Goutsos, D. (1997). *Modeling discourse topic: Sequential relations and strategies in expository text*. Norwood, NJ: Ablex.

Greenberg, B. S., & Hofschire, L. (2000). Sex on entertainment television. In D. Zillmann & P. Vorderer (Eds.), *Media entertainment: The psychology of its appeal* (pp. 93–111). Mahwah, NJ: Lawrence Erlbaum Associates.

Grice, H. P. (1975). Logic and conversation. In P. Cole & J. L. Morgan (Eds.), *Syntax and semantics III: Speech acts* (pp. 41–58). New York: Academic.

Grimes, J. E. (1982). Topics within topics. In D. Tannen (Ed.), *Georgetown University roundtable on language and linguistics, 1981* (pp. 164–176). Washington, DC: Georgetown University Press.

Gruber, H. (1995). Computer-mediated communication and scholarly discourse: Forms of topic-initiation and thematic development. *Pragmatics, 8*, 21–45.

Guerrero, L. K., & Afifi, W. A. (1995a). Some things are better left unsaid: Topic avoidance in family relationships. *Communication Quarterly, 43*, 276–296.

Guerrero, L. K., & Afifi, W. A. (1995b). What parents don't know: Topic avoidance in parent-child relationships. In T. J. Socha & G. H. Stamp (Eds.), *Parents, children, and communication: Frontiers of theory and research* (pp. 219–245). Hillsdale, NJ: Lawrence Erlbaum Associates.

Haas, A. (1979). Male and female spoken language differences: Stereotypes and evidence. *Psychological Bulletin, 86*, 616–626.

Haas, A., & Sherman, M. A. (1982). Reported topics of conversation among same-sex adults. *Communication Quarterly, 30*, 332–342.

Halliday, M. A. K. (1970). Language structure and linguistic function. In J. Lyons (Ed.), *New horizons in linguistics* (pp. 140–165). Harmondsworth, England: Penguin.

Haviland, J. B. (1977). *Gossip, reputation and knowledge in Zinacantan*. Chicago: University of Chicago Press.

Hemphill, L. (1989). Topic development, syntax, and social class. *Discourse Process, 12*, 267–286.

Heritage, J., & Greatbatch, D. (1991). On the institutional character of institutional talk: The case of news interviews. In D. Boden & D. H. Zimmerman (Eds.), *Talk and social structure: Studies in ethnomethodology and conversation analysis* (pp. 93–137). Berkeley: University of California Press.

Hinkel, E. (1994). Topic appropriateness in cross-cultural social conversations. *Pragmatic and Language Learning, 5*, 163–179.

Hjelmquist, E. (1984). Memory for conversations. *Discourse Processes, 7*, 321–336.

Hjelmquist, E., & Gidlund, Å. (1985). Free recall of conversations. *Text, 5*, 169–185.

Hockett, C. F. (1958). *A course in modern linguistics*. New York: Macmillan.

Holdgrafer, G., & Campbell, T. F. (1986). Children's comprehension of intonation as a marker for discourse topic collaboration. *Applied Psycholinguistics, 7*, 373–384.

Housel, T. J. (1985). Conversational themes and attention focusing strategies: Prediction comprehension and recall. *Communication Quarterly, 33*, 236–253.

Howe, M. (1991). Collaboration on topic change in conversation. *Kansas Working Papers in Linguistics, 16*, 15.

Janis, I. (1982). *Groupthink: Psychological studies of policy decisions and fiascoes.* Boston: Houghton Mifflin.

Janis, I. (1989). *Crucial decisions: Leadership in policy making and crisis management.* New York: Free Press.

Janis, I., & Mann, L. (1977). *Decision making: A psychological analysis of conflict, choice and commitment.* New York: Free Press.

Jefferson, G. (1984). On stepwise transition from talk about a trouble to inappropriately nextpositioned matters. In J. M. Atkinson & J. Heritage (Eds.), *Structures of social action: Studies in conversation analysis* (pp. 191–222). Cambridge, England: Cambridge University Press.

Jefferson, G. (1993). Caveat speaker: Preliminary notes on recipient topic-shift implicature. *Research on Language and Social Interaction, 26,* 1–30.

Kavanaugh, R. D., Whittington, S., & Cerbone, M. J. (1983). Mothers' use of fantasy in speech to young children. *Journal of Child Language, 10,* 45–55.

Keenan, E. O., & Schieffelin, B. B. (1976). Topic as a discourse notion: A study of topic in the conversations of children and adults. In C. N. Li (Ed.), *Subject and topic* (pp. 335–384). New York: Academic.

Kellermann, K. (1989). The negativity effect in interaction: It's all in your point of view. *Human Communication Research, 16,* 147–183.

Kellermann, K. (1991). The conversation MOP. II. Progression through scenes in discourse. *Human Communication Research, 17,* 385–414.

Kellermann, K. (1995). The conversation MOP: A model of patterned and pliable behavior. In D. E. Hewes (Ed.), *The cognitive bases of interpersonal communication* (pp. 181–221). Hillsdale, NJ: Lawrence Erlbaum Associates.

Kellermann, K., Broetzmann, S., Lim, T., & Kitao, K. (1989). The conversation MOP: Scenes in the stream of discourse. *Discourse Processes, 12,* 27–61.

Kellermann, K., & Lim, T. (1989). Conversational acquaintance: The flexibility of routinized behavior. In B. Dervin, L. Grossberg, B. J. O'Keefe, & E. Wartella (Eds.), *Rethinking communication. Vol. 2. Paradigm exemplars* (pp. 172–187). Newbury Park, CA: Sage.

Kellermann, K., & Lim, T. (1990). The conversation MOP. III. Timing of scenes in discourse. *Journal of Personality and Social Psychology, 59,* 1163–1179.

Kellermann, K., & Palomares, N. A. (2004). Topical profiling: Emergent, co-occurring, and relationally-defining topics in talk. *Journal of Language and Social Psychology, 23,* 308–337.

Kellermann, K., & Park, H. (2001). Situational urgency and conversational retreat: When politeness and efficiency matter. *Communication Research, 28,* 3–47.

Kellermann, K., & Sleight, C. (1989). Coherence: A meaningful adhesive for discourse. In J. A. Anderson (Ed.), *Communication yearbook 12* (pp. 95–129). Newbury Park, CA: Sage.

Kertoy, M. K., & Vetter, D. K. (1995). The effect of conversational setting on topic continuation in mother-child dyads. *Journal of Child Language, 22,* 73–88.

Kipers, P. S. (1987). Gender and topic. *Language in Society, 16,* 543–557.

Klein, J. (1971). The family in "traditional" working-class England. In M. Anderson (Ed.), *Sociology of the family* (pp. 70–77). Baltimore: Penguin.

Komarovsky, M. (1967). *Blue-collar marriage.* New York: Vintage.

Koriat, A., Goldsmith, M., & Pansky, A. (2000). Toward a psychology of memory accuracy. *Annual Review of Psychology, 51*, 481–537.

Kuder, S. J., & Bryen, D. N. (1993). Conversational topics of staff members and institutionalized individuals with mental retardation. *Mental Retardation, 31*, 148–153.

Landis, C. (1927). National differences in conversation. *Journal of Abnormal and Social Psychology, 21*, 354–357.

Landis, M. H., & Burtt, H. E. (1924). A study of conversations. *Journal of Comparative Psychology, 4*, 81–89.

Langer, E. (1970a, March 12). Inside the New York telephone company. *New York Review of Books, 14*(5), 14, 16–22.

Langer, E. (1970b, March 26). The women of the telephone company. *New York Review of Books, 14*(6), 16, 18, 20–24.

Laudan, L. (1977). *Progress and its problems*. Berkeley: University of California Press.

Levin, J., & Arluke, A. (1985). An exploratory analysis of sex differences in gossip. *Sex Roles, 12*, 281–286.

Lin, M.-C., Harwood, J., & Bonnesen, J. L. (2002). Conversation topics and communication satisfaction in grandparent-grandchild relationships. *Journal of Language and Social Psychology, 21*, 302–323.

Lucariello, J. (1990). Freeing talk from the here-and-now: The role of event knowledge and maternal scaffolds. *Topics in Language Disorders, 10*, 14–29.

Lunt, P. K. (1991). The perceived causal structure of loneliness. *Journal of Personality and Social Psychology, 61*, 26–34.

Maass, A., Salvi, D., Arcuri, L., & Semin, G. R. (1989). Language use in intergroup contexts: The linguistic intergroup bias. *Journal of Personality and Social Psychology, 57*, 981–993.

Malamuth, N. M., & Impett, E. A. (2001). Research on sex in the media: What do we know about effects on children and adolescents? In D. G. Singer & J. L. Singer (Eds.), *Handbook of children and the media* (pp. 269–287). Thousand Oaks, CA: Sage.

Marlin, M., & Barron, N. (1972). Topic and redundancy of discourse sequences. In D. G. Hays & D. M. Lance (Eds.), *From soundstream to discourse: Papers from the 1971 mid-America linguistics conference* (pp. 125–134). Columbia: The University of Missouri.

Martin, R. (1997). "Girls don't talk about garages!" Perceptions of conversation in same- and cross-sex friendships. *Personal Relationships, 4*, 115–130.

Marvin, C. A. (1994). Cartalk! Conversational topics of preschool children en route home from preschool. *Language, Speech, and Hearing Services in Schools, 25*, 146–155.

Marvin, C. A., Beukelman, D. R., Brockhaus, J., & Kast, L. (1994). "What are you talking about?" Semantic analysis of preschool children's conversational topics in home and preschool settings. *AAC: Augmentative and Alternative Communication, 10*, 75–86.

Maynard, D. W. (1980). Placement of topic changes in conversation. *Semiotica, 30*, 263–290.

Maynard, D. W., & Zimmerman, D. H. (1984). Topical talk, ritual and the social organization of relationships. *Social Psychology Quarterly, 47*, 301–316.

McKerrow, R. E., Gronbeck, B. E., Ehninger, D., & Monroe, A. H. (2002). *Principles and types of public speaking* (15th ed.). Boston: Allyn & Bacon.

McLaughlin, M. L. (1984). *Conversation: How talk is organized.* Beverly Hills, CA: Sage.

McLaughlin, M. L., Louden, A. D., Cashion, J. L., Altendorf, D. M., Baaske, K. T., & Smith, S. W. (1985). Conversational planning and self-serving utterances: The manipulation of topical and functional structures in dyadic interaction. *Journal of Language and Social Psychology, 4*, 233–251.

McShane, M. K. (1990). *Topic management in the conversation of four-year-olds.* Unpublished master's thesis, University of California, Santa Barbara.

Mentis, M. (1991). Topic management in the discourse of normal and language-impaired children. *Journal of Childhood Communication Disorders, 14*, 45–66.

Mentis, M. (1994). Topic management in discourse: Assessment and intervention. *Topics in Language Disorders, 14*, 29–54.

Mentis, M., Briggs-Whittaker, J., & Gramigna, G. D. (1995). Discourse topic management in senile dementia of the Alzheimer's type. *Journal of Speech and Hearing Research, 38*, 1054–1066.

Moerk, E. L. (1975). Verbal interactions between children and their mothers during the preschool years. *Developmental Psychology, 6*, 788–794.

Monge, P. R. (1977). The systems perspective as a theoretical basis for the study of human communication. *Communication Quarterly, 25*, 19–29.

Monge, P. R., & Contractor, N. S. (2003). *Theories of communication networks.* Oxford, England: Oxford University Press.

Moore, H. T. (1922). Further data concerning sex differences. *Journal of Abnormal Psychology, 17*, 210–214.

Mulcahy, G. A. (1973). Sex differences in patterns of self-disclosures among adolescents: A developmental perspective. *Journal of Youth and Adolescence, 4*, 343–356.

Murphy, G. L., & Shapiro, A. M. (1994). Forgetting of verbatim information in discourse. *Memory & Cognition, 22*, 85–94.

Myers, G. (1998). Displaying opinions: Topics and disagreement in focus groups. *Language in Society, 27*, 85–111.

Ng, S. H., & Bradac, J. J. (1993). *Power in language: Verbal communication and social influence.* Newbury Park, CA: Sage.

Nofsinger, R. E. (1988/89). "Let's talk about the record": Contending over topic redirection in the Rather/Bush interview. *Research on Language and Social Interaction, 22*, 273–292.

Nofsinger, R. E. (1990). Rethinking "topic." *Communication Reports, 3*, 45–47.

O'Hair, D., & Stewart, R. (1998). *Public speaking: Challenges and choices.* New York: Bedford/St. Martin's.

Öhlschlegel, S., & Piontkowski, U. (1997). Topic progression and social categorization. *Journal of Language and Social Psychology, 16*, 444–455.

Orletti, F. (1989). Topic organization in conversation. *International Journal of the Sociology of Language, 76*, 75–85.

Palmer, M. T. (1989). Controlling conversations: Turns, topics, and interpersonal control. *Communication Monographs, 56,* 1–18.

Palmer, M. T., & Badzinski, D. M. (1986, May). *Topics as natural discourse processing units.* Paper presented at the meeting of the International Communication Association, Chicago, IL.

Palomares, N. A. (2004). Gender schematicity, gender identity salience, and gender-linked language use. *Human Communication Research, 30,* 556- 588.

Parker, J. H. (1980). Conversational topics: What do you say after you say hello. *International Journal of Contemporary Sociology, 17,* 112–131.

Petronio, S., & Martin, J. N. (1986). Ramification of revealing private information: A gender gap. *Journal of Clinical Psychology, 42,* 499–506.

Planalp, S., & Tracy, K. (1980). Not to change the topic but . . . : A cognitive approach to the management of conversation. In D. Nimmo (Ed.), *Communication yearbook 4* (pp. 237–258). New Brunswick, NJ: Transaction.

Postmes, T., & Spears, R. (2002). Behavior online: Does anonymous computer communication reduce gender inequality? *Personality & Social Psychology Bulletin, 28,* 1073–1083.

Prince, E. F. (1981). Towards a taxonomy of given-new information. In P. Cole (Ed.), *Radical pragmatics* (pp. 223–255). New York: Academic.

Raffaelli, M., & Duckett, E. (1989). "We were just talking. . .": Conversation in early adolescence. *Journal of Youth and Adolescence, 18,* 567–582.

Reichman, R. (1978). Conversational coherency. *Cognitive Science, 2,* 283–327.

Reinhart, T. (1981). Pragmatics and linguistics: An analysis of sentence topics. *Philosophica, 27,* 53–94.

Ridley, J., Radford, J., & Mahon, M. (2002). How do teachers manage topic and repair? *Child Language Teaching and Therapy, 18,* 43–58.

Roloff, M. E., & Ifert, D. (1998). Antecedents and consequences of explicit agreements to declare a topic taboo in dating relationships. *Personal Relationships, 5,* 191–205.

Roloff, M. E., & Ifert, D. E. (2000). Conflict management through avoidance: Withholding complaints, suppressing arguments, and declaring topics taboo. In S. Petronio (Ed.), *Balancing the secrets of private disclosures* (pp. 151–164). Mahwah, NJ: Lawrence Erlbaum Associates.

Roloff, M. E., & Johnson, D. I. (2001). Reintroducing taboo topics: Antecedents and consequences of putting topics back on the table. *Communication Studies, 52,* 37–50.

Rosch, E. (1978). Principles of categorization. In E. Rosch & B. B. Lloyd (Eds.), *Cognition and categorization* (pp. 27–48). Hillsdale, NJ: Lawrence Erlbaum Associates.

Rudolph, U., & Forsterling, F. (1997). The psychological causality implicit in verbs: A review. *Psychological Bulletin, 12,* 192–218.

Ruscher, J. B., & Hurley, M. M. (2000). Off-target verbosity evokes negative stereotypes of older adults. *Journal of Language and Social Psychology, 19,* 141–149.

Sacks, H., Schegloff, E., & Jefferson, G. (1974). A simplest systematics for the organization of turn taking for conversation. *Language, 50,* 696–735.

Samter, W., Burleson, B. R., Kunkel, A. W., & Werking, K. J. (1994, July). *Gender and beliefs about communication in intimate relationships: Moderating effects of type of* communication and type of relationship *(or, when gender differences make a differ-ence—and when they don't)*. Paper presented at the meeting of the International Communication Association, Sydney, Australia.

Sargent, J. (2002). Topic avoidance: Is this the way to a more satisfying relationship? *Communication Research Reports, 19,* 175–182.

Schaffer, D. (1984). The role of intonation as a cue to topic management in conversa-tion. *Journal of Phonetics, 12,* 327–344.

Schank, R. C. (1977). Rules and topics in conversation. *Cognitive Science, 1,* 421–441.

Schlobinski, P., & Schütze-Coburn, S. (1992). On the topic of topic and topic conti-nuity. *Linguistics, 30,* 89–121.

Schober-Peterson, D., & Johnson, C. J. (1989). Conversational topics of 4-year-olds. *Journal of Speech and Hearing Research, 32,* 857–870.

Scollon, R., & Wong-Scollon, S. (1991). Topic confusion in English-Asian discourse. *World Englishes, 10,* 113–125.

Semin, G. R., & Fiedler, K. (1988). The cognitive functions of linguistic categories in describing persons: Social cognition and language. *Journal of Personality and Social Psychology, 54,* 558–568.

Sirois, P., & Dorval, B. (1988). The role of returns to a prior topic in the negotiation of topic change: A developmental investigation. *Journal of Psycholinguistic Research, 17,* 185–210.

Song, K. (1996). Topic management strategies in spoken discourse: Cognitive and social aspects of topic shift in Korean. In H. Bates (Ed.), *The twenty-second LACUS forum 1995* (pp. 239–250). Chapel Hill, NC: Linguistic Association of Canada & United States.

Stafford, L., Waldron, V. R., & Infield, L. L. (1989). Actor-observer differences in con-versational memory. *Human Communication Research, 15,* 590–611.

Sternberg, R. J., Conway, B. E., Ketron, J. L., & Bernstein, M. (1981). People's con-ceptions of intelligence. *Journal of Personality and Social Psychology, 41,* 37–55.

Stoke, S. M., & West, W. D. (1930). The conversational interests of college students. *School and Society, 32,* 567–570.

Stuart, S., Vanderhoof, D., & Beukelman, D. R. (1993). Topic and vocabulary use patterns of elderly women. *AAC: Augmentative and Alternative Communication, 9,* 95–110.

Svennevig, J. (1999). *Getting acquainted in conversation: A study of initial interactions.* Philadelphia: J. Benjamins.

Tannen, D. (1990a). Gender difference in conversational coherence: Physical alignment and topical cohesion. In B. Dorval (Ed.), *Conversational organization and its devel-opment* (pp. 167–206). Norwood, NJ: Ablex.

Tannen, D. (1990b). Gender differences in topical coherence: Creating involvement in best friends' talk. *Discourse Processes, 13,* 73–90.

Thomas, L., & Wareing, S. (1999). *Language, society and power: An introduction.* London: Routledge.

Tracy, K. (1982). On getting the point: Distinguishing "issues" from "events," an aspect of conversational coherence. In M. Burgoon (Ed.), *Communication yearbook 5* (pp. 279–301). New Brunswick, NJ: Transaction.

Tracy, K. (1983). The issue-event distinction: A rule of conversation and its scope condition. *Human Communication Research, 9*, 320–334.

Tracy, K. (1984a). Staying on topic: An explication of conversational relevance. *Discourse Process, 7*, 447–464.

Tracy, K. (1984b). The effect of multiple goals on conversational relevance and topic shift. *Communication Monographs, 51*, 274–287.

Tracy, K. (1985). Conversational coherence: A cognitively grounded rules approach. In R. L. Street & J. N. Cappella (Eds.), *Sequence and pattern in communicative behaviour* (pp. 30–49). London: Edward Arnold.

Tracy, K. (1993). It's an interesting article! *Research on Language and Social Interaction, 26*, 195–201.

Tracy, K., & Moran, J. P. (1983). Conversational relevance in multiple-goal settings. In R. T. Craig & K. Tracy (Eds.), *Conversational coherence* (pp. 116–135). Beverly Hills, CA: Sage.

Turnbull, W. (1994). Thematic structure of designs of violent events influences perceptions of responsibility: A thematic structure effect. *Journal of Language and Social Psychology, 13*, 132–157.

van Dijk, T. A. (1977). *Text and context*. London: Longman.

van Dijk, T. A. (1980). *Macrostructures: An interdisciplinary study of global structures in discourse, interaction and cognition*. Hillsdale, NJ: Lawrence Erlbaum Associates.

Vangelisti, A. L. (1994). Family secrets: Forms, functions and correlates. *Journal of Social and Personal Relationships, 11*, 113–135.

Vangelisti, A. L., & Caughlin, J. P. (1997). Revealing family secrets: The influence of topic, function, and relationships. *Journal of Social & Personal Relationships, 14*, 679–705.

Wanska, S. K., & Bedrosian, J. L. (1985). Conversational structure and topic performance in mother-child interation. *Journal of Speech and Hearing Research, 24*, 579–584.

Wanska, S. K., & Bedrosian, J. L. (1986). Topic and communicative intent in mother-child discourse. *Journal of Child Language, 13*, 523–535.

Wanska, S. K., Bedrosian, J. L., & Pohlman, J. C. (1986). Effects of play materials on the topic performance of preschool children. *Language, Speech, and Hearing Services in Schools, 17*, 152–159.

Wasserman, S., & Faust, K. (1994). *Social network analysis*. Cambridge, England: Cambridge University Press.

Watson, J., Breed, W., & Posman, H. (1948). A study of urban conversations: Samples of 1,001 remarks overheard in Manhattan. *Journal of Social Psychology, 28*, 121–133.

Watzlawick, P., Beavin, J. H., & Jackson, D. D. (1967). *Pragmatics of human communication*. New York: W. W. Norton.

West, C., & Garcia, A. (1988). Conversational shift work: A study of topical transitions between women and men. *Social Problems, 35*, 551–575.

Wiener, M., & Mehrabian, A. (1967). *Language within language: Immediacy, a channel in verbal communication*. New York: Appleton-Century-Crofts.

Wilson, B., Kunkel, D., Linz, D., Potter, W. J., Donnerstein, E., Smith, S., et al. (1997). Violence in television programming overall: University of California Santa Barbara study. In *National Television Violence Study, Vol. 1* (pp. 3–268). Thousand Oaks, CA: Sage.

Yamada, H. (1990). Topic shifts in American and Japanese business conversation. *Georgetown Journal of Languages and Linguistics, 1*, 249–256.

Zhao, X., & Gantz, W. (2003). Disruptive and cooperative interruptions in prime-time television fiction: The role of gender, status, and topic. *Journal of Communication, 53*, 347–362.

CHAPTER CONTENTS

3 Blurring the Boundaries: Historical Developments and Future Directions in Organizational Rhetoric

REBECCA J. MEISENBACH
University of Missouri-Columbia

JILL J. McMILLAN
Wake Forest University

This chapter provides a concise but thorough view of organizational rhetoric. We review how work in organizational rhetoric spans research on propaganda analysis, organizational communication, public relations, and rhetorical social movements, highlighting connections and differences among these perspectives and outlining what organizational rhetoric has borrowed from and contributed to each. We then consider issues of concern to organizational rhetoric scholars: crisis communication, maintenance communication, power relationships, and ethics. In discussing these areas, we address individual theories of organizational rhetoric, including legitimacy, apologia, issue management, identification, and corporate social responsibility. Finally, by reflecting on existing work, we offer our predictions for the future of research in organizational rhetoric. Overall, we call attention to thinking about all organizations as "inherently rhetorical" so that communication scholars and practitioners can understand and explore the utility of applying a rhetorical perspective to their work in various communication contexts.

In 2005, Harvard University's then-president, Larry Summers, came under fire for asking a question in a conference speech about whether men perform better than women in the sciences because of innate differences. Amid the uproar, Richard Freeman, one of the conference organizers, argued that the conference planners did not invite the president as the president, suggesting that Summers was to speak as an individual. Harvard's Standing

Correspondence: Rebecca J. Meisenbach, 115 Switzler Hall, Department of Communication, University of Missouri-Columbia, Columbia, MO 65211-2310; phone: (573) 882-4431

Communication Yearbook 30, pp. 99–141

Committee on Women responded with a letter arguing that "the president of a university never speaks entirely as an individual, especially when that institution is Harvard" (Fish, 2005, ¶12). This situation highlights the importance of organizational affiliations in today's society and how both rhetors and message receivers participate in creating identifications between organizations and individuals (Cheney & McMillan, 1990). In this way, rhetors are increasingly understood and interpreted as organizational beings, speaking about or on behalf of organizations (Crable, 1990).

At the same time, organizations are increasingly positioned as rhetors through messages such as "the White House announces policy," "US Air reassures customers," "the AMA endorses legislation," and "the Methodist church denies homosexuality." These virtually taken-for-granted phrases actually involve complicated use of synecdoche and personification that demonstrate the subtle ways in which organizations penetrate and influence our public discourse (Cheney, 1992; McMillan, 1987). Organizations—whether they make widgets, care for the sick, educate children, or oversee our religious and spiritual lives—constitute major players in today's rhetorical landscape. In fact, some have argued persuasively (Crable, 1990; Greider, 1992, 2003) that organizations have usurped the rhetorical ground that individual rhetors and spokespersons have vacated. Some scholars suggest that organizations belong in this landscape (see Boyd, 2001a), whereas others insist that organizations overpower public discourse in unproductive and even harmful ways (Deetz, 1992; Schiller, 1990). From either position, it seems clear that, if modern organizations are "inherently rhetorical" (Crable, 1990, p. 115), then communication scholars have a unique responsibility to explore the rhetorical commonality of all collectivities and what it means for message makers and message receivers in organizations of all ilks.

Since the early 1980s, a growing group of scholars has formally addressed such issues and questions through study of the concept *organizational rhetoric,* but a cursory review of their work indicates that, with some exceptions, they have stayed fairly close to their organizational communication roots where for-profit business organizations were the central focus of attention. For instance, Crable and Vibbert (1983) studied Mobil Oil as a corporate rhetor that spoke through Sunday newspaper advertisements. Sproule (1988) introduced the idea of a managerial rhetoric and how it can and should be analyzed in comparison with traditional individual rhetoric. In 1990, an issue of the *Journal of Applied Communication Research* was devoted to introducing and developing organizational rhetoric as an area of theoretical and practical investigation in communication research (see Jablonski, 1990). At the same time, public relations scholars have promoted the investigation of corporate advocacy through work that studies public relations from a rhetorical perspective (e.g., Boyd, 2004; Heath, 1980). Although editors increasingly include organizational rhetoric in currently popular handbooks (Cheney & Christensen, 2001; Cheney, Christensen, Conrad, & Lair, 2004), one could argue that those scholars who understand the "inherently rhetorical" nature of *all* human collectivities have failed to make the case to their colleagues in related communication fields such as health communication, mass communication, political communication, small-group communication, and intercultural communication. Clearly, it is time to cross those boundaries with an understanding of the utility of a rhetorical perspective.

Despite this scholarly attention, the spark of interest in organizational rhetoric has not yet built into a flame. In a panel at the National Communication Association's 2004 convention celebrating Roderick Hart's influence on scholars of organizational rhetoric, researchers lamented this stagnation or leveling off of the work in this area when they envisioned so much more yet to be done.[1] In scholarly circles, organizational rhetoric is relegated to the edges of research in organizational communication, rhetoric, and public relations, never fully belonging in any one area. The development and study of organizational rhetoric are spread widely across a variety of journals and subfields in the discipline, yet (or perhaps because of this diversity) we lack the development of cohesive and basic theoretical models.[2] The area may also have progressed more slowly in creating such models because of the scope and complexity of the issues involved in handling and explaining the phenomenon: When an organizational representative speaks, who is responsible? At whose feet do we lay blame when organizations offend us? Whose interests are truly represented in organizational messages, and whose perspectives are marginalized, silenced, or contradicted? Can we believe what organizations "say" publicly and privately? Can individuals speak as independent agents, distinct from organizational memberships and identifications? In short, the wide-ranging relevance of such questions calls the communication discipline to a rigorous and thorough consideration of when, how, and the consequences with which organizations and organizational beings speak, listen, respond to, and generally participate in public and private discourse.

We frame this chapter with the following questions: What counts as "organizational rhetoric"? How has the study of organizational rhetoric developed out of a variety of communication subfields? What is the unique function of organizational rhetoric within our discipline? What are the major concerns and issues that are being and can be addressed from this perspective? What theories are useful to gaining understanding of and critiquing organizational rhetoric as product and process? What future directions of study will contribute to a metatheoretical model of organizational rhetoric? We believe that asking and answering these questions will yield a thorough review of the origins, issues, and potential of organizational rhetoric. In a volume predicated on "crossing boundaries," we trust that colleagues in other communication contexts will recognize the utility of a rhetorical perspective in speaking and enacting *organization* as it applies to their unique perspectives.

IDENTIFYING ORGANIZATIONAL RHETORIC

A major question involves understanding what counts as organizational rhetoric. The study of rhetoric, which can be defined as "the use of language as a symbolic means of inducing *cooperation* [italics added] in beings that by nature respond to symbols," offers a particular way of investigating and considering discourse (Burke, 1950/1969, p. 43). Burke's use of the term "cooperation" in this definition leads naturally to issues of organizing and organizations within discussions of rhetoric. Crable (1990) described organizational rhetoric as the discourse of organizations presented through organizational beings. Cheney and McMillan (1990) referred to it as organizational persuasion and as collectively created and/or presented discourse. Overall, an organizational rhetoric perspective means focusing on messages created within and/or on behalf of organizations that seek to create identifications, solicit cooperation, and/or persuade.

Such understandings invite questions about the relationships and distinctions between the study of organizational rhetoric and the study of organizational discourse. Putnam and Fairhurst (2001) broadly defined discourse analysis as "the study of words and signifiers, including the form or structure of these words, the use of language in context and the meanings of interpretation of discursive practices" (p. 79). In fact, a rhetorical perspective is one of eight categories of language analysis that Putnam and Fairhurst reviewed, describing it as centering "on the text of discourse and the ways that meaning intertwines with function to shape messages and message responses" (p. 103). This shaping represents the persuasive process, a distinctive area of focus for organizational rhetoric. From this perspective, organizational discourse constitutes a broader concept than rhetoric, since discourse may be studied without its persuasive and rhetorical nature being highlighted. We acknowledge that organizational messages may be studied nonrhetorically. For example, Clair (1993) examined institutional discourse in her consideration of the sexual harassment policies of Big Ten universities without taking an explicitly rhetorical perspective. Yet her analysis targeted the texts of these policies and how they generate oppressive and emancipatory discourses through particular techniques or strategies, matching Putnam and Fairhurst's description of a rhetorical perspective. Critical scholars may fault a rhetorical approach for not focusing adequately on the power-laden nature of discourse. However, scholars of organizational rhetoric, as we will discuss later, argue that rhetoric and persuasion inherently involve power (Cheney, Garvin-Doxas, & Torrens, 1998; McMillan, 1990), making them particularly potent tools for the exploration of the uneven symbolic playing field of the typical organization.

Scholars of organizational rhetoric contend that all discourse contains persuasive elements and that all individuals are now organizational beings

(Crable, 1990), representing and speaking through a variety of shifting and competing organizational identities (Cheney, 1991). This position suggests that all discourse involving human collectivities remains open to consideration from an organizational rhetoric perspective. Thus, we do not claim discourse and its study as the exclusive domain of organizational rhetoric. Rather, we suggest that a rhetorical perspective can be used to explain, critique, and transform a wide range of organizationally created and influenced discourses and meaning-making processes. As such, the study of organizational rhetoric is relevant to many of the communication discipline's areas of study, including organizational communication, rhetoric, public relations, political communication, mass communication, and health communication.

EMERGENCE OF ORGANIZATIONAL RHETORIC AS AN AREA OF STUDY

We begin by tracing lines of investigation that feed into the study of organizational rhetoric. Rather than presenting a unitary, linear, and coherent history (indeed, we do not believe that one exists), we offer a look at various, competing, and disparate origins of organizational rhetoric research, with a goal of showing connections and overlaps that may not have been recognized or heeded until now. For example, the earliest work in this area can be attributed to classical rhetoric, World War I propaganda analysis, public relations research, or students of W. Charles Redding, Phillip Tompkins, and Roderick Hart. By articulating these diverse influences, we identify similarities and make sense of a wide range of work in the area.[3] Thus, in this section, we explore rhetorical tendencies in the mass communication tradition (with attention to propaganda analysis), the organizational communication tradition, the public relations tradition, and the rhetorical tradition (with attention to social movements), before concluding with consideration of the specific contributions of organizational rhetoric.

Propaganda Analysis

Some of the earliest modern research in communication ties directly to the roots of the mass communication research tradition (Rogers, 1994; Simpson, 1994; Sproule, 1997). In his history of communication study, Everett Rogers acknowledged that he did not cover and include much of the humanistic and, specifically, rhetorical origins of communication study. However, elements of mass communication history that are relevant to organizational rhetoric focus on the creation and study of propaganda. The term *propaganda* originated with the Catholic church's formation of the *congregatio de propaganda fide*, or the congregation for propagating the faith, in 1622 (*Merriam-Webster's Collegiate Dictionary*, 1993).

Critical public attention to the use of propaganda developed in the early twentieth century in the United States. Sproule (1997) addressed the role of the muckrakers during this time in questioning relationships between propaganda and democracy. For example, according to Sproule, Ray Stannard Baker ran a series of five articles between November 1905 and April 1906 that challenged the railroad companies' business practices and influence on public opinion.

Although scholars note the use of propaganda in the early 1900s, analysis of propaganda really accelerated during and after World War I (see Rogers, 1994; Sproule, 1987 for a full review of this body of research). Rogers noted that, whereas propaganda had once been understood as neutral dissemination or propagation of an idea, after World War I, the term evoked connotations of manipulation and brainwashing. Lasswell (1927/1938) argued that propaganda dealt with "the management of opinions and attitudes by the direction manipulation of social suggestion" and referred to "the control of opinion by significant symbols" (p. 9).

During the war, the United States formed the Committee on Public Information (CPI) to coordinate wartime communication (Sproule, 1987). The propaganda messages created during World War I (1914–1918) became the focus of Lasswell's dissertation (originally published in 1927 as *Propaganda Technique in the World War*). He used specific textual examples to identify propaganda techniques being used in the campaigns, leading Rogers (1994) to label Lasswell's work as "qualitative and critical in tone" (p. 213). Lasswell's work included content analysis of leaflets dropped from the air and military recruiting posters (see Kitch, 2001, for pictures and analysis of World War I recruiting posters that used images of women). Research on propaganda flourished during the 1920s and 1930s as a group of scholars investigated propaganda's effects, and it eventually culminated in the formation of an Institute for Propaganda Analysis, which was intended to help citizens recognize and analyze propaganda.

However, propaganda analysis faded away during the 1940s and gave way to the social scientific research that formed the basis of contemporary mass communication research focusing on social influence and media effects (see Sproule, 1987, for a discussion of this transition). During this time, research on propaganda shifted away from qualitative, rhetorical leanings, as researchers, including Lasswell (e.g., Lasswell & Blumenstock, 1939), concentrated on developing rigorous statistical content analysis methodologies and on determining the persuasive effects of propaganda messages. Sproule noted how the scientific persuasive studies tended to overlook questions about the ethics and motives of the persuaders, questions that had been raised through the historical-critical studies. By World War II, the same scholars who once critiqued and questioned propaganda messages turned to analyzing and creating such messages for the United States. Today, propaganda analysis may be seen in the work of individuals such as Bagdikian (2000), who has long followed and questioned the ever-shrinking number of corporations that control media outlets in the United States.

Sproule's (1987) suggestion that propaganda analysis suffered from its interdisciplinary nature is particularly important for organizational rhetoric. Since others viewed propaganda analysis as an outgrowth or extension of other disciplines, such as political science, sociology, psychology, and journalism, "propaganda analysis lacked a coherent body of theory capable of withstanding the challenge of a competing paradigm" (p. 71). Just as early mass communication scholars appeared unaware of or unmotivated by the rich tradition of rhetorical theory from which they could draw, current organizational rhetoric scholars may be only marginally aware of the rich and relevant history of propaganda analysis.

Organizational Communication Tradition

Organizational communication research arrived on the scene as propaganda analysis was falling out of favor. As a well-established field today, organizational communication's history has been detailed and critiqued by a number of scholars (see Redding, 1985; Redding & P. K. Tompkins, 1988; Taylor, Flanagin, Cheney, & Seibold, 2000, for general histories; see Cheney, 2004, for a discussion of the sociological roots of organizational communication, and see Clair, 1999, for a critique of such histories). In this section, we focus on the connections of organizational communication research to rhetorical study.

Those who trace the origins of organizational communication scholarship describe the period from the 1900s to the 1940s as a time in which scholars taught communication skills to people in organizations (Redding, 1985; Redding & P. K. Tompkins, 1988; Taylor et al., 2000).[4] Redding particularly noted how business English and Dale Carnegie's work from this period drew from rhetorical principles, leading him to argue that "[o]ne of the most important 'roots,' then, of the field of organizational communication is unquestionably what we call today 'rhetorical theory'" (p. 17). Indeed, the philosophical and rhetorical origins of the field are numerous (see Clair, 1999).

Redding (1985) referred to the period from 1942 to 1947 as the seminal years in organizational communication. With the advent of World War II, academic, military, and industrial organizations discovered the importance of communication skills. Aligning with the trend in propaganda analysis, work from the 1940s to the 1970s tended to adopt a neutral and supposedly objective stance toward communication in organizations. This applied-scientific phase once again moved scholarship away from rhetorical theory, focusing instead on measurement, variables, and experimental research designs (Taylor et al., 2000).

The 1980s brought in a renewed focus on rhetorical aspects of organizing. In 1985, Putnam and Cheney identified a rhetorical perspective as one of four new directions in organizational communication research. They undoubtedly based this conclusion on work such as P. K. Tompkins's (1984) contribution to an edited volume on rhetorical and communication theory, in which he took a decidedly rhetorical stance toward his review of organizational communication literature. P. K. Tompkins reviewed the root organizational theories of Fayol (1925/1949), Taylor (1912/1947), and Weber (1978) and interpreted them for communication, and, in particular, for rhetorical scholars. He contended that "the appeal for organizational *persuasion*, [italics added] as opposed to compulsion . . . underscores the observation . . . that organizational communication should be concerned at least as much with influence or persuasion as with information processing" [which was the predominant model of the day] (p. 667). P. K. Tompkins (1987) translated Weber's systems of authority (charismatic, traditional, and legal-rational) into rhetorical terms, discussing the relationship of Weber's ideal types of authority with Aristotle's modes of proof: *ethos, pathos,* and *logos.* In addition, two different bibliographic reviews of organizational communication literature from this time period mentioned areas related to rhetorical study of organizing. The analysis by Wert-Gray, Center, Brashers, and Meyers (1991) mentioned public organizational communication, and the review by Allen, Gotcher, and Seibert (1993) of 17 different areas covered in existing research included categories of power and influence, organizational-environmental communication interfaces, and studies of language and message content. By the end of the 1990s, supported by two successful special NCA seminars on the subject, a small group of organizational scholars formally articulated and defined the study of organizational rhetoric (Cheney & McMillan, 1990; Crable, 1990). However, before we review this work, we turn our attention to two other areas, public relations and social movements, from which relevant scholarship also has emerged.

Public Relations Tradition

Public relations is an often overlooked area in the communication discipline. Reviews of public relations are split between research and practice in a manner that we believe to be unique within communication; that is, practice and application are as important and often take precedence over research and theory. As an example, Vasquez and Taylor (2000) argued that the essence of public relations research and practice is "the building and maintenance of strategic ethical relationships" (p. 319). This description reflects the area's historical focus on the "production of strategic organizational messages" more than on critique and questioning of these practices (Botan & Taylor, 2004, p. 651). Indeed, critiques of public relations tend to come from journalists and journalism scholars (e.g., Soley, 1995; Stauber & Rampton, 1995). Perhaps the marriage of the practical and theoretical in public relations hinders much internal critique of the practice, inasmuch as such critique calls into question the jobs of over half the field. Despite these difficulties, Botan and Taylor contended that public relations research and theory (focusing particularly on public-organization relationships) are developing quickly, and, most importantly for this chapter, this area remains extremely relevant to organizational rhetoric.

In this section, we discuss rhetorical public relations scholarship, showing connections among public relations research and the other areas already reviewed. The origins of public relations practice are tied to a variety of times and places ranging from ancient Greece to the American Revolutionary War (e.g., Cutlip, Center, & Broom, 1999). One important moment of modern public relations practice in the United States deals with the big railroad companies in the late 1800s. These organizations enjoyed large but troubled reputations, creating a need to defend their actions against negative public opinion (Cheney & Vibbert, 1987). The Association of American Railroads used the term *public relations* to describe these actions in 1897 (Cutlip et al., 1999), setting up understandings of public relations as reactive and defensive.

Heath (2001) suggested that public relations originated from mass communication research, and, indeed, the development of public relations practice and research is connected to the propaganda work discussed above. Edward Bernays, who is considered to be the father of modern public relations (Cheney & Vibbert, 1987), worked for the CPI during World War I (Sproule, 1987). During this time, the field of public relations operated largely out of an assumption that propaganda, publicity, and public information were good for democracy and society (Sproule, 1997). The end of World War I and the start of the 1920s brought the development of public relations firms and two different types of public relations practice. Bernays took what he viewed as a scientific approach to public relations practice, aligning with the post–World War I trends in propaganda analysis. This approach has undoubtedly led to much of the social scientific public relations research that we witness in contemporary times (see Vasquez & Taylor, 2000, for a review).

Meanwhile, the Rockefellers' celebrated press agent, Ivy Lee, advocated an approach that at least implicitly was more rhetorical in nature. Although Lee described his job as being about publicity, he suggested that his role was to interpret the railroads to the public and the public to the railroads (Cheney & Vibbert, 1987). Lee's understanding of public relations resembles Bryant's (1953) definition of rhetoric as "adjusting ideas to people and people to ideas" (p. 413), as well as more recent definitions of public relations as "the adjustment of organizations to environments and environments to organizations" (Crable & Vibbert, 1986, p. 394). This adjustment, of course, is accomplished rhetorically, inviting rhetorical theory to assist in the examination and understanding of public relations practice.

Although these practical origins of public relations are at least 100 years old, public relations research and theory have mostly developed during the last 25 years (Botan & Taylor, 2004). A growing body of research in public relations embraces a rhetorical perspective, although it still remains secondary to the social scientific approach in the area (Hazleton & Botan, 1989; Vasquez & Taylor, 2000). As just one indication of rhetoric's secondary status in public relations research, a 2004 NCA public relations panel grouped papers with critical, postmodern, and rhetorical perspectives under the title "Alternative views in public relations." However, Robert Heath, the editor of the *Handbook of Public Relations*, has long advocated a rhetorical approach to public relations (e.g., Heath, 1992, 2001), and several edited volumes discuss rhetorical approaches to public relations (Elwood, 1995; Toth & Heath, 1992). As an example of this approach, Boyd (2001b) explored the development of questions about Standard Oil's practices as a monopolistic trust during the early 1900s and the company's response as an example of public relations apologia (see Benoit, 1995a). Boyd argued that a rhetoric of arrogance, one that was aloof and suggested self-importance, contributed to the dissolution of Standard Oil Company in 1911. Thus, some scholars in public relations have demonstrated the value of addressing organizational messages through a rhetorical lens.

The Pivotal Role of Social Reform Movements

The rhetorical tradition encompasses 2500 years of scholarship and history. Thus far, organizational rhetoric has invoked only a small portion of the theories and ideas developed within rhetorical theory. Here we detail an important shift of rhetorical studies to a focus on collectivities that occurred about mid-twentieth century. Before the Civil War, higher education in the United States concentrated on oratory and rhetoric, but afterward, educational foci moved away from citizen rhetors to written and technical communication (Sproule, 1997). Rhetoricians continued to study individual orators such as Daniel Webster and the Lincoln-Douglas debates, but rhetoricians had little to no role in the propaganda analysis discussed earlier. The earliest modern rhetorical studies emphasized the individual "great men" rhetors (Cheney, 1991). Examples of these works can be found in early volumes of the *Quarterly Journal of Public Speaking* (e.g., Doyle, 1916; Gislason, 1917).

Although general rhetorical studies and theorizing can and do inform organizational rhetoric, the study of historical movements has particular relevance.

Griffin (1952) was one of the first to suggest that we "turn our attention from the individual 'great orator'" toward the rhetorical study of "a multiplicity of speakers, speeches, audiences, and occasions" (p. 184). He argued for positioning the rhetorical movement within the historical context and challenged the rhetorician to interrogate the message, while considering the rhetorical theory of the time. Interestingly, Griffin highlighted a connection to the mass communication tradition when he mentioned that scholars studying rhetoric from the period 1920–1950 must acknowledge and consider propaganda strategies. Furthermore, he established an early foundation for organizational rhetoric with his suggestion that the "great orators" rarely speak apart from a movement.

Study of the rhetoric of social movements continued to flourish, particularly in light of the tumultuous 1960s and 1970s in the United States (see Simons, Mechling, & Schreier, 1984, for a review). Social movement scholars distinguished their work from organizational communication and "more institutionalized collectivities," including business organizations, established religious denominations, and interest-group lobbies (Simons et al., 1984, p. 794). Organizational rhetoric scholars note that social movements tend to be characterized by their limited life spans, identifiable spokespeople, and antiestablishment nature, distinguishing them from traditional organizations (Cheney, 1992; Cheney & McMillan, 1990). Yet Cheney acknowledged social movement research as the "first systematic study of the rhetoric of collectivities" (p. 168).

So while the early study of collectivities stressed the attempts at influence by insurgency groups that sought to promote change from the bottom up and from the margins of society, scholars largely ignored the old established institutions that had endured. However, as the field of speech communication expanded into the organizational arena, some scholars began to ask a question posed by McMillan (1982) in one of the early studies of organizational rhetoric: "If insurgent collectivities, which usually have limited life and utility, have significant and well defined rhetorical markers, do not long-term, established, formal organizations also demonstrate distinctive rhetorical characteristics? . . . Are there perhaps even rhetorical correlates to organizational survival which remain untapped within the limited confines of movement study?" (p. 2).

Two important theories were pivotal during this transitional period of the 1970s and 1980s. Systems theory suggested a framework that considered the organization as embedded in a physical context of discourse that included both internal environments (workers, physical plant, management, etc.) and external environments (competitors, raw materials, cultural and political institutions, etc.) (Katz & Kahn, 1978). Furthermore, exchanging and transforming energy (resources, personnel, ideas) into a product or a service begged for an analysis of how such transactions were symbolically negotiated, both inside and between boundaries. Katz and Kahn were organizational sociologists, with no particular communication slant to their work; the fact that systems theory was replete with communication implications had to be explored and pointed out by one of the communication field's own.

Herbert Simons did just that when he took what social movement scholars knew about campaigns and overlaid it upon the tasks of more formal collectivities to stake out a theoretical perspective of rhetorical systems— whether institutionalized or ad hoc. In his important transitional article, Simons (1972) also provided a much-needed critical methodology for judging the leadership of collectivities by assessing the degree to which it succeeds in managing the "requirements, problems, and strategies" of the group that it leads. Notably, because of its grounding in systems theory, this piece addressed *any* formally or informally organized group that must mobilize those on the inside to work and convince those outside to accept the "product" of the group's labors, despite its explicit focus on social movement study. Much like the tenets of general systems theory, which puts an organism in contact and interaction with its environment, Simons's work reminds us that nothing short of organizational survival depends on compelling persuasion by organizational leadership.

Contemporary work in social movements increasingly blends with research in organizational communication, as the boundaries of what constitutes organizations and social movements expand and shift. Pezzullo (2003) employed participant observation (frequently used in organizational research) as her methodology for studying the competing messages of two counterpublics addressing both breast cancer and each other. Cloud (2001) called for further rhetorical attention to organizationally related issues of class and power in pursuit of social change. Critical and feminist organizational scholars pursue issues of class (e.g., Kirby, Golden, Medved, Jorgenson, & Buzzanell, 2003), but few of these studies have taken a rhetorical perspective (see Lair, Sullivan, & Cheney, 2005; Meisenbach et al., 2003, for exceptions), and even fewer have adopted a social movements perspective.

As an example of the kind of disciplinary boundary-blending that is present and possible in contemporary social movement studies, Brimeyer, Eaker, and Clair (2004) considered the rhetorical strategies employed by both Complete Grains Grocery management and United Grocery Workers union organizers during a contentious period. They found a complex overlap and interplay of the strategies and messages created by the two groups that may have been missed through separate consideration of either the union or the corporation's rhetoric. This study could be classified as belonging within organizational communication, social movement, and public relations bodies of work. We argue that it can also be usefully understood as contributing to another growing area of study—organizational rhetoric.

Birth of the Subfield of Organizational Rhetoric

History and development. Parallel with the rhetorical turn to the study of the discourse of collectivities, other rhetorical work was also breaking ground for this new and fledgling area of study. Some of the most immediate precursors to organizational rhetoric include several studies from the 1970s. Bormann (1972, 1982, 1983) developed symbolic convergence theory to examine how organizational members create and interpret events through fantasy chains. P. K. Tompkins, Fisher, Infante, and E. L. Tompkins (1975) began the work of applying Burke's theorizing to the characteristics of formal organizations, and Sharf (1978) offered a rhetorical analysis of leadership communication in small-group settings.

A particular pocket of interest in the academy emerged, specifically at Purdue University, in the study of organizations as rhetorical entities that served as an important catalyst for the young field. The development of organizational rhetoric is particularly associated with students of W. Charles Redding, Phillip Tompkins, and Roderick Hart at Purdue University and the University of Texas–Austin, perhaps beginning with Carol Jablonski's 1979 dissertation on institutional rhetoric and change in the Catholic church. Hart moved from Purdue to the University of Texas–Austin in 1982, bringing an awareness of and interest in organizational rhetoric to his new department. During this time, Jill McMillan (1982) wrote her dissertation, which explored a variety of organizations as both products and sources of rhetorical influence. George Cheney's dissertation and early work (e.g., 1983a, 1983b, 1991) adapting Burkean rhetorical concepts to organizations also contributed significantly to theorizing about organizational rhetoric. The development and use of the term *identification* in these publications highlight the subtle and covert nature of organizational persuasion. P. K. Tompkins and Cheney (1985) demonstrated how organizations exert subtle decision-making control (unobtrusive control) through their use of enthymematic arguments. Thus, one of the important contributions of organizational rhetoric consists of a focus on the subtle methods of identification as a form of persuasion.

Two successive preliminary conferences at NCA in 1988 and 1989 brought together a diverse group of scholars and resulted in the 1990 special issue of the *Journal of Applied Communication Research,* edited by Jablonski. Cheney and McMillan (1990) provided the groundwork for considering organizational rhetoric as an area of study. Crable (1990) detailed implications of understanding organizational rhetoric as a fourth great system of rhetoric, succeeding the grammatical, psychological, and sociological systems (see Ehninger, 1968). Hegstrom (1990) considered the presence and tolerance of dissent in organizations. Sproule (1990) discussed the ways in which social science perspectives on managerial influence relate to "how organizational rhetoric contributes to a rational-democratic society that is based on a lively public sphere" (p. 130). Heath (1990) explored how the asbestos industry convinced itself that its product was acceptable, and Peterson (1990) illustrated how religious organizational leaders used a rhetorical-historical argument "to ease member identification with organizational change" (p. 181). In the next year, Cheney (1991) published *Rhetoric in an Organizational Society*, characterizing organizational rhetoric as "the management of multiple identities" (p. 2). These examples of scholarship constitute a basis for work and research in organizational rhetoric.

By way of summary, we would like to suggest what the new subfield extracted from its predecessors and then specify its contributions to organizational theory and research. From social movement theory, we learned to enlarge the unit of analysis of criticism from one individual and his/her social influence to a group of people (Griffin, 1952). From the public relations perspective, we learned that, for an organization to survive and thrive, it must communicate well with the environment outside its boundaries to secure necessary resources and to "sell" its product or service (Cheney & Vibbert, 1987; Crable & Vibbert, 1986). From organizational communication, we discovered that differences exist between the rhetoric of insurgency groups and of formal organizations and institutions and that the workplace, with its constituent power and hierarchy, offers a unique environment of interpersonal and group influence-peddling (Cheney, 1991). From propaganda analysis and early mass communication, we observed that sometimes discourse migrates from face-to-face settings (i.e., beyond superior/subordinate and workgroup communication) to expanded, mediated conditions, and in the absence of the possibility of direct feedback with the source of those messages, audiences must learn how to "read" such messages wisely and well (Sproule, 1988).

Contributions of organizational rhetoric. Though organizational rhetoric "borrowed" a great deal from the four traditions mentioned above, it also has made some important contributions. Perhaps its most critical contribution involves a reconsideration of the notion of *power* within the organization. Early organizational literature seemed to indicate that power in the organization was concentrated at the top, and thus "orders" from management and bosses marked the most efficient way to pass communication to underlings (P. K. Tompkins, 1984). Organizational rhetoric scholars examined early organizational texts (e.g., the Hawthorne studies and early decision-making models), and they determined that something more complex was happening within organizations (Conrad, 1983; P. K. Tompkins & Cheney, 1985). Indeed, power in organizations was more widespread and ubiquitous than we had imagined.

Furthermore, when power is widespread, workers are not inclined to be coerced, forced, or ordered; they must be persuaded (McMillan, 1990; Redding, 1987; P. K. Tompkins, 1984) and adjusted or adjusted to; these are rhetorical imperatives that have greatly expanded and enriched the communicative terrain of organizational study.

Another unique aspect of work in organizational rhetoric involves its tendency to *blur boundaries*—in other words, to consider simultaneously both the internal and external rhetoric of organizations and their relationship. Traditionally, organizational communication research has focused on internal communication, such as employee handbooks, newsletters, and memos (Cheney & Vibbert, 1987). It has taken a long time for organizational scholars to look outside organizational boundaries and to analyze the interrelations among organizations and environments (Cheney, 2004; Cheney & Christensen, 2001). In parallel fashion, Cheney and Vibbert observed that scholars have tended to treat internal organizational documents and communication as beyond the scope of public relations research.

Such distinctions and boundaries have recently begun to blur as organizational scholars increasingly examine the interplay of organizational, environmental, and societal discourses (e.g., Cheney, 1999; Knight & Greenberg, 2002; Livesay, 2002) and as public relations scholars explore the organizational identity and reputational impacts of internal employee communication (Cheney & Christensen, 2001; see also Cheney, 2004, for a chart representation of studies that cross these internal/external borders). According to Cheney and Christensen, organizational communication that "can be described as self-referential communication or auto-communication" can also speak to external audiences (p. 252). For example, Ulmer's (2001) study showed how Aaron Feuerstein's postcrisis communication, which was directed internally toward his Malden Mills employees, also "spoke" to external audiences about the values of the organization and its leader.

Although scholars have come to question the solidity of organizational boundaries, especially in a technological age (Cheney & Christensen, 2001), the interplay between the audiences and organizations may be uniquely understood and appreciated by organizational rhetoric scholars with their focus on "the management of multiple identities" (Cheney, 1991, p. 2). Organizational rhetoric scholars show how internal and external environments check and balance one another and operate simultaneously. For example, in the study of a religious denomination's attempt to make a policy change concerning sexist language, McMillan (1988) demonstrated the importance of spokespersons' attention to language and persuasive strategies when they talk to present members as well as to those they hope to recruit.

Finally, organizational rhetoric also has facilitated the study of organizations by privileging their *public* words and record. Organizational scholars know well that organizations are more than just a little paranoid about admitting researchers, analysts, even consultants, into their inner sanctums. Rhetorical scholars, however, believing in the "inherent sociability of organizations" of systems theory say, "no problem, we'll wait," because most of those decisions, the important ones at least, made "behind closed corporate doors are destined to face the glaring light of public scrutiny" (McMillan, 1987, p. 24). Once those words become public, they are fair game. Furthermore, assessing the organization's public, written record affords researchers the opportunity to study organizations as they are meant to be studied, longitudinally.

Organizational rhetoric owes much to the fields that preceded it and those that continue to coexist with and to inform it. However, it has contributed some important theoretical and methodological wrinkles itself: a different way to conceive of organizational power and discourse, a loosening of the rigid parameters around the internal and external boundaries of the organization, and a way to honor and to leverage the publicity and longevity of organizational words and actions. In part, this review is intended to invite other scholars to the table, but, on the other hand, it also reveals that many diverse scholars have long been sitting at the table without recognition of one another. We hope that we can reenergize and move forward in studying and theorizing about organizational rhetoric by highlighting a wide variety of contributions and bringing them together. In the next section, we note issues that have attracted organizational rhetoric scholars and some of the key theories that have guided their work.

ISSUES FOR ORGANIZATIONAL RHETORIC

The previous section considered the historical antecedents and development of organizational rhetoric. Next, we outline four vital issues that have been and continue to be investigated through organizational rhetoric: crisis communication, maintenance communication, power and voice, and corporate social responsibility. With regard to each issue, we outline existing theories that help scholars in their investigations.

Crisis Communication

First, a great deal of rhetoric-based research in recent years has focused on organizational crises. A crisis can be defined as "a specific, unexpected and nonroutine event or series of events that create[s] high levels of uncertainty and threaten[s] or [is] perceived to threaten an organization's high priority goals" (Seeger, Sellnow, & Ulmer, 1998, p. 233). Some early examples of this kind of research include the discussion by Benoit and Lindsey (1987) of Tylenol's strategic management of its bottle-tampering crisis, the exploration by Dionisopoulos and Crable (1988) of the importance of the rhetoric of definition in the Three Mile Island incident, and Foss's (1984) consideration of Chrysler's corporate rhetoric during a financial crisis. Building on Burke's understanding of the rhetoric of redemption, Foss argued that Chrysler and other organizations can use symbols to create a new identity as a path to redemption.[5] Scholars have also explored how organizations may speak as epideictic (Crable & Vibbert, 1983) and deliberative rhetoricians (Johnson & Sellnow, 1995) during times of crisis. Within the crisis communication literature (see Lee, 2005; Seeger et al., 1998, 2001, 2003, for full reviews), two particular areas of concentration have developed that deserve separate attention for their rhetorical natures: legitimacy research and image restoration/apologia research.

Legitimacy. In their work on the rhetorical management of organizational crises, scholars frequently invoke the concept of legitimacy. *Organizational legitimacy* generally refers to the process of justifying or supporting an organization's existence (e.g., Allen & Caillouet, 1994; Coombs, 1992; Francesconi, 1982; Goldzwig & Sullivan, 1995; Maurer, 1971; Metzler, 2001; Meyer & Scott, 1983). It has been studied in a variety of disciplines, including philosophy (Habermas, 1973), politics (Stillman, 1974), sociology (Dowling & Pfeffer, 1975; Suchman, 1995), and management (Deephouse, 1996), where definitions emphasize the degree of congruence between societal values and an organization's actions. Hearit (1995b) offered an explicitly rhetorical definition of legitimacy when he argued that corporate social legitimacy is "the rhetorically constructed and publicly recognized congruence between the values of a corporation and those of a larger social system in which it operates" (p. 3).

Scholars have devised ways of describing and categorizing legitimation processes, and we briefly review two of the best-known categorizations with a goal of identifying strengths and future directions. Dowling and Pfeffer (1975) argued that legitimacy can be measured by examination of societal values and norms, which can be compared with organizational values and norms. First, scholars determine relevant societal values through systematic surveys of written and spoken communication. They then compare those values with an organization's method of operating, output, and goals. If the societal values do not match an organization's norms, then the organization has legitimacy problems.

Dowling and Pfeffer (1975) offered three basic strategies that organizations can use to obtain legitimacy when a problem exists. First, an organization may change and adapt its output, methods, and goals to match societal values and norms. Second, the organization can alter societal values and norms to align with the organization's output, methods, and goals. Finally, Dowling and Pfeffer contended that organizational members can work to establish connections between their organization and symbols, values, and other organizations that already have strong bases of legitimacy (see Sethi, 1977, for a nearly identical set of strategic options).

Coombs (1992) proposed a broader approach to understanding legitimacy. He asserted that, for publics to support an organization's position, they must believe in the legitimacy of the issue, its manager, and the proposed policy. He then described 10 strategies or bases for supporting legitimacy: a) tradition, charisma, and bureaucracy (from sociology literature); b) values, symbols, de-legitimacy (from social movement literature), and c) credibility, rationality, emotionality, and entitlement (from persuasion literature). Coombs suggested determining the strategies that an organization uses during each aspect of legitimacy (issue, issue manager, policy) and then evaluating their effectiveness by assessment of public responses.

These two approaches provide excellent starting points for analysis of organizational legitimation. However, both models stop at description. They do not explain *why* an organization's attempt at use of a strategy may fail. Organizations frequently claim to be credible, but why do some claims work and some fail? Second, these models also stop short of considering whether and when an organization should engage in these strategies. In essence, both methods discussed reveal a managerial and functional perspective, asking how organizations can best manage challenges to legitimacy, while leaving questions of power and ethics unaddressed. Some scholars seek a redress of those concerns. For example, Bonewits and Meisenbach (2004) outlined how Habermas's discussion of validity claims can assist scholars in questioning and understanding public reactions to legitimacy-building efforts.[6] Such efforts begin to address legitimation from a critical perspective. Meanwhile, Cheney and Christensen (2001) maintained that legitimacy is an ethical issue, yet existing studies of legitimacy rarely consider such implications. One exception is Hearit's (1995b) argument that a legitimation message must articulate both the usefulness or competence of an organization and its community responsibility. In short, his orientation to legitimacy highlights the rhetorical justification of the utility and responsibility of an organization.

We also believe that scholars can and should turn their attention toward understanding how the legitimation process works outside of times of crisis. Boyd (2000) argued for further refinement of legitimacy research by distinguishing between *institutional* legitimacy, in which the existence of the entire organization is being challenged, and more common *actional* legitimacy, when various publics challenge particular policies and actions of an organization. We encourage scholars to investigate moments of actional legitimacy as one way of investigating day-to-day versus crisis management of legitimacy in organizations.

Image restoration and apologia. A second major area of crisis research within organizational rhetoric scholarship is image restoration and apologia studies (see Benoit, 1995a; Hearit, 2001; Ihlen, 2002, for full reviews). Much of this work extends from Ware and Linkugel's (1973) discussion of apologetic discourse strategies used by individual speakers facing criticism.[7] Ware and Linkugel offered four strategies: denial, bolstering, differentiation, and transcendence. In 1991, Schultz and Seeger argued for applying and considering the use of these apologia strategies in corporate-centered rhetoric.

Benoit (1995a) provided one comprehensive application in his book *Accounts, Excuses, and Apologies*, which articulates a theory of image restoration that has spurred a growing body of research on corporate apologia (e.g., Benoit, 1995b, 1997; Benoit & Czerwinksi, 1997; Burns & Bruner, 2000; Coombs & Schmidt, 2000; Sellnow, Ulmer & Snider, 1998). He suggested five basic categories of image restoration strategies: denial, evasion of responsibility, decreasing the offensiveness of an event, corrective action, and mortification (see Brinson & Benoit, 1999, for a useful table presenting all of Benoit's image restoration strategies).

Although scholars frequently employ Benoit's categorization of image restoration strategies, there are other perspectives and even some challenges to his work (see Coombs, 1999b; Hearit, 2006). Burns and Bruner (2000) questioned how Benoit's theory tends to suggest that apologia is a linear process that can result in a restoration of the original state and reputation for an organization. Indeed, Benoit (2000) acknowledged his preference in hindsight for describing his work as focusing on image repair rather than on image restoration for this very reason. Fishman (1999) combined Benoit's articulation of image restoration strategies with Fink's (1986) stage theory in one attempt to offer richer understanding of complex crisis events, such as the ValuJet Flight 592 crash. Coombs (1998, 1999a, 1999b) recently developed a typology of crisis communication strategies that includes attacking, denying, excusing, justifying, ingratiating, correcting, and apologizing. Recent research highlights the occasions and the kinds of combinations in which certain strategies are used (see Allen & Caillouet, 1994; Ihlen, 2002).

Hearit has generated a considerable body of research addressing rhetorical aspects of apologia and image restoration (e.g., 1995a, 1995b, 1996, 1997, 1999, 2001, 2006). Hearit (1996) offered *kategoria*, or the counterattack strategy, as an addition to apologia research. His paradigmatic example is how General Motors responded to *Dateline NBC*'s accusations that GM trucks were prone to explosion. Upon learning that *Dateline* producers had attached explosive devices to the GM trucks used in the segment footage, GM responded by attacking the credibility of its accuser. Hearit (2001) also noted four sources of corporate criticism or types of alleged wrongdoing: accidents, scandals and illegalities, product safety incidents, and social irresponsibility. He called for greater attention to possible connections between the use of certain strategies and the types of wrongdoing of which organizations are accused. Most recently, Hearit (2006) featured the inherently public and corporate nature of apologia, contending that the public act of engaging in apologia is essential in the management of accusations of wrongdoing.

These various typologies reveal opportunities for future research. One area in which we see a particular need for increased scholarly attention is the crisis communication of nonprofit organizations (Hearit, 2006). Although apologia and crisis scholars undoubtedly intend to include nonprofit organizations in their discussions of "corporate" crises, a review of existing case studies indicates an overwhelming focus on for-profit organizations (e.g., AT&T, Daimler-Benz, Dow Corning, Johnson & Johnson, Sears, USAir, and Texaco). Scholars can also address situations such as the handling by the American Red Cross of the Liberty Fund after the September 11, 2001, attacks, and the many other nonprofit organizations whose actions and policies have been questioned. Another growing concern in apologia work considers the constraint that legal liability creates in the process (Hearit, 2006; Tyler, 1997). Overall, scholars still need to test, refine, and question these various categorizations and typologies of legitimacy, apologia, and image repair strategies as they are employed by all genres of organizational actors.

Maintenance Communication

In the 2004 NCA panel discussion on organizational rhetoric, Roderick Hart challenged organizational rhetoric scholars to pull back from their investigation of crisis rhetoric, asking how one can really explain and understand a deviation from the norm (a crisis) before one grasps its everyday complexity and character. He advocated focusing more on day-to-day rhetorical practices of organizations. The fact that these actions are common and continuous suggests that these examples of rhetoric are at least as powerful as (or more powerful than) those generated in crisis. In terms of organizational rhetoric, these arguments highlight the need for increased focus on everyday rhetorical moments, such as those found in mundane organizational documents and conversations.

Quiescence and issue management. Hart (2004) correctly asserted that scholars of organizational rhetoric have been slower to address noncrisis moments. In a rare exception, McMillan's (1982) dissertation devoted a chapter to the function of maintenance rhetoric. In a study of four sociologically diverse organizations, McMillan learned that, despite their different goals, membership, and technology, these organizations—a church, an educational organization, a national business, and a political organization—exhibited some common rhetorical markers. In what she called the "rhetoric of quiescence," each organization mobilized its rhetorical forces around creating and maintaining an image, internal support of its people and tasks, and an interface with an environment "outside" that contained vital resources and markets. This "business as usual" rhetoric eschewed the highly charged, often defensive posture of a company in conflict, but McMillan reasoned that it enabled "the trains to run on time" and that no company would remain around to defend without solid maintenance discourse.

McMillan's (1982) work connects with an emerging maintenance-oriented area within rhetorical public relations scholarship—the issue management literature (e.g., Heath, 1997). These studies theorize about the life cycle of issues, offering suggestions for how to guide issues through the cycle without creating or encountering a full crisis (Gaunt & Ollenburger, 1995; Jones & Chase, 1979). This research pursues successful issue management by an organization and its public relations department, taking a managerial perspective.

Of course, issue management research still blends with issues of crisis. Ulmer (2001) highlighted how, in the case of Aaron Feuerstein and Malden Mills, effective pre-crisis leadership communication helped the company weather a major crisis in 1995. Knight and Greenberg (2002) discussed how Nike's discussions with anti-sweatshop advocates created a dialectic of issue and crisis management. Such initial investigations can be expanded to question the managerial perspective of public relations crisis management studies and to better explore everyday organizational messages.

Identification and identity. The significant body of research on identification also addresses everyday maintenance issues within organizational rhetoric. Identification can be understood as "the process through which people bond themselves with a particular value-based identity and subsequently make sense of the world through that discursive formation" (Larson & Pepper, 2003, p. 532). Burke (1950/1969) argued that "identification is compensatory to division" (p. 22). Individuals seek to distinguish themselves from others and to create connections with individuals and organizations. Cheney and Christensen (2001) noted that "the ongoing rhetorical struggle for organizations of most kinds is to establish a clearly distinctive identity and at the same time connect with more general concerns so as to be maximally persuasive and effective" (p. 233). This balance is pursued by the rhetorical creation of unique organizational identities that build identifications with various individuals.

On the macro level, all of these identifications are designed to coalesce around a sense of an organization's identity (see Cheney & Christensen, 2001, for a full review of organizational identity). Organizations increasingly focus on their overall images and impressions, and this pursuit of desirable public and internal images motivates organizations to participate in public dialogue (Boyd, 2001a). Cheney and McMillan (1990) asserted that organizational communication emphasizes gaining support for the organization (and it does so by fostering identifications between individuals and the organization).

On the micro level, identification is both a process and outcome, and, as such, it remains central to discussions of persuasion, rhetoric, and identity. As discussed above, work on organizational identification is part of the earliest body of research in organizational rhetoric. Kenneth Burke (e.g., 1950/1969) developed the construct of identification, and Cheney (e.g., 1983a, 1983b) applied and expanded Burke's notion of identification for the study of the rhetoric of organizations. Although Burke wrote explicitly about how an individual rhetor fosters identification with an audience, he addressed rhetoric associated with the process of organizing in his explication of administrative rhetoric. Although a great deal of recent research has centered on identification (e.g., Apker, Zabava Ford, and Fox, 2003; Barker & Tompkins, 1994; DiSanza & Bullis, 1999; Kuhn & Nelson, 2002; Larson & Pepper, 2003; Scott et al., 1999; Scott, Corman, & Cheney, 1998), in this review, we emphasize its rhetorical nature, highlighting a few aspects of identification that have not yet received significant attention from organizational rhetoric scholars.

Cheney's (1983a, 1983b) early work on identification relies on the strategic side of identification that Burke (1972) covered in *Dramatism and Development* (see p. 28). Cheney formalized this passage into three strategies of identification, providing a guide for criticism of organizational rhetoric. Burke suggested three ways in which identification may be generated strategically by rhetors. First, he offered the example of the politician who tells a humble people of his/her own humble origins. Cheney called this strategy "common ground." It makes a direct association between similar people, ideas, concepts, etc. Next, Burke and Cheney discussed the power of identification through *antithesis*, in which a rhetor, through the articulation of a common enemy, unites those who might otherwise be opposed to one another. Finally, Cheney assessed use of Burke's the *assumed* or *transcendent we*, in which a rhetor articulates disparate groups, people, or ideas as working together. This subtle strategy associates dissimilar groups and articulates them as simultaneously present, transcending the differences. Thus, extending from Burke, Cheney described three ways that organizations and their individual rhetors may attempt to get individuals and publics to identify with an organization.[8] DiSanza and Bullis (1999) later articulated four additional identification substrategies that they saw as fitting within the strategy of building common ground: global recognition of individuals' contributions, recognition of individuals' contributions outside the organization, invitation, and bragging.

Scholars have also expanded rhetorical identification research to consider how the espousal of values can foster identification with and approval for an organization (Bostdorff & Vibbert, 1994; Cheney & Frenette, 1993; O'Connor, 2004; Vaughn, 1997). For example, Bostdorff and Vibbert explained how organizations articulate and promote values in order to enhance the organization's image, deflect criticisms, and establish premises from which future decisions can be made by stakeholders. Vaughn noted how common values articulated in high-tech industry recruiting materials foster identification and socialize newcomers.

Future research in organizational rhetoric could concentrate more on how the audiences of organizational messages do or do not perceive themselves as identified with organizations. DiSanza and Bullis (1999) provide an excellent example of this kind of research in their consideration of four diverse ways in which employees respond to attempts to foster organizational identification within U.S. Forest Service newsletters: nonidentification, textual identification, contextual identification, and disidentification (see also Larson & Pepper, 2003). Most recently, Boyd (2004) developed Burke's principle of the oxymoron as an element in explaining the success or failure of organizational identifications.

We also direct the attention of organizational rhetoric scholars to Burke's (1966) suggestion that the less conscious one is of an identification, the more effective the identification will be in eliciting a response. Conversely, as one's consciousness of an identification increases, the power of the identification decreases. This point highlights the power of what P. K. Tompkins and Cheney (1985) called "unobtrusive control" or the manner in which employees and other publics are subtly led to fill in enthymematic arguments in ways consistent with the desires and interests of an organization.

Overall, identification constitutes a powerful concept that plays a significant role in the identities and the day-to-day success of organizations and individuals. Organizational scholars (e.g., Papa, Auwal, & Singhal, 1997; Scott et al., 1998) have continued to explore the role of identification in organizational processes, including consideration of interactions among multiple targets of identification. Organizations attempt to get individuals to align and identify with the organization through messages, but these identifications constantly shift, and much more may still be learned. In the future, we hope that scholars will further pursue the possibilities of less strategic and less conscious aspects of identification, which are perhaps the key characteristics that distinguish identification as a particular form of persuasion.

Power and Voice in Organizational Rhetoric

Rethinking power on the inside of the organization. Whereas early organizational communication theory seemed to present managerial power as virtually absolute, critical organizational rhetoric scholars reminded us that spokespersons for organizations may expect some reciprocal verbal reaction when they "speak" power to employees and other constituencies (Brown & McMillan, 1990). This simple point foregrounded some important insights about power and voice that organizational communication theorists had neglected: 1) voice *is* power in the organization and is governed accordingly by the hierarchy; 2) truly committed workers and stakeholders must be *persuaded,* not coerced, and 3) these stakeholders also can "talk back." This section begins by considering how these three primarily internal insights, which are rhetorically derived, have affected organizational theory and research, and it then concludes with a consideration of the organization itself as a social rhetor.

Redding (1987) was one of the first to note a fundamental relationship between influence and rhetoric, characterizing it as complicated by the management of organizational voices, identities, and identifications by organizational beings. Whereas early guild organizing was done to offer individual workers a collective voice that equated the church and government (Coleman, 1974), more contemporary corporate organizational voices frequently seem to be irrelevant to, if not working against, the interests of organizational members (Mumby, 1988). The power of organizational rhetoric can be viewed as accessible by relatively few elite members, whereas low-status organizational members may lack access to necessary resources or may lack permission to speak on behalf of the organization (McMillan, 1990). Furthermore, organizational interests often seem to take precedence over individual interests (Hegstrom, 1990).

Influenced by the work of Redding and, no doubt, the insights of the humanist movement, P. K. Tompkins (1984) forced us also to reconsider what sorts of messages motivate workers. As we mentioned earlier, traditional organizational theory assumed that workers did as they were told (see Fayol, 1925/1949; Taylor, 1912/1947; Weber, 1978)—a sort of verbal coercion—and that when downward communication failed, it was a matter of misunderstanding. (This tenet was entirely consistent with the information processing model of organizational communication that dominated at the time.) P. K. Tompkins made the provocative observation that the widespread ineffectiveness of downward communication might rather be a failure of persuasion— that indeed, rather than failing to comprehend what they had been told to do, the workforce just might not have been *convinced* that it was in its best interests to follow the order. This rhetorical turn was significant in suggesting that the traditional manager, who was previously a "cop," "referee," "devil's advocate," and "naysayer" (Peters & Austin, 1985, p. 265), must now become a "wordsmith," a "manager of eloquence" (Weick, 1980, p. 18), as he or she seeks to persuade toward a desired end (see Fairhurst, 1993; Gardner &

Cleavenger, 1998; Zorn, 2001, for examples of studies that have explored the symbolic influence of leaders).

Final reinforcement for the relationship between power and rhetoric came with the growing understanding that rhetoric is one of the few organizational resources that is abundant and free to all. Even if management possesses the privilege and responsibility to lead with symbols, symbols can also be deployed throughout the organization; indeed, workers and other stakeholders can "talk back" through formal channels (such as participative decision making, self-directed work teams, and suggestion boxes) *or* informal ones, and sometimes more dangerous venues, such as gossip, withholding or distorting information, or even whistle-blowing (see, for example, Hegstrom, 1999; Kassing, 1997; Sprague & Ruud, 1988). An example of research that examined the reciprocal rhetorical power of subordinates is Murphy's (1998) study of flight attendants who devised a range of strategies to counter what they believed to be excessive organizational control. Also, Brown and McMillan (1990) described how nursing home employees created a counter-narrative to resist the official organizational position that workers believed to be duplicitous and untrue. In an organizational world where stakeholders possess the potential for reciprocal symbolic power, it behooves organizational spokespersons to employ strategy and savvy rather than verbal force.

The power of the collective organizational voice. Notably, the notion of widespread, reciprocal power of individuals in the organization has been contested, especially by scholars who argue that the individual has been "de-centered" in the contemporary organization to the point that the only significant agency is that of organization as actor (Meisenbach et al., 2003). That admonition encourages us to consider "who" is really speaking when the organization makes a public announcement or participates in a social debate as well as whose interests are being served as it does so.

Crable (1990), for example, made a distinction between a rhetor being a Hollywood actor or a Burkean actor. The Burkean actor uses some means (agency) to act in order to achieve a purpose amid a particular scene. In contrast, the Hollywood actor simply reads lines written by someone else, the Burkean actor. Crable posed the question of whether an organizational individual in contemporary society is a Hollywood actor, articulating the words and representing the interests of the larger organization. Crable's question has been echoed by many other critical scholars who fear the potential of corporate hegemony (Bagdikian, 2000; Deetz, 1992; Habermas, 1981/1984, 1981/1987; Schiller, 1990).

Boyd (2001a), however, maintained that corporations constitute legitimate participants in public dialogue, that they have a right to their influence and participation in the public sphere. He also challenged Cheney and McMillan's (1990) criticism of organizations that advance their own interests over those of the general public, by noting that corporations may appropriately represent their own interests, just as individual rhetors do. Boyd's argument assumes that corporations contribute to public discourse rather than overwhelm and destroy it. Indeed, Waltzer (1988) argued that it could be dangerous and irresponsible not to give voice to organizational concerns, that perhaps "more of a risk is incurred by not joining the dialogue than by entering the fray" (p. 55).

We develop this debate by encouraging study of the extent to which and ways in which individuals, nonprofits, and government organizations are invited and able to participate in contemporary public dialogue. In so doing, we actually echo a concern raised by Ray S. Baker in the early 1900s, who, according to Sproule (1990), "saw managerial rhetoric as undemocratic because the unorganized public lacked its own publicity agents" (p. 130). From a critical perspective, it may be less important whether organizations are allowed to "speak" than whether they welcome other rhetors to the table. Manheim (1991) offered at least one instance in which this welcome did not occur, when Mobil Oil refused to talk to the *Wall Street Journal* and its reporters for three years after the paper wrote a negative editorial about the company.[9] In his study of paid advocacy advertising in the Op-Ed page of the *New York Times*, the *Washington Journalism Review*, and the *Columbia Journalism Review*, Waltzer (1988) noted that, although unions and other organizations can use these spaces, they are overwhelmingly used by corporations. Corporations are also overrepresented in organizational rhetoric research. Whereas Cheney (1991) emphasized the term "corporate" to refer to any group or collectivity, organizational rhetoric studies tend to focus on for-profit organizations. Of course, these nonprofits and government agencies may lack the resources to participate in what Burke (1950/1969) called "the wrangle in the marketplace," making their involvement difficult to study. Social movement studies tend to focus on how one kind of noncorporate organization finds and uses its voice, but we might consider many other nonprofit and government organizations whose voices and participation in the public sphere are often muted or missing altogether.

In summary, this section has considered the admonition of Charles Redding (1987) that "when we begin to study influence, we inevitably encounter . . . rhetoric" (p. 17). Whether that influential message comes from a manager attempting to justify a decision or from the organization "struggling just to be heard" in the wider public sphere (Cheney, Christensen, Zorn, & Ganesh, 2004, p. 118), the work of organizational rhetoric scholars has helped us to rethink how communicative power works in organizational contexts. Through a rhetorical lens, what once appeared to be "simple" control (P. K. Tompkins & Cheney, 1985) or essentially top-down, straightforward orders, now appears more complex, nuanced, and egalitarian; what once appeared just to be a "marketplace" in which to sell wares now seems to be an exquisite symbolic contest for the hearts and minds of an audience. Still, not all voices, whether on the shop floor or in the marketplace, are created equal.

Corporate Social Responsibility and Business Ethics

Closely related to the issues of organizational legitimacy, identification, and power mentioned here remains the question of an organization's responsibilities. In the wake of recent corporate scandals, critical questions about corporations must be asked not only by stakeholders but also by the academics and scholars who have been studying these organizations for years. Some scholars have asserted that corporations are, in fact, held more accountable today than they have been in the past (Boyd, 2001a; Heath, 1997; Judd, 1995). However, what is the nature of *corporate social responsibility* (CSR)[10] in today's society, and how, if at all, are organizations discursively fulfilling and altering these responsibilities? The rhetorical messages of organizations attempt to define these standards and influence judgments. Thus far, we have foreshadowed the potential for ethical violations against individuals by organizational power brokers; the characteristics of collective organizational voices "complicate issues of responsibility and accountability" (Cheney, 1991, p. 4) as well. Therefore, it is important to consider the emerging research on corporate social responsibility and business ethics from a rhetorical perspective (see Daugherty, 2001, for a review of social responsibility and public relations).

Scholarly and practical interest in organizational ethics seems to ebb and flow, based on whether corporate misdeeds appear in the news headlines, and until very recently the entire area of corporate social responsibility has been overlooked in communication research (see May & Zorn, 2003, and their forum on CSR). In particular, we call attention to the fact that neither the CSR special forum in *Management Communication Quarterly*, introduced by May and Zorn, nor its separate special issue, edited by Charles Conrad (2003), on the recent corporate meltdown, addresses these issues *explicitly* from a rhetorical perspective, though rhetoric is often implied.

Overall, organizational rhetoric scholarship thus far has rarely focused on ethical issues. A review by Allen et al. (1993) found that only 28 of 889 articles on organizational communication published between 1980 and 1991 addressed ethical issues. Johannesen's (2002) coverage of ethics in organizational communication revealed two conference papers addressing ethical implications of identification (Cheney, 1986; Cheney & P. K. Tompkins, 1984), but we discovered no record of their publication.

A few scholars have explained and interpreted ethical implications of organizational rhetoric. In addition to the various essays in the May and August

2003 issues of *Management Communication Quarterly*, Conrad's (1993) edited book, *The Ethical Nexus*, considered relations among ethics, values, and organizational decision making, with several authors taking a rhetorical approach (e.g., Cheney & Frenette, 1993, discussed how corporate discourse establishes value premises; Vibbert & Bostdorff, 1993, described how the insurance industry promoted certain values). McMillan and Hyde (2000) explored the existence and formation of an "institutional conscience, greater and more complex than the sum of its parts" (p. 32). They contended that Levinas's (1991) "call of conscience" applies to organizations as well as individuals, noting also that many organizations fail to answer this call. Roberts (2003) also extended the work of Levinas to develop two contrasting paths for human beings and collectivities: "the reflexive 'encrustation' of the self or the 'denuding of the self in responsibility for my neighbor'" (p. 251). Roberts recommended the latter as an admonition for corporations that "act" and "speak" altruistically. Furthermore, McMillan and Hyde suggested that a coherent, unitary, and consensual outcome to a troublesome ethical dilemma is less important than an organization's willingness to engage in the *process* of conscience formation or adaptation, and, for these authors, that process is rhetorical to the core. In one possible extension of this argument, Meisenbach (in press) detailed a process for organizational moral deliberation based on Habermas's (1983/1990) articulation of a discourse ethic. Hearit's (2006) new book takes an in-depth look at the ethical implications of corporate apologia, reinforcing McMillan and Hyde's assertion that participation in the process is valuable in and of itself. Finally, whereas studies such as these at least start discussion, Cyphert and Saiia (2004) argued that recent corporate malfeasance indicates that we should now "reconceptualize the discourse of organizational citizenship" (p. 241). They proposed a vocabulary of "corporate ecology," which allows corporations to "create discursive communities that reflect both the complexity of business relationships and the centrality of corporations in the resource allocation process of modern society" (p. 241).

Organizational scholars George Cheney, Steve May, and Juliet Roper are taking a significant step in addressing the paucity of rhetorical research in CSR by launching an edited volume to be published by Oxford University Press, titled *The Debate over Corporate Social Responsibility*. This volume will be interdisciplinary in nature, calling on scholars from organizational communication, public relations, management, law, and economics, and it will feature the creation of meaning and discourses around the contested terrain of CSR and business ethics that we have discussed here. Consistent with the argument of this review, it seeks to "blur boundaries" between related fields to determine how corporations can be encouraged to do their part, not just to feed their bottom line, but also to "accommodate the modern struggle for existence" that is common to us all (Cyphert & Saiia, 2004, p. 254).

PREDICTIONS ABOUT THE FUTURE DIRECTION OF THEORY AND STUDY IN ORGANIZATIONAL RHETORIC

Based on our review of the historical antecedents of, the development of, and issues in organizational rhetoric, we offer four predictions about the future direction of theory and study in organizational rhetoric.

First, future theory and study in organizational rhetoric will work to tease out and explain ways in which organizational rhetoric is unique. For example, because the audiences of organizational rhetoric are complex and ubiquitous (Cheney, Christensen, Conrad, et al., 2004), future theory must *locate* and describe those various audiences and, in particular, determine how they are specifically compelled by the messages of the organization. A particular challenge for scholars will be the exploration of the organization's persuasive potential and problems when it must convince multiple and diverse audiences with one message alone (which often occurs in advertising and even in such benign and supposedly neutral message forms as public service announcements). Related to problems of audience is the simultaneous interpersonal and public function of organizational rhetoric (Cheney & McMillan, 1990). Because organizational persuasion can take place in the coffee room or through a health communication campaign covered in the local newspaper and carried over national news, future theory must encompass all venues. Furthermore, organization members who sit on the boundaries of both the internal and external environment are positioned to "overhear" (McMillan, 1988). Thus, although an organization naturally wants to tailor its messages to target audiences, as Cheney, Christensen, Conrad, et al. contended, the public nature of organizational rhetoric behooves spokespersons to strive for some degree of consistency and to consider strategy carefully, and future theory must explore how rhetors walk this tightrope. Finally, in contrast to the study of transient social movements, organizational rhetoric scholars must explore deeply, as we suggested earlier, the message strategies of maintenance and survival. How do organizations that endure "talk differently" from those that do not? How do these institutional survivors construct and maintain a discursive environment that protects them from the winds of change and adversity?

Second, aligning with critical and poststructuralist work, future theory and study will explore ontology vis-à-vis the organization, specifically seeking to better understand and perhaps reposition the individual organizational rhetor, identifying and helping him or her to find and use a voice. Scholars have argued that organizational rhetoric and its rhetors have more power than individuals and individual rhetoric (Cheney, 1991; Cheney & McMillan, 1990). Poststructuralist scholars understand that individuals' identities and identifications shift and are shifted through macro-, meso-, and micro-level discourses and practices (Ashcraft & Mumby, 2004). According to some theorists, individuals have corporate identities that work together and/or clash at different times. For example, Burke (1937) noted, "The so-called 'I' is merely a unique combination of partially conflicting 'corporate we's'" (p. 140). In turn, this positioning of the "I" as a combination of "corporate we's" leads to the argument that individuals speak as organizational beings (Crable, 1990). Such theorizing raises questions that remain to be answered about the potential and/or existence of individual rhetors. Does an individual now have to speak as an organizational representative in order to participate in public discourse? The status as organizational beings decenters the individual speaking self or, stated alternatively, recognizes that individual speakers never have been centered, problematizing distinctions between individual and organizational voices. Furthermore, if scholars believe that corporations, in particular, have gained harmful control over and power in society through their participation in the public sphere (e.g., Deetz, 1992; Schiller, 1990), then we predict that scholars of organizational rhetoric will direct their attention toward understanding how all kinds of organizations (not just for-profits) can have voices and find ways of speaking in the public sphere.[11]

Third, future theory and study will also explore how an organization operates from its often obscure and uncertain agency. Organizational rhetoric traditionally has been characterized by a sleight of hand that can make it difficult for receivers of organizational messages to decide who is responsible for the rhetoric and whom to praise or to blame. We have noted that Crable (1990) envisions this characteristic as standing Burkean dramatism and agency on its head; in particular: "When a spokesperson 'appears' for an organization . . . we are witnessing magic: The actor or agent is not really the ACTOR; the words we hear are someone else's. . . . The actor in the Hollywood sense 'appears' and the ACTOR in Burke's sense [the organization] remains behind the SCENES (p. 123)."

A degraded corporate climate has made stakeholders less tolerant of such verbal and actional duplicity (Boyd, 2001a; Heath, 1997; Judd, 1995). Thus future investigations will make more transparent the "magical," behind-closed-doors quality of corporate rhetoric and find critical tools to unpack it. At present, it is difficult to gauge an organizational text *frontally* because the organization's past and present discursive history, actions, and alliances may be difficult to obtain and discern (McMillan, 1987). Social movement study and traditional rhetorical criticism have taught us the value of in-depth investigation of the historical record, even if it is challenging to uncover. Future organizational scholars will seek legitimate ways to establish context so that an organization's consistency and veracity can be judged, and in the present climate of public suspicion, wary organizations may be more willing to cooperate.

Fourth, future theory and study will feature the axiological, or value-laden, function of organizational rhetoric. Just as Crable (1990) positioned the organizational age of rhetoric as following Ehninger's (1968) three great rhetorical systems (classical, psychological, and sociological), so will the organizational age morph into an axiological mode to characterize the near future. As described in this review, fledgling research in organizational rhetoric has succeeded in describing rhetorical strategies such as legitimacy, and so it is naturally time to move to critical and ethical assessment of these strategies. This shift occurs not only at the prerogative of critics but from the actions of organizations themselves. The corporate colonization of the life world (Deetz, 1992; Habermas, 1981/1984, 1981/1987) and the decline of countervailing institutional influences (such as the church, home, and school) have left a void in the focus on values that will help to define the rhetorical agenda for the next decade. Also, the corporate malfeasance that has accompanied such unabated exercise of power forces rhetorical scholars to examine those instances of abuse and to apply the most stringent criteria for ethics and corporate social responsibility to them. Furthermore, we believe that, when ethical issues are considered in concert with the organizational nature of individual identities, scholars will ask more questions about organizational versus individual values.

We base these predictions on our assessment of gaps in the current literature and signals from the cultural landscape. We do not seek to limit potential directions of work in organizational rhetoric with our predictions; rather, we look forward to seeing how our predictions are or are not realized during the coming decades.

CONCLUSION

In short, this chapter provides a concise but thorough view of organizational rhetoric. We have shown how work in organizational rhetoric spans research on propaganda analysis, organizational communication, public relations, and rhetoric, highlighting connections and differences among these perspectives and outlining what organizational rhetoric has borrowed from and contributed to each. Current major issues of concern to organizational rhetoric scholars include crisis and maintenance communication, power relationships, and ethics. In discussing these areas, we considered individual theories of organizational rhetoric, including legitimacy, apologia, issue management, identification, and corporate social responsibility. Finally, by reflecting on existing work, we offered our predictions for the future of research in organizational rhetoric. This future extends beyond the areas of organizational communication and rhetoric. For example, political communication scholarship faces questions about intersections between organizational and individual status of politicians as rhetors, and that research increasingly needs effective critical tools to assess the symbolic renderings of the powerful organizations—both institutional and insurgent—that vie for public allegiance. An organizational rhetoric approach can also sit at the nexus of the health care debate in this country to offer critical mediation among organizational actors (e.g., the AMA, hospitals, HMOs, insurance providers, drug lobbies, the AARP, and other patient rights groups) as they "wrangle" (Burke, 1969) over health care practices, treatments, and diseases—indeed, ultimately over such a high-stakes issue as life and death. In essence, scholars throughout the communication discipline already share the interests of organizational rhetoric; it has been the purpose of this chapter to share its utility. To that end, we have called attention to different ways of thinking about, investigating, and creating organizational rhetoric so that scholars and practitioners can understand how the study of organizational rhetoric crosses borders in the communication discipline, enabling us to synthesize findings, determine new directions for study, and move closer to powerful explanatory theories of communication in general and organizational rhetoric in particular.

ACKNOWLEDGMENTS

The authors would like to thank the anonymous reviewers, editor Christina Beck, and her excellent staff for their helpful suggestions and support throughout this project.

NOTES

1. Panelists included John T. Llewellyn, Carol Jablonski, and Jill J. McMillan.

2. Articles on organizational rhetoric can be found in *Quarterly Journal of Speech, Management Communication Quarterly, Journal of Applied Communication Research, Argumentation and Advocacy, Public Relations Review, Journal of Public Relations Research, Journal of Business Communication, Western Journal of Communication, Communication Studies* (formerly *Central States Communication Journal*), and *Southern Journal of Communication*.

3. We recognize that other areas could have been traced and tied in to organizational rhetoric, including advertising and sociology studies.

4. Although it is clear that the field of organizational communication has moved beyond this focus, it is worth noting that, like public relations, organizational communication once had a practitioner orientation and focus.

5. See Bobbitt's (2004) *The Rhetoric of Redemption: Kenneth Burke's Redemption Drama* and Martin Luther King, Jr.'s "I Have a Dream" speech for a discussion of the rhetoric of redemption.

6. Habermas (1983/1990) explained how utterances are judged on their truth, rightness, and sincerity and how attempts to build legitimacy can be explored in relation to how each validity claim is received and interpreted by publics.

7. See Burns and Bruner (2000) for a more thorough listing of theoretical antecedents to image restoration theory.

8. Cheney (1983b) also offered and discussed a fourth identification tactic, unifying symbols, which he felt did not arise directly from Burke's discussion of identification.

9. In an even more recent example of how corporations may be silencing rather than inviting other voices into public discourse, in April 2005, General Motors pulled all of its advertising from the *Los Angeles Times,* citing factual errors and misrepresentations in the paper as its rationale. The decision came only two days after the newspaper published an unfavorable editorial about General Motors and its CEO (Miller & Mateja, 2005). Such decisions may silence dissent in the public sphere.

10. One is hard pressed to locate a clear-cut, universal definition for "corporate social responsibility." In fact, the same phenomenon is often represented as "business for social responsibility," "business for sustainability," "corporate citizenship," etc. It is the case, however, that CSR is widely used, as do May and Zorn in their 2003 *Management Communication Quarterly* forum, as synonymous with "business ethics." Although it goes beyond the scope of this essay to present an exhaustive review of this important new area of study, we hope that the issues we unpack in this section suggest the parameters of CSR for the reader.

11. One example of this attention is found in the study of "out-law discourse," in which the smaller of two organizations in conflict breaks traditional rules of argument to gain ground in public dialogue (Boyd, 2002; Sloop & Ono, 1997).

REFERENCES

Allen, M. W., & Caillouet, R. H. (1994). Legitimation efforts: Impression management strategies used by an organization in crisis. *Communication Monographs, 61,* 44–62.

Allen, M. W., Gotcher, J. M., & Seibert, J. H. (1993). A decade of organizational communication research: Journal articles 1980–1991. In S. A. Deetz (Ed.), *Communication yearbook 16* (pp. 252–330). Newbury, CA: Sage.

Alternative views in public relations. (2004, November). Panel session conducted at the meeting of the National Communication Association, Chicago, IL.

Apker, J., Zabava Ford, W. S., & Fox, D. H. (2003). Predicting nurses' organizational and professional identification: The effect of nursing roles, professional autonomy, and supportive communication. *Nursing Economics, 21,* 226–231.

Ashcraft, K. L., & Mumby, D. K. (2004). *Reworking gender: A feminist communicology of organization.* Thousand Oaks, CA: Sage.

Bagdikian, B. H. (2000). *The media monopoly.* Boston: Beacon.

Barker, J. R., & Tompkins, P. K. (1994). Identification in the self-managing organization: Characteristics of target and tenure. *Human Communication Research, 21,* 223–240.

Benoit, W. L. (1995a). *Accounts, excuses, and apologies: A theory of image restoration strategies.* Albany: State University of New York Press.

Benoit, W. L. (1995b). Sears' repair of its auto service image: Image restoration discourse in the corporate sector. *Communication Studies, 46,* 89–105.

Benoit, W. L. (1997). Image repair discourse and crisis communication. *Public Relations Review, 23,* 177–186.

Benoit, W. L. (2000). Another visit to the theory of image restoration strategies. *Communication Quarterly, 48*, 40–43.

Benoit, W. L., & Czerwinksi, A. (1997). A critical analysis of USAir's image repair discourse. *Business Communication Quarterly, 60*, 38–57.

Benoit, W. L., & Lindsey, J. J. (1987). Argument strategies: Antidote to Tylenol's poisoned image. *Journal of American Forensic Association, 23*, 136–146.

Bobbitt, D. A. (2004). *The rhetoric of redemption: Kenneth Burke's redemption drama and Martin Luther King, Jr.'s "I have a dream" speech.* Lanham, NJ: Rowman & Littlefield.

Bonewits, S. L., & Meisenbach, R. J. (2004, November). *Analyzing organizational legitimacy from a Habermasian perspective.* Paper presented at the meeting of the National Communication Association, Chicago, IL.

Bormann, E. G. (1972). Fantasy and rhetorical vision: The rhetorical criticism of social reality. *Quarterly Journal of Speech, 58*, 396–407.

Bormann, E. G. (1982). Symbolic convergence theory of communication: Applications and implications for teachers and consultants. *Journal of Applied Communication Research, 10*, 50–61.

Bormann, E. G. (1983). Symbolic convergence: Organizational communication and culture. In L. L. Putnam & M. E. Pacanowsky (Eds.), *Communication and organization: An interpretive approach* (pp. 99–122). Beverly Hills, CA: Sage.

Bostdorff, D. M., & Vibbert, S. L. (1994). Values advocacy: Enhancing organizational images, deflecting criticism, and grounding future arguments. *Public Relations Review, 20*, 141–158.

Botan, C. H., & Taylor, M. (2004). Public relations: State of the field. *Journal of Communication, 54*, 645–661.

Boyd, J. (2000). Actional legitimation: No crisis necessary. *Journal of Public Relations Research, 12*, 341–353.

Boyd, J. (2001a). Corporate rhetoric participates in public dialogue: A solution to the public/private conundrum. *Southern Communication Journal, 66*, 279–292.

Boyd, J. (2001b). The rhetoric of arrogance: The public relations response of the Standard Oil Trust. *Public Relations Review, 27*, 163–178.

Boyd, J. (2002). Public and technical interdependence: Regulatory controversy, out-law discourse, and the messy case of Olestra. *Argumentation and Advocacy, 39*, 91–109.

Boyd, J. (2004). Organizational rhetoric doomed to fail: R. J. Reynolds and the principle of the oxymoron. *Western Journal of Communication, 68*, 45–71.

Brimeyer, T. M., Eaker, A. V., & Clair, R. P. (2004). Rhetorical strategies in union organizing: A case of labor versus management. *Management Communication Quarterly, 18*, 45–75.

Brinson, S. L., & Benoit, W. L. (1999). The tarnished star: Restoring Texaco's damaged public image. *Management Communication Quarterly, 12*, 483–510.

Brown, M. H., & McMillan, J. J. (1990). Culture as text: The development of an organizational narrative. *Southern Communication Journal, 57*, 49–60.

Bryant, D. (1953). Rhetoric: Its function and its scope. *Quarterly Journal of Speech, 39*, 401–424.

Burke, K. (1937). *Attitudes toward history.* New York: New Republic.

Burke, K. (1966). *Language as symbolic action: Essays on life, literature, and method.* Berkeley: University of California Press.

Burke, K. (1969). *A rhetoric of motives.* Berkeley: University of California Press (original work published in 1950).

Burke, K. (1972). *Dramatism and development.* Barre, MA: Clark University Press.

Burns, J. P., & Bruner, M. S. (2000). Revisiting the theory of image restoration strategies. *Communication Quarterly, 48,* 27–39.

Cheney, G. (1983a). On the various and changing meanings of organizational membership: A field study of organizational identification. *Communication Monographs, 50,* 343–363.

Cheney, G. (1983b). The rhetoric of identification and the study of organizational communication. *Quarterly Journal of Speech, 69,* 143–158.

Cheney, G. (1986, November). *Coping with bureaucracy: Ethics and organizational relationships.* Paper presented at the meeting of the Speech Communication Association, Chicago, IL.

Cheney, G. (1991). *Rhetoric in an organizational society: Managing multiple identities.* Columbia: University of South Carolina Press.

Cheney, G. (1992). The corporate person (re)presents itself. In E. L. Toth & R. L. Heath (Eds.), *Rhetorical and critical approaches to public relations* (pp. 165–183). Hillsdale, NJ: Lawrence Erlbaum Associates.

Cheney, G. (1999). *Values at work: Employee participation meets market pressure at Mondragon.* Ithaca, NY: Cornell University Press.

Cheney, G. (2004). Theorizing about rhetoric and organizations: Classical, interpretive, and critical aspects. In S. K. May & D. K. Mumby (Eds.), *Engaging organizational communication theory and research: Multiple perspectives* (pp. 55–84). Thousand Oaks, CA: Sage.

Cheney, G., & Christensen, L. T. (2001). Organizational identification: Linkages between internal and external communication. In F. M. Jablin & L. L. Putnam (Eds.), *The new handbook of organizational communication: Advances in theory, research, and methods* (pp. 231–269). Thousand Oaks, CA: Sage.

Cheney, G., Christensen, L., Conrad, C., & Lair, D. J. (2004). Corporate rhetoric as organizational discourse. In D. Grant, C. Hardy, C. Oswick, N. Phillips, & L. L. Putnam (Eds.), *Handbook of organizational discourse* (pp. 79–103). London: Sage.

Cheney, G., Christensen, L. T., Zorn, T.E. Jr., & Ganesh, S. (2004). *Organizational communication in an age of globalization: Issues, reflections, practices.* Prospect Heights, IL: Waveland.

Cheney, G., & Frenette, G. (1993). Persuasion and organization: Values, logics, and accounts in contemporary corporate public discourse. In C. Conrad (Ed.), *The ethical nexus* (pp. 49–73). Norwood, NJ: Ablex.

Cheney, G., Garvin-Doxas, K., & Torrens, K. (1998). Kenneth Burke's implicit theory of power. In B. Bock (Ed.), *Kenneth Burke for the 21st century* (pp. 133–150). Albany: State University of New York Press.

Cheney, G., May, S. K., & Roper, J. (in press). *The debate over corporate social responsibility.* New York: Oxford University Press.

Cheney, G., & McMillan, J. J. (1990). Organizational rhetoric and the practice of criticism. *Journal of Applied Communication Research, 18*, 93–114.

Cheney, G., & Tompkins, P. K. (1984, March). *Toward an ethic of identification.* Paper presented at the Burke Conference, Philadelphia, PA.

Cheney, G., & Vibbert, S. L. (1987). Corporate discourse: Public relations and issue management. In F. M. Jablin, L. L. Putnam, K. H. Roberts, & L. W. Porter (Eds.), *Handbook of organizational communication: An interdisciplinary perspective* (pp. 165–194). Newbury Park, CA: Sage.

Clair, R. P. (1993). The bureaucratization, commodification, and privatization of sexual harassment through institutional discourse. *Management Communication Quarterly, 7*, 123–157.

Clair, R. P. (1999). Standing still in an ancient field: A contemporary look at the organizational communication discipline. *Management Communication Quarterly, 13*, 283–293.

Cloud, D. L. (2001). Laboring under the sign of the new: Cultural studies, organizational communication, and the fallacy of the new economy. *Management Communication Quarterly, 15*, 268–278.

Coleman, J. S. (1974). *Power and the structure of society.* New York: Norton.

Conrad, C. (1983). Organizational power: Faces and symbolic forms. In L. Putnam & M. Pacanowsky (Eds.), *Communication and organizations* (pp. 173–194). Beverly Hills, CA: Sage.

Conrad, C. (Ed.). (1993). *The ethical nexus.* Norwood, NJ: Ablex.

Conrad, C. (2003). Setting the stage: Introduction to the special issue on the "corporate meltdown." *Management Communication Quarterly, 17*, 5–19.

Coombs, W. T. (1992). The failure of the Task Force on Food Assistance: A case study of the role of legitimacy in issue management. *Journal of Public Relations Research, 4*, 101–122.

Coombs, W. T. (1998). An analytic framework for crises situations: Better responses from better understanding of the situation. *Journal of Public Relations Research, 10*, 177–191.

Coombs, W. T. (1999a). Information and compassion in crisis response: A test of their effects. *Journal of Public Relations Research, 11*, 121–142.

Coombs, W. T. (1999b). *Ongoing crisis communication: Planning, managing, and responding.* Thousand Oaks, CA: Sage.

Coombs, T., & Schmidt, L. (2000). An empirical analysis of image restoration: Texaco's racism crisis. *Journal of Public Relations Research, 12*, 163–178.

Crable, R. E. (1990). "Organizational rhetoric" as the fourth great system: Theoretical, critical, and pragmatic implications. *Journal of Applied Communication Research, 18*, 115–128.

Crable, R. E., & Vibbert, S. L. (1983). Mobil's epideictic advocacy: Observation of Prometheus bound. *Communication Monographs, 50*, 38–394.

Crable, R. E., & Vibbert, S. L. (1986). *Public relations as communication management.* Edina, MN: Bellweather.

Cutlip, S. M., Center, A. H., & Broom, G. M. (1999). *Effective public relations* (8th ed.). Upper Saddle River, NJ: Prentice Hall.

Cyphert, D., & Saiia, D. H. (2004). In search of the corporate citizen: The emerging discourse of corporate ecology. *Southern Communication Journal, 69*, 241–256.

Daugherty, E. L. (2001). Public relations and social responsibility, In R. L. Heath (Ed.), *Handbook of public relations* (pp. 389–402). Thousand Oaks, CA: Sage.

Deephouse, J. L. (1996). Does isomorphism legitimate? *Academy of Management Journal, 39*, 1024–1039.

Deetz, S. (1992). *Democracy in an age of corporate colonization: Developments in communication.* Albany: State University of New York Press.

DiSanza, J. R., & Bullis, C. (1999). "Everybody identifies with Smokey the Bear": Employee responses to newsletter identification inducements at the U.S. Forest Service. *Management Communication Quarterly, 12*, 347–399.

Dionisopoulos, G., & Crable, R. E. (1988). Definitional hegemony as a public relations strategy: The rhetoric of the nuclear power industry after Three Mile Island. *Central States Speech Journal, 39*, 134–145.

Dowling, J., & Pfeffer, J. (1975). Organizational legitimacy: Social values and organizational behavior. *Pacific Sociological Review, 18*, 122–135.

Doyle, J. H. (1916). The style of Wendell Phillips. *Quarterly Journal of Public Speaking, 2*, 331–339.

Ehninger, D. (1968). On systems of rhetoric. *Philosophy and Rhetoric, 1*, 131–144.

Elwood, W. N. (Ed.). (1995). *Public relations as rhetorical criticism: Case studies of corporate discourse and social influences.* Westport, CT: Praeger.

Fairhurst, G. T. (1993). The leader-member exchange patterns of women leaders in industry: A discourse analysis. *Communication Monographs, 60*, 321–351.

Fayol, H. (1949). *General and industrial management.* New York: Pitman (original work published 1925).

Fink, S. (1986). *Crisis management: Planning for the inevitable.* New York: American Management Association.

Fish, S. (2005, February 23). Clueless in academe. *The Chronicle of Higher Education.* Retrieved February 23, 2005, from http://chronicle.com/jobs/2005/02/2005022301c .htm

Fishman, D. A. (1999). ValuJet Flight 592: Crisis communication theory blended and extended. *Communication Quarterly, 47*, 345–375.

Foss, S. (1984). Retooling an image: Chrysler corporation's rhetoric of redemption. *Western Journal of Speech Communication, 48*, 75–91.

Francesconi, R. A. (1982). James Hunt, the Wilmington 10, and institutional legitimacy. *Quarterly Journal of Speech, 68*, 47–59.

Gardner, W. L., & Cleavenger, D. (1998). The impression management strategies associated with transformational leadership at the world-class level. *Management Communication Quarterly, 12*, 3–41.

Gaunt, P., & Ollenburger, J. (1995). Issues management: A tool that deserves another look. *Public Relations Review, 21*, 199–210.

Gislason, H. G. (1917). Elements of objectivity in Wendell Phillips. *Quarterly Journal of Public Speaking, 3*, 125–134.

Goldzwig, S. M. & Sullivan, P.A. (1995). Post-assassination newspaper editorial eulogies: Analysis and assessment. *Western Journal of Communication, 59*, 126–150.

Greider, W. (1992). *Who will tell the people.* New York: Simon & Schuster.

Greider, W. (2003). *The soul of capitalism: Opening paths to moral economy.* New York: Simon & Schuster.

Griffin, L. M. (1952). The rhetoric of historical movements. *Quarterly Journal of Speech, 38*, 184–188.

Habermas, J. (1973). *Legitimation crisis* (T. McCarthy, Trans.). Boston: Beacon.

Habermas, J. (1984). *The theory of communicative action, vol. 1: Reason and the rationalization of society.* (T. McCarthy, Trans.). Boston: Beacon (original work published 1981).

Habermas, J. (1987). *The theory of communicative action, vol. II: Lifeworld and system: A critique of functionalist reason.* (T. McCarthy, Trans.). Boston: Beacon (original work published 1981).

Habermas, J. (1990). *Moral consciousness and communicative action* (C. Lenhardt & S. W. Nicholson, Trans.). Cambridge, MA: MIT Press (original work published 1983).

Hart, R. P. (2004, November). Respondent. In C. E. Carroll (Chair), *Looking back: The silver anniversary of the study of organizational rhetoric, Part 1—The contributions of Rod Hart.* Panel session conducted at the meeting of the National Communication Association, Chicago, IL.

Hazleton, V., Jr., & Botan, C. H. (1989). The role of theory in public relations. In C. H. Botan & V. Hazleton, Jr. (Eds.), *Public relations theory* (pp. 3–15). Hillsdale, NJ: Lawrence Erlbaum Associates.

Hearit, K. M. (1995a). "From we didn't do it" to "It's not our fault:" The use of apologia in public relations crises. In W. Elwood (Ed.), *Public relations inquiry as rhetorical criticism* (pp. 117–131). New York: Greenwood.

Hearit, K. M. (1995b). "Mistakes were made": Organizations, apologia, and crises of social legitimacy. *Communication Studies, 46*, 1–17.

Hearit, K. M. (1996). The use of counter-attack in public relations crises: The case of General Motors vs. NBC. *Public Relations Review, 22*, 233–248.

Hearit, K. M. (1997). Transcendence as apologia strategy: The case of Johnson controls. *Public Relations Review, 23*, 217–231.

Hearit, K. M. (1999). When the organization's image becomes the issue: The corporate apologia of the Intel Corporation in defense of its Pentium chip. *Public Relations Review, 25*, 291–308.

Hearit, K. M. (2001). Corporate apologia: When the organization speaks in defense of itself. In R. L. Heath (Ed.), *Handbook of public relations* (pp. 501–511). Beverly Hills, CA: Sage.

Hearit, K. M. (2006). *Crisis management by apology: Corporate response to allegations of wrongdoing.* Mahwah, NJ: Lawrence Erlbaum Associates.

Heath, R. L. (1980). Corporate advocacy: An application of speech communication perspectives and skills—and more. *Communication Education, 29*, 370–377.

Heath, R. L. (1990). Effects of internal rhetoric on management response to external issues: How corporate culture failed the asbestos industry. *Journal of Applied Communication Research, 18*, 153–167.

Heath, R. L. (1992). The wrangle in the marketplace: A rhetorical perspective of public relations. In E. L. Toth & R. L. Heath (Eds.), *Rhetorical and critical approaches to public relations* (pp. 17–36). Hillsdale, NJ: Lawrence Erlbaum Associates.

Heath, R. L. (1997). *Strategic issues management: Organizations and public policy challenges.* Thousand Oaks, CA: Sage.

Heath, R. L. (2001). Shifting foundations: Public relations as relationship building. In R. L. Heath (Ed.), *Handbook of public relations* (pp. 1–9). Beverly Hills, CA: Sage.

Hegstrom, T. G. (1990). Mimetic and dissent conditions in organizational rhetoric. *Journal of Applied Communication Research, 18,* 141–152.

Hegstrom, T.G. (1999). *Reasons for rocking the boat: Principles and personal problems.* In H. K. Geissner, A. F. Herbig, & E. Wessela (Eds.), *Business communication in Europe* (pp. 179–194). Tostedt, Germany: Attikon Verlag.

Ihlen, O. (2002). Defending the Mercedes A-Class: Combining and changing crisis-response strategies. *Journal of Public Relations Research, 14,* 185–206.

Jablonski, C. J. (1979). *Institutional rhetoric and radical change: The case of the contemporary Roman Catholic church in America, 1947–1977.* Unpublished doctoral dissertation, Purdue University, West Lafayette, IN.

Jablonski, C. J. (Ed.). (1990). Organizational rhetoric [Special issue]. *Journal of Applied Communication Research, 18*(2).

Johannesen, R. L. (2002). *Ethics in human communication* (5th ed.). Prospect Heights, IL: Waveland.

Johnson, D., & Sellnow, T. (1995). Deliberative rhetoric as a step in organizational crisis management: Exxon as a case study. *Communication Reports, 8,* 54–60.

Jones, B., & Chase, H. (1979). Managing public policy issues. *Public Relations Review, 5,* 3–20.

Judd, L. R. (1995). An approach to ethics in the information age. *Public Relations Review, 21,* 35–44.

Kassing, J. W. (1997). Articulating, antagonizing, and displacing: A model of employee dissent. *Communication Studies, 48,* 311–322.

Katz, D., & Kahn, R. L. (1978). *The social psychology of organizing.* New York: Wiley.

Kirby, E., Golden, A., Medved, C., Jorgenson, J., & Buzzanell, P. M. (2003). An organizational communication challenge to the discourse of work and family research: From problematics to empowerment. In P. J. Kalbfleisch (Ed.), *Communication yearbook 27,* (pp. 1–44). Mahwah, NJ: Lawrence Erlbaum Associates.

Kitch, C. (2001). *The girl on the magazine cover: The origins of visual stereotypes in American mass media.* Chapel Hill: University of North Carolina Press.

Knight, G., & Greenberg, J. (2002). Promotionalism and subpolitics: Nike and its labor critics. *Management Communication Quarterly, 15,* 541–570.

Kuhn, T., & Nelson, N. (2002). Reengineering identity: A case study of multiplicity and duality in organizational identification. *Management Communication Quarterly, 16,* 5–38.

Lair, D. J., Sullivan, K., & Cheney, G. (2005). Marketization and the recasting of the professional self: The rhetoric and ethics of personal branding. *Management Communication Quarterly, 18,* 307–343.

Larson, G. S., & Pepper, G. L. (2003). Strategies for managing multiple organizational identifications: A case of competing identities. *Management Communication Quarterly, 16,* 528–557.

Lasswell, H. D. (1938). *Propaganda technique in the world war.* New York: Peter Smith (originally published 1927).

Lasswell, H. D., & Blumenstock, D. (1939). *World revolutionary propaganda.* New York: Knopf.

Lee, B. K. (2005). Crises, culture, community. In P. K. Kalbfleisch (Ed.), *Communication yearbook 29* (pp. 275–309). Mahwah, NJ: Lawrence Erlbaum Associates.

Levinas, E. (1991). *Otherwise than being or beyond essence* (A. Lingis, Trans.). Dordrecht: Kluwer Academic.

Livesay, S. M. (2002). The discourse of the middle ground: Citizen Shell commits to sustainable development. *Management Communication Quarterly, 15*, 313–349.

Manheim, J. B. (1991). *All of the people all the time: Strategic communication and American politics.* Armonk, NY: Sharp.

Maurer, J. G. (1971). *Readings in organization theory: Open-systems approaches.* New York: Random House.

May, S. K., & Zorn, T. E. (2003). Forum introduction. *Management Communication Quarterly, 16*, 95–598.

McMillan, J. J. (1982). *The rhetoric of the modern organization.* Unpublished doctoral dissertation, University of Texas, Austin.

McMillan, J. J. (1987). In search of the organizational persona: A rationale for studying organizations rhetorically. In L. Thayer (Ed.), *Organization—Communication: Emerging perspectives II* (pp. 21–45). Norwood, NJ: Ablex.

McMillan, J. J. (1988). Institutional plausibility alignment as rhetorical exercise: A mainline denomination's struggle with the exigence of sexism. *Journal for the Scientific Study of Religion, 27*, 326–344.

McMillan. J. J. (1990). Symbolic emancipation in the organization: A case of shifting power. In J. A. Anderson (Ed.), *Communication yearbook 13* (pp. 203–214). Newbury Park, CA: Sage.

McMillan, J. J., & Hyde, M. J. (2000). Technological innovation and change: A case study in the formation of organizational conscience. *Quarterly Journal of Speech, 86*, 19–47.

Meisenbach, R. J. (in press). Habermas' discourse ethics and principle of universalization as a moral framework for organizational communication. *Management Communication Quarterly.*

Meisenbach, R. J., Remke, R. V., Buzzanell, P. M., Liu, M., Bowers, V. A., & Conn, C. (2003, May). *"We were allowed": Investigating the presence of a bureaucratic pentad in women's maternity leave discourse.* Paper presented at the meeting of the International Communication Association, San Diego, CA.

Merriam-Webster's collegiate dictionary (10th ed.). (1993). Springfield, MA: Merriam-Webster.

Metzler, M. S. (2001). The centrality of organizational legitimacy to public relations practice. In R. L. Heath (Ed.), *Handbook of public relations* (pp. 321–333). Thousand Oaks, CA: Sage.

Meyer, J. W., & Scott, W. R. (1983). Centralization and the legitimacy problems of local government. In J. W. Meyer & W. R. Scott (Eds.), *Organizational environments: Ritual and rationality* (pp. 199–215). Beverly Hills, CA: Sage.

Miller, J. P., & Mateja, J. (2005, April 8). GM, unhappy with coverage, won't advertise in Los Angeles Times. *Chicago Tribune,* Retrieved June 17, 2005, from InfoTrac OneFile database.

Mumby, D. K. (1988). *Communication and discourse in organizations: Discourse, ideology and domination.* Norwood, NJ: Ablex.

Murphy, A. G. (1998). Hidden transcripts of flight attendant resistance. *Management Communication Quarterly, 11*, 499–535.

O'Connor, A. (2004). *In the boardroom of good and evil: An assessment of the persuasive premises and social implications of corporate values advocacy messages.* Unpublished dissertation, Purdue University, West Lafayette, IN.

Papa, M. J., Auwal, M. A., & Singhal, A. (1997). Organizing for social change within concertive control systems: Member identification, empowerment, and the masking of discipline. *Communication Monographs, 64,* 219–249.

Peters, T. J. & Austin, N. (1985). *A passion for excellence.* New York: Random House.

Peterson, T. R. (1990). Argument premises used to validate organizational change: Mormon representations of plural marriage. *Journal of Applied Communication Research, 18,* 162–184.

Pezzullo, P. C. (2003). Resisting "national breast cancer awareness month": The rhetoric of counterpublics and their cultural performances. *Quarterly Journal of Speech, 89,* 345–365.

Putnam, L. L., & Cheney, G. (1985). Organizational communication: Historical development and future directions. In T. W. Benson (Ed.), *Speech communication in the 20th Century* (pp. 130–156). Carbondale: Southern Illinois University.

Putnam, L. L., & Fairhurst, G. T. (2001). Discourse analysis in organizations: Issues and concerns. In F. M. Jablin & L. L. Putnam (Eds.), *The new handbook of organizational communication: Advances in theory, research, and methods* (pp. 78–136). Thousand Oaks, CA: Sage.

Redding, W. C. (1985). Stumbling toward identity: The emergence of organizational communication as a field of study. In R. D. McPhee & P. K. Tompkins (Eds.), *Organizational communication: Traditional themes and new directions* (pp. 15–54). Beverly Hills, CA: Sage.

Redding, W. C. (1987, May). *Communication implications of Mintzberg's "Power in and around the organization."* Paper presented at the meeting of the International Communication Association, Montreal, Canada.

Redding, W. C., & Tompkins, P. K. (1988). Organizational communication: Past and present tenses. In G. M. Goldhaber & G. A. Barnett (Eds.), *Handbook of organizational communication* (pp. 5–33). Norwood, NJ: Ablex.

Roberts, J. (2003). The manufacture of corporate social responsibility: Constructing corporate sensibility. *Organization, 10,* 249–265.

Rogers, E. M. (1994). *A history of communication study: A biographical approach.* New York: Free Press.

Schiller, H. I. (1990). *Culture inc.: The corporate takeover of public expression.* New York: Oxford University Press.

Schultz, P. D., & Seeger, M. W. (1991). Corporate centered apologia: Iaccoca in defense of Chrysler. *Speaker and Gavel, 28,* 50–60.

Scott, C. R., Connaughton, S. L., Diaz-Saenz, H. R., Maguire, K., Ramirez, R., Richardson, B., et al. (1999). The impacts of communication and multiple identifications of intent to leave: A multimethodological exploration. *Management Communication Quarterly, 12,* 400–435.

Scott, C. R., Corman, S. R., & Cheney, G. (1998). Development of a structurational model of identification in the organization. *Communication Theory, 8,* 298–336.

Seeger, M. W., Sellnow, T. L., & Ulmer, R. R. (1998). Communication, organization, and crisis. In M. Roloff (Ed.), *Communication yearbook 21* (pp. 230–275). Thousand Oaks, CA: Sage.

Seeger, M. W., Sellnow, T. L., & Ulmer, R. R. (2001). Public relations and crisis communication: Organizing and chaos. In R. L. Heath (Ed.), *Handbook of public relations* (pp. 155–165). Thousand Oaks, CA: Sage.

Seeger, M. W., Sellnow, T. L., & Ulmer, R. R. (2003). *Communication and organizational crisis*. Westport, CT: Praeger.

Sellnow, T. L., Ulmer, R. R., & Snider, M. (1998). The compatibility of corrective action in organizational crisis communication. *Communication Quarterly, 46*, 60–74.

Sethi, S. P. (1977). *Advocacy advertising and large corporations*. Lexington, MA: Lexington Books.

Sharf, B. F. (1978). A rhetorical analysis of leadership emergence in small groups. *Communication Monographs, 45*, 156–172.

Simons, H. W. (1972). Requirements, problems, and strategies: A theory of persuasion for social movements. In D. Ehninger (Ed.), *Contemporary rhetoric* (pp. 190–198). Glenview, IL: Scott Foresman.

Simons, H. W., Mechling, E. W., & Schreier, H. N. (1984). The functions of human communication in mobilizing for action from the bottom up: The rhetoric of social movements. In C. Arnold & J. Bowers (Eds.), *Handbook of rhetorical and communication theory* (pp. 792–867). New York: Allyn & Bacon.

Simpson, C. (1994). *Science of coercion: Communication research and psychological warfare 1945–1960*. New York: Oxford University Press.

Sloop, J. M., & Ono, K. A. (1997). Out-law discourse: The critical politics of material judgment. *Philosophy and Rhetoric, 30*, 50–69.

Soley, L. C. (1995). *Leasing the ivory tower: The corporate takeover of academia*. Boston: South End Press.

Sprague, J., & Ruud, G. L. (1988). Boat-rocking in a high technology culture. *American Behavioral Scientist, 32*, 169–193.

Sproule, J. M. (1987). Propaganda studies in American social science: The rise and fall of the critical paradigm. *Quarterly Journal of Speech, 73*, 60–78.

Sproule, J. M. (1988). The new managerial rhetoric and the old criticism. *Quarterly Journal of Speech, 74*, 468–486.

Sproule, J. M. (1990). Organizational rhetoric and the rational-democratic society. *Journal of Applied Communication Research, 18*, 129–140.

Sproule, J. M. (1997). *Propaganda and democracy: The American experience of media and mass persuasion*. Cambridge, England: Cambridge University Press.

Stauber, J., & Rampton, S. (1995). *Toxic sludge is good for you! Lies, damn lies, and the public relations industry*. Monroe, MA: Common Courage.

Stillman, P. G. (1974). The concept of legitimacy. *Polity, 7*, 32–56.

Suchman, M. (1995). Managing legitimacy: Strategic and institutional approaches. *Academy of Management Review, 20*, 571–610.

Taylor, F. W. (1947). *Principles of scientific management*. New York: Harper Bros. (original work published 1912).

Taylor, J. R., Flanagin, A. J., Cheney, G., & Seibold, D. R. (2000). Organizational communication research: Key moments, central concerns, and future challenges.

In W. B. Gudykunst (Ed.), *Communication yearbook 24* (pp. 99–137). Thousand Oaks, CA: Sage.

Tompkins, P. K. (1984). The functions of communication in organizations. In C. Arnold & J. Bowers (Eds.), *Handbook of rhetorical and communication theory* (pp. 659–719). New York: Allyn & Bacon.

Tompkins, P. K. (1987). Translating organizational theory: Symbolism over substance. In F. M. Jablin, L. L. Putnam, K. H. Roberts, & L. W. Porter (Eds.), *Handbook of organizational communication: An interdisciplinary perspective* (pp. 70–122). Newbury Park, CA: Sage.

Tompkins, P. K., & Cheney, G. (1985). Communication and unobtrusive control in contemporary organizations. In R. D. McPhee & P. K. Tompkins (Eds.), *Organizational communication: Traditional themes and new directions* (pp. 179–210). Beverly Hills, CA: Sage.

Tompkins, P. K., Fisher, J. Y., Infante, D. A., & Tompkins, E. L. (1975). Kenneth Burke and the inherent formal characteristics of organizations: A field study. *Speech Monographs, 42*, 135–142.

Toth, E. L., & Heath, R. L. (Eds.). (1992). *Rhetorical and critical approaches to public relations.* Hillsdale, NJ: Lawrence Erlbaum Associates.

Tyler, L. (1997). Liability means never being able to say you're sorry: Corporate guilt, legal constraints, and defensiveness in corporate communication. *Management Communication Quarterly, 11*, 51–73.

Ulmer, R. R. (2001). Effective crisis management through established stakeholder relationships: Malden Mills as a case study. *Management Communication Quarterly, 14*, 590–615.

Vaughn, M. A. (1997). Organizational identification strategies and values in high technology industries: A rhetorical-organizational approach to the analysis of socialization processes in corporate discourse. *Journal of Public Relations Research, 9*, 119–139.

Vasquez, G. M., & Taylor, M. (2000). Public relations: An emerging social science enters the new millennium. In W. B. Gudykunst (Ed.), *Communication yearbook 24* (pp. 319–342). Thousand Oaks, CA: Sage.

Vibbert, S. L., & Bostdorff, D. M. (1993). Issue management in the "lawsuit crisis." In C. Conrad (Ed.), *The ethical nexus* (pp. 103–120). Norwood, NJ: Ablex.

Waltzer, H. (1988). Corporate advocacy advertising and political influence. *Public Relations Review, 14*, 41–55.

Ware, B. L., & Linkugel, W. A. (1973). They spoke in defense of themselves: On the general criticism of apologia. *Quarterly Journal of Speech, 59*, 273–283.

Weber, M. (1978). *Economy and society.* Berkeley: University of California Press.

Weick, K. (1980). The management of eloquence. *Executive, 6*, 18–21.

Wert-Gray, S., Center, C., Brashers, D. E., & Meyers, R. A. (1991). Research topics and methodological orientations in organizational communication: A decade in review. *Communication Studies, 42*, 141–154.

Zorn, T. E. (2001). Talking heads: The CEO as spokesperson. In P. J. Kitchen & D. E. Schultz (Eds.), *Raising the corporate umbrella: Corporate communications in the 21st century* (pp. 23–42). New York: St. Martin's.

CHAPTER CONTENTS

4 Work-Life Research from Both Sides Now: An Integrative Perspective for Organizational and Family Communication

ANNIS G. GOLDEN
University at Albany, State University of New York

ERIKA L. KIRBY
Creighton University

JANE JORGENSON
University of South Florida

This article uses work-life interrelationships as a lens through which to identify communication concepts that span the traditional "division divide" between organizational and family communication and to identify potential substantive contributions to work-life research that might be made from integrative perspectives. We review extant work-life research within the communication discipline to identify themes and methodological approaches represented to date; we also identify lines of research in both organizational and family communication that have not yet been tied to work-life research but that have strong potential connections. We explore three theoretical perspectives for bridging workplace and private-life frames of reference: structuration, systems, and relational dialectics. Within each perspective, we identify integrative directions for future research. We conclude with metadiscursive reflections on obstacles to and pathways for spanning division divides.

I n the communication discipline, research on organizations and families rarely intersect. Yet a growing body of communication research on work-family/work-life[1] interrelationships suggests a potentially fruitful arena for integration. Within the larger context of the social sciences and organiza-

Correspondence: Annis G. Golden, Dept. of Communication, University at Albany, State University of New York, Albany, NY 12222; email: agolden@albany.edu

Communication Yearbook 30, pp. 143–195

tional studies, the literature on work-life interrelationships can be broadly divided into studies that focus on the workplace and its response to workers with families and studies that focus primarily on the family and the effects of work on the family. Thus, although scholars acknowledge interaction effects between private life and the world of work, the primary emphasis remains "short- and long-term *consequences of work* [italics added] for the quality of family life and the development of family members" (Perry-Jenkins, Repetti, & Crouter, 2000, p. 981). The primacy of work in the work-life relationship is reflected throughout the evolution of work-life research over the past three decades, which, according to Gilbert (1993), has evolved from an early emphasis on individual role conflict created by women's entry into the workforce, to resolution of inequities in domestic responsibilities for dual-earner couples (created by women's work roles), to the function of workplace practices and policies in the management of work-life conflict.

In the context of this trajectory, and given the communication discipline's relatively recent entry into the domain of work-life research, not surprisingly, more research has been generated that takes the organization as its primary frame of reference, rather than the family (e.g., Buzzanell, 2000; Kirby, Golden, Medved, Jorgenson, & Buzzanell, 2003; Kirby & Krone, 2002). However, research studies that take the family as their primary frame of reference have also identified important substantive areas in which communication scholars can contribute to the interdisciplinary dialogue on work-life issues while advancing communication research agendas more generally (e.g., Golden, 2000b; Jorgenson, 1995; Medved, 2004; Medved & Kirby, 2005). Moreover, some of these scholars' publications include both studies that use organizational frames and studies that use family frames, pointing to an unrealized potential for integration: a more explicit acknowledgment of the bidirectionality of work and personal life interactions and influences.

Kirby et al. (2003) argued that the communication discipline is particularly well positioned among the social sciences to contribute to the understanding of the experience of work-life interrelationships through a meaning-centered and process-oriented rather than an outcome-oriented perspective. Yet they self-identify their review and synthesis of the literature as an "organizational communication challenge to the discourse of work and family research" (p. 1). Imagine how much more productive our discipline's contribution to work-life research could be with the integration of organizational and family communication perspectives. From this integrative perspective, working women and men are "border crossers" (Clark, 2000, p. 748), engaged in a continuous process of sense-making with partners in the workplace (co-workers, supervisors, and other organizational voices) and in the home space (relational partners, parents, and children). Work-life researchers from organizational and family communication then become subdisciplinary border-crossers, much like those whose lives they study.

Work-life research, in all of its many forms, has now succeeded in establishing itself as a well-defined area of inquiry in communication studies. Consequently, we believe that we have reached an optimum moment—when a significant body of research has been accumulated and yet while the area is still relatively young—to consider how to avoid reproducing (at least implicitly) in our own research the "separate spheres" discourse that we so frequently criticize. Indeed, while many humanistic social scientists in diverse areas of inquiry value integrative rather than narrowly focused research, an integrationist orientation is particularly compelling for work-life researchers who now problematize segmentationist constructs.

We find the "balance" metaphor that pervades so much work-life research particularly problematic. First, "balance" implies a zero-sum game where "the energy invested in one side of the scales requires taking energy away from the other side" (Hattery, 2000, p. 3). Moreover, balance can be identified with normative assumptions about the equality of investment and separation of domains. Finally, balance suggests stasis, a final state to be achieved and then maintained. Hattery offered "weaving" as a metaphor to encourage viewing more seamless integration of work and family, and the idea of weaving meshes with our integrationist perspective toward work-life research. At the same time, however, we do not wish to prescribe integration rather than alternation as the more desirable mode of managing work-life interrelationships.

As we argue in this chapter, future research that positions itself at the intersections of organizational and family communication will contribute substantially to dereifying the public-private divide in the discourse of work and personal life and problematizing the much vaunted notion of work-life "balance." Whereas Kirby et al. (2003) positioned the communication perspective on work-life interrelationships within the *interdisciplinary* literature and identified the distinctive differences and potential contributions of the communication discipline, the analytic framework of this essay is more discipline-specific. We not only consider what the communication discipline can contribute to work-life interrelationships as a substantive area of research; we also use work-life as a lens through which to bring into focus communication concepts that span the traditional division divide between organizational and family communication research. For example, like Kirby et al., we contend that one of these "spanning" concepts is gender; gender is a macrodiscourse inasmuch as organizations and families are gendered institutions. Therefore, we assume work-life practices and processes as addressed in organizational and family communication are embedded within discourses of gender—"the meaning of gender is constantly (re)negotiated within everyday family and organizational interactions" (Kirby et al., p. 5).

Through this review, we present an explicit essay in "border crossing" and "weaving" to create an integrative perspective as well as to point the way toward future research. We begin by reviewing the existing body of communication research on work-life relationships from both organizational and family perspectives to provide a cumulative picture of our discipline's contributions. As part of the project of specifying integrating constructs across subdisciplines, we also indicate research streams in organizational and family communication that have not yet been linked to work-life research but have strong potential connections. We make explicit the theoretical and methodological commonalities of work-life research that has already been completed in both family and organizational settings. Our goal is to create a more inclusive framework that may suggest new research questions for both beginning scholars and researchers already working in these areas. Ideally, this integrative paradigm may also be suggestive for integrating diverse strands of other areas of communication research.

Following this review, we detail three alternative theoretical frameworks that can bridge the public/private dualism and correct the unidirectional modes of influence implied in much work-life research. Like Kirby et al. (2003), we contend that "daily micro-level discourses as well as macro-discourses of organizations and families creat[e] the current processes, structures and relationships surrounding work and family" (p. 1). We attempt to elucidate these processes through structuration, systems, and relational dialectics theories. We offer structuration theory (Giddens, 1979, 1984), often used in organizational communication research, but seldom in family communication, as an integrating framework for organization- and family-based research on work-life interrelationships. We argue that systems theories, though well employed in both organizational and family communication research, provide a potentially rich and as-yet unexploited theoretical framework for understanding work and personal-life interrelationships when we frame organizations and families (or other personal relationship networks) as loosely coupled systems. Finally, we consider relational dialectics, which has provided a fruitful "meta-theoretical perspective" (Baxter & Montgomery, 1997, p. 326) in family and interpersonal communication, and which offers a potential integrative framework from which to view work and personal-life interrelationships, beginning from within either the home or the workplace.

Inasmuch as we begin by noting a lack of integration of organizational and family communication research on work and personal-life interrelationships (and we wish to remedy this division), we consider obstacles to integration from a metadiscursive perspective and provide a self-reflexive examination of the potential barriers to integrative research as our first purpose. We focus on the professional need for scholars (especially more junior ones) to establish well-defined subdisciplinary identifications and the professional challenges of mastering and integrating diverse bodies of research literature in an age of information proliferation.

ORGANIZATIONAL APPROACHES TO WORK AND PERSONAL LIFE

The commitment of communication scholars working from an organizational perspective to work-life research is indicated by the steady accumulation of publications since the thematic issue of *The Electronic Journal of Communication/La Revue Electronique de Communication* (Golden, 2000a), which served as the first focal point for work-life research as such in the communication discipline.[2] (Four of the six articles appearing in that journal took the workplace as their primary frame of reference.[3]) Interest in the area has continued to grow since that publication, attracting the attention of both new and established scholars. Another special issue of *The Electronic Journal of Communication* on "Communication and the Accomplishment of Personal and Professional Life" is forthcoming (Kirby, in press). The programs for the 2004 National Communication Association convention and the 2005 International Communication Association convention featured six competitive papers and five panels centering on issues of work and family, including a roundtable-style discussion panel on "Bringing Family Forward in Work-Family/Work-Life Research," where ten family communication and organizational communication scholars "came together" to identify productive directions for research.

Variation and Commonalities in Existing Organizational Work-Life Research

The substantive areas focused on by scholars taking work as their primary frame of reference encompass maternity leave (Ashcraft, 1999; Buzzanell, 2003; Buzzanell & Ellingson, 2005; Buzzanell & Liu, 2005; Liu & Buzzanell, 2004; Miller, Jablin, Casey, Lamphear-Van Horn, & Ethington, 1996); implementation of family-friendly policies in the workplace (Kirby, 2000; Kirby & Krone, 2002); the social construction of worker identity and commitment through the lenses of gender in the workplace (Jorgenson, 2000, 2002); employees' decisions to talk or not talk about family in the workplace and their consequences (Farley-Lucas, 2000; Kirby, 2001); the impact of new information and communication technologies on managing work-life interrelationships (Edley, 2001, 2004; Edley, Hylmö & Newsom, 2004; Ellison, 2005; Golden &

Geisler, 2005); the impact of race, ethnicity, and (dis)ability on positioning within organizations and the management of work-life interrelationships (Buzzanell, 2003; Liu & Buzzanell, 2006); supervisory communication regarding the (un)boundedness of work (Kirby, 2000); faculty communication with students regarding the (un)boundedness of school (Medved & Heisler, 2002), and workplace practices and structures that promote organizational inclusion and employees' strategies for resistance (Farley-Lucas, 2000; Golden & Geisler, 2005; Hylmö & Buzzanell, 2002).

In their 2003 review, Kirby and colleagues observed that much research to that point privileged the "voice" of (a) managerial/corporate interests, (b) traditional families (creating a heterosexist bias), and (c) the (upper) middle-class, white, professional woman. Since then, research has begun to emerge to challenge this position, including studies that address heteronormative assumptions (Young, 2004), expand the focus from professional white women (Patterson, 2004; Petroski & Edley, 2004; Simpson & Kirby, 2004), and bring in international perspectives (Hylmö, 2004a; Liu, 2004).

These diverse studies are united, first, by an orientation to workplaces as sites of human social life as well as sites of economic production, a concern with the quality of life at work, and a recognition of the tension between technical and practical modes of rationality (Mumby & Stohl, 1996) in workplace experiences and activities. Second, they are connected by a common theoretical and methodological commitment to the centrality of discourse in constituting identity, relationships, and organizational structures, or the "constitutive role of communication in shaping organizational reality" (Mumby & Stohl, p. 57). The range of specific methods and theories invoked in these studies is rich, encompassing explicitly structurational research (Kirby & Krone, 2002), discourse analytic research in the tradition of interpretative repertoires (Golden & Geisler, 2005), and research in the discursive psychology tradition of discursive positioning (Jorgenson, 2002), among other approaches. However, all underscore the interplay between discourse in interpersonal interaction, workplace structures, and macrodiscourses of gender, work, and family.

Extant work-life research from the organizational perspective demonstrates the significant contribution that organizational communication scholars are positioned to make. For example, they emphasize the affective domain of the experience of work; the centrality of gender, race, ethnicity, and (dis)ability to the experience of work, and the relationship between the individual and the organization. However, they also enrich the interdisciplinary literature on work-life interrelationships that has been oriented more toward outcomes than toward processes (Kirby et al., 2003). We hasten to add, however, that the communication discipline holds no monopoly on meaning-centered approaches and that many scholars outside of communication take meaning-centered perspectives on work-life issues within the context of organizations. For example, Runté and Mills (2004) asserted that popular discourses of bridging work and family (especially the term *work-family conflict*) actually privilege organizational notions of the effective use of time and speed to resolve the conflict. Likewise, Clark (2000) described the management of boundaries through communication, and Perlow (1998) referenced spousal negotiations over employees' work patterns.

Further Potential Connections between Organizational Communication and Work-Life Research

Several streams of research within organizational communication, which we can loosely group under research that investigates the more "human" side of organizational life, have not yet made explicit connections to work-life issues, but they are well positioned to make further contributions to this body of research. For example, studies on resistance to organizational domination, organizational attachment and identification, emotion and stress in the workplace, workplace relationships, constructions of time in the workplace, and the public-private divide all have the potential to intersect with work-life interrelationships. In the process, such work could expand the scope of organizational communication research in these areas while, at the same time, introducing new perspectives into the interdisciplinary discourse.

Domination, resistance, attachment, and identification. The research findings on organizational dominance and resistance (see Murphy, 1998; Trethewey, 1997), for example, suggest micro-discursive mechanisms through which individuals can resist dominant organizational and macrocultural discourses about the "proper" interrelationships between work and personal life. Research on organizational attachment and identification (see Cheney, 1983; Cheney & Tompkins, 1987; Kuhn & Nelson, 2002; Russo, 1998; Scott, Corman, & Cheney, 1998) points to processes that promote the individual's inclusion in organization life and which could be counterposed with processes of acceptance of and resistance to both organizational and family inclusion.

Emotion and stress. The concept of emotion as an integral aspect of work (Morgan & Krone, 2001; Mumby & Putnam, 1992; Shuler & Sypher, 2000; S. Tracy & K. Tracy, 1998) and the problematizing of technical rationality as the dominant mode of understanding the workplace have great potential as lenses through which to explore how individuals experience work-life tensions in the workplace and how they make decisions when the demands of work and personal life come into conflict. There is already some research in this area in the context of dual-career couples (see Buzzanell, 1997); however, given the rich diversity of studies in workplace emotion, many more potential contributions can be made. For example, on the positive side, this research could point the way toward emotional synergy between work and personal life experiences. Furthermore, organizational literature on stress (Ray & Miller, 1994; S. Tracy, 2004) complements this focus on emotion. Specifically, Mattson, Clair, Chapman Sanger, and Kunkel (2000) illustrated the potential for new understandings to arise when we reframe what counts as work/organization and as family. They offered the story of a stressed-out stay-at-home mother, Rose, and her struggle to "hold it together" as an example of what might be considered organizational stress, showing an integrated approach to the work-life relationship.

Workplace relationships and time. Research on workplace relationships (Bridge & Baxter, 1992; Cahill & Sias, 1997; Sias & Cahill, 1998) and their ties to social support also hold strong relevance for work-life research, perhaps shedding light on the role of common personal-life commitments in developing workplace friendships among co-workers and building superior-subordinate relationships. Increasingly in organizational communication, time has been explored as a construct that structures our professional lives (Ballard & Seibold, 2003, 2004). This research does acknowledge the possible impact of organizational time policies on work-life interrelationships; however, the contribution of family members to the intersubjective construction of time and the related differences between "being orientations" and "doing orientations" (Clark, 2000) to time have yet to be explored. Furthermore, time spent doing work outside of the workplace can "colonize" (Deetz, 1992) the home space (Edley, 2001; Edley et al., 2004; Hylmö & Buzzanell, 2002); thus, as we gain control over the place of work, we may lose control over time.

Public-private divide. Finally, research on the public-private divide as it plays out in organizational programs and policies constitutes another area that, although not always explicitly characterized as work-life, poses strong implications for it. For example, questions surrounding the "boundaries" between personal life and organizational life emerge with the creation of employee assistance programs (May, 2004), the implementation of corporate wellness programs (Zoller, 2003, 2004), the creation of corporate volunteer programs (Gibson & Schullery, 2000) and requirements for corporate adventure-based training, such as mountain climbing (Kirby, 2006). In addition, an emerging body of research examines how organizations utilize (and/or co-opt) spirituality (see Rodriguez, 2001). Such research agendas illustrate the ways in which issues that were formerly framed as "personal" or "private" concerns have now become the purview of organizations.

FAMILY-BASED APPROACHES TO
WORK AND PERSONAL LIFE

Published studies of work-life interrelationships from the perspective of the family are somewhat less numerous than those from the organizational perspective; nonetheless, they constitute a significant portion of disciplinary research in this area and suggest ways in which the unidirectional bias of work to home and the micro-macro dualisms reflected in much of the interdisciplinary research can be overcome. As Clark (2002) noted, we should not lose a focus on family in the work-family/life relationship because work hours and stress at work can affect the family unit's cohesiveness, functionality, and integration, and individuals who talk with family about work and talk with co-workers/supervisors about life have greater work satisfaction, higher work functioning, and higher satisfaction with home and family activities. Lucas and Buzzanell (2006) argued that, within the context of work-life relationships, the very definition of "family" has profound implications: Individuals with configurations of private life that do not fit traditional definitions of "family" may be marginalized when it comes to managing work-life interrelationships, and an unjust distribution of workplace accommodations and benefits may be the result.

Variation and Commonalities in Existing
Family-Based Work-Life Research

The substantive areas addressed in studies that consider work-life concerns from the perspective of the family include the multifaceted functions of dual-earner couples' communication in managing work and family (Golden, 2000b, 2001, 2002), the communicative integration of home-based work into the fabric of family life (Edley, 2004; Ellison, 2005; Jorgenson, 1995), the everyday accomplishment of work and family routines (Medved, 2004), the utilization of organizational/corporate language to represent work performed in the home and family (Medved & Kirby, 2005), and the influence of workplace experiences on family communication patterns (Ritchie, 1997)—including how job loss affects communication and emotion work in the family (Buzzanell & Turner, 2003).

In general, communication approaches to the family emphasize everyday interactions among members as constitutive of relationships and roles. A large part of the family's daily interchange involves the exchange of implicit relationship messages. A particular family's symbolic "currencies" (Galvin, Bylund, & Brommel, 2004) include those locally meaningful gestures, artifacts, and behaviors whose significance is embedded in the particular history of their interactions. This symbolic content holds meanings that are important to a family's collective identity or "culture" (Galvin & Brommel, 1996; Whitchurch & Dickson, 1999). The notion of family culture presupposes the existence of common values and cognitive orientations that provide family members with a more or less shared definition of the situation. A family culture approach often seeks to identify dimensions along which couples and families can be differentiated and which reflect distinct ways in which families have organized their relationships (Yerby & Stephen, 1986).

Several studies that emphasize how families socialize their children for the broader culture and its conceptions of "work" fit with and extend this family culture perspective. For example, Ritchie (1997) linked families' childrearing orientations to parents' work environments. He argued that parents who emphasize conformity and obedience to authority with their children are likely to work in jobs requiring deference to authority, whereas those who prioritize autonomy and self-direction with their children are more likely to work in (white collar) environments where initiative and autonomy are valued. Outside of the communication discipline, yet still coming from a family socialization perspective, Paugh (2005) examined how children are socialized into work through routine social interaction with family members during dinnertime conversations in middle-class working families. Roy (2004) explored the construction of paternal provider roles, and he found that his male interviewees were socialized through family communication as children into roles of needing to be the provider for their family—whether or not they achieved this position successfully as adults.

Golden's work on dual-earner couples (2000b, 2001, 2002) underscores the importance of couples' communication in the management of work and family, given the many aspects of this process that must be managed by couples themselves, even those with the most family-friendly employers. Golden's work particularly highlights the identity-building and maintenance functions served by dual-earner spouses' communication in the context of a post-traditional society, where the validity of individuals' choices with respect to managing work and family is continually open to question and renegotiation. Buzzanell and colleagues have also pursued how managerial women create their identities as "good working mothers" when they return to work after maternity leaves (Buzzanell et al., 2005). Other communication research on dual-earner couples includes the typology of dual-career marriages by Rosenfeld, Bowen, and Richman (1995), an assessment of communication variables embedded in the dual-career literature (Heacock & Spicer, 1986), and studies of role structuring (Wood, 1986), decision making (Krueger, 1986), and self-disclosure (Rosenfeld & Welsh, 1985).

An emerging body of interdisciplinary literature focuses on the family itself as a site for domestic work and, in particular, on the role of communication in accomplishing family care and household chores (see Perry-Jenkins, Pierce, & Goldberg, 2004, for a review). In some cases, the home serves as a setting for the performance of both paid work and domestic work or childcare. Jorgenson's (1995) research on the coordination of work and family activities by women artists who are also mothers supplies an explicitly communicative perspective on this phenomenon. She discovered a variety of ways in which these mothers incorporated their children into their professional work so that the work served as an expression of family relatedness. In such cases, the performance of paid work at home becomes a vehicle for "doing family." Medved and Kirby (2005) illustrated the ways in which stay-at-home mothers frame the performance of their domestic work as a profession where they function as "family CEOs," ironically appropriating the language of organizations.

Parallel to the "discursive turn" in organizational studies, studies conducted by work-life family scholars outside of the communication discipline also take a discourse-centered approach, often informed by symbolic interactionism. For example, Doucet (2004) explored constructions of hegemonic masculinity in the interview discourse of 70 stay-at-home fathers. She found that fathers remain connected to traditionally masculine sources of identity, such as paid work, even when they have temporarily or permanently left a career to care for children. Similarly, Daly's (2001) analysis of family members' discourse revealed contradictions between the ideal and the typical experience of "family time."

Potential Connections between Family Communication and Work-Life Research

As we noted earlier, fewer work-life research studies use the family or personal life more generally as their primary frame of reference than use organizations as their primary frame. This fact points to a wide-open field of inquiry for family communication scholars. Potential areas of intersection between the studies already described here and well-established streams of family communication research span the management of conflict and decision making, issues of power and control, parent-child communication, family life-cycle research, family rituals, and the emerging field of new information and communication technologies and their impact on the family.

Conflict and control. The issues of conflict, decision making, and power and control in marital and family relationships and how they are communicatively expressed and managed (see Noller & Fitzpatrick, 1993) have enormous relevance to the management of work-life interrelationships. The apportionment of care-giving and wage-earning responsibilities across the transition to parenthood is the most obvious aspect, but day-to-day negotiations must also be accomplished to accommodate transient circumstances like care for sick children. Research on parent-child communication has largely centered on such topics as conflict patterns across different life-cycle stages and within diverse family structures (e.g., Noller, Feeney, Peterson, & Sheehan, 1995), discipline styles (Prusank, 1995; Wilson & Morgan, 2004), and emotional socialization (Fitness & Duffield, 2004). However, in her research on work and family, Galinsky (1999) documented surprising discrepancies between parents' perceptions of their children's attitudes toward parental work and attitudes reported by the children themselves (with children generally viewing their parents' work more positively than expected by the parents). The work-life research agenda could pursue how parents communicate the importance of their work to their children and how this situating of work affects family relationships and anticipatory socialization to the workplace.

Family rituals. The concept of family ritual has been an evocative resource for researchers seeking to understand how families create meanings and reinforce traditions, values, and religious/ethnic identifications (Jorgenson & Bochner, 2004). Although "family ritual" connotes the idea of a celebratory and formal occasion, some authors have expanded the definition to include more mundane and routinized procedures, ranging from family dinners to bedtime stories, by which a family's daily life is organized. Auslander (2002) argued that the work-family boundary may be "among the most intensively ritualized domains of modern society" (p. 1); some families, for example, regularly turn off cell phones and beepers during meals or otherwise restrict work-related activities during joint family activities. According to Auslander, further research is needed to identify such forms of "ritual innovation" through which families creatively manage the frontiers of work and non-work life.

Technology, work, and the family. Technology clearly plays an important role in shaping these boundaries, and an emerging body of research addresses the use of digital technology within the family setting, exploring how family practices and relationships are modified in response to new influences in the household. For example, in their study of families taking part in a digital divide initiative in rural Florida, Bird and Jorgenson (2002) found marital strains emerging around the acquisition of a home computer; wives wanted their husbands to take advantage of online tutorials to advance their educations, whereas the husbands did not feel a compelling need to explore such resources, nor did they see the computer as particularly relevant to their lives.

Teleworking brings together the issues of the family as a site for paid employment, the impact of new information and communication technologies (ICTs) on work-life boundaries, and the role of communication among family members or relationship partners in managing work-life relationships in this context (Mallia & Ferris, 2000). Hylmö (2004b) examined gender differences in the experience of telecommuting, finding that women who wished to preserve their promotable status within the organization tended to reproduce traditionally masculine values in their work patterns and boundary maintenance behaviors. Ellison (2005) learned that teleworkers used ICTs to "calibrate" the permeability of the work-life boundary as they negotiated boundary preferences with relationship partners and family members. Edley's (2004) research on entrepreneurial home-based mothers, whose work also made heavy use of ICTs, provided positive evidence of home-based work resulting in perceptions of increased autonomy and flexibility, as well as more time for leisure and family interactions through a variety of integrative strategies.

INTEGRATING ORGANIZATIONAL AND FAMILY COMMUNICATION APPROACHES TO WORK AND FAMILY

In their 2003 review, Kirby and colleagues offered the problematic of boundary as a way to think about the "ways transitions are negotiated symbolically, emotionally and practically between the worlds of work and family" (p. 5) and to examine the container metaphor that is often implicit where the organization and the family are characterized as concrete entities with discrete boundaries. In this piece, we struggled not only with boundaries as they have been constructed in the literature, but also with disciplinary boundaries, so that even attempting a review of both organizational and family literatures was complex. As noted earlier, any strategies for integrating subdisciplinary areas of research must first account for the forces that keep them apart. When we consider the relationship between organizational and family communication research on work-life interrelationships, several issues come into focus, such as substantive matters concerned with the way that work and personal life are understood, methodological orientations, and finally (but not least important), professional issues for researchers.

Questioning Work-Life Dualisms

The study of work-life interrelationships is riddled with dualisms: integration/segmentation, relational/instrumental, being/doing. These dualisms have their roots in the doctrine of separate spheres that has been evolving since the Industrial Revolution but that assumed the particular form we know today in the last third of the twentieth century (Kirby et al., 2003). In brief, the doctrine of separate spheres traditionally associates the workplace with (masculine) rational instrumentality and the home with (feminine) caring. Whereas scholars (see Kirby et al. for a review) criticize this distinction as unreflective of the lived experiences of working women and men, as instrumental in disadvantaging women, and as creating obstacles to the further humanization of the workplace, at the same time, research that does not explicitly connect the supposedly dominant modes of being in the two domains of experience misses an opportunity to undermine this ideological divide.

For example, whereas we hear a good deal about the need for recognizing the operation of practical rationality (against the dominant mode of technical rationality) in the workplace (Mumby & Stohl, 1996), we hear less about the potentially productive tension between a technical mode of rationality against the assumed dominant mode of practical rationality in the home (see Medved & Kirby, 2005, for a notable exception). Moreover, when this issue is raised, research generally frames the tension as negative rather than as potentially productive (see, for example, Hochschild, 1997, 2003). However, work must be done in the home, and just as the workplace has its affective and humane dimension, so, conversely, planning, coordination, and various forms of labor take place in the home. Although there are good reasons to be careful of the importation of business metaphors for coordination into the family, we risk trivializing the important social contributions and achievements of organization that occur in the home when we consistently privilege home-based emotion work over home-based instrumentality.

Arguably, the construct of "balance," which both scholarly and popular discourse often heralds as the most desirable state of work-life interrelationships, is rooted in this binary opposition. However, both the well-established tradition of research on dialectical tensions in interpersonal communication (Baxter, 1988) and the more recent work on paradoxes in organizational communication (Ashcraft & Trethewey, 2004; Trethewey & Ashcraft, 2004) offer us a way out of this oppositional framework of balance. First, they free us from the expectation of resolution. Consistent with Golden's (2000b) research on dual-earner couples, which demonstrated that working parents' accounts of their arrangements contain positively framed dual investments in the self and others (i.e., spouse and child), dialectical and paradoxical perspectives hold open the possibility of productive tension rather than destructive conflict. Moreover, as Golden discovered, working parents also report synergy between work and parental roles; similarly, Jorgenson (1995) found successful integration of work and family in the context of home-based work.

Integrating Through Meaning-Centered Methodologies

With respect to methodology, at the most basic level, work-life research from both organizational and family perspectives stresses a discursive approach to the construction of shared meanings as well as the importance of those meanings for personal identities, interpersonal and family relationships, and coordinated activity. However, disconnects emerge between the two frames of reference. For example, although the importance of the connections between the family and its environment (including the organizations at which family members work) is implied in the very nature of the research, scholars seldom make it explicit. Likewise, research that foregrounds the organization seldom incorporates specific consideration of the families of the organizational members and the potential impact of their sense-making on organizing in the workplace. These disconnects could be addressed through the application of three theoretical approaches that help to foreground the relationships of mutual influence between home and the workplace and explore productive tensions while, at the same time, addressing the structure-agency dualism on which the assumption of the workplace as primary influence rests.

USING STRUCTURATION THEORY TO INTEGRATE AND FURTHER WORK-LIFE COMMUNICATION RESEARCH

Structuration theory, as articulated by sociologist Anthony Giddens (1979, 1984), offers a possible integrating framework for organization- and family-based research on work-life interrelationships that concomitantly emphasizes agency and structure. Though historically associated more with organizational communication than with family communication as a theoretical lens, structuration is adaptive for either communication context. The structurational perspective focuses on social practices ordered across space and time; it links individual discursive micropractices to macro-level social and institutional change as well as meso-level organizational change (Krone, Schrodt, & Kirby, 2006).

Structuration is the process by which social systems are (re)produced by agents' use of rules and resources in their routinized, day-to-day interactions (Giddens, 1984). Giddens defines social systems as the patterns of relationships among individuals that serve to constrain interaction and defines structures as the rules and resources members use to create and sustain the system, so that "in and through their activities agents reproduce the conditions that make these activities possible" (p. 2). A structurational perspective allows a process orientation of looking at structures as being constructed and reconstructed on a daily basis as individuals call upon "recipes" for action (Giddens, 1984; Poole, Seibold, & McPhee, 1996).

A key concept in structuration theory is the duality of structure: structures are the medium of action that members draw on to interact, and yet they are the outcome of action because rules and resources exist only by virtue of being used in interaction. Thus, structure both constrains and enables. Human agents created structures that "exist," and so individuals possess the ability/agency to change them. Yet when people experience structures as constraining, they often forget this agency because they take the structure for granted. Another facet of the duality of structure is power. The bases of power are the resources that agents possess to control other people (authoritative) or material supplies (allocative) within the social context (Banks & Riley, 1993; Giddens, 1984). While the dominant interests typically structure the changing availability of resources, Giddens articulates the dialectic of control to help explain the two-way character of power.

Structuration also addresses human agency; organizations and families "only exist insofar as they are continually created and recreated in every encounter" (Giddens, 1979, p. 118). Structuration theory assumes that human actors are skilled and knowledgeable beings who monitor their activities as they engage in social interaction. Human agents maintain a sense of security in their everyday life through routines and routinization, and human agency is bounded by factors that constrain action (i.e., the structures they created) as well as by the unintended consequences of action. Finally, individuals have the ability to "appropriate" (use/adapt) a structure to create a situated version that meets their needs (DeSanctis & Poole, 1994). While human agents can create structures unique to their workplace or family, typically such structures are "appropriated . . . from pre-existing social institutions, such as larger political, economic, religious, or cultural institutions" (Krone et al., 2006, p. 298).

Inasmuch as Giddens (1984) suggests the key to understanding the reproduction of social structures lies in the routinized, day-to-day interactions of agents, structuration directs attention at daily communicative practices and how these practices enable or constrain experiences as individuals accomplish their work and personal/family lives on a daily basis. In organizational communication research using structuration, scholars stress the use of rules and resources as they relate to power (Mumby, 1987) as well as the creation of organizational standards (Browning & Beyer, 1998), cultures (Witmer,

1997), and identification (Scott et al., 1998). The longest trajectory of structuration has been examined in the context of small groups (see Seyfarth, 2000, for a review), including the research agenda of Poole and his colleagues regarding *adaptive structuration theory* and group decision making (e.g., DeSanctis & Poole, 1994; Poole et al., 1996).

The Structuration of Work-Life Interrelationships

In this context, structuration assumes that the micropractices of individuals' discursive interactions are the means of (re)production (and evolution) of macrosocietal discourses and institutional practices of work and personal life. Kirby and Krone (2002) utilized structuration to explore the ways in which co-worker talk about work-family benefits guided and constrained utilization, and they found that co-workers allocated resources to control others in the form of communicating positively or negatively about benefits and those who used them. As a result, widespread use of the policies did not occur—multiple work-family benefits were available on paper, but "you can't *really* use [them]" (italics added) (Kirby & Krone, 2002, p. 50). Perlow (1995) also employed structuration to explain barriers to successful implementation of work-family policies by examining the unintended consequences of rewarding a crisis mentality. Both studies illuminate how structuration can further understandings of work-life interrelationships, yet they still treat work and the organization as central.

In contrast to the burgeoning use of structuration in organizational communication, the theory has not been embraced in family communication. Based on our review, the only utilization of structuration in family communication appears in Schrodt, Baxter, McBride, Braithwaite, and Fine (2004). Schrodt et al. studied the ways in which communication among adults in stepfamilies structured the divorce decree as a meaningful basis for action in co-parenting relationships. They located structures of signification (Giddens, 1984) within participants' discourse that framed the divorce decree as either a legal document that dictated the rights and responsibilities of parenting or as a negotiating guide/backdrop for more informal co-parental decision-making processes. Their study echoes the assertion of Krone et al. (2006) that a "structuration approach to family interaction would focus not on surface-level behaviors or family functions, but rather on the *structures and structuring processes that support them*" (italics added) (p. 8).

Krone et al. (2006) provided a detailed review of how structurational concepts intersect with family communication. They highlighted the utility of this theory for family communication in that structuration allows scholars to (a) look across levels of analysis, (b) illustrate the production and reproduction of social structures, and (c) explore the dualities between agency and structure. As they noted, "discourse from multiple levels—including intrapersonal, interpersonal, family, organizational, and macro-societal—can impact how families 'manage' the interrelated realms of working life and family life" (p. 301). This framework treats couple and family discourses regarding the "proper" relationship between work and family as part of the resources that individuals draw on as they enact their roles within the workplace and in the home space (and these discourses, in turn, are framed by other influences).

To illustrate how discourse from across levels may affect work-life interrelationships, Harter, Kirby, McClanahan, and Edwards (2003, 2005) critiqued the discourse (and campaigns) of age-related infertility regarding its narration as a story of women who made selfish choices to work in the child-bearing years rather than have children. For women who choose both (paid) work and children, another set of discourses emerges: stay-at-home mothers "do the right thing" by sacrificing their career for their children (cf. Belkin, 2003; Schlessinger, 2001). Douglas and Michaels (2004) called this macrodiscourse the "new momism," and they described how it has been structured by 30 years of media imagery of mothers—including the "mommy wars" and sensationalist coverage of day care. New momism operates as a structure that constrains behavior: "[Insisting] that no woman is truly complete or fulfilled unless she has kids, that women remain the best caretakers of children, and that to be a remotely decent mother, a woman has to devote her entire physical, psychological, emotional and intellectual being, 24/7, to her children" (p. 4).

From a structurational perspective, how does this gendered macrodiscourse of new momism affect the routine daily interactions of women who work in the paid labor force? Are they able to go to work without guilt on a daily basis, or do they constantly need to be reassured that they are making an acceptable choice? In addition to affecting women, the macrodiscourse of new momism can also influence men. If "society" has structured the role of men as providers and breadwinners, if and when a father chooses to be a full-time caregiver, a plethora of issues could arise from a structurational perspective, including the intended and unintended consequences (both inside and outside the family) of challenging this macro-level expectation about who works and who nurtures (Krone et al., 2006).

As an example of structuration in practice, we now revisit the work of Doucet (2004) and her exploration of stay-at-home fathers. She illuminated how the "long shadow of hegemonic masculinity" hung over the men who she studied in their identity struggles over staying at home (p. 277). From a structurational perspective, hegemonic masculinity operates as a structure or a recipe for action for men regarding work and family, and the result is mostly constraining for these stay-at-home fathers. Yet, as the dialectic of control illustrates, although dominant interests (e.g., breadwinner stereotypes) have more power to structure, human agents possess the power to manage resources in such a way as to exert control over the more powerful. Thus, these men enacted agency by discursively reconfiguring work, care, and masculinity. In some ways, these fathers resisted the structure of hegemonic masculinity by reconfiguring their own definitions, but in other ways, they reproduced it by remaining connected to masculine sources.

A Structurational Research Agenda for Work-Life Interrelationships

We previously addressed family communication scholarship on issues of conflict, decision-making, and power/control in marital and family relationships in terms of its connections to work-life research. When viewing these concepts through the lens of a structurational perspective toward work-life relationships, research questions might include the following:

In the realm of couples' communication, how do dual-career couples resolve "conflicts" concerning the daily accomplishment or management of work and family life?

What structures operate as they decide who will pick up children, stay home when a child is sick, etc.—what recipes for action emerge, or do they continually renegotiate such situations?

If one parent does choose to stay at home, how do both parents treat "work" done in the home space?

Does the partner who engages in paid work discursively construct (structure) the domestic labor as "work" or merely as "staying at home"? What relationship does this discursive construction have to power and control, and what could be the unintended consequences?

Outside the "traditional" nuclear family structure, how do single parents and children co-construct work and family?

We also reviewed research on family cultures and socialization. If we view family cultures as the way that things are done in a family and the way children are socialized into that knowledge, several possibilities emerge for structurational research. How do parents communicate the importance of their work to their children? As Mumby (1987) illustrated, narrative is a symbolic form through which ideology and power structures are both expressed and constituted. In the family, narratives (both formal and informal) often teach children lessons about work and family. The fable of how the ants work hard while the grasshopper is lazy certainly begins to socialize children into the structure of the Protestant work ethic. Krone et al. (2006) encouraged scholars to explore family communication that "reproduces the privileging of work (i.e., 'not now kids, I have to finish this work.')" (p. 303). Although the literature we reviewed on the role of family cultures in socializing children to work (Paugh, 2005; Roy, 2004) did not explicitly utilize a structurational frame, certainly concepts such as "routine social interaction" are echoed in Giddens (1984), and, depending on children's responses (appropriation or resistance), other concepts may also emerge.

Finally, the intersection of family ritual and technology provides fruitful possibilities for structurational research. If the work-family boundary is an "intensively ritualized domain" (Auslander, 2002) that families seek to protect, what recipes for action emerge? How do families decide what constitutes "family time" (Daly, 2001)? What structures do families then enact to protect that time from working life? This research should explore not only structures that parents enact, but also those of their children. For example, children who loudly talk to their parents when they take a work-related call on the weekend probably recognize their actions should result in getting Mom or Dad off of the phone more quickly—and when these tactics work, they then become a recipe for future action (structure). Inasmuch as technology has made it possible for paid work to ever increasingly bleed into family and private life, how do individuals resist (and enable) blurring of previously distinct boundaries? How can these technologies (re)produce either enablement/empowerment or constraint/exploitation in the family (Giddens, 1984)?

In sum, a structurational perspective allows for an examination of the ways in which the family, the workplace, and their intersections are produced and reproduced on a daily basis through routine interaction. This theoretical perspective offers great potential for integrating organization-based and family-based communication scholarship on the work-life interrelationship. We now discuss systems theory as a second potential theoretical frame with which to bridge these subdisciplines.

USING SYSTEMS THEORY TO INTEGRATE AND FURTHER WORK-LIFE COMMUNICATION RESEARCH

Systems theory represents a second potentially fruitful theoretical framework for integration, because, by its nature, it encourages the exploration of interrelationships and contexts. When organizations and families are conceptualized as coupled systems characterized by resonant exchanges, we foreground their interdependency and their mutuality. Systems thinking has been described as transdisciplinary in the sense that it engages knowledge from a plurality of disciplines to understand the principles common to complex entities of many kinds (Whitchurch & Constantine, 1993). To think systemically about a family or an organization is to focus on the whole as constituted by the relations between the parts, rather than to reduce and simplify by isolating ever smaller units from their contexts.

As we look across the spectrum of systems perspectives in organizational and family communication, we see that different translations of the ideas configure the relation of "part" to "whole" in different ways. Some approaches are based on images of cellular organisms, whereas others seem to emphasize a unified "field" of interdependent influences (Morgan, 1986). Yet, taken together, systems approaches help to integrate organizational and family perspectives on work-life by problematizing the "container" metaphor for organizations and families and emphasizing system-environment linkages. As systems models develop means of accounting for processes of meaning creation and the observer-dependent nature of systems, they provide a particularly promising vantage point for work-life research.

Open Systems as a Metaphor for Organizations and Families

Systems-theoretic concepts such as boundary permeability and interdependence often appear as organizing constructs in the academic literature on work-life and work-family. The imagery of families and organizations as open systems facilitates our thinking about the everyday practices through which individuals manage conflicting commitments as they strive to achieve a desired degree of integration between work and home. The notion that system boundaries are selectively permeable alerts us to the ways in which the activities and choices associated with each domain condition those of the other. Much of the empirical research exploring the spatial, temporal, and behavioral connections between work and family accords with the idea that individuals are "partially included" in organizations, with their commitments and identifications dispersed between the employing organization and extra-organizational realms (Weick, 1979). Companies and other entities "are not aggregates of whole persons, but aggregates of parts of persons," as Gregory Bateson put it, and their organizational behavior is heavily influenced by considerations that spring from various other parts (Bateson, 1991, p. 160).

How a person manages "organizational inclusion" is a complex process. As noted earlier, traditional divisions between "work" and "home" are currently in flux, as employers move toward new work arrangements characterized by temporal and spatial flexibility. A variety of studies shows how workers mediate their levels of inclusion and preserve multiple affiliations through resourceful boundary management (Clark, 2000; Golden & Geisler, 2005; Mirchandani, 1998; Perlow, 1998). Information and communication technologies increasingly influence this process. According to Clark, with the help of wireless access, cellular telephones, and other innovations, individuals "mold the parameters and scope of their activities" so as to cope with competing claims on their time and energy (p. 750).

Partial inclusion affords one way of punctuating the relationship among systems and parts, and it fits with Weick's (1995) overall notion of the organization as a transactional network comprising interlocking routines. More commonly, scholars present organizations and families as neatly nested within an environmental surround (Bertalanffy, 1968; Keeney & Sprenkle, 1982; Morgan, 1986). In these translations of open systems ideas, *system* and *environment* stand in a figure-ground relationship, such that the environment, by definition, *lies outside* the system boundary. The hierarchical ordering of system-within-system appears prominently in early family systems theorizing, when researchers and clinicians began to consider the implications of seeing individual patients "as existing in a special kind of ecological system, namely his or her family" and disturbed behavior as an adaptive response to a dysfunctional family environment (Bavelas & Segal, 1982, p. 101; see also Watzlawick, Bavelas, & Jackson, 1967). Family systems theory came to emphasize the process of defining boundaries (i.e., establishing patterns of separateness and connectedness) as crucial to the maintenance of stability (Kantor & Lehr, 1975). Boundaries occur at various levels; according to Keeney and Sprenkle, subsystems (sibling, spousal, etc.) are enfolded within nuclear and extended family systems, which are, in turn, encompassed by communities, and so on, in an image of cascading "Chinese boxes" (see also Galvin et al., 2004; Yerby, Buerkel-Rothfuss, & Bochner, 1995).

The definition of environment as external to the system has led to a conceptual asymmetry in work-life research in that such scholars view the work environment as having enormous consequences for family systems, while they less clearly articulate the complementary influences of family on work. The idea of mutual (or circular) influence remains central to a systems approach, but an appreciation of mutual influences becomes particularly difficult to sustain when the family or the organization is represented as a "'here and now' self-contained entity," as some critics of family systems theory have argued (Leslie & Glossick, 1992, p. 258). Discussions of systems and boundaries overlook the elusive nature of boundaries, constituted by communicative rules and interaction patterns and often differently perceived and defined by various participants (Rosenblatt, 1994). Some family systems therapists (Anderson, Goolishian, & Winderman, 1986) speak of the *problem-determined system* in recognition of the idea that the definition of a system involves a choice made by an observer to influence the way that problems are resolved.

A small body of research on family-owned businesses illustrates how taking a more constructionist, sense-making-based systems perspective can deepen understanding of work-family dynamics. The family business provides unique access to boundary phenomena and mutual causality, inasmuch as task and family processes overlap. Often the company becomes an arena for acting out family agendas, and interpersonal issues among family members or between family and nonfamily employees form the basis for alliances and coalitions (Davis & Stern, 1980; Weigel & Ballard-Reisch, 1997). In an early paper, Miller and Rice (1967/1990) explored the connections between diminished effectiveness and the tangled boundaries of the various family business subsystems. They applied the distinction between *task* and *sentient* systems, in which the *task system* is defined by the operational activities of the business process, whereas the *sentient system* is defined by loyalties and personal bonds among members. As the authors acknowledged, the assignment of specific interactions and processes to one or the other system often depends on the standpoint of the observer. Davis and Stern also concentrated on the interpretive ambiguity in family business settings. They noted a tendency for both family and nonfamily participants to see "family" issues as motivating the most "businesslike" of decisions (for example, whether to establish a marketing department in the company), so that the search for a unified legitimizing framework is made difficult. The family business vividly exemplifies a process relevant to many other settings, in which "work" and "family" operate jointly as framing contexts. It highlights the need for more complex conceptualizations that recognize how family *and* organization operate as co-determining environments for each other.

Rethinking "Figure" and "Ground" in Work-Life Research

One of the key contributions of systems theories is the perspective that it provides for thinking about the survival potential of a given system. The viability of any living system depends on its ability to maintain constancy in the face of environmental change along with the ability to adapt in response to changed environmental conditions (Hoffman, 1981). The idea that families can be differentiated according to their levels of adaptability and other system-wide variables has been central in the development of various family typologies (Galvin et al., 2004; Kantor & Lehr, 1975; Olson, Sprenkle, & Russell, 1979).

In work-life research, researchers introduce considerations of viability and adaptability mainly in the context of crisis conditions as they investigate stress-producing aspects of work situations and family systems. As Kanter (1977) explained, such studies pursue "how tension and illness-producing features of one system affect the likelihood of a member's successful adjustment to the other system" (p. 84). Although such knowledge is crucial, as Kanter noted, it may obscure the ways in which systems change in response to opportunities, not simply when their essential variables are threatened. Cybernetic notions of variety and constraint are helpful in the identification of other positive mutualities between home and work. We think here of how family identities and traditions can serve as a potential resource for enlarging the vocabulary of responses needed by the organization to cope with a complex environment.

As one example, consider the story of a food chemist named Linda, an Asian-American woman employed by a food company as part of a product development group (Thomas & Ely, 1996). She and her colleagues faced a problem concerning the flavoring of a new soup. After the group made several scientific attempts to solve the problem, Linda came up with a family-inspired solution "by setting aside my chemistry and drawing on my understanding of Chinese cooking" (p. 89). Linda chose not to share the real source of her ideas with her colleagues, for fear that it would set her apart or that they might consider her unprofessional. After solving the problem, she simply went back to the so-called "scientific way of doing things" (p. 89). As Thomas and Ely detailed, Linda engaged in several boundary violations as a woman doing ethnic cooking in a chemistry lab—boundaries based not only on ethnicity but also gender and the associated distinction between public and private spheres. Linda's story constitutes one example of how particularistic ties and competencies might enhance a person's organizational contributions and how, when such knowledges are devalued, critical sources of variety are lost.

The choices that Linda and others make in how they enact the work-family relationship can be seen as a sense-making process (Buzzanell et al., 2005; Weick, 1995). According to Buzzanell et al., the impetus for sense-making often presents itself as a challenge to one's identity—as a "good worker" in Linda's case or "good parent" or even "good working mother." At such moments, when everyday routines and procedures fail and identities are called into question, participants revise their accounts of themselves, often transforming organizational thinking in the process. A sense-making-based systems perspective invites further study of those critical moments when participants engage work-home dilemmas to see how "variety" is perhaps mobilized and organizational flexibility is safeguarded.

USING RELATIONAL DIALECTICS TO INTEGRATE AND FURTHER WORK-LIFE COMMUNICATION RESEARCH

Last, we turn to relational dialectics, a perspective that has been primarily, though not exclusively (see Bridge & Baxter, 1992), associated with family and relational communication contexts and a potentially fruitful and under-exploited perspective for spanning the divide between organization- and family-based studies of work and personal-life interrelationships. Dialectical scholarship, according to Baxter and Montgomery (1998), "tends to cohere around four core concepts: *contradiction, change, praxis,* and *totality"* (p. 3). Each of these concepts has significant implications for integrating organizational and family communication approaches to the study of work-life interrelationships.

Contradiction

Baxter and Montgomery (1997) defined contradiction as "the dynamic interplay between unified opposites" and asserted that this "unity in opposition" is manifested in two ways: as a "unity of identity," in which "each oppositional tendency presupposes the existence of the other for its very meaning," and as "interdependent unity," which is the condition of the two oppositions, each constituting part of a larger whole (p. 327). Contradiction also entails "dynamic interplay or tension between the unified opposites" but without any negative connotation, a characteristic that "distinguishes a dialectical perspective from a dualistic one" (p. 327). Baxter and Montgomery explained that this characteristic gives dialectical contradictions a quality of "both/and" in contrast to "either/or" (p. 327). Thus, the "relationship [between the opposites] is an improvised, fluid boundary of unity and difference" (p. 340). However, a dialectic is more than a simple binary opposition. Baxter and Montgomery argued that the conception of dialectics should be expanded to embrace a "more complex view in which multiple voices of opposition function at once, a phenomenon we call 'multivocal contradiction'" (p. 340).

When applied to work and personal-life interrelationships, and the project of integrating organizational and family perspectives, we can observe that the work-life interrelationship displays all of the characteristics delineated by Baxter and Montgomery. In fact, some work-life research from the family perspective (see Golden, 2000b) has characterized working parents' management of their concerns for themselves and their children as dialectical in nature. The fit is particularly clear if we understand the work-life relationship as a manifestation of an underlying tension between what Dinnerstein (1976), in her classic treatise on gender and identity, termed *enterprise* and *embodiment.* The concept of contradiction fits Dinnerstein's enterprise/embodiment in both of the senses of "unity in opposition" delineated by Baxter and Montgomery (1997). Enterprise/embodiment exhibits "unity of identity" (Baxter & Montgomery, p. 327) insofar as embodiment (the experience of *being* in the world) is not meaningful without its complement, enterprise (the experience of *doing* in the world). The dualism exhibits "interdependent unity" (Baxter & Montgomery, p. 327) insofar as embodiment and enterprise represent two modes of experience, both of which, according to Dinnerstein, are needed to be fully human.

The enterprise/embodiment dialectic also demonstrates multivocal contradiction in the context of work-life interrelationships, pointing the way toward an integrative paradigm for home- and work-based approaches to work and personal-life interrelationships. Within a framework of multivocal contradiction, we can see that work is not entirely instrumental (or associated with enterprise and autonomy) and personal life is not entirely relational (or associated with embodiment and interdependence). Rather, these dualisms represent modes of experience that are encountered across time and space and in the context of interactions with both work partners and relational partners.

Totality

Defined by Baxter and Montgomery (1997) as the "assumption that phenomena can be understood only in relation to other phenomena" (p. 330), the concept of totality relates to (a) where we locate contradictions, (b) how we contextualize contradictory interplay, and (c) interdependencies among contradictions. By "interdependencies among contradictions," Baxter and Montgomery meant the distinction between primary and secondary contradictions. For example, they observed that "the interplay between autonomy and interdependence has often been identified by dialectical theorists as the most central of all relational contradictions" (p. 331). As indicated above, we see the work-life interrelationship as representing a variation on this pervasive contradiction, in which work is associated primarily with autonomy (or a doing orientation) and personal life is associated with interdependence (or a being orientation). However, we must also recognize that this dialectic is experienced in both work and personal life.

The issue of where we locate contradictions has profound implications for understanding work and personal-life interrelationships and for the integration of home and work-based approaches (and organizational and family communication). If, as we argue above, we experience both of the oppositions (whether we express them as doing and being, or enterprise and embodiment) in both spatiotemporal realms (work and home)—we implicitly locate the conflict that exists in work and personal life between the two halves of the dialectic rather than between the domains themselves or between roles associated with those domains. Such a positioning contributes to the dereification of work and personal life as separate spheres, and it shifts the focus to how individuals experience tensions between the two halves of the dialectic across domains and how these tensions are interactionally realized and communicatively managed.

Contextualizing contradictory interplay, another aspect of totality, refers to the distinction between internal and external contradictions, another very useful concept in terms of understanding how work and personal life relate to each other, and it cuts across workplace and home space interactions. Relational dialectics theory treats internal and external contradictions as the way in which societal expectations of relationships may contrast with individuals' desires for defining their relationship at the same time as the individuals struggle with internal contradictions like the autonomy/interdependence dialectic (Baxter & Montgomery, 1997). Work-life interrelationships can be similarly understood; that is, different social expectations of the way in which individuals should manage work and personal-life interrelationships may clash with individuals' local goals and experiences. Moreover, societal expectations may evidence contradiction among themselves; for example, what have come to be known as "the mommy wars" manifest the cultural contradictions of motherhood in late twentieth and early twenty-first century America (Hays, 1996).

As we noted earlier in the context of the structurational approach to work-life interdependencies, cultural discourses (for example, on career planning, personal growth, effects of maternal employment on child development) represented in mediated communication constitute a symbolic environment that includes a set of external contradictions that individuals may draw upon and incorporate or defend against in their own sense-making processes. Other external contradictions that could influence the negotiation of internal dialectics include industry-specific expectations regarding work practices—for example, the practice of valorizing long work hours within the high-tech field (see Perlow, 1999) and work values at the level of national culture (Bernstein, 1997). The internal and external contradiction phenomenon could also be applied in a more integrative manner—orienting toward work and personal life as interpenetrating systems such that each one constitutes an environment for the other, as we have suggested in the systems perspective.

Change

Within the context of relational dialectics, the emphasis on change shifts attention away from homeostasis as the goal of relationship development and toward evolution and growth. When applied to work-life interrelationships, this construct foregrounds how shifts over time—within the context of relational development, individual growth and development, career development, and the family life cycle—all need to be taken into consideration in the construction of integrative accounts of how individuals experience and manage work and personal life. This perspective directly confronts and dismantles the stasis implications of the metaphor of "finding balance," as well as its implications for equality of distribution between the two domains of experience. The change construct underscores the principle that one size does not fit all in terms of work-life proportions, and, furthermore, for varying reasons, the proportions may shift over time in both work and personal life.

Stamp & Banski's (1992) work on the impact of the first-time transition to parenthood on couples' experiences of autonomy and connection (and their communicative strategies for managing newfound constraints on autonomy) exemplifies family communication research that takes an explicitly dialectical perspective while foregrounding the "chronotopic" (Baxter & Montgomery, 1997, p. 341) nature of dialectical experiences. This research, as well as Stamp's work (1994) on how the parental role is appropriated by first-time parents, suggests research that might be done on how the work-life dialectic evolves across the family life cycle, which has been explored by Golden (2000b) from a dialectical perspective in the context of the first-time transition to parenthood.

Praxis

Baxter and Montgomery (1997) defined *praxis* as the "joint actions of relationship parties in response to the dialectical exigencies of the moment" (p. 343) and noted that this aspect of dialectical tensions has thus far received limited attention. They identified two forms of *dys*functional praxis—denial (in which the attempt is made to ignore one half of the dialectic) and disorientation (in which contradictions are recognized but seen as intractable and negative)—as well as six functional patterns, including such strategies as spiraling alternation, segmentation, and integration. Denial reflects the position adopted in many workplaces, and disorientation characterizes much work-life research itself, with its emphasis on conflict and the elusiveness of "balance." Baxter and Montgomery also observed that the research on dialectical praxis, in addition to being limited, tends to focus on the "molar level of analysis," and they called for a "finer-grained dialogic perspective" (p. 345) focusing on situated discourse.

This call affords enormous possibilities for discourse-based research on work-life interrelationships; indeed, most of the research cited in our initial literature review is discourse-based in one form or another, although the "situatedness" of the discourse is relative. Capturing "meaning that is constructed in the moment-to-moment discourse between interlocutors" (Baxter & Montgomery, 1997, p. 345) constitutes a substantial challenge for researchers. However, interview-based discourse analytic studies can tell us a great deal about the construction of meaning and the management of dialectical contradictions. Lindlof (1995) argued, "The qualities of disclosure and tact that characterize most relationships can be cultivated within the frame of the interview. The effect of this is to simulate the features of a relationship" (p. 167), including co-construction of accounts that function to manage dialectical tensions. Thus, it can be plausibly argued that interview responses also count as situated instances of communicative practice. Joint interviews with relationship partners (see Golden, 2000b, 2001, 2002; Stamp, 1994; Stamp & Banski, 1992) also offer rich opportunities to capture dialogic sense-making.

In addition to these microdialogic forms of praxis, the ritual constitutes another form of praxis referenced by Baxter and Montgomery (1997) and represented in dialectical relationship research (Braithwaite, Baxter, & Harper, 1998). Braithwaite et al. contended that blended family rituals provide a means of achieving a "both/and" state in the context of managing the dialectic of "old family" and "new family." Rituals have already been suggested in the work-life literature as a technique for role transitioning (Nippert-Eng, 1996), which corresponds to the form of praxis labeled *alternation* by Baxter and Montgomery at the molar level of praxis. The potential of rituals for accomplishing other forms of praxis, such as integration (as in the description by Braithwaite et al. of rituals of stepfamilies, in which elements of two families are blended), has yet to be explored in work-life research from a dialectical perspective. However, as we noted earlier, the attention to family rituals in the research literature indicates that such an approach would be fruitful, especially in terms of expanding the field of view from rituals narrowly defined as boundary maintenance strategies to include integrative forms of praxis. For example, families or couples may ritualize the sharing of daily life events outside the home upon coming together over an evening meal. Some communication researchers have focused on the special challenges presented when individuals' work and home are co-located, including how they use rituals to manage role transitions (see Ellison, 2005; Shumate & Fulk, 2004); as Baxter and Montgomery argued, a dialectical approach could further enrich this line of research by considering forms of praxis other than alternation, such as integration and reaffirmation.

Dialectics, Identity, and Work-Life Interrelationships

Clearly, relational dialectics intersects with all four of the central problematics identified by Kirby and colleagues: boundaries, identity, rationality, and voice (Kirby et al., 2003). It has especially strong resonance, however, for the identity problematic. We have argued here that work-life interrelationships cannot be defined by interaction (and potentially conflict) between two domains that are unequivocally associated with instrumentality or affective relations. That is, work-life interrelationships represent a more complex "knot" (Baxter

& Montgomery, 1997, p. 331) of dialectical contradictions, not just a binary opposition between two domains of activity and experience, each with a single dimension that conflicts with the other. Rather, our experiences of both work and personal life contain oppositions of being and doing, enterprise and embodiment, technical and practical rationality.

The implication for the identity problematic is that role, as commonly understood—a discrete compartment of the self defined by a set of patterned behaviors and social interactants—is an inadequate construct for understanding work-life interrelationships and conflicts. It fails to capture the manner in which the underlying dialectics of being and doing and enterprise and embodiment cut across domains of experience. Thus, conflict, when it arises, may derive not from incompatibilities between roles per se but from tensions between two different modes of experience (Golden, 2000b; Kirby et al., 2003).

The research on relational dialectics that explicitly examines tensions between roles is instructive from this standpoint. This research reveals that apparent conflicts between roles such as spouse/parent (Stamp, 1994) or spouse/stepparent role conflicts (Cissna, Cox, & Bochner, 1990) can also be framed as tensions between different modes of being. For example, in his research on how first-time parents appropriate their new roles as mothers and fathers and integrate them into their existing identities (including their roles as spouses), Stamp provided a conversation between a husband and wife with their baby present, in which the wife shifts back and forth between the more "doing" stance of sharing information with her husband and the almost purely relational work of spontaneously responding with "motherese" to her baby's smiles. Stamp observed an "instantaneous movement from one role to another thereby facilitating successful enactment of both roles, while compromising neither" (p. 100). This effortless shifting from a being mode of relaxation to the doing mode of engagement with work has also been noted in the context of individuals' use of mobile information and communication technologies (see Golden & Geisler, 2005). Likewise, Cissna et al. (1990) examined the dialectical tension between the stepparent's roles as relationship partner and parent—each of which includes both instrumental and affective demands.

This research points to a much more fluid concept of identity than provided by more conventionally atomistic notions of roles (Marks & MacDermid, 1996), as well as to personal identity as the site of dialectical contradictions that are nonetheless necessary parts of the whole person existing in productive tension, rather than a fragmented set of roles enacted in response to changes in setting or interactants. By reframing identity in this way, we find a different and more complex set of tensions that includes not only cross-domain conflicts but also within-domain conflicts—though still with the same set of dialectical contradictions—as well as productive tensions in the sense of one half of a dialectic producing the other (such as a friendship that develops in the course of a workplace project or a joint parent-child decision to cultivate a family garden).

Thus, research on work and personal life from a dialectical perspective is rich with possibilities. Generally, a dialectical perspective highlights the importance of studies that incorporate data from both domains and that employ dialectical oppositions as the unit of analysis rather than the roles involved. Although none of the work-life research by communication scholars in this review adopted a cross-domain approach, models for this approach appear in the work of management scholars whose research emphasizes discourse and the interactional negotiation of meaning, such as Perlow's (1998) study of engineers and their spouses and Bailyn's (1993) networked case study approach (although this research, in turn, does not display an explicitly dialectical perspective). Likewise, research undertaken by anthropologist English-Lueck (2002) on work-life issues in a high-tech community utilized observations at work and home. The dialectical perspective also invites us as researchers to focus not just on dysfunctional conflict but also on potentially productive tensions and to reject the normative implications of the balance metaphor for stasis and proportion.

ADDITIONAL POSSIBILITIES FOR INTEGRATIVE RESEARCH THROUGH THE LENS OF WORK-LIFE INTERRELATIONSHIPS

A Fourth Perspective: Critical/Feminist Approaches

As noted earlier, our choice of structuration, systems, and dialectics as theoretical approaches was informed by our view that they are particularly well suited to foreground relationships of mutual influence between personal life and work-life rather than assuming work as the dominant force in the individuals' life worlds, and, as such, they represent particularly promising frameworks for bringing together family and organizational communication perspectives on work-life interrelationships. Of course, all theoretical frameworks include their own "blinders" and limitations, so that what is revealed about work-life and personal life through a particular theoretical frame may be concealed in another. Furthermore, the fact that systems, dialectics, and structuration generally share a more interpretive than critical metatheoretical orientation means that explicitly critical approaches to integrating family and organizational communication in the context of work-life research have not occupied the foreground in our discussion here.

At the same time, several of the examples of extant communication-based work-life research referenced earlier are informed by critical—more specifically, feminist—perspectives (e.g., Buzzanell & Liu, 2005; Farley-Lucas, 2000); moreover, our discussion of structurational approaches to work-life references gender as a macro-discourse that serves as a resource in everyday interactions. Furthermore, all of the work-life research cited here shares, either explicitly or implicitly, the critical approach's general commitment to identifying and raising awareness of social practices that undermine individual well-being and to contributing to positive social change. Although space limitations preclude as thorough a treatment of this perspective as the others, we nonetheless feel that our project would be incomplete without at least some explicit (albeit brief) consideration of what at least one type of critical perspective—feminist approaches—offers in terms of integrating family and organizational communication perspectives on work-life interrelationships.

Feminist approaches encompass a broad range of perspectives—liberal feminism, standpoint feminism, poststructuralist feminism—but all share two concerns that are also central to work-life research: the centrality of gender in shaping human experience and social arrangements and a commitment to seeking broader social and structural explanations for individual experiences or, in other words, to the inextricable intertwining of public and private worlds. Feminist standpoint and poststructuralist perspectives, in particular, have sought to reconceptualize gender from an individual characteristic of workers to a constitutive feature of families, jobs, and organizing processes (Alvesson & Billing, 1997).

Empirical research from a standpoint perspective attempts to make visible the suppressed gender conflicts that characterize these everyday settings by examining women's subjectivities and day-to-day experiences and pursuing their ways of coping with and negotiating perceived constraints. Poststructuralist-oriented research seeks to challenge the taken-for-granted categories of "family," "work," and "organization" by recognizing how they are communicatively constituted (see, for example, Martin, 1990). A key direction within the emerging body of feminist organization studies is to advocate for changes that will speed up women's organizational advancement and decrease the rates at which women exit certain fields relative to men due to work-family conflicts.

Various strands of feminist theory converge in their attempt to challenge the inevitable gender division of labor known as the ideology of "separate spheres" (see Ferree, 1990; Rosaldo, 1974). This work seeks to make explicit the ways in which the assumed natural divisions between "private" concerns of sexuality, pregnancy, and family and "public" workplace concerns have functioned to rationalize discrimination against female workers. Furthermore, feminist scholars argue that, as long as work-family problems are cast as private problems that must be solved individually, collective action is defused (Martin, 1990).

An interesting newer strain of research in sociologically oriented studies of work-life interrelationships, which has not yet been taken up by the communication discipline but holds great promise, involves the migration of traditionally feminine caretaking behaviors into the workplace as women have entered the workforce themselves (Brannen, 2005; Philipson, 2002a, 2002b). This research examines how women's gendered enactment of caretaking crosses the boundaries between work and personal life and holds the potential to systematically disadvantage women in the context of work cultures that have abandoned an ethic of mutual commitment while, at the same time, holding out the possibility for transforming the workplace. In addition to feminist research that highlights the choices and roles of women, the constraints that men face regarding work and family in a patriarchal society are also in the infancy of exploration (see Kirby, 2003; Petroski & Edley, 2004). Space considerations preclude a lengthier discussion of the possibilities for new directions in communication research on work-life interrelationships from a feminist perspective. Clearly, however, although our society has witnessed significant role convergence along gender lines in recent years (see Golden, 2002), gender remains an intensely meaningful category, making feminist approaches especially appropriate for the study of this area of human social life.

Social Support, Health Communication, and Work-Life Interrelationships

In addition to offering this fourth theoretical approach to integrating home-based and workplace-based perspectives on work-life interrelationships, in keeping with the spirit of inclusiveness and integration that informs this project (while not wishing to stray too far from our primary focus on integrating organizational and family communication), we would like to briefly identify some additional subdisciplinary intersections that come into view through the lens of work-life research. Earlier, in the context of specifying substantive areas within organizational communication that have not yet connected to work-life research, but which have strong potential to do so, we cited research on workplace relationships (e.g., Sias & Cahill, 1998), stress (e.g., S. Tracy, 2004), and emotion (Shuler & Sypher, 2000). These concerns intersect with research in health communication that concerns itself with stress, burnout, and coping mechanisms among health-care and human service professionals (e.g., Miller, Birkholt, Scott, & Stage, 1995) and have been integrated into the organizational communication literature (Miller, 2006).

Research on communication and work-life interrelationships could be significantly enriched by the further integration of health and organizational communication research in this area, consistent with the approach of Ray and Miller (1994) in their study of nurses' use of social support in coping with stresses associated with managing work and personal life. As these authors observed, most research on stress and the buffering effects of social support focus on stress that is rooted in the workplace, but scholars do not speak to stress that may have an extra-organizational source or that results from the interaction of work and non-work domains. The integration of health communication research on stress, burnout, and coping with organizational communication research on relationships, stress, and emotion has the potential to provide insights into managing work-life interrelationships, both in a general organizational context and in terms of the special work-life management challenges of health-care organizations. Such research should examine not only interpersonal support, but also organizational support systems such as EAPS and workplace wellness programs. Furthermore, the recent call for health communication and organizational communication scholars to embrace spirituality as a factor in personal life that influences health and work outcomes constitutes another promising area of intersection (in health communication, see Egbert, Mickley, & Coeling, 2004; Parrott, 2004; in organizational communication, see Rodriguez, 2001).

Intercultural Communication and Work-Life Interrelationships

A second set of potential subdisciplinary intersections clusters around the construct of "culture." Earlier in this essay, in the context of summarizing new directions in communication-specific organization-based work-life research, we called attention to work that has expanded the focus from mainstream white, middle-class American culture to include the experiences of individuals of color and their families (Patterson, 2004), challenge heteronormative assumptions (Young, 2004), and introduce international perspectives (Hylmö, 2004a; Liu, 2004). We also discussed the usefulness of culture as a construct in understanding work and personal-life interrelationships in the context of research that takes the family as its primary frame of reference. We could further deepen our understanding of work-life interrelationships by identifying and developing intersecting insights about culture and communication from intercultural, organizational, and family communication research.

One area, for example, that is rich with possibilities is the examination of the effects of matches and mismatches between family cultures and work cultures. Kanter's (1977) early agenda for work and family research targets the meanings that families assign to workplace events as a key factor in understanding how families respond to and adapt to the requirements of family members' work. Kanter also cited evidence from early research to support the argument that some family cultures—for example, those whose "roles were flexible and life philosophy was not dominated materialism" (p. 86)—are more adaptable to workplace stressors.

Another dimension of family culture that intersects with working and adaptation to organization life is work values. Research demonstrates that such values are not only shaped by the family but by national history (Bernstein, 1997), and they can also be a significant component of ethnic identity, which is displayed in communicative conduct (Aoki, 2000). The complexity of possibilities for interaction between family and organizational cultures is further complicated by the prevalence of dual-earner couples in American society. Moreover, spouses/relationship partners in the same family may be employed by organizations with very different cultural requirements for participation, a situation that poses other challenges for managing work and personal life; consider, for example, a corporate employee with conventional hours coordinating child-care arrangements with a partner who works in a health-care organization where rotating shift work is the norm. In a sense, these two distinct organizational cultures intersect with each other through the individuals, who must educate their co-workers regarding the expectations of their partners' work environments.

Cross-cultural and intercultural perspectives also have much to contribute to our understanding of work-life interrelationships. Comparative cross-cultural work-life research, though primarily the province of management scholars up to now (Bailyn, 1992; Etzion & Bailyn, 1994), has the value of problematizing our assumptions about the nature of work-life interrelationships, and it could be greatly enriched by a communication perspective focusing on the role of discourse in the construction of meaning. Taking a more intercultural perspective, Stohl's (2001) review of interdisciplinary research related to multinational and global organizing identifies multiple dimensions of cultural variability—such as orientation to authority (hierarchical versus egalitarian) and orientation to community (individualistic versus collectivistic)—and their implications for organizational communication practices. This matrix could readily be extended to the implications of these constructs for orientations to work-life interrelationships. For example, if collectivist cultures value relationships over tasks, might they also accommodate more penetration of personal life into work life?

Intercultural communication research on interactions among individuals of different cultures in multinational organizations or organizations doing business globally (e.g., Stage, 1999; Zaidman, 2001) can be extended to an examination of how norms for work-life interrelationships—for example, inclusion of talk about family and private life in workplace interactions or availability for work-related exchanges outside of regular business hours—are communicatively enacted, as well as to a consideration of the challenges of managing work and personal life that arise when workers are transplanted into a "foreign" culture or even just communicating with individuals and organizations in other parts of the world. With respect to expatriate workers, Stohl's (2001) review references research that documents the impact of the family's overall adjustment to a new cultural environment on the worker's adaptation to the organizational culture. However, the tensions that might result more particularly from cross-cultural differences in norms for work-life interrelationships, which have been identified for at least some national groups, have yet to be explored and represent a potentially fruitful avenue for investigation. Moreover, the discourse analytic approaches employed in the intercultural research referenced here highlights the importance of attending to the daily experiences of workers to understand cultural interactions and underscores the goodness of fit between communicative approaches and the study of various dimensions of work-life interrelationships.

Media Representations of Work-Life Interrelationships

Another "subdisciplinary intersection" emerging in communication scholarship is the exploration of mediated representations of work and personal life. One area of scholarship critiques the ways in which "work-family choices" are constructed for women through the media, such as when choice is bifurcated and women are told they must choose between work and family through macrosocietal discourses such as those of age-related infertility (see Harter et al., 2003, 2005) and the "new momism" (Douglas & Michaels, 2004). In addition, mediated artifacts often imply that all women are able to make choices about work and family in a world that is unconstrained by finances. A recent NCA panel used lenses of cultural studies (Japp, 2004) and social class/white privilege (Simpson & Kirby, 2004) to analyze the "opt-out revolution" (Belkin, 2003), where many well-educated, white, formerly professional mothers are choosing to exit the paid labor force to spend time with their families. Panelists argued that the underlying implication of choice ignores many women for whom paid labor is not a matter of choice but a matter of survival (also see Medved & Kirby, 2005).

Edley and Kirby (2003) examined, in *Working Mother* magazine, the idealized construction of women who have made the choice to work outside the home and found that working moms are largely defined through the products they should consume to be "good" mothers. Even in mediated sources that are not explicitly about mothers, issues of mothering inevitably result when women and work are discussed, as Shuler (2003) discovered in her analysis of *Fortune* magazine's list of the "50 Most Powerful Women in American Business." Mediated portrayals of the changing roles and expectations of men have also been explored by communication scholars. For example, Vavrus (2002) analyzed *Mr. Mom* as an exemplar of "domesticating patriarchy," and Hendricks and Kirby (2003) critiqued the ways in which the film *One Fine Day* sets up the character of the working father as endearing, whereas the working mother is often portrayed as annoying.

CONCLUSIONS: DISCIPLINARY "BOUNDARIES" AND BARRIERS—AND PATHWAYS— TO INTEGRATIVE RESEARCH

Finally, we consider potential barriers to integrative research from a metadiscursive professional perspective. As indicated earlier, these barriers take two forms: professional identification requirements and information management. Scholars (particularly those in the earlier stages of their careers) need to establish well-defined subdisciplinary identifications, and—partly as a consequence of this specialization—mastering and integrating diverse bodies of research literature presents a formidable challenge. This challenge of keeping current with relevant inter(sub)disciplinary research is made even more thorny by the frequent disconnects between theoretical frameworks.

For example, as we indicated earlier, structuration theory has been associated primarily with organizational communication research; thus, someone undertaking work-life research from a family communication perspective might question the relevance of extant work-life research grounded in this approach. Conversely, work-life research from a dialectical perspective may appear foreign to someone working primarily from an organizational communication perspective. Furthermore, systems approaches, though used extensively in both organizational and family communication research, have tended to emphasize different constructs and draw upon different bodies of literature. Our aim here has been to open windows into these perspectives for scholars who may not have previously considered their usefulness to their research and to encourage their application in studies that cross boundaries to follow border-crossers as they negotiate work and personal life.

Thus, our goal has been twofold. First, we seek to advance work-life research by suggesting new approaches for both organizational and family communication scholars, and second, we hope to advance this research through a more integrative paradigm—one that is grounded not in a metaphor of "balance" with its implications of stasis, proportion, and separation but rather in the recognition of the "both/and" fluidity of experience in both work and personal life, the duality of structure, and the mutual influence of work and personal life. Therefore, the theoretical perspectives that we have outlined here point to ways of integrating organizational and family based approaches to work-life research, at the same time that work-life research itself—since, by definition, that work deals with the two domains—prompts us to search for possible intersections between organizational and family communication. Perhaps by bringing together organizational and family communication research, we can also promote more productive engagements between work and personal life in the world outside of the academy.

As a community of scholars, we collectively applaud integration and deplore fragmentation; however, we seldom explicitly acknowledge the professional pressures to self-identify with a subdiscipline and thus keep our research relatively narrowly focused. As we considered the body of research that constitutes the communication discipline's contribution to work-life inquiry thus far, we found ourselves reflecting on the ways in which our own research has evolved within and across subdisciplinary boundaries and the difficulty of categorizing some of it as either organizational or family. Although some of the research may seem more organizationally than family oriented or vice versa, it never completely focuses on one or the other because of the intersections of the workplace and personal-life networks in which all individuals have membership. Moreover, in the course of our reflections, an irony became apparent: we pursue work-life research (and we suspect that others do as well) because it has deep personal resonance for us as human beings and scholars, and yet, we may have felt constrained at some points by our own professional considerations in terms of how we framed our questions. While we acknowledge that intersubdisciplinary research does occur, we wonder how much of its relative infrequency can be ascribed to the perceived rigidity of division divides. If we identify ourselves as organizational communication scholars and attempt to integrate family frameworks of understanding, will we be credible to family communication researchers? If we win credibility with another group of subdisciplinary scholars, will our research accomplishments then be recognized in our home subdiscipline? Thus, as researchers, what we "bracket" for attention (as either Karl Weick or Gregory Bateson would say, depending on whether we have on our organizational or family hat) is influenced by professional concerns and identifications. Here we offer a few personal reflections in the interest of further illuminating this issue.

Thoughts from Erika: As an organizational communication graduate student in the late 1990s, I chose to dissertate on the role of workplace supports on work-life interrelationships; this choice came from a very personal place after I had a child as a graduate student (and another while ABD). I begrudgingly tackled the enormous interdisciplinary work-family literature in order to build an argument. (Today, this endeavor would not be necessary because communication scholars have now created reviews of this literature; see Kirby et al. (2003) and this article.) I remember that, in the library, I felt more comfortable in the "organizational" periodicals than in the mysterious "family" section. Even as an emerging work-life scholar, I viewed the literature predominately through the lens of my training in organizational communication, and upon (forced) reflection, I felt that I would be stepping out of my "training" to explicitly recognize the family dynamics—I had never had a class in family communication, so what did I know?

Even now, I am still not confident that I can do justice to the work in family communication; just last year, I asked a colleague in family communication to join me on an invited book chapter on work-life conflict to help me with "that side of things" (see Kirby, Wieland, & McBride, in press). In the context of this review, that request seems a little ridiculous, but it serves to prove our point: we can become so entrenched in subdisciplines that we feel we cannot speak to "outside" research, and we may not do work that makes sense if it is not "an area" within our subdiscipline. To conclude my reflection, two moments of truth have come rather recently to illustrate for me that work-life issues do indeed constitute subdisciplinary border crossing. First, a recent article that I co-authored with Caryn Medved on the appropriation of corporate titles and language by stay-at-home mothers truly served as an example to me of the fuzziness of the edges between work and family (see Medved & Kirby, 2005). Then, in a recent review, I was asked, "Why do you identify Kirby and Krone as organizational communication scholars? Can't their work also be considered family communication?" Hmmmm . . . maybe it can.

Thoughts from Jane: My interest in work-family relationships developed from the interplay of personal and professional experiences over many years. During graduate school, I worked as a research assistant at a child guidance clinic, where I was drawn to the study of the family as a meaning-making system. I later focused my dissertation research on the communicative processes by which families construct a definition of "family." I remember that, as a graduate student, I first began to get a sense of how certain academic cultures devalue caregiving when I attended a residential conference on cybernetics with my husband and two-month-old son. This conference took place in the mid-1980s, and the rules prohibited children from attending any sessions. To join in lunch and dinner discussions, we had to park the stroller on the patio outside the dining room and keep an eye on him through the window—the image reminds me of the work-family bifurcation that still subtly characterizes many work settings.

As the trailing spouse of an academic, I held adjunct positions for several years while conducting research on women in different occupational environments, including engineering and professional art, each with its own culture,

values, and orientations to the meaning of work and the work-family relationship. Because I was outside of a full-time tenure-track position, I think
that I may have been less burdened by a sense of the disciplinary "rules" and
agendas that establish what topics do or don't belong. Since then, opportunities to collaborate with Annis, Erika, and others on shared questions have
continued to nourish my interests in work-life issues.

Thoughts from Annis: Like both of my co-authors, my research interests
had their roots in personal-life events, starting with the birth of my son while
I was still thinking about a dissertation topic. My interests have evolved, along
with changes in my family and career, from identity and the transition to parenthood, to work and transition to parenthood, to work and family more generally, and ultimately to work and personal life more broadly defined. At the
same time, my primary frame of reference has shifted from individuals and
couples across organizations to more organization-based inquiry. The common threads, however, have been a consistent interest in how individuals manage the autonomy/interdependence dialectic—whether in the context of an
employee's relationship to an organization or in the context of individuals'
connections to relationship partners and families—and an interest in how discourse enables participants to produce identity as well as the organizing properties of communication, whether in the home or in the workplace.

Doing research positioned at the intersection of two subdisciplinary
domains has sometimes proved challenging for me from the standpoint of
professional identity. Interestingly, this project has afforded me the opportunity to notice how (paradoxically?) *at home* I now feel in the literature of *work*
as well as to reconnect with the family communication literature that bears
upon the work-life dialectic.

Collective Reflections

To slip back into our collective voice, we conclude by noting that work-life
research is fundamentally about intersections—about both/and experiences—
about the unity of identity that individuals experience as computer program-
mers, administrative assistants, teachers, nurses, spouses, parents, children of
aging parents, gardeners, pet owners, and rock climbers. Thus, an important
substantive challenge in doing this research involves doing justice to that
both/and quality, deciding where to start from and what to include, and reconciling ourselves to the fact that the picture we provide and our understanding of it are always incomplete.

We also struggle with another type of challenge—the challenge of locat-
ing one's research and oneself in this interstitial space—determining who,
within our community of scholars, our work speaks to. Clark's (2000) work on
border crossing between work and personal life instructed us that border

crossers' success in managing their moves across boundaries depends on the centrality of the border crossers themselves to the domains they move between. The literature referenced in this review, the steady accumulation of published research on work-life issues by communication scholars working from both family and organizational perspectives, and the recognition of our peers offer clear evidence of the growing centrality of this research. We hope that this review leads scholars to feel freer to pursue more integrative approaches in the future.

While recognizing the difficulties of overcoming traditional divisions, we remain committed to the integration of organizational and family communication perspectives on work-life research. In part, we sought to assist in the project of dereifying the public-private divide, while, at the same time, recognizing the utility of self-managed boundaries. Myriad possibilities now present themselves to many working women and men in terms of configuring the interrelationships between their work and personal lives. This diversity of possibilities places us at a crucial juncture for increasing researcher reflexivity on the potentials that new arrangements and understandings of those arrangements have for empowering working women and men. This situation also invites us to identify channels for contributing to increased reflexivity, or awareness, on the part of those women and men themselves in order to ensure that they recognize potential pitfalls, but above all, to promote the recognition that, with agency and the liberation from constraining traditional roles and arrangements, comes ambiguity and indeterminacy, and sometimes anxiety.

ACKNOWLEDGMENTS

The authors wish to thank Christina Beck and two anonymous reviewers for their insightful comments and suggestions on drafts of this chapter.

NOTES

1. Throughout the rest of this essay, we use the terminology "work-life" rather than "work-family" or "work and family." Although we address and identify ways of bridging subdisciplinary division divides between organizational and family communication, we prefer the inclusiveness of "work-life." While we acknowledge that much of private life is concerned with family, it is not always family in the sense in which family is being defined in everyday (and in a good deal of scholarly) discourse on work-life issues. In keeping with family communication scholars' more inclusive definitions of "family" (e.g., Whitchurch & Dickson, 1999), we do not wish to privilege forms of personal life involvements that do not fit traditional definitions of family. At the same time, we feel that work-life is not an entirely satisfactory descriptor, since it may imply that "work" is not "life," a view that we do not support.

2. In 1986, *The Southern Speech Communication Journal* featured a special report titled "Careers and Relationships: The Interpersonal Intricacies of Maintaining a Dual-Career Relationship" that included an introductory overview by Christopher Spicer and three papers by Heacock and Spicer, Wood, and Krueger. This collection differed from the theme issue of *The Electronic Journal of Communication/La Revue Electronique de Communication* that appeared in 2000, in that it was a special report within an issue, and that it was focused on interpersonal communication issues in couples who were linked to their dual-career status, whereas the theme issue of EJC addressed a broader range of communication issues related to managing work and personal life interrelationships from both organizational and family perspectives (see below).

3. Four of the six articles appearing in this issue of *The Electronic Journal of Communication/La Revue Electronique de Communication* (Vol. 10, nos. 3 and 4) took the workplace as their primary frame of reference (see Farley-Lucas, 2000; Jorgenson, 2000; Kirby, 2000; Mallia & Ferris, 2000), whereas two took the home and/or family as their primary frame (see Avery & Baker, 2000; Golden, 2000b).

REFERENCES

Alvesson, M., & Billing, Y. D. (1997). *Understanding gender and organizations.* London: Sage.

Anderson, H., Goolishian, H., & Winderman, L. (1986). Problem determined systems: Towards transformation in family therapy. *Journal of Strategic and Systemic Therapies, 5,* 1–14.

Aoki, E. (2000). Mexican American ethnicity in Biola, CA: An ethnographic account of hard work, family, and religion. *Howard Journal of Communications, 11,* 207–227.

Ashcraft, K. L. (1999). Managing maternity leave: A qualitative analysis of temporary executive succession. *Administrative Science Quarterly, 44,* 240–280.

Ashcraft, K., & Trethewey, A. (2004). Special issue introduction. *Journal of Applied Communication Research, 32,* 81–89.

Auslander, M. (2002). Rituals of the family. A Sloan Work and Family Encyclopedia entry. Retrieved February 14, 2003 from http://www.bc.edu/bc_org/avp/wfnetwork/rft/wfpedia/wfpROFent.html

Avery, G. C., & Baker, E. (2000). Understanding technology use within Australian households. *Electronic Journal of Communication/La Revue Electronique de Communication, 10*(3). Retrieved March 13, 2005 from http://www.cios.org/www/ejcrec2.htm

Bailyn, L. (1992). Issues of work and family in different national contexts: How the United States, Britain, and Sweden respond. *Human Resource Management, 31,* 201–208.

Bailyn, L. (1993). *Breaking the mold: Women, men, and time in the new corporate world.* New York: Free Press.

Ballard, D. I., & Seibold, D. R. (2003). Communicating and organizing in time: A meso-level model of organizational temporality. *Management Communication Quarterly, 16,* 280–415.

Ballard, D. I., & Seibold, D. R. (2004). Organizational members' communication and temporal experience: Scale development and validation. *Communication Research, 31*, 135–172.

Banks, S. P., & Riley, P. (1993). Structuration theory as an ontology for communication research. In S. A. Deetz (Ed.), *Communication yearbook 16* (pp. 167–196). Newbury Park, CA: Sage.

Bateson, M. C. (1991). *Our own metaphor*. Washington, DC: Smithsonian Institution Press.

Bavelas, J., & Segal, L. (1982). Family systems theory: Background and implications. *Journal of Communication, 32*, 99–107.

Baxter, L. A. (1988). A dialectic perspective on communication strategies in relationship development. In S. W. Duck (Ed.), *Handbook of personal relationships: Theory, research, and interventions* (pp. 257–273). Chicester, England: Wiley.

Baxter, L. A., & Montgomery, B. M. (1997). Rethinking communication in personal relationships from a dialectic perspective. In S. Duck (Ed.), *Handbook of personal relationships* (pp. 325–349). New York: John Wiley.

Baxter, L. A., & Montgomery, B. M. (1998). A guide to dialectical approaches to studying personal relationships. In B. M. Montgomery and L. A. Baxter (Eds.), *Dialectical approaches to studying personal relationships* (pp. 1–16). Mahwah, NJ: Lawrence Erlbaum Associates.

Belkin, L. (2003, October 26). The opt-out revolution. *New York Times*, p. 42.

Bernstein, P. (1997). *American work values: Their origin and development*. Albany: State University of New York Press.

Bertalanffy, L. von. (1968). *General systems theory*. New York: George Braziller.

Bird, E., & Jorgenson, J. (2002). Extending the school day: Gender, class and the incorporation of technology in the home. In M. Consalvo & S. Paasonen (Eds.), *Women and everyday uses of the internet* (pp. 255–274). New York: Peter Lang.

Braithwaite, D. O., Baxter, L. A., & Harper, A. M. (1998). The role of rituals in the management of the dialectical tension of "old" and "new" in blended families. *Communication Studies, 49*, 101–120.

Brannen, J. (2005). Time and the negotiation of work-family boundaries: Autonomy or illusion? *Time & Society, 14*, 113–131.

Bridge, K., & Baxter, L. A. (1992). Blended relationships: Friends as work associates. *Western Journal of Communication, 56*, 200–225.

Browning, L. D., & Beyer, J. M. (1998). The structuring of shared voluntary standards in the U.S. semiconductor industry: Communicating to reach agreement. *Communication Monographs, 65*, 220–243.

Buzzanell, P. M. (1997). Toward an emotion-based feminist framework for research on dual career couples. *Women and Language, 20*, 40–48.

Buzzanell, P. M. (2000). The promise and practice of the new career and social contract: Illusions exposed and suggestions for reform. In P. M. Buzzanell (Ed.), *Rethinking organizational and managerial communication from feminist perspectives* (pp. 209–235). Thousand Oaks, CA: Sage.

Buzzanell, P. M. (2003). A feminist standpoint analysis of maternity and maternity leave for women with disabilities. *Women and Language, 26*, 53–65.

Buzzanell, P. M., & Ellingson, L. (2005). Contesting narratives of workplace maternity. In L. M. Harter, P. Japp, & C. S. Beck (Eds.), *Constructing our health: The implications of narrative for enacting illness and wellness* (pp. 277–294). Mahwah, NJ: Lawrence Erlbaum Associates.

Buzzanell. P. M., & Liu, M. (2005). Struggling with maternity leave policies and practices: A poststructuralist feminist analysis of gendered organizing. *Journal of Applied Communication Research, 33*, 1–25.

Buzzanell, P. M., Meisenbach, R., Remke, R., Bowers, V., Liu, M., & Conn, C. (2005). The good working mother: Managerial women's sensemaking and feelings about work-family issues. *Communication Studies, 56*, 261–285.

Buzzanell, P. M., & Turner, L. (2003). Emotion work revealed by job loss discourse: Backgrounding-foregrounding of feelings, construction of normalcy, and (re)instituting of traditional masculinities. *Journal of Applied Communication Research, 31*, 27–57.

Cahill, D. J., & Sias, P. M. (1997). The perceived social costs and importance of seeking emotional support in the workplace: Gender differences and similarities. *Communication Research Reports, 14*, 231–241.

Cheney, G. (1983). On the various and changing meanings of organizational membership: A field study of organizational identification. *Communication Monographs, 50*, 342–362.

Cheney, G., & Tompkins, P. K. (1987). Coming to terms with organizational identification and commitment. *Central States Speech Journal, 38*, 1–15.

Cissna, K. N., Cox, D. E., & Bochner, A. P. (1990). The dialectic of marital and parental relationships within the stepfamily. *Communication Monographs, 57*, 44–61.

Clark, S. C. (2000). Work/family border theory: A new theory of work/family balance. *Human Relations, 53*, 747–770.

Clark, S. C. (2002). Communicating across the work/home border. *Community, Work & Family, 5*, 23–48.

Daly, K. J. (2001). Deconstructing family time: From ideology to lived experience. *Journal of Marriage and the Family, 63*, 283–294.

Davis, P., & Stern, D. (1980). Adaptation, growth and survival of the family business: An integrated systems perspective. *Human Relations*, 207–224.

Deetz, S. A. (1992). *Democracy in an age of corporate colonization: Developments in communication and the politics of everyday life.* Albany: State University of New York Press.

DeSanctis, G., & Poole, M. S. (1994). Capturing the complexity in advanced technology use: Adaptive structuration theory. *Organization Science, 5*, 121–147.

Dinnerstein, D. (1976). *The mermaid and the minotaur.* New York: HarperCollins.

Doucet, A. (2004). "It's almost like I have a job, but I don't get paid": Fathers at home reconfiguring work, care, and masculinity. *Fathering, 2*, 277–303.

Douglas, S., & Michaels, M. W. (2004). *The mommy myth: The idealization of motherhood and how it has undermined women.* New York: Free Press.

Edley, P. P. (2001). Technology, employed mothers, and corporate colonization of the lifeworld: A gendered paradox of work and family balance. *Women and Language, 24*, 28–35.

Edley, P. P. (2004). Entrepreneurial mothers' balance of work and family: Discursive constructions of time, mothering, and identity. In P. M. Buzzanell, H. Sterk, & L. H. Turner (Eds.), *Gender in applied communication contexts* (pp. 255–274). Thousand Oaks, CA: Sage.

Edley, P. P., Hylmö, A., & Newsom, V. A. (2004). Alternative organizing communities: Collectivist organizing, telework, home-based Internet businesses, and online communities. In P. J. Kalbfleisch (Ed.), *Communication yearbook 28* (pp. 87–126). Thousand Oaks, CA: Sage.

Edley, P. P., & Kirby, E. L. (2003, October). *What constitutes a working mother? A Third Wave discursive analysis.* Paper presented at the meeting of the Organization for the Study of Communication, Language, and Gender, Cincinnati, OH.

Egbert, N., Mickley, J., & Coeling, H. (2004). A review and application of social scientific measures of religiosity and spirituality: Assessing a missing component in health communication research. *Health Communication, 16*, 7–27.

Ellison, N. B. (2005). *Telework and social change: How technology is reshaping the boundaries between home and work.* Westport, CT: Praeger.

English-Lueck, J. A. (2002). *Cultures@SiliconValley.* Stanford, CA: Stanford University Press.

Etzion, D. & Bailyn, L. (1994). Patterns of adjustment to the career/family conflict of technically trained women in the United States and Israel. *Journal of Applied Social Psychology, 24*, 1520–1549.

Farley-Lucas, B. (2000). Communicating the (in)visibility of motherhood: Family talk and the ties to motherhood with/in the workplace. *The Electronic Journal of Communication/La Revue Electronique de Communication, 10*(3). Retrieved March 13, 2005 from http://www.cios.org/www/ejcrec2.htm.

Ferree, M. M. (1990). Beyond separate spheres: Feminism and family research. *Journal of Marriage and the Family, 52*, 866–884.

Fitness, J., & Duffield, J. (2004). Emotion and communication in families. In A. Vangelisti (Ed.), *Handbook of family communication* (pp. 473–494). Mahwah, NJ: Lawrence Erlbaum Associates.

Galinsky, E. (1999). *Ask the children: What America's children really think about working parents.* New York: Morrow.

Galvin, K., & Brommel, B. (1996). *Family communication: Cohesion and change* (4th ed.). New York: HarperCollins.

Galvin, K., Bylund, C., & Brommel, B. (2004). *Family communication: Cohesion and change* (6th ed.). Boston: Pearson.

Gibson, M. K., & Schullery, N. M. (2000). Shifting meanings in a blue-collar worker philanthropy program. *Management Communication Quarterly, 14*, 189–236.

Giddens, A. (1979). *Central problems in social theory: Action, structure and contradiction in social analysis.* Berkeley: University of California Press.

Giddens, A. (1984). *The constitution of society: An outline of the theory of structuration.* Cambridge, MA: Polity.

Gilbert, L. A. (1993). *Two careers/one family.* Newbury Park, CA: Sage.

Golden, A. G. (Ed.). (2000a). Communication perspectives on work and family [Special issue]. *Electronic Journal of Communication/La Revue Electronique de Communication, 10*(3–4).

Golden, A. G. (2000b). What we talk about when we talk about work and family: A discourse analysis of parental accounts. *Electronic Journal of Communication/La Revue Electronique de Communication, 10*(3–4). Retrieved March 13, 2005 from http://www.cios.org/www/ejc/v10n3400.htm.

Golden, A. G. (2001). Modernity and the communicative management of multiple role-identities: The case of the worker-parent. *The Journal of Family Communication, 1*, 233–264.

Golden, A. G. (2002). Speaking of work and family: Spousal collaboration on defining role-identities and developing shared meanings. *Southern Communication Journal, 67*, 122–141.

Golden, A. G., & Geisler, C. (2005). *Work-life boundary management and the personal digital assistant: Practical activities and interpretative repertoires.* Manuscript submitted for publication.

Harter, L. M., Kirby, E. L., McClanahan, A., & Edwards, A. (2003, October). *A third wave discursive analysis of age-related infertility: Historical connections and contemporary contradictions surrounding choices about work and family.* Paper presented at the meeting of the Organization for the Study of Communication, Language, and Gender, Cincinnati, OH.

Harter, L. M., Kirby, E. L., McClanahan, A., & Edwards, A. (2005). Time, technology and meritocracy: Narratively constructing age-related infertility. In L. M. Harter, P. M. Japp, & C. S. Beck, (Eds.), *Narratives of health and healing* (pp. 83–106). Mahwah, NJ: Lawrence Erlbaum Associates.

Hattery, A. J. (2000). *Women, work, and family: Balancing and weaving.* Thousand Oaks, CA: Sage.

Hays, S. (1996). *The cultural contradictions of motherhood.* New Haven: Yale University Press.

Heacock, D., & Spicer, C.H. (1986). Communication and the dual career: A literature assessment. *Southern Speech Communication Journal, 51*, 260–266.

Hendricks, M., & Kirby, E. L. (2003, November). *Viewing One Fine Day as a reflection of gendered work-family expectations.* Paper presented at the meeting of the National Communication Association, Miami Beach, FL.

Hochschild, A. R. (1997). *The time bind: When work becomes home and home becomes work.* New York: Metropolitan.

Hochschild, A. R. (2003). *The commercialization of intimate life.* Berkeley: University of California Press.

Hoffman, L. (1981). *Foundations of family therapy.* New York: Basic.

Hylmö, A. (2004a, November). *Negotiating time and balancing life: Discursive constructions among Swedish academics viewed through a generational lens.* Paper presented at the meeting of the National Communication Association, Chicago.

Hylmö, A. (2004b). Women, men, and changing organizations: An organizational culture examination of gendered experiences of telecommuting. In P. M. Buzzanell, H. Sterk, & L. H. Turner (Eds.), *Gender in applied communication contexts* (pp. 47–68). Thousand Oaks, CA: Sage.

Hylmö, A., & Buzzanell, P. M. (2002). The phenomenon of telecommuting and changing organizations: An organizational culture examination. *Communication Monographs, 69*, 329–356.

Japp, P. M. (2004, November). *A cultural studies response to the "opt-out revolution."* Paper presented at the meeting of the National Communication Association, Chicago.

Jorgenson, J. (1995). Marking the work-family boundary: Mother-child interaction and home-based work. In T. Socha and G. Stamp (Eds.), *Parents, children and communication: frontiers of theory and research* (pp. 203–216). Hillsdale, NJ: Lawrence Erlbaum Associates.

Jorgenson, J. (2000). Interpreting the intersections of work and family: Frame conflicts in women's work. *The Electronic Journal of Communication/La Revue Electronique de Communication, 10*(3). Retrieved March 13, 2005 from http://www.cios.org/www/ejcrec2.htm.

Jorgenson, J. (2002). Engineering selves: Negotiating gender and identity in technical work. *Management Communication Quarterly, 15*, 350–381.

Jorgenson, J., & Bochner, A. (2004). Imagining families through stories and rituals. In A. Vangelisti (Ed.), *Handbook of family communication* (pp. 513–538). Mahwah, NJ: Lawrence Erlbaum Associates.

Kanter, R. M. (1977). *Work and family in the United States: A critical review and agenda for research and policy.* New York: Russell Sage Foundation.

Kantor, D., & Lehr, W. (1975). *Inside the family: Toward a theory of family process.* San Francisco: Jossey-Bass.

Keeney, B., & Sprenkle, D. (1982). Ecosystemic epistemology: Critical implications for the aesthetics and pragmatics of family therapy. *Family Process, 21*, 1, 1–20.

Kirby, E. L. (2000). Should I do as you say, or do as you do? Mixed messages about work and family. *Electronic Journal of Communication/La Revue Electronique de Communication, 10*(3). Retrieved March 13, 2005 from http://www.cios.org/www/ejcrec2.htm.

Kirby, E. L. (2001, May). *Blurring personal and professional boundaries: Perceptions of men and women regarding talking about family and personal life at work.* Paper presented at the annual meeting of the International Communication Association, Washington, DC.

Kirby, E. L. (2003). Bob's dilemma. In J. Keyton & P. Shockley-Zalabak (Eds.), *Organizational communication: Understanding communication processes* (pp. 287–294). Los Angeles, CA: Roxbury.

Kirby, E. L. (2006). Your attitude determines your altitude: Reflections on a company-sponsored mountain climb. In J. Keyton & P. Shockley-Zalabak (Eds.), *Organizational communication: Understanding communication processes* (2nd ed., pp. 99–108). Los Angeles, CA: Roxbury.

Kirby, E. L. (Ed.). (in press). Communication and the accomplishment of personal and professional life [Special issue]. *Electronic Journal of Communication/La Revue Electronique de Communication.*

Kirby, E. L., Golden, A. G., Medved, C. E., Jorgenson, J., & Buzzanell, P. M. (2003). An organizational communication challenge to the discourse of work and family research: From problematics to empowerment. In P. J. Kalbfleisch (Ed.), *Communication yearbook 27* (pp. 1–43). Thousand Oaks, CA: Sage.

Kirby, E. L., & Krone, K. J. (2002). "The policy exists but you can't really use it": Communication and the structuration of work-family policies. *Journal of Applied Communication Research, 30*, 50–77.

Kirby, E. L., Wieland, S. M., & McBride, M. C. (2006). Work/life conflict. In J. Oetzel and S. Ting-Toomey (Eds.), *Handbook of conflict communication* (pp. 327–357). Thousand Oaks, CA: Sage.

Krone, K. J., Schrodt, P., & Kirby, E. L. (2006). Structuration theory: Promising directions for family communication research. In D. O. Braithwaite & L. Baxter (Eds.), *Family communication theories* (pp. 293–308). Thousand Oaks, CA: Sage.

Krueger, D. L. (1986). Communication strategies and patterns in dual-career couples. *Southern Speech Communication Journal, 51*, 274–281.

Kuhn, T., & Nelson, N. (2002). Re-engineering identity: A case study of multiplicity and duality in organizational identification. *Management Communication Quarterly, 16*, 5–38.

Leslie, L.A., & Glossick, M.L. (1992). Changing set: Teaching family therapy from a feminist perspective. *Family Relations, 41*, 256–263.

Lindlof, T. R. (1995). *Qualitative communication research methods.* Thousand Oaks, CA: Sage.

Liu, M. (2004, November). *Deconstructing the concept of work-family balance for Chinese women: Looking back and moving forward.* Paper presented at the meeting of the National Communication Association, Chicago.

Liu, M., & Buzzanell, P. M. (2004). Negotiating maternity leave expectations: Perceived tensions between ethics of justice and care. *Journal of Business Communication, 41*, 323–349.

Liu, M., & Buzzanell, P. M. (2006). When workplace pregnancy highlights difference: Openings for detrimental gender and supervisory relations. In J. H. Fritz & B. L. Omdahl (Eds.), *Problematic relationships in the workplace* (pp. 47–68). New York: Peter Lang.

Lucas, K., & Buzzanell, P. M. (2006). Employees "without families": Discourses of family as an external constraint to work-life balance. In L. H. Turner & R. West (Eds.), *The family communication sourcebook* (pp. 335–352). Thousand Oaks, CA: Sage.

Mallia, K. L., & Ferris, P. S. (2000). Telework: A consideration of its impact on individuals and organizations. *Electronic Journal of Communication/La Revue Electronique de Communication, 10*(3). Retrieved March 13, 2005 from http://www.cios.org/www/ejcrec2.htm.

Marks, S. R., & MacDermid, S. M. (1996). Multiple roles and the self: A theory of role balance. *Journal of Marriage and the Family, 58*, 417–432.

Martin, J. (1990). Deconstructing organizational taboos: The suppression of gender conflict in organizations. *Organization Science, 4*, 339–360.

Mattson, M., Clair, R. C., Chapman Sanger, P. A., & Kunkel, A. D. (2000). A feminist reframing of stress: Rose's story. In P. M. Buzzanell (Ed.), *Rethinking organizational and managerial communication from feminist perspectives* (pp. 157–176). Thousand Oaks, CA: Sage.

May, S. (2004). A question of boundaries. In G. Cheney, L. T. Christensen, T. E. Zorn, & S. Ganesh (Eds.), *Organizational communication in an age of globalization: Issues, reflection, practices* (p. 410). Prospect Heights, IL: Waveland.

Medved, C. E. (2004). The everyday accomplishment of work and family: Exploring practical actions in daily routines. *Communication Studies, 55*, 128–145.

Medved, C. E., & Heisler, J. (2002). Critical student-faculty interactions: Non-traditional students manage multiple roles. *Communication Education, 51*, 105–120.

Medved, C. E., & Kirby, E. L. (2005). Family CEOs: A feminist analysis of corporate mothering discourses. *Management Communication Quarterly, 18*, 435–478.

Miller, E., & Rice, A.K. (1990). Task and sentient systems and their boundary controls. In E. Trist & H. Murray (Eds.), *The social engagement of social science: A Tavistock anthology, Vol. 1. The socio-psychological perspective* (pp. 259–271). Philadelphia: University of Pennsylvania Press (original work published 1967).

Miller, K. (2006). *Organizational communication: Processes and approaches.* Belmont, CA: Thomson/Wadsworth.

Miller, K. I., Birkholt, M., Scott, C., & Stage, C. (1995). Empathy and burnout in human service work: An extension of the communication model. *Communication Research, 22*, 123–147.

Miller, V. D., Jablin, F. M., Casey, M. K., Lamphear-Van Horn, M., & Ethington, C. (1996). The maternity leave as a role negotiation process. *Journal of Managerial Issues, 8*, 286–309.

Mirchandani, K. (1998). Protecting the boundaries: Teleworker insights on the expansive concept of "work." *Gender & Society, 12*, 168–187.

Morgan, G. (1986). *Images of organization.* Beverly Hills, CA: Sage.

Morgan, J. M., & Krone, K. J. (2001). Bending the rules of "professional" display: Emotional improvisation in caregiver performances. *Journal of Applied Communication Research, 29*, 317–340.

Mumby, D. K. (1987). The political function of narrative in organizations. *Communication Monographs, 54*, 113–127.

Mumby, D. K., & Putnam, L. (1992). The politics of emotion: A feminist reading of bounded rationality. *Academy of Management Review, 17*, 465–486.

Mumby, D. K., & Stohl, C. (1996). Disciplining organizational communication studies. *Management Communication Quarterly, 10*, 50–72.

Murphy, A. G. (1998). Hidden transcripts of flight attendant resistance. *Management Communication Quarterly, 11*, 499–535.

Nippert-Eng, C. E. (1996). *Home and work.* Chicago: University of Chicago Press.

Noller, P., Feeney, J., Peterson, C., & Sheehan, G. (1995). Learning conflict patterns in the family: Links between marital, parental and sibling relationships. In T. Socha and G. Stamp (Eds.), *Parents, children and communication: Frontiers of theory and research* (pp. 273–298). Hillsdale, NJ: Lawrence Erlbaum Associates.

Noller, P., & Fitzpatrick, M. A. (1993). *Communication in family relationships.* Englewood Cliffs, NJ: Prentice Hall.

Olson, D. H., Sprenkle, D., & Russell, C. (1979). Circumplex model of marital and family systems I: Cohesion and adaptability dimension, family types, and clinical applications. *Family Process, 18*, 3–28.

Parrott, R. (2004). "Collective amnesia:" The absence of religious faith and spirituality in health communication research and practice. *Health Communication, 16*, 1–5.

Patterson, L. (2004, November). *You just do it: African American women managing work and family.* Paper presented at the meeting of the National Communication Association, Chicago.

Paugh, A. L. (2005). Learning about work at dinnertime: Language socialization in dual-earner American families. *Discourse & Society, 16,* 55–78.

Perlow, L. A. (1995). Putting the work back into work/family. *Group and Organization Management, 20,* 227–239.

Perlow, L. A. (1998). Boundary control: The social ordering of work and family time in a high-tech corporation. *Administrative Science Quarterly, 43,* 328–357.

Perlow, L. A. (1999). The time famine: Toward a sociology of work time. *Administrative Science Quarterly, 44,* 57–81.

Perry-Jenkins, M., Pierce, C., & Goldberg, A. (2004). Discourses on diapers and dirty laundry: Family communication about childcare and housework. In A. Vangelisti (Ed.), *Handbook of family communication* (pp. 541–562). Mahwah, NJ: Lawrence Erlbaum Associates.

Perry-Jenkins, M., Repetti, R. L., & Crouter, A. C. (2000). Work and family in the 1990s. *Journal of Marriage and the Family, 62,* 981–998.

Petroski, D. J., & Edley, P. P. (2004, November). *Stay-at-home fathers: Masculinity, family, work, and gender stereotypes.* Paper presented at the meeting of the National Communication Association, Chicago.

Philipson, I. (2002a). *Married to the job: Why we live to work and what we can do about it.* New York: Free Press.

Philipson, I. (2002b). *Bringing the second shift to work.* The Working Paper Series: Center for Working Families, University of California, Berkeley. Working paper No. 50. Retrieved June 16, 2005, from University of California, Berkeley Web site: http://www.bc.edu/bc_org/avp/wfnetwork/berkeley/workingpapers.html

Poole, M. S., Seibold, D. R., & McPhee, R. D. (1996). The structuration of group decisions. In R. Y. Hirokawa & M. S. Poole (Eds.), *Communication and group decision-making* (2nd ed., pp. 114–146). Newbury Park, CA: Sage.

Prusank, D. (1995). Studying parent-child discipline from a communication perspective. In T. Socha and G. Stamp (Eds.), *Parents, children and communication: Frontiers of theory and research* (pp. 249–272). Hillsdale, NJ: Lawrence Erlbaum Associates.

Ray, E. B., & Miller, K. I. (1994). Social support, home/work stress, and burnout: who can help? *Journal of Applied Behavioral Science, 30,* 357–373.

Ritchie, L. D. (1997). Parents' workplace experiences and family communication patterns. *Communication Research, 24,* 175–187.

Rodriguez, A. (Ed.). (2001). *Essays on communication and spirituality: Contributions to a new discourse on communication.* New York: University Press of America.

Rosaldo, M. (1974). Women, culture, and society: A theoretical overview. In M. Rosaldo & L. Lamphere (Eds.), *Women, culture, and society* (pp. 17–42). Palo Alto, CA: Stanford University Press.

Rosenblatt, P. (1994). *Metaphors of family systems theory: Toward new constructions.* New York: Guilford.

Rosenfeld, L. B., Bowen, G. L., & Richman, J. M. (1995). Communication in three types of dual-career marriages. In M. A. Fitzpatrick & A. L. Vangelisti (Eds.), *Explaining family interactions* (pp. 257–289). Thousand Oaks, CA: Sage.

Rosenfeld, L. B., & Welsh, S. M. (1985). Differences in self-disclosure in dual career and single-career marriages. *Communication Monographs, 52*, 253–263.

Roy, K. M. (2004). You can't eat love: Constructing provider role expectations for low-income and working-class fathers. *Fathering, 2*, 253–276.

Runté, M., & Mills, A. J. (2004). Paying the toll: A feminist post-structural critique of the discourse bridging work and family. *Culture & Organization, 10*, 237–249.

Russo, T. C. (1998). Organizational and professional identification. *Management Communication Quarterly, 12*, 72–112.

Schlessinger, L. (2001). *Stupid things parents do to mess up their kids: Don't have them if you won't raise them.* New York: Quill.

Schrodt, P., Baxter, L. A., McBride, M. C., Braithwaite, D. O., & Fine, M. A. (2004, November). *The divorce decree, communication, and the structuration of co-parenting relationships in stepfamilies.* Presented at the meeting of the National Communication Association, Chicago.

Scott, C. R., Corman, S. R., & Cheney, G. (1998). Development of a structurational model of identification in the organization. *Communication Theory, 8*, 298–336.

Seyfarth, B. (2000). Structuration theory in small group communication: A review and agenda for future research. In M. E. Roloff (Ed.), *Communication yearbook 23* (pp. 341–379). Thousand Oaks, CA: Sage.

Shuler, S. (2003). Breaking the glass ceiling without breaking a nail: Women executives in Fortune magazine's "Power 50" list. *American Communication Journal, 6*(2). Retrieved March 21, 2004 from http://www.acjournal.org/holdings/vol6/iss2/

Shuler, S., & Sypher, B. D. (2000). Seeking emotional labor: When managing the heart enhances the work experience. *Management Communication Quarterly, 14*, 50–89.

Shumate, M., & Fulk, J. (2004). Boundaries and role conflict when work and family are colocated: A communication network and symbolic interaction approach. *Human Relations, 57*, 55–74.

Sias, P. M., & Cahill, D. J. (1998). From co-workers to friends: The development of peer friendships in the workplace. *Western Journal of Communication, 62*, 273–299.

Simpson, J. L., & Kirby, E. L. (2004, November). *A white privileged communication response to the "opt-out revolution."* Paper presented to the meeting of the National Communication Association, Chicago.

Spicer, C. H. (1986). Special report: Careers and relationships: The interpersonal intricacies of maintaining a dual-career relationship. *Southern Speech Communication Journal, 51*, 256–259.

Stage, C. (1999). Negotiating organizational communication cultures in American subsidiaries doing business in Thailand. *Management Communication Quarterly, 13*, 245–280.

Stamp, G. H. (1994). The appropriation of the parental role through communication during the transition to parenthood. *Communication Monographs, 61*, 89–112.

Stamp, G. H., & Banski, M. A. (1992). The communicative management of constrained autonomy during the transition to parenthood. *Western Journal of Communication, 56*, 281–300.

Stohl, C. (2001). Globalizing organizational communication. In F. M. Jablin and L. L. Putnam (Eds.), *The new handbook of organizational communication: Advances in theory, research, and methods* (pp. 323–378). Thousand Oaks, CA: Sage.

Thomas, D., & Ely, R. (1996). Making differences matter: A new paradigm for managing diversity. *Harvard Business Review, 7*(5), 79–91.

Tracy, S. J. (2004). Dialectic, contradiction, or double bind? Analyzing and theorizing employee reactions to organizational tension. *Journal of Applied Communication Research, 32,* 119–146.

Tracy, S. J., & Tracy, K. (1998). Emotion labor at 911: A case study and theoretical critique. *Journal of Applied Communication Research, 26,* 390–411.

Trethewey, A. (1997). Resistance, identity, and empowerment: A postmodern feminist analysis of clients in a human service organization. *Communication Monographs, 64,* 281–301.

Trethewey, A., & Ashcraft, K. (2004). Special issue synthesis. *Journal of Applied Communication Research, 32,* 171–182.

Vavrus, M. D. (2002). Domesticating patriarchy: Hegemonic masculinity and television's "Mr. Mom." *Critical Studies in Media Communication, 19,* 352–375.

Watzlawick, P., Bavelas, J. B., & Jackson, D. (1967). *Pragmatics of human communication.* New York: Norton.

Weick, K. (1979). *The social psychology of organizing.* New York: Random House.

Weick, K. (1995). *Sensemaking in organizations.* Thousand Oaks, CA: Sage.

Weigel, D., & Ballard-Reisch, D. S. (1997). Merging family and firm: An integrated systems approach to process and change. *Journal of Family and Economic Issues, 18*(1), 7–31.

Whitchurch, G., & Constantine, L. (1993). Systems theory. In P. Boss, W. Doherty, R. LaRossa, W. Schumm, & S. Steinmetz (Eds.), *Sourcebook of family theories and methods: A contextual approach* (pp. 325–352). New York: Plenum.

Whitchurch, G., & Dickson, F. C. (1999). Family communication. In M. B. Sussman, S. K. Steinmetz, & G. W. Peterson (Eds.), *Handbook of marriage and the family* (2nd ed., pp. 687–704). New York: Plenum.

Wilson, S. R., & Morgan, W. M. (2004). Persuasion and families. In A. Vangelisti (Ed.), *Handbook of family communication* (pp. 447–471). Mahwah, NJ: Lawrence Erlbaum Associates.

Witmer, D. F. (1997). Communication and recovery: Structuration as an ontological approach to organizational culture. *Communication Monographs, 64,* 324–349.

Wood, J. T. (1986). Maintaining dual-career bonds: Communicative dimensions of internally structured relationships. *Southern Speech Communication Journal, 51,* 267–273.

Yerby, J., Buerkel-Rothfuss, N., & Bochner, A. (1995). *Understanding family communication.* (2nd ed.). Scottsdale, AZ: Allyn & Bacon.

Yerby, J., & Stephen, T. (1986, November). *The development and application of an instrument to measure the family's communication environment.* Paper presented at the meeting of the Speech Communication Association, Chicago.

Young, C. (2004, November). *Work-life balance: Looking back at heteronormative assumption, moving forward to inclusivity.* Paper presented at the meeting of the National Communication Association, Chicago.

Zaidman, N. (2001). Cultural codes and language strategies in business communication: Interactions between Israeli and Indian businesspeople. *Management Communication Quarterly, 14*, 208–441.

Zoller, H. M. (2003). Working out: Managerialism in workplace health promotion. *Management Communication Quarterly, 17*, 171–205.

Zoller, H. M. (2004). Manufacturing health: Employee perspectives on problematic outcomes in a workplace health promotion initiative. *Western Journal of Communication, 68*, 278–301.

CHAPTER CONTENTS

5 Collaborative Interaction: Review of Communication Scholarship and a Research Agenda

LAURIE K. LEWIS
University of Texas at Austin

It appears that collaborative interaction is nearly everywhere, including our dyadic relationships, our schools, our doctors' offices, our workplaces, and our local and international communities. Furthermore, mounting evidence points to the conclusion that collaborative interaction has great promise as a tool across contexts. Unfortunately, despite the growing use and recognition of effective collaboration, very little synthesis exists across various domains of literature about how collaborative interaction works and its critical components. This chapter serves as a means to examine these disparate sets of literature, with an eye toward creating synthesis across the various domains. This chapter reviews 80 sources published within the last decade that concern collaboration in various contexts, including developmental/learning, interpersonal relationships, conflict, group problem solving and decision making, health (spanning the micro-macro range from doctor-patient communication, health-care teams, and community health alliances), community groups, and interprofessional and interorganizational settings. Themes found across the literature, as well as definitional issues related to key constructs, are developed and discussed. Finally, a descriptive and heuristic model of collaborative interaction is presented that encompasses the key features and issues raised in the review. Research and theory-building agendas are also offered to stimulate more investigations of this phenomenon.

- An older married couple works together to recall a moment in their shared history. One spouse fills in facts and details that the other cannot remember until they've recreated the memory collaboratively.
- A group of children collaborate to create a map of their local town. Each child adds some creative idea, helps implement the ideas of the other children, and discusses the merits of contributions. In the end, they create something completely new.

Correspondence: Laurie K. Lewis, Department of Communication Studies, University of Texas at Austin, 1 University Station A1105, Austin, TX 78712-0115; email: lklewis@mail.utexas.edu

Communication Yearbook 30, pp. 197–247

- A doctor and her patient collaboratively decide on the best treatment for the patient's cancer. The doctor provides expertise, and the patient offers knowledge of her body, her life style, and her goals.
- Two friends in conflict talk with each other to maximize a "win-win" strategy, making sure that both of them will get what they want, and they resolve their conflict.
- A group of co-workers gathers together in a meeting room once a week to share what they've learned about a new technology. They take turns in conversation about what is most exciting and perplexing about this new technology. They commiserate, laugh, solve problems, and learn together.
- A set of local charities, health and human service providers, and county agencies meet to coordinate case management and work together to provide emergency shelter and relief services for survivors of Hurricane Katrina.

Each of these examples claims some legitimate ground as a type of "collaborative interaction." All have been empirically investigated in the literature exploring communication and collaboration. It appears that collaborative interaction is nearly everywhere, including our dyadic relationships, our schools, our doctors' offices, our workplaces, and our local and international communities (for a related review, see Heath & Frey, 2004). The contexts in which individuals enact collaborative approaches are limitless; the expansive research examining those uses includes health care (DiMatteo, Reiter, & Gambone, 1994; Ellingson & Buzzanell, 1999; Medved et al., 2001; Young & Flower, 2001), small groups (Barron, 2000; Iverson & McPhee, 2002; Kuhn & Poole, 2000), scientific research (Levine & Moreland, 2004), community and interorganizational alliances (Keyton & Stallworth, 2003; Zoller, 2004), negotiation (Taylor & Donald, 2004), and conflict resolution (Canary, Cupach, & Serpe, 2001; Lakey & Canary, 2002; Weider-Hatfield & Hatfield, 1996). Other contexts in which we can observe collaboration span family interactions (from everyday scheduling discussions to crisis decision making), task collaborations at work, political coalitions and alliances in service of party or legislative goals, national and international relief efforts (e.g., hurricane preparation efforts, coordinating major disaster relief), police investigations (e.g., the Amber Alert system, FBI co-investigations with local and state police), and homeland security operations that involve CIA, FBI, and intelligence operations of other nations.

Along with the proliferation of collaboration across contexts, various concepts describe collaborative practices. Terms like *dialogue, communities of practice,* and *integrative conflict style* are well-known constructs in the communication discipline that draw from the collaboration ideology. Less well known concepts, such as *collaborative spirit* (Heath & Sias, 1999), *peer col-*

laboration (Kumpulainen & Kaartinen, 2003), *collaborative learning* (Wilczenski, Bontrager, Ventrone, & Correia, 2001), and *collaborative interpretation* (Young & Flower, 2001), also describe important practices and processes within this domain of activity. As Huxham and Vangen (2003) noted, "The last decade has seen a worldwide movement toward collaborative governance, collaborative public service provision, and collaborative approaches to addressing social problems" (p. 1159).

Collaborative interaction appears to have great promise as a tool across several contexts. Tschannen (2004) argued that dire consequences may follow from ignoring trends toward collaboration in health care. According to Tschannen, patient mortality in hospitals using collaborative communication was reported to be 41% lower than the predicted number of patient deaths, whereas hospitals recognized for lack of collaborative communication exceeded their predicted number of patient deaths by 58%. Similarly, findings from the mental health profession indicate that collaborative efforts between providers and families of the mentally ill have been effective in reducing the morbidity and mortality of those patients and that families permitted to collaborate with professionals about the health of their ill relatives reap benefits in terms of their own psychological and physical well-being (Kaas, Lee, & Peitzman, 2003).

Furthermore, evidence from conflict research overwhelmingly supports the use of integrative communication practices that focus on "win-win" strategies (Gross, Guerrero, & Alberts, 2004) to foster positive interpersonal relationships. Literatures in the areas of aging and development/learning have also asserted benefits of collaboration, including coping (Berg, Meegan, & Deviney, 1998), problem solving (Strough, Berg, & Meegan, 2001; Wilczenski et al., 2001), and learning (Kumpulainen & Kaartinen, 2003). Barron (2000) advocated teaching collaborative skills to young people, such as developing students' capacities to notice their own and others' attentional engagement, strategies for achieving common focus, persistence in the face of resistance, and steadfastness in remaining engaged during moments of confusion and lack of joint understanding. She also pointed out that learning to collaborate and engage in successful teamwork is among the educational goals expressed in most new educational reform documents, including the National Science Education Standards. As work becomes "more knowledge-based, interdisciplinary, and distributed across time and space, the ability to recognize and repair problems in communication is becoming more highly valued" (Barron, p. 433).

In sum, evidence quickly accumulates regarding the success of various forms of collaborative activity. Unfortunately, despite the growing use and recognition of effective collaboration, very little synthesis exists across various domains of literature about how collaborative interaction works and its critical components. Several authors have noted the lack of integration of collaboration literatures in general. For example, Lawrence, Phillips, & Hardy (1999) explained this problem: "Although the study of collaboration has examined many aspects of its dynamics, these results remain somewhat diffuse. Divergent theoretical perspectives seem to examine similarly divergent empirical phenomena, such that the results are largely noncumulative" (p. 483). Keyton and Stallworth (2003) also highlighted the problem within the community context: "Although communities perceive collaboration as an innovative, positive means for addressing social problems, researchers and practitioners alike are still trying to discover the most effective means to create and sustain collaborative efforts" (p. 235). Although collaboration and related concepts are threaded throughout the communication discipline (and others), publications reveal little integration of the theory, conceptualizations, and/or empirical evidence concerning collaboration in general or collaborative interaction specifically. This chapter provides a necessary step in bringing these disparate literatures together to explore collaboration from a communication perspective.

This chapter serves as a means to examine these disparate sets of literature, with an eye not toward theory building in any single area, but toward creating synthesis across the various domains. Essentially, the major guiding questions of this chapter include the following:

What are key themes in common across these different treatments of collaborative interaction?

What are the unique pockets or points of departure?

What is being missed, and what directions ought to be pursued to further the communication discipline's understanding of collaborative interaction?

This review sought to locate scholarship within the last decade (1995–2005) to ascertain and describe current approaches to collaborative interaction.

SCOPE OF THE REVIEW

Although the term *collaboration* is widely and rather loosely applied across disciplines—meaning everything from simply sharing information/opinions or "working together" to striving to arrive at win-win outcomes of conflict to a specific means of regarding relational partners in interaction—this review focused on unearthing current literature most reflective of a more restricted sense of *collaborative interaction*. The review process for this chapter began with searches for scholarly works published within the last decade (1995–2005) that are labeled with certain titles or key words, including *collaboration, collaborative communication, collaborative groups/teams, collaborative problem solving, collaborative decision making*, and the like. As the review progressed, I increasingly employed other related terms (e.g., *integrative communication, integrative bargaining*, and *dialogue*) to produce a more expansive set of works that might enlighten the discussion of collaborative interaction. Some works were identified through citation in other located works. Colleagues representing various areas within the communication discipline were consulted for ideas about related constructs within their expertise domains.

In the end, the scholarly works retained for this review include several characteristics. First, all works attended significantly to communicative interaction and/or process among participants. Whereas, in some cases, this emphasis entails a close interactional analysis of talk, turns, or utterances (e.g., Bonito & Sanders, 2002; Drake, 2001; Kuhn & Poole, 2000), in others, it encompasses a more macro-analysis of the general process of collaborations (e.g., how communicative relationships developed over time) (e.g., Lawrence et al., 1999; Zoller, 2004). In some instances, publications detail how collaborations will or should evolve, and others report participants' own understandings or recollections of collaborative interaction or processes.

Collaborations that are less dependent on communicative interactions among participants, or are completely void of such interactions, were not the object of this review. For example, collaborative writing that does not require much interaction from the participants, scientific collaboration in which the involved scientists may be aware of one another only through published works but whose combined work on scientific problems effectively amounts to collaborative processes, or a musical or physical collaboration that might be experienced by a jazz band or a football team were not sought for this review. In addition, I initially considered some works for this review that used the term *collaboration* to refer to their context. However, they simply did not focus on the processes of collaborating, but rather on the inputs (characteristics of group, structures in which the collaboration was embedded), tools (technologies and their characteristics), or outcomes (e.g., satisfaction, achievement of goals) of collaboration, and thus they were excluded.

A second criterion used to define this review specified that these works concern situations wherein participants embrace a joint purpose (or at least a pretense of joint purpose) and/or the mutual achievement of individual goals. Although shared goals and/or mutually valued individual goals of collaborations were examined or discussed in some cases (e.g., Gross et al., 2004; Lakey & Canary, 2002; Meiners & Miller, 2004), it was more implicit in others (e.g., Coopman, 2001; DiMatteo et al., 1994). Although idealized definitions of collaboration seemingly include both a high regard for joint goals *and* mutual regard for individual goals, this assumption does not appear consistently in all of the relevant literature. Thus, for this review, as long as works noted one or the other of these types of goal allegiance, they were included. Some works concerned with general participative practices (e.g., participative organizational practices, increasing community voice) were not sought for inclusion under this criterion because such processes need not always imply joint purpose or mutual support of individual goals of participants; some stressed competition of goals and contention over the joint purpose of collectives. To that extent, the process would not be considered "collaborative interaction" in this perspective. Certainly, some forms of participative governance or empowerment practices in other contexts might be collaborative, but they need not be.

I employed a third criterion in this review to isolate a more specific case of communication than simply "working together." This review focuses on collaborative interaction involving a special form of interdependence among the participants. To help discern this criterion, I drew from a now-classic text, *Organizations in Action* (Thompson, 1967), on organizational structure. Thompson articulated three types of interdependence (which he applied to work structures in organizations, not to collaboration specifically). In some cases of working together, participants share a mutual end goal and count on one another to make individual contributions to the whole in order to ensure the joint goal is accomplished, a situation termed *pooled interdependence* by Thompson. Individuals do not truly depend on one another. In a second case, participants working together require individuals to do their respective parts to achieve a joint goal, and the order of the contributions make individuals serially interdependent—person A cannot do his or her part until person B does his or her part. In this case, *sequential interdependence*, both participants experience pooled interdependence (i.e., counting on one another to do his or her part) and rely individually on other participants to be enabled to make individual contributions to the whole. A third type, which encompasses the first two types of interdependence, is represented in the situation where the outputs of *each* participant become the inputs for other participants. In such a relationship, the work of an individual participant is necessitated by the work of another. Furthermore, the products of individual work provide input back to the original propagator of the work. Thompson labeled this looped relationship *reciprocal interdependence*.

In the context of collaborative interaction, participants tied together in merely pooled or sequentially interdependent relationships do not share the same interactional necessities as those partnered in reciprocally interdependent ones. As Thompson (1967) argued, reciprocally interdependent participants must coordinate through mutual adjustment (rather than simply changing one end of the partnership). According to Thompson, mutual adjustment requires more sophisticated communication and decision-making activity than do coordination tools appropriate to pooled or sequential interdependence (i.e., standardization, planning).

Some team and group literature might not meet this criterion. Basic team behavior does not necessitate reciprocal interdependence. An effective team might accomplish its team and individual goals in any number of ways (e.g., going with the best contributor, dividing tasks by skill, dividing tasks equally, taking turns, majority rules voting), and members may experience only pooled or sequential interdependence. Thus, teams may or may not exhibit collaborative interaction as it is conceptualized here.

Fourth, the works included in this review concern collaborations where participants actively and mindfully engage one another, selecting this type of interaction over others. Thus, coincidentally or mindless coordinated behavior or coerced collaboration (e.g., a mediated circumstance wherein participants were only following the rules laid down by an outside force) were not included. Under this criterion, a larger category of *cooperative*—as opposed to competitive—forms of communication was not automatically subsumed as collaborative interaction. Although more submissive and passive forms of communication might be thought of as cooperative rather than competitive, they would not be termed "collaborative" in the sense embraced by this review because they lack the requirement of active contribution. Those who merely submit to higher authority or power are not active collaborators. Collaborative relationships that are mandated (e.g., agencies mandated to work together to coordinate a disaster relief effort) might be included under this criterion if the *nature of the collaborative interaction* was selected by the participants. In other words, the circumstances that bring collaborative participants together might be coerced, mandated, purely voluntary, or ambiguous/mixed, but the choice to engage one another in a collaborative way must be volitional under this conceptualization.

The criteria described above did not allow for inclusion of literature addressing coordination of speech patterns (usually out of awareness), interorganizational literature that does not detail communication processes, collaborative technologies literature that focused on a set of tools used to do collaboration more so than the process of communication within collaboration, and collaboration literature that dealt with either motivations for joining collaborative partnerships or the outcomes of those collaborations without consideration of the communicative interactions or processes involved. Some literature was not included because it was published before 1995.[1] It should be noted here that a great deal of literature exists across these omitted categories. Readers who want a fuller picture of antecedents and outcomes of collaboration as well as structural issues and case studies that highlight other issues aside from communication (e.g., membership, resources, typologies of collaborations, benefits of collaboration) should read more widely than the works cited in this review. This review is representative and not comprehensive of all study and scholarship concerning collaborative interaction.

SAMPLE FOR THIS REVIEW

This search resulted in the collection of 80 scholarly works. Approximately 56% of these works were either published in communication journals or books (usually edited books) or authored by communication scholars in journals from other disciplines. The remainder were authored by noncommunication scholars (as far as could be determined) in noncommunication journals. The collaborative contexts examined by these sources vary and include developmental/learning, interpersonal relationships, conflict (mostly dyadic), group problem solving and decision making, health (spanning the micro-macro range from doctor-patient communication, health-care teams, and community health alliances), community groups, and interprofessional and interorganizational settings. The vast majority (68%) of the sources included in this review are empirical (see Table 5–1). Works did not need to be empirical to be included, but it appears to be a trend in the scholarship. The remaining articles are conceptual essays and theory-building efforts. I did not discover any literature reviews (that focused on communication) or research agendas.

I devote the rest of this chapter to examining the content of these sources and specifying themes within them to generate a research agenda for communication scholars interested in collaborative interaction. To begin, the issue of definitions is most paramount. This chapter initially turns to the complex problem of how to define collaborative interaction and related terms used in the reviewed literature, and it then examines the themes throughout this literature.

DEFINITIONS

As Huxham and Vangen (1996) observed, many definitions of collaboration exist, and much alternative terminology has been used at times interchangeably with it, including *cooperation, coordination, coalition, partnership,* or, on the darker side, *collusion* or *co-option*. In the current review, each source was examined to extract any explicit definitions of collaboration and related constructs. In several cases, a set of authors within a certain literature cited the same definition. For example, Barbara Gray's (1989) definition is commonly cited in the interorganizational literature. According to Gray, collaboration constitutes "a process through which parties who see different aspects of a

TABLE 5-1

Key Communication Variables Studied in Collaboration Empirical Literature

Authors by area	Method	Key communication variables/constructs
Developmental/Learning		
Berg, Johnson, Meegan, & Strough (2003)	Experiment and open-ended interviews	High/low affiliation exchanges during decision making and errand tasks; communication about division of labor and delegation
Dixon & Gould (1998)	Experiment	Retelling a complex story
Kumpulainen & Kaartinen (2003)	Qualitative case study	Social interaction problem-solving strategies; mathematical language use; negotiation; shared understanding
Strough, Berg, & Meegan (2001)	Qualitative observation and questionnaire	Salience of social and task problems collaborative problem-solving
Wilczenski, Bontrager, Ventrone, & Correia (2001)	Experiment	Collaborative problem solving; facilitative behaviors
Conflict / negotiation		
Bonito & Sanders (2002)	Interaction analysis	Establishment of "footings" in collaborative writing task; conflict resolution
Cai, Wilson, & Drake (2000)	Questionnaires and interaction analysis	Information sharing; heuristic trial and error; distributive tactics
Canary, Cupach, & Serpe (2001)	Longitudinal panel study w/ questionnaires	Integrative tactics; distributive tactics
Drake (2001)	Interaction analysis and questionnaire	Anticipated competition; information exchange
Gross, Guerrero, & Alberts (2004)	Questionnaire following interaction	Conflict strategies (nonconfrontational, solution-oriented, control); communication competence

(continued)

TABLE 5-1 (*Continued*)

Authors by area	Method	Key communication variables/constructs
Kuhn & Poole (2000)	Observation of natural groups	Group conflict styles; group decision making
Lakey & Canary (2002)	Questionnaires	Conflict strategies; effectiveness and appropriateness of strategies; communication competence of partner; sensitivity to partner's goals in interaction
Meiners & Miller (2004)	Questionnaires	Integrative negotiation behaviors (elaboration, directness, mutual concessions); formality of interaction setting; relational tone (e.g., friendliness, warmth, affiliation)
Oetzel & Ting-Toomey (2003)	Questionnaires	Conflict styles (integrative, dominating); self-construal; face concerns (self and other)
Pavitt & Kemp (1999)	Experimental-scenarios	Preference and feasibility of negotiation strategies
Rudawsky, Lundgren, & Grasha (1999)	Questionnaires	Degree of negativity of peer feedback; importance of feedback; negative affective responses of receiver; choice of conflict resolution strategies (i.e., collaborative, competitive)
Taylor (2002)	Content analysis of transcriptions	Integrative bargaining; levels of interaction (i.e., avoidance, distributive, integrative); styles of communication (i.e., identity, instrumental, relational); intensity of communication

Taylor & Donald (2004)	Content analysis of transcribed crisis negotiations	Integrative bargaining; levels of interaction (i.e., avoidance, distributive, integrative); styles of communication (i.e., identity, instrumental, relational); intensity of communication
Ting-Toomey, Oezel, & Yee-Jung (2001)	Questionnaire	Self-construal; conflict management styles (i.e., integrating, compromising, dominating, avoiding, obliging)
Weider-Hatfield & Hatfield (1995, 1996)	Questionnaires	Conflict management styles (integrating, compromising, dominating, avoiding, obliging); levels of conflict
Yoshimura (2004)	Scenario experiment	Emotion intensity; target's responses to jealous expressions (integrative communication, attack, concession/agreement, minimization)
Groups Barge (2002) Barron (2000)	Case study Case study and interaction analysis	Dialogue process; Mutuality of exchanges; achievement of joint attentional engagement; alignment of group members' stated goals
Breu & Hemingway (2002)	Individual and focus group interviews in single case	Use of facilitator; networking use of channels for communication
Franz & Jin (1995)	Interaction analysis of taped group discussions	Group conflict levels (high/low); conflict management behaviors (i.e., integrative, cooperative, distributive, and competitive)
Keyton & Stallworth (2003)	Case study	Communication structures
Lammers & Krikorian (1997)	Observation, archival, and interviews	Nature of personal interactions Network centrality

(continued)

TABLE 5–1 (Continued)

Authors by area	Method	Key communication variables/constructs
Mangrum, Fairley, & Wieder (2001)	Longitudinal case study	Self-perceptions of communication patterns; multimodal communication; problem-solving communication; ad hoc gatherings
Health		
Akhavain, Amaral, Murphy, & Uehlinger (1999)	Case study (treatment teams)	Sharing of knowledge, expertise, insights
Brashers, Haas, Klingle, & Neidig (2000)	Participant observation, interviews, open-ended questionnaires	Patient assertiveness with doctors; patient-physician communication quality
Coopman (2001)	Questionnaires	Perceptions of participation in decision-making
Ellingson (2003)	Ethnographic observation and interviews	Backstage / informal communication practices; relationship-building talk; information sharing
Ellingson & Buzzanell (1999)	Interviews	Negotiating communication with physicians; characteristics of satisfying communication with physicians; patient communication styles; communication satisfaction
Hermansen & Wiederholt (2001)	Interviews and questionnaires	Patient's collaborative willingness; interpersonal relationship quality w/ pharmacist
Higgins (1999)	Questionnaires	Nurses' perceptions of collaborative nurse-physician transfer decision-making

Author	Method	Focus
W. L. Holleman, Bray, Davis, & M.C. Holleman (2004)	Case study	Communicative aspects of patient care in AIME program
Jameson (2004)	Interviews	Critical incidents of anesthesiologists and nurse anesthetists conflict; face-saving strategies; politeness
Kaas, Lee, & Peitzman (2003)	Questionnaires	Barriers to mental health professionals' collaboration with families of patients
Maseide (2003)	Discourse analysis	Medical and moral order of collaborative discourse
Medved et al. (2001)	Questionnaires, interviews, content analysis, observation	Homophily tension (people's preferences for communication with those similar to them); problems associated with diverse membership and communication; information dissemination
Mizrahi & Abramson (2000)	Questionnaires	Satisfaction with physician-social worker collaboration
Street, Krupat, Bell, Kravitz, & Haidet (2003)	Questionnaires	Active communicative participation of patients
Street & Millay (2001)	Interaction analysis of physician-patient interactions	Doctor-patient partnership building; Patient participation behaviors (i.e., asking questions, expressing concerns, and assertive utterances); physician partnership building and supportive talk
Tschannen (2004)	Questionnaires	Collaborative problem solving (doctors-nurses)

(continued)

TABLE 5-1 *(Continued)*

Authors by area	*Method*	*Key communication variables/constructs*
Young & Klingle (1996)	Questionnaires	Patient assertiveness (w/ physician) before and after appointment; patient communicative efficacy before and after appointment; patient participation; physician feedback
Interprofessional Bouman (2002)	Interviews	Influence and power in communicative interactions; differences in communication cultural norms; strategies for communicating across professional lines
Clark et al. (1996)	Participant observation and case studies	Challenges in gaining equality in collaboration (researchers and teachers); perspective taking; sharing information; shared dialogue
Macduff & Netting (2000)	Participant case study	Relational issues (i.e., trust-building, familiarity); models of collaboration (dialogic, hierarchical)
Interorganizational Austin (2000)	Case studies through interviews, and questionnaires	Communicating about value and purpose; social partnerships created in collaborations; shared visioning; characteristics of beneficial communication practices (forthrightness, constructive criticism, openness, norms for communication speed)

Browning & Beyer (1998)	Case study through interviews, observations, archival	Overcoming conflict and building trust through communication; setting standards
Browning, Beyer, & Shetler (1995)	Case study through interviews, observations, archival	Cooperation and competition embedded in a complex organizational consortium in a competitive industry
Hardy & Phillips (1998)	Case studies	Cooperation and conflict; four strategies of engagement (collaboration, compliance, contention, and contestation)
Hardy, Phillips, & Lawrence (2003)	Longitudinal case study through interviews and archival	Interaction among organizations (bridging roles); flows of information; level of involvement (interaction "deep" or "shallow"); embeddedness (i.e., breadth of interaction)
Heath & Sias (1999)	Case study through interviews and textual analysis of documents	Communication of shared mission; communication of shared power; collaborative spirit
Huxham & Vangen (2003)	Case studies	Leadership behaviors (e.g., encouraging sharing of information, developing common understandings)
Jones & Bodker (1998)	Case study with archival, interviewing and interaction analysis	Conflict over identity and membership; negotiation of authority; Inclusion and participation
Lawrence, Hardy, & Phillips (2002)	Case study through interviews and archival	Development of common understandings and practices; norms of interaction
Lawrence, Phillips, & Hardy (1999)	Case study through interviews	Discursive activity that underlies collaboration and its social structures; stakeholders' discursive resources; discourse as a means to change the conception of collaboration

(continued)

TABLE 5-1 (*Continued*)

Authors by area	Method	Key communication variables/constructs
Miller, Scott, Stage, & Birkholt (1995)	Interviews	Coordination methods (referrals, use of technologies); focus of coordination (e.g., advocacy, funding, image)
Mohr, Fisher, & Nevin (1996)	Questionnaires	Characteristics of collaborative communication (e.g., frequency, bidirectionality, formality, coerciveness); governance (i.e., in terms of ownership and decision-making involvement)
Stone (2000)	Case study through interviews and archival	Density of relationships; strategic decision-making
Zoller (2000)	Observational case study	Communication practices
Zoller (2004)	Case study	Strategic use of dialogue structures

problem can constructively explore their differences and search for solutions that go beyond their own limited visions of what is possible" (p. 5). However, many sources offered no definition of collaboration (e.g., Austin, 2000; Bouman, 2002; Stone, 2000), and they simply applied the term in such a way that its meaning was assumed to be understood. Others created unique definitions or built upon earlier work in emphasizing a definition. Thirty-four definitions related to collaboration were collected in this review (see Table 5–2). Given the conditions for inclusion in this review, it is not surprising to see that most of these definitions emphasize shared goals, shared activity, or joint production.[2] However, other similarities and differences are more notable. I draw the reader's attention to five points of convergence and three points of divergence in these definitions.

Points of Convergence

The definitions nearly always focused on action and doing: recalling (Gould, Osborn, Krein, & Mortenson, 2002); problem solving (Barron, 2000; Berg et al., 1998; Kumpulainen & Kaartinen, 2003; Rudawsky, Lundgren, & Grasha, 1999; Young & Flower, 2001); working, playing, and creating (Macduff & Netting, 2000; Wilczenski et al., 2001); discussion (Barge, 2002; Wilczenski et al., 2001); decision making (Keyton & Stallworth, 2003; Young & Klingle, 1996); learning (Barge, 2002; Ellingson, 2003; Lesser & Storck, 2001; Wilczenski et al., 2001), and sharing knowledge/resources/expertise (Breu & Hemingway, 2002; Gross et al., 2004; Kumpulainen & Kaartien, 2003; Wenger & Snyder, 2000; Wilczenski et al., 2001; Young & Flower, 2001). Thus, it appears that the definitions used by these authors construct collaboration as an activity rather than a state or an object. We don't *have* a collaboration, nor *are* we a collaboration; we *engage in* collaboration. It seems also that collaboration might be thought of as *a way of doing* something communicative. We can learn collaboratively, collaboratively solve problems, decide collaboratively, or discuss collaboratively, etc. To collaborate, for many of these authors, means to do some other communicative activity in a collaborative way.

A second common thread in these definitions concerns the recurrent notation of the relation between self and other(s) as a fundamental part of the definition. Several works refer to "working together" or "working jointly" (Henneman, 1995; Macduff & Netting, 2000), "nonhierarchical" relationships (Hardy, Phillips, & Lawrence, 2003; Tschannen, 2004), "reciprocal relationship" (Young & Flower, 2001), sharing "turf" (Ellingson, 2003), and uses of the terms "partner" (Lakey & Canary, 2002; Mohr, Fisher, & Nevin, 1996) and "autonomy" (Stohl & Walker, 2002) as well as avoidance of "domination" (Mintzberg, Dougherty, Jorgensen, & Westley, 1996). Akhavain, Amaral,

TABLE 5–2
Definitions of Collaboration-Related Terms

Developmental/Learning	
Barron (2000, p. 407), citing the work of Forman and Cazden, described cooperative interactions as "those in which children constantly monitored each other's work and played complementary roles in completing the problems."	Barron (2000)
Peer collaboration: "coordinated activity during which participants collectively process and solve problems toward a joint outcome . . . students working jointly on the same task to negotiate shared meanings that may challenge the subjective understandings of the participants or go beyond what they already know individually" (Kumpulainen & Kaartinen, 2003, pp. 333–334).	Kumpulainen & Kaartinen (2003)
Wilczenski et al. (2001, pp. 269–270), citing the definition developed by Clark and colleagues, defined collaboration as "a dialogue or discussion with emphasis on group process and full participation of group members . . . include[s] exchanging ideas, giving and receiving help from others, clarifying strategies, resolving conflict, and encouraging others to participate." Wilczenski et al. (2001) further defined collaborative learning as "students working together without immediate teacher supervision in groups small enough that all students can participate collectively on a task" (p. 270).	Wilczenski et al. (2001)
"Collaborative problem-solving strategies entail a greater degree of involvement with others in actual coping efforts and include negotiation, joint problem solving, division of labour, influence and control, compensation for others' deficits, and transactive dialogues which move the coping efforts forward" (Berg et al., 1998, p. 251).	Berg et al. (1998)
"Collaborative recall occurs when two or more individuals work together and cooperatively on a memory task" (Gould et al., 2002, p. 36).	Gould et al. (2002)
Negotiation and Conflict	
Integrative negotiation: "As negotiations progress, hostage takers may be persuaded that both sides working together will ultimately lead to a satis-	Taylor (2002)

(*continued*)

TABLE 5–2 (*Continued*)

factory solution, so they place greater emphasis
on normative and cooperative communication as
a way of reconciling the parties' divergent interests" (Taylor, 2002, p. 10).

Meiners & Miller (2004, p. 304) adopted Walton &   Meiners & Miller (2004)
McKersie's definition of integrative negotiation:
"the process by which the parties attempt to
increase the size of the joint gain without respect
to the division of the payoffs." Meiners and
Miller argued that "[w]here a distributive model
of negotiation emphasizes competition over
scarce resources, those in integrative negotiation
generally assume a more collaborative and cooperative orientation" (p. 304).

"Integrative conflict strategies (also called solution-   Gross et al. (2004)
oriented, collaborating, and problem-solving
strategies) are direct, prosocial, and focus on
mutual goals. People using integrative strategies
generally engage in open communication, information sharing, and problem solving" (Gross
et al., 2004, p. 252).

Collaboration: "a mutual problem solving orienta-   Rudawsky et al. (1999)
tion toward conflict where both parties' interests
are taken into account" (Rudawsky et al., 1999,
p. 173).

"Interpersonal communication competence is an   Lakey & Canary (2002)
impression formed by an interaction partner of
an actor's communication behaviors that are performed to achieve his/her goals while also to
respect the partner's goals" (Lakey & Canary,
2002, p. 221).

Integrative conflict tactics: "those that work toward
the other person and promote relational objectives" (p. 222).

Health

Collaboration: "to involve individuals with varying   Tschannen (2004)
backgrounds and expertise communicating effec-
tively with one another in a nonhierarchical fashion. Together they are able to search for solutions
that cannot be determined with an individual's
limited scope of knowledge" (Tschannen, 2004,
p. 313).

(*continued*)

TABLE 5–2 (*Continued*)

Henneman (1995, p. 360) cited Coluccio & Maguire's definition of collaboration as it relates to health care: "The joint communicating and decision-making process with the expressed goal of satisfying the patient's wellness and illness needs while respecting the unique qualities and abilities of each professional."	Henneman (1995)
"Collaboration in Bowen theory terms means working in a system while giving *of* oneself but not giving *up* oneself. It is the ability to combine assertiveness and cooperativeness and to remain true to individual principles while working toward a common goal. It is a balance between autonomy and togetherness" (Akhavain et al., 1999, p. 4).	Akhavain et al. (1999)
Collaborative willingness: "a patient's likelihood to engage in social exchange and self-disclosure activities with his or her provider (pharmacist)" (Hermansen & Wiederholt, 2001, p. 311).	Hermansen & Wiederholt (2001)
Collaborative relationship (doctor-patient): "in which patients actively seek information and participate in mutual decision-making with the health professional" (Young & Klingle, 1996, p. 31).	Young & Klingle (1996)
Collaborative interpretation: "CI allows providers and patients to develop a reciprocal relationship, where the exchange of information, identification of problems, and development of solutions is an interactive process. CI is a multifaceted construct that includes dialogue, problem solving, and knowledge building as modes of inquiry, analysis and persuasion" (Young & Flower, 2001, p. 71).	Young & Flower (2001)
Ellingson (2003) adopted Wieland, Kramer, Waite, & Rubenstein's definition of transdiciplinary teams, in which "members have developed sufficient trust and mutual confidence to engage in teaching and learning across disciplinary boundaries" (p. 95). Ellingson also noted that these teams "comfortably share their turf as they work toward common goals" (p. 95).	Ellingson (2003)

(*continued*)

TABLE 5-2 (*Continued*)

Group/community	
Stohl & Walker (2002, p. 240) adopted Walker, Craig, & Stohl's definition of collaboration: "the process of creating and sustaining a negotiated temporary system which spans organizational boundaries involving autonomous stakeholders with varying capabilities including resources, knowledge and expertise and which is directed toward individual goals and mutually accountable and innovative ends."	Stohl & Walker (2002)
Keyton and Stallworth (2003, p. 237) adopted Stallworth's definition of collaborative process as "a process in which two or more organizations engage in shared decision-making and coordinated, joint action to address a common goal" Collaboration: "the group of stakeholders or organizational representatives that engage in a collaborative process" (Keyton & Stallworth, p. 237).	Keyton & Stallworth (2003), Stallworth (1998)
"Dialogue is, thus, a collective and collaborative communication process whereby people explore together their individual and collective assumptions and predispositions. In so doing, dialogue moves individuals and groups from engaging in single-loop to double- and triple-loop learning" (Barge, 2002, p. 168). Barge (2002) adopted Barret's definition of collaborative competence as "an ability to 'create forums in which members engage in ongoing dialogue and exchange diverse perspectives" (Barge, p. 175).	Barge (2002)
"Community of Practice [is] a group whose members regularly engage in sharing and learning, based on their common interests. . . . a group of people playing in a field defined by the domain of skills and techniques over which the members of the group interact" (Lesser & Storck, 2001, p. 831).	Lesser & Storck (2001)
Breu and Hemingway (2002, p. 148), citing the work of Brown and Duguid, defined community of practice as "informal, self organizing networks of people dedicated to sharing knowledge in an area of common interest or expertise."	Breu & Hemingway (2002)

(*continued*)

TABLE 5–2 (*Continued*)

Breu and Hemingway (2002, p. 148) further elaborated, citing Wenger: "CoPs tend to assemble practitioners who have worked together and, through extensive communication and interaction, have developed a common sense of purpose, and a desire to share work-related knowledge and experience."	Breu & Hemingway (2002)
Communities of practice: "groups of people informally bound together by shared expertise and passion for joint enterprise . . . people in communities of practice share their experiences and knowledge in free-flowing, creative ways that foster new approaches to problems" (Wenger & Snyder, 2000, pp. 139–140).	Wenger & Snyder (2000)

Interorganizational/interprofessional

"Collaboration is viewed as a process in which two or more persons work and play together to achieve some result or create some product in which they are jointly invested and about which they care enough to pool their strengths. These persons may be from the same or different fields, disciplines or professions" (Macduff & Netting, 2000, p. 48).	Macduff & Netting (2000)
"Rather than solidify alternatives and lock us into either/or situations, collaboration allows us to avoid unnecessary compromise or domination, and to use integration and synthesis to invent third ways" (Mintzberg et al., 1996, p. 61).	Mintzberg et al. (1996)
"Dialogue requires collaboration that does not rule out disagreement and debate but presumes a focus on joint sense making and a willingness to be vulnerable to being changed through the interaction" (Zoller, 2004, p. 214).	Zoller (2004)
Collaboration: "a cooperative, interorganizational relationship that is negotiated in an ongoing communicative process, and which relies on neither market nor hierarchical mechanisms of control" (Hardy et al., 2003, p. 323).	Hardy et al. (2003)
Collaborative spirit: "the general principles regarding acceptable goals, values and behavior that underlie and guide the collaborative alliance" (Heath & Sias, 1999, p. 358).	Heath & Sias (1999)
Collaboration: "a mutual engagement strategy in which all partners voluntarily participate" (Hardy & Phillips, 1998, p. 224).	Hardy & Phillips (1998)

(*continued*)

TABLE 5–2 (*Continued*)

"Collaborative Communication relies on the development of cooperative attitudes and processes to guide and administer the relationship . . . which creates an atmosphere of mutual support and respect. By highlighting shared interests and common goals, collaborative communication can create volitional compliance between partners" (Mohr et al., 1996, p. 103).	Mohr et al. (1996)

Murphy, & Uehlinger (1999) defined collaboration as "working in a system while giving of oneself but not giving up oneself . . . a balance between autonomy and togetherness" (p. 4). Wenger and Snyder (2000) described "groups of people informally bound together by shared expertise and passion for joint enterprise" (p. 139). Thus, the ways in which participants in collaboration regard one another seems to be a further defining characteristic. Such orientation to the other(s) is not structural in these definitions, but it relates to the perceptions and behaviors that participants have of/with one another. This perspective implies that collaboration cannot be formally convened, but rather, it emerges when the participants choose to engage one another in a certain way or manner. While formal collaborations may exist in name, collaborative interaction, by this definition, is not truly present until a specific type of relationship between participants develops. Scholars define that type of relationship differently, but, as illustrated in the discussion of the third point of convergence in what follows, they tend to emphasize equality.

The third point of definitional convergence involves equalization of the participants in collaborative interactions. This aspect of the definition goes beyond the basic condition of "joint activity." In several cases, these definitions speak directly to the need to avoid status and power differences by ensuring equality. Equality is raised in terms of roles (Barron, 2000), status (Tschannen, 2004), and value/respect for expertise or contributions (Henneman, 1995; Lakey & Canary, 2002). Although not always present in the definitions, much of the focus on status difference reduction appears in the health communication literature. Throughout this literature, a chief perceived problem that collaboration is meant to overcome concerns the dysfunctional communication between high-status (e.g., doctors) and low-status (e.g., patients, nurses) individuals (e.g., Akhavain et al., 1999; Coopman, 2001; Young & Flower, 2001). In these situations, collaborative processes may level the field so that lower-status participants' wisdom, knowledge, concerns, and ideas can become a part of the decision-making process. This theme is also fairly prevalent in the interorganizational context where partner organizations (that, by virtue of resources or legitimacy or network centrality, are higher in status) may contaminate a collaborative process by wielding status over weaker partners (e.g., Mintzberg et al., 1996; Stone, 2000; Zoller, 2004) . In sum, equalizing practices constitute a valued component of collaboration in some contexts where status differences are highly salient and likely to be prominent.

A fourth point of convergence across these definitions concerns the emphasis on process. Several of these definitions imply that collaborative activities involve processes with beginning, middle, and end components and, thus, should be expected to develop or change over time. The term *process* is used in several of the definitions (Barge, 2002; Hardy et al., 2003; Henneman, 1995; Keyton & Stallworth, 2003; Macduff & Netting, 2000; Meiners & Miller, 2004; Mohr et al., 1996; Stohl & Walker, 2002; Young & Flower, 2001). In addition, Berg et al. (1998) noted "moving the coping efforts forward" (p. 251), and Taylor (2002) depicted hostage negotiations as progressing. Thus, we might expect these conceptualizations of collaboration to propose that collaborative activity will look different at various points along the process. Collaboration is less like a single action (e.g., kicking a ball) and more like an organized activity (e.g., a ball game). In particular, it features characteristics (presumably) of the beginning, middle, and end of the activity; different expected behaviors and roles need to be fulfilled at particular points, and assorted important milestones at diverse points and the value of those milestones (e.g., a field goal) vary throughout the process.

A fifth and final point of convergence across these definitions regards their nature as emergent, informal, and volitional. Although this theme runs more thinly through this literature, scholars imply this treatment of collaboration. In one case (Hardy et al., 2003), the authors declared that collaboration occurs outside of "market" and "hierarchical" mechanisms of control. There are also references to "self-organizing" (Breu & Hemingway, 2002), informality (Wenger & Snyder, 2000), and volitional participation (Hardy & Phillips, 1998; Mohr et al., 1996). Each of these references bolsters an image of collaboration as something entered into freely and without coercion. Furthermore, the process appears to be conceived as owned and constructed by the actions of the participants.

Points of Divergence

Some interesting contrasts within this set of definitions can also be noted. First, definitions explicitly or implicitly consider a dimension of time. Stohl and Walker (2002), quoting Walker, Craig, and Stohl, stated that collaboration "is the process of creating and sustaining a negotiated *temporary* system" (italics added) (p. 240), whereas the definition of Lesser and Storck (2001) suggests that a community of practice engages in regular and ongoing activity. Definitions that imply more temporariness include the focus by Gould et al. (2002) on specific tasks and the treatment by Wilczenski et al. (2001) of dialogue/discussion as an event—both of which appear to refer to relatively short-lived interaction. The communities of practice literature (Breu & Hemingway, 2002; Lesser & Storck, 2001; Wenger & Snyder, 2000) promotes a sense of ongoing activity with a long-term time horizon. Most of the definitions do not address a time dimension, suggesting that collaborative activity may take place over long or short time spans. Important differences between short and long-running collaborations may exist, but they have not been the subject of communication scholarship yet. Issues such as participant commitment in multiparty collaborations, continuity of participation, short- and long-range goals and planning, and communicative characteristics across the life span of collaborations lack empirical evidence.

In a second point of divergence, some definitions assume a starting point of difference among the participants in the process. In such cases, collaboration is used as a method to bring the parties closer together. The conflict literature provides the best example. Taylor (2002) described "reconciling parties' divergent interests" (p. 10). Lakey and Canary (2002) emphasized "working toward the other person" (p. 222), implying original separation, and Barge (2002) included "exchanging diverse perspectives" (p. 175). The alternative view offered in some definitions integrates assumptions of shared starting points of participants that are then nurtured through collaborative interaction, exemplified best in the communities of practice (COP) literature. Lesser and Storck (2001), Breu and Hemingway (2002), and Wenger and Snyder (2000) all suggested that shared interests bring people together initially in COPs and keep the collaboration going. Most of the definitions examined in this review lack explicitness about the assumptions of initial difference or similarity. Again, collaborative interaction likely serves as a tool to highlight and consider difference in a productive way as well as to celebrate and take advantage of similarity or commonality.

The third and final point of divergence noted in this examination concerns the explicit focus on "payoffs" or getting individual needs met versus an exclusive emphasis on joint/collective goals. Several of the definitions explicitly acknowledge the importance of individual participants' interests/goals that should be considered and met (Akhavain et al., 1999; Lakey & Canary, 2002; Rudawsky et al., 1999; Stohl & Walker, 2002; Taylor, 2002) as well as an initial desire for "payoffs" (Meiners & Miller, 2004). Other definitions highlight joint/shared goals and needs without mentioning individual goals or interests (Breu & Hemingway, 2002; Gross et al., 2004; Henneman, 1995; Keyton & Stallworth, 2003; Kumpulainen & Kaartinen, 2003; Macduff & Netting, 2000; Mohr et al., 1996). This review indicates that some scholars conceive collaborative interaction as a means to satisfy individual goals through a joint process with a concurrent shared goal or purpose. For other scholars, collaboration concentrates solely on shared goals without consideration of individual goals.

Critique of Definitions

Many of the definitions included in this review suffer from one or more of the following problems: (a) lack of precision, (b) lack of discernment of related key constructs, and (c) focus on idealized versions of collaboration rather than minimal qualifications. Definitions that do not lend themselves to clear operationalization will likely not serve the scholarly community well. In order to accumulate results about collaboration or collaborative interaction across the discipline (and perhaps others), we must specify more closely what we mean by the core terminology and then use terms consistently across theoretical and empirical works. One huge problem in the larger literature on this general topic is that researchers treat *collaboration* both as a noun (e.g., "We have a collaboration.") and a verb (e.g., "We are collaborating."). Whereas one phenomenon may have more to do with the structures surrounding the participants and the roles, rights, and responsibilities of "membership," the other may have more to do with the behaviors engaged in by the participants and the way of interacting (although overlaps certainly occur between these orientations).

Perhaps we cannot narrow all perspectives on collaboration into a single construct. It may be more useful to discern a typology of "collaborisms." For example, it may be helpful to develop a scheme of authority-reducing collaboration, problem-solving collaboration, creative collaboration, etc. On the other hand, creating some new terms that more accurately portray central phenomena (and that are not as loaded with lay interpretations and misuse as *collaboration*) would be a good resolution to the problem of precision. One colleague, after hearing about this review chapter, recommended the terms *collabrocation* and *collabrocating* as ways of describing how we communicate in collaborative ways. Whichever route scholars go—to create more context-specific language or new, more comprehensive language—we need to enhance the precision with which we define the core concept(s) here, so that, at least, we can use a common language to compare findings and theoretical ideas about the phenomenon.

In part, definitional precision involves delineating related constructs from one another. Definitions that list sets of behaviors without distinguishing which ones are necessary or sufficient to qualify cases of collaboration are useful only as guideposts, not to clearly discern collaborative constructs from related ones. For example, what differentiates basic problem solving, recall, and working together from doing these things collaboratively? In the instances of integrative conflict/bargaining definitions, we see a comparison with what is *not* included (i.e., avoidance and distributive) (cf. Drake, 2001; Kuhn & Poole, 2000; Oetzel & Ting-Toomey, 2003). It would be useful if other domains creating definitions of collaboration would follow suit and more clearly specify the boundaries of these constructs by detailing opposites or alternatives.

The further problem of describing collaboration (or its variants) in terms of the idealized version obfuscates readers' abilities to distinguish what is merely desirable from what is basic to this phenomenon. From these definitions, it is hard to imagine what doing collaboration in a mediocre or baseline case would look like. Much of the literature seems to focus on healthy examples of collaborations and on promoting such interactions. Thus, some definitions reflect a bias toward the ideal. The baseline of collaboration ought to define the necessary and sufficient behaviors, attitudes, activities, and participants that indicate the presence of this phenomenon. Aspects of the activity and its participants that enhance the basic activity and discern good from bad execution marks another level of definition, but they should not be confused with the root definition. We can observe and make distinctions between decision making and vigilant decision making, persuasion attempts and effective persuasion, feedback and motivational feedback, media use and strategic media use, and so on. We should also be able to differentiate from the baseline collaborative activity and the idealized and less effective versions.

THEMES ACROSS THE LITERATURE

Method of Analysis

The main intent of this chapter is to review and synthesize research on collaboration across the various domains in communication. In order to accomplish this goal, I read each of the 80 sources at least three times. First, I examined the works against the criteria laid out for inclusion. (At this point, some of the originally located sources were eliminated for one reason or another, mostly because they did not go into any detail about communication.) At this first reading, the article or chapter was scanned for key definitions related to collaboration as well as for categorization by domain/context. Six domains or contexts for the examination of collaboration were groundedly determined: developmental/learning (which included collaboration across the life span), conflict/negotiation, health, groups, interprofessional, and interorganizational. Obviously, overlaps exist between these categories (e.g., some health articles addressed conflict; some group articles described groups of kids and thus were categorized under "developmental"). Through this categorization, I strived to determine the main context of the authors' work. The second reading of the articles involved a more careful examination of the arguments, methods, and findings. I read all articles within a domain/context one after another to provide some sense of the continuity of ideas and approaches within contexts. I took notes on the key findings related to communication and the major theoretical perspectives used to explain findings and to make propositions. In a third reading, I focused on the methodologies employed in the reviewed works and isolated key communication variables studied. Although searching for synthetic themes across domains was always on my mind as I read the various articles and chapters, I determined themes across domains after this reading.

This method of reviewing the communication collaboration literature resulted in the development of four themes of collaborative communication research and theory. These themes represent dominant approaches to the study and discussion of communication in collaborative activities that run across at least a few different contexts (although not necessarily across all of the contexts identified in this review). I arrived at themes by a method similar to qualitative analysis of unstructured data. I identified several potential points of commonality across the literatures, and I then compared and recombined those threads into the most parsimonious set of themes that would still preserve the ideas expressed in the original reading of the works reviewed. I discuss the nature of each theme next and cite the sources that exemplify particular themes.

Constructing Self and Others Through Collaborative Communication

In much of the literature reviewed for this chapter, issues of identity, role, and relationships between self and other(s) were raised or invoked in empirical studies. In many cases, these constructions of self and other impeded or enabled collaboration to take place; in other cases, it was viewed by authors as an antecedent to or necessary component of collaboration.

One prominent dimension of constructing self-other identities concerns relative power as it is constructed in communication. As I noted earlier, equality is presumed to be a necessary or preferred characteristic of much collaborative activity. Some authors emphasized this characteristic strongly (Akhavian et al., 1999), and others questioned whether it is even possible (Stohl & Walker, 2002). Where equality is lacking, usually power is in play. Much of the literature in the health context raised the issue of relative power related to the professional status of doctors relative to patients or nurses or of health professionals in relation to patients or families (cf. Akhavain et al., 1999; Coopman, 2001; Young & Flower, 2001). In communicating collaboratively, doctors and other high-status health professionals are asked to give up or share some power through their communication practices. The study by

Brashers, Haas, Klingle, and Neidig (2000) of AIDS activists' self-advocacy in their doctor-patient interactions provided a good example:

> When I first began seeing my physician 7 years ago I was a "yes" patient. I never asked questions, I did whatever the doctor said. The doctor was an authority figure and I was afraid to question his decisions or report how I really felt. I've since learned the importance of communication with my doctor. He's a human being just like me, he doesn't always know what's best for me. (p. 385)

Doctors who listen to lower-status communication partners and who may even seek their input and/or permission become collaborative partners in health care, and their identities as "experts" are reconstructed. Brashers et al. exemplified this transformation:

> Since my physician had so little to do with my early care, and because I have become a well-known proponent of self empowerment, she is careful with her suggestions. I tend to educate her as much as she educates me. I'm probably the longest-lived full-blown PWA [person with AIDS] in this city, so who is to argue with my success? . . . My physician and I are partners in learning how to win this fight. (p. 389)

In another example from the health communication literature, Ellingson and Buzzanell (1999) depicted such episodes as a dialogic of power and control. According to Ellingson and Buzzanell, "the process of continually negotiating a balance between retaining and sharing control with the physician is crucial to patient communication satisfaction. When control is shared, participants feel as though they are in partnerships" (p. 168).

The weaker partner does not always push the more powerful partner to relinquish power in order to collaborate. The study by Hermansen and Wiederholt (2001) of pharmacist-patient communication examined what pharmacists could do interpersonally to encourage patients' collaborative willingness (the patient's likelihood to engage in social and self-disclosure activities with his or her provider). They found that pharmacists presenting themselves in caring, trustworthy and respectful ways to patients was related to collaborative willingness of patients.

This exploration of defining relative power through communication occurs in other contexts as well. Bouman's (2002) description of an interprofessional collaboration between health communication professionals and television professionals serves as a case in point. This collaboration involved the creation of health campaign messages. Bouman detailed the contradictions between the idealized form of collaboration (equal roles) and the real-life reality where the "television world was perceived as far more powerful" (p. 233). The television professionals viewed the health communication professionals as the "visiting" or dependent party in the collaboration. Bouman's analysis showed that the constructions of relative power in these two groups of professionals changed across the course of the collaboration. To reconstruct the power in their own roles, the health communication professionals learned to take on tasks during production to appear to be more in service of the television professionals. This shift necessitated moving from a more formal role (in which formal approval would be needed) to informal communication strategies that positioned themselves as more useful to the television professionals, thus resulting in more control over the project. This turn of communication strategy also empowered the health professionals to become more collaborative.

In interorganizational contexts, simply defining who is "in" and who is "out" and trying to define oneself as "in" raises identity and power issues. In the study by Lawrence et al. (1999) of the whale watching community of stakeholders in the northwest, some actors struggled to explain their role in the collaboration. According to Lawrence et al., "In negotiating roles in some collaborative activity, actors may successfully present themselves as important to the resolution of an issue and still remain excluded or marginal in the network of representation" (p. 494). Struggles to specify the boundaries of membership were also described in the account by Jones and Bodker (1998) of team collaboration between U.S. and South African conflict specialists and educators. The social justice project and the past experiences of the South African participants, in particular, created such discomfort with defining team membership and issues of control that the group essentially agreed not to resolve them, opting instead to simply work toward coordinated action (e.g., reporting processes, limited decision-making structures) without really denoting the governance and membership issues.

In other contexts, definitions of "member" are much more fluid. The bona fide group perspective considers membership boundaries to be permeable and somewhat unstable (Lammers & Krikorian, 1997; Putnam & Stohl, 1996). The communities of practice literature tends to treat membership as completely volitional and fluid, as determined by self-interest and self-definition (Lesser & Storck, 2001; Wenger & Snyder, 2000). An even more fluid example of collaborative communication is presented in the study by Mangrum, Fairley, and Wieder (2001) of informal problem-solving (IPS) meetings in an information technology firm. Collaborative participants in IPS meetings are determined by the nature of the problem being solved, the availability of employees to add to the conversation, and the numbers of individuals whose work is affected by the problem. The "membership" in these meetings changes as the group encounters new and different problems.

In another domain concerning construction of identities through collaboration, the conflict literature deals with issues of self-construal (Oetzel & Ting-Toomey, 2003; Ting-Toomey, Oetzel, & Yee-Jung, 2001), face of self and others (Jameson, 2004; Oetzel & Ting-Toomey, 2003), and construction of partner as "competent" (Lakey & Canary, 2002). This research recognizes that the ways in which individuals construct parts of their own identity and those of their interaction partners can fundamentally shape the collaborative interactions. In fact, when construction or maintenance of certain identities or roles is overwhelmingly strong (e.g., support face of other), it may inhibit collaborative communication. Oetzel and Ting-Toomey found that high regard for another's face was related to avoidance styles of conflict. In a study of buyer-seller role taking in a negotiation study, Drake (2001) discovered that the role taken was a stronger predictor of integrative versus distributive tactics than the culture of the participant. In their work on self-construal, Ting-Toomey et al. learned that construal of oneself as "independent" or "interdependent" within the context of a relationship affected the use of integrative and distributive conflict styles.

In other approaches, identity shifts over the course of collaborations. In his discussion of dialogue, Barge (2002) argued that a defining feature of dialogue involves the move from breaking things into parts and emphasizing difference to seeing things holistically and creating space for learning. In this move, the participants must recreate their construction of one another from "opponent" to "partner." Mintzberg et al. (1996) mentioned this dynamic of converting the "enemy" into a partner:

> In tightly knit groups, outsiders are often the enemy. And so anyone who enjoys his or her collaborative partnership with an outsider can become suspect. Indeed, people who do this often or long can get treated as traitors—the enemy. They become "collaborators." (p. 67)

In another example, Stone (2000) examined the effects of collaboration on strategic planning processes of individual nonprofits. Identity issues became very salient for one participant who described a shift from perceiving himself as the sole producer and marketer of a new program to seeing himself as a coproducer with others. Stone interpreted this report as "not only a shift in how he views his management responsibilities but a more fundamental shift in self-identity relative to the collective resources of the community" (p. 110).

In their model of social-contextual coping with everyday problems, Berg and colleagues (1998, 2003) argued that we reconstruct identities of strangers and enemies as well as those of our friends. In this conceptualization, in some cases, individuals use others to cope with everyday problems by assigning roles relative to the problem situation. Others might be designated as co-problem solvers or delegates to solve some portion of the problem. Thus, these relationships go beyond supportive communicative relationships. The study by Berg, Johnson, Meegan, and Strough (2003) of young and older married couples illustrated that collaboration provides a means of accomplishing everyday tasks and decision making. Interestingly, the reconstruction of identities in married pairs during collaboration sometimes involved creating a temporary power imbalance. Berg et al. asserted:

> Collaboration was also described as one person directing the problem solving and consulting with the other partner, potentially involving more control by one member of the couple. Collaboration was described by eight individuals as one person taking the lead, formulating a plan, and then allowing the other person to refine the plan. (p. 49)

In sum, a strong theme throughout the reviewed literature, and across most of the contexts, suggests that collaboration invokes issues of identity construction for self and collaborative partners. At times, this literature indicates that identity reconstruction may be necessary to create true collaborative interaction. Limits on one's ability or willingness to construct one's own or another's identity or to be defined differently by others (e.g., as a partner, as assertive) may hinder one's willingness or ability to interact collaboratively.

Collaborative Communication as Mutual Exchange

An overarching characteristic of collaboration, as defined for this review and elsewhere, involves the sharing of goals, resources, and means to a common goal. One theme in this literature concerns the mutual exchange of communication resources. As Berg et al. (1998) asserted, collaborative problem solving entails exchanging (among other things) different perspectives, guidance, hints, strategies, and praise and encouragement. Kumpulainen & Kaartinen (2003) found in their study of peer collaboration that students' verbal interactions encompass exchanging reasoning, hypothesizing, arguing, questioning, and equal participation. They contended that "collaboration between peers seemed to be supported by reciprocal attempts to create a joint meaning" (p. 366). In another investigation, the description by Clark et al. (1996) of their joint research collaboration (teachers with academic researchers) emphasized not doing the same task (i.e., research work) together, but "understanding the [different] work of one another" (p. 196). For Clark et al., this crucial distinction avoids privileging the work of one group (researchers) over the work of the others (teachers). They stressed dialogue, rather than work, to become the shared focus in collaboration.

In the health context, the equal *value* for expertise, opinion, and information exchanged is as important as the exchange itself. Akhavian et al. (1999) maintained that "each contribution [of collaborative partners in a treatment team] is of equal importance and value and each contribution affects the outcome" (p. 4). The explicit reason given for prioritizing equal value of resources brought to the common task is the decrease in the "potential for blame" (p. 4).

The pattern of talk between physicians and their patients also highlights this notion of equal exchange. Ellingson and Buzzanell (1999) noted how the feminine style of talk desired by the cancer patients in their study induced the notion of "equality" (p. 173). According to Ellingson and Buzzanell, "Equality is fostered through matching experiences to indicate that others are not alone in their experiences . . . our participants sought give and take in their conversations with their physicians" (p. 173). Furthermore, in their study of physician-patient communication, Street, Krupat, Bell, Kravitz, & Haidet (2003) underscored that physicians and patients "can use their own communication to help the other be a more effective communicator. For example, if they are not receiving sufficient information, support, and personalized care, patients can engage in simple, but powerful communication tactics (asking questions, expressing concerns, offering opinions) that often will elicit more of these resources from physicians" (p. 614). Young and Flower (2001) argued for the notion of reciprocity between physicians and patients, and they created *collaborative interpretation* as a tool to encourage providers and patients to "develop a reciprocal relationship, where the exchange of information, identification of problems, and development of solutions is an interactive process" (p. 71).

In some contexts, concerns over ownership of communicative resources and trust must be overcome before collaboration, involving the exchange of resources, can succeed. Medved et al. (2001) described one version of this problem as the "information use tension" (p. 146), in which leaders must build coalitions through information dissemination (within collaborations) while, at the same time, protecting information for use in the marketplace. Medved et al. found that "in order to succeed in the [collaborative] the community leaders had to possess highly context sensitive communication skills" (p. 146). Browning, Beyer, & Shetler (1995) detailed similar problems at Sematech (a high-tech consortium). Members of the consortium struggled over how much proprietary information from their home organizations that they could share with other consortium members. As Browning et al. reported, "members felt they had to keep such information secret, and long periods of silence characterized meetings" (p.135). The group finally realized that the unspoken "secrets" weren't really secrets at all, and the differences between firms were primarily cultural, not technological. The Sematech case raises an interesting set of issues about collaboration among competitors. In the case of Sematech, the participants had motivations to work together. In the case of the whale watching community surrounding Vancouver Island and the San Juan Islands, stakeholders sometimes had contentious and competitive stances toward one another. For this group, sharing their "discursive resources" to negotiate even the meaning of the social object of collaboration is problematic.

Of the literature presented here, the communities of practice (COPs) liter-ature is probably the most focused on collaboration through the sharing of informational resources. Iverson & McPhee (2002) used Wenger's (1998) three features of COP to explain how they facilitated knowledge management. These authors describe how COP members share their interaction (i.e., through ideas, stories, knowledge, insights, questions, critiques, and frustra-tions). COPs also share a repertoire for negotiating meaning (i.e., through sto-ries, jokes, jargon, theories, forms, and other communicative techniques). Iver-son and McPhee illustrated how these features of COPs constitute an organization's informal and emergent knowledge management structure. In line with this more open mutual exchange of information, Monge et al. (1998) argued for a model of production of public goods (communication) in alliances. They discussed the sharing of connectivity (the ability of partners to directly communicate with each other through the information and commu-nication system of the alliance) and communality (the availability of a com-monly accessible pool of information to alliance partners). The exchange of these public goods is a key feature and benefit of belonging to such alliances.

In sum, collaborative communication involves mutual exchange of com-municative resources like those discussed above. These sources depict collabo-rations as fundamentally concerned with exchanging such resources, and in some cases (COPs), such negotiation may be the bulk of the activity or work of the collaborative. For other collaborations, exchange of ideas and contribu-tions to decision making may be more featured in the talk. In all cases, some sense of reciprocity is embedded in the process of collaboration, although the importance of equality of contributions from partners varies with perspectives.

Collaborative Communication as Skill

These articles do not present collaboration as "natural" or easy. Many selected publications assume that one must master some skills in order to accomplish collaboration. Although none actually talk about collaborative skills, several recommended or provided evidence of skill-like communication competen-cies. To be a skilled collaborator, one likely needs to build communicative competencies in integrative behaviors (Canary et al., 2001; Gross et al., 2004; Meiners & Miller, 2004), like showing concern for others, reasoning with oth-ers, expressions of trust, using elaboration, directness and mutual concessions, showing support for partner's conflict goals (Lakey & Canary, 2002), provid-ing face support (Jameson, 2004; Oetzel & Ting-Toomey, 2003), maintaining a warm and friendly tone (Ellingson & Buzzanell, 1999; Hermansen & Wiederholt, 2001; Meiners & Miller, 2004; Street & Millay, 2001), assertive-ness (e.g., asking questions, providing opinions) (Brashers et al., 2000; Street & Millay, 2001; Young & Klingle, 1996), use of effective communication structures (DiMatteo et al., 1994; Keyton & Stallworth, 2003; Young & Flower, 2001), group integrative conflict skills (Kuhn & Poole, 2000), and mastery over informal group repertoires (Iverson & McPhee, 2002), among others. This orientation toward skills suggests that collaboration may be something that can be learned and mastered. As indicated in the learning approach to collaboration explained earlier (Barron, 2000), educators of young children are attempting to train kids to collaborate. Interestingly, little scholarship exists about learning of these skills at other points in the life span or in particular contexts.

Literature embracing this skills approach to collaboration also tends to assume that different skills are likely suitable at various points during collaboration or in diverse contexts. In three studies among those reviewed here (Franz & Jin, 1995; Taylor, 2002; Taylor & Donald, 2004), collaboration was depicted as a process wherein partners begin in more avoidance or dominating modes of interaction and progress toward more integrative interactions. Furthermore, Rudawsky et al. (1999) found that competition and collaboration might be used in combination (especially by women). Gross et al. (2004) discovered that controlling strategies were considered effective, even if not always as appropriate, and Weider-Hatfield and Hatfield (1996) contended that superiors in work settings sometimes did better with a dominating style of conflict management. Therefore, this skills approach implies that situational contingencies operate on these skill sets.

In summary, this literature typically presents collaboration in terms of skills that can be learned, mastered, and then applied situationally. Unfortunately, this review indicates little convergence on a specific set of skills that are paramount to collaboration, although themes of a cooperative orientation run through many of them.

Communicative Alternatives to Collaboration

A final theme running through this literature on communication and collaboration concerns alternatives to collaborative communication. Several authors discuss the alternative communication behaviors and activities that are juxtaposed with collaborative ones. Distributive behaviors (marked by competitive, aggressive, and dominant communication patterns) and avoidance behaviors (where engagement with partners is not made) are opposed to integrative ones (Cai, Wilson, & Drake, 2000; Canary et al., 2001; Franz & Jin, 1995; Gross et al., 2004; Kuhn & Poole, 2000; Lakey & Canary, 2002; Meiners & Miller, 2004; Oetzel & Ting-Toomey, 2003; Ting-Toomey et al., 2001; Weider-Hatfield & Hatfield, 1995). Some authors have argued that alternatives to collaboration may be preferable in some instances. According to evidence presented by Weider-Hatfield and Hatfield, dominant conflict styles might be more effective than collaborative ones in particular contexts and circumstances. Moreover, we should remember that collaboration is not really a polar opposite of competitive/dominating behaviors but, rather, occasionally even a companion strategy in some cases (Taylor, 2002).

A useful way to consider alternatives to collaboration is to examine the portraits of situations examined in these sources of the absence of collaboration. For nurses and patients, the absence of collaboration with physicians underscores the reality of a status-based relationship in which physicians direct and control interactions and lower-status individuals have very little say in decision making. On the other hand, the constraining forces connected to belonging to a collaboration may make it more advantageous, at times, to act independently. Stone (2000) and Miller, Scott, Stage, and Birkholt (1995) provided some evidence that coordination among agencies can become costly in terms of autonomy. Kumpulainen and Kaartinen (2003) also observed that less competent collaborative partners may sometimes be equally likely to persuade others to take their stand on a matter in question, leading the group to negative outcomes. Hardy and Phillips (1998) detailed the dangers of giving up too much independence to collaborative causes. In their study of a UK refugee system, they explained how systems of "compliance" may masquerade as collaboration. In compliance systems, "power is neither shared nor is participation, strictly speaking, voluntary. Instead of reciprocal relations we find in collaboration, the dominant partner uses its power to regulate weaker parties which have no choice but to cooperate" (Hardy and Phillips, p. 224). Stone also acknowledged that members may feel pressure to continue in collaborations for fear of what will happen in their absence. In her study of a welfare-to-work partnership, members considered the payoffs relative to costs of participation, but they also professed concern "that they could not afford to be absent from partnership meetings because decisions might be made that would materially affect their organizations" (p. 106). In this way, independence becomes less optional, and collaboration participation becomes coercive.

In sum, there are numerous alternatives to collaboration, and, to some extent, these other choices underscore the voluntary nature of collaborative communication. However, we can also see that at least in some contexts—those that involve more than two partners—coercive forces may penalize noncollaborators for lack of participation. Alternatives also likely offer benefits over collaboration in some circumstances, and it is wise to learn the limits of collaborative communication in terms of appropriateness and effectiveness.

RESEARCH AGENDA

Considerable work has been done across these domains in explicating collaborative interaction and its contexts. The final task for this chapter is to suggest some directions for future research and theory building, particularly some directions of research across the communication discipline that could further our understanding of collaborative interaction in general. So, in that mode of synthesis, I offer the following directions for future research in the areas of theory, topics and context, and methods.

Theory

Many theoretical perspectives have been invoked in the works presented in this review, including public goods theory (Monge et al., 1998), structuration (Browning & Beyer, 1998), institutionalization (Lawrence, Hardy, & Phillips, 2002; Phillips, Lawrence, & Hardy, 2000), theories of organizational environment (Miller et al., 1995), discourse perspectives (Lawrence et al., 1999), critical dialogic perspectives (Zoller, 2004), communicative competence (Canary et al., 2001), face-negotiation theory (Oetzel & Ting-Toomey, 2003), and cultural individualism-collectivism (Oetzel & Ting-Toomey, 2003), among others. Only a few of these theoretical lenses are centrally communicative, and we have seen no truly cross-domain theory of collaborative interaction emerge. The obvious recommendation is that we ought to develop one.

My argument here will first concern why we ought to build one comprehensive theory of collaborative interaction rather than work in theoretical isolation within narrow domain areas. First, as we can see from this review, much about collaborative interaction has been shared across contexts. Building on what appear to be emerging dimensions of collaboration across areas, we may be able to create a powerful explanatory framework to account for the effects of and contingencies related to collaborative interaction as well as a communication theory that is central enough to tie great segments of the discipline together, thus enabling needed integration.

Second, as we acknowledge the need for communication theory, in general, and the trends across disciplines that treat collaboration as a chief element of other processes and domains (e.g., education, management, health provision, knowledge creation and transfer, decision making, political processes, and intercultural exchange), communication scholars enjoy an opportunity to produce theory that other disciplines will find relevant and useful in explaining their own phenomena. That opportunity ought not to be missed. Communication scholars have legitimate grounds to claim expertise on this topic, and working together is most likely to produce a high-quality integrated theoretical development that may be easily adopted by other disciplines.

Third, collaboration is already a highly applied concept in many diverse contexts. Learning more about collaborative interaction and formulating a powerful covering theory concerning its operation positions communication scholars to speak authoritatively on many applied questions related to health care, service integration, organizational structures for decision making, marital counseling, training communication competencies for young and old alike, and many others. Arming the discipline with powerful theory that explains a highly regarded activity across many domains affords potential for applied work, grant-funded research, and contributions to society in a larger sense. In sum, therefore, working together (collaboratively) will make possible larger wins for the knowledge domain, the discipline, and the variety of real-world contexts to which such theory can be applied.

A Theoretical Model of Collaborative Interaction across Contexts

A more difficult question to answer than whether we ought to have a comprehensive theory of collaborative interaction entails what such a theory might look like. Figure 5–1 depicts a theoretical model that derives its components and relationships from the review of the literature presented above, and it advances directions for theorizing and research. I propose this model to help synthesize what current research and other scholarly works consistently point to as central issues in collaborative interaction across contexts.

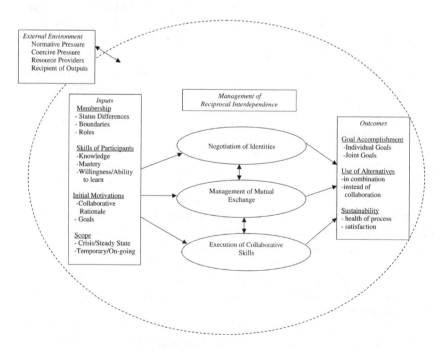

FIGURE 5–1.   Theoretical model of collaborative interaction across contexts.

External environment. As the model depicts, collaborative interaction (regardless of context) is embedded in larger environmental contexts. Although researchers acknowledge external environments in the interorganizational and group communication literature, descriptions do not appear much anywhere else. Stohl and Walker (2002) and Putnam and Stohl (1996) used bona fide group perspective to highlight the importance of external environments to internal communicative processes. Stohl and Walker asserted:

> [It] recognizes that groups and organizations are not only positioned within multiple contexts but are also constantly interacting with and through those environments, which results in changes for both the acting group and contexts. In short, to understand what is going on "inside" any group we must also understand what is going on "outside" it and the relation between these two spaces. (p. 242)

External environments are important for couples, doctor-patient pairs, classrooms, professionals working together, and any other collaborative context that can be imagined. External pressures, resources, norms, and coercive forces all matter. So, when we examine any collaborative phenomenon, we ought to be sensitive to the larger systems in which those collaborations are embedded. Married couples collaborate in the context of families; kids solve problems in larger contexts of schools and friendship networks; health-care providers and their patients interact within the structures of hospitals, insurance provision systems, legal systems, and larger cultural understandings of "health care." All of these external environments certainly exert some degree of influence over the collaborative interactions of the smaller groupings or pairings, and reciprocal effects back to the larger environmental systems likely depend on the outcomes and processes of the collaboration.

Important research directions for further unpacking of environmental influences in collaborative interactions include examining how external environments offer either support or barriers to collaboration, the importance of overarching structural arrangements (e.g., decision making, power, and role structures) to how collaborative interactions take form, the types of coercive and normative pressures from external environments that bear on would-be collaborative partners, and the expectations that various stakeholders in the environment place on collaborations.

Inputs. A variety of inputs to collaborative interaction have been identified and emphasized within the literature reviewed in this chapter. Among the most central are the characteristics of and relationships among participants (i.e., membership), initial skills, initial motivation, and the intended scope and life span of the collaborative interaction.

Membership in a collaboration constitutes a seemingly less complex matter in dyadic forms of collaborative interaction (e.g., members are defined by those in conflict). However, even though the identification of participants may be straightforward, other issues complicate consideration of the members and what is afforded by their membership in the collaborative interaction. For instance, the means of determining the partners and how the rights and responsibilities of membership are distributed may be complicated even in dyadic collaborative settings. For example, when a patient and doctor are defined as a collaborative team, membership issues might range from types of membership (e.g., If we are equals, what does that mean?) to who can withdraw or advance the partnership domain (e.g., Are we collaborating about only a single decision or all care decisions about this patient?), to what membership implies about confidentiality, information sharing, resource sharing, and/or to how we mutually mark the exclusion of outsiders (e.g., do patients and doctors mark the boundaries of their collaborative partnership to exclude family members or specialists?).

Initial skills of collaborative interactants are also critical inputs. Examining the learning of collaborative interaction skills and processes should not be examined solely by developmental scholars and should not focus primarily on young people. We ought to be assessing the degree to which these skills concordant with collaborative processes can be learned at later points in life and whether learning in one context can be transferred to others. If one learns to collaborate on a team at work, can he or she take those lessons home and collaborate with family in decision making? Such questions require answers as we develop interventions for applied contexts. The health communication scholarship is way ahead of some other domains on the issue of training individuals in collaborative skills. We should not be satisfied with describing the collaborative experiences, tools, and behaviors of individuals, groups, and organizations. We must also learn how to translate best practices, learning, and mastery of collaborative communication skills if we hope to reap the most benefit from them.

The purpose(s) of collaborative interaction as viewed from multiple perspectives also has high potential for influencing their progress. Much of the literature reviewed in this chapter suggests that the foregrounding of either individual or joint goals is one likely determinant of the processes embraced by the interactants in collaboration. In addition, the degree to which individual goals, if embraced at all, are mutually regarded as important by all participants constitutes another determinant of the processes engaged in by collaborating partners. That is, collaborations differ in the degree to which each participant perceives value in shared and individual goals. In some cases, members consider only joint goals to be legitimate, and they view individual goals as irrelevant or even dysfunctional. However, different processes for engagement are likely when mutual regard for individual goals is also considered important to all participants. Future research should unpack whether the different regard for these levels of goals reflects varying types of collaborative practice/interaction or diverse levels of collaboration (e.g., less to more advanced).

Finally, the intention for collaborative partnerships to endure over time or adopt a more ad hoc nature (e.g., IPS meetings) will affect the attentiveness that participants pay to some aspects of process. Enduring collaborative relationships likely involve attending to more aspects of interactional structure and membership than groups whose purpose and function are only intended to achieve short-term results and then dissolve. Whether the same types of collaborative interaction are useful in both long-term and short-term collaborations remains an open question. Future research should explore the frequency and purpose of collaborations of different life spans as well as the collaborative practices that work to maintain each type. Short-term collaborations may be critical in times of crisis where not much time can be spent on setting up rules of engagement, membership understandings, and structure. Having effective means of establishing quick collaborative practices might be a tremendous advantage for unexpected, disastrous, or emergent situations, such as the recent relief and recovery efforts of collaborating agencies during hurricanes Katrina and Rita.

Management of reciprocal interdependence. Although the tools and means used by collaborative interactants across contexts to achieve desired outcomes certainly vary greatly, this review indicates that all such interactions need to deal with three major process issues: negotiation of identities, management of mutual exchange, and execution of collaborative skills. How participants regard one another; the manner in which they manage exchange of resources, work product, information, and communicative resources (e.g., floor time, decision making, leadership), as well as the execution and evaluation of critical collaborative skills (e.g., face management, integrative communication tactics, dialogue) give rise, ultimately, to their outcomes. The model in Figure 5–1 asserts common issues faced in collaborative interactions and positions them as central in accounting for outcomes. Thompson (1967) argued that dealing with reciprocal interdependence mandates mutual adjustment and that simpler and easily controllable strategies (for dealing with pooled and sequential interdependence) like standardization and planning are not sufficient for coordination. This review provides evidence that much of that mutual adjustment involves communication skills—mutual adjustments of identity and mutual regard for partners, face saving and construction, give and take of bargaining, and information sharing.

Future research in each of these three areas can help us to develop a clear theoretical understanding of the generative mechanism of collaborative interaction. Such a mechanism serves as the driving force of collaborative inter-action and accounts for how inputs are translated into outcomes. Research into the concept of mutual adjustment will likely lead to consideration of uncertainty reduction, equity, negotiation, and other related constructs as ways to account for how collaborating participants regard one another and interact. In these reciprocally interdependent relationships, issues of inde-pendence and mutuality may be addressed in a synergistic exchange. Research needs to further analyze just how participants in collaboration manage this type of interaction, how they recognize it as appropriate, and how they eval-uate their experiences with it. We have noted evidence that, in several contexts, individuals express preferences for this type of interaction. However, its con-tingencies and constitutive components have not yet been identified.

Outcomes. Numerous outcomes are possible for consideration in collabo-rative interaction. Goal accomplishment (whether at the joint or individual levels) may be the most obvious outcome, but the use of alternatives to col-laboration (e.g., distributive communication, avoidance, hierarchy, power) has been considered an outcome in the sense that failed or stalled collaborative efforts sometimes revert to these alternatives. Furthermore, we have observed instances where alternatives have been used in combination with collaborative interaction styles. The degree to which members employ collaborative inter-action versus other types of interaction should be examined and theorized. Perhaps failure to manage some aspects of reciprocal interdependence more strongly relates to the use of some alternatives. For example, when identities cannot be satisfactorily sorted out to enable collaboration, we may observe more use of hierarchy or avoidance.

Sustainability of collaborative interaction speaks in part to the goal of ongoing relationships. Whereas some collaborations may be able to manage interdependence successfully for short periods, different strategies may be important for sustaining collaborations over time.

In sum, the model represented in Figure 5–1 provides a guidepost for the specification of a theory that will encompass many of the common features of collaborative interaction across contexts. This model integrates important inputs, processes, and outputs that appear to be critical in all collaborative interactions. A general theory of collaboration, once thoroughly developed, will be able to specify the connections among these elements and to describe the key generative mechanism that drives those relationships.

New Topics and Contexts

The topics and contexts to which collaborative communication can be applied are limitless. The current work on collaboration in the communication discipline has only scratched the surface of what can be done. This review has not been able to reveal any piece of literature dealing with collaboration-like processes in the communication literatures on families, political settings, ethics, or instructional development. Some contributions from these areas may have been missed, but the fact that none surfaced in this review suggests an abundance of opportunity. The first general recommendation concerning expanding topics for study would be for each area of the discipline to consider where collaboration fits into its own communicative phenomena and see if exploring this construct would benefit other theories and concepts within particular areas.

Second, much of the collaboration literature centers on assumptions of more "western" communication styles and characteristics. At the very least, little comparative work has been conducted across contexts to determine how collaborative interaction varies significantly among cultures. Exceptions to this claim include the conflict and negotiation research (cf. Cai et al., 2000; Drake, 2001). Those exceptions exemplify how culture appears to matter regarding how participants interact and regard the collaborative process. Less attention has been given to the cultural aspects of this type of interaction in other contexts. Collaborative interactions in cross-cultural work groups, international relief agencies and crisis coordination efforts, and doctor-patient interactions where participants do not share a common language or culture are all examples where more understanding of the cultural aspects of collaborative interaction would be warranted. The few studies that have been conducted attest to the importance and salience of cultural aspects of identity issues (e.g., face and national identification) in collaborative interactions. Cultural differences may bear upon the assumptions of "skillfulness" in these contexts and the management of exchange (e.g., values for honesty, sharing, give-and-take, trust). Processes involving key issues in the management of reciprocal interdependence most assuredly collide with cultural practice, value, and belief. These processes should be explored more in work on collaborative interaction.

Third, as recent efforts at coordination and collaboration during hurricane relief and recovery efforts have demonstrated well, researchers should attend more to situations of crisis. Although the circumstances that bring these organizations and agencies together are clearly not voluntary (e.g., some agencies are mandated to work together), they have an array of choices about how to interact (e.g., authority-based, sequentially), including collaborative interaction as it has been defined here. Taylor (2002) and Taylor and Donald (2004) called our attention to one context of crisis collaboration (i.e., hostage negotiation), but we have very few other examples. Collaboration is necessary in many crisis situations, from dyadic to more macro levels. Examples include families in crisis because of death, divorce, or dysfunctional behavior of children or parents; friendship pairs in crisis because of fractured relationships; medical crises such as emergency room decision making or battle triage; work teams in crises because of serious error or outside contingency (e.g., New York firefighters and police during on September 11, 2001), and organizational partners in crisis because of unexpected events or rapidly changing contingencies. Frequently, crises are marked by conditions of urgency, high stakes, high emotion, lack of immediately available resources, lack of available expertise, unknown and unfamiliar stakeholders and participants, and high levels of outside scrutiny during and/or after the crisis. These internal and external pressures doubtlessly affect the collaborative interaction of participants and their perceived and real options for communicating. Work across contexts ought to investigate how crises affect collaborative interaction.

Methods

A survey of Table 5–2 reveals a wide range of methods being used to study collaboration in various settings. Questionnaires have been used most frequently across domains, followed by interviews, some sort of observation/interaction analysis, and experiments. This table suggests that most of the empirical knowledge about collaboration comes from self-report data and that observation of collaboration, especially in naturalistic settings, is the thinnest slice of data. These trends indicate a few possibilities.

For researchers to establish causal relationships and build theories of collaborative communication, experiments will likely need to be in the mix. In the current literature, experiments are limited to group and dyadic contexts, and they suffer from the same critiques of most experimental literature in the communication discipline in that they primarily involve undergraduate students doing contrived tasks for extra credit. It seems prudent to explore the use of quasi-experimental designs in more naturalistic settings to further our understanding of the processes of collaborative communication practices and their effects. Comparing the results of collaborating groups (different groups with varying collaborating methods, collaborating groups versus groups led with noncollaborative methods) working on tasks that matter to them (in systems of politics, knowledge networks, expertise networks, and with natural pressures for performance) would provide information that would be immensely valuable to an understanding of collaboration. Experiments assigning natural dyads (roommates, married couples, superior-subordinate pairs) to work in a collaborative or in hierarchical manner for a single task in their normal work or personal life and then recording outcomes and process variables would also yield important insights into the relative benefits of both styles.

Second, researchers should look for new ways to observe collaborative behaviors as they naturally occur. At this point, we have very little in the way of useful schemes that compare findings about collaborative behaviors (see Anderson, Martin, and Infante, 1998, for a notable exception). Although there are standard markers of "integrative" communication behaviors, we lack a standardized measure of degree of collaboration that might be used across domains and contexts. Creating an inventory of collaborative communication behaviors and attitudes would enable researchers to compare results of verbal, nonverbal, structural, and affective/attitudinal measures of collaboration that have a history of validation and reliability. Such a tool would be immensely valuable in a program of work that explores important contingencies that affect collaboration's effectiveness and appropriateness across contexts. An extension of this idea would be to create a "collabrocation audit." Such a tool would provide researchers, across contexts, with a powerful set of tools—observation categories, interview protocols, survey instrument—that could be applied to comparatively audit the collaborative interactions of various pairs and groups of participants. The existence of such a tool could make it possible to more easily accumulate research results within this domain and thus lead to more powerful and covering claims about the phenomenon in general.

Finally, although much self-report work has already been done concerning collaboration, we can benefit from additional work with these methods by expanding the perspectives from which self-reports are taken. Often self-reports are taken from only one perspective in a study (e.g., nurses or patients). In addition, self-reports of collaborative interaction are usually obtained only from the collaborating partner as opposed to involved observers. Combining these multiple perspectives could enrich the understandings to be gained from self-report methods. One example of the knowledge to be gained in this approach involves determining whether one's own sense of collaborating is received that way by interactional partners. Is my "collaborating" perceived by you as "argumentativeness"? Can collaboration be engaged in without announcement? If patients enter a doctor's examination room primed to collaborate, will they be perceived as doing so? Similar questions could be asked about members to multiparty groups and interorganizational collaborations. Is there a threshold proportion of members that must view the interaction as collaborative before good things can happen? If 50% view a collaboration as collaborative and 50% perceive it as debate, what are the consequences for the communicative process and the outcomes? Such questions cannot be answered well by single reports of collaborative behaviors.

CONCLUSION

Collaboration is likely to be a hallmark of the century. We see calls for it in nearly every aspect of life and a need for it in many contexts. Collaboration has the potential to be empowering, egalitarian, energizing, and satisfying. Probably most importantly, it serves as a doorway to a vast sea of previously wasted input, ideas, creativity, cross-fertilization, insight, and experience. Fortunately for the communication discipline, the phenomenon is fundamentally communicative. This review has illustrated the many and varied ways that we can explore collaboration from a communication perspective, but I hope its major contribution has been to inspire readers to envision all that remains to be done—truly, a vast possibility.

NOTES

1. The past decade was chosen as a time frame for this review because it allows us to focus on the most current literature and thus provides a review of current scholarship. It also appeared through my efforts to locate materials for this review that most of the collaboration scholarship fitting the scope defined here occurred within the last decade.

2. Although choosing an a priori set of definitional parameters for this review was useful in limiting the review to a conceptually similar terrain, it also certainly had the disadvantage of not permitting inclusion of every article that employed the term *collaboration* or a similar term. At a point in this review process, I felt it necessary to set some conceptual boundaries around the review so that apples, oranges, and every other conceivable intellectual fruit wasn't being inappropriately lumped together. The scope conditions of the review certainly had influence over the themes and the definitional trends I observed—which is true of all sampling methods in any study. However, these scope conditions, in my mind, locate the most interesting and conceptually distinct territory.

REFERENCES

Note: Asterisks indicate scholarly works included in this review that appear only in tables.

Akhavain, P., Amaral, D., Murphy, M., & Uehlinger, K. C. (1999). Collaborative practice: A nursing perspective of the psychiatric interdisciplinary treatment team. *Holist Nurse Practitioner, 13*(2), 1–11.
Anderson, C. M., Martin, M. M., & Infante, D. A. (1998). Decision-making collaboration scale: Tests of validity. *Communication Research Reports, 15*, 245–255.
Austin, J. E. (2000). Strategic collaboration between nonprofits and businesses. *Nonprofit and Voluntary Sector Quarterly, 29*, 69–97.
Barge, J. K. (2002). Enlarging the meaning of group deliberation. In L. R. Frey (Ed.), *New directions in group communication* (pp. 159–177). Thousand Oaks, CA: Sage.
Barron, B. (2000). Achieving coordination in collaborative problem-solving groups. *Journal of the Learning Sciences, 9*, 403–436.
Berg, C. A., Johnson, M. M. S., Meegan, S. P., & Strough, J. (2003). Collaborative problem-solving interactions in young and old married couples. *Discourse Processes, 35*, 33–58.

Berg, C. A., Meegan, S. P., & Deviney, F. P. (1998). A social-contextual model of coping with everyday problems across the lifespan. *International Journal of Behavioral Development, 22,* 239–261.

Bonito, J. A., & Sanders, R. E. (2002). Speakers' footing in a collaborative writing task: A resource for addressing disagreement while avoiding conflict. *Research on Language and Social Interaction, 35,* 481–514.

Bouman, M. (2002). Turtles and peacocks: Collaboration in entertainment-education television. *Communication Theory, 12,* 225–244.

Brashers, D. E., Haas, S. M., Klingle, R. S., & Neidig, J. L. (2000). Collective AIDS activism and individuals' perceived self-advocacy in physician-patient communication. *Human Communication Research, 26,* 372–402.

Breu, K., & Hemingway, C. (2002). Collaborative processes in knowledge creation in communities-of-practice. *Collaborative Processes and Knowledge Creation, 11,* 147–153.

Browning, L., & Beyer, J. M. (1998). The structuring of shared voluntary standards in the U.S. semiconductor industry: Communicating to reach agreement. *Communication Monographs, 65,* 220–243.

Browning, L. D., Beyer, J. M., & Shetler, J. C. (1995). Building cooperation in a competitive industry: SEMATECH and the semiconductor industry. *Academy of Management Journal, 28,* 113–151.

Cai, D. A., Wilson, S. R., & Drake, L. E. (2000). Culture in the context of intercultural negotiation: Individualism-collectivism and paths to integrative agreements. *Human Communication Research, 26,* 591–617.

Canary, D. J., Cupach, W. R., & Serpe, R. T. (2001). A competence-based approach to examining interpersonal conflict. *Communication Research, 28,* 79–104.

Clark, C., Moss, P.A., Goering, S., Herter, R.J., Lamar, B., Leonard, D., et al. (1996). Collaboration as dialogue: Teachers and researchers engaged in conversation and professional development. *American Educational Research Journal, 33,* 193–231.

Coopman, S. J. (2001). Democracy, performance, and outcomes in interdisciplinary health care teams. *Journal of Business Communication, 38,* 261–284.

DiMatteo, M. R., Reiter, R. C., & Gambone, J.C. (1994). Enhancing medication adherence through communication and informed collaborative choice. *Health Communication, 6,* 253–265.

*Dixon, R. A., & Gould, O. N. (1998). Younger and older adults collaborating on retelling everyday stories. *Applied Developmental Science, 2,* 160–171.

Drake, L. E. (2001). The culture-negotiation link: Integrative and distributive bargaining through an intercultural communication lens. *Human Communication Research, 27,* 317–349.

Ellingson, L. L. (2003). Interdisciplinary health care teamwork in the clinic backstage. *Journal of Applied Communication Research, 31,* 93–117.

Ellingson, L. L., & Buzzanell, P. M. (1999). Listening to women's narratives of breast cancer treatment: A feminist approach to patient satisfaction with physician-patient communication. *Health Communication, 11,* 153–183.

Franz, C. R., & Jin, K. G. (1995). The structure of group conflict in a collaborative work group during information systems development. *Journal of Applied Communication Research, 23,* 108–127.

Gould, O. N., Osborn, C., Krien, H., & Mortenson, M. (2002). Collaborative recall in married and unacquainted dyads. *International Journal of Behavioral Development, 26*, 36–44.

Gray, B. (1989). *Collaborating: Finding common ground for multiparty problems.* San Francisco: Jossey-Bass.

Gross, M. A., Guerrero, L. K., & Alberts, J. K (2004). Perceptions of conflict strategies and communication competence in task-oriented dyads. *Journal of Applied Communication Research, 32*, 249–270.

Hardy, C., & Phillips, N. (1998). Strategies of engagement: Lessons from the critical examination of collaboration and conflict in an interorganizational domain. *Organization Science, 9*, 217–230.

Hardy, C., Phillips, N., & Lawrence, T. B. (2003). Resources, knowledge and influence: The organizational effects of interorganizational collaboration. *Journal of Management Studies, 40*, 321–347.

Heath, R. G., & Frey, L. R. (2004). Ideal collaboration: A conceptual framework of community collaboration. In P. Kalbfleisch (Ed.), *Communication yearbook 28* (pp. 189–232). Mahwah, NJ: Lawrence Erlbaum Associates.

Heath, R. G., & Sias, P. M. (1999). Communicating spirit in a collaborative alliance. *Journal of Applied Communication Research, 27*, 356–376.

Henneman, E. A. (1995). Nurse-physician collaboration: A poststructuralist view. *Journal of Advanced Nursing, 22*, 359–363.

Hermansen, C. J., & Wiederholt, J. B. (2001). Pharmacist-patient relationship development in an ambulatory clinic setting. *Health Communication, 13*, 307–325.

*Higgins, L. W. (1999). Nurses' perceptions of collaborative nurse-physician transfer decision-making as a predictor of patient outcomes in a medical intensive care unit. *Journal of Advanced Nursing, 29*, 1434–1443.

*Holleman, W. L., Bray, J. H., Davis, L., & Holleman, M.C. (2004). Innovative ways to address the mental health and medical needs of marginalized patients: Collaborations between family physicians, family therapists, and family psychologists. *American Journal of Orthopsychiatry, 74*, 242–252.

Huxham, C., & Vangen, S. (1996). Working together: Key themes in the management of relationships between public and non-profit organizations. *International Journal of Public Sector Management, 9*(7), 5–17.

Huxham, C., & Vangen, S. (2003). Leadership in the shaping and implementation of collaboration agendas: How things happen in a (not quite) joined-up world. *Academy of Management Journal, 43*, 1159–1175.

Iverson, J. O., & McPhee, R. D. (2002). Knowledge management in communities of practice: Being true to the communicative character of knowledge. *Management Communication Quarterly, 16*, 259–266.

Jameson, J. K. (2004). Negotiating autonomy and connection through politeness: A dialectical approach to organizational conflict management. *Western Journal of Communication, 68*, 257–277.

Jones, T. S., & Bodker, A. (1998). A dialectical analysis of a social justice process: International collaboration in South Africa. *Journal of Applied Communication Research, 26*, 357–373.

Kaas, M. J., Lee, S., & Peitzman, C. (2003). Barriers to collaboration between mental health professionals and families in the care of persons with serious mental illness. *Issues in Mental Health Nursing, 24,* 741–756.

Keyton, J., & Stallworth, V. (2003). On the verge of collaboration: Interaction processes versus group outcomes. In L. R. Frey (Ed.), *Group communication in context: Studies of bona fide groups* (2nd ed, pp. 235–260). Mahwah, NJ: Lawrence Erlbaum Associates.

Kuhn, T., & Poole, M. S. (2000). Do conflict management styles affect group decision-making? Evidence from a longitudinal field study. *Human Communication Research, 26,* 558–590.

Kumpulainen, K., & Kaartinen, S. (2003). The interpersonal dynamics of collaborative reasoning in peer interactive dyads. *Journal of Experimental Education, 71,* 333–370.

Lakey, S. G., & Canary, D. J. (2002). Actor goal achievement and sensitivity to partner as critical factors in understanding interpersonal communication competence and conflict strategies. *Communication Monographs, 69,* 217–235.

Lammers, J. C., & Krikorian, D. H. (1997). Theoretical extension and operationalization of the bona fide group construct with an application to surgical teams. *Journal of Applied Communication Research, 25,* 17–38.

Lawrence, T. B., Hardy, C., & Phillips, N. (2002). Institutional effects of interorganizational collaboration: The emergence of proto-institutions. *Academy of Management Journal, 45,* 281–290.

Lawrence, T. B., Phillips, N., & Hardy, C. (1999). Watching whale watching: Exploring the discursive foundations of collaborative relationships. *Journal of Applied Behavioral Science, 35,* 479–502.

Lesser, E. L., & Storck, H. J. (2001). Communities of practice and organizational performance. *IBM Systems Journal, 40,* 831–841.

Levine, J. M, & Moreland, R. L. (2004). Collaboration: The social context of theory development. *Personality & Social Psychology Review, 8,* 164–173.

Macduff, N., & Netting, F. E. (2000). Lessons learned from a practitioner-academic collaboration. *Nonprofit and Voluntary Sector Quarterly, 29,* 46–60.

Mangrum, F. G., Fairley, M. S., & Wieder, D. L. (2001). Informal problem solving in the technology-mediated work place. *Journal of Business Communication, 38,* 315–336.

*Maseide, P. (2003). Medical talk and moral order: Social interaction and collaborative clinical work. *Text, 23,* 369–403.

Medved, C. E., Morrison, K., Dearing, J. W., Larson, S., Cline, G., & Brummans, B. H. J. (2001). Tensions in community health improvement initiatives: Communication and collaboration in a managed care environment. *Journal of Applied Communication Research, 29,* 137–152.

Meiners, E. B., & Miller, V.D. (2004). The effect of formality and relational tone on supervisor/subordinate negotiation episodes. *Western Journal of Communication, 68,* 302–321.

Miller, K., Scott, C. R., Stage, C., & Birkholt, M. (1995). Communication and coordination in an interorganizational system: Service provision for the urban homeless. *Communication Research, 22,* 679–699.

Mintzberg, H., Dougherty, D., Jorgensen, J., & Westley, F. (1996). Some surprising things about collaboration—Knowing how people connect makes it work better. *Organizational Dynamics, 25*(1), 60–71.

*Mizrahi, T., & Abramson, J. (2000). Collaboration between social workers and physicians: Perspectives on a shared case. *Social Work in Health Care, 31*(3), 1–24.

Mohr, J. J., Fisher, R. J., & Nevin, J. R. (1996). Collaborative communication in inter-firm relationships: Moderating effects of integration and control. *Journal of Marketing, 60*, 103–115.

Monge, P. R., Fulk, J., Kalman, M. E., Flanagin, A. J., Parnassa, C., & Rumsey, S. (1998). Production of collective action in alliance-based interorganizational communication and information systems. *Organization Science, 9*, 411–433.

Oetzel, J. G., & Ting-Toomey, S. (2003). Face concerns in interpersonal conflict: A cross-cultural empirical test of the face negotiation theory. *Communication Research, 30*, 599–624.

*Pavitt, C., & Kemp, B. (1999). Contextual and relational factors in interpersonal negotiation strategy choice. *Communication Quarterly, 47*, 133–150.

Phillips, N., Lawrence, T. B., & Hardy, C. (2000). Inter-organizational collaboration and the dynamics of institutional fields. *Journal of Management Studies, 37*, 23–43.

Putnam, L. L., & Stohl, C. (1996). Bona fide groups: An alternative perspective for communication and small group decision making. In R. Y. Hirokawa and M.S. Poole (Eds.), *Communication and group decision making* (2nd ed., pp. 147–178). Thousand Oaks, CA: Sage.

Rudawsky, D. J., Lundgren, D. C., & Grasha, A. F. (1999). Competitive and collaborative responses to negative feedback. *International Journal of Conflict Management, 10*, 172–190.

*Stallworth, V. (1998). *Building a model of interorganizational nonprofit collaboration.* Unpublished master's thesis, University of Memphis, TN.

Stohl, C., & Walker, K. (2002). A bone fide perspective for the future of groups. In L. R. Frey (Ed.), *New directions in group communication* (pp. 237–252). Thousand Oaks, CA: Sage.

Stone, M. M. (2000). Exploring the effects of collaborations on member organizations: Washington County's welfare-to-work partnership. *Nonprofit and Voluntary Sector Quarterly, 29*, 98–119.

Street, R. L., Krupat, E., Bell, R. A., Kravitz, R. L., & Haidet, P. (2003). Beliefs about control in the physician-patient relationship: Effect on communication in medical encounters. *Journal of General Internal Medicine, 18*, 609–616.

Street, R. L., & Millay, B. (2001). Analyzing patient participation in medical encounters. *Health Communication, 13*, 61–73.

Strough, J., Berg, C. A., & Meegan, S. P. (2001). Friendship and gender differences in task and social interpretations of peer collaborative problem solving. *Social Development, 10*, 1–22.

Taylor, P. J. (2002). A cylindrical model of communication behavior in crisis negotiations. *Human Communication Research, 28*, 7–48.

Taylor, P. J., & Donald, I. (2004). The structure of communication behavior in simulated and actual crisis negotiation. *Human Communication Research, 30*, 443–478.

Thompson, J. D. (1967). *Organizations in action.* New York: McGraw-Hill.

Ting-Toomey, S., Oetzel, J. G., & Yee-Jung, K. (2001). Self-construal types and conflict management styles. *Communication Reports, 14,* 87–104.

Tschannen, D. (2004). The effect of individual characteristics on perceptions of collaboration in the work environment. *MEDSURG Nursing, 13,* 312–318.

Weider-Hatfield, D., & Hatfield, J. D. (1995). Relationships among conflict management styles, levels of conflict, and reactions to work. *Journal of Social Psychology, 135,* 687–698.

Weider-Hatfield, D., & Hatfield, J. (1996). Superiors' conflict management strategies and subordinate outcomes. *Management Communication Quarterly, 10,* 189–208.

Wenger, E. C. (1998). *Communities of practice: Learning, meaning, and identity.* Cambridge, England: Cambridge University Press.

Wenger, E. C., & Snyder, W. M. (2000, January/February). Communities of practice: The organizational frontier. *Harvard Business Review, 78*(1), 139–145.

Wilczenski, F.L., Bontrager, T., Ventrone, P., & Correia, M. (2001). Observing collaborative problem-solving processes and outcomes. *Psychology in the Schools, 38,* 269–281.

*Yoshimura, S. M. (2004). Emotional and behavioral responses to romantic jealousy expressions. *Communication Reports, 17,* 85–101.

Young, A., & Flower, L. (2001). Patients as partners, patients as problem-solvers. *Health Communication, 14,* 69–97.

Young, M., & Klingle, R. S. (1996). Silent partners in medical care: A cross-cultural study of patient participation. *Health Communication, 8,* 29–53.

*Zoller, H. M. (2000). A place you haven't visited before: Creating the conditions for community dialogue. *Southern Communication Journal, 65,* 191–208.

Zoller, H. M. (2004). Dialogue as global issue management: Legitimizing corporate influence in the transatlantic business dialogue. *Management Communication Quarterly, 18,* 204–240.

CHAPTER CONTENTS

6 Bullying at School and in the Workplace: A Challenge for Communication Research

MAILI PÖRHÖLÄ
SANNA KARHUNEN
SINI RAINIVAARA
University of Jyväskylä, Finland

In this chapter, previous literature concerning school bullying and workplace harassment is reviewed from a communication perspective. The chapter details the seriousness and extensiveness of bullying, among both children at school and adults at work. We intend to provoke discussion of how communication research and theory might help us in understanding and explaining bullying. As elaborated here, bullying appears in interaction situations, mostly in the forms of verbal and nonverbal communication; it exists in the interpersonal relationship of bully and victim, and it can be associated with group communication processes and the structuration of groups, as well as with organizational and cultural communication processes. The benefits of applying communication theories and constructs to research focusing on bullying are demonstrated, and suggestions for future studies are made.

*B*ullying, mobbing, and *harassment* are examples of the terms used to describe negative, aggressive, and unjust behavior directed either at peers in school or at workmates, subordinates, or superiors in the workplace. The purpose of these intentionally aggressive or hurtful forms of behavior is to harm, subjugate, or humiliate the victim. Scholars regard bullying as a systematic and long-lasting subjection process, in which the participants are not equally matched (e.g., Einarsen, 2000; Hazler & Miller, 2001; Leymann, 1986; Naylor & Cowie, 1999; Olweus, 1978, 1993; Salmivalli, 1998; Vartia-Väänänen, 2003).

Although, as we demonstrate in the following section, there are some differences between the terms used to refer to this kind of behavior, we employ

---

Correspondence: Maili Pörhölä, Department of Communication, University of Jyväskylä, FI-40014, University of Jyväskylä, Finland; email: maili.porhola@jyu.fi

Communication Yearbook 30, pp. 249–301

the term *bullying* in this chapter as an umbrella term covering physical, verbal, and nonverbal attacks directed toward the victim or victims, as well as the direct and indirect forms of hurting, abusing, or socially excluding a peer or peers, a superior, or subordinates. In order to avoid annoying repetition, however, we also use the term *harassment* synonymously with *bullying* to refer to these phenomena.

In this chapter, our first goal is to detail the seriousness and extensiveness of bullying among both children at school and adults at work. We examine bullying in the two contexts of school and workplace side by side in order to demonstrate the similarities and differences in the behavior of children and adults in various bullying processes.

The second goal of this chapter is to demonstrate the ways in which bullying is realized in the processes of interaction between the parties and to show that it relates closely to various communication processes taking place between individuals and within groups. We claim that bullying is a communication phenomenon that can and should be examined by means of communication constructs and theories. As we elaborate in this chapter, bullying appears in interaction situations, mostly in the forms of verbal and nonverbal communication. It exists in the interpersonal relationship of bully and victim, and it can be associated with group communication processes and the structuration of groups. As our third goal, we intend to provoke discussion of how communication research and theory might help us in understanding and explaining bullying.

The literature reviewed in this chapter represents research conducted within several disciplines, including psychology, communication, and management. This research has been reported in disciplinary-specific as well as in multidisciplinary books and journals. Although we did not set out to offer cross-cultural comparisons, the literature reviewed has been conducted in various countries and in a variety of cultures, such as in Europe (especially in the Nordic countries), the United States, Canada, Australia, and Asia, and, for this reason, it should provide a broad perspective on issues related to bullying. Perhaps most importantly, it illustrates the universality of bullying, both at school and in the workplace.

Since the research into workplace bullying and bullying at school originated in and has been strongly promoted in Scandinavia, the greater part of the literature examined in this chapter represents the research carried out by Scandinavian researchers. Notably, because of space constraints, this chapter cannot provide an overview of all of the extensive research on bullying at school and in the workplace, but rather, we quite selectively introduce some of the more important issues and problems, the understanding of which may be able to make a significant contribution to communication research in the future.

In the following sections, previous literature concerning school bullying and workplace harassment is reviewed from a communication perspective by raising issues central to communication research, such as the exchange and appraisal of messages, the establishment and maintenance of interpersonal relationships, the processes of group formation, organizational communication processes, and the effects of communication. The benefits of applying communication theories to research focusing on bullying are demonstrated by an examination of some well-known communication theories and concepts as examples of the communicative understanding available. Throughout the chapter, suggestions for future studies will be made, investigations that involve treating bullying as a communication phenomenon.

DEFINING BULLYING AT SCHOOL AND IN THE WORKPLACE

We begin with an examination of the concepts used in previous literature to describe bullying at school and in the workplace. A large number of terms have been used to label this phenomenon. A closer review of these labels indicates that some terms resemble each other very closely; they can be (and have been) used synonymously. In the following, we offer a short review of these terms.

Einarsen, Hoel, Zapf, and Cooper (2003) investigated bullying at work in Europe; Einarsen (2000) researched the concept in Scandinavian countries, and Keashly and Jagatic (2003) analyzed the corresponding American perspective. The concept of school bullying has also been considered broadly in previous literature (see, for example, Smith et al., 1999). Since extensive analyses of this kind are available, we do not seek to repeat those summaries in this chapter. Instead, we will briefly identify the most dominant similarities of (and differences between) the terms broadly used in the literature concerning bullying at school and in the workplace.

Therefore, we focus on three kinds of issues. First, we describe common features shared by several broadly used definitions describing bullying both at school and in the workplace. Second, we highlight fundamental differences between the concepts of bullying at school and in the workplace, and third, we underscore the role of communication in prior definitions of bullying.

Concepts Most Closely Related to Each Other

Whereas the terms *bullying* and *victimization* have become general in studies focusing on aggressive and abusive behavior demonstrated by children and adolescents at school (Olweus, 2003), a great number of different labels have been applied to the corresponding behavior of adults at the workplace. These terms include *harassment* (Brodsky, 1976), *scapegoating* (Thylefors, 1987), *mobbing* (Leymann, 1990, 1996; Zapf, 1999), *psychological terror* (Leymann, 1996), *work harassment* (Björkqvist, Österman, & Hjelt-Bäck, 1994), *bullying* (Adams, 1992; Einarsen & Skogstad, 1996; Hoel & Cooper, 2001; Salin, 2001), *workplace aggression* (Baron & Neuman, 1996), *abusive behavior* and *emotional abuse* (Keashly, 1998; Keashly, Trott, & MacLean, 1994). Terms such as *petty tyranny* (Ashforth, 1994) and *workplace trauma* (C. B. Wilson, 1991) have most clearly referenced the hostile behaviors of employers and supervisors directed at their subordinates. Additional terms for this kind of mental violence at work include *employee mistreatment* (Meares, Oetzel, Torres, Derkacs, & Ginossar, 2004), *employee abuse* (C. B. Wilson, 1991), and *employee emotional abuse* (Lutgen-Sandvik, 2003). (For reviews, see Einarsen, 2000; Vartia-Väänänen, 2003.) *Sexual harassment* (Fitzgerald & Shullman, 1993) can also constitute one form of bullying occurring at the workplace.

   Bullying. According to Olweus (2003), "[a] student is being bullied or victimised when he or she is exposed, repeatedly and over time, to negative actions on the part of one or more other students" (p. 62). Very similarly, Smorti, Menesini, and Smith (2003) described bullying as "a subcategory of aggressive behavior, but of a particularly vicious kind, inasmuch as it is directed, often repeatedly, toward a particular victim who is unable to effectively defend himself or herself" (p. 417). Olweus added that bullying behavior often occurs without apparent provocation, and it can be considered a form of abuse. He has also used the term *peer abuse* as a label for this phenomenon. According to Olweus, the abusive context and the relationship characteristics of the interacting partners set bullying apart from other forms of abuse, such as child abuse and spouse abuse.
   Including the same elements as featured in the definitions given by Olweus (2003), as well as by Smorti and colleagues (2003), Batsche and Knoff (1994) defined bullying as "a form of aggression in which one or more students physically and/or psychologically (and more recently, sexually) harass another student repeatedly over a period of time" (p. 165), and Hoover, Oliver, and Hazler (1992) described it as "attempts by stronger students to harm a weaker victim, presumably in the absence of provocation. The attempted harm can be of either a physical or psychological nature and is longitudinal in nature" (p. 5). In the Peer Relations Questionnaire of Rigby and Slee, bullying is characterized as what happens when "someone is deliberately hurting or frightening someone weaker than themselves for no good reason. This may be done in dif-

ferent ways: by hurtful teasing, threatening actions or gestures, name-calling or hitting or kicking" (as cited in Peterson & Ribgy, 1999, p. 482).

Although *bullying* has widely been adopted in scientific literature as a term to denote the kind of behavior of children described above, the complexity of this term has posed several problems for researchers. One of the first problems in empirical studies has been translating the term from English into other languages. An equivalent word that covers exactly the same meaning is impossible to find. As Smorti and colleagues (2003) observed, some terms are more specific in describing the negative actions of peers toward another peer, while others refer to social exclusion and psychological bullying or to group episodes, and yet others refer to direct physical types of bullying.

In Japan, for example, a largely independent research tradition focusing on *ijime* has emerged. Morita, H. Soeda, K. Soeda, and Taki (1999) argued that *ijime* refers more to psychological than to physical aggression, and it is often perpetrated by the whole class against a victim (e.g., by collective ignoring or social exclusion) rather than by one or a few pupils, as in situations called *bullying* elsewhere. In Japan, exclusion and the shunning of a classmate are much more typical forms of bullying than physical and verbal forms.

Bullying in the workplace has been defined by several researchers. For example, Einarsen (1999) contended that "the concept refers to a rather specific phenomenon where hostile and aggressive behaviours, be it physical or non-physical, are directed systematically at one or more colleagues or subordinates leading to stigmatisation and victimisation of the recipient" (p. 17). In an earlier definition, Einarsen and his colleagues paid special attention to the imbalance of power in the relationships of the parties, asserting that "[a] person is bullied or harassed when he or she feels repeatedly subjected to negative acts in the workplace, acts that the victim may find it difficult to defend themselves against" (Einarsen, Raknes, & Matthiesen, 1994, p. 383). Similarly, Vartia-Väänänen (2003) employed *workplace bullying* to specify "a situation in which one or more individuals are subjected to persistent and repetitive negative acts by one or more co-workers, supervisors or subordinates, and the person feels unable to defend him/herself" (p. 11).

To summarize, in these definitions, scholars agree on three criteria for bullying, 1) It is aggressive behavior or intentional doing of harm, 2) which is carried out repeatedly and over time, 3) in an interpersonal relationship characterised by an imbalance of power. In addition to the researchers and studies already mentioned, the term *bullying* has been used by different researchers in a large number of studies (e.g., Adams, 1992; Cooper, Faragher, & Hoel, 2004; Crawford, 1999; Niedl, 1995; Rayner, Sheehan, & Barker, 1999; Salmivalli, Karhunen, & Lagerspetz, 1996; Salmivalli, Lagerspetz, Björkqvist, Österman, & Kaukiainen, 1996; Vartia, 1996; Zapf, 1999).

Mobbing. Leymann (1996) recommended *bullying* as the appropriate term for activities between children and teenagers at school and the use of *mobbing* for adult behavior. He argued that much of this disastrous communication among adults does not have the characteristics of bullying. Instead, quite often, adults bully in a very sensitive manner, though still with highly stigmatizing effects. According to Leymann, the connotation of *bullying* is physical aggression and threat, a characteristic feature for bullying at school. In contrast, physical violence is very seldom found in mobbing behavior at work. Leymann emphasized that mobbing involves much more sophisticated behaviors, such as socially isolating the victim. According to Leymann, mobbing means "harassing, ganging up on someone, or psychologically terrorizing others at work" (p. 165).

Leymann (1996) used *mobbing* synonymously with *psychological terror in working life*:

> Psychological terror in working life involves hostile and unethical communication, which is directed in a systematic way by one or a few individuals mainly towards one individual who, due to mobbing, is pushed into a helpless and defenceless position, being held there by means of continuing mobbing activities. (p. 168)

Although Zapf (1999) employed *bullying* and *mobbing* interchangeably, he construed them differently, although not in the same way as Leymann (1996). Zapf treated mobbing as "psychological aggression that often involves a group of 'mobbers' rather than a single person. Theoretically, mobbing is an extreme type of social stressor at work. Unlike 'normal' social stressors, however, mobbing is a long-lasting, escalated conflict with frequent harassing actions systematically aimed at a target person" (p. 70). In turn, Zapf argued that *bullying* implies physical aggression by a single person, mostly by a supervisor, which is rare in the working context. Leymann and Zapf agree that mobbing involves less physical aggression and threat than bullying. Recently, however, this kind of distinction between the two terms seems to have fallen away, and the terms have been used synonymously by researchers (e.g., Niedl, 1996; Zapf & Einarsen, 2001).

Harassment and sexual harassment. According to Björkqvist and his colleagues (1994), *harassment* refers to repeated activities that have the aim of causing mental (sometimes also physical) pain and are directed toward one or more individuals who, for one reason or another, are not able to defend themselves. Quite similarly, by *scapegoats*, Thylefors (1987) meant one or more persons who, over a period of time, are exposed to repeated, negative actions from one or more other individuals. These two definitions stress the same characteristics that are relevant to the various definitions of bullying.

In pioneering work on harassment at work, Brodsky (1976) identified five types of work harassment: name calling, scapegoating, physical abuse, work pressures, and sexual harassment. Brodsky described harassment as repeated and persistent attempts by a person to torment, wear down, frustrate, or get a reaction from another person, as well as treatment that persistently provokes, pressures, frightens, intimidates, or otherwise brings discomfort to the recipient. In contrast to the definitions of harassment presented earlier, Brodsky emphasized the effect of negative behavior on the target. He also specified sexual harassment as one type of work harassment.

Interestingly, on one hand, it seems that the etiological development of workplace bullying has followed the same path across the Scandinavian countries and the United States, where social scientists examined the concept first, followed by the legal system picking up on it and passing laws to protect individuals from harm in the workplace. On the other hand, Scandinavian laws regarding workplace bullying and sexual harassment protect all workers, while the laws in the United States protect certain classes of "protected" workers (minorities and women). One potential reason for this difference in outcomes may be due to a sense that the legal and political systems in the United States are correcting for past wrongdoings. However, in the Scandinavian countries there is no need to create classes of individuals who are protected because the history of discrimination is not as salient.

According to Pryor and Fitzgerald (2003), two general types of sexual harassment have been distinguished: 1) unwelcome sexual or gender-related behavior that creates a hostile environment, and 2) "quid pro quo" behavior, where the unwelcome behavior becomes a term or condition of employment or advancement. They explained that, in the legal analysis of sexual harassment, sexual coercion often constitutes "quid pro quo" sexual harassment, where sexual or gender-related behavior comprises a term or condition of employment or advancement. Unwanted sexual attention and gender harassment often constitute what is termed *hostile environment sexual harassment*, where the sexual or gender-related behavior creates an intimidating, offensive, or hostile work environment. It may be argued that unwanted sexual attention constitutes a form of quid pro quo sexual harassment, if toleration of such behavior becomes a term or condition of employment (Fitzgerald, Gelfand, & Drasgow, 1995). According to Pryor and Fitzgerald, gender harassment comprises the most common form of sexually harassing experience, followed by unwanted sexual attention and then by sexual coercion.

The legal understanding of sexual harassment in the United States focuses upon potential employment consequences for victims. Sexual harassment is illegal because it represents a potential barrier to equal employment. Whether the perpetrator intends the behavior to be offensive or not is not the issue, according to the law. The main consideration includes the incident unwelcome behavior. Perspectives of unwelcome sexual or gender-related behaviors obviously vary from person to person and across circumstances. Perhaps the crucial feature distinguishing sexual harassment from bullying is that plaintiffs in sexual harassment lawsuits in the United States must prove that the harassment is somehow based upon gender (Pryor & Fitzgerald, 2003). (For a review of the research on sexual harassment, see, for example, Fitzgerald & Shullman, 1993; Kreps, 1993.)

Finally, it should be noted that a growing area of research in the United States focuses especially on sexual harassment established at school. Batsche and Knoff (1994), for example, have paid attention to sexual harassment in their definition of bullying at school. In the European tradition, sexual harassment at school has not usually been distinguished as a concept, but instead, the various forms of sexual harassment have been included in the concept of school bullying in the sense of name-calling, physical harassment, or insulting remarks concerning one's physical appearance, for example.

Characteristics of Bullying at School and in the Workplace

In the following pages, we compare the main characteristics of the concepts reviewed thus far and identify their most visible similarities and differences. Most definitions include common features of bullying, both at school and in the workplace, but in some respects, scholars treat the concept of bullying differently in school contexts and in working-life contexts.

The nature of hurtful behavior. In most of these definitions, bullying, mobbing, and harassment are depicted as negative behaviors directed at the target. However, while the direct forms of bullying seem to be clearly established in the existing definitions as negative actions, aggressive behavior, a form of aggression, hostile and aggressive behavior, deliberate hurting and frightening, and hostile and unethical communication, the indirect forms of this behavior have rarely been noticed explicitly at the definitional level. Indirect bullying (e.g., social exclusion and the spreading of rumors) is not addressed directly to the target; the target might be totally unaware that this kind of behavior is taking place. Yet indirect forms of bullying can be even more hurtful and long-lasting than direct forms because, in the case of indirect bullying, the victim might not even be afforded any logical situations to stand up and defend him- or herself. Although the victim clearly experiences the consequences of bullying, he or she might not even know the identity of his or her most influential bully or bullies. However, also in these cases, the role of victim is created and maintained by means of communication, which could be explicated in the definition of bullying.

In the school context among children and adolescents, empirical studies have shown that bullying behaviors include both physical (e.g., hitting, kicking, and pushing) and verbal (e.g., shouting, threatening) as well as direct (i.e., directly addressed at the target) and indirect (e.g., spreading of rumors, social exclusion) forms of violence and hurtful communication (e.g., Olweus, 1993; Salmivalli, 1998; Sharp & Smith, 1991). In work contexts, bullying consists of negative and hurtful verbal messages, both direct and indirect forms of bullying, as well as various kinds of work-related activities designed to hamper the target in the performance of his/her duties, whereas the various forms of physical violence do not usually occur in the work environment (e.g., Björkqvist et al., 1994; Einarsen & Raknes, 1997; Meek, 2004; Vartia, 1993). Hence, empirical findings suggest that the characteristics of bullying become more sophisticated in working life compared with school. However, this developmental course cannot be traced in the definitions of bullying.

Furthermore, very exceptionally, Leymann (1996) defined *mobbing* as hostile and unethical communication. As communication scholars, we would, with pleasure, move the focus from negative acts and aggressive behaviors more specifically to the negative and hurtful communication that seems to be the most typical form of bullying among both children and adults. The various forms of communication in bullying situations can be unintentionally ignored by researchers if they ask respondents to describe and evaluate the negative acts or behaviors of which they have been targets. The definitions of *bullying* should explicitly include negative and hurtful communication that is either directed toward the target or has significant reference to him or her, as in the case of indirect bullying.

Finally, instead of being examined only as the behavior of one person or a few persons directed toward another person/persons, bullying should be examined as a communication relationship between bully/bullies and victim/victims and, as such, be envisioned as an ongoing interaction process consisting of a continuous flow of exchanging and appraising messages. The nature of a bullying relationship changes all the time, according to the outcomes of this interaction. The parties involved in this interaction process (bully/bullies, victim/victims, and bystanders) have a significant role in changing the course of the bullying relationship. Definitions of bullying should recognize the relational nature of this phenomenon.

The frequency and duration of hurtful behavior. The terms *bullying* (e.g., Batsche & Knoff, 1994; Einarsen, 1999; Hoover et al., 1992; Olweus, 2003; Smorti et al., 2003; Vartia-Väänänen, 2003), *mobbing* (e.g., Leymann, 1996; Zapf, 1999), and *harassment* (Björkqvist et al., 1994; Brodsky, 1976) all refer to negative behavior that is repeated, persistent, and long-term. Hence, these definitions do not include occasional aggressive or insulting behavior in the context of either school or the workplace. The concept of mobbing offered by Leymann, for example, excludes temporary conflicts and focuses on a point in time where the psychosocial situation begins to result in a psychiatrically or psychosomatically pathological condition. Thus, he considered the distinction between *conflict* and *mobbing* to be a question not of *what* is done or *how* it is done but of the *frequency* and *duration* of what is done. Leymann even provided statistical indicators for frequency and duration by determining that, in order to be classified as mobbing, hurtful activities need to occur on a very frequent basis (statistical indicator: at least once a week) and over a long period of time (statistical indicator: at least six months).

Adherence to a temporal criterion has been criticized particularly in the school context. Ross (1996), for example, argued that it is not in the best interests of effective management of bullying because interventions should be introduced at the earliest point, when it is easiest to stop the bullying and the least damage has been caused to the victim. Our suggestion is, however, that we reserve the terms *bullying* and *mobbing* to determine the repeatedly occurring hurtful behavior and use labels such as *aggressive behavior* and *hurtful communication* to refer to occasional insulting and unethical behavior directed at a target. We want to emphasize that, in a practical sense, any hurtful incident between pupils requires intervention as soon as it occurs, in order to prevent bullying relationships from developing.

Although sexual harassment can also represent a pattern of behavior in the workplaces where it exists, single episodes of behavior may cross a threshold of severity so as to be considered sexual harassment in a legal sense, particularly in instances of blatant "quid pro quo" sexual harassment (Pryor & Fitzgerald, 2003). Hence, sexual harassment is an exception to the criterion of repetition.

The imbalance of power between the parties. An obvious imbalance in the power relationships between the parties has been clearly emphasized in the definitions focusing on bullying at school (Hoover et al., 1992; Olweus, 2003; Peterson & Rigby, 1999) as well as the work environment (e.g., Einarsen et al., 1994; Hoel & Cooper, 2001; Leymann, 1996; Vartia-Väänänen, 2003). Olweus, for example, stressed that bullying requires an imbalance in strength (an asymmetrical power relationship), which means that the student who is exposed to the negative actions has difficulty in defending himself or herself and is somewhat helpless against the student or students who harass. Similarly, Naylor and Cowie (1999) characterized bullying as being based on the systematic abuse of power. It is typified by the inequality of access to power by the bully and victim. As such, bullying does not occur when two schoolchildren of about the same strength have the odd fight or quarrel (Peterson & Rigby, 1999) nor should a conflict situation where an equal balance of power exists between the employees involved be regarded as bullying, mobbing, or harassment.

Among children, the imbalance of power might result from the target of the bullying actually being physically weaker, or he or she might simply perceive himself or herself as physically or mentally weaker than the perpetrator. Imbalances could also encompass a difference in numbers (with several students ganging up on a single victim) or when the "source" of the negative actions is difficult to identify or confront (as in the cases of social exclusion from a peer group, talking behind the victim's back, or sending anonymous mean notes) (Olweus, 2003).

In the workplace, the imbalance of power might originate from an individual's hierarchical position within the organization or society, experience and previous knowledge, or personal contacts. Hoel and Cooper (2001) presumed that knowledge of an opponent's vulnerabilities could also be a source of informal power.

Hence, the imbalance of power constitutes one of the clearest characteristics of bullying both at school and in the workplace, but the sources of power differ between children and adults. Among children, perceived or anticipated physical predominance and the inability of the victim to defend him/herself are the most obvious sources of the imbalance of power, whereas professional status likely plays a significant role as a source of power differences among adults at work. As communication researchers, we would consider differences in communication skills between the parties as well as the communication networks of individuals to be further sources of power both at school and in the workplace.

Intentionality and interpretability of hurtful behavior. The intentional attempt of a bully to hurt and cause harm to his or her target remains central to the concept of school bullying (e.g., Hoover et al., 1992; Olweus, 2003; Peterson & Rigby, 1999). Olweus stated:

> [a]lthough children or youth who engage in bullying very likely vary in their degree of awareness of how the bullying is perceived by the victim, most or all of them probably realise that their behaviour is at least somewhat painful or unpleasant to the victim. (p. 62)

In the concept of workplace bullying, on the other hand, intentionality becomes more problematic. Scholars disagree concerning the usefulness of including intentionality in the defining characteristics. For example, the behavior of a person who is considered a bully might not always be meant to harm the target, but the experience of having been bullied might be formed as a nonintended side-effect of this behavior (Hoel & Cooper, 2001). Similarly,

Einarsen (1999) argued that hurtful actions can be performed either deliberately or subconsciously, but they clearly have negative consequences for the target. Hence, the hurtful behavior might sometimes be intended to be hostile, but, in some cases, it might merely be perceived as hostile by the recipient.

Furthermore, according to Leymann (1996), hostile activity consists of quite normal interactive behaviors to a great extent, but when they happen very frequently and longitudinally in order to harass, their content and meaning change, consequently turning them into dangerous, communicative weapons. Hence, their systematic use in this type of interaction triggers the development of the mobbing process.

Scholars emphasize that the definitional core of bullying at work rests on the subjective perception by the victim that the repeated acts are hostile, humiliating, and intimidating and that they are directed at him/her, and the subjective experience of being bullied can manifest itself in mental and physical health problems (e.g., Einarsen, Raknes, Matthiesen, & Hellesöy, 1996). According to this view, being exposed to a behavior that can be construed as bullying is not harmful if the recipient does not perceive it as such. On the other hand, however, Cooper and colleagues (2004) asserted that becoming a target of bullying, regardless of whether participants label the experience as bullying, has a considerable detrimental effect on targets, seriously affecting their health and well-being.

In the concept of sexual harassment, intent has mostly been excluded as a defining feature (Pryor & Fitzgerald, 2003). Therefore, the subjective interpretation of the target as having been sexually harassed is enough to determine a hurtful behavior as sexual harassment.

To conclude, intentionality and interpretability of the behavior or communication of an individual constitute critical issues in the definition and examination of bullying. It seems contradictory that children, who are usually less conscious of their communication behavior than adults, are presumed by researchers to be aware of the harm that they cause to the victim by bullying (e.g., Hoover et al., 1992; Olweus, 2003; Peterson & Rigby, 1999), whereas adults are presumed to be not necessarily conscious of their bullying behavior (e.g., Einarsen, 1999; Hoel & Cooper, 2001). The explanation for this contradiction lies in the different forms taken by bullying among children and adults. The physical and verbal forms of bullying directly addressed to the target (e.g., hitting, pushing, shouting, and threatening the target), which have been shown in empirical studies to be typical of children at school, may easily be recognized and identified as bullying even by children. These acts cannot be undertaken without a conscious design to hurt the target. Instead, the indirect and work-related forms that characterize bullying among adults at work (e.g., criticizing or ignoring the victim's work or ideas, giving feedback in a hurtful manner, or excluding someone from the social group to which he or she should belong), as well as the various forms of sexual harassment and the harm that these behaviors cause to the victim, are much more difficult to perceive and label as bullying, even though the target of this behavior clearly experiences harassment. This kind of hurting can be either intentionally or unintentionally produced.

However, we think that paying more attention to the indirect forms of school bullying, both conceptually and empirically, might show that indirect bullying is as typical as direct bullying among pupils. Instead of expressing power (as in the cases of direct bullying), the forms of indirect bullying (e.g., spreading rumors or socially excluding someone from a group) basically function constructively in the processes of establishing interpersonal relationships and group structuring, as we detail later in this chapter. As such, these processes could be positive for most of the individuals involved, but, for those who are used as "tools" to serve others' social goals, they become destructive. Bullying, which is produced as a "side-effect" of these processes, might often be unconsciously generated.

The definitions given to bullying at school reflect more general tendencies, such as paying attention to easily observable forms of bullying (see, for example, Batsche & Knoff, 1994; Hoover et al., 1992; Olweus, 2003; Peterson & Rigby, 1999; Smorti et al., 2003), whereas the studies of workplace bullying and sexual harassment (and the concepts used to refer to these phenomena) focus mainly on the victim's subjective experience of having been bullied (e.g., Brodsky, 1976; Einarsen et al., 1994; Pryor & Fitzgerald, 2003; Vartia-Väänänen, 2003). The subjective experience of the victim always extends from interpretations given to others' behavior by the victim. This fact emphasizes the need to examine the interpretative nature of communication in bullying situations, which is discussed more closely in the following sections.

THE PREVALENCE OF BULLYING AT SCHOOL AND IN THE WORKPLACE

The hurtful and abusive behavior described in the previous section unfortunately occurs commonly both at school and in the workplace. In this section, we examine the general prevalence of bullying at school and in the workplace in different cultures, and we then move on to identify the bullies and their victims, according to differences in gender and organizational status.

Although the ways in which school bullying is defined and assessed vary across individual studies, thus making direct comparison of results difficult, 5–20% of school children have been reported to be victims of repeated bullying (see, for example, Björkqvist, Ekman, & Lagerspetz, 1982; Espelage &

Holt, 2001; Kannas & Brunell, 2000; Kannas, Välimaa, Liinamo, & Tynjälä, 1995; Lagerspetz, Björkqvist, Berts, & King, 1982; Olweus, 1993, 2003; D. G. Perry, Kusel, & L. C. Perry, 1988; Rigby & Slee, 1991; Salmivalli, Lager-spetz, et al., 1996; Whitney & Smith, 1993). About the same percentage of pupils usually report acting as bullies on a weekly or more frequent basis (Olweus, 1999; O'Moore, 1989; Rigby, 1997; Smith & Sharp, 1994; Vikat, 1998). Bullying likely decreases in the upper grades, with the highest incidence occurring in grades 5 to 9 (corresponding to ages 11 to 15, approximately) (Espelage & Holt, 2001; Smith & Madsen, 1999). According to Espelage and Holt, boys self-report more bullying and are nominated as bullies more often than girls.

The proportion of children involved in bullying in primary schools, either in the role of bully or in that of victim, or both, fluctuates from 41% in Italy to 27% in England, 20% in Portugal, 18% in Spain, 11% in Japan, and 9% in Norway, in studies conducted in these countries with similar methodologies (see Smith et al., 1999). Based on their study of retrospective data collected from adolescent students, Hoover and colleagues (1992) concluded that vic-timization by bullies can be even more prevalent in the United States than in European countries, perhaps as a function of the overall higher rate of vio-lence in the United States. In their study, 76.8% of the respondents reported experiencing bullying at some point in their student careers. However, Smorti and colleagues (2003) suggested that, rather than indicating cultural differ-ences in the prevalence of bullying, varying frequencies between studies more likely reflect the variety of the meanings given to bullying by respondents in different cultures and languages.

At work, bullying is as widespread a problem as it is at school. A study con-ducted in Britain by Hoel, Cooper, and Faragher (2001) revealed that 10.6% of the respondents (N = 5,288) had been bullied within the preceding six months. The number increased to 24.7% when the respondents were asked about having been bullied within the last five years. Additionally, 46.5% reported indirect experiences of workplace bullying (i.e., having witnessed or observed bullying) within the previous five years. Another study demonstrated that as many as 53% in a sample of 1,137 part-time students at an English uni-versity reported that they were bullied at work (Rayner, 1997).

In Scandinavian countries, similar frequencies have been reported. In a study of Norwegian employees (N = 7,986) representing a broad array of organizations and professions, 8.6% had experienced bullying and harassment at work during the preceding six months (Einarsen & Skogstad, 1996). In a study conducted in Sweden, using a scale on which bullying was operational-ized as exposure to any one of 45 predefined negative acts on a weekly basis for more than six months, 3.5% of a representative sample of the working population were found to be victims of bullying at work (Leymann, 1992).

Furthermore, in a survey of Finnish university employees (N = 726), 24% of females and 17% of males were regarded as victims of harassment at work (Björkqvist et al., 1994), and among the personnel of Finnish health-care units (N = 984), Vartia (1991) determined 10% of respondents to be victims of bullying. According to the latest Working Condition Survey conducted in Finland, as many as 22% of 4,000 respondents claimed to be (or have been) a target of bullying in the workplace (Lehto & Sutela, 2004).

Similarly, among the employees of an Australian public hospital, 26.6% reported that they had been subjected to one or more hostile acts once a week during the preceding six months (Niedl, 1995), and in a survey of 806 employees at an American university, 23% revealed mistreatment during the previous 18 months (Spratlen, 1995).

Although these studies suggest some cultural differences in the prevalence of workplace bullying, variance in definitions and measurement and types of samples employed make national comparisons difficult, as Einarsen (2000) emphasized. However, bullying at work has clearly been established as a serious problem at workplaces in all of the examined countries.

Some cultural differences, however, emerge regarding the prevalence of sexual harassment at work. More than half of all Finns, for example, suffer from it at some point in their lives (Heiskanen & Piispa, 1998; Melkas, 2001). Investigations in the United States indicate very similar numbers of victims (Einarsen, Raknes, & Matthiesen, 1993). However, in a survey focusing on cultural differences, Norwegian women working in male-dominated industrial organizations were exposed less to recurrent unwanted sexual attention (27%), compared with American women in a similar situation (60%). Furthermore, whereas 36% of the American women reported being victims of sexual harassment, only 5% of Norwegian women disclosed the same experience (Einarsen & Sørum, 1996). This difference has been attributed to the androgynous sex roles and feminine values more characteristic of Norwegian than of American culture (Einarsen, 2000).

Previous research conducted in several countries indicates that the majority of bullies tend to be individuals with organizational authority who hold superior positions relative to their victims (e.g., Hoel et al., 2001; Lutgen-Sandvik, 2003). However, Scandinavian studies suggest that the number of superiors and peers perceived to be bullies are approximately equal (Einarsen & Skogstad, 1996; Leymann, 1992). Furthermore, based on a study investigating bullying among business professionals holding predominantly managerial or expert positions, Salin (2001) concluded that individuals in managerial positions are also likely to be bullied. Of those classifying themselves as managers, 2% had experienced bullying during the previous 12 months, whereas 9.6% of middle managers, 7.2% of experts, and 17.5% of officials/clerks experienced bullying during the same time period. According to Salin, the percentage of victims was significantly higher among female than among male managers and experts, and the percentage of bullied female managers was higher than the percentage of bullied females in other positions.

Concerning gender differences, data from surveys of 7,986 Norwegian employees within 13 different organizational settings exhibited no difference in the prevalence of bullying among men and women (Einarsen & Skogstad, 1996). The British male workers surveyed by Hoel and colleagues (2001), however, were more likely to be bullied than women, but this finding was reversed in the study of middle and senior management. Of the female senior management, 15.5% reported having been bullied, just about twice as many, in percentage terms, as the male managers. Based on this research, women become more vulnerable to negative behaviors as they progress through the organizational hierarchy and penetrate the hierarchical barriers. Men who feel threatened by women might use bullying to exclude women from the higher positions (Davidson & Cooper, 1992; Veale & Gold, 1998).

These findings indicate that gender and organizational status do explain the division of bullies and victims, to some extent. Whereas boys take the role of bully more often than girls in peer groups at school, no clear gender differences have been identified among employees working at the lower levels of organizational hierarchy. However, women with more organizational authority become more vulnerable to bullying than men in corresponding positions.

These findings emphasize the need to examine the issue of power in bullying incidents. Who has the power in bullying relationships, and how is this power communicated? How is power achieved, and how is it revealed in the relationship? How is it distributed in the group and the organization in which bullying occurs? What is the role of communication in the processes of the distribution of power? What kind of communication is used to increase or decrease the power differences between individuals? Can power (e.g., the professional power of a female manager) be neglected or ignored in the interaction of individuals involved in bullying? Finding answers to these questions would be important in the promotion of the development of impartial communication relationships at school and in workplaces.

Another issue arising from the findings described above underscores the role of cultural learning. In socialization processes, children learn and adopt from their parents, and particularly in their peer groups, such behavior that is characteristic of their gender in their own culture (e.g., Harris, 1995). If girls at school and women with more organizational authority are more vulnerable to bullying than boys and men in the same circumstances, then we should examine the kind of gender-related communication expectations and norms that direct our behavior at school and in the workplace, the way in which they relate to bullying, and how they are taught and shared in society.

PROCESSES OF BULLYING AS THE EXCHANGE
AND APPRAISAL OF MESSAGES

In this section, we explore bullying as a communication process consisting of the exchange of hurtful messages delivered by the bully and strategies of defense produced by the target. Both of these components have been researched, but their connections to each other in actual communication situations have not been demonstrated. In this section, we stress the need for future communication studies to focus on these connections and, in so doing, on the interaction processes and communication relationships in which bullying appears. We begin with a review of investigations that describe characteristics of hurtful messages and various strategies of defense, and we conclude the section by offering some ideas as to how future studies might profitably approach bullying as a communication process.

Hurtful Messages

Bullying among children and adolescents at school occurs in many different forms, as we already demonstrated in the discussion concerning the defining of bullying. It can be direct or indirect. Scholars consider bullying to be direct when it includes fairly open attacks directed against the victim. Direct forms of bullying include various kinds of physical violence (such as kicking, beating, and pushing) and assorted verbal attacks, such as insulting, name-calling, and threatening. Coercion, blackmail, and the destruction of the other student's work also comprise forms of direct bullying (Olweus, 1993). Name-calling, denigration, and threatening are the most common forms of bullying among both boys and girls (Salmivalli, 1998).

Indirect bullying takes forms like isolating someone from the group, spreading rumors, and revealing secrets (Olweus, 1993; Salmivalli, 1998). A person using strategies of this kind to hurt might not be punished for his or her actions because indirect bullying is not easy to identify. Previous research has reported a general decline in direct, physical bullying with increase in age/grade, whereas the level of verbal harassment remains constant (Perry et al., 1988).

Most previous empirical research suggests that, whereas boys more often resort to physical and verbal attacks and threats than girls, girls tend to prefer more subtle and indirect ways of bullying, such as slander, or manipulation of others to make them avoid talking to or playing with the victim (Björkqvist, Lagerspetz, & Kaukiainen, 1992; Olweus, 1978, 1993; Rigby, 1997; Salmivalli, Kaukiainen, & Lagerspetz, 2000; Sharp & Smith, 1991). However, conflicting results concerning gender differences in the aggressive behavior of children and adolescents have also been widely reported (for a discussion of these conflicting findings, see, for example, Salmivalli & Kauki-ainen, 2004; Underwood, Galen, & Paquette, 2001; Underwood, Scott, Galperin, Bjornstad, & Sexton, 2004). These contradictory findings can be attributed to differences in participant's age, sample sizes, methods and mea-surement scales, and cultural characteristics of communication. Expectations concerning the expression of aggression by females and males may vary from one culture to another; males and females may be encouraged to move in the same direction in one culture and in different directions in another culture. Notably, patterns of behavior do change with time, which can be seen, for example, in some Western cultures where the frequency of physical violence demonstrated by girls has clearly increased (Lagerspetz, 1998).

Although different researchers vary in their classification of the forms of bullying at work (see, e.g., Björkqvist et al., 1994; Einarsen & Raknes, 1997; Hoel et al., 2001; Keashly & Jagatic, 2003; Meek, 2004; Vartia, 1993), similar types of direct, indirect, and work-related harassment have been identified in several studies. The methods of harassment that occur at work very much resemble those occurring at school, although the former tend to be more sophisticated, including more developed enactments of indirect bullying. Indeed, the most common forms of aggression at the workplace have been reported to be indirect in nature (Björkqvist et al., 1994) and encompass dif-ferent kinds of work-related harassing activities.

Just as with school bullying, the direct forms of bullying at work range from intimidation (Einarsen & Raknes, 1997; Hoel et al., 2001) to threats or acts of physical violence (Meek, 2004; Vartia, 1993). However, more typical types of direct bullying include verbal utterances such as insulting or offensive remarks (Hoel et al., 2001; Meek, 2004), personal derogation, humiliation and personal criticism (Einarsen & Raknes, 1997), accusations (Björkqvist et al., 1994), and insinuations about a person's mental state (Vartia, 1993) or per-sonal life (Björkqvist et al., 1994).

Like the forms of bullying that occur at school, the forms of indirect bully-ing in the workplace span social exclusion (Einarsen & Raknes, 1997; Meek, 2004), slander (Vartia, 1993), the spreading of rumors (Björkqvist et al., 1994; Hoel et al., 2001; Vartia, 1993), and "the silent treatment" (i.e., shunning; Björkqvist et al., 1994; Meek, 2004). However, work-related forms of harass-ment, such as the withholding of information, causing work overload, or hav-ing one's responsibilities removed (Einarsen & Raknes, 1997; Hoel et al., 2001; Meek, 2004; Vartia, 1993), and continuous criticism of people's work and its results (Björkqvist et al., 1994; Hoel et al., 2001; Vartia, 1993) occur most typ-ically in work contexts. Commonly, targets of bullying at work have limited opportunities to express themselves or influence their tasks or be taken seriously or listened to (Björkqvist et al., 1994). Pupils at school might also confront such constraints, but there is no empirical evidence to support such a claim.

Keashly and Jagatic (2003) demonstrated the multifaceted nature of bullying by summarizing the research results of several scholars and proposing a distinction between verbal and physical aggression in the workplace, between the directness or indirectness of the behavior, and the activeness or passiveness of the behavior in question. Name-calling, insulting jokes, and yelling are examples of active, direct, verbal aggression occurring in the workplace. The indirect version of this active aggression could be false accusations and the spreading of rumors. Passive ways to directly and verbally affect the target include ignoring and silent treatment. With indirect verbal behavior, the aggression manifests itself when the person is excluded from necessary work-related information in several ways. Aggression in the workplace can also take physical, active, and direct forms when the target is exposed to physical assaults and harassment (e.g., sexual, racial). Indirectly, the physical assault can be directed to, for example, the property of the target. Work overloading can also be construed as an active physical assault, yet an indirect form of that assault. However, the severe attempts to sabotage the targets' possibilities to do their tasks by cutting the resources necessary or offering impossible resources can be perceived as passive and indirect physically aggressive behaviors.

Research findings hint at some cultural and situational variation in the forms of bullying, although this issue has not been systematically examined. In Japan, for example, where the prevalence of workplace bullying dramatically increased in the early 1990s, victims reported extremely destructive forms of bullying, such as being a target of physical violence, having superiors and peers refuse to talk to the victim or greet him or her, not being allowed to attend meetings or receive memos, having office furniture and equipment taken away, being required to do excessively late and all-night work, and sexual harassment (Meek, 2004). As interpreted by Meek, this trend corresponded with the economic crisis faced by Japan in the 1990s; the purpose of workplace bullying was to drive out employees without technically violating the lifetime employment principle characteristic of Japan.

The comparison of bullying experiences at different organizational levels illustrates the fact that workers are exposed to insults or offensive remarks and excessive teasing more often than are managers. Managers, however, disclosed exposure to unmanageable workloads and unreasonable deadlines more frequently than workers (Hoel et al., 2001).

Kinney (2003) categorized sexual harassment messages into five groups, according to the theme of the message: (1) hostile and aggressive sexual demands (statements that include sexual demands, often using vulgarities and threats), (2) sexual condescension (statements that disparage the intellect or competence of the recipient), (3) sexual desirability and undesirability (statements that refer to the sexual potential of the recipient), (4) sexual willingness and readiness (statements that make reference to the perceived sexual willingness of the recipient), and (5) sexual dissection/objectification (statements that referenced specific aspects of the recipient's body that were sexualized). In a research interview conducted by Ryynänen (2003), ten sexually harassed women reported that their experiences of sexual harassment were based not only on the meanings carried by the verbal messages of the harasser, but also on the appraisals and interpretations given to nonverbal messages (e.g., tone of voice, use of silence, facial expressions, use of gaze or smile, physical distance between communicators, and touching), the personality of the harasser, his/her expected intentions in the communication situation, and his/her responses to the target's signals of rejection. Hence, perceived sexual harassment may be based not only on the harasser's communication behavior as such, but also on the interpretations given to this behavior by the target.

To summarize, previous research has clearly demonstrated the multiplicity of the forms of bullying. It has also revealed various ways in which communication is involved in bullying, either in the form of messages directly addressed to the target or concerning his or her work or personal affairs, or as interaction that hinders the target's ability to perform his or her tasks in a desirable manner or makes it more difficult for him or her to establish good relationships with colleagues or peers. However, we do not know much about the interaction processes in which bullying messages are produced and interpreted, with or without the parties being simultaneously present.

In the target's evaluation of the significance of negative acts directed at him or her, the target presumably tries to understand why he or she has been chosen as a target and estimate his or her chances of preventing the bully from proceeding. The target could possibly find the reason for bullying in the characteristics or behavior of him/herself or in those of the bully, the relationship of the parties, or the interaction that has taken place between them. Potentially, the target can then use this interpretation in the production of his or her self-defense.

Strategies of Defense

When a person feels that he or she has been attacked or victimized by individuals with whom s/he shares a substantial part of his/her daily life, s/he must choose how to respond to this abuse and how to defend him/herself. Previous research indicates that victims of bullying employ a variety of defensive strategies to survive.

According to Salmivalli, Karhunen, et al. (1996), the victims of school bullying tend to use three different kinds of strategy to defend themselves. These strategies include aggression, trying to show that one doesn't care about the bullying, and responding with helpless behavior. Children who use aggression as a strategy to cope with bullying try to hit back as hard as needed. Pupils who try not to care about the whole situation attempt to stay calm and avoid showing any interest in the bullying acts being performed. Helpless victims, rather than face the bully, strive to escape from the critical situation. Their response is to exhibit their powerlessness. It should be noted that these categories only describe the observable behavior of the victims, not their subjective feelings or thoughts.

Furthermore, Smith, Talamelli, Cowie, Naylor, and Chauhan (2004) coded the coping strategies reported by pupils into seven discrete categories: (1) talk to someone (teacher, counselor, parents, tutor), (2) ignore the bullying, (3) stick up for oneself (take care of myself, get more mature, sort it out with bully), (4) avoid, stay away from the bully, (5) get more and different friends, make an effort to become more popular, (6) fight back, and (7) initiate different behavior/attitude (try to be happier, behave normally, mind one's own businesses, don't cry). Overall, the most common strategy was talking to someone about bullying. However, the escaped victims (i.e., those who had been, but no longer were, bullied) more frequently reported disclosing talking to someone about the bullying and trying to have more or different friends and be more popular, whereas those who had not managed to escape from the bullying more often reported trying to ignore the bullying.

Research suggests that defensive acts in bullying situations improve when children get older. Younger pupils are more likely to react to bullying by crying. Defensive strategies become more complex with age, and, for example, not paying attention to bullying becomes a more common defensive strategy (Smith & Madsen, 1999). Crick and Dodge (1994) also contended that, as children age, their ability to perceive social information, produce more complex responses, and enact strategies improves. If the improvement of defensive acts further continues in adulthood, we can assume that the strategies used by adults in cases of workplace bullying are quite well developed.

In studies of bullying at work, the term *coping* has usually been used instead of *strategies of defense* to refer to the efforts made by the victim in bullying processes. *Coping* refers to the "constantly changing cognitive and behavioral efforts to manage specific external and/or internal demands that are appraised as taxing or exceeding the resources of the person" (Folkman & Lazarus, 1984, p. 141). Hence, coping in bullying processes can be regarded as including the behavioral strategies of defense used by the victim in actual bullying situations as well as the cognitive efforts of the victim to master or overcome bullying.

In their interviews of bullying victims, Zapf and Gross (2001) identified four conflict management strategies. The exit category includes active behavior that might at the same time be regarded as destructive, since, in bullying cases, exit behavior often means, for example, the ultimate solution—quitting the job. On the other hand, for the victim, leaving a difficult working environment is not necessarily a destructive thing. The voice category refers to active and constructive problem-solving behavior, and the loyalty category consists of the silent and passive hope that the problem will be solved. The fourth strategy is neglect, which refers to passive and thus destructive behavior such as reduction of commitment to the working organization. Zapf and Gross found that most of the bullying victims changed their strategy several times during the bullying process.

Several other researchers have examined the coping strategies used by the victims in bullying processes at work (e.g., Alberts, Lutgen-Sandvik, & Tracy, 2005; Hogh & Dofradottir, 2001; Niedl, 1996; Zapf & Gross, 2001), getting similar results regarding the developmental courses of these strategies. Very often, victims of bullying faced with a conflict situation start off with a more active and constructive strategy (e.g., advancing arguments against the accusations of the bully or openly talking about the distressing situation with him or her). If this strategy fails to succeed, victims tend to change their behavior, and the majority avoid conflicts, if possible. One way of trying to avoid conflict is to adapt to the other party and give up one's own interests. Even this approach is not always a successful strategy, and thus, most victims end up trying to escape the conflict or to direct their efforts toward becoming "invisible." According to Zapf and Gross, leaving the organization and seeking support are the strategies most often recommended by bullying victims to other bullying victims. However, seeking support by making a complaint against the perceived bully, for example, can be regarded by the bully as provocative or hurtful behavior, which, in turn, can result in the escalation of the conflict and lead to a situation that the victim cannot control.

With regard to sexual harassment, Clair (1993) concluded that women do not openly complain about sexual harassment because organizations rarely encourage open discussion of this issue and prefer confidentiality when dealing with complaints. Furthermore, Clair suggested that women avoid going through formal channels to report sexual harassment because they expect (and fear) that their complaints could be ignored or trivialized and that they may face a lack of protection from future retaliation, as well as opposition from the male-dominated hierarchy. Hence, their time will be wasted because of the ineffective sexual harassment policy of the organization. Instead, they choose to avoid or escape conflicts with their harasser and to discuss harassment only with their family members or best friends.

Even talking to one's family members about sexual harassment can be difficult in some cultures. In Malay societies, for example, women avoid reporting sexual harassment incidents to their fathers and brothers, out of fear that they would be accused of having invited the harassment by being insufficiently reticent and modest, or that, by reporting these incidents, they would oblig-ate their male family members to react aggressively (e.g., by taking a revenge to the harasser) to being shamed by the harassment of their female family members (Collins & Bahar, 2000).

To summarize, on the basis of previous research, we already know some-thing about the kinds of defensive or coping strategies victims choose in bul-lying processes. However, we do not know why victims choose a particular strategy, what factors direct the selection of the strategy, or what the possible consequences of different strategies might be for the bullying. To increase understanding of why the processes of interaction sometimes lead to a situa-tion where the victim finds it difficult to defend him/herself, growing attention should be paid not only to the forms of bullying, but also to the intensity of hurtful messages and the communication strategies used in bullying as well as to the relationship between hurtful communication and the characteristics of the strategies of defense.

Communication research offers some initial insight as to how these ques-tions might be approached. For example, Kinney (1994) provided a model for the classification of hurtful messages. By means of this model, verbal attacks can be described as based on conscious selection of the power and content of the attack as well as on the method of delivering it. Our assump-tion is that the bully can choose how deeply he or she wants to hurt the tar-get by varying these elements. In addition to taking advantage of this varia-tion, the bully might construct his or her verbal attack so skillfully as to make it almost impossible for the victim to respond and for an outsider to identify it as an attack. For group members, the insults are usually easier to interpret because the hurtful messages extend from meanings shared within the group. A skillful bully can identify these shared meanings, although the victim might be unaware of them. The bully may also be adept at resisting possible defen-sive acts of the victim. Hence, although the victim may try to respond to hurt-ful messages with the same intensity, responses can be deterred because of the well-developed strategies used by the bully.

The concept of *face* can be traced back for centuries in Chinese culture (e.g., Ho, 1976; Hu, 1944), and the theory of face work (Goffman, 1967) pro-vides a further tool for analyzing the relationship between hurtful messages and the strategies of defense. Brown and Levinson (1987) defined the con-cept of face (which they derived from the work of Goffman) as "the public self-image that every member wants to claim for himself" (p. 61). According to Cupach and Metts (1994), the theory of face work is useful in challenging, threatening, paradoxical, difficult, or awkward situations. While speakers usu-ally base interaction upon respect and the preference for mutual face preser-vation, in bullying situations, the interaction involves hurting and threatening the partner's face. Bullying can certainly be regarded as a face threat to the target, and in order to save or return his or her face, the target must engage in defensive and protecting acts. Hence, we should investigate the possibility that the defensive strategies chosen by the victim will be related to the threat of face experienced by him or her.

Furthermore, interpretations of (and the different kinds of clues used to identify) hurtful communication can trigger specific defensive responses. The Social Information-Processing model, introduced by Crick and Dodge (1994), clarifies children's creation of behavioral enactment in situations where social adjustment is needed. Crick and Dodge found that aggressive children are more likely interpret other's intentions as deliberately hostile and concentrate more on aggressive clues. Aggressive children also generate more hostile strategies and goals than prosocial children, and they tend to believe that the use of aggression can lead to positive outcomes. Suggesting that personal characteristics direct defensive strategies, this research invites further investigation in order to determine the various interpretations made of others' communication behavior and the strategies generated on the basis of these interpretations by individuals with different kinds of personal characteristics (e.g., shy or reticent, assertive, and supportive individuals).

On the other hand, from the victim's perspective, a bullying relationship can be examined as an unwanted relationship in which the bully is the stronger party and the victim is always the clear loser in the exchange. Hess (2003) suggested that unwanted relationships cause stress, and stress demands some sort of coping by the individual. He identified the different tactics that people use to deal with unwanted relationships. Primarily, Hess asserted that people try to avoid closeness and self-disclosure with an unwanted person. According to Hess, tactics include avoidance, ignoring and inattention, discounting the hurtful messages, deception, humor, and degrading (i.e., perceiving the other person as less than human).

According to Hess (2003), a behavior that seems universal in unwanted relationships is the effort to distance oneself from the unwanted communication partner. Distance can be created, for example, through making interactions shorter in duration, staying away from the other person as much as possible, or simply ignoring the other. The defensive strategies found by Salmivalli, Karhunen, et al. (1996), as well as by Smith and colleagues (2004), share many features with the distancing strategies introduced by Hess, suggesting that the selection of the defensive strategy stems from the characteristics of the relationship between bully and victim. Most challenging for the victims of bullying is to maintain a minimum level of closeness with the unpleasant partner while preserving the relationship with that person (or, at least, maintaining membership in the peer group). Distancing can be a successful strategy at school, but in the contexts of working life, this tactic can make the victim's work even more difficult, since good employees cannot hide from their supervisors and co-workers.

Communication studies should aim at improving our ability to identify mentally violent communication behaviors and processes as well as to identify the communicative strategies that form an effective defense against them. In addition, we should examine production of hurtful communication and the strategies of defense, as well as the relationship between them. Theoretical and conceptual frameworks from the discipline of communication offer particularly useful resources for explicating such factors.

On the intrapersonal level, communication theories describe, for example, the cognitive processes of individuals in which they set goals for interaction with others and construct communication strategies, produce, perceive and interpret verbal and nonverbal messages, and give meanings and interpretations to messages (i.e., theories of information processing, e.g., the constructivist approach, see Burleson, 1989; Delia, B. O'Keefe, & D. O'Keefe, 1982). Understanding the intrapersonal dynamics of bullying could also be enhanced through communication research on verbal aggressiveness (Infante & Wigley, 1986), communication apprehension (McCroskey, 1982), willingness to communicate (McCroskey & Richmond, 1987), and cognitive complexity (e.g., Burleson & Caplan, 1998), which direct the cognitive processes, perceptions, and communication behavior of individuals. In addition, significant studies focus on the communication skills and communication competence of individuals (e.g., Cupach & Spitzberg, 2002; Greene & Burleson, 2003; Malcom, 1994; Spitzberg, 1994; S. R. Wilson & Sabee, 2003). The knowledge concerning communication orientations and communication skills, together with the theories of message production, facilitates understanding of why and how some individuals create more complex and sophisticated communication strategies than others to achieve their communication goals (e.g., get social approval from others, gain compliance, affect others' interpersonal relationships, or get a leading position in a group), whereas others might find it almost impossible to get a single reliable friend or express their opinions in the presence of others.

ANTECEDENTS OF BULLYING AT SCHOOL AND IN THE WORKPLACE

Previous studies have examined the antecedents of bullying at school and in the workplace on three primary levels: (1) personal characteristics or conditions of an individual, either of a bully or of a victim, (2) dynamic functions of a group, and/or (3) organizational (and cultural) level variables. Since this area of research is large, we have restricted our review to those studies and findings which intersect most with communication theory and research. In this section, we will argue that communication research can make a significant contribution in enlarging understanding of associations of bullying with the development of communication relationships between individuals, within groups, and within organizations.

Individual Differences in Communication Behavior

In the case of school bullying, individual-level factors examined as antecedents of bullying have included physical appearance (e.g., over- or underweight, clumsiness, and physical strength), self-esteem, shyness, insecurity, social withdrawal, anxiety, depression, loneliness, social intelligence, aggressiveness (both reactiveness and proactiveness), the family relationships of an individual (e.g., attachment relationships, family-management practices, and the structural aspects of families), and practices used in upbringing at home. As previous research attests, the most powerful predictors of victimization at the individual level are low self-esteem, shyness or timidity, insecurity, sensitivity, and anxiousness on the part of a child (e.g., Olweus, 1993; Salmivalli, 2003). This research emphasizes, however, that features of this kind might not only be causes of bullying, but they might also develop as a consequence of repeated harassment (e.g., Pikas, 1990).

The most typical characteristic of a bullying boy is aggressiveness (e.g., Olweus, 1993), whereas a girl who bullies others is not necessarily aggressive. Instead, she might possess a very high level of social intelligence that she uses against her victim by means of indirect bullying and the manipulation of peer relationships (Kaukiainen, 2003). According to Olweus, a bully usually does not have low self-esteem and does not express insecurity. Rather, he or she most probably has a strong need for self-assertion and to be at the center of attention (Salmivalli, 1998).

However, previous studies have yielded conflicting results regarding the characteristics of bullies and their victims. On the one hand, bullies have appeared to be aggressive individuals (e.g., Olweus, 1993) with inadequate communication skills, especially in relation to self-control, cooperation, and empathy (Kaukiainen, 2002, 2003). On the other hand, a bully might as easily be a pupil with normally developed communication skills. He or she might even have exceptionally good communication skills, especially in persuasion, and she or he might be highly perceptive about his/her social environment and the relationships existing among others. He or she might be very competent in establishing friendships, knowing how the other person feels, and making others laugh; in other words, the bully might be very competent in the kinds of communication skills that make him or her a skillful manipulator (see Kaukiainen, 2002, 2003; Weir, 2001).

Kaukiainen (2003) reported a significant relationship between social intelligence and indirect bullying. Social intelligence enables the practice of indirect bullying. Girls tend to be more socially intelligent than boys. As such, they hold the potential to make precise interpretations of the surrounding social reality and influence other people in a tactful way. Usually, social intelligence positively affects relationships, but it can be used in negative ways as well. Future research should explore children's skills in argumentation, persuasion, and relational attachment, and the relationships of these skills with bullying.

According to previous studies conducted among schoolchildren, the victims of bullying can be classified into three categories: (1) passive victims, who are typically sensitive, shy, anxious, insecure, and careful and have low self-esteem and a negative communicator image (Olweus, 1993); (2) provocative victims, who are aggressive and irritating to others and might simultaneously be bullies (Olweus, 1993), and (3) ordinary pupils, whom others, for some reason, have selected as a victim (Salmivalli, 1998). Hence, very different kinds of individual-level factors characterize both bullies and their victims.

Corresponding findings have been obtained in working-life contexts. In working life, the individual-level characteristics examined as antecedents of bullying have included differences in the age and gender of the individuals; dissimilarity in thinking, behavior, and values between the individuals; inflexibility of the victim in adapting to the norms and rules of the working community; aggressiveness and inability to communicate in constructive ways; self-esteem of the bully; the tendency of an individual to criticize others' work, and envy and jealousy.

Previous research characterizes the bully or harasser as either an incompetent communicator with a low tolerance of criticism directed against himself/herself or a skillful "player" in interpersonal relationships (Lindroos, 1996; Tasala, 1997). Rainivaara (2004) interviewed individuals who had experienced bullying at their place of work. Respondents described their bullies as dominant, overly self-confident, competitive, and verbally aggressive communicators who had deficiencies in their argumentation and listening skills as well as in their ability to take the role of the other and show empathy. At the same time, however, the bullies were adept at protecting their own position by creating a good impression of themselves to others in the work community.

The victim of workplace bullying, in turn, tends to be someone who is rather different, when compared with the others around him. As suggested by Vartia-Väänänen (2003), the "difference" of the victim might be a matter of, for example, having the courage to express one's opinions, unusual diligence, or creativity, or it might be simply a matter of being the only representative of one's own sex, age, or area of expertise. On the other hand, previous studies also suggest that victims can lack sensitivity concerning the implicit rules and norms of the working community, and therefore, they might irritate others (Vartia & Perkka-Jortikka, 1994).

Studies of bullying rarely focus on the interpersonal relationships between bully and victim. One exception is Einarsen (1999), who divides the origins of bullying into two categories. By *dispute-related bullying*, Einarsen referred to harassment that develops as a result of an unresolved conflict between individuals. By *predatory bullying*, on the other hand, Einarsen treated harassment as the means by which the bully tries to achieve some personal advantage at the victim's expense. Einarsen stated:

> Predatory bullying refers to cases where the victim personally has done nothing provocative that may reasonably justify the behaviour of the bully. In such cases the victim is accidentally in a situation where a predator either is demonstrating power or in other ways is trying to exploit an accidental victim into compliance. (p. 22–23)

According to Einarsen, a bullying case typically is triggered by a work-related conflict. Additional research should explore the communication processes where work-related conflict turns into bullying.

In one study, sexually harassed women described two kinds of men. Some men sent sexually harassing verbal and nonverbal messages and seemed to send those messages deliberately in order to increase their power over the target in situations without bystanders present, and other harassers did not seem to have any other kind of model or form of behavior when communicating with women and, therefore, perhaps did not even realize that their behavior was experienced as intrusive (Ryynänen, 2003). The first kind of sexual harassment behavior involves adequate communication skills and goal orientation, whereas the latter kind of behavior suggests insufficient communication skills. In both cases, however, the negative interpretation given to the behavior of the harassers resulted from some kind of violation of communication norms or expectations.

As a general conclusion to the survey of this area of research, the personal characteristics and communication skills examined in previous studies are associated to some extent, at the least, with involvement in bullying, either in the role of bully or as a victim. However, they do not explain the variance in its entirety. In addition, in some cases, the results are even contradictory. In other words, we have so far identified a number of "types" of individuals who are at risk of becoming involved in bullying, but we do not know for sure that they will. Therefore, we should examine the developmental courses of *bullying relationships* more closely in order to determine what kinds of interaction result in the formulation of a bullying relationship. We claim that, rather than being casually formed, the roles of bully and victim are formulated in communication processes taking place between individuals and within groups over a longer period of time. Therefore, we should pursue what actually happens in the processes of interaction that take place between different kinds of persons before and during the development of their relationship into a bullying relationship.

Communication theories that describe the development of interpersonal relationships include uncertainty reduction theory (see Berger, 1987; Berger & Bradac, 1982), social penetration theory (see Altman & Taylor, 1973; Taylor & Altman, 1987), and expectancy violations theory (see Burgoon and Hale, 1988). Each of these theories could facilitate understanding of, in particular, why and how bullying between two individuals starts at the beginning of their acquaintanceship. These theories describe how interpersonal relationships develop in repeated interactions between the partners, how knowledge of the other person deepens by gradually moving on toward more and more intimate issues in discussions, and how partners build trust and mutual understanding of important issues. These theories, together with message-production theories and constructs of communication orientation, could be valuable for expressing how, on some occasions, a close and supportive friendship springs up between certain individuals, whereas a bullying relationship develops between others, in which only one partner benefits while the other one loses.

Furthermore, the concept of *verbal aggression* has been applied in communication research to describe violent and hostile communication behavior as a traitlike or statelike orientation of an individual (for related review, see Morgan & Wilson, 2005). Verbally aggressive messages attack an individual's self-concept in order to make the person feel less favorably about himself (Infante & Wigley, 1986). They can consist of character attacks, competence attacks, insults, maledictions, teasing, ridicule, profanity, threats, and nonverbal indicators (Infante, 1987).

For an individual who constantly expresses aggression with his or her communication behavior, establishing friendships with others than those of the same kind might be difficult because his or her offensive communication style does not tempt others to expose their personal and intimate concerns to him or her. Research suggests that bullies usually hang out with other bullies (Salmivalli, 1998), and they nominate fellow bullies as their friends (Espelage & Holt, 2001). As a result, instead of learning friendly and supportive forms of communication from other kinds of children and adolescents, they reinforce aggressive forms of communication.

Communication theories and concepts provide potentially useful theoretical and conceptual frameworks for learning how different communication orientations and communication skills relate to interaction processes as well as typical communication patterns for critical situations where the roles of bully and victim are formulated. In future studies, we should examine the individual, relational, and situational factors that increase the probability that an interpersonal relationship will turn into a bullying relationship.

Bullying and Harassment as Group Processes

In this section, we focus on the role of group communication in bullying processes. After providing a review of previous literature in which bullying has been examined as a group process, we advance some communication theories as examples of the tools that the communication discipline has to offer for the examination of the goals and purposes that bullying serves in groups and of the formulation of the roles of bully and victim within the group structure.

Previous research suggests that bullying at school quickly expands into a group process, with several persons involved in different roles. In addition to the bullies and their victims, Olweus (1973), Salmivalli (1998) and O'Connell, Pepler, and Craig (1999) identified various other roles in bullying situations. Some children eagerly join in the bullying when someone initiates it, and they act as "assistants" to the bully. "Reinforcers" provide an audience for the bully, for example, by laughing and giving positive feedback to him/her. Furthermore, a remarkable number of children remain aloof, as "outsiders," from actual bullying situations, but they still allow bullying to go on through their silent approval. Finally, as Salmivalli argued, a few "defenders" linger to support the victim by comforting and taking sides with him/her and by trying to make the others stop bullying.

The roles of individuals in bullying situations have been explained, for example, in terms of group norms and status hierarchies within a group. First, bullying occurs more commonly in school classes where the group norms concerning bullying are rather positive and bullying is seen as acceptable behavior (Salmivalli & Voeten, 2004). Second, the status of an individual within a group sets limits to the individual's behavior and role in the group. Whereas a pupil with low status (i.e., is not liked, and clearly rejected by peers) most often ends up a victim, a person with high status in the group (i.e., is liked and not rejected by peers) is more freely allowed to choose the role of a defender of the victim, and acting in this role might actually raise his/her status. The status of a bullying boy is usually quite low, whereas bullying girls are either very much liked or very clearly rejected by their peers (Salmivalli, Lagerspetz, et al., 1996).

Other group-level explanations for bullying have been asserted by, for example, Olweus and Pikas. Olweus (1993) suggested that bullying can result from following the behavioral model of an admired person, weakened control of one's own aggressive tendencies after seeing that the negative behavior of a bully is rewarded (in terms of "overcoming" the victim) rather than punished (by peers, teachers, or parents, for example), perceptual changes after continual attacks and hurtful comments, resulting in an increased tendency of adolescents to see the victim as a person of no value, and diffusion of individual responsibility when the whole group is involved in bullying. Janis recognized this phenomenon in the theory of Groupthink (see Janis, 1982). The theory suggests that, since responsibility for the decisions made by the group is diffused, a group can end up approving a decision that no single member of the group would have approved on his own. The whole group kicking someone in the school yard or destroying his or her personal property could result from a decision made in this way. We already know that school bullying appears most often in the presence of a larger group. At work, a decision concerning the dramatic cutting of employee resources or increasing his/her work load can be done more easily by an executive group than by an individual employer.

An additional explanation given for school bullying is that the group follows the model of the bully because the members are afraid of becoming victims too, if they resist him/her (Slee, 1994). Furthermore, Pikas (1990) contended that bullying might result from cognitive dissonance caused by the dissimilarity between the victim and others. After this dissonance occurs, members of a group start to "test" the victim in order to classify him/her according to categories that they can recognize. Pikas also argued that members of the group could develop a view of the victim as an enemy. This perception might be completely irrational and independent of the victim's behavior, or it might be caused by a threat from the victim that really has been experienced by the bully.

In work contexts, participant roles in bullying processes have not been empirically examined. However, based on research in school settings, we should investigate the possibilities that, in workplaces where people often form both official and unofficial teams and groups, the harassment of one or several individuals can also take the form of a group phenomenon, with individuals participating in different roles (as bullies, victims, assistants, reinforcers, and defenders).

Indeed, several group phenomena have been proposed as explanations of why individuals in workplaces approve the bullying of their workmates or even participate in that bullying. First, the existence of unresolved problems or continuous competition in the working community can result in the employees choosing a victim as a scapegoat whom they can blame for all the problems occurring at the workplace (e.g., Einarsen, 1999; Lindroos, 1996; Thylefors, 1987; Vartia & Perkka-Jortikka, 1994). As Thylefors detailed, a second explanation for bullying is that a new or somehow different employee becomes rejected by others because of an anticipated (or potential) threat to the working practices or interpersonal relationships of the group. Third, members of a working community may not try to prevent the bullying of their workmates because they fear sharing the victim's fate and be rejected by others.

On the basis of previous research, we already know that, in addition to bully and victim, bystanders play significant roles in bullying processes, and most of these roles serve to support the purposes of the bully instead of the victim. Thus, we can conclude that bullying seems to have a particular purpose in a group, and most of the children and adolescents at school, as well as adults at work, are committed to proceeding toward this purpose. In addition to searching for an explanation of bullying by asking about bully motivations, we must ask what goals and purposes are served in a group by bullying (Kaukiainen, 2002; Salmivalli, 2002) and how members of the group choose their own role in bullying processes. We should also explore the ways in which the roles of bully and victim are produced and reinforced in the interaction processes of the group members. Are these roles developed in the actual bullying situations or based on longer and more extensive processes of group formation?

On the group level, a large amount of communication research has focused on understanding how roles, norms, rules, and status hierarchies develop within groups and how the communication characteristics of individuals affect these processes (for a review, see Haslett & Ruebush, 1999). In addition, existing communication literature describes how groups are developed, how interpersonal relations are established and reinforced in groups, how group cohesion is strengthened or weakened in interaction processes, and how groups are structured and restructured through communication (see, for example, Anderson, Riddle, & Martin, 1999; Keyton, 1999; Mabry, 1999).

Structuration theory, developed by Giddens (1984) and later applied to small group communication by Poole, provides one example of a useful theoretical framework about the processes of group formation. Structuration theory (see Giddens, 1984; Poole, 1999; Poole, Seibold, & McPhee, 1996) focuses on the processes by which the formation and reproduction of groups occur and the factors that influence these processes. The theory rests on a distinction between system and structure. A system constitutes a social entity, such as a group, pursuing various practices that give rise to an observable pattern of relations within the group. Structures involve the rules and resources that members use to generate and sustain the group system. Structures provide a kind of "recipe" for acting that comprises a configuration of rules as well as the material and social resources used to bring about the action.

In the theory, *structuration* serves the central concept representing the nature of structures and the relationship between structure and system. It refers to "the process by which systems are produced and reproduced through members' use of rules and resources" (Poole et al., 1996, p. 117). Thus, on the one hand, members of a group draw on rules and resources (structures) to interact, and, on the other hand, structures exist only by virtue of rules and resources being used in practice.

When the question of accepting a new member of the group arises, the group has to weigh the costs and benefits of accepting the newcomer. The members must evaluate how much pressure accepting a new member will bring for the group to change its structures and rules. Notably, a newcomer might also have significant resources to bring to the group in the form of his/her characteristics, abilities, and knowledge. If a group accepts the new employee, the structures of that group will be rebuilt. In a situation of this kind, the group might (often subconsciously) come to the conclusion that the benefits to be gained from accepting the new person are less than the costs that it will entail in the sense of changing the system and structures of the group. Because they perceive the newcomer as a threat to the system and structures of the group, the group members might end up mobbing, or approving the mobbing, of this person.

Why do some groups resort to extreme antisocial actions, such as bullying, while other groups choose to show the boundaries of the group in a friendly way and try to get along with the outsiders, even though they are not willing to risk change to the existing system and structures of the group by accepting them as members? A closer examination of some naturally occurring groups on the basis of the structuration theory might help to answer this question.

Another advantage of structuration theory is that it considers factors that could have an effect on the processes of bullying. The theory states that several factors influence structuration, for example, by differential distributions of resources among group members and between the group and external actors. Actors with special expertise or privileged positions in a group can control structuration more than novices or individuals with few resources. Potentially, resources that individuals can offer to the group increase or decrease over time, which can affect the restructuration processes.

In the processes of group structuration, communication plays a significant role (Poole, 1999; Poole et al., 1996). By means of communication, the resources of the possible members of a group become identified; structures and rules of the group become negotiated, and group cohesion becomes strengthened. Communication also facilitates the processes of social exclusion. By means of effective persuasion, the members of a group can be convinced that someone deserves to be rejected by others or should be treated in negative and humiliating ways. For example, in a study conducted by Teräsahjo and Salmivalli (2002), pupils explained why particular individuals were bullied in their school. Participants described victims of bullying as strange or somehow odd and, therefore, deserving to be bullied. These kinds of attributions given to bullying reflect the narrative nature of interpersonal persuasion, which has been described in the symbolic convergence theory developed by Bormann (1996). This theory sheds light on the ways in which members of a group integrate themselves into the group by sharing fantasies, which also involves them in sharing common values and ideals, and a common model of reality. The attributions given by children to the bullying of someone seem to represent the fantasies shared in a peer group about victims.

To summarize, bullying can be constructive for those individuals who belong to a particular group but extremely destructive for someone perceived as an "unworthy" person or even as a threat and who, therefore, instead of being accepted, functions as a tool to serve the cohesive purposes of the group. Future studies should especially focus on how bullying relationships between individuals intersect with other interpersonal relationships as well as the structures of the group where the bullying relationship exists.

Organizational and Cultural Level Antecedents of Bullying and Harassment

In this section, we summarize and compare research that has focused on organizational-level factors presumed to be antecedents of bullying at school and in workplace. We also advance some theoretical perspectives to enlarge understanding of bullying as an organizational and cultural communication phenomenon.

As Salmivalli (2003) summarized, organizational-level determinants of school bullying have been pursued in the physical environment of the school (e.g., the size, location, and coziness of the school as well as level of control exercised during breaks), school culture and climate, clarity of the school rules, goal orientation and general motivation in school work, and involvement of school personnel in preventing bullying. Class-level investigations of bullying have included, among other things, the management of the class by teachers and the social structure of the class, both of which have been associated with the prevalence of bullying in class (Roland & Galloway, 2002).

The norm climate of the school comprises an important factor in bullying at school. A study of bullying-related classroom norms in grades 4, 5, and 6 revealed that, with increasing age, a decrease in anti-bullying norms appears. Defending the victim becomes less approved, whereas joining in bullying becomes more accepted in the upper classes (Salmivalli & Voeten, 2004).

On the subject of bullying in working life, Leymann (1993) found four factors that could have a significant effect on the occurrence of workplace bullying: 1) deficiencies in the way in which the worker's tasks are defined and organized by management, 2) deficiencies in leadership behavior, 3) a socially exposed position of the victim, and 4) a low moral standard. In a Finnish study, victims of bullying described their workplace as a highly stressful and competitive environment, full of interpersonal conflicts and lacking a supportive atmosphere, subject to organizational changes, and managed with an authoritarian leadership style (Vartia, 1996). Furthermore, organizational-level antecedents of work harassment have included a high level of role conflicts and the lack of any opportunity for self-monitoring of one's work (Einarsen et al., 1994), deficiency in information flow, the lack of mutual discussions concerning tasks and goals, and a low level of influence in matters concerning oneself (Vartia, 1996) as well as job content, social environment, and the lack of control over one's own time combined with high cooperation requirements (Zapf, Knorz, & Kulla, 1996).

In summary, although organizational-level antecedents of bullying at school and in the workplace appear to include many similar features (e.g., weaknesses in the style of leadership and social structure of a class or organization and failings in the norms or moral standards adopted by members), bullying at work seems to be more clearly associated with task-related antecedents than it is in school contexts. Thus, in the move from school to working life, the number of organizational risk factors that might lead to bullying increases rather than decreases. Communication practices utilized in the distribution of work, in decision-making, in conflict resolution, and in the giving of feedback become critical factors of the organizational culture (see, for example, Hoel & Salin, 2003; Vartia, 1996).

The meaning of culture in the workplace can also be viewed from a wider perspective. In the communication literature, culture has been examined as a criterion used at workplaces to discriminate against the representatives of certain groups, such as women (e.g., Clair, 1993; Leets & Giles, 1999; Meares et al., 2004), homosexuals (e.g., Lim, 2003), and ethnic and racial minorities (e.g., Leets & Giles, 1999; Meares et al., 2004). Discrimination directed against a whole group of people because of their visible difference from the surrounding majority, devalued social identity, or presumed character flaws is sometimes also called stigmatization (see, for example, Miller & Kaiser, 2001).

Although a large number of organizational and cultural factors affect bullying and harassment at school and in the workplace, we lack a theory that might combine all of these factors to explain what organizational and cultural purpose bullying serves in institutions like schools and workplaces. What kind of societal order or structure does bullying create in these institutions?

Studies have employed muted group theory (Kramarae, 1981) to address the societal purpose of bullying and harassment (see, for example, Clair, 1993, 1994; Hack & Clair, 1996; Lutgen-Sandvik, 2003; Meares et al., 2004). This theory focuses on lack of voice and resistance to silencing. As summarized by Meares and colleagues, muted group theory is based on four main premises. The first premise is that the members of different groups have varied experiences and, therefore, diverse perceptions of the world. The second premise suggests that each society privileges some groups over others, though individuals at the top of the social hierarchy determine the dominant discourse for that society, reinforcing their own worldview. In this discourse, groups that are not privileged have fewer opportunities to express their experiences and worldviews. The dominant discourse mutes other perspectives. According to the third premise, in order to get their concerns recognized, those belonging to the subordinate groups must use the language and communication style of those in the dominant group. The fourth premise states, however, that resistance and change are possible.

On the basis of this theory, Clair (1993) analyzed women's interviews concerning their experiences of sexual harassment at work. Paying attention to the ways in which these women told their stories, she found that the framing of sexual harassment stories portrayed the harassment as a hegemonic device that served to maintain the interests of the dominant group. Clair identified six types of framing device: accepting dominant interests, simple misunderstanding, reification, trivialization, denotative hesitancy, and public/private expression—public/private domain. We advise interested readers to examine the work of Clair more specifically in order to familiarize themselves with all six types of framing device; we limit our review here to consideration of those techniques that might explain the framing of sexual harassment as well as the framing techniques of bullying at school and in the workplace.

As described by Clair (1993), the *simple misunderstanding* framing device can be noted in the frequent explanation that women may have misconstrued flirting as sexual harassment. If we apply this framing to the work contexts more generally, it might be identified in a case where a superior who has been accused of harassment explains that the steps taken to reorganize the work of an employee were necessary for the organization, but the employee simply took it too personally. At school, pupils can often be heard to say that "We were just teasing him/her, but he/she was offended because he/she does not have any sense of humor." For the victimized individual, however, the experience remained serious and damaging. Along the same lines as the simple misunderstanding framing device, *trivialization* may take place, invalidating the abusive situation and denying the experience of the target by turning the event into a joke. Students may assert that "We were teasing him/her just for fun; it was nothing else but play," or "I was not referring to his/her sexual orientation with my comment. Can't he/she take a joke?"

Denotative hesitancy refers to the constraints that the subjugated group feels in expressing itself because the existing vocabulary of the institution defines the institution's reality only from the perspective of the dominant group. Therefore, the members of the subjugated group may not have the means of expression necessary to convey their own narrative or define their own experience. Clair (1993) argued that, when new terms (e.g., sexual harassment) are introduced into a language system, their definitions must be contested before language users reach consensus about their denotative meaning. Hence, as long as bullying and harassment as concepts and phenomena are not generally identified (and their existence at school and in the workplace is, therefore, not admitted and openly discussed), the subjugated groups remain confused and without the means to recognize the nature of their experience. This circumstance can be observed in the accounts of previous victims, when they explain in later years that, during their schooldays, they never understood that what they experienced was school bullying.

As we pointed out earlier in the chapter, the imbalance of power between the parties is one of the main characteristics of bullying, as identified by researchers in various definitions. Lutgen-Sandvik (2003) applied muted group theory in explaining bully's and victim's inequality of access to power in the superior-subordinate-relationship. She argued that individuals who have access to structural (hierarchical) power dominate organizational language in the workplace. As a result, the dominant language likely reflects productivity or other organizational goals and might not reveal subordinate employees' workplace experiences. Applying muted group theory, she proposed an extension of Leymann's (1990) linear model of workplace mobbing to describe the developmental phases of employee emotional abuse. Furthermore, Meares and colleagues (2004) examined employee mistreatment through the perspectives of employees with different cultural backgrounds in order to understand how some voices are muted and others are privileged in an organization.

If we regard victims of bullying and harassment as members of the muted group, new questions arise. What features characterize the members of the muted group and members of the dominant group, at school and in workplaces of different kinds? What kinds of individual characteristics, skills, and behavioral features are used to "justify" the bullying of one person and privilege another to bully, and how are these justifications negotiated in the interaction processes of the individuals involved? Answers to these questions might be found through investigation of the attributions that are given to bullying of others or to being bullied. Previous studies suggest that children at school, both victims and others, tend to find justification for bullying in the characteristics and behavior of the victim (Hoover et al., 1992; Teräsahjo & Salmivalli, 2002), rather than in those of the bully.

Bullying might also be regarded as a way of teaching an individual to follow the norms and rules of the organization, as could be presumed to occur in the cases of bully-victims where pupils start to bully an individual who acts aggressively toward others. However, bullying others seems to be acceptable behavior in the case of some students, whereas for others, it is not. Are there certain characteristics of individuals that privilege them to bully others, or are these individuals just employing more acceptable forms of bullying?

Muted group theory constitutes one example of the communication perspectives that can be applied to bullying. Previous studies of organizational communication (see, for example, Hoel & Salin, 2003; House, Hanges, Javidan, Dorfman, & Gupta, 2004; Taylor, Flanagan, Cheney, & Seibold, 2001; Vartia, 1996), conflict management (see, for example, De Dreu & Van de Vliert, 1997; Hample, 1999; Keashly & Nowell, 2003; Kellet & Dalton, 2001), leadership (see, for example, Connaughton & Daly, 2005), and feedback (see, for example, Kluger & DeNisi, 1996; Lizzio, Wilson, Gilchrist, & Gallois, 2003) shed light on the communicative factors that direct the communication climate of the workplace, the development of conflicts, organizing of tasks, and the developmental courses of bullying processes. This research could help in understanding the organizational-level risk factors in the processes of bullying as well as in finding tools for directing organizations in a more supportive and less violent direction.

MANAGING THE COSTS OF BULLYING
WITH SOCIAL SUPPORT

For the victim, bullying or harassment comprises a traumatic experience that markedly reduces the quality of life. At school, the anxiety and fear experienced by bullied children often lead to serious motivation and learning difficulties, negative attitudes toward schooling, and impaired academic achievement (Mottet & Thweatt, 1997). According to the literature, bullying can lead to lowered self-esteem and feelings of loneliness, anxiety, and depression (Boulton & Smith, 1994; Callaghan & Joseph, 1995; Hodges & Perry, 1996; Kaltiala-Heino, M. Rimpelä, Rantanen, & A. Rimpelä, 2000), and over time, to psychosomatic symptoms of stress, such as increased somatic complaints and more illnesses (Boulton & Smith, 1994; Kaltiala-Heino et al., 2000; Rigby, 1998) as well as mental health problems such as eating disorders (Kaltiala-Heino et al., 2000). Surprisingly, recent studies have demonstrated that victims and bullies both suffer from depressive symptoms (Kaltiala-Heino, M. Rimpelä, Rantanen, & A. Rimpelä, 1998; Roland, 2002a), and they experience suicidal thoughts (Kaltiala-Heino et al., 1998; Roland, 2002b) and psychosomatic symptoms (Vikat, 1998) more often than pupils who are not involved in bullying at school.

Similarly, hostile behavior in the workplace significantly affects victims on individual and organizational levels. Keashly and Jagatic (2003) detailed the effects of workplace bullying. They divided the effects of workplace bullying into *direct* and *indirect* effects. Direct effects encompass negative mood (anger, resentment, anxiety) as well as fear of violence and cognitive distraction (depressed mood, fear, loss of concentration). Indirect effects decrease the psychological well-being of the target. These include lowered self-esteem and life satisfaction, problem drinking, depression, overall emotional health, and symptoms of post-traumatic stress disorder (PTSD) (see also Björkqvist et al., 1994; Leymann, 1992; C. B. Wilson, 1991). Indirect effects also include poor psychosomatic functions of the target (physically weak health) and reduced organizational functioning, at least partially signified through decreased job satisfaction, greater turnover of workers, increased absenteeism, decreased productivity, and greater intention to leave. Further consequences of bullying are insomnia, various nervous symptoms, melancholy, apathy, and sociophobia (Björkqvist et al., 1994), as well as social isolation, stigmatization, social maladjustment, psychosomatic illnesses, compulsions, helplessness, and despair (Leymann, 1990). Sexual harassment leads especially to a decreased level of self-esteem, the feeling of not being professionally appreciated, fear of the opposite sex, feelings of shame, and suspicion of employers (Alemay et al., 1999; Timmerman & Bajema, 1999).

To conclude, in addition to the suffering during actual threatening communication situations, bullying and harassment can have long-lasting effects on an individual's overall psychosocial well-being, personal relationships, and career development. Furthermore, bullying is not only a personal problem for the individual victim. It can have serious consequences for the bully as well as for families, friends, and relatives of both the victim and the bully and the whole community where the problem exists.

Social support has a central role in an individual's coping processes. A growing body of research demonstrates that supportive interpersonal relationships buffer the negative consequences of peer rejection and victimization at school (e.g., Hodges, Boivin, Vitaro, & Bukowski, 1999; Parker & Asher, 1993). According to Einarsen (2000), victims with high social support at work or off work probably feel less vulnerable when faced with aggression because social support can reduce the emotional and physiological activation of the victim, hence reducing the health effects of long-term bullying.

Previous studies suggest, however, that the victims of bullying seldom receive support from their peers in a concrete and perceivable way. In cases of school bullying, the number of individuals who defend victims is small (Salmivalli, 1998; Salmivalli, Lagerspetz, et al., 1996). Similar findings characterize cases of workplace harassment. Lutgen-Sandvik (2003), for example, described the final stages of the communicative cycle of employee emotional abuse. During these final stages, fear and intimidation silence both the targets and the other employees. Most co-workers do not speak up in the face of collegial abuse, so targets are silenced and separated from support. In addition to fearing reprisal, providing support for a bullied co-worker drains energy from peers, and they can become emotionally exhausted and withdraw support from a colleague who seems to be too demanding or takes too much of their energy. Even the family members of the victim can become emotionally exhausted and withdraw their support.

In communication studies, social support and supportive communication have been investigated in several other contexts: in health-care, family, and close relationships (see, for example, Burleson, Albrecht, & Sarason, 1994; Gardner & Cutrona, 2004), but not in the context of bullying and harassment.

The communication processes and interpersonal relationships in which social support is given to the individuals involved in bullying should be examined both among children and adults. Important questions remain: Who are the best providers of support in bullying cases, and what kind of social support and supportive communication is expected and needed by the victims from different sources (e.g., parents, siblings, mates, friends, teachers and other school personnel, superiors, and workmates)? Is the mate at home expected to provide a different kind of support from that required from the superior at work, and is the support needed from parents different from the support required from teachers at school? Further, do individuals differ in their need of social support in cases of bullying, and how does support affect different kinds of victim? What kinds of differences exist in the availability of support between victims or victim groups? Finally, researchers should pursue the kinds of support that bullies need and receive; how does a bully communicate his or her need to others, and what are the effects of support received by the bully?

CONCLUSION

Although bullying has been studied both in school and working-life contexts, research combining these two areas is rare. We already know that, although the extent of bullying can be reduced by means of effective interventions by highly-committed personnel involved at school (see, for example, Olweus, 2003; Roland, Bjørnsen, & Mandt, 2003; Salmivalli, 2003), the roles of bullies and victims seem to be quite permanent at school. We also know that, the older children get, the more likely they are to accept bullying behaviors directed toward others (Espelage & Holt, 2001; Salmivalli, 2003). Similarly, at the workplace, once harassment begins, it tends to continue until the victim leaves his or her work.

Research suggests that the forms of both bullying and self-defense become more skilled and sophisticated as the participants grow older. Simultaneously, while the forms of indirect bullying increase, the meanings and interpretations given to communication behavior become more significant, and outsiders face increasing difficulty in recognizing bullying when it occurs. As a result, the examination of bullying grows even more challenging, since the subjective aspects of the phenomenon increasingly predominate.

Verbally and nonverbally hurtful messages, and the meanings given to them, as well as their effects in bullying situations have not received much attention in communication research. Further, research focusing on the strategies of defense as communication acts in actual bullying situations is rare in studies concerning workplace bullying, while in the studies of school bullying, less attention has been paid to the long-term coping strategies of victims.

Communication studies should aim to improve our ability to identify mentally violent communication behaviors and processes as well as to specify the communicative strategies (both immediate and long-term) that form an effective defense against them.

However, labeling an individual's behaviors as bullying or harassment could be difficult because the meanings and interpretations given to communication behavior vary from one person to another. The same phrase, gesture, laughter, or touch might be interpreted quite differently by various recipients who will assess that phrase, etc. in light of the interpersonal relationship that they have with the sender and their history of interactions with him/her. Therefore, the same kind of message can be received as a spontaneous, harmless joke by one person and as a repeated, painful insult by another. Similarly, the ability of an individual to defend himself might be estimated from the verbal and nonverbal messages he sends, and they must also be interpreted in the light of the previous knowledge gained of the sender and the relationship that he or she has with the bully. In future research, more attention should be paid to the factors directing the production of hurtful communication and the strategies of defense as well as to the relationship between them. Here, communication theories and concepts provide useful tools for researchers.

In the beginning of the chapter, we examined definitions given to bullying and related concepts. We suggested that, in addition to the tradition of previous research which approached bullying as the behavior of an individual directed to another individual or individuals, we should pay more attention to the bullying relationship as an interpersonal relationship taking place between individuals within groups and organizations. This perspective means making the interaction and relationships of individuals the center of attention and moving the characteristics of the individuals involved into the background (without forgetting them). The benefits of this kind of approach could be found in an increased understanding of the interpersonal, organizational, and group processes leading to bullying. On the basis of this approach, several questions call for the contribution of communication scholars.

Future research should focus, first, on the developmental courses of bullying relationships and on the variation to be found in them, both in the contexts of school and working life. By means of this research, we should learn to identify bullying relationships and interpersonal relationships which are at risk of becoming such as well as individuals who are at risk of falling into bullying relationships.

Second, the different participant roles which have been specified in studies of school bullying should also be studied in the contexts of working life. We have presumed that these roles are formed in the communication processes of a group during a longer period of time, and their existence serves mainly constructive purposes in the group (e.g, the strengthening of group cohesion as well as group structuring and restructuring), although, simultaneously, it may become extremely destructive for the "outsider" of the group who has been chosen as victim. The development of these roles in the interaction of the group needs further examination.

Third, research into school bullying, in turn, would benefit from applying theories of organizational and cultural communication, such as muted group theory. This kind of research could reveal the typically muted groups among children and detail how their voices become muted. Is the subjugation of these children groups based on racial, ethnic, or gender-related discrimination, the physical appearance of these children (e.g., obesity, physical unattractiveness, or a visible disability), or their communication skills and orientations, such as shyness or reticence, low levels of assertiveness, or insufficient relational skills? If certain groups of children are more vulnerable than others to becoming subjugated, we should investigate how the rules governing subjugation and the assigning of privilege are transferred from adults to children. Do adults at home and at school participate in the subjugating process? Are the same individuals and groups at risk of becoming victimized or becoming bullies, first at school and then later in the workplace?

In searching for an understanding of bullying among children and adults, the benefits of the core theories of information processing and interpersonal and group communication have been ignored so far. Communication theories can help in understanding bullying and harassment, and their advantages can be easily recognized. However, empirical research applying these theories to explain bullying and harassment processes is almost entirely lacking.

In what ways can knowledge concerning bullying be used in order to get a better understanding of the socio-communicative nature of humans? What can be done to make a change in existing conditions and in the behavior of individuals? Increasing understanding of the communication processes involved in school bullying and workplace harassment will certainly enhance our understanding of human communication behavior in other kinds of contexts and relationships where mentally and/or physically violent behavior appears. This behavior might be realized as verbal and physical abuse in domestic surroundings, coercion and subjection in romantic relationships, bullying and harassment in the out-of-school activities of adolescents, ethnic and racial harassment and rejection among individuals or groups representing different cultures or subcultures, or as hostile behavior in the conflicts between nations. Crawford (1999), for example, broadened the term bullying to include incidents on an international level, as phenomena occurring between nations. The accumulation of armaments or the testing of nuclear weapons can be regarded as nations demonstrating their power to attack each other. In addition, the methods of prevention, intervention, and the provision of support in one context of bullying are often obviously transferable to other contexts of the same kind. The study of bullying in human relationships is a great challenge for communication theory and research.

ACKNOWLEDGMENTS

This chapter was prepared within the research project no. 107301, "Mental violence in communication relationships at school and in the workplace", funded by the Academy of Finland. The authors wish to thank Dr. Christina Beck, the editor of *Communication Yearbook 30*, and the three anonymous reviewers for their most valuable comments and suggestions on the manuscript.

REFERENCES

Adams, A. (1992). *Bullying at work: How to confront and overcome it?* London: Virago Press.

Alberts, J. K., Lutgen-Sandvik, P., & Tracy, S. J. (2005, May). *Workplace bullying: A case of escalated incivility.* Paper presented at the annual meeting of the International Communication Association, New York.

Alemay, M.-C., Boyer, J., Cattaneo, N., Paparriga-Costavara, C., Bergamaschi, M., & Campino, M. M. (1999). Sexual harassment at work in five Southern European Countries. In *Sexual harassment at the workplace in the European Union* (pp. 155–233). Luxembourg, Luxembourg: Office for Official Publications of the European Communities.

Altman, I., & Taylor, D. (1973). *Social penetration: The development of interpersonal relationships.* New York: Holt.

Anderson, C. M., Riddle, B. L., & Martin, M. M. (1999). Socialization processes in groups. In L. R. Frey, D. S. Gouran, & M. S. Poole (Eds.), *The handbook of group communication theory and research* (pp. 139–166). Thousand Oaks, CA: Sage.

Ashforth, B. (1994). Petty tyranny in organizations. *Human Relations, 47*, 755–778.

Baron, R. A., & Neuman, J. H. (1996). Workplace violence and workplace aggression: Evidence on their relative frequency and potential causes. *Aggressive Behavior, 22*, 161–173.

Batsche, G. M., & Knoff, H. M. (1994). Bullies and their victims: Understanding a pervasive problem in the schools. *School Psychology Review, 23*, 165–175.

Berger, C. R. (1987). Communicating under uncertainty. In M. Roloff & G. Miller (Eds.), *Interpersonal processes: New directions in communication research* (pp. 39–62). Newbury Park, CA: Sage.

Berger, C. R., & Bradac, J. J. (1982). *Language and social knowledge: Uncertainty in interpersonal relations.* London: Edward Arnold.

Björkqvist, K., Ekman, K., & Lagerspetz, K. (1982). Bullies and victims: Their ego picture, ideal ego picture and normative ego picture. *Scandinavian Journal of Psychology, 23*, 307–313.

Björkqvist, K., Lagerspetz, K., & Kaukiainen, A. (1992). Do girls manipulate and boys fight? Developmental trends in regard to direct and indirect aggression. *Aggressive Behavior, 18*, 117–127.

Björkqvist, K., Österman, K., & Hjelt-Bäck, M. (1994). Aggression among university employees. *Aggressive Behavior, 20*, 173–184.

Bormann, E. G. (1996). Symbolic convergence theory and communication in group decision making. In R. Y. Hirokawa & M. S. Poole (Eds.), *Communication and group decision making* (2nd ed., pp. 81–113). London: Sage.

Boulton, M., & Smith, P. K. (1994). Bully/victim problems in middle-school children: Stability, self-perceived competence, peer perceptions and peer acceptance. *British Journal of Developmental Psychology, 12*, 315–329.

Brodsky, C. M. (1976). *The harassed worker*. Toronto, Canada: Lexington Books, DC Health.

Brown, P., & Levinson, S. (1987). *Politeness: Some universals in language usage* (2nd ed.). Cambridge, England: Cambridge University Press.

Burgoon, J. K., & Hale, J. (1988). Nonverbal expectancy violations: Model elaboration and application to immediacy behaviors. *Communication Monographs, 55*, 58–79.

Burleson, B. R. (1989). The constructivist approach to person-centered communication: Analysis of a research exemplar. In B. Dervin, L. Grossberg, B. J. O'Keefe, & E. Wartella (Eds.), Rethinking communication (Vol. 2, pp. 29–36). Newbury Park, CA: Sage.

Burleson, B. R., Albrecht, T. L., & Sarason, I. G. (Eds.). (1994). *Communication of social support: Messages, interactions, relationships, and community*. Thousand Oaks, CA: Sage.

Burleson, B., & Caplan, S. (1998). Cognitive complexity. In J. McCroskey, J. Daly, & M. Martin (Eds.), *Communication and personality: Trait perspectives* (pp. 233–286). Cresskill, NJ: Hampton Press.

Callaghan, S., & Joseph, S. (1995). Self-concept and peer victimization among school-children. *Personality and Individual Differences, 18*, 161–163.

Clair, R. P. (1993). The use of framing devices to sequester organizational narratives: Hegemony and harassment. *Communication Monographs, 60*, 113–136.

Clair, R. P. (1994). Resistance and oppression as a self-contained opposite: An organizational communication analysis of one man's story of sexual harassment. *Western Journal of Communication, 58*, 235–262.

Collins, E. F., & Bahar, E. (2000). To know shame: *Malu* and its uses in Malay societies. *Crossroads, 14*, 35–69.

Connaughton, S. L., & Daly, J. A. (2005). Leadership in the new millennium: Communication beyond temporal, spatial, and geographical boundaries. In P. J. Kalbfleisch (Ed.), *Communication yearbook 29* (pp. 203–218). Mahwah, NJ: Lawrence Erlbaum Associates.

Cooper, C., Faragher, B, & Hoel, H. (2004). Bullying is detrimental to health, but all bullying behaviours are not necessarily equally damaging. *British Journal of Guidance and Counselling, 32*, 367–387.

Crawford, N. (1999). Conundrums and confusion in organisations: The etymology of the word "bully." *International Journal of Manpower, 20*, 86–93.

Crick, N., & Dodge, K. (1994). A review and reformulation of social information-processing mechanism in children's social adjustment. *Psychological Bulletin, 115,* 74–101.

Cupach, W. R., & Metts, S. (1994). *Facework.* Thousands Oaks, CA: Sage.

Cupach, W. R., & Spitzberg, B. H. (2002). Interpersonal skills. In M. L. Knapp & J. A. Daly (Eds.), *Handbook of interpersonal communication* (3rd ed., pp. 564–612). Thousand Oaks, CA: Sage.

Davidson, M. J., & Cooper, C. L. (1992). *Shattering the glass ceiling.* London: Paul Chapman.

De Dreu, C., & Van de Vliert, E. (Eds.). (1997). *Using conflict in organizations.* London: Sage.

Delia, J., O'Keefe, B., & O'Keefe, D. (1982). The constructivist approach to communication. In F. E. X. Dance (Ed.), *Human communication theory* (pp. 147–191). New York: Harper & Row.

Einarsen, S. (1999). The nature and causes of bullying at work. *International Journal of Manpower, 20,* 16–27.

Einarsen, S. (2000). Harassment and bullying at work: A review of the Scandinavian approach. *Aggression and Violent Behavior, 5,* 379–401.

Einarsen, S., Hoel, H., Zapf, D., & Cooper, C. (Eds.). (2003). *Bullying and emotional abuse in the workplace: International perspectives in research and practice.* London: Taylor & Francis.

Einarsen, S., & Raknes, B. I. (1997). Harassment in the workplace and the victimization of men. *Violence and Victims, 12,* 247–263.

Einarsen, S., Raknes, B. I., & Matthiesen, S. B. (1993). *Seksuell trakassering* [Sexual harassment]. Bergen, Norway: Sigma Forlag.

Einarsen, S., Raknes, B. I., & Matthiesen, S. B. (1994). Bullying and harassment at work and their relationships to work environment quality: An exploratory study. *European Work and Organizational Psychologist, 4,* 381–401.

Einarsen, S., Raknes, B. I., Matthiesen, S. B., & Hellesöy, O. H. (1996). Bullying at work and its relationships with health complaints. Moderating effects of social support and personality. *Nordisk Psykologi, 48,* 116–137.

Einarsen, S., & Skogstad, A. (1996). Bullying at work: Epidemiological findings in public and private organizations. *European Journal of Work and Organizational Psychology, 5,* 185–201.

Einarsen, S., & Sørum, D. (1996). Arbeidskamerat eller sex-objekt? En krysskulturell studie av seksuell trakassering [Co-worker or sex-object? A cross-cultural study on sexual harassment at work]. *Nordisk Sexologi, 14,* 17–33.

Espelage, D. L., & Holt, M. K. (2001). Bullying and victimization during early adolescence: Peer influences and psychosocial correlates. In R. A. Geffner, M. Loring, & C. Young (Eds.), *Bullying behavior: Current issues, research, and interventions* (pp. 123–142). New York: Haworth Press.

Fitzgerald, L. F., Gelfand, M. J., & Drasgow, F. (1995). Measuring sexual harassment: Theoretical and psychometric advances. *Basic and Applied Social Psychology, 17,* 425–445.

Fitzgerald, L. F., & Shullman, S. L. (1993). Sexual harassment: A research analysis and agenda for the 1990s. *Journal of Vocational Behavior, 42,* 5–27.

Folkman, S., & Lazarus, R. S. (1984). Stress, appraisal, and coping. New York: Springer.

Gardner, K. A., & Cutrona, C. E. (2004). Social support communication in families. In A. L. Vangelisti (Ed.), Handbook of family communication (pp. 495–512). Mahwah, NJ: Lawrence Erlbaum Associates.

Giddens, A. (1984). The constitution of society: Outline of the theory of structuration. Cambridge, England: Polity Press.

Goffman, E. (1967). Interaction ritual: Essays on face-to-face behavior. New York: Pantheon Books.

Greene, J. O., & Burleson, B. R. (Eds.). (2003). Handbook of communication and social interaction skills. Mahwah, NJ: Lawrence Erlbaum Associates.

Hack, T. J., & Clair, R. P. (1996). Sexual harassment: Raising consciousness and sharing solutions. In E. B. Ray (Ed.), Case studies in communication and disenfranchisement: Applications to social health issues (pp. 151–162). Mahwah, NJ: Lawrence Erlbaum Associates.

Hample, D. (1999). The life space of personalized conflicts. In M. E. Roloff (Ed.), Communication yearbook 22 (pp. 171–208). Thousand Oaks, CA: Sage.

Harris, J. R. (1995). Where is the child's environment? A group socialization theory of development. Psychological Review, 102, 458–489.

Haslett, B. B., & Ruebush, J. (1999). What differences do individual differences in groups make? The effects of individuals, culture, and group composition. In L. R. Frey, D. S. Gouran, & M. S. Poole (Eds.), The handbook of group communication theory and research (pp. 115–138). Thousand Oaks, CA: Sage.

Hazler, R. J., & Miller, D. L. (2001). Adult recognition of school bullying situations. Educational Research, 43, 133–146.

Heiskanen, M., & Piispa, M. (1998). Usko, toivo, hakkaus. Kyselytutkimus miesten naisille tekemästä väkivallasta [Faith, hope, hitting. A survey of the violence directed towards women by men] (Justice, No. 12). Helsinki, Finland: Statistics Finland: Council for Equality (Edita).

Hess, J. A. (2003). Maintaining undesired relationships. In D. J. Canary & M. Dainton (Eds.), Maintaining relationships through communication: Relational, contextual, and cultural variations (pp. 103–126). Mahwah, NJ: Lawrence Erlbaum Associates.

Ho, D. Y. (1976). On the concept of face. American Journal of Sociology, 81, 867–884.

Hodges, E. V. E., Boivin, M., Vitaro, F., & Bukowski, W. M. (1999). The power of friendship: Protection against an escalating cycle of peer victimization. Developmental Psychology, 35, 94–101.

Hodges, E. V. E., & Perry, D.G. (1996). Victims of peer abuse: An overview. Journal of Emotional and Behavioral Problems, 5, 23–28.

Hoel, H., & Cooper, C. L. (2001). Origins of bullying. Theoretical frameworks for explaining workplace bullying. In N. Tehrani (Ed.), Building a culture of respect: Managing bullying at work (pp. 3–19). London: Taylor & Francis.

Hoel, H., Cooper, C. L., & Faragher, B. (2001). The experience of bullying in Great Britain: The impact of organizational status. European Journal of Work and Organizational Psychology, 10, 443–465.

Hoel, H., & Salin, D. (2003). Organizational antecedents of workplace bullying. In S. Einarsen, H. Hoel, D. Zapf, & C. Cooper (Eds.), Bullying and emotional abuse *in the workplace: International perspectives in research and practice* (pp. 203–218). London: Taylor & Francis.

Hogh, A., & Dofradottir, A. (2001). Coping with bullying in the workplace. *European Journal of Work and Organizational Psychology, 10*, 485–495.

Hoover, J. H., Oliver, R., & Hazler, R. J. (1992). Bullying: Perceptions of adolescent victims in the midwestern USA. *School Psychology International, 13*, 5–16.

House, R. J., Hanges, P. J., Javidan, M., Dorfman, P. W., & Gupta, V. (Eds.). (2004). *Culture, leadership, and organizations: The GLOBE study of 62 societies.* Thousand Oaks, CA: Sage.

Hu, H. C. (1944). The Chinese concepts of "face." *American Anthropologist, 46*, 45–64.

Infante, D. A. (1987). Aggressiveness. In J. C. McCroskey & J. A. Daly (Eds.), *Personality and interpersonal communication* (pp. 157–192). Newbury Park, CA: Sage.

Infante, D. A., & Wigley, C. J. (1986). Verbal aggressiveness: An interpersonal model and measure. *Communication Monographs, 53*, 61–69.

Janis, I. L. (1982). *Groupthink: Psychological studies of policy decisions and fiascos* (2nd ed.). Boston: Houghton Mifflin.

Kaltiala-Heino, RK., Rimpelä, M., Rantanen, P., & Rimpelä, A. (1998). Koulukiusaaminen, masentuneisuus ja itsetuhoajatukset [School bullying, depression, and suicidal thoughts]. *Suomen Lääkärilehti, 53*(26), 2799–2808.

Kaltiala-Heino, RK., Rimpelä, M., Rantanen, P., & Rimpelä, A. (2000). Bullying at school–an indicator of adolescents at risk for mental disorders. *Journal of Adolescence, 23*, 661–674.

Kannas, L., & Brunell, V. (Eds.). (2000). *Subjektiv hälsa, hälsovanor och skoltrivsel. Jämförelse mellan svensk- och finskspråkiga elever 1994–1998* [Subjective health, health behaviour and school satisfaction. A comparative study of Finnish- and Swedish-speaking schoolchildren in Finland in 1994–1998] (Terveystieteiden laitoksen julkaisusarja, No. 10) [Publication reports of the Department of Health Sciences, No. 10]. Jyväskylä, Finland: University of Jyväskylä, Department of health sciences.

Kannas, L., Välimaa, R., Liinamo, A., & Tynjälä, J. (1995). Oppilaiden kokemuksia kouluviihtyvyydestä ja kuormittuneisuudesta sekä koulukiusaamisesta Euroopassa ja Kanadassa [School children's experiences of school satisfaction and stress and bullying at school in Europe and Canada]. In L. Kannas (Ed.), *Koululaisten kokema terveys, hyvinvointi ja kouluviihtyvyys. WHO-koululaistutkimus* [Perceived health, well-being and school satisfaction among school children. The HBSC-study] (pp. 131–149). Helsinki, Finland: National Board of Education.

Kaukiainen, A. (2002). Onko aggressio ja kiusaaminen aina sosiaalisen kompetenssin puutetta? [Do aggression and bullying always indicate a lack of social competence?] *Psykologia, 37*, 115–123.

Kaukiainen, A. (2003). *Social intelligence as a prerequisite of indirect aggression: Some manifestations and concomitants of covert forms of aggression* (Annales Universitatis Turkuensis, Ser. B-257). Turku, Finland: University of Turku.

Keashly, L. (1998). Emotional abuse in the workplace: Conceptual and empirical issues. *Journal of Emotional Abuse, 1*, 85–117.

Keashly, L., & Jagatic, K. (2003). By any other name: American perspectives on workplace bullying. In S. Einarsen, H. Hoel, D. Zapf, & C. L. Cooper (Eds.), *Bullying* and emotional abuse in the workplace: International perspectives in research and practice (pp. 31–61). London: Taylor & Francis.

Keashly, L., & Nowell, B. L. (2003). Conflict, conflict resolution and bullying. In S. Einarsen, H. Hoel, D. Zapf, & C. Cooper (Eds.), Bullying and emotional abuse in the workplace: International perspectives in research and practice (pp. 339–358). London: Taylor & Francis.

Keashly, L., Trott, V., & MacLean, L. M. (1994). Abusive behavior in the workplace: A preliminary investigation. Violence and Victims, 9, 125–141.

Kellet, P. M., & Dalton, D. G. (2001). Managing conflict in a negotiated world: A narrative approach to achieving dialogue and change. Thousand Oaks, CA: Sage.

Keyton, J. (1999). Relational communication in groups. In L. R. Frey, D. S. Gouran, & M. S. Poole (Eds.), The handbook of group communication theory and research (pp. 192–224). Thousand Oaks, CA: Sage.

Kinney, T. A. (1994). An inductively derived typology of verbal aggression and its association to distress. Human Communication Research, 21, 183–222.

Kinney, T. A. (2003). Themes and perceptions of written sexually harassing messages and their link to distress. Journal of Language and Social Psychology, 22, 8–28.

Kluger, A. N., & DeNisi, A. (1996). The effects of feedback interventions on performance: A historical review, a meta-analysis, and a preliminary feedback intervention theory. Psychological Bulletin, 119, 254–284.

Kramarae, C. (1981). Women and men speaking. Rowley, MA: Newbury House.

Kreps, G. L. (Ed.). (1993). Sexual harassment: Communication implications. Cresskill, NJ: Hampton Press.

Lagerspetz, K. (1998). Naisten aggressio [Female aggression]. Helsinki, Finland: Tammi.

Lagerspetz, K., Björkqvist, K., Berts, M., & King, E. (1982). Group aggression among school children in three schools. Scandinavian Journal of Psychology, 23, 45–52.

Leets, L., & Giles, H. (1999). Harmful speech in intergroup encounters: An organizational framework for communication research. In M. E. Roloff (Ed.), Communication yearbook 22 (pp. 91–138). Thousand Oaks, CA: Sage.

Lehto, A.-M., & Sutela, H. (2004). Uhkia ja mahdollisuuksia. Työolotutkimusten tuloksia 1977–2003 [Threats and possibilities. Results from the Finnish working conditions research made in 1977–2003]. Helsinki, Finland: Statistics Finland (Edita).

Leymann, H. (1986). Vuxenmobbning. Om psykiskt vÅld i arbetslivet [Adultmobbing. About mental violence in working life]. Lund, Sweden: Studentlitteratur.

Leymann, H. (1990). Mobbing and psychological terror at workplaces. Violence and Victims, 5, 119–126.

Leymann, H. (1992). Från mobbning till utslagning i arbetslivet [From mobbing to expulsion in work life]. Stockholm, Sweden: Publica.

Leymann, H. (1993). Mobbing–Psychoterror am Arbeitsplatz und wie man sich dagegen wehren kann [Bullying–Psycho-terror at work and how one might protect oneself]. Rowolt, Germany: Reinbeck.

Leymann, H. (1996). The content and the development of mobbing at work. European Journal of Work and Organizational Psychology, 5, 165–184.

Lim, V. K. G. (2003). Managing HIV at the workplace: An empirical study of HIV and HR managers in Singapore. *Journal of Occupational Health Psychology, 8*, 235–246.

Lindroos, R. (1996). *Kiusaamisen kurjuus yhteisöissä ja työyhteisöissä* [The misery of harassment in society and at work] (Labour Policy Studies No. 164). Helsinki, Finland: Ministry of Labour.

Lizzio, A., Wilson, K. L., Gilchrist, J., & Gallois, C. (2003). The role of gender in the construction and evaluation of feedback effectiveness. *Management Communication Quarterly, 16*, 341–379.

Lutgen-Sandvik, P. (2003). The communicative cycle of employee emotional abuse: Generation and regeneration of workplace mistreatment. *Management Communication Quarterly, 16*, 471–501.

Mabry, E. A. (1999). The systems metaphor in group communication. In L. R. Frey, D. S. Gouran, & M. S. Poole (Eds.), *The handbook of group communication theory and research* (pp. 71–91). Thousand Oaks, CA: Sage.

Malcom, R. P. (1994). Communicative competence and interpersonal control. In M. L. Knapp & G. R. Miller (Eds.), *Handbook of interpersonal communication* (pp. 589–618). Thousand Oaks, CA: Sage.

McCroskey, J. C. (1982). *An introduction to rhetorical communication* (4th ed). Englewood Cliffs, NJ: Prentice Hall.

McCroskey, J. C., & Richmond, V. (1987). Willingness to communicate. In J. C. McCroskey & J. A. Daly (Eds.), *Personality and interpersonal communication* (pp. 129–156). Newbury Park, CA: Sage.

Meares, M. M., Oetzel, J. G., Torres, A., Derkacs, D., & Ginossar, T. (2004). Employee mistreatment and muted voices in the culturally diverse workplace. *Journal of Applied Communication Research, 32*, 4–27.

Meek, C. B. (2004). The dark side of Japanese management in the 1990s: Karoshi and ijime in the Japanese workplace. *Journal of Managerial Psychology, 19*, 312–331.

Melkas, T. (2001). *Tasa-arvobarometri 2001* [The equality-assessment rating made in 2001] (Tasa-arvojulkaisuja No. 9) [Publications on Equality No. 9). Helsinki, Finland: Statistics Finland: Council for Equality (Edita).

Miller, C. T., & Kaiser, C. R. (2001). Implications of mental models of self and others for the targets of stigmatization. In M. R. Leary (Ed.), *Interpersonal rejection* (pp. 189–212). New York: Oxford University Press.

Morgan, W. M., & Wilson, S. R. (2005). Nonphysical child abuse: A review of literature and challenge to communication scholars. In P. Kalbfleisch (Ed.), *Communication yearbook 29* (pp. 1–34). Mahwah, NJ: Lawrence Erlbaum Associates.

Morita, Y., Soeda, H., Soeda, K., & Taki, M. (1999). Japan. In P. K. Smith, Y. Morita, J. Junger-Tas, D. Olweus, R. Catalano, & P. Slee (Eds.), *The nature of school bullying: A cross-national perspective* (pp. 309–323). London: Routledge.

Mottet, T. P., & Thweatt, K. S. (1997). The relationship between peer teasing, self-esteem, and affect for school. *Communication Research Reports, 14*, 241–248.

Naylor, P., & Cowie, H. (1999). The effectiveness of peer support system in challenging school bullying: The perspectives and experiences of teachers and pupils. *Journal of Adolescence, 22*, 467–479.

Niedl, K. (1995). *Mobbing/bullying am arbeitsplatz* [Mobbing/bullying at work]. München, Germany: Rainer Hampp Verlag.

Niedl, K. (1996). Mobbing and well-being: Economic and personnel development implications. *European Journal of Work and Organizational Psychology, 5,* 239–249.

O'Connell, P., Pepler, D. & Craig, W. (1999). Peer involvement in bullying: Insights and challenges for intervention. *Journal of Adolescence, 22,* 437–452.

Olweus, D. (1973). *Hackkycklingar och översittare. Forskning om skolmobbning* [Victims and bullies. Research on school bullying]. Stockholm, Sweden: Almqvist & Wicksell.

Olweus, D. (1978). *Aggression in the schools: Bullies and whipping boys.* Washington, DC: Hemisphere (Wiley).

Olweus, D. (1993). *Bullying at school: What we know and what we can do.* Oxford, England: Blackwell.

Olweus, D. (1999). Sweden. In P. K. Smith, Y. Morita, J. Younger-Tas, D. Olweus, R. F. Catalano, & P. Slee (Eds.), *The nature of school bullying: A cross-national perspective* (pp. 7–27). New York: Routledge.

Olweus, D. (2003). Bully/victim problems in school: Basic facts and an effective intervention programme. In S. Einarsen, H. Hoel, D. Zapf, & C. L. Cooper (Eds.), *Bullying and emotional abuse in the workplace: International perspectives in research and practice* (pp. 62–78). London: Taylor & Francis.

O'Moore, A. M. (1989). Bullying in Britain and Ireland: An overview. In E. Roland & E. Münthe (Eds.), *Bullying: An international perspective* (pp. 3–21). London: David Fulton.

Parker, J. G., & Asher, S. R. (1993). Friendship and friendship quality in middle childhood: Links with peer group acceptance and feelings of loneliness and social dissatisfaction. *Developmental Psychology, 29,* 357–389.

Perry, D. G., Kusel, S. J., & Perry, L. C. (1988). Victims of peer aggression. *Developmental Psychology, 24,* 807–814.

Peterson, L., & Rigby, K. (1999). Countering bullying at an Australian secondary school with students as helpers. *Journal of Adolescence, 22,* 481–492.

Pikas, A. (1990). *Irti kouluväkivallasta* [Getting away from violence in schools] (2nd ed.). (E. Pilvinen, Trans.). Espoo, Finland: Weilin+Göös.

Poole, M. S. (1999). Group communication theory. In L. R. Frey, D. S. Gouran, & M. S. Poole (Eds.), *The handbook of group communication theory and research* (pp. 37–70). Thousand Oaks, CA: Sage.

Poole, M. S., Seibold, D. R., & McPhee, R. D. (1996). The structuration of group decisions. In R. Y. Hirokawa & M. S. Poole (Eds.), *Communication and group decision making* (2nd ed., pp. 114–146). Thousand Oaks, CA: Sage.

Pryor, J. B., & Fitzgerald, L. F. (2003). Sexual harassment research in the United States. In S. Einarsen, H. Hoel, D. Zapf, & C. L. Cooper (Eds.), *Bullying and emotional abuse in the workplace: International perspectives in research and practise* (pp. 79–100). London: Taylor & Francis.

Rainivaara, S. (2004, November). *Communication culture of the workplace and communication behavior as a form of mental violence.* Paper presented at the annual meeting of the National Communication Association, Chicago.

Rayner, C. (1997). The incidence of workplace bullying. *Journal of Community and Applied Social Psychology, 7,* 199–208.

Rayner, C., Sheehan, M., & Barker, M. (1999). Theoretical approaches to the study of bullying at work. *The International Journal of Manpower, 20*, 11–15.

Rigby, K. (1997). Attitudes and beliefs about bullying among Australian school children. *Irish Journal of Psychology, 18*, 202–220.

Rigby, K. (1998). The relationship between reported health and involvement in bully/victim problems at school among male and female secondary schoolchildren. *Journal of Health Psychology, 3*, 465–476.

Rigby, K., & Slee, P. T. (1991). Bullying among Australian school children: Reported behavior and attitudes toward victims. *Journal of Social Psychology, 131*, 615–627.

Roland, E. (2002a). Aggression, depression and bullying others. *Aggressive Behavior, 28*, 198–206.

Roland, E. (2002b). Bullying, depressive symptoms and suicidal thoughts. *Educational Research, 44*, 55–67.

Roland, E., Bjørnsen, G., & Mandt, G. (2003). Taking back adult control: A report from Norway. In P. K. Smith (Ed.), *Violence in schools. The response in Europe* (pp. 200–215). London: Routledge.

Roland, E., & Galloway, D. (2002). Classroom influences in bullying. *Educational Research, 44*, 299–312.

Ross, D. M. (1996). *Childhood bullying and teasing: What school personnel, other professionals, and parents can do.* Alexandria, VA: American Counseling Association.

Ryynänen, S. (2003). *Sukupuolinen häirintä vuorovaikutustilanteena* [Sexual harassment as a communication situation]. Unpublished master's thesis, University of Jyväskylä, Jyväskylä, Finland.

Salin, D. (2001). Prevalence and forms of bullying among business professionals: A comparison of two different strategies for measuring bullying. *European Journal of Work and Organizational Psychology, 10*, 425–441.

Salmivalli, C. (1998). *Koulukiusaaminen ryhmäilmiönä* [Bullying as a group process]. Tampere, Finland: Gaudeamus.

Salmivalli, C. (2002). Suhdeskeemat, sosiaaliset tavoitteet ja sosiaalinen käyttäytyminen [Relational schemas, social goals, and social behavior]. *Psykologia, 37*, 84–92.

Salmivalli, C. (2003). *Koulukiusaamiseen puuttuminen: kohti tehokkaita toimintamalleja* [Interventions in bullying: towards effective practices]. Jyväskylä, Finland: PS-kustannus.

Salmivalli, C., Karhunen, J., & Lagerspetz, K. (1996). How do the victims respond to bullying? *Aggressive Behavior, 22*, 99–109.

Salmivalli, C., & Kaukiainen, A. (2004). "Female aggression" revisited: Variable- and person-centered approaches to studying gender differences in different types of aggression. *Aggressive Behavior, 30*, 158–163.

Salmivalli, C., Kaukiainen, A., & Lagerspetz, K. (2000). Aggression and sociometric status among peers: Do gender and type of aggression matter? *Scandinavian Journal of Psychology, 41*, 17–24.

Salmivalli, C., Lagerspetz, K., Björkqvist, K., Österman, K., & Kaukiainen, A. (1996). Bullying as a group process: Participant roles and their relations to social status within the group. *Aggressive Behavior, 22*, 1–15.

Salmivalli, C., & Voeten, M. (2004). Connections between attitudes, group norms, and behaviors associated with bullying in schools. *International Journal of Behavioral Development, 28,* 246–258.

Sharp, S., & Smith, P. K. (1991). Bullying in UK schools. The DES Sheffield bullying project. *Early Child Development and Care, 77,* 44–55.

Slee, P. T. (1994). Situational and interpersonal correlates of anxiety associated with peer victimization. *Child Psychiatry and Human Development, 25,* 97–107.

Smith, P. K., & Madsen, K. (1999). What causes the age decline in reports of being bullied at school? *Educational Research, 41,* 267–286.

Smith, P. K., Morita, Y., Junger-Tas, J., Olweus, D., Catalano, R., & Slee, P. (Eds.). (1999). *The nature of school bullying: A cross-national perspective.* London: Routledge.

Smith, P. K., & Sharp, S. (Eds.). (1994). *School bullying: Insights and perspectives.* London: Routledge.

Smith, P. K., Talamelli, L., Cowie, H., Naylor, P., & Chauhan, P. (2004). Profiles of non-victims, escaped victims, continuing victims and new victims of school bullying. *British Journal of Educational Psychology, 74,* 565–581.

Smorti, A., Menesini, E., & Smith, P. K. (2003). Parents' definitions of children's bullying in a five-country comparison. *Journal of Cross-Cultural Psychology, 34,* 417–432.

Spitzberg, B. H., (1994). The dark side of (in)competence. In W. R. Cupach & B. H. Spitzberg (Eds.), *The dark side of interpersonal communication* (pp. 25–50). Hillsdale, NJ: Lawrence Erlbaum Associates.

Spratlen, L. P. (1995). Interpersonal conflict which includes mistreatment in a university workplace. *Violence and Victims, 10,* 285–297.

Tasala, M. (1997). *Työpaikkakiusaamisen noidankehät* [The vicious circles of workplace bullying]. Jyväskylä, Finland: Gummerus.

Taylor, D., & Altman, I. (1987). Communication in interpersonal relationships: Social penetration processes. In M. Roloff & G. Miller (Eds.), *Interpersonal processes: New directions in communication research* (pp. 257–277). Newbury Park, CA: Sage.

Taylor, J. R., Flanagan, A. J., Cheney, G., & Seibold, D. R. (2001). Organizational communication research: Key moments, central concerns & future challenges. In W. B. Gudykunst (Ed.), *Communication yearbook 24* (pp. 99–138). Thousand Oaks, CA: Sage.

Teräsahjo, T., & Salmivalli, C. (2002). "Se tavallaan haluu olla yksin". Koulukiusaamisen tulkintarepertuaarit ala-asteen oppilaiden puheissa ["In a way he wants to be alone". The repertoires of interpretation concerning school bullying in the talk of primary-school pupils]. *Psykologia, 37,* 101–114.

Thylefors, I. (1987). *Syndabockar. Om utstötning och mobbning i arbetslivet* [Scapegoats. On expulsion and bullying in working life]. Stockholm, Sweden: Natur och Kultur.

Timmerman, G., & Bajema, C. (1999). Sexual harassment in European workplaces. In *Sexual harassment at the workplace in the European Union* (pp. 1–154). Luxembourg, Luxembourg: Office for Official Publications of the European Communities.

Underwood, M., Galen, B., & Paquette, J. (2001). Top ten challenges for understanding gender and aggression in children: Why can't we all just get along? *Social Development, 10,* 248–266.

Underwood, M. K., Scott, B. L., Galperin, M. B., Bjornstad, G. J., & Sexton, A. M. (2004). An observational study of social exclusion under varied conditions: Gender and developmental differences. *Child Development, 75,* 1538–1555.

Vartia, M. (1991). Bullying at workplaces. In S. Lehtinen, J. Rantanen, P. Juuti, A. Koskela, K. Lindström, P. Rehnström, & J. Saari (Eds.), *Towards the 21st century. Proceedings from the international symposium on future trends in the changing working life* (pp. 131–135). Helsinki, Finland: Institute of Occupational Health.

Vartia, M. (1993). Psychological harassment (bullying, mobbing) at work. In K. Kauppinen-Toropainen (Ed.), *OECD panel group on women, work, and health* (pp. 149–152). Helsinki, Finland: Ministry of Social Affairs and Health.

Vartia, M. (1996). The sources of bullying–Psychological work environment and organizational climate. *European Journal of Work and Organizational Psychology, 5,* 203–214.

Vartia, M., & Perkka-Jortikka, J. (1994). *Henkinen väkivalta työpaikoilla. Työyhteisön hyvinvointi ja sen uhat* [Mental violence in workplaces. The well-being of the working community and the threats facing it]. Tampere, Finland: Gaudeamus.

Vartia-Väänänen, M. (2003). *Workplace bullying: A study on the work environment, well-being and health* (People and work, Research reports No. 56). Helsinki, Finland: Finnish Institute of Occupational Health.

Veale, C., & Gold, J. (1998). Smashing into the glass ceiling of women managers. *Journal of Management, 17,* 17–26.

Vikat, A. (1998). Kiusaamisen yleisyys ja riskitekijät [The prevalence and risk-factors of bullying] (Abstract). *Kouluterveys 2002, 6,* 30–32.

Weir, E. (2001). The health impact of bullying. *Canadian Medical Association Journal, 165,* 1249–1252.

Whitney, I., & Smith, P. K. (1993). A survey of the nature and extent of bullying in junior/middle and secondary schools. *Educational Research, 35,* 3–25.

Wilson, C. B. (1991, July). U.S. businesses suffer from workplace trauma. *Personnel Journal, 70,* 47–50.

Wilson, S. R., & Sabee, C. M. (2003). Explicating communicative competence as a theoretical term. In J. O. Greene & B. R. Burleson (Eds.), *Handbook of communication and social interaction skills* (pp. 3–50). Mahwah, NJ: Lawrence Erlbaum Associates.

Zapf, D. (1999). Organisational, work group related and personal causes of mobbing/bullying at work. *International Journal of Manpower, 20,* 70–85.

Zapf, D., & Einarsen, S. (2001). Bullying in the workplace: Recent trends in research and practice–an introduction. *European Journal of Work and Organizational Psychology, 10,* 369–373.

Zapf, D., & Gross. C. (2001). Conflict escalation and coping with workplace bullying: A replication and extension. *European Journal of Work and Organizational Psychology, 10,* 497–522.

Zapf, D., Knorz, C., & Kulla, M. (1996). On the relationships between mobbing factors, and job content, social work environment and health outcomes. *European Journal of Work and Organizational Psychology, 5,* 215–238.

CHAPTER CONTENTS

7   Forgiveness: Communicative
Implications for Social
Relationships

DOUGLAS L. KELLEY
VINCENT R. WALDRON
Arizona State University

In the last decade, psychologists, philosophers, and, most recently, communication scholars generated a significant body of research focusing on responses to relational injury. Forgiveness is one such response that has profound possibilities for affecting relationships of couples, groups, families, organizations, and nations. The following essay overviews the extant literature on forgiveness, from historical understandings to more recent social science-based and philosophical conceptualizations. We specifically emphasize the role of communication in the forgiveness process and offer a communication-based definition of forgiveness. The essay concludes by developing a necessary research agenda focusing on the communication implications of studying forgiveness.

As humankind enters a new millennium, "we bid farewell to the bloodiest century in human history" (McCullough, Pargament, & Thoresen, 2000, p. xiii). Indeed, public calls for forgiveness and reconciliation have grown louder in recent years, embedded in highly publicized conflict resolution efforts, such as restitution for slavery in the United States, recovery from a racist government in South Africa, and resolution of religious and political conflict in Northern Ireland. Scholars of communication have responded by examining the role of public discourse in framing and apologizing for past injustices (Augoustinos, Lecouter, & Soyland, 2002) and exploring the rhetorical dimensions of reconciliation (Doxtader, 2003).

The communication behaviors used to negotiate forgiveness in families and romantic relationships have begun to receive attention as well (Kelley, 1998). Indeed, it can be argued that interest in the role of forgiveness is even more

Correspondence: Douglas L. Kelley, Communication Studies #3251, P.O. Box 37100, Arizona State University, Phoenix, AZ 85069-7100; email: drdoug@asu.edu

Communication Yearbook 30, pp. 303–341

acute among those who study the private realm of personal relationships. A quick check of any major metropolitan newspaper reveals a culture plagued by relational stress. The relational injuries that accompany divorce, absentee parents, blended family conflicts, psychological and physical abuse, and adultery intensify the need for positive alternatives to feelings of alienation, hostility, or revenge. The process of forgiveness may offer hope to those seeking relational reconciliation and psychological recovery.

Thinking about forgiveness, while rooted deeply in religious, philosophical, and rhetorical texts, has only in the last decade begun to emerge in social scientific literature as a response to this need for relational restoration and psychological health. Like other complex topics, such as love and friendship, social scientists have been slow to examine what may have seemed too difficult to measure or conceptualize. However, recent research on forgiveness has "mushroomed" (Kearns & Fincham, 2004) and achieved "rapid progress" (Zechmeister, Garcia, Romero, & Vas, 2004). For example, in their examination of extant empirical studies, Worthington and Scherer (2004) found that the number of articles about forgiveness quadrupled after 1997, when only 58 articles (McCullough, Exline, Baumeister, 1998) on forgiveness could be found. In addition, the last decade has witnessed a cavalcade of new social science-based forgiveness books for the general public (e.g., Luskin, 2002; McCullough, Sandage, & Worthington, 1997) and from other specialists such as theologians (e.g., Smedes, 1996). The trend toward a positive psychology is partly behind this movement. For example, Peterson and Seligman (2004) include a chapter on forgiveness and mercy in their recent book on *Character Strengths and Virtues*. In addition, forgiveness research is emerging during a time that has produced considerable work focusing on relational repair and maintenance processes (see Canary & Dainton, 2003).

This surge in attention begs for continued research of the forgiveness process at several different levels of analysis. Researchers must recognize forgiveness as a process that can be both intrapersonal and between parties. Intrapersonal foci tend to emphasize psychological processes, whereas intergroup (e.g., Catholics and Protestants in Northern Ireland) or interpersonal (e.g., a husband and wife; Afifi, Falato, & Weiner, 2001; Kelley & Waldron, 2002) perspectives place focus on issues of relational repair and reconciliation. Furthermore, we must recognize that the forgiveness process always involves issues of embedded power, justice, and mercy. These issues may be made manifest as social distinctions between gender, race, or organizational status (e.g., superior and subordinate) or between individuals in personal relationships, such as parents and children, husbands and wives, and friends.

We focus this essay on forgiveness processes within personal relationships while, at the same time, providing direction to researchers who study communication in other contexts, such as international relations and organization studies. Even as we focus our review on the social scientific study of forgiveness, we broaden the discussion to issues of social justice and mercy, which may be of particular interest to critical scholars and those who examine the rhetorical and ethical dimensions of forgiving communication. Our intent is to examine the totality of the interpersonal forgiveness process. That is, we are interested in the larger social phenomena that influence the giving and receiving of forgiveness, as well as its enactment in personal relationships.

To accomplish these goals, we propose a communication-based definition of forgiveness. Specifically, our definition focuses attention on symbolic processes of forgiveness seeking and granting and the means by which partners negotiate these processes over time. Because the forgiveness concept is highly contested, we follow our definition by documenting alternative conceptualizations of forgiveness and explaining how they influence our own approach. The essay then proceeds to an overview of historical and interdisciplinary perspectives, with an emphasis on the rhetorical roots of forgiveness. Subsequently, we examine extant communication research that focuses specifically on forgiveness. That is, what do we know so far regarding forgiveness as a communication process? We end the essay with final thoughts as to how communication scholars can usefully contribute to this growing area of inquiry. In particular, we propose theoretical perspectives that may be useful in guiding future research and identify unanswered questions regarding the seeking and granting of forgiveness in various social contexts.

CONCEPTUALIZING FORGIVENESS

As communication scholars, we are interested in the symbolic process by which individuals seek and offer forgiveness. As such, we understand forgiveness as *a relational process whereby harmful conduct is acknowledged by one or both partners; the harmed partner extends undeserved mercy to the perceived transgressor; one or both partners experience a transformation from negative to positive psychological states, and the meaning of the relationship is renegotiated, with the possibility of reconciliation.* This relationally based definition emphasizes both the psychological and communicative aspects of the forgiveness process. Defined in this way, forgiveness should be of interest to communication scholars who focus on international and intergroup relations, organization studies, conflict and mediation processes, and gender, class, and race relations, as well as those who study the negotiation of personal relationships. To help the reader appreciate how a communicative approach is distinct, we examine alternative conceptualizations of forgiveness.

Existing Forgiveness Definitions

Although social science research on forgiveness has been on the rise during the last decade, no central definition of forgiveness has emerged. As Kearns and Fincham (2004) acknowledged, "no consensus exists on the dimensions of forgiveness or the steps and processes that it involves" (p. 838), at least partly because of the relative infancy of this area of research. Yet the lack of conceptual clarity may also be a result of the nature of the phenomena being studied. Kearns and Fincham argued that the classical manner of defining concepts is inappropriate for forgiveness phenomena:

> This classical view of defining concepts assumes that category membership is an all or none phenomenon; any instance that meets the criteria is a member and all others are not. Because each member must possess the same set of attributes that is the criterion for category inclusion, all members of a category are assumed to be equally representative. This, however, does not appear to be true of the concepts of forgiveness where researchers, and their research participants, recognize degrees of forgiveness. (p. 841)

Kearns and Fincham (2004) recommended a prototype approach for defining forgiveness, similar to that used in studying such ill-defined phenomena as love and commitment (Fehr, 1988) and romantic jealousy (Sharpsteen, 1993). Drawing from Rosch (1975, 1978), they focused on central features rather than critical features. Thus, not all manifestations of a concept are expected to demonstrate all of the components of the prototype. In a similar vein, Prager (1995) grappled with the difficulty of defining the fuzzy construct of intimacy, proposing five functions that such a definition should serve. These guidelines prove useful in our effort to define forgiveness.

Prager (1995) indicated that a useful definition should, first, integrate current conceptualizations of the construct. Second, it should identify the relationship between various loci. Is the phenomenon an "individual capacity, a property of interactions, or a characteristic of a relationship" (p. 13)? A definition of forgiveness requires recognition of both psychological and interpersonal perspectives. Third, the definition should distinguish between the concept under study and similar concepts. For example, forgiveness must be differentiated from related concepts such as condonation, excuse, and reconciliation. Fourth, Prager argued that the ultimate definition is unobtainable; it is characterized by a "shifting template of features" (p. 13). For example, it may not be possible to clearly delineate between forgiveness, relationship maintenance, and relationship repair. Finally, Prager identified the need to reconcile lay and scholarly definitions. It may be this consideration, in part, that further makes the definition of forgiveness a fuzzy one. For example, in a study that we recently completed with married couples (Waldron & Kelley, 2002), some couples identified forgiveness as a routine relational occurrence, whereas others reserved the term *forgiveness* for major relational transgressions, like affairs.

Integration of Existing Definitions

A consensus definition of forgiveness has yet to emerge from researchers who focus on intrapersonal and interpersonal processes. However, certain characteristics surface with some regularity. After a review of both early and current psychological perspectives, McCullough et al. (2000) defined forgiveness as "intraindividual, prosocial change toward a perceived transgressor that is situated within a specific interpersonal context" (p. 9). Their definition highlights five important characteristics of the forgiveness process. First, it is intraindividual. That is, forgiveness always involves a cognitive component. Second, forgiveness involves prosocial change toward a perceived offender. Third and fourth, one person perceives that another has injured them in some way. That is, forgiveness is perception based, and individuals recognize that a *wrong* has occurred. Finally, forgiveness occurs within interpersonal relationships.

Consistent with McCullough et al. (2000), Enright, Eastin, Golden, Sarinopoulos, and Freedman (1992) offered the following definition based on a review of both ancient and modern perspectives on forgiveness. They asserted that "[forgiveness involves] the casting off of deserved punishments, the abandonment of negative reactions, the imparting of love toward the other person, self-sacrificial nature, the potential restoration of the relationship, and positive benefits for the forgiver" (p. 88). This definition assumes that harmed individuals believe they have the "right" to seek revenge in proportion to the harm experienced. Forgiveness lays aside the right to *equal the score* or punish the other person. Enright, Gassin, and Wu (1992) posited that forgiveness involves a decrease in negative affect, cognition, and behavior toward the injurer and an increase in positive affect, cognition, and behavior toward the same. This gradual move to neutral and more positive reactions may include the production of prosocial behavior toward the offender (e.g., expressions of love) (Enright, Eastin, et al., 1992; Enright, Gassin, et al., 1992). This process opens the door for potential reconciliation with the offender and results in positive benefits for the forgiver, which may include positive physical and psychological effects.

What Forgiveness Is Not

Although it is unclear what forgiveness is, there is general consensus that forgiveness is not pardoning, forgetting, condoning, excusing, denying, or reconciliation (McCullough et al., 2000). Pardon is associated with legal settings; the judge who pardons does not experience a personal offense (Enright, Eastin, et al., 1992). The old adage "forgive and forget" is problematic for two reasons. First, individuals are not able to remove memories simply by will; people keep painful memories for years (Enright & Fitzgibbons, 2000). As such, forgive and forget, if taken literally, places the offended party in an impossible situation. Second, because perceiving a transgression is what initially sets the condition for forgiveness to take place (E. Scobie & G. Scobie, 1998), even if one could forget, by implication, forgiveness would no longer be necessary.

Enright, Eastin, et al. (1992) argued that condonation and excuse are distinct from forgiveness. One who *condones* an offense "puts up with" it, often because of mitigating circumstances (p. 89). This approach removes responsibility from the perceived offender and thus lessens the need for forgiveness. So, too, *excusing* eliminates the need for forgiveness because it legitimizes the offensive act (Enright & Fitzgibbons, 2000). *Denying* is even more clearly distinct from forgiveness. By denying that any wrongdoing occurred, one also eliminates the need to grant forgiveness.

Acceptance has also been distinguished from forgiveness (Smedes, 1984). Smedes stated that "we accept people for the good they *are*, we forgive them for the bad they *did*" (p. 67). As such, like the other concepts just discussed, acceptance is distinct from forgiveness in that it fails to acknowledge a wrongdoing or views a wrongdoing as inconsequential, compared with the value of the person or the relationship, to warrant forgiveness.

Two other terms associated with forgiveness deserve specific attention: *justice* and *reconciliation*. Enright and the Human Development Study Group (1991) claimed that harmed individuals face a basic choice between justice and mercy. Those choosing justice tend to focus on issues of fairness and equity. In contrast, mercy responses forgo revenge and punishment (both of which "balance" the pain experienced by the partners). As Pingleton (1989) recognized, forgiveness involves choosing to give "up one's right to hurt back" (p. 27). However, mercy may not preclude other kinds of consequences for the offender. Mercy may be exercised through passive strategies, such as condonation and simple acceptance, or active strategies such as forgiveness.

Finally, forgiveness must be carefully distinguished from *reconciliation*. Hargrave and Sells (1997) emphasized reconciliation when they defined forgiveness as "the release of blame and reconciliation" (p. 43). They based this conceptualization on Hargrave's (1994) forgiveness model, which is organized around the reactions of *exoneration* and *forgiveness*. Exoneration involves insight into the transgression and understanding or reframing the offender's actions. The *forgiveness* category is in essence what many scholars would call reconciliation (Enright & Fitzgibbons, 2000). For Hargrave, forgiveness involves the *opportunity for compensation* and an *overt act of forgiveness*. Specifically, forgiveness often encompasses apology and a renegotiation of the relationship.

Importantly, Hargrave's (1994) conceptualization was developed in the context of marital therapy, where reconciliation is often the goal. Most researchers distinguish between forgiveness and reconciliation (McCullough et al., 2000). For example, it may not be possible or desirable to reconcile with an ex-spouse (Rye, Folck, Heim, Olszewski, & Traina, 2004). Conceptualizing reconciliation as a *necessary* component of forgiveness empowers the offender to stop the process. Recognizing this stipulation, Enright and Fitzgibbons (2000) contended that forgiveness can be unconditional—independent from the offender's actions. According to Enright and Fitzgibbons, "Whenever an offended person wishes, he or she can commence forgiving. Whenever that same person wishes reconciliation, he or she must await the negotiation, the discussion, and the cooperation of the other party" (p. 41).

For Enright and Fitzgibbons (2000), reconciliation requires the reestablishment of trust. Worthington (2001) agreed, noting that "reconciliation is the restoration of trust in a relationship where trust has been violated, sometimes repeatedly. Reconciliation involves not just *forgiveness* but also many other ways of reducing *unforgiveness*" (p. 176). Unforgiveness consists of an emotional complex of resentment, bitterness, hatred, hostility, residual anger, and fear. Unforgiveness intensifies when people ruminate about the transgression. Forgiveness is but one way of managing unforgiveness and moving toward reconciliation. Other ways of managing unforgiveness include justice strategies, conflict resolution, psychological mechanisms such as denial, and simply forbearing or accepting.

Reconciling Lay and Researcher Definitions

A number of forgiveness researchers have implemented Prager's (1995) suggestion to reconcile lay and researcher definitions. This process is essential to the development of therapeutic and educational programs that can benefit laypeople (Kearns & Fincham, 2004). Two studies have examined layperson' self-generated notions of forgiveness. Zechmeister and Romero (2002) instructed participants to write two narratives that described an event in which they had committed a relational transgression and were forgiven or not. Consistent with the definition of Enright et al. (1991), forgiveness narratives, compared with unforgiveness narratives, included more positive affect. In addition, forgiveness narratives revealed more positive outcomes and more event closure.

Kelley (2001) asked participants to write forgiveness narratives drawn from their romantic relationships. Participants described situations in which they forgave, were forgiven, or requested forgiveness. Judges identified two themes relevant to our discussion of lay definitions. *Elements of Forgiveness* included words that were used synonymously with forgiveness by some participants, such as *trust, apology, sincerity, remembering* and *forgetting*, and *understanding*.

These words coincide with Hargrave's (1994) conceptualization, which includes understanding, overt displays of forgiveness (e.g., apology and sincerity), and concepts related to reconciliation (e.g., trust).

Kelley's (2001) participants also identified *Forgiveness Types*, including intellectual and emotional forgiveness, conditional forgiveness, and unilateral and bilateral forgiveness. The intellectual/emotional distinction has been proposed by therapists (e.g., Worthington, 2001). Conditional forgiveness is based on if/then propositions (e.g., "I will forgive you if you don't do it again."). The unilateral and bilateral types are distinguished by the degree of partner reciprocation.

Several additional studies contrast lay and researcher definitions. Kantz (2000), using a series of yes/no questions created from a review of previous forgiveness research, found strong similarities between lay and researcher conceptualizations of forgiveness. For example, both researchers and laypeople believed that anger dissipates during forgiveness. Interestingly, only laypersons believed that reconciliation was an essential part of forgiveness. These findings have practical import for therapists, who may find that clients resist forgiveness-based interventions because of their reluctance to reconcile with an offender.

Similarities between laypersons and researchers were reported by French researchers (Mullet, Girard, & Bakhshi, 2004). Participants indicated level of agreement with 93 definitional statements extracted from the forgiveness literature. A representative statement read, "To forgive someone who has done you wrong necessarily means to start feeling affection toward him again" (p. 82). Factor analysis yielded four definitional dimensions: forgiveness is a change of heart; forgiveness is immoral (e.g., humiliation of the forgiven, approval of the offense); forgiveness can encourage repentance, and forgiveness is a more-than-dyadic process (that is, forgiveness can be given to institutions and groups, in the name of other people, and even to distant or dead people). According to Mullet et al., nearly 23% of respondents believed forgiveness involves a change of heart; 33% saw forgiveness as encouraging repentance; 46% believed forgiveness could be more than a dyadic process, and only 4% saw forgiveness as immoral in any way.

Kearns and Fincham (2004), through five separate studies, supported the idea that laypeople use a forgiveness prototype similar to that suggested by researchers. Both acknowledged that (1) forgivers' responses toward the offender become less negative and (2) forgiveness involves cognition, affect, and behavior. However, some differences between researcher and lay conceptualizations were noted regarding the following concepts, which researchers do not typically consider to be part of forgiveness: 12% of lay participants listed condoning and excusing as an attribute of forgiveness; 28% believed that forgetting was important to forgiveness, and 21% believed that reconciliation is a central feature of forgiveness. In addition, only laypeople believed that negative aspects of forgiveness include feelings of weakness, being a pushover, and giving the other person permission to hurt you again. Based on this work, we can conclude that a small but notable minority of lay definitions differ from those offered by forgiveness researchers.

A Psychosocial Definition of Interpersonal Forgiveness

As we have indicated, significant debate still surrounds the definition of forgiveness, and yet certain elements can be agreed upon. Virtually all researchers describe forgiveness as a cognitive process of managing the negative emotions that result from a perceived transgression by a relational partner. McCullough et al. (2000) claimed:

> A consensual definition might be more feasible than one might initially imagine. All existing definitions seem to be built on one core feature: When people forgive, their responses toward . . . people who offended or injured them become more positive and less negative. (p. 9)

Definitions of forgiveness also typically position the construct as social. The context may involve relationships between countries, organizations, or other types of groups. Most pertinent to this review, however, transgressions take place within the social context of interpersonal relationships. Although significant questions remain regarding the role of interpersonal relationships in the forgiveness process (e.g., clearly, many researchers view reconciliation as a process that is distinct from, but related to, forgiveness; see Enright & Fitzgibbons, 2000; Worthington, 2000), it is important to recognize the interpersonal nature of forgiveness. As McCullough et al. (2000) explained, "forgiveness has a dual character; it is interpersonal as well as intrapersonal. . . . Perhaps it is most comprehensive to think of forgiveness as a *psychosocial* construct" (p. 9).

Toward a Communicative Definition

In light of the ongoing dialog regarding the defining features of forgiveness, the definition that we offered at the beginning of this section draws three important distinctions. First, it focuses on *both* intrapersonal and relational processes. That is, it acknowledges the possibilities for psychological transformation in individuals as well as relational renegotiation (even reconciliation) by the partners. Second, it makes overt recognition of harmful behavior a central component of forgiveness. Third, our definition is clearly communicative with its emphasis on partners' efforts to *acknowledge* harm, *extend* mercy, and *negotiate meaning*.

Before moving on, we note that the conceptual dialog should continue. Cross-cultural communication scholars can contribute to the discussion by exploring how forgiveness is manifested in different cultural contexts. Gender researchers may find that women, who more often experience abuse in personal relationships, will define forgiveness differently than men (see Cann & Baucom, 2004). Scholars of religious discourse may be particularly helpful in discerning how various theological conceptions of forgiveness are manifested in public debates about such issues as capital punishment and restorative justice.

HISTORICAL AND
INTERDISCIPLINARY PERSPECTIVES

Apologia: The Rhetorical Roots of Forgiveness Seeking

The interest of communication scholars in the topic of forgiveness traces to the study of *apologia*, perhaps the most enduring of rhetorical genres (Ware & Linkugel, 1973). Today's focus of apology and apologia on seeking forgiveness and making accounts for one's actions (Cody & McLaughlin, 1988; McCullough, Worthington, & Rachel, 1997) comes from a long rhetorical history. As Ryan (1982) observed, Plato contrasted apology and accusation as two fundamental types of discourse. In the *Rhetoric*, Aristole (1954) identified *apologia* as a kind of defensive discourse designed to protect the speaker from accusation. Among the most notable "apologies" was the defense offered by Socrates. In the classical tradition, apologia constituted a carefully crafted form of public discourse, typically presented in a formal context, usually with the objective of convincing the audience to exonerate the speaker (Downey, 1993).

As the genre evolved, its rhetorical objectives multiplied (Downey, 1993). During the medieval period, guilt was frequently predetermined by the church, so apologists rarely attempted exoneration. Rather, their discourse was frequently confessional, as the accused admitted past mistakes and sought divine forgiveness (if not intervention). During this period, sincere apology was linked explicitly to the possibility of forgiveness and possible reconciliation with God. Later, during the modern period, rebellious leaders recurrently employed apologia to energize audiences and advance their causes. Downey noted this strategy in the apologia of abolitionist John Brown, who claimed that it may be necessary to "forfeit my life" on behalf of the slaves "whose rights are disregarded by wicked, cruel, and unjust enactments" (p. 51). Like many apologists, Brown saw himself as a scapegoat for his cause.

Contemporary apologia has focused on increasing audience identification with the accused, obscuring the speaker's responsibility for unethical behavior, and increasing the speaker's chances of political survival after an ethical lapse. For example, Simons (2000) highlighted the use of ambiguity in President Clinton's apology for the Monica Lewinsky affair and subsequent cover-up. Downey (1993) went so far as to claim that deception is a primary function of modern apologia. In fact, contemporary critiques of apologetic discourse often criticize speakers' efforts to seek forgiveness without fully accepting responsibility for their actions. In analysis of apologies offered by the Catholic Church for sex abuses committed by clergy, Dunne (2004) found that the church uses mystification and distancing language to avoid direct responsibility. Tellingly, Dunne argued that the church uses *apologia* rather than *apology*. Critical and feminist scholarship will be helpful in examining discourses of this type, especially in terms of how pleas for forgiveness may advance certain institutional interests while disadvantaging less powerful parties.

With Dunne (2004), we would argue that apologia, at least in its classical defensive form, should not be confused with forgiveness-seeking communication. Moreover, the contemporary practice of using ambiguity or deception to preserve a relationship with the audience also fails to qualify. Rather, forgiveness seeking is marked by communication that accepts responsibility, expresses genuine remorse, and asks the listener for mercy that only a wounded party can provide. These criteria may be particularly useful as scholars of rhetoric and communication ethics examine the efforts of corporate and government leaders to seek forgiveness for their transgressions.

Theological Foundations

Whereas the roots of apologia can be traced back to Plato and Aristotle (Ryan, 1982), the idea of granting forgiveness may be found back as far as certain early Hindu texts (Rye et al., 2000), though substantive conceptual development did not occur in early Jewish and Christian traditions. For both Christians and Jews, forgiveness is foremost something that takes place between God and humankind. As such, the emphasis of forgiveness is on creating a way to reconcile separated parties. In the Pentateuch, Moses prayed to God, "forgive our wickedness and our sin, and take us as your inheritance" (Exodus 34:9). In the Hebrew scriptures, God ordained a sacrificial system in which a priest might intercede for the people and gain God's forgiveness. Early and more contemporary Jewish writings stress the importance of forgiveness-seeking behaviors as they underscore the importance of repentance in gaining forgiveness and subsequent reconciliation with God.

In the Christian New Testament, Jesus emphasized the importance of God's forgiveness of humanity, but he also linked the idea of God's forgiveness to the importance of human beings forgiving one another. Jesus taught his disciples to ask God to "forgive us our debts, as we also have forgiven our debtors" (Matthew 6:12). Perhaps the most magnanimous example of forgiveness comes from Jesus when he prayed for his persecutors while being crucified: "Father forgive them, for they know not what they do" (Luke 23:34).

Other religious traditions have also emphasized the importance of forgiveness. Islam views forgiveness as important between God and people and between people, and it indicates that Muhammad, as a leader of the state, is seen to forgive people (Rye et al., 2000). Both Buddhist and Hindu writings stress karma as the means by which justice is maintained, releasing followers of these religious traditions to act in more forgiving ways. Although Buddhist writings typically do not reference forgiveness specifically, they do focus on the virtues of *forbearance* and *compassion*. Rye et al. asserted that "the chief function of compassion is to ease pain and suffering in others, while the chief function of forbearance is to desist from causing more suffering, both for oneself and others" (p. 17).

These perspectives, while primarily formed from ancient texts, have relevance today. Research suggests that people frequently draw on religious teaching when trying to forgive and that religious people value forgiveness more than less religious people (Rye et al., 2000). Of specific interest to communication scholars, religious perspectives have been utilized to better understand both interpersonal and intergroup conflict. For example, Kirkup (1993) employed religious principles to provide practical guidelines for mediation processes, and Helmick (2001) made an extensive argument for the potential usefulness of religion to the healing of international conflicts through *track two* diplomacy. Finally, Rye et al. contended that religious-historical perspectives may help guard against an oversimplification of the forgiveness process by social scientists. For example, religious perspectives offer important insights into the relationship between forgiveness and reconciliation, and they provide an understanding of how repentance is enacted in the forgiveness process. The role of religion in granting and receiving forgiveness should remain a fruitful field of study, as should the role of forgiveness in processes of mediation and intergroup conflict.

Philosophical Debates

Philosophers have also argued the meaning of forgiveness since ancient times. For example, in the *Rhetoric* (1954), Aristotle suggested that seeking forgiveness is an appropriate response to behavior that is involuntary and inconsistent with the actor's character. In contrast, apologia is called for when the actor is accused of intentional and unacceptable behavior (see Ryan, 1982). Hegel (1977) also indicated concern for the philosophy of human action in the *Phenomenology of Spirit.* A central question for Hegel and later Arendt (1958) was: What can be forgiven? Given that human action often leads to unforeseen and tragic consequences, when is it possible to hold actors accountable and to whom should/can forgiveness be granted? Arendt elevated the importance of forgiveness in the following statement:

> The possible redemption from the predicament of irreversibility—of being unable to undo what was done though one did not, and could not, have known what he was doing—is the faculty of forgiving. . . . Without being forgiven, released from the consequences of what we have done, our capacity to act would, as it were, be confined to one single deed from which we could never recover; we would remain the victims of its consequences forever. . . . (p. 237)

Philosophers have also explored the issue of whether forgiveness is a good thing or even possible. For example, Derrida (2001) argued that pure forgiveness, the unconditional kind, is impossible and perhaps not truly good. In the practice of politics, forgiveness must be linked to conditions if it is to result in just outcomes. Furthermore, he contended that the granting of forgiveness requires sovereignty, or the capacity to grant pardon to another person. Those who must forgive are not sovereign. Instead, harm-doers can initiate the process of forgiveness as a means of evading justice. Yet, Derrida implied that the political peace that sometimes follows from forgiveness may (or may not) be preferable to continued hostility.

Indeed, the important role of forgiveness in preserving human solidarity may be a primary reason for forgiving unconditionally (McNaughton, 1992). Similarly, a consequentialist philosophy argues that the process of forgiveness is valuable because it can lead to positive outcomes, such as democracy in countries previously wracked by injustice and civil strife (Pope, 2003). In analyzing "political forgiveness" in El Salvador, where religious leaders and civilians were murdered by government-affiliated thugs, Pope maintained that forgiveness need not imply forgetting or a willingness to forgo justice. Rather, forgiveness should be part of a larger process of truth telling and the bearing of responsibility. From this point of view, forgiveness is predicated on a full accounting of the wrongs of the past. It is an important step in establishing a just system of human relationships.

This body of research should be of particular interest to communication scholars who concern themselves with issues of social justice and political communication. How is forgiveness used in the discourse of those who make or respond to claims of wrongdoing? How (if at all) is forgiveness integrated into public processes of reconciliation or truth-telling? In public discourse, how is forgiveness linked to goodness, truth-telling, forgetting, mercy, and justice?

International Perspectives

Attempts to respond justly to transgressions while seeking reconciliation have been well documented. Perhaps best known is Tutu's (1999) account of the Truth and Reconciliation processes in South Africa. The title of Tutu's book, *No Future Without Forgiveness*, provides a summary of the challenge presented to the South African people: pursue justice with great time and cost by trying to bring the guilty to trial, grant everyone amnesty or, through confession and truth-telling, grant forgiveness and amnesty. Tutu movingly recounted the hearing for the Bisho Massacre. Four officers were ushered into a room filled with tension from previous testimony, and their spokesman said:

> "Yes, we gave the orders for the soldiers to open fire." Ho! It was combustible! And then he turned to the audience, this angry audience, seething, and he said, "Please, forgive us. Please accept my colleagues back into the community." And do you know what that audience, that angry audience, did? It broke out into deafening applause. (p. xii)

Forgiveness may be of particular interest to scholars of postcolonialism; for example, da Silva (2001) reviewed three cases of nonviolent resistance in India that helped move conflicting parties toward reconciliation. Reconciliation for da Silva has commonalities with four dimensions of forgiveness as identified by Shriver (1995): moral judgment, forbearance, empathy, and repairing of broken relationships. Smyth (2001), a Dominican theologian from Belfast, described events that opened the door to forgiveness and reconciliation in Ireland. One such event, "Counting the Cost," involved Christians from Northern Ireland and the Irish Republic in a ritual that was televised throughout the country on Good Friday, 1995. Likewise, Bartoli (2001) identified forgiveness as a key element in the peace processes that ended 30 years of armed struggle in Mozambique.

Finally, a discussion of forgiveness beyond personal relationships cannot be complete without reference to Wiesenthal's (1997) book *The Sunflower*, which chronicled Wiesenthal's own experience in a Nazi concentration camp and the request made of him to forgive a Nazi SS officer who was dying. *The Sunflower* summarizes this event, but it then asks experts in religion, the military, and politics to discuss the question of whether forgiveness should have been given. This marvelous dialogue about forgiveness reminds us that, although the intergroup level is concerned with a Jew forgiving a Nazi, forgiveness is often simultaneously negotiated at the interpersonal level. That is, Wiesenthal recognized that he and the SS officer were individuals thrown together in a moment in time, in which one man was asking forgiveness of another.

Psychological Research Traditions

Psychologists have studied forgiveness from three overlapping points of view. First, research psychologists have examined the personality traits and psychological states that facilitate or inhibit the forgiveness process. Second, the role of forgiveness in the preservation of nonclincial personal relationships has been a growing area of research. Finally, clinicians have examined forgiveness-based interventions with distressed couples and families.

Psychological traits and states. *Willingness to forgive* has been conceptualized as an enduring disposition in recent studies (Brown & Phillips, 2005; Hebl & Enright, 1993). The scales used by these authors measure individual reactions to various hypothetical transgressions. Measures of more generalized forgiveness orientation have also been offered by Mauger et al. (1992); Berry, Worthington, Parrot, O'Connor, and Wade (2001); Rye et al. (2001); and others. However, a recent review noted that existing measures tend to be idiosyncratic to original study conditions and to be rarely used (Ross, Kendall, Matters, Wrobel, & Rye, 2004).

One response to this criticism is to link forgiveness with more familiar personality traits. Ross and colleagues (2004) examined the pervasive five-factor model (FFM) of personality and its association with forgiveness in a study of 147 undergraduates. These traits included neuroticism-emotional stability, extraversion-introversion, openness-closedness, agreeableness-antagonism, and conscientiousness-undirectedness. Forgiveness of others was positively related to the dimensions of agreeableness and extraversion (warmth and positive emotions subscale). It was negatively associated with the hostility facet of the neuroticism scale as well as the order dimension of the conscientiousness subscale. In general, known personality traits appear to be modestly successful in predicting forgiveness responses.

Research on sociocognitive responses to transgressions, such as situational empathy, rumination, and attribution, seems still more promising. McCullough, Worthington, et al. (1997) argued that empathy was essential if the offended partner was to shift from a self-focused concern with emotional hurt to an other-focused care for the partner and the relationship. Recent research confirms that empathy is an independent predictor of forgiveness in marital couples (Paleari, Regalia, & Fincham, 2005). On the other hand, rumination, the tendency to dwell on the transgression, has been associated with unforgiveness (Worthington & Wade, 1999). Rumination was negatively associated with forgiveness in a recent study of 87 married couples (Kachadourian, Fincham, & Davila, 2005). Finally, attributions about the motives of the offender have been important in several studies. For example, it appears that the degree of blame attributed to the offender shapes the forgiveness response (Zechmester et al., 2004). Before forgiving, the offended partner may consider the degree to which the offense was intentional, mitigated by external forces, or likely to be part of an enduring pattern (Kearns & Fincham, 2005).

Another sociocognitive process closely related to forgiveness is altruism. S. L. Smith et al. (2005) defined altruism as a "voluntary action (independent of motive) that is intended to benefit others beyond simple sociability or duties associated with a [helping] role" (p. 4). They excluded simple acts of cooperation. They operationalized altruistic acts at two levels: helping and sharing. They also measured the extent to which actors express concern for others and empathy. They argued that the degree to which an actor is able to escape the obligation to help should also be considered. The issue here seems to be the degree to which helping constitutes a contextual obligation or a choice made by the actor. To fully understand the degree to which an act is altruistic these authors further contended that the costs incurred by the actor (because of the altruistic action) must be considered, as well as the actual benefits to the recipient. Acts that involve more costs to the actor and more benefit to the recipient are more altruistic.

As we define it, forgiveness could be considered an instance of altruistic relational behavior. Notably, empathy is prominent in both processes. In addition, Worthington (2001) lists altruism as part of a prescriptive process of forgiving. Worthington uses the acronym REACH to identify five steps in the forgiveness process: Recall, Empathy, Altruistic Gift, Commit, and Hold On to forgiveness. Altruistic gift refers to the fact that the forgiver gives an unwarranted gift, forgiveness, to the offender. Although altruism can be seen here as a step in the forgiveness process, it is probably more useful to understand altruism as an umbrella concept for understanding forgiving acts. That is, forgiveness can be considered a type of altruistic behavior because it may serve to benefit the other, and yet, forgiveness is narrower in scope than altruism, as it includes only cases that have been preceded by a transgression. Other forms of nonforgiveness, such as acceptance and tolerance, may be considered less active altruistic acts toward a transgressing partner.

Relationship quality. Relationship quality has also been associated with forgiveness in a growing number of studies, many of which are reported by psychologist Frank Fincham and colleagues (e.g., Fincham, 2000; Fincham & Beach, 2002). Generally, this research indicates that wounded partners are more forgiving in the context of romantic relationships that are close, committed, and satisfying. Apparently, satisfied partners may be more willing to offer apologies when they commit transgressions, and they are more likely to respond with empathy (McCullough, Worthington, et al., 1997). A recent study of 177 undergraduates provided support for a causal model in which positive relationship quality led to more benign interpretations of transgressions, which, in turn, fostered feelings of forgiveness (Kearns & Fincham, 2005). However, Fincham's study indicated that the decision to forgive a partner seems to affect behavior toward that partner, independent of marital satisfaction. Partners who avoid forgiveness may experience less positive outcomes to conflict (Fincham, Beach, & Davila, 2004).

Research in this developing tradition seems likely to clarify the causal sequencing of these largely psychological dimensions of forgiveness. A recent longitudinal study (six months) of Italian couples revealed that empathy and rumination independently predicted marital forgiveness, but it also suggested that forgiveness and marital quality had reciprocating effects over time (Paleari et al., 2005).

Clinical interventions. Clinical applications of forgiveness now appear frequently in counseling and therapeutic publications. The literature consists of experimental studies documenting the effects of forgiveness-based interventions as well as clinical reports describing therapeutic techniques. In a recent example of the latter, Barnett and Youngberg (2004) described a technique for ritualizing forgiveness in couple therapy. Using metaphorical reenactment, the therapists use a "flowerpot, potting soil, and bulbs" (p. 14) to help couples implement the concepts of forgiveness and growth. Fincham and Beach (2002) provided a valuable survey of the experimental work. The authors noted that therapeutic claims for the value of forgiveness-based therapies are more frequent than well-conducted studies of the issue. However, a review of 12 group interventions (Worthington, Sandage, & Berry, 2000) concluded that therapies that encourage clients to think about forgiveness are successful in that clients report more forgiving attitudes.

Fincham and Beach (2002) obtained mixed evidence for the claim that, once established, forgiveness leads to positive relational outcomes. Hebl and Enright (1993) studied older females in forgiveness therapy, finding that placebo and treatment groups both showed reductions in symptoms of depression. In contrast, Al-Mabuk, Enright, and Cardis (1995) found significant increases in hope and anxiety for college students who were counseled to use forgiveness in a hurtful parenting relationship. In a carefully conducted study (Freedman & Enright, 1996) of adult survivors of sexual abuse, significant improvements resulted from forgiveness-based therapy on measures of hope, self-esteem, and anxiety (as compared with a wait-listed control group). Although intervention-based research on forgiveness has been conducted for only a decade or so, Fincham and Beach (2002) viewed the trend as positive. However, more rigorous experimental studies are needed to supplement valuable clinical accounts.

FORGIVENESS AS A
COMMUNICATIVE PHENOMENON

Our proposed definition of forgiveness, at the beginning of this chapter, encourages further development of communication perspectives on forgiveness. As such, we devote the remainder of this essay to identifying how forgiveness research can both inform and be benefited by communication theories and perspectives.

Communication Research on Forgiveness:
What Do We Know So Far?

Few studies have looked explicitly at how forgiveness is communicated, although communication researchers have studied forgiveness-related concepts (e.g., apology). For example, the accounts literature suggests that more mitigating strategies, such as concession (of which apology is one type), may lead to conciliatory responses from offended partners (Cody & McLaughlin, 1988). More recently, Emmers and Canary (1996) conceptualized forgiveness and apology as related "interactive" strategies of relationship repair (p. 174). Interestingly, psychological researchers have proposed that communication is instrumental in determining forgiveness outcomes. McCullough, Worthington, et al. (1997) found strong evidence for the relationship between apology and forgiveness. Focusing on family relationships, Hargrave (1994) suggested that an appropriate apology is needed before relationships can be renegotiated. Walters (1984) conceptualized a *follow-through* process, which at times requires discussion between the aggrieved party and the offender. Despite these isolated studies, researchers have only recently conceptualized forgiveness as a communicative process.

Kelley (1998) explicitly addressed communication in an exploratory study of forgiveness processes in nontherapeutic relationships. His participants provided narratives of times when they granted, received, and/or sought forgiveness. Findings from 304 narratives were organized around four central components of the forgiveness process: situational elements, motivations, strategies, and relational consequences.

Situational elements: Relational type and severity of transgression. Kelley (1998) identified key situational elements such as relationship type and severity of the infraction. The forgiveness narratives concerned the following relationship types: family (primarily parent-child, followed by spouse, sibling, and extended family), friendships, dating relationships, and a few instances of work and stranger/acquaintance relationships. Chi-square analyses indicated that forgiveness was exercised differently in these relational contexts.

The nature of the transgression is a critical element in nearly every discussion of forgiveness processes. Worthington and Wade (1999) noted that "transgressions are particularly destructive when they are repeated, heavily charged with negative emotion, severe, and unaccompanied by transgressor guilt or apology" (pp. 389–390). Metts (1994) argued that transgression severity is a major factor shaping the communicative choices and relationship outcomes experienced in personal relationships. Confirming this claim, Waldron and Kelley (2005) asked participants to rate the relationship infractions they experienced in terms of severity, damage to the relationship, and threat to the relationship. Higher scores on this summative measure were associated with negative relationship outcomes, although forgiveness strategies appeared to mitigate the effects, even when transgressions were most severe.

Motivation for forgiveness. Kelley (1998) culled forgiveness narratives for the motives reported by forgiveness seekers and forgivers. Both reported using forgiveness as a means of restoring emotional well-being to the self or partner. Some employed forgiveness to rebuild the damaged relationship. These individuals mentioned the need to restore trust, a desire for relationship restoration, and feelings of obligation as motives for initiating forgiveness. Often they linked motivation to reframing the infraction. Motivation was increased by framing of the offense as unintentional or lower in severity. If the offender didn't "really mean" to be hurtful or wasn't completely responsible for the infraction, aggrieved partners were more motivated to forgive. Some forgave only after the offender offered an appropriate account, such as an apology, demonstration of remorse, or restitution.

Kelley's (1998) findings on motivation link to previous work on psychological dimensions of forgiveness. Some of his forgiveness motivations are viewed as internal forgiveness strategies in psychological models. For example, consonant with Kelley's notion of reframing severity, intent, and responsibility of the transgression, E. D. Scobie and G. E. Scobie (1998) identified reinterpreting the event as a strategy of response to a damaging transgression. For these authors, reinterpreting is passive acceptance. In contrast, Enright, Eastin, et al. (1992) envisioned reframing as part of the "therapeutic regimen" (p. 97) of a psychologically based forgiveness. Such a regimen seeks to develop a richer understanding of the event and of the perpetrator. Reframing begins a process that leads to empathy, compassion, realization of past and current truths, and awareness of decreased negative affect and emotional release.

If one views forgiveness as an interpersonal process, these internal forgiveness strategies become motivations for engaging in the kinds of communication that move partners through the process of forgiveness. Consistent with this characterization, Hargrave (1994) distinguished between forgiveness and exoneration. Exoneration, a first step toward forgiveness, involves two elements: 1) insight into what caused the pain and 2) understanding of the offender's own limitations. Understanding essentially reframes the offender by seeing him or her as fallible (though still responsible). This first step establishes the psychological conditions that may lead to forgiveness-granting communication. Kelley's (1998) study also confirmed that motivation to forgive can be linked to the performance of communication behavior by the offender. That is, study participants identified the offender's response (e.g., apology) as one of the reasons that they were willing to forgive. This finding coincides with religious perspectives reviewed previously, particularly the Jewish tradition.

Finally, Kelley (1998) found that relationship type influences forgiveness motivation. In the context of family relationships, some forgiveness motives were rarely reported, including restoring the relationship, love, and the offender's communication strategy. In contrast, dating and friendship partners were more motivated to restore the relationship. Apparently, the nonvoluntary nature of family relationships makes the restorative function less salient (e.g., "I don't need to forgive you in order to restore the relationship; you will always be my sister."). Also, compared with friends, dating partners were more motivated by love, well-being, and the strategy of their partner. Compared with family and friendship bonds, dating relationships are more subject to social sanction (Rawlins, 1989) and may be perceived as relatively fragile by the partners (Owen, 1984). In this more difficult relational environment, forgiveness processes may be particularly important if partners are to maintain feelings of love and well-being.

Interestingly, the partner's forgiveness-seeking strategy was more important in dating relationships than in friendships. Rawlins (1989) argued that best friendships can often endure "even without identifiable rewards and interaction" (p. 169). As such, close friends may have less need for certain partner behaviors (e.g., apology) when making decisions regarding forgiveness and reconciliation of the relationship.

Forgiveness-seeking strategies. Worthington and Wade (1999) noted that "the victim's perception of the transgressor's account is crucial to forgiveness or unforgiveness" (p. 402). Yet few researchers (e.g., Schmitt, Gollwitzer, Forster, & Montada, 2004) have examined the role of the offender's communication in the forgiveness process. (Table 7–1 summarizes the results of a series of studies conducted by Kelley and Waldron on communication strategies

TABLE 7–1
Self-Reported Forgiveness Strategies and Romantic Relationship Outcomes

Strategy	Examples	Outcome
Forgiveness-seeking strategies		
1. Explicit acknowledgment	Apology; remorse	Positive
2. Nonverbal Assurance	Eye contact; hugs	Positive
3. Compensation	Gifts; repeated efforts	Positive
4. Explanation	Reasons; discuss offense	None
5. Humor	Joking; humoring	None
Forgiveness-granting strategies		
1. Explicit	"I forgive you"	Positive
2. Nonverbal displays	Facial expressions; touch	Positive
3. Conditional	I forgive you, but only if . . .	Negative
4. Discussion	Talking about the offense	Positive
5. Minimize	"No big deal"; "don't worry"	None

Kelley & Waldron (2005); Waldron & Kelley (2005).

and their relational consequences; see Kelley, 1998; Kelley & Waldron, 2005; Waldron & Kelley, 2005). Kelley's study of forgiveness narratives revealed three general communication strategies used by forgiveness-seeking partners. *Direct* strategies were characterized by requests for forgiveness, apology, taking responsibility for one's actions, explanations, and showing remorse. When using the *conditional* strategy, offenders pledged to change or improve their future behavior in exchange for forgiveness. Forgiveness would be withdrawn if the conditions were not met.

Kelley's (1998) discussion of indirect strategies was unique in the forgiveness literature. Indirect approaches to securing forgiveness involved humor, nonverbal behaviors and displays of emotion, using the social network to communicate the offender's feelings to the forgiver, ingratiation, and resuming "normal" behavior patterns. Through all of these tactics, the offender and offended do not ever specifically talk about the transgression or forgiveness.

Kelley and Waldron (2005) elaborated on Kelley's (1998) taxonomy, with the use of factor analytic techniques and a larger sample of romantic partners. Their findings paralleled Kelley's, but they expanded his direct/indirect dichotomy to five categories of behavior. The factors were explicit acknowledgement, nonverbal assurance, compensation, explanation, and humor. Explicit acknowledgement included behaviors commonly reported in previous research, such as apology, expression of remorse, and direct requests for forgiveness. The nonverbal assurance factor was characterized by behaviors such as eye contact and giving hugs. When combined, these approaches likely demonstrate honesty and sincerity. As E. D. Scobie and G. E. Scobie (1998) observed, cultural norms demand a sincere apology and expression of remorse if forgiveness is to be considered. Compensation, the third factor, involved making an investment of time and effort, repeated attempts to gain forgiveness, or gift giving. The fourth factor, explanation, included discussing the situation, circumstances, and reasons for the transgression. The final strategy, humor, may distract the offended partner or lighten the mood.

Kelley and Waldron (2005) connected forgiveness-seeking strategies with transgression severity. Compensation tactics were more frequently reported and minimization tactics less frequently reported when transgressions were rated most severe. Explicit acknowledgement (including apology), discussion-based approaches, and nonverbal assurances were offered extensively across all levels of transgression severity. When respondents reported on the relational consequences of the communication strategies, explicit acknowledgment and nonverbal assurance were positively correlated with relationship change and increases in post-transgression satisfaction, intimacy, and stability. Importantly, Kelley and Waldron's findings indicate that forgiveness-seeking communication is associated with positive relational outcomes beyond the effects of transgression severity alone.

Forgiveness-granting strategies. Most studies of forgiveness have focused on the forgiver's behavior. Kelley (1998) reported direct, indirect, and conditional approaches to granting forgiveness. *Direct* strategies included discussion designed to understand the offender's position, statements of forgiveness (e.g., "I forgive you"), and use of third-party mediators. *Indirect* strategies involved using humor, diminishing the perceived effect of the infraction (e.g., "It was no big deal"), enacting nonverbal behaviors and emotional displays, allowing a "return to normalcy," an intuitive sense that the other was forgiven, and feeling that the situation was now "understood." *Conditional responses* were characterized by if/then propositions (e.g., "I'll forgive you if . . .").

Waldron and Kelley (2005) reexamined the Kelley (1998) taxonomy, with the use of factor analytic techniques and a larger sample of romantic partners. Table 7–1 includes their five forgiveness-granting strategies and their associations with relational outcomes. Nonverbal displays involved employing facial expressions and touching to convey forgiveness and sincerity. *Conditional responses* were characterized by directives ("Don't let it happen again . . ."), promises ("If you promise . . ."), and if/then propositions ("If you change, then . . ."). Minimizing responses included messages such as "It's no big deal." Discussion-based approaches explored motives, emotions, and solutions. Discussion-based approaches were included originally in Kelley's direct category. However, they are direct only in the sense that individuals explicitly discuss the transgression. They do not imply that forgiveness was explicitly granted.

Waldron and Kelley (2005) did include explicit forgiveness-granting as a distinct fifth approach. In open-ended responses, some partners explicitly used the phrase, "I forgive you" (explicit forgiveness). This language was incorporated into one Likert-type item. Although this strategy didn't load cleanly on any one factor, it is obviously conceptually important and did account for significant variance in a number of their analyses.

The findings concerning explicit forgiveness are interesting in light of the fact that Hargrave's (1994) forgiveness model requires an overt expression to the offended party; for Hargrave, this response differentiates forgiveness from exoneration. In Kelley's (1998) data, only a little over one-half of the scenarios describing a forgiver strategy mentioned the forgiver using direct strategies. If Hargrave is correct, "true forgiveness" was not experienced, or at least not reported, by almost half of Kelley's participants. This finding further emphasizes the importance of understanding the distinctions between lay and researcher definitions of forgiveness. These differences have important ramifications for research design and clinical implementation of forgiveness-based programs.

Waldron and Kelley (2005) found these forgiveness-granting strategies to be related to perceived transgression severity. Conditional forgiveness-granting was positively associated with severity. Apparently, for severe transgressions, individuals feel the need to place parameters on their relationship if forgiveness is to lead to reconciliation of the relationship. Conditions may be used to secure the relationship until trust has redeveloped. Minimizing and nonverbal strategies were negatively associated with severity. Regarding minimizing and nonverbal displays, as one might suspect, telling someone, "It's no big deal," or giving a hug may be appropriate responses to a ding on a new car but likely not to an extramarital affair.

Forgiveness-granting strategies also had significant associations with relational outcomes (Waldron & Kelley, 2005). Strategies of discussion, nonverbal display, and explicit forgiveness were all positively correlated with relationship strengthening; stepwise regression analyses showed explicit forgiveness and nonverbal displays to be most significant. These behavioral responses may work together to reduce uncertainty and show sincerity. Interestingly, the only strategy associated with relationship deterioration was conditional forgiveness. Although setting conditions on the relationship may empower the offended party, at the same time it may signal a lack of trust or signal severe damage to the relationship. Finally, the relationship outcome of "returning to normal" was significantly, but somewhat weakly, related to nonverbal displays of forgiveness. Under some circumstances, saying nothing may save face for both parties or simply ease the process of forgiveness. Particularly when transgressions were of modest severity, nonverbal acknowledgments sufficed for some partners. If confirmed, this finding would contradict claims about the importance of explicit messages of forgiveness (Hargrave, 1994).

Relational consequences. Although psychological models often focus on individual cognitive, emotional, and physical benefits of forgiveness, we must also consider forgiveness as a strategy for relational repair that unfolds over time. Kelley (1998) described the central dimensions of relational consequences as change and return to normalcy. Participants' narratives revealed that relationships change in type, strengthen, deteriorate, or develop new behavior or rules in response to forgiveness. As reported above, in romantic relationships, both forgiveness-granting and forgiveness-seeking strategies are associated with the quality of post-transgression relationships in preliminary studies. It appears that the process of forgiveness, at times, allows partners to let go of negative emotion and bitterness. In fact, the data suggest that forgiving communication may actually strengthen and deepen relationships.

The conditions determining whether relationships are strengthened or weakened vary by relationship type. For example, Kelley's (1998) early work exploring relational outcomes found differences across family, dating, and friendship relationships. Deterioration in the relationship was most often reported by friends, whereas dating couples changed relationship type more than did other types of relationships. Potentially, without as many social constraints as other relationships, friendships are easier to let go, whereas dating couples may use the proverbial "Let's just be friends" to signal a change in relationship type.

Pertinent to our forgiveness definition, these examples remind us that, although forgiveness may open the door for reconciliation, reconciliation is not always wise or warranted. For reasons of psychological safety or a sense that the transgression will be repeated, a harmed partner may forgive while also choosing to end or change the nature of the relationship. In such cases, individual outcomes like peace of mind or psychological well-being may be as important as relational consequences.

A final issue regarding relational outcomes demonstrates the complexity of understanding human behavior. Across studies, returning the relationship to normal served as both a relational consequence and a type of indirect strategy of forgiveness (Kelley, 1998; Kelley & Waldron, 2005; Waldron & Kelley, 2005). This factor exemplifies the difficulty in assessing causal relationships between strategies and outcome; that is, individuals might begin acting normally in a relationship as a way of giving forgiveness or, after receiving forgiveness, might return to acting normal.

POTENTIAL RESEARCH DIRECTIONS

In coming years, communication researchers will have the opportunity to shape the development of the forgiveness literature, if only because the communicative aspects of the process have been least studied. In this section, we provide some preliminary research directions. We begin by suggesting that the already impressive communication research on relationship repair be extended to the realm of forgiving communication. We then discuss how certain communication theories might be particularly applicable to the study of forgiveness. Finally, we examine how forgiveness research can be expanded to several contextualized areas of communication research, including health communication, organizational communication, and personal relationships.

Communication and Relationship Repair

For many years, therapists have argued that forgiveness can repair broken relational bonds. For example, Hargrave (1994) claimed that forgiveness can result in a new (and possibly) improved relationship "covenant" (p. 346), a claim that coincides with Kelley's (1998) findings that roughly half of respondents who experienced relationship changes actually reported relationship improvement once forgiveness was granted to a transgressing partner. For their part, communication researchers have studied communication behaviors used to repair and maintain relationships for several decades, as evidenced by the publication of a comprehensive edited volume on the subject (Canary & Dainton, 2003). Early studies of relationship repair tactics largely ignored forgiveness (Dindia & Baxter, 1987). However, in a later study of relationship repair tactics, young couples described "forgiveness" as one way to recover from a negative relational event (Emmers & Canary, 1996).

More recent work provides substantive guidance to researchers who want to better understand how forgiveness is implicated in relationship repair. We would argue (with Gordon, Baucom, & Snyder, 2000) that partners must accomplish three communicative tasks during the forgiveness process, if they hope to repair the relationship after a severe transgression (see Waldron & Kelley, 2005). First, the emotional impact of the offense must be absorbed and acknowledged. Recent applications of face-management theory (e.g., Afifi et al., 2001) suggest that communication that affirms the emotional reaction of the offended partner and places blame on the self should be most helpful. Metts (1994) asserted that acknowledging and apologizing for relational harm may have an emotionally transformative effect, making it more likely that feelings of affection can be restored. If these claims are true, researchers should find that "successful" forgiveness discourse is characterized by expressions of remorse or regret, acknowledgment of harm, and a willingness to accept emotion-charged criticism. These behavioral patterns can be contrasted with avoidant, minimizing, or defensive discourse. The second communicative task requires partners to "make sense of" the relational situation. Causes, motives, and relational implications of the offense must be vented and interpreted. This stage helps both parties to evaluate the severity of the transgression. Before engaging in relationship repair, the offended partner may need to reevaluate the character of the partner and assess the psychological safety of the relationship. Explanations and accounts may be requested and offered, questions may be asked, and assurances and promises may be exchanged as partners accomplish this task (Kelley & Waldron, 2005).

Third, having progressed on the emotional and cognitive tasks, partners may co-construct a relational future. Metts (1994) drew on Newell and Stutman's (1991) social confrontation episode to show how relationships can be repaired through reaffirmation or relegislation of rules. Similarly, forgiveness theorists suggest that partners may renegotiate the "relationship covenant" (Hargrave, 1994), a process characterized in part by the negotiation of new rules/conditions (e.g., restrictions on dating others). An offender who pledges compliance with relational conditions may increase the margin of psychological safety perceived by the damaged partner. Rule-related communication may be the means by which relational trust is gradually restored (Kelley & Waldron, 2005). Meta-communicative behavior (Dindia & Baxter, 1987) might be particularly useful as partners consciously "rescript" their patterns of relational communication.

Related Communication Frameworks

Several theoretical frameworks used in the study of communication could be particularly useful as researchers pursue questions pertinent to the enactment of forgiveness.

Face Management

This theoretical approach links forgiveness to the face-management activities of relational partners (e.g., Afifi et al., 2001). Rooted in the early work of Erving Goffman (1955, 1959), this approach conceives of forgiving communication as a process of managing self-presentation in the presence of threatening relational transgressions. For example, upon discovery, the act of adultery threatens the reputation of the adulterer, and the partner, mutual friends, and family members are likely to disapprove. As well, a victim of adultery may feel embarrassment, shame, or anger in part because his/her positive face (e.g., I am a valued and exclusive mate) is threatened. Researchers adopting this theoretical perspective may address the behaviors that mitigate or redress these face threats. For example, a private confession and earnest request for forgiveness would be less face-threatening to the victimized partner than an approach that implied shared blame. In fact, Affifi and colleagues found that such forgiveness-seeking behavior could have some ameliorating effects on the partner's perceptions of the event, but not on relational outcomes.

In addition to examining identities of individual partners, identity researchers should examine the role of forgiveness in forging relational identity. The fact that partners have forgiven past transgressions (or chosen not to) may be an important part of their present identity ("the kind of couple we are") or their definition of marriage. Forgiveness may be implicit in some couples' definition of "real" marriage (Waldron & Kelley, 2002), particularly if they practice marriage within the definitions of some Christian churches. Analysis of individual and jointly told relational narratives may reveal the role of forgiveness in the construction of couple identity.

Rules

Metts (1994) used rules theories to explain how relational transgressions are assessed and new relational agreements are constructed. As Kelley (1998) reported, aggrieved partners sometimes set new conditions as part of the forgiveness process (e.g., "I forgive you as long as you don't do it again"). Presumably, this kind of communication restores relational rules or imposes new ones in order to redefine or stabilize the relationship.

Uncertainty Management

Berger's work on uncertainty management (e.g., Berger, 1987) was adapted by Emmers and Canary (1996) to study the relationship repair tactics used by young couples. Although forgiveness was not a primary focus, their work indicates that seeking forgiveness serves as one way for partners to manage the relational uncertainty that stems from serious transgressions. Under such circumstances, offended partners find it difficult to explain and predict the behavior of their mate. As such, individuals may seek to reduce uncertainty levels by monitoring communication closely. For example, the perceived sincerity of an apology may be utilized to gauge the likelihood of a repeat offense. From this theoretical perspective, offers of conditional forgiveness (e.g., "I will forgive you but only if you promise to do [not do] X") may be attractive to offended parties because they specify boundaries for future behavior, thus adding predictability to the relationship (Waldron & Kelley, 2005). Researchers embracing this perspective should examine the communication processes that manage uncertainty and the extent to which psychological judgments of forgiveness are related to their use.

Account-Making Frameworks

Conversational analysts have long examined the discourse by which accounts are offered, accepted, and rejected (e.g., Antaki, 1994). Accounting is the way in which failure events are managed between social interactants (Cody & McLaughlin, 1988). The account process begins with the experience of a transgression or failure event. Failure events can include transgressions of omission or commission. A second phase involves communication by the offended party to the offender that a transgression has occurred. The actual account-giving phase takes place when the perceived offender responds in some way to being reproached in phase two. Finally, the offended party evaluates the account, the offense in light of the account, and the characteristics of the perceived offender. This process terminates with restoration of the relationship or with increased conflict and possible relationship termination (Schonbach & Kleibaumhuter, 1990). This last stage of the process corresponds with the description by Enright et al. (1991) of release and reconciliation in the forgiveness process.

Hargrave's (1994) inclusion of apology as a prerequisite for relationship renegotiation can be understood in light of existing accounts research. When offenders use more mitigating strategies, such as concession (of which apology is one type), to manage their transgression, the injured party will more likely also respond with a mitigating response (Cody & McLaughlin, 1988), such as forgiveness of the offense. In fact, the relationship between apology and forgiveness has been well established (McCullough, Worthington, et al., 1997).

Dialectical Theory

Dialectical theory suggests that relationships are in constant flux, moving back and forth between polar opposite characteristics, such as openness and closedness (Baxter, 1990). Behavior that communicates forgiveness may be the means by which dialectical tensions are managed. For example, an offended partner who communicates willingness to forgive a transgression initiates a move away from separateness and toward togetherness. Perhaps more interestingly, forgiveness dialogue reveals dialectical tensions unique to the forgiveness process. For example, couples sometimes verbalize a tension between "remembering and forgetting." Forgetting of the intense emotional pain associated with past transgressions may be an indicator that the forgiveness process is progressing. However, couples often value the wisdom gained from past mistakes and vow not to repeat the past. Another tension involves counterbalancing urges to "hash out" the details of a relational offense and to "move on" or return to normal. The dialectical framework should prove useful as researchers analyze forgiveness discourse more closely.

Turning Points

A variety of researchers have investigated turning points as a means for understanding how significant events shape relationships (Barge & Musambira, 1992; Baxter & Bullis, 1986). Baxter and Bullis defined a turning point as "any event or occurrence that is associated with change in a relationship" (p. 470). As such, turning point research can be pursued in one of two ways. The first method seeks to provide a broad picture of how turning points influence relationship progress. For example, Baxter and Bullis identified 26 turning points in romantic relationships, with respondents generally listing 9.5. A second method focuses on individual turning points. For example, Siegert and Stamp (1994) investigated couples' first major conflict as a relational turning point in order to determine what led up to the fight, the effects of the fight, and what distinguished couples who survived the fight from those who did not. Similar approaches to forgiveness research may result in identifying turning points in forgiveness processes that take significant amounts of time or may identify forgiveness as a significant turning point in overcoming significant relational transgressions.

Contextual Applications

As noted previously in this essay, forgiveness research has been conducted across numerous contexts, including international contexts (e.g., Bartoli, 2001), mediation settings (Kirkup, 1993), apologia (e.g., Downey, 1993) and apology (e.g., Cody & McLaughlin, 1988) situations, and family communication (Kelley & Waldron, 2002). This existing research will be enriched when forgiving communication is studied in additional relational contexts.

Organizational Contexts

In organizational settings, forgiveness research has obvious application, particularly in the area of crisis communication. Crisis communication scholars have analyzed the discourse of *apologia* used when, for example, Jack-in-the-Box served tainted meat (Ulmer & Sellnow, 2000) or Exxon spilled oil (Sellnow, 1993). Typically, this discourse is characterized by efforts to evade responsibility, express mortification, repair a damaged public image, or offer compensation to the victims (Benoit, 1995). In other words, few companies seek forgiveness after making mistakes. However, an alternative "discourse of renewal" recently emerged from a detailed case study of executive responses to catastrophic fires at two different wood products companies (Seeger & Ulmer, 2002). The authors described potential benefits of a more honest response to negative events, including improved relationships with stockholders and the emergence of organizational heroes. The authors use Weick's (1995) sense-making theory as the basis for exploring how crisis discourse creates meaning, particularly in times of high uncertainty and ambiguity. Obviously, this work parallels our earlier discussion of how forgiveness manages uncertainty in personal relationships.

In addition, relational transgressions at work may be the most cited sources of emotional distress among American workers (Waldron, 2000). A study of emotional events at work revealed that lingering resentment and hostility were common even years after the transgressions, which included betrayals of trust and public embarrassments (Waldron & Krone, 1991). Waldron contends that revenge, withdrawal, and bitterness rather than forgiveness may be the favored response to workplace injustices. Organizational researchers should examine the organizational practices and structures that hinder forgiveness and the interventions that might help co-workers mend their relationships.

Health Communication

Forgiveness has long been linked to improved health and well-being in the self-help literature. Medical research reveals at least modest support for some of these claims (Berry & Worthington, 2001). In a thoughtful summary of this research, Witvliet (2001) concluded that more experimental research is needed, but "in general, levels of forgiveness are positively correlated with indicators of mental health and negatively correlated with indicators of dysfunction and distress" (p. 216). Those who forgive may be less likely to remain angry, depressed, and bitter after a transgression. To date, relatively few researchers have used experimental designs in studying causal connections between these variables; however, forgiveness/health research raises questions about the biological effects of forgiving communication that should interest health communication researchers. Other health communication issues are suggestive as well. For instance, to what degree might forgiving communication facilitate reconnection to social support networks, including family members who reinforce healthy behavior, and to what extent is forgiving communication recommended or modeled by health professionals for clients? Issues of sexual abuse, domestic violence, and excessive alcohol use are other important areas of study.

Processes in Personal Relationships

Forgiveness processes unfold over time, sometimes over years or decades. Kelley and Waldron's series of studies suggest that time influences the forgiveness process at virtually all stages: motivation, strategy, relational consequences. Communication researchers should increasingly ask questions about the behavioral sequences and long-term communication patterns that culti-vate forgiveness in personal relationships. We present some examples next, based on data that we have collected from interviews with long-term married couples (Kelley & Waldron, 2002).

Persistence. It is unlikely that initial efforts to seek forgiveness will be suc-cessful, given the intense emotional pain and hostility experienced after seri-ous transgressions. Potentially, multiple forgiveness-seeking attempts (e.g., repeated apologies) and multiple efforts to grant forgiveness may be required to repair relationships.

Distancing. Partners may delay communication or remain silent for long periods of time as a means of managing intense emotion. Our interviews reveal that some happily married partners avoid discussion of certain events, even decades after they were experienced.

Rule renegotiation. Partners may propose, modify, reject, and endorse new rules of relational behavior immediately after a transgression. How are these agreements modified, eased, or reinforced as the transgression becomes a dis-tant memory?

Identity management. Surviving a serious transgression may be part of the relational identity shared by a couple. The means by which transgressions are integrated into relational narratives require investigation. For example, how does a couple recount an incident of infidelity, and how does the retelling apportion blame for the offense, manage shame and embarrassment of the partners, and factor into the couple's definition of their present commitment? How are individual and relational identities differently or similarly affected by the ongoing process of forgiveness?

Emotion management. Forgiveness provides partners with the opportunity to express negative emotions and to legitimize emotional reactions (Gordon & Baucom, 1999). How long do these emotions last? What relational rules are developed to manage them? At what point do emotional expressions become a hindrance in the forgiveness process? What are the long-term consequences if emotions are not expressed early in the process?

Relational learning. To what extent does the process of forgiveness result in improved understanding of the partner, his or her values and expectations, and communication behaviors that facilitate long-term relationship success? If forgiveness results in strengthened relationships for some partners, what mechanisms account for this improvement?

Uncertainty management. As part of the forgiveness process, partners may provide evidence of future intentions and attempt to predict the likelihood of future transgressions. How successful are partners in predicting future inten-tions? Do partners vary in their tolerance for relational risk? What behaviors escalate or calm anxieties about what the future holds for relational partners?

Mutual planning. When committing to forgive, partners may collaborate to construct a plan for relational recovery, which might include gradual reintroduction of intimate activity and managing public knowledge of the transgression. What does this planning process look like? Is it explicitly discussed? Monitored? Are third parties (friends, family members) part of the process?

Trust restoration. How do partners rebuild trust after major transgressions? How is the decision to forgive linked to trust? How long does it take for trust to be reestablished? Does it typically return to previous levels? If not, what communication mechanisms compensate for diminished trust?

CONCLUDING REMARKS

Forgiveness constitutes a rich social phenomenon with important implications for the relationships of couples, groups, families, organizations, and nations. Although rhetoricians were among the first to examine how forgiveness was enacted in public discourse, communication researchers have largely sidestepped the growing wave of forgiveness research. We urge our colleagues to rectify this situation because some of the most pressing research questions involve the communicative elements of the forgiveness process. As communication researchers immerse themselves in this literature, they will need to negotiate at least three dialectical tensions that are surfacing in the research. The first involves the religious and the secular. Much recent forgiveness research is fueled by the important role of forgiveness in theology, particularly Judeo-Christian traditions. However, the role of forgiveness in the secular realm has received increasing attention from social science researchers. Forgiveness is a concept with the potential to cross or reframe the secular/sacred divide.

A second tension involves the relationship between the individual and the social. As we have noted in this essay, forgiveness is frequently conceptualized as a psychological process, but more research is needed on the means by which it is enacted in a greater variety of social contexts. Existing social research is heavily weighted toward the psychosocial adjustments made by distressed romantic partners and, to some extent, family members.

Finally, the literature requires a rebalancing, such that additional critical scholarship is added to the rapidly growing body of therapeutic and prescriptive work. Researchers are making impressive progress in documenting the potentially positive effects of forgiveness-based interventions. At the same time, popular interest in the topic has resulted in numerous books for practitioners and the general public. Only recently have scholars begun to question, for example, the relationship between forgiveness processes and power structures of couples, families, and larger collectives or the extent to which the act of forgiveness facilitates or inhibits social justice. The study of forgiving communication can only be invigorated by these kinds of critical inquiry.

ACKNOWLEDGMENTS

The authors acknowledge Lisa Sandeno for her input on this work.

REFERENCES

Afifi, W., Falato, W., & Weiner, J. (2001). Identity concerns following a severe relational transgression: The role of discovery method for relational outcomes of infidelity. *Journal of Social and Personal Relationships, 18*, 291–308.

Al-Mabuk, R. H., Enright, R. D., & Cardis, P. A. (1995). Forgiveness education with parentally love-deprived late adolescents. *Journal of Moral Education, 24*, 427–444.

Antaki, C. (1994). *Explaining and arguing: The social organization of accounts.* Thousand Oaks, CA: Sage.

Arendt, H. (1958). *The human condition.* Chicago: University of Chicago Press.

Aristotle (1954). *Rhetoric* (W. R. Roberts, Trans.). New York: Modern Library.

Augoustinos, M. & Lecouter, A. & Soyland, J. (2002). Self-sufficient arguments in political rhetoric: Constructing reconciliation and apologizing to the Stolen Generations. *Discourse and Society, 13*, 105–142.

Barge, J. K., & Musambira, G. W. (1992). Turning points in chair-faculty relationships. *Journal of Applied Communication Research, 20*, 54–77.

Barnett, J. K., & Youngberg, C. (2004). Forgiveness as a ritual in couples therapy. *Family Journal Counseling and Therapy for Couples and Families, 12*(1), 14–20.

Bartoli, A. (2001). Forgiveness and reconciliation in the Mozambique peace process. In R. G. Helmick & R. L. Petersen (Eds.), *Forgiveness and reconciliation* (pp. 361–381). Philadelphia: Templeton Foundation Press.

Baxter, L. A. (1990). Dialectical contradictions in relationship development. *Journal of Social and Personal Relationships, 4*, 261–280.

Baxter, L. A., & Bullis, C. (1986). Turning points in developing romantic relationships. *Human Communication Research, 12*, 469–493.

Benoit, W. (1995). *Accounts, excuses, and apologies.* Prospect Heights, IL: Waveland.

Berger, C. R. (1987). Communicating under uncertainty. In M. E. Roloff & G. R. Miller (Eds.), *Interpersonal processes. New directions in communication research* (pp. 39–62). Newbury Park, CA: Sage.

Berry, J. W., & Worthington, E. L. (2001). Forgiveness, relationship quality, stress while imagining relational events, and physical and mental health. *Journal of Counseling Psychology, 48*, 447–455.

Berry, J. W., Worthington, E. L., Parrot, L., O'Connor, L. E., & Wade, N. G. (2001). Dispositional forgiveness: Development and construct validity of the Transgression Narrative Test of Forgiveness (TNTF). *Personality and Social Psychology Bulletin, 27*, 1277–1290.

Brown, R. P., & Phillips, A. (2005). Letting bygones be bygones: Further evidence for the validity of the tendency to forgive scale. *Personality and Individual Differences, 38*, 627–638.

Canary, D. J., & Dainton, M. (Eds.). (2003). *Maintaining relationships through communication: Relational, contextual, and cultural variations.* Mahwah, NJ: Lawrence Erlbaum Associates.

Cann, A., & Baucom, T. R. (2004). Former partners and new rivals as threats to a relationship: Infidelity type, gender, and commitment as factors related to distress and forgiveness. *Personal Relationships, 11*, 305–318.

Cody, M. J., & McLaughlin, M. L. (1988). Accounts on trial: Oral arguments in traffic court. In C. Antaki (Ed.), *Analyzing everyday explanation: A casebook of methods* (pp. 113–126). London: Sage.

da Silva, A. (2001). Through nonviolence to truth: Gandhi's vision of reconciliation. In R. G. Helmick & R. L. Petersen (Eds.), *Forgiveness and reconciliation* (pp. 305–327). Philadelphia: Templeton Foundation Press.

Derrida, J. (2001). *On cosmopolitanism and forgiveness.* New York: Routledge.

Dindia, K. & Baxter, L. (1987). Strategies for maintaining and repairing marital relationships. *Journal of Personal and Social Relationships, 4*, 143–158.

Downey, S. D. (1993). The evolution of the rhetorical genre of apologia. *Western Journal of Communication, 57*, 42–64.

Doxtader, E. (2003). Reconciliation—a rhetorical concept/ion. *Quarterly Journal of Speech, 89*, 267–292.

Dunne, E. A. (2004). Clerical child sex abuse: The response of the Roman Catholic church. *Journal of Community and Applied Social Psychology, 13*, 490–494.

Emmers, T. M., & Canary, D. J. (1996). The effect of uncertainty reducing strategies on young couples' relational repair and intimacy. *Communication Quarterly, 44*, 166–182.

Enright, R. D., Eastin, D. L., Golden, S., Sarinopoulos, I., & Freedman, S. (1992). Interpersonal forgiveness within the helping professions: An attempt to resolve differences of opinion. *Counseling and Values, 36*, 84–103.

Enright, R. D., & Fitzgibbons, R. P. (2000). *Helping clients forgive: An empirical guide for resolving anger and restoring hope.* Washington, DC: American Psychological Association.

Enright, R. D., Gassin, E. A., & Wu, C. R. (1992). Forgiveness: A developmental view. *Journal of Moral Education, 21*, 99–114.

Enright, R. D., & the Human Development Study Group. (1991). The moral development of forgiveness. In W. Kurtines & J. Gewirtz (Eds.), *Handbook of moral behavior and development* (Vol. 1, pp. 123–152). Hillsdale, NJ: Lawrence Erlbaum Associates.

Fehr, B. (1988). Prototype analysis of the concepts of love and commitment. *Journal of Personality and Social Psychology, 5*, 557–579.

Fincham, F. D. (2000). The kiss of the porcupines: From attributing responsibility to forgiving. *Personal Relationships. 7*, 1–23.

Fincham, F. D., & Beach, S. R. (2002). Forgiveness in marriage: Implications for psychological aggression and constructive communication. *Personal Relationships, 9*, 239–251.

Fincham, F. D., Beach, S. R., & Davila, J. (2004). Forgiveness and conflict resolution in marriage. *Journal of Family Psychology, 18*, 72–81.

Freedman, S. R., & Enright, R. D. (1996). Forgiveness as an intervention goal with incest survivors. *Journal of Consulting and Clinical Psychology, 64*, 983–992.

Goffman, E. (1955). On face-work: An analysis of ritual elements in social interaction. *Psychiatry: Journal for the Study of Interpersonal Processes, 18*, 213–231.

Goffman, E. (1959). *The presentation of self in everyday life.* Garden City, NY: Doubleday.

Gordon, K. C., & Baucom, D. H. (1999). A multitheoretical intervention for promoting recovery from extramarital affairs. *Clinical Psychology: Science and Practice, 6*, 382–399.

Gordon, K. C., Baucom, D. H., & Snyder, D. K. (2000). The use of forgiveness in marital therapy. In M. C. McCullough, K. I. Pargament, & C. E. Thoresen (Eds.), *Forgiveness: Theory, research, and practice* (pp. 203–227). New York: Guilford.

Hargrave, T. D. (1994). Families and forgiveness: A theoretical and therapeutic framework. *The Family Journal: Counseling and Therapy for Couples and Families, 2*, 339–348.

Hargrave, T. D., & Sells, J. M. (1997). The development of a forgiveness scale. *Journal of Marital and Family Therapy, 23*, 41–62.

Hebl, J. H., & Enright, R. D. (1993). Forgiveness as a psychotherapeutic goal with elderly females. *Psychotherapy, 30*, 658–667.

Hegel, G. W. F. (1977). *Phenomenology of spirit* (A. V. Miller, Trans.). Oxford, England: Clarendon.

Helmick, R. G. (2001). Does religion fuel or heal conflicts? In R. G. Helmick & R. L. Petersen (Eds.), *Forgiveness and reconciliation* (pp. 81–95). Philadelphia: Templeton Foundation Press.

Kachadourian, L., Fincham, F. D., & Davila, J. (2005). Attitudinal ambivalence, rumination and forgiveness of partner transgressions in marriage. *Personality and Social Psychology Bulletin, 31*, 334–342.

Kantz, J. E. (2000). How do people conceptualize and use forgiveness? The Forgiveness Attitudes Questionnaire. *Counseling and Values, 44*, 174–186.

Kearns, J. N., & Fincham, F. D. (2004). A prototype analysis of forgiveness. *Personality and Social Psychology Bulletin, 30*(7), 838–855.

Kearns, J. N., & Fincham, F. D. (2005). Victim and perpetrator accounts of interpersonal transgressions: Self-serving or relationship-serving biases? *Personality and Social Psychology Bulletin, 31*, 321–333.

Kelley, D. L. (1998). The communication of forgiveness. *Communication Studies, 49*, 1–17.

Kelley, D. L. (2001, November). *Common perspectives of forgiveness.* Paper presented at the meeting of the National Communication Association, Atlanta.

Kelley, D. L., & Waldron, V. R. (2002, November). Forgiveness in long-term marriage. Presented at the annual meeting of the National Communication Association, New Orleans, LA.

Kelley, D. L., & Waldron, V. R. (2005). An investigation of forgiveness-seeking communication and relational outcomes. Communication Quarterly, 53, 339–358.

Kirkup, P. A. (1993). Some religious perspectives on forgiveness and settling differences. Mediation Quarterly, 11, 79–94.

Luskin, F. (2002). Forgive for good: A proven prescription for health and happiness. New York: HarperCollins.

Mauger, P. A., Perry, J. E., Freeman, T., Grove, D. C., McBride, A. G., McKinney, K. E., et al. (1992). The measurement of forgiveness: Preliminary research. Journal of Psychology and Christianity, 11, 170–180.

McCullough, M. E., Exline, J. J., and Baumeister, R. F. (1998). An annotated bibliography of research on forgiveness and related topics. In E. L. Worthington, Jr. (Ed.), Dimensions of forgiveness: Psychological research and theological speculations (pp. 193–317). Philadelphia: Templeton Foundation Press.

McCullough, M. E., Pargament, K. I., & Thoresen, C. E. (Eds.). (2000). Forgiveness: Theory, research, and practice. New York: Guilford.

McCullough, M. E., Sandage, S. J., & Worthington, E. L. (1997). To forgive is human: How to put your past in the past. Downers Grove, IL: InterVarsity.

McCullough, M. E., Worthington, E. L., & Rachal, K. C. (1997). Interpersonal forgiving in close relationships. Journal of Personality and Social Psychology, 73, 321–336.

McNaughton, D. (1992). Repentance and atonement. Religious Studies, 28, 129–144.

Metts, S. (1994). Relational transgressions. In W. R. Cupach & B. H. Spitzberg (Eds.), The dark side of interpersonal communication (pp. 17–34). Hillsdale, NJ: Lawrence Erlbaum Associates.

Mullet, E., Girard, M., & Bakhshi, P. (2004). Conceptualizations of forgiveness. European Psychologist, 9(2), 78–86.

Newell, S. E., & Stutman, R. K. (1991). The social confrontation episode. Communication Monographs, 55, 266–285.

Owen, W. F. (1984). Interpretive themes in relational communication. Quarterly Journal of Speech, 70, 274–287.

Paleari, F. G., Regalia, C., & Fincham, F. D. (2005). Marital quality, forgiveness, empathy, and rumination: A longitudinal analysis. Personality and Social Psychology Bulletin, 31, 368–378.

Peterson, C., & Seligman, M. E. P. (2004). Character strengths and virtues: A handbook and classification. Washington, DC: American Psychological Association.

Pingleton, J. P. (1989). The role and function of forgiveness in the psychotherapeutic process. Journal of Psychology and Theology, 17, 27–35.

Pope, S. J. (2003). The convergence of forgiveness and justice: Lessons from El Salvador. Theological Studies, 64, 812–835.

Prager, K. (1995). The psychology of intimacy. New York: Guilford.

Rawlins, W. K. (1989). A dialectical analysis of the tensions, functions, and strategic challenges of communication in young adult friendships. In J. Anderson (Ed.), *Communication yearbook 12* (pp. 157–189). Newbury Park, CA: Sage.

Rosch, E. (1975). Cognitive representations of semantic categories. *Journal of Experimental Psychology: General, 104*, 192–233.

Rosch, E. (1978). Principles of categorization. In E. Rosch & B. B. Lloyd (Eds.), *Cognition and categorization* (pp. 22–71). Hillsdale, NJ: Lawrence Erlbaum Associates.

Ross, S. R., Kendall, A. C., Matters, K. G., Wrobel, T. A., & Rye, M. S. (2004). A personological examination of self and other-forgiveness in the Five Factor model. *Journal of Personality Assessment, 82*, 207–214.

Ryan, H. R. (1982). Kategoria and apologia: On their rhetorical criticism as a speech set. *Quarterly Journal of Speech, 68*, 254–261.

Rye, M. S., Folck, C. D., Heim, T. A., Olszewski, B. T., & Traina, E. (2004). Forgiveness of an ex-spouse: How does it relate to mental health following a divorce? *Journal of Divorce and Remarriage, 41*(3–4), 31–51.

Rye, M. S., Loiacono, D. M., Folck, C. D., Olszewski, B. T., Heim, T. A., & Madia, B. (2001). Evaluation of the psycho-metric properties of two forgiveness scales. *Current Psychology, 20*, 260–277.

Rye, M. S., Pargament, K. I., Ali, M. A., Beck, G. L., Dorff, E. N., Hallisey, C., et al. (2000). Religious perspectives on forgiveness. In M. E. McCullough, K. I. Pargament, & C. E. Thoresen (Eds.), *Forgiveness: Theory research, and practice* (pp. 17–40). New York: Guilford.

Schmitt, M., Gollwitzer, M., Forster, N, & Montada, L. (2004). Effects of objective and subjective account components on forgiving. *Journal of Social Psychology, 144*, 465–485.

Schonbach, P., & Kleibaumhuter, P. (1990). Severity of reproach and defensiveness of accounts. In M. J. Cody & M. L. McLaughlin (Eds.), *The psychology of tactical communication* (pp. 229–243). Philadelphia: Multilingual Matters.

Scobie, E. D., & Scobie, G. E. (1998). Damaging events: The perceived need for forgiveness. *Journal for the Theory of Social Behavior, 28*, 373–401.

Seeger, M. W., & Ulmer, R. R. (2002). A post-crisis discourse of renewal: The cases of Malden Mills and Cole Hardwoods. *Journal of Applied Communication Research, 30*, 126–142.

Sellnow, T. (1993). Scientific argument in organizational crisis communication: The case of Exxon. *Argumentation and Advocacy, 30*, 28–42.

Sharpsteen, D. J. (1993). Romantic jealousy as an emotion concept: A prototype analysis. *Journal of Social and Personal Relationships, 10*, 69–82.

Shriver, D. Jr. (1995). *An ethic for enemies: Forgiveness in politics.* New York: Oxford University Press.

Siegert, J. R., & Stamp, G. H. (1994). Our first big fight: As a milestone in the development of close relationships. *Communication Monographs, 61*, 345–360.

Simons, H. W. (2000). A dilemma-centered analysis of Clinton's August 17th apologia: Implications for rhetorical theory and method. *Quarterly Journal of Speech, 86*, 438–453.

Smedes, (1984). *Forgive and forget.* San Francisco: HarperCollins.

Smedes, L. B. (1996). *The art of forgiving.* New York: Ballantine.

Smith, S. L., Smith, S. W., Yoo, J. H, Ferris, A., Downs, E., Pieper, K. M., et al. (2005, May). *Altruism on American television: Examining the prevalence of and context surrounding such acts.* Paper presented at the meeting of the International Communication Association, New York.

Smyth, G. (2001). Brokenness, forgiveness, healing, and peace in Ireland. In R. G. Helmick & R. L. Petersen (Eds.), *Forgiveness and reconciliation* (pp. 329–359). Philadelphia: Templeton Foundation Press.

Tutu, D. (1999). *No future without forgiveness.* New York: Image.

Ulmer, R. R., & Sellnow, T. L. (2000). Consistent questions of ambiguity in organizational crisis communication: Jack in the Box as a case study. *Journal of Business Ethics, 25,* 143–155.

Waldron, V. R. (2000). Relational experiences and emotion at work. In S. Fineman (Ed.), *Emotion in organizations* (2nd ed., pp. 64–82). London: Sage.

Waldron, V. R., & Kelley, D. L. (2002, November). *Forgiveness in long-term marriage.* Paper presented at the meeting of the National Communication Association, New Orleans, LA.

Waldron, V. R., & Kelley, D. L. (2005). Forgiving communication as a response to relational transgressions. *Journal of Social and Personal Relationships.*

Waldron, V. R., & Krone, K. J. (1991). The experience and expression of emotion in the workplace: A study of a corrections organization. *Management Communication Quarterly, 4,* 287–309.

Walters, R. P. (1984). Forgiving: An essential element in effective living. *Studies in Formative Spirituality, 5,* 365–374.

Ware, B. L., & Linkugel, W. A. (1973). They spoke in defense of themselves: On the generic criticism of apologia. *Quarterly Journal of Speech, 59,* 273–283.

Weick, K. E. (1995). *Sensemaking in organizations.* Thousand Oaks, CA: Sage.

Wiesenthal, S. (1997). *The sunflower: On the possibilities and limits of forgiveness.* New York: Schocken.

Witvliet, C. V. (2001). Forgiveness and health: Review and reflections on a matter of faith, feelings, and physiology. *Journal of Psychology and Theology, 29,* 212–224.

Worthington, E. L. (2000). Is there a place for forgiveness in the justice system? *Fordham Urban Law Journal, 27,* 1721–1734.

Worthington, E. L. (2001). Unforgiveness, forgiveness, and reconciliation and their implications for societal interventions. In R. G. Helmick & R. L. Petersen (Eds.), *Forgiveness and reconciliation* (pp. 171–192). Philadelphia: Templeton Foundation Press.

Worthington, E. L., Sandage, S. J., & Berry, J. W. (2000). Group interventions to promote forgiveness: What researchers and clinicians ought to know. In M. E. McCullough, K. Pargament, & C. Thoreson (Eds.), *Forgiveness: Theory, research, and practice* (pp. 228–253). New York: Guilford.

Worthington, E. L., & Scherer, M. (2004). Forgiveness is an emotion-focused coping strategy that can reduce health risks and promote health resilience: Theory, review, and hypotheses. *Psychology and Health, 19,* 385–405.

Worthington, E. L., & Wade, N. G. (1999). The psychology of forgiveness and unforgiveness and implications for clinical practice. *Journal of Social and Clinical Psychology, 18*, 385–418.

Zechmeister, J. S., Garcia, S., Romero, C., & Vas, S. N. (2004). Don't apologize unless you mean it: A laboratory investigation of forgiveness and retaliation. *Journal of Social and Clinical Psychology, 23*, 532–564.

Zechmeister, J. S. & Romero, C. (2002). Victim and offender accounts of interpersonal conflict: Autobiographical narratives of forgiveness and unforgiveness. *Journal of Personality and Social Psychology, 82*, 675–686.

CHAPTER CONTENTS

8   From the Roots to the Shoots: A Hawaiian Case Study of Language Revitalization and Modes of Communication

MIKAELA L. MARLOW
HOWARD GILES
University of California at Santa Barbara

Throughout history, multiple indigenous groups have had their cultural, linguistic, and communicative identities supplanted by the norms of dominant groups. Nonetheless, the communication discipline has given minimal attention to the preservation and revitalization of minority languages. This article begins to redress this oversight by means of a case study of the Hawaiian language. In the last 200 years, the Hawaiian Islands have been significantly affected by Western influence, a process that has severely endangered the Hawaiian language. Beginning in the 1980s, scholars and community activists developed language immersion education programs to reverse this decline. In light of globalization forces and interview data, and drawing on the ethnolinguistic vitality framework, our integrative analysis uniquely assesses the history and status of the Hawaiian language as it is currently being revitalized through demographic support, media, and educational immersion programs. In addition to discussing future challenges to these efforts, we offer an agenda for research across an array of communication domains.

> *I ka ʻōlelo nō ke ola, I ka ʻōlelo nō ka make.*
>
> *In the language there is life, in the language there is death.*
>
> —*Hawaiian proverb*

Throughout history, numerous cultural groups have been irreversibly affected by the influence of dominant groups imposing cultural and communicative practices—sometimes to the extent of strategic linguistic annihilation. For instance, Fishman (2001) discussed Western culture and

Correspondence: Mikaela L. Marlow, 5843 Ellison Hall, Santa Barbara, CA 93106; email: mmarlow@umail.ucsb.edu

Communication Yearbook 30, pp. 343–385

its powerful effect on indigenous peoples, cultures, and languages. He suggested: "Today, the worldwide process of globalization of the economy, communication, and entertainment media . . . have threatened to sweep away everything locally authentic and different that may stand in their way . . . progress is revealed as taking three steps forward and two steps back . . . the struggle against language-in-culture decimation still goes on with little likelihood of early and clear triumph" (pp. xiii–xiv). Recent literature has established that indigenous languages have been rapidly decreasing, and current estimates suggest that, by 2100, nearly half of the world's 6,500 languages may be extinct (Hotz, 2000). On the other hand, and in parallel with (if not, in some ways, in reaction to) increasing patterns of globalization, we have witnessed the resurrection and revitalization of many languages that have increased in their usage and prestige of late: Luxembourgish, Welsh, Irish, Estonian, Inuktitut, Faroese, and Catalan, to name a few.

This chapter examines one such effort that is taking place in the United States but is rarely recognized as such internally, let alone elsewhere in the world, namely, the revitalization of the Hawaiian language. Over the years, regular sojourners to Hawai'i may have noticed changes in the linguistic landscape (Dailey, Giles, & Jansma, 2004; Landry & Bourhis, 1997), such that they have encountered an ever-increasing use of Hawaiian, in greetings and expressions of gratitude (e.g., *aloha* and *mahalo*) and on street signs, store signs, bumper stickers, and so forth. Through our integrative analysis of the Hawaiian example, we wish not only to provide a unique voice for this important language movement—analyzed infrequently in other disciplines (see Hinton & Hale, 2001; W. H. Wilson & Kamanā, 2001)—but also to draw communication scholars' attention to the enormous potential in representing language maintenance through educational and communication practices (see also Barker et al., 2001).

To accurately depict the Hawaiian language revitalization movement, this research draws significantly from unique cultural values that have influenced the immersion paradigm. From the Hawaiian perspective, knowledge transmission is often deeply rooted in traditional, mythic representations that bridge the past to the globalized present. In this sense, and as the title of this chapter indicates, Hawaiian language and culture may be understood as *shoots* that rise from the *roots* of previous generations, like the kalo or taro, a mythic plant that has always sustained the Hawaiian people and continues to serve as a living symbol of Hawaiian identity and continuity (Meyer, 2003).

Communication theory has addressed the significant impact of modern globalization phenomena on economic, political, social, and cultural communication interactions (e.g., Stohl, 2005). For instance, based upon the necessity for uniform language and ideology among worldwide corporations, processes of "production, exchange, distribution, and consumption" (p. 231) have been modified to better meet the requirements of a common global communication code. Politically, governments and organizations have responded to the necessity for global communication norms by developing employment climates that are often rooted in "coercion, surveillance, and control" (p. 231) tactics to ensure reliable and predictable results in routine interactions.

Considering that English is the official language of 52 countries (Crystal, 2005; Wallraff, 2005), it seems evident that it has been established as a global communicative norm (de Swaan, 2001). Scholarly evaluations further attest that "English has in fact become the European Union's lingua franca" (House, 2003, p. 561). Sociolinguistic research (e.g., Cope & Kalantzis, 2000; Fairclough, 1992) acknowledges the impact that globalization has had on language patterns, variation, and changes (Cameron, 2000; Coupland, 2003), suggesting that, in the future, international interactions will contribute to "the intensification of global consciousness, reflexivity, perceptions of risk . . . struggles for identity, and community" (Stohl, 2005, p. 231).

Although House (2003) suggested that the spread of English as a global lingua franca "may stimulate members of minority languages to insist on their own local language for emotional binding to their own culture, history, and tradition" (p. 561), this claim seems to disregard the actual inequity, in agency and power, among various ethnic and language groups within existing global exchange processes. For example, Wallerstein (1983, 2001) purported that the emerging world system is based upon established hierarchical divisions between central and marginalized populations who often have varying levels of access to opportunities and resources. Similarly, Heller (2003) argued that emerging research should explicate how values, actors, and resources influence the relationship between language and identity in the global economy.

Drawing from such arguments, research assessing the communicative implications inherent in globalization should investigate issues salient for groups that attempt to maintain their unique linguistic and cultural identities. Although ample sociolinguistic research has explicated the experiences of indigenous groups seeking language revitalization (e.g., England, 2003; Mansoor, 2004), less work in our discipline has examined language loss and revitalization (see, however, Garrett, Giles, & Coupland, 1989; Leets & Giles, 1995). Monge (1998) asserted that "the global imperative requires no less than that we apply our communication theories to address practical human issues" (p. 150), reinforcing the notion that communicative principles should be utilized to explore global interactions (see also Thurlow & Jaworski, 2003).

In this chapter, we examine how language has recently emerged as a valuable communication commodity in the global context and briefly discuss challenges that various groups confront in attempting to maintain authentic linguistic and cultural agency. We then assess current efforts of marginalized language groups that have worked toward revitalization and review the history of the Hawaiian people and the status of their language as it is being revitalized through demographic, media, and educational support. The scholarly research that does exist on the current state of language in Hawai'i does not emanate from the communication discipline. Given this state of affairs, we have been privileged to augment our analysis with interview data from local experts who have been key (and quite accomplished) leaders in forging new vistas in the Hawaiian language movement. Moreover, with the increasing interest in the societal and communicative consequences of changing patterns of non-English use in recent years in the United States (see Barker & Giles, 2003; Barker et al., 2001) and globally, we draw attention to this fascinating context by adopting (for the first time in this domain) the ethnolinguistic group vitality framework to structure dynamics for locals and tourists alike (e.g., Giles, 2001; Giles, Bourhis, & Taylor, 1977).

LANGUAGE AS A COMMUNICATIVE COMMODITY IN THE NEW GLOBAL ECONOMY

The emerging international economic order has mandated transformations of identity, language, and communication (Castells, 2000; Giddens, 1990) due to local, national, and worldwide interactions and the resulting demand for linguistic and cultural uniformity. For example, Gee, Hull, and Lankshear (1996) maintained that emerging organizational practices are based on standardization (implementing identical speech and behavioral conduct in organizational communication) and typically require competence in English, a language that is rapidly becoming prevalent in most business transactions (Tagliabue, 2005).

Addressing the international proliferation of corporate telephone call centers, Cameron (2000) described how standardization has modified linguistic variation among employees to ensure predictable and profitable communication interactions with U.S.-based clientele. She referred to standardization as "the practice of making and enforcing rules for language-use with the intention of reducing optional variation in performance" (p. 324). J. Milroy and L. Milroy (1998) similarly asserted that corporations often mandate that employees operate within preferred norms in interactive discourse (e.g., speech performance, norms of address, and politeness procedures). Many organizations now view language as a commodity requiring management, even in what may be considered the most trivial elements of employee speech (du Gay, 1996). Organizations can effectively communicate across regional and national boundaries by accommodating Western language and speech norms through employee training, monitoring, and surveillance, therefore maintaining a competitive advantage in the global marketplace. Heller (2003) specified the role that language plays in determining social and political privilege among individuals and reviewed how industrialization in southern Canada (Ontario) contributed to social unrest among speakers of French and English. Heller concluded that "ethnic stratification (anglophone owners and francophone and immigrant workers) and residential segregation . . . [of] parishes and neighborhood schools served important functions of social and cultural reproduction, including the persistence of ethnolinguistic identities and practices" (p. 481).

This circumstance exemplifies how community members encountered varying degrees of social and economic prestige, inclusion, or exclusion based on their position in a commodified cultural and language system. Individuals who were unable to assume the marketable identity were relegated to less advantageous positions in education, society, and politics. In the 1970s, the highly educated francophone community promoted its interests through political mobilization and by drawing from discourse about ethno-national identity and language to access political rights.

The effective political organization of the francophones in Canada resulted in the establishment of a French-language high school. This facility has now become the primary resource for multinational employers seeking to recruit bilingual labor for corporate telephone call centers. In the 1980s, when the community sought to rebuild its economy through communication and tourism industries, bilingual (English and French) speakers, who had previously been marginalized within the dominant English-speaking community, solidified employment in call center organizations. People of this particular community viewed their bilingual skills primarily as a tool for "privileged access to poorly paid, non-unionized and mainly dead-end jobs" (Heller, 2003, p. 483). In this town, although call center employment was perceived as an opportunity to continue their French language and identity, people admitted that they maintained bilingual skills primarily based on market motives, hoping for employment in service-related jobs.

Coupland, Bishop, and Garrett (2003) assessed the ethnolinguistic vitality (see Giles et al., 1977) of the Welsh language and concluded that "Welsh is an increasingly core facet of public life in Wales and all major institutions play a part in the revitalization of the language" (p. 157). However, in assessing the use of Welsh in an American newspaper, the authors suggested that "Welsh is literally commodified when it is packaged and sold by the language teaching and learning institutions that bring American tourists to Wales" (p. 174). Authentic Welsh ethnic and traditional identities were depicted through limited linguistic and cultural reference. Articulating the complexity involved in modern cultural and language revitalization, Coupland et al. (2003) argued, "In an era of increasing global flow and interdependence, it might necessarily be through the iconisation of minority languages that their local values are established in complex, global sociolinguistic ecologies" (p. 174).

In a similar context, Le Menestrel (1999) addressed how Cajun identity in Louisiana has been commodified, inciting debate over what constitutes authentic identity by those who considered themselves to be Cajun ethnically yet struggle with language proficiency. Despite initial setbacks, middle-class Cajuns reestablished authentic identity and language through educational programs that were instilled to "recoup lost ground through the revitalization of language via schooling, that is, by trying to regain what is meant to count as authentic linguistic capital through institutionalized means" (p. 475).

Each of these examples suggest that difficulties related to individual and social identity may emerge when language, culture, and ethnicity are transformed from authentic to commodified entities. In support of this claim, Hedetoft (1999) contended, "The globalization of culture (whether American or not) in this threat scenario is invested with a normatively negative sign value; it comes to stand for and represent the transnational imperatives that in turn are interpreted as eroding the nation-state and its identity (p. 79) . . . [and] the structuration of identities, loyalties and mental geographies" (p. 83). The ideology of globalization, in many cases, has transformed the cultural and national identities of participants after its own (Western) image. Considering these issues, as other nations continue to adopt English as the communicative language of business, educational, media, and global discourse, their identities may also begin to resemble that of Western individuals, cultures, and nations (Friedman, 1999; Giddens, 1999)

Amidst the global proliferation of the English language and Western culture (see Crystal, 2005; Wallraff, 2005), language revitalization movements have developed in a variety of contexts, with varying levels of accomplishment. For instance, Kashoki (2003) described how modern beliefs about linguistic freedom in postcolonial South Africa and Zimbabwe inspired efforts at multilingual language policy formation. However, this process has been extremely complicated because of sociohistorical attitudes of indigenous populations who "regard a single language—English—as the language of prestige, social mobility and economic empowerment" (p. 193). Verhoef (1998) found that, in the North West Province, South African teenagers minimally developed multilingual skills, instead demonstrating an inclination toward English because they viewed it as economically and administratively advantageous.

Similarly, Yagmur and Kroon (2003) reviewed ethnolinguistic vitality perceptions of Bashkir, a revitalized language used primarily in Bashkortostan, a former republic of the Soviet Union. During the Soviet era, the region endured complete Russification, and Bashkir was banned in educational and public spheres and allowed primarily in domestic contexts. This process contributed to the adoption of Russian by younger generations and the simultaneous lowering of the Bashkir language's status and functional values. More recently, however, language activists have noted that citizens in the region of Bashkortostan have realized the importance of authentic revitalization and have worked toward cultural and linguistic survival by instituting language programs and schools. Yagmur and Kroon assessed this specific revitalization movement and suggested, "To further advance the vitality of the native languages in Bashkortostan, Bashkir medium universities and Bashkir teacher training programs are essential. For multiculturalism to take root in the community, ethnic groups should be encouraged to learn each other's language and culture" (p. 333). Despite increasing utilization of Bashkir and other languages in educational contexts, Yagmur and Kroon asserted that "the shift to a Latin script [is] a very difficult task" (p. 333), given that Russian is the official language and all public documents are still in the dominant language. Although Yagmur and Kroon could not determine non-linguistic outcomes of revitalization in schools, Taylor and Wright (2003) demonstrated that Inuit children in artic Quebec (Nunavik) who were immersed in their native language outperformed their peers schooled in English or French, scored higher in self-esteem, and maintained more positive images of their ethnic group.

Fishman (2004) reviewed several unique languages that have been successfully maintained in the United States. For instance, Spanish speakers in rural communities in Arizona, New Mexico, and Texas have continued their language for between six and eight generations. Similarly, French speakers within northern areas (close to Quebec) of Maine, Vermont, and New Hampshire have retained authentic linguistic expression, in addition to German speakers in Pennsylvania who attained linguistic and cultural survival by establishing communities separate from mainstream interaction. During the 1960s and 1970s, favorable attitudes toward non-English language survival in the United States grew substantially, as evidenced by young adults who celebrated ethnic pride and their non-English native tongues. Within this 10-year period, radio and television broadcasts, printed sources, community centers, and religious organizations were instituted to facilitate native language survival.

More recently, Fishman (2004) observed the negative response to "English-only" laws in the United States, and he argued that "[the] laws foster suspicions, divisiveness, and recriminations that discourage individuals and businesses from public use of languages other than English and, doubtlessly, have again helped undercut non-English mother tongue transmission in the country as a whole" (p. 414). Although diverse language and cultural groups in the United States should have the right to express authentic identities, the implementation of English-only policies in organizations, schools, and public contexts will likely contribute to decreasing numbers of people who maintain native languages.

In assessing Hawaiian language revitalization and the role of immersion education in reestablishing and sustaining language vitality, we emphasize that, in contrast to other languages that originate from a specific country (which may continue to utilize that language), the Hawaiian language is indigenous to the Islands. Therefore, indigenous immersion should be "clearly differentiated from foreign language immersion (for learning languages unconnected to the personal identity of students) and from heritage immersion (for immigrant groups with thriving languages elsewhere)" (Wilson & Kamanā, 2001, p. 156). In the following sections, we review ethnolinguistic vitality theory and provide a brief historical backdrop to the Hawaiian language example. We then analyze its dynamics in terms of the ethnolinguistic vitality model, draw on interview data from Hawaiian language experts where appropriate, outline challenges for the future of this language movement, and provide a research agenda across different domains of inquiry. In doing so, we present readers with an overview of the processes inherent in one language preservation initiative and discuss educators' perceptions of its positive impact on students' language identity and communicative vitality.

LANGUAGE, CULTURE, AND ETHNOLINGUISTIC VITALITY

Ample research on intergroup communication (see Harwood & Giles, 2005) has focused on interethnic interactions, a large portion of which has been driven by communication accommodation theory (see the recent review by Gallois, Ogay, & Giles, 2005). Notably, communication accommodation theory has been ranked as the most influential framework in the social psychology of language and communication (Tracy & Haspel, 2004), and it has served as the springboard for a number of satellite models, including ethnolinguistic identity theory (ELIT). ELIT articulates (see also Tajfel and Turner, 1986, for a related discussion of social identity theory) the conditions under which group members differentiate from outgroup members by maintaining, emphasizing, and revitalizing their own distinctive communicative codes (Giles & Johnson, 1981, 1987).

Besides a strong sense of ingroup allegiance and beliefs about injustices perpetrated by the outgroup, another important construct in ELIT is ethnolinguistic (or group) vitality (Giles, 1977; Harwood, Giles, & Bourhis, 1994). Over the decades, this theoretical framework has spawned considerable exploration across different continents (see Giles, 2001), and it has been invoked in other intergroup contexts, such as intergenerational interactions (e.g., Giles, Kutchukhides, Yagmur, & Noels, 2003). ELIT has been amenable to conceptual refinements (e.g., Allard & Landry, 1986; Evans, 1996) and theoretically related to or inherent in an array of other models, constructs, and processes, including acculturation (e.g., Sayahi, 2005). The theory maintains that the more vitality a group has—or, rather, the more its individual members believe it has relative to a comparative outgroup—the more likely it is that members will invest significant effort into identifying with the ingroup and engage in collective actions and messages on its behalf.

The ethnolinguistic vitality model was originally developed to measure the combined influence of three factors, namely, status (e.g., economic and historical conditions), demography (e.g., numbers of in- and outgroup speakers, birthrates, etc.), and institutional support (e.g., media and educational representation of the group) across various cultural, intergroup, and multilingual contexts (Giles, 1977). *Objective vitality* may be investigated, for example, by measurement of the amount of newsprint and television representation marginalized groups maintain relative to dominant groups. However, *subjective vitality* explores how members of ethnic collectivities themselves judge ("rightly or wrongly") the societal conditions impinging on their own and relevant outgroups (see subjective vitality scale of Bourhis, Giles, & Rosenthal, 1981). Research suggests that the survival of indigenous and minority languages may depend upon the prevalence of their use, speaker status, and perceived vitality levels (e.g., Cenoz & Valencia, 1993). Group members may demonstrate "visible vitality . . . interaction networks (and) . . . employ them . . . for one or more vital functions" (Fishman, 1972, p. 21). Those who perceive their group vitality as strong may use native language skills more frequently than those who view it as weak (Bourhis & Sachdev, 1984). Groups that are low in vitality may compromise native languages and undergo linguistic assimilation, whereas groups demonstrating high vitality often maintain unique linguistic and cultural characteristics. Furthermore, high ingroup vitality may also be an important predictor of nonlanguage outcomes, such as satisfaction with home life, educational achievements, and occupational aspirations (Currie & Hogg, 1994). Hence, language identification and utilization may significantly influence social cohesion, esteem, and language survival among diverse indigenous groups.

Although research has established that group vitality may influence perceptions, attitudes, and behaviors in various multilingual environments, this framework has not been adopted to analyze the Hawaiian language situation. Considering that increasing numbers of indigenous peoples are in various stages of reclaiming and preserving cultural and linguistic identities (England, 2003; House, 2003; Kashoki, 2003; Mansoor, 2004; Taylor & Wright, 2003; Yagmur & Kroon, 2003), it merits further investigation. Given the history of Hawaiian colonization and existing progress toward cultural and linguistic reclamation, research should explicate the pivotal role of communication within this matrix. Ideally, this research will afford language and cultural advocates an understanding of the challenges and complexity inherent in revitalization and assist future preservation initiations and movements. Therefore, this chapter provides an overview of the diverse structural, social, and communicative conditions that attend the history and current condition of Hawaiian language dynamics.

BRIEF HISTORY OF THE HAWAIIAN LANGUAGE

Within the last 200 years, Western influence has contributed to extreme social, political, and linguistic changes that have significantly compromised the ability of Hawaiian people to maintain authentic expressions of culture and language. For example, diseases introduced by foreigners significantly reduced the Hawaiian population from an estimated 300,000 in 1778 to approximately 50,000 by 1878 (Reinecke, 1969; Wilson, 1998). This alarming decline in the Hawaiian presence, and the concomitant lowering of linguistic capital, is undisputedly related to the overthrow of the Hawaiian monarchy and the resulting banishment of Hawaiian as an educational and social medium. K. Silva (personal communication, January 8, 2004) described the impact of foreign influence on the Hawaiian people. He confirmed that "[t]he oppression led to the decline of our language and our culture and . . . in important ways, led to the decline in the status of Hawaiian people in our own country . . . our own view or perspective of the world and ourselves changed dramatically because of the lack of the ability to use our own language in our own schools." As a consequence, Wilson (1998) contended that the Hawaiian language became associated with "an irretrievable past, and a lack of power in the educational, economic, and political spheres" (p. 124). In accordance with the salience of language as a core aspect of identity among many cultural groups (e.g., Cargile, Giles, & Clément, 1996; Giles, 1977), Hawaiian beliefs emphasize the profound importance of language as a communicative medium to facilitate understanding and expression. According to Wilson, cultural members treat communication and language as "a procreative force" (p. 124), utilized by people to establish and determine their social reality. For example, elderly Hawaiians may be hesitant to use words referring to death because of the inherent connection between the spoken word and actual life events. The centrality of language in cultural revitalization can also be understood by assessing the phrase *I ka 'ōlelo Hawai'i ke ola*, translated as "Life rests in the Hawaiian language." Meyer (2003) emphasized the importance of language in Hawaiian interaction by referring to the view of Pukui, Haertig, and Lee (1972) that " 'Ōlelo, 'word' or 'speech,' was far more than a means of communicating. To the Hawaiian, the spoken word did more than set into motion forces of destruction and death, forgiveness, and healing. The word itself was a force" (p. 124). This research documents that many Hawaiians view language as a force that creates, defines, and reifies reality.

Before interactions with European explorers in 1778, the Hawaiian language and culture were transmitted orally through storytelling and performance rituals, hula, or chanting. In the nineteenth century, literacy among the native people flourished when Hawai'i became an independent kingdom with a parliamentary style of government. After their arrival in 1820, missionaries developed a written alphabet for the Hawaiian language, which contributed to the establishment of printed publications by missionaries.

At this time, the Hawaiian people began to publish various literatures, including the first Hawaiian newspaper, *Ka Lama Hawai'i*, in 1834. Local newspapers served an important purpose in furthering the discussion and preservation of Hawaiian traditions and perspectives. Several religious and literary works were also translated into Hawaiian, enabling people to record cultural and linguistic information that had previously been maintained through oral transmission (Warschauer & Donaghy, 1997). In order to instill literacy in the Hawaiian language for Hawaiians and others, missionaries established schools in the Islands. As Wilson (1998) wrote, "Hawaiian was the language of government, religion, retail business, the media, education and interethnic communication during the monarchy" (p. 127). During the initial century of consistent interaction with European culture, Hawai'i was a "multiracial nation using Hawaiian both as a lingua franca and as an official language of government" (Wilson & Kamanā, 2001, p. 148).

Upon contact, the influence of missionaries and commerce profoundly affected the culture and livelihood of Hawaiians. For example, within a generation, the Hawaiian language completely vanished from the schools. In 1880, 150 schools taught their curricula in Hawaiian, and 60 in English, but by 1902, all 203 schools in the Islands instructed in English (Schutz, 1994). According to W. H. Wilson (personal communication, December 18, 2004), the Hawaiian language was outlawed in schools in 1896. Monastersky (2004) similarly discussed legal sanctions that enforced English-only policies and their impact on Hawaiian language. He reported that "[s]tate law actually prohibited teachers from using Hawaiian as the classroom language in elementary and secondary school—a holdover from the colonial rules imposed by Americans after they wrestled control of the islands from the original Polynesian inhabitants in 1893. That law and the cultural dominance of the United States nearly succeeded in killing off the native language" (p. 8). By the twentieth century, Hawaiian language use among locals almost completely disappeared, seriously disrupting Hawaiians' social, spiritual, and political values and stability. Meyer (2003) addressed the negative impact of language loss on Hawaiian vitality:

> What began as an altruistic and well-meaning effort has, in fact, ended . . . [by] scarring the cultural beliefs, vitality, and strength of a race. Hawaiians suffered in their belief that their missionary tutors of Western culture were indeed superior which left them feeling inferior and insignificant. (p. 29)

Based on growing commercial interests in Hawai'i, agricultural labor immigration expanded to support the increasing demands of various industries. Prior to the annexation of the Islands by the U.S., Hawai'i Creole English (also known as Hawaiian Pidgin) originated, based upon the English, Hawaiian, Japanese, Chinese, Portuguese, and Filipino languages (Bickerton, 1983; Reinecke, 1969). W. H. Wilson (personal communication, December 18, 2004) confirmed that Hawaiian Creole English greatly assisted communication among culturally diverse plantation workers, and Hawaiians and locals in the Islands still utilize it. Current statistics estimate that there are at least 600,000 speakers of Hawaiian Creole English, indicating that this variety still maintains social and political significance (Grimes, 1992) despite its low prestige in comparison with standard English (see Ohama, Gotay, Pagano, Boles, & Craven, 2000).

Corresponding with international preservation movements (see Hsiau, 2000; Hung, 1992; Li & Lee, 2004; Liu, 2000; Midori, 2001; Pu, 1996; Siddle, 1995) and in response to the endangerment of the Hawaiian language and culture, concerned scholars and community activists developed educational revitalization programs to facilitate increased awareness, involvement, and perpetuation of Hawaiian culture in social, educational, and performance contexts. Celebrations of music, dance, land, and political rights abounded, and traditional canoe voyaging activities also were reestablished (Wilson, 1998). Fortunately, recent movements toward cultural revitalization among Hawaiians have helped to reify Hawaiian "culture, confidence, and achievement" (p. 124), increasing the ability of natives and interested others to maintain the Hawaiian language.

ANALYSIS OF THE ETHNOLINGUISTIC VITALITY OF THE HAWAIIAN LANGUAGE

Social and Historical Status

Historically, the Hawaiian language and culture were relegated to a low socioeconomic status, a process that seriously compromised their survival. For example, Warschauer and Donaghy (1997) noted that missionaries perceived traditional language and art negatively and discouraged such native expression. At the end of the nineteenth century, English began to replace Hawaiian as the dominant language, because of political influence in the state. The Hawaiian language was abolished in favor of English and banned from scholastic interactions through legal mandates and severe physical punishment. However, the recent emergence of the Hawaiian language and cultural movement appears to be increasing language vitality.

For instance, the population of Hawaiians who now learn or speak their native language has increased significantly in the last 20 years, a trend that seems to represent the importance of maintaining the language among Hawaiians and interested others. Describing their role in the establishment of the Hawaiian language education program, Wilson and Kamanā (2001) reported that "contemporary Hawaiian-medium education at the University of Hawai'i at Hilo began when we were hired in the late 1970s to establish a Bachelor of Arts degree in Hawaiian Studies" (p. 148). In 1983, after the Board of Education approved Hawaiian-medium education, several language and cultural specialists, including Larry Kimura, William H. Wilson, Kauanoe Kamanā, and Kalena Silva, developed the 'Aha Pūnana Leo (language nest gathering). In the following excerpt, Wilson and Kamanā described the pivotal role of family involvement in language reclamation: "[the 'Aha Pūnana Leo] has focused on developing education for native speakers of Hawaiian and the expansion of the native-speaker group by including other families interested in developing children who are dominant-Hawaiian speakers rather than simply teaching Hawaiian as a second-language skill" (p. 149).

Educational immersion and Hawaiian language/studies programs have enabled students to learn through the language and culture of Hawai'i, and research suggests that "immersion students have a high regard for Hawaiian language and culture and for themselves as speakers of the Hawaiian language" (Slaughter, 1997, p. 124). Furthermore, Hawaiian language scholars K. Silva (personal communication, January 8, 2004) and W. H. Wilson (personal communication, December 18, 2004) asserted that immersion programs positively correspond to increased enrollment in Hawaiian studies courses and greater numbers of language students at university campuses. According to K. Silva, in 2003, 100 students majored in Hawaiian studies at the University of Hawai'i at Hilo, and an additional estimated 100 individuals majored in Hawaiian language and studies at the University of Hawai'i at Manoa. By the fourth year of study, many students in these programs are fluent in Hawaiian, and following graduation, they often become established within immersion schools as educators, translators, or other positions related to Hawaiian language and cultural preservation. Some students pursue graduate degrees in Hawaiian studies or in other areas of related interest. In 1996, the Board of Regents of the University of Hawai'i at Hilo approved a graduate (M.A.) program in Hawaiian language, and, according to W. H. Wilson, this represents the "only program in a specific native American language" in the United States. The first cohort graduated in 1998, and graduates currently serve in positions of immersion education, higher education, and community leadership. The University of Hawai'i at Hilo is currently working to develop a Ph.D. program in Hawaiian and indigenous language and culture revitalization, and although still in the early stages of formation and approval, its potential is receiving international attention.

Thus, in the last 100 years, the Hawaiian language has endured low social and economic status. However, recent developments in political, social, educational, and cultural trends indicate that the status of the Hawaiian language may be increasing.

Demographic Support

The 2000 United States Census Bureau Report suggested that only 9.4% (or approximately 118,215 of a population of 1,257,608) of the people of the Islands were Native Hawaiians, compared with a U.S. presence of 1%, or 12,576 (of an estimated U.S. population of 209,809,777). However, the same report indicates that 41% of people identify as Asian, 25% as Caucasian, and 21.3% as belonging to two or more racial groups (United States Census Bureau, 2000). Addressing this discrepancy between assessed and actual ethnic presence in Hawai'i, Malone and Corry (2004) contended that, upon closer examination, United States Census Bureau estimates indicate that between 300,000 and 400,000 individuals in the state identify with Hawaiian ethnicity, although two-thirds of these citizens belong to multiple racial groups. Based on recent changes in the 2000 United States Census Bureau measurement of race and ethnicity, for the first time, people could select more than one race group. Malone and Corry acknowledged a "noticeable increase in the Native Hawaiian population reported in the United States, rising from only 211,014 in 1990 to 401,162 in 2000" (p. 4). Clearly, the population of Native Hawaiians would not likely double within a 10-year period, indicating that the presence of Native Hawaiians in the Islands is actually much higher than the United States Census Bureau estimated.

By the 1980s, the Hawaiian language was threatened with extinction because fewer than 2,000 native speakers of the language reportedly remained, with only a few dozen cf them under the age of 18 (Warschauer & Donaghy, 1997). Of nearly 200,000 Native Hawaiians in Hawai'i, the 1990 United States Census Bureau listed roughly 9,000 speakers of Hawaiian (Kamana & W. H. Wilson, 1996). Approximately 26% of people in Hawai'i speak languages other than English in the home, in comparison with roughly 18% of the overall U.S. population. Monastersky (2004) confirmed: "When the Hawaiian professors started their work, only 32 people under the age of

18 spoke the language at home. Now some 2,000 children are enrolled in Hawaiian immersion schools, and as many as 6,000 people have some fluency in the language" (p. 9).

Currently, estimates of Hawaiian speakers range between 6,000 and 9,000, but Hawaiian language schools and colleges continue to train students who have a strong command of Hawaiian; hence, there is a great likelihood that the number of Hawaiian language speakers will continue to increase in the future (Monastersky, 2004). Despite the apparent discrepancy between academic and United States Census Bureau estimates of how many people currently speak the language, clearly, substantial demographic support increasingly emerges for the perpetuation and survival of the Hawaiian language.

Political Support

Political support for Hawaiian language and cultural preservation also seems to be increasing. For instance, a recent poll conducted by the Office of Hawaiian Affairs revealed that 86% of 303 Native Hawaiians and 78% of 301 non-Hawaiians believe that Native Hawaiians should be recognized by the United States as a distinct group, similar to the special recognition given to American Indians and Alaska Natives (Staton, 2003). Slaughter (1997) examined the political endorsement of immersion programs and concluded:

> The legislative mandate that created the initial pilot program was the result of lobbying by parents and a few Hawaiian-language educators for recognition of (1) the validity of the Hawaiian language as a medium suitable for instruction, (2) the importance of preserving and maintaining the Hawaiian language and culture, (3) the concomitant belief that total immersion was the best way to accomplish that goal, and (4) the desire of parents that their children's linguistic gains during preschool years, in terms of fluency in Hawaiian, not be lost in elementary school. (p. 105)

In addition, several different groups within Hawai'i have initiated correspondence with Hawaiian language professors regarding the translation of literature from English to Hawaiian and from Hawaiian to English. K. Silva (personal communication, January 8, 2004) affirmed that political activists within the state have also begun discussing the potential of establishing the requirement that all state government documents be written in both Hawaiian and English:

> At political . . . (and) governmental levels . . . we can estimate how Hawaiian is beginning to emerge as a language that . . . is embraced by more . . . of our own people, and others . . . by its use in society today . . . [Several] groups want translations in Hawaiian from English, from Hawaiian into English . . . These kinds of organizations are both private and state run . . . A Legislative

[representative] . . . is interested in having everything in Hawaiian government be bilingual . . . all of the documents, marriage certificates, death certificates, so if people wanted them they could request a document in Hawaiian.

Such information supports the claim that Hawaiian language preservation and utilization efforts have assisted in developing substantial support within a variety of government and political contexts. Although political support should not be equated with social status and support of a language and culture, endorsement within political contexts does suggest that the Hawaiian language currently possesses higher levels of social status than a few decades ago. Furthermore, increasing political support has empowered Hawaiians to establish and maintain cultural and linguistic presence in social, educational, and political contexts.

In 2005, legislators proposed the Native Hawaiian Government Reorganization Act. If approved, it would grant sovereignty to Hawaiians and provide them with legal opportunities similar to those of American Indians and native Alaskans, including the development of a governing body that would represent the interests of 400,000 Native Hawaiians in the United States. If established, this governing collective would assist in negotiating the distribution of 1.2 million acres of land claimed by the U.S. government in 1959, when Hawai'i was acquired in statehood. Murphy (2005) reported that a recent survey conducted on behalf of the State Office of Hawaiian Affairs demonstrated substantial support for the bill, whereas findings from the Grassroot Institute of Hawai'i suggested that two out of three Hawai'i residents opposed the bill. Hawai'i Governor Linda Lingle and Senators Daniel K. Akaka and Daniel K. Inouye support the bill, in addition to the multitudes of Hawaiian rights activists who have worked for an equitable government for Native Hawaiians.

In a separate but related state of affairs, on August 2, 2005, Kamehameha Schools[1] were significantly challenged by the U.S. Federal Court, which ruled that current admission policies that favor Native Hawaiians violate civil rights and antidiscrimination laws. Describing the event, Kobayashi and Pang (2005) wrote that: "A federal appeals court delivered a devastating blow to Kamehameha Schools' practice of giving admission preference to students of Hawaiian blood . . . the admissions policy violates federal civil rights laws first passed in 1966 barring private institutions from discriminating on the basis of race" (p. A1). Based on the court's recent decision, some suggest that rejecting the race-based admissions policy at Kamehameha Schools may threaten other Native Hawaiian programs, increasing the urgency of a Native Hawaiian federal recognition bill (DePledge, 2005).

Although the U.S. federal government has demonstrated that it will mandate Kamehameha Schools to modify current practices, media representation of the public's reaction to the ruling in the Islands affirms that there is significant social support for allowing Kamehameha Schools' admission policies to remain intact. For instance, following the court ruling, Native Hawaiians and non-Hawaiian supporters gathered on Oahu (in front of Iolani Palace, the final resting place of Princess Bishop) and the Big Island (in Hilo and Kailua-Kona) to march in protest. In Honolulu, between 12,000 and 15,000 people filled the streets to demonstrate opposition, and 300–400 individuals walked on Aliʻi Drive in Kailua-Kona. According to Sur (2005), "Amid the blaring of car and truck horns, some 130 people, including alumni, students and parents of students, stood on the sidewalk, waving signs and yelling, 'Educate Hawaiians!' to passing motorists" (p. A1).

Local activists and community organization members also expressed opposition to the recent ruling. Kobayashi and Pang (2005) referred to a statement by Vicki Holt Takamine, president of the Ilioulaokalani Coalition, who described her evaluation of the U.S. Federal Court system: "Those courts were not set up to protect the rights of Native Hawaiians. The courts were not set up to protect the rights of indigenous people. The courts were set up to protect the white men who wrote that constitution—and it is a white men's policy" (p. A16). In response to the ruling, Lilikala Kameʻeleihiwa, former director of Hawaiian studies at the University of Hawaiʻi at Mānoa, petitioned non-Hawaiians to assist in the aid of Hawaiians as they seek to solidify their resources and build collective solidarity. She stated that "[t]he good non-Hawaiians would never try to steal from us by applying to Kamehameha Schools for anything because they know that we have children who need to have that money to go to school and for education" (DePledge, 2005, p. A17). Bishop (2005) reported the response of Robert Kihune, a Hawaiian rights activist who has encouraged the people of Hawaiʻi to maintain their stance about the Kamehameha Schools' policy. Bishop wrote:

> Kamehameha Schools may have lost a battle, but the war to preserve the schools' Hawaiians-first admission policy will go on, retired Navy Vice-Admiral Robert Kihune vowed Saturday (p. A1) . . . Kihune cautioned the near-full gymnasium that the fight is not against non-Hawaiians, most of whom understand that the preference policy is good for all Hawaiʻi, he said. The policy was never intended to be racial, he said, but to correct past actions taken against Native Hawaiians, who "lost their identity and self esteem long ago . . . . Let us not raise our fists, but our voices to let people throughout the nation know the history," Kihune said. (A5)

As these incidents suggest, despite political policies that undermine the admission practices of Kamehameha Schools, significant social support has been demonstrated by Hawaiians and non-Hawaiians for the institutions' ability to maintain autonomy. Although the literature indicates that political support for the Hawaiian language has increased tremendously in the last few decades, the U.S. Federal Court system continues to negate the ability of Hawaiians to procure resources that have been specifically designated for them. This affair also demonstrates that, although there may be significant public social support for Hawaiian interests, political agendas may threaten Hawaiians' social status as a distinct cultural group. Given that social status is one factor influencing language vitality and utilization (Giles, 1977), it seems possible that compromising the social standing of Hawaiian culture (through legal rulings that erode Hawaiian autonomy, interests, and resources) may decrease the status of the language and, in effect, actually disrupt current progress toward linguistic preservation.

Institutional Support via Media

As research attests, the level of institutional promotion for a given language constitutes an essential element contributing to its vitality (Giles, 2001). Institutional support for the revitalization of the Hawaiian language and immersion programs has also been established in a variety of media contexts.

Although Henningham (1992) argued that commercial broadcasters have dominated the media agenda—ultimately contributing to the dissolution of the Hawaiian language—and that native Hawaiian cultural development has been restricted to minimally viewed public-access television channels, current trends indicate that media endorsement of Hawaiian language may be increasing. For instance, Hawaiian language expression has been promoted through a variety of contexts, including newsprint, television, radio, and web media (see Abrams, Eveland, & Giles, 2003).

During the 1960s, authentic media representation of the Hawaiian language and perspectives was featured in Hawaiian-language radio programs. Describing such initiatives, K. Silva (personal communication, January 8, 2004) noted:

> Larry Kimura [University of Hawai'i at Hilo faculty member] . . . beginning in the 1960s . . . interviewed his family and expanded . . . to his own Hawaiian language program (Ka Leo Hawai'i) . . . on KCCN Radio in Honolulu . . . for . . . 17 years . . . [and] interviewed hundreds of people. . . . [Because of this] we have an oral record . . . of ideas, thoughts, and feelings of people . . . from the late 1800s, many of them, born then. . . . This kind of information is extremely valuable to us, as we Hawaiians seek to reclaim our identity . . . along with our language and culture. . . . Several newspapers currently represent past and present Hawaiian perspectives.

The Hawaiian Nūpepa Collection consists of historic newspapers that were developed between 1834 and 1948 and includes approximately 120,000 news pages extracted from 100 distinct periodicals, also available on microfilm and in digital form. This collection is available at the University of Hawai'i at Mānoa Library and has been sponsored by 'Aha Pūnana Leo, Alu Like Incorporated, and the Hawai'i Community Foundation. Historically speaking,

K. Silva asserted that prolific Hawaiian writers have amassed a wealth of literary records, starting in 1860:

> Our Hawaiian ancestors, from 1800s . . . into the 20th century, developed a huge repository of literature mainly published in Hawaiian language newspapers. People like Kepelino, Kamakau, and of course, before them, Malo, those kinds of writers of Hawaiian culture began writing in our language and left this huge legacy of material written in our language, about our culture, about our views of the world, and . . . of other people who were coming to Hawai'i at the time. . . . Some people think that this literary repository is the largest for any indigenous people in the world, which is staggering. . . . Hundreds of thousands of pages are yet to be uncovered, yet to be viewed, and yet to be gleaned for the kind of material that can be used to assist us in the work that we do today.

Students have utilized the Hawaiian language to read and transcribe Hawaiian-language newspapers that were developed by prolific Hawaiian writers during the time of the Hawaiian monarchy. Currently, the University of Hawai'i at Hilo Hawaiian Collection includes newspapers, journals, monographs, periodicals, maps, pamphlets, and reprints about information related to the Islands and Hawaiians. Moreover, *'Ōiwi: The Journal of Artistic Expression* presents journal articles addressing play excerpts, poems, songs, and short stories relating to the Hawaiian experience. The Hamilton Language Newspapers provide electronic resources that are available about Hawaiian newsprint to students in the state of Hawai'i who do not have access to microfilms, a service sponsored primarily by the Bishop Museum and Alu Like Incorporated through the University of Hawai'i at Hilo, Hawaiian Language College.

Television also affords invaluable opportunities for Hawaiians and interested others to learn about Hawaiian language and culture. For instance, the Public Broadcasting Station frequently airs various shows dealing with Hawaiian history, myths, and geography, in addition to information assessing language, education, performance, and revitalization issues. One popular show that has recently emerged is *Ke Kupu Nei* (Sprouting Forth), which airs twice weekly. This program features local activists, musicians, and celebrities such as Manuwai Peters, Leilani Poli'ahu, and Keali'i Reichel. This Hawaiian language interview show has been labeled as the "Jay Leno and Oprah Winfrey" of Hawaiian language television and is conducted entirely in Hawaiian.

Informed local opinion suggests that Hawaiian cultural and language vitality expressed through music is another interesting area of media endorsement (see Mattern, 1998). For instance, in the state of Hawai'i, several radio stations play Hawaiian music, although fewer radio stations broadcast interactive conversation in the Hawaiian language. KWXX radio, on the Big Island, is one progressive radio station that conducts a weekly show entirely through Hawaiian language and music. W. H. Wilson (personal communication, December 18, 2004) verified that the show, *Alana I Kai Hikina*, is sponsored through the 'Aha Pūnana Leo and broadcast locally through FM radio and on-line. Hawaiian music stations are also popular on neighboring islands and receive widespread attention among Hawaiians and non-Hawaiians alike (see Chebatoris, 2005; Namuo, 2004). Interested listeners can utilize several online Hawaiian music radio stations that are broadcast from Alaska, California, Nevada, Oregon, Washington, and British Columbia, demonstrating that media support for Hawaiian language and music spans domestic and international contexts (Berger, 2001).

Internet information resources also positively affect the objective vitality of Hawaiian culture and language. For instance, several Hawaiian language web links address various issues related to language acquisition and learning. The 'Ahahui 'Ōlelo Hawai'i, a private, nonprofit organization dedicated to the perpetuation of the Hawaiian language, sponsors one such website, http://hawaiian language.com/o-linkpage.html. The resource offers links to basic alphabet, pronunciation, diacriticals, grammar, phrases, essays, and lessons. In addition, other links on this website permit access to learning materials, resources, classes, institutions, and supporting organizations. Through web-based information dissemination, the objective vitality of Hawaiian culture and language can continue to develop and progress. A plethora of media resources accurately represent authentic Hawaiian experiences, demonstrating that widespread media support for Hawaiian language and culture preservation is developing and gaining momentum.

Institutional Support via Educational Immersion Programs

Recalling the collective action of University of Hawai'i faculty (of the 'Aha Pūnana Leo), who advocated the reestablishment of Hawaiian as a state language, K. Silva (personal communication, January 8, 2004) asserted that legal restrictions were removed in 1986 when it was reinstated alongside standard English. Monastersky (2004) explained the process that the faculty has undergone in reviving the Hawaiian language:

> Along the way, they have established language-immersion schools reaching from pre-kindergarten all the way through to a master's degree. They have testified before Congress, changed state laws, and are now establishing the country's first doctoral program in indigenous languages. And they have created a small but burgeoning community of fluent Hawaiian speakers, some of whom are becoming the next generation of educators. (p. 9)

Through the efforts of the 'Aha Pūnana Leo, immersion programs were developed that would provide an educational environment for students by teaching the language and culture of Hawai'i. For example, scholars like L. Kimura, W. H. Wilson, K. Silva, K. Kamanā, and others participated in the planning and implementation of immersion education and university Hawaiian language education. In the following excerpt, W. H. Wilson (personal communication, December 18, 2004) described the importance of sustaining the Hawaiian language and the benefit of immersion education on language, culture, and identity:

> To us it is intrinsically valuable to know the Hawaiian language and culture. Like in English, it's intrinsically valuable to know about Shakespeare, or English history, because they have lessons for life. Well, it's the same thing with Hawaiian culture or history. There are lessons for life, no matter what your identity is. It's also much easier to learn both Hawaiian and English, by going to school in Hawaiian, in today's world. You can take someone in an English medium school, who is taught Hawaiian with a very good teacher one hour a day from kindergarten through high school, and our students, in Hawaiian immersion, will still speak Hawaiian better and English at the same level of fluency and literacy, as that other person. So as far as languages, the students in Hawaiian immersion are way ahead.

Johnson and Swain (1997) also addressed the invaluable potential of immersion education programs in the reestablishment of cultural and linguistic expression of marginalized groups. They suggested that any language community that endures decreasing numbers of native speakers will likely require immersion as an essential step in reversing language extinction. Slaughter (1997) highlighted positive impacts of immersion education:

> [T]here has been an upsurge of enrollment in Hawaiian language and Hawaiian studies on the university campuses. Recent graduates are perceived as having a higher command of the Hawaiian language. . . . As some of the younger generation of university students become immersion teachers, they will be more adequately prepared to contribute to immersion and reconstructing the Hawaiian language and culture. (p. 127)

Such findings are especially important, considering previous literature suggesting that children's attitudes may become less favorable toward languages that are not perceived to be "standard" as they mature and become influenced by dominant social conditioning (e.g., Day, 1982).

Children in immersion programs do not have to be Hawaiian, but over 90% of them are, many with one non-Hawaiian parent (Wilson, 1998). Warschauer and Donaghy (1997) asserted that the development of Hawaiian language schools represents a promising possibility of increasing the number of fluent Hawaiian speakers. Slaughter (1997) also described immersion classrooms as unique environments that reflect the *'ohana* (Hawaiian word for family) and *aloha* of the culture of Hawai'i.

As a result of innovative educational initiatives, the Hawaiian Language College University laboratory schools have received attention, both nationally and internationally, from visitors and educators who are curious about reviving and maintaining indigenous languages within their communities. Because of widespread interest in Hawaiian immersion education, the Ford Foundation, a private advocate, recently funded a new immersion consortium project, Hale Kipa 'Ōiwi. This name references the hospitality that has been extended to visitors of the 'Aha Pūnana Leo and indicates how successful working relationships may ensue from private and public interests in indigenous cultural and language preservation (Kawaihae, 2003).

As the Hawaiian language programs at the University of Hawai'i at Hilo and the 'Aha Pūnana Leo expanded, the two schools established a consortium to collaboratively solidify funding, coordinate activities, and maximize resources. In addition to K–12 education and university language and cultural programs, "the consortium also provides books, videos, radio programming, computer services, newspapers, or scholarships to another 5,000 to 7,000 people in Hawai'i and elsewhere" (Wilson & Kamanā, 2001, p. 150). K. Kawai'ae'a (personal communication, September 13, 2004) confirmed that immersion education has long recognized the importance of media-facilitated communication as an essential tool in bridging the distance between immersion children in Hawai'i and other indigenous groups in the United States and internationally. Media interactions among students and instructors also allow Hawaiian language immersion programs to overcome certain challenges. For example, video recording provides educational and cultural advocates with the opportunity to secure and preserve the language and perspectives of native Hawaiian speakers. K. Kawai'ae'a confirmed that, since the 1990s, Hale Kuamo'o, at the University of Hawai'i at Hilo's Center for Hawaiian-Medium Education and Culture, has developed computer programs in Hawaiian, which enable immersion students to become technologically skilled in their native language. Primary software has been utilized through Apple Computers, permitting the addition of diacritical markings within the Hawaiian language, once a source of concern among translators. Apple Macintosh Hawaiian language fonts programs are available to Hawaiian immersion schools and other institutions addressing issues of Hawaiian language education.

Warschauer and Donaghy (1997) assessed the positive impact of technological resources, and they referred to Keiki Kawai'ae'a, Programs Director at Hale Kuamo'o, who contended that immersion education enables children to view Hawaiian as a living and valuable language through their use of Hawaiian in traditionally based curricula (science and math) and innovative computer or media programs. For instance, one kindergarten class at an immersion school in Keaukaha, on the Big Island, utilizes traditional Hawaiian customs of learning and communication with the assistance of a computer program called Leokï (Powerful Voice), provided by the Hawaiian Language College and the ʻAha Pūnana Leo. The first global bulletin board system based solely on the indigenous Hawaiian language, this innovation allows students and schools to employ services, including electronic mail (*leka uila*), chat lines (*laina kolekole*), open forums (*haʻina uluwale*), news lines (*kuʻi ka lono*), marketplace (*hale kūʻai*), vocabulary lists (*papa huaʻōlelo*), and current and back issues of the *Nā Maka o Kana* newspaper for Hawaiian immersion programs, materials, songs, and stories (*noiʻi nowelo*). In addition, the program provides contact information about Hawaiian language offices and services related to coursework and immersion programs (*nā keʻena ʻōlelo Hawaiʻi*).

K. Silva (personal communication, January 8, 2004) suggested that the development of immersion education has been significantly reinforced through interactions with other indigenous groups that have encountered similar difficulties related to Western colonialism.

> We have a very close relationship, for example, with the Maoris in New Zealand . . . in terms of the work we've been doing in the past several years to reclaim and revitalize our languages. From the very beginning, when we first started our work twenty years ago, we'd share stories about the trials and tribulations the old people went through . . . they were the first to be forced to be educated through English and the kinds of punishment . . . they endured . . . because they spoke Hawaiian at school. . . . We've heard the same stories and worse, in some instances from Native Americans in North America, some of whom were forced to live away from their families at boarding schools. They were taught only in English, and to separate themselves from their people, their culture, and their language. It's just tragic. So, all of us who have families and ancestors who have gone through this can relate and we share these stories and it just shows you what many of us have gone through.

According to Wilson (1998), Hawaiians are increasingly striving to make connections with other indigenous peoples. Most recently, correspondence between diverse cultures and countries has facilitated "curriculum sharing and cooperative lexicon enrichment" (p. 133). Interacting with other indigenous groups allows immersion students to share similar experiences and understand how culture and language revitalization may be achieved. For example, the Hawaiian tradition of "talking story," which emphasizes the exchange of personal experiences, has brought students from throughout the state together within a virtual classroom environment named the Pāhana Haku Mele (Compose a Song Project). This program is one such media-based opportunity that links children in geographically dispersed immersion programs (Warschauer & Donaghy, 1997).

K. Kawaiʻaeʻa (personal communication, September 13, 2004) has observed that children who utilize technological tools to communicate with students in various locations demonstrate high levels of Hawaiian language esteem and proficiency. Leokï has now been installed in all immersion schools. ʻAha Pūnana Leo preschools also utilize Leokï for primary communication between schools and among administrative offices. Other exciting technological innovations include the development of online chat rooms, hosted by mainstream Internet services like Yahoo. Eventually, the people behind Leokï would like to increase interaction among students and fulfill the goal of reaching larger populations of Hawaiian-speaking communities, like those on the island of Niʻihau (Warschauer & Donaghy, 1997).

K. Silva (personal communication, January 8, 2004) emphasized that various indigenous groups have inquired about Hawaiʻi's model of immersion education. He reported:

> There has been a lot of interest in our model from North America . . . from different Native American Indian tribes. People are saying, we'd like to do more of this at the higher academic level, so we developed a program that would allow us to help folks . . . achieve the best for their own peoples . . . to . . . point them in directions and to provide them with the kind of framework that allows them to develop their own programs for their own communities, wherever they are from.

Such facts suggest that language vitality and cultural preservation among various indigenous cultural groups is inspiring widespread interest and action, which indicates that language preservation movements may gain momentum in the future.

ETHNOLINGUISTIC VITALITY, IMMERSION EDUCATION, AND BEYOND

Various scholars have asserted that the existence of immersion programs demonstrates progress toward the preservation of the language and culture of indigenous groups. For instance, Johnson and Swain (1997) suggested that the existence of a language immersion curriculum indicates that the cultural identity of a particular marginalized group has been acknowledged. Such movements contribute to the belief—among Hawaiians and interested others— that indigenous people have the right to be educated in their own language (see Skutnabb-Kangas & Cummins, 1988).

Slaughter (1997) found that immersion education is increasing the ethnolinguistic vitality of Hawaiian children, adults, and interested students. For instance, Slaughter argued that "immersion students have a high regard for

Hawaiian language and culture and for themselves as speakers of the Hawaiian language" (p. 124). K. Silva (personal communication, January 8, 2004) verified that Hawaiian students at the University of Hawai'i at Hilo laboratory schools demonstrate proficiency in standard English and Hawaiian, yet they often choose to utilize Hawaiian, rather than Hawai'i Creole English (Pidgin). He explained:

> We're finding . . . this is an interesting social [situation]. . . . Ethnically, Hawaiian students are reticent sometimes, especially if there is a lot of very strong Hawaiian background in the family, to speak Standard English because they associate Pidgin with who they are as Hawaiians, which I think is so unfortunate. I have nothing against Pidgin, I can speak it myself . . . but why accept Pidgin English . . . as my language, rather than Hawaiian, a legitimate language that has a huge repository of literary materials and hundreds of years of thought and tradition behind it. . . . Immersion school [children] . . . more often than not, don't feel reticent about speaking standard English because they do speak Hawaiian as well.

The 'Aha Pūnana Leo have also implemented an educational model that differs significantly from the dominant Western paradigm. For instance, K. Kawai'ae'a (personal communication, September 13, 2004) discussed the importance of maintaining Hawaiian as the exclusive communicative norm in the immersion education until the fifth grade:

> The whole pace of immersion is different. The goal isn't to create excellent monolingual speakers; it really is a bilingual movement. And for a lot of us, we really see it as a multilingual movement. . . . Because of that, it's not about trying to follow and shadow the regulations of the English movement . . . you need to make sure that the language development in the target language is strong enough before you bring in English because English is everywhere. We don't formally introduce English reading until fifth grade, but they've had reading, writing, speaking, and listening, all areas of language development in Hawaiian. So it's just a different kind of pace and pattern sequence of learning.

Furthermore, in contrast to the dominant educational paradigm, which develops the academic/intellectual, physical, and affective/emotional character of children, immersion education also emphasizes socialization and spirituality. Describing this style of education, K. Kawai'ae'a stated:

> The whole issue of holistic human development is a part of the immersion movement. We focus on academic/intellectual, affective/emotional, and physical development, but there are also two other areas. One is social development and . . . social consciousness. . . . Immersion . . . and indigenous education also promote spiritual development. Spiritual development has to do

with the connection between people, places, and things all around you. It has to do with connecting and relating to and honoring the purpose of education and the things that help you to be more mentally, physically, socially, emotionally, spiritually prepared, as well as acknowledging those parts that are present visually, and not present, that help you stay focused as a learner.

Immersion education schools typically begin with students and teachers chanting in unison, a spiritual ritual that builds cohesion and encourages students to respect the educational environment, their teachers, and other students. K. Kawai'ae'a (personal communication, September 13, 2004) commented: "All of our schools start with the chant, in unison, to get the students focused and connect the teachers with the students. You don't see the bell ring and the kids just running into the classrooms. Schools start in a different way and are closed in a different way. So that it is an example of how spiritualism is woven into the immersion experience." This example demonstrates that immersion students draw from unique cultural, linguistic, and communicative advantages in routine interactions. At times, children may desire more involvement with mainstream popular culture, like that on MTV; however, once the students progress, they realize the importance of immersion education. K. Kawai'ae'a asserted that Hawaiian language education contributes to a stable sense of identity among children because they feel connected to their language, culture, and history:

> All the subjects and courses are developed through the Hawaiian language so the children . . . want, at times, to feel more like they are the youth on MTV, because the media has a huge amount of power on the students' attitudes about who they are as young people. . . . But if you ask them, maybe a year after that, they see things very much in a different light. It's been a tremendous advantage for them.

Children educated through immersion programs feel a deep sense of connection to their Hawaiian culture and language and typically continue to serve the tradition of immersion education through professional or community involvement. For example, K. Kawai'ae'a (personal communication, September 13, 2004) discussed the advantages that her own children have experienced, as a result of being educated through immersion:

> My eldest right now is going into teaching 7th and 8th graders. . . . She has a real edge ahead of many other students her age, I think, because of immersion education. [She is] well grounded, and her choice to go into education was because she felt that she had to continue the legacy. Nobody told her that, but she feels that. And you see a lot of our students doing that, in all kinds of different areas, not necessarily in education. But they kind of grew up with the belief that taking the language into all venues is very important in terms of stimulating the vitality of the culture. I think it is very important.

From a communication perspective, this issue could be addressed on a broader level, with other indigenous education and language programs, to determine how immersion affects students' attitudes and behavior toward the ethnolinguistic vitality of their own group and others. For instance, M. A. Meyer (personal communication, September 11, 2004) asserted that immersion education positively affects the identity reclamation and development of immersion students:

> Immersion and language reclamation is a blessing and a gift to our evolution as a culture . . . because it gives us an option and it gives families an option, it gives communities an option . . . to be bound by culture to each other, and that's liberating, and we need that option. Language is a doorway, and the process of language revitalization is a cultural re-awakening. It allows us to express and experience our own identities. . . . [T]hey begin to know who they are historically and in the present time.

Such immersion programs, therefore, enable students to experience education from a unique perspective, one that honors history, culture, language, and the individual.

CHALLENGE, RESISTANCE, AND TRIUMPH

Although immersion education has established a reputation for providing students access to a quality education through the Hawaiian language, W. H. Wilson (personal communication, December 18, 2004) described the social and political challenges that his family endured in establishing and enrolling their children in immersion education:

> To me the most important thing is the Hawaiian language and culture. That's why we started the schools [and] put our children in the schools, because we thought it was valuable . . . we risked lots of things, because . . . there is . . . pressure in Hawai'i to go to private schools. So, we chose Hawaiian, over the dominant paradigm. . . . People were saying, if you do this they're going to be educationally smashed, they're not going to speak English, it will really hurt them. And politically, what we said is we should have the right to make that choice. And if we don't, then that's linguistic and cultural genocide. So, the State agreed. . . . But we said, let us have the choice to choose this. . . . Hawaiian is our official language, why can't we speak Hawaiian?

Individuals in immersion education were able to establish a system to educate their children in Hawaiian, yet W. H. Wilson reported that, on more than one occasion, the Department of Education placed teachers in Hawaiian immersion programs who were not able to speak the language. Because the ability to speak Hawaiian is incontestably essential for the success of immersion education, the 'Aha Pūnana Leo responded by hiring their own Hawaiian language teachers from nonprofit funds and not allowing unqualified teachers to work with the children. Eventually, local immersion administrators hired those fluent in Hawaiian, but initially, staffing presented a substantial challenge. W. H. Wilson explained the process of resistance that was necessary in establishing immersion education:

> We try to make sure that people who can speak Hawaiian are the teachers . . . if they [the Department of Education] hired a teacher that could not speak Hawaiian, then we ['Aha Pūnana Leo] would hire a teacher with our nonprofit [funds] and put them in the classroom and let the one who speaks English sit in the corner. . . . So we fulfilled the Department of Education thing. But I would tell them [English-speaking teachers], you cannot teach, don't you dare try and teach. . . . You just collect your paycheck. . . . We did that until we got people out.

Although current movements toward revitalizing the Hawaiian language are encouraging, K. Silva (personal communication, January 8, 2004) stated that "we [the Hawaiian people] are not out of the woods yet." Given that immersion schools are typically geographically separated, they may not sustain regular contact with each other, especially if they lack access to the valuable technological resources that we detailed earlier in this chapter. This condition may contribute to physical and social fragmentation among language immersion communities, which may further challenge the cognitive, social, and cultural cohesion of students and educators in the program.

Social attitudes also hinder Hawaiian immersion education. Because immersion programs remain relatively small in size, many have been placed within larger English-medium educational environments. Individuals within the programs may struggle with institutional challenges that can compromise the effectiveness and success of immersion education (Warschauer & Donaghy, 1997). For instance, some programs, established in larger public schools, have been placed next to special education classrooms, separated from the main area of classrooms. K. Kawai'ae'a (personal communication, September 13, 2004) reported:

> It's just amazing to get people to change their attitudes. For example, they put the special education kids in the very different building, apart from everybody else. That's where they chose to put immersion. And all the regular kids, are all in the healthy area of the school, that kind of attitude. . . . [What is needed] is getting people to look at you . . . getting people to make those

shifts in their thinking in terms of really wanting better for the children . . .
because their mindset is based on a whole different paradigm. That has been
a big challenge for many immersion teachers. They feel like lone warriors.
They have to fight for their budget. They have to fight the attitudes and the
prejudice, but you know, I would say that's par for the course if it's worth-
while and if it's going against the flow of traffic. That's what immersion does.
It's gotten easier with the years.

This statement suggests that the immersion education movement in Hawai'i
has endured challenges related to negative social attitudes; however, through
the commitment and perseverance of key individuals, the movement has successfully established an alternative educational model to revitalize the language and culture.

Immersion programs have also encountered obstacles related to the variable use of Hawaiian by parents in the home. Often, immersion children
attend school for about six to seven hours per day, yet despite the prevalent
use of Hawaiian in immersion environments, some parents are not fluent
enough in Hawaiian to engage children in useful dialogue at home. In order to
increase language fluency among the families of immersion students, Wilson
(1998) recommended "expanding 'Aha Pūnana Leo parent-class requirements
. . . and developing Hawaiian-speaking settlements with intensive live-in modeling" (p. 134). K. Silva (personal communication, January 8, 2004) also contended that family and parental involvement are essential for the success of
children in immersion programs:

> The family's involvement . . . in the education of the child is crucial. . . . It
> reflects on the family's desire for that child, and the child picks this up very
> quickly. . . . If parents show indifference, or are not as supportive or involved
> . . . the child realizes that. But if parents are involved . . . to nurture the use of
> language and nurture the education of the child through Hawaiian language
> . . . the child, very keenly, understands that as well . . .

Although many of the parents of immersion students are successfully acquiring the language, others encounter difficulty, especially because most young
immersion students develop their Hawaiian language ability at a rapid pace.
W. H. Wilson (personal communication, December 18, 2004) argued: "The
parents of the children in immersion have to go to class . . . and suddenly [the
parents] feel this is hard . . . and my kid is going [developing Hawaiian] so
fast. And the kids, when they are real young, they don't know [how difficult
it is to learn a language]." The challenge of language acquisition may also
be an issue with some college students in the Hawaiian language and studies
program who have not had formal language training in the past and struggle to acquire the necessary skills. For instance, W. H. Wilson (personal com-

munication, December 18, 2004) discussed the circumstances surrounding this issue:

> In the university system we have to teach students to speak Hawaiian very fluently, after they come in, as freshman educated in the Hawai'i Public School System, or a private school. . . . They come in not really knowing anything about languages . . . they can't speak the languages, so then we have to teach them really hard, and it goes against what they are used to, and they [say], "How come Hawaiian is so hard? Hawaiian is supposed to be Aloha and just get it easy." . . . They think of their identity as Hawaiian, but to learn that the language is more structured than standard English. That's a huge emotional wall for people to deal with and people do conquer it but it's difficult. . . . Students get mad at us for that. But then, we get them through.

These examples demonstrate the conflict that may emerge in internal, familial, and social communication among students and parents of immersion education. Although those who successfully learn the language seem to exhibit high levels of language and cultural vitality and esteem, the acquisition process may challenge people cognitively, emotionally, and socially.

Immersion education has also struggled with a shortage of resources (i.e., textbooks and teaching materials in the Hawaiian language and perspective). Certain programs, such as the Ānuenue School on O'ahu, have enlisted parents and volunteers from the community to record Hawaiian translations of English-language textbooks in order to alleviate curriculum shortages. Warschauer and Donaghy (1997) referred to Laiana Wong, a Hawaiian language educator and member of the Hawaiian Language Lexicon Committee, who underscored that "the main problem [with using Western translations] is that this imposes a perspective from outside of the Islands. We need to develop original materials in Hawaiian that can reflect our own culture, perspective, and reality" (p. 353). Ideally, immersion students and educators should be able to communicate in Hawaiian from an orientation that is based upon authentic ethnic, cultural, and traditional values.

Within the Hawaiian language and cultural education community, an ongoing dialogue has emerged about the importance of written literacy in comparison with oral practice. Clearly, literacy constitutes an extremely important element in the ability of indigenous cultures to preserve language and culture in the modern world. However, educational practitioners M. A. Meyer, K. Kawai'ae'a, and others maintain that the establishment of oral immersion programs may be more congruent with historical Hawaiian cultural traditions and more accessible to the larger population. Educational specialists who endorse drawing from the oral tradition of language acquisition and maintenance assert that literacy and the process of learning through a symbolic language, like the alphabet, is a relatively new and even somewhat foreign experience for some indigenous cultures. For example, historically speaking, Hawaiians (in addition to most groups) were an oral culture until contact with Western influences contributed to the establishment of an alphabet and written language. In the past, cultures with oral traditions have preserved authentic stories, legends, rituals, and history through the use of memorized chants, verse, dance, and song, a type of oral communication that represented the highest evocative tradition in indigenous cultures.

Experts who identify with this orientation support the promotion of language preservation and utilization through oral interaction, as well as literacy, because this method may be more consistent with historical and cultural traditions. For instance, K. Kawai'ae'a (personal communication, September 13, 2004) maintained that the oral element of communication is essential to perpetuating the Hawaiian language within a variety of contexts:

> The root of our language is oral . . . oral literacy is key to the rest of the literacy, especially since this is a second language for a majority of students. . . . We need to do a lot more . . . of oral literacy in the quality of literacy. Literacy [also] means reading and writing, but oral literacy is very important. . . . If your levels of oral literacy are low, then your levels of writing are going to also be low. . . . We have to have more contexts that are community driven, so then you get more vocabulary, and sophistication of language in those contexts . . . we need to spend a lot more time with, things as simple as storytelling. . .

M. A. Meyer (personal communication, September 11, 2004) also emphasized the importance of oral communication in addition to written literacy:

> . . . language is a doorway, but it is only one doorway . . . and it gets shut once they [students] leave. . . . I want the oracy to be more than a metaphor of deepening knowledge. It needs to be a practice to . . . revitalize that animated principle of truth found in present moment practice and . . . articulation . . . and play a pivotal role in the reclamation of that because of the rolling nature, the beauty of it, the rounded drama of its capacity . . . Let's shape our language differently and not only writing, but oracy combined with literacy. I think this is our future.

Hawaiian language oracy advocates, such as K. Kawai'ae'a and M. A. Meyer, endorse a valid perspective by emphasizing traditional learning processes of Hawaiians and other indigenous groups. However, the reality of the twenty-first century seems to demand that immersion educators prepare students to be effective within dominant political and education models. Hawaiian language and immersion programs, which attempt to instill both written and oral literacy, assist students by equipping them to operate within the lingua franca of the dominant realm and, therefore, position them at the forefront for deal-ing with emerging issues directly. When students and faculty in Hawaiian lan-guage programs are required to have oral and written literacy, they are likely better prepared to represent individual and collective interests in the dominant paradigm. However, is it possible that the expectation of literacy, as we cur-rently understand it, is in fact a reinvention of a colonial model in a post-colonial Western world? Oral cultures throughout the world likely face the impending risk of linguistic, cultural, and political extinction if they cannot maintain and express culture, at least in part, through the ideology of Western norms. Clearly, future examination and research are warranted in the methods and processes by which modern scholars define themselves, their traditions, and their life aspirations. As this review suggests, immersion education has already contributed profoundly to the collective esteem, identity, and subjec-tive vitality of Hawaiian students, and it will likely continue to do so in the future. However, these empirical issues should incite future research, and we turn to such prospects in our epilogue.

CONCLUSION AND RESEARCH AGENDA

This case study extends from global communication (Monge, 1998; Stohl, 2005) and ethnolinguistic vitality (Giles, 1977) frameworks in representing selected language revitalization movements worldwide, while emphasizing Hawaiian historical events that have contributed to the endangerment of the Hawaiian language amidst "the global expansion of European culture" (Wilson & Kamanā, 2001, p. 148). Moreover, we analyze the ethnolinguistic vitality of the Hawaiian language as it is currently being revitalized through demo-graphic, political, media, and educational support. Furthermore, this analysis addresses the current challenges, resistance, and triumphs of the Hawaiian language movement through incorporation of the opinions of immersion and education experts. As the proliferation of globalization continues to influ-ence communication among diverse individuals and cultures, issues of cul-tural and language preservation will likely continue to stimulate research in a multitude of communicative contexts. Indeed, social identity theory (Tajfel & Turner, 1986) predicts that, as contrastive in- and outgroups become more similar, they increasingly strive to differentiate from each other. As an illus-tration, anecdotal evidence indicates that the ever-increasing English linguis-tic landscape in some cities in China is being frowned upon, with police offi-cers cautioning shopkeepers whose signs do not display Chinese characters. Relatedly, and for even decades earlier, Japanese scholars and institutions have been concerned about the global influence of English in constituting and marketing communication technologies, business, and finance to the exclusion—and hence the decrease—of Japanese language use both abroad and at home (see Hildebrandt & Giles, 1983).

Given that previous research indicates that global communication phenomena may play a pivotal role in individual, social, and educational interactions, it would be useful to explore how the issues identified in this case study apply to other immersion education movements worldwide. Research could assess challenge, resistance, and outcomes of various movements to specify common themes that characterize language revitalization processes. Ng and Bradac (1993), in their seminal work on the relationships between power and language, drew from Harwood et al. (1994), who suggested that strength in numbers may be utilized as a legitimizing force to empower groups with the institutional control required to define and reify collective identity. In the next excerpt, K. Kawaiʻaeʻa (personal communication, September 13, 2004) emphasized that Hawaiian speakers must maintain their language, even in contexts where others may not speak Hawaiian:

> One of the elements of language is communication. So every time we go to a place and are amongst Hawaiian speakers, we turn around and speak English because one person can't speak Hawaiian . . . we dis-empower our own attitudes toward our language and the use of our language. . . . Empowerment about our language is in using it and not being afraid to use it. If it's going to be a vibrant living language, it has to be used as much as possible.

As this research documents, the vitality of the Hawaiian language has increased over the years and empowered people to develop and maintain authentic language traditions, despite dominant-language use. Future research should determine the types of individual, social, or political circumstances that facilitate maintenance of the Hawaiian language, in contrast to English. For example, in close familial or social circles, using Hawaiian may be accepted and condoned, whereas other situations (organizational or political) may naturally curb authentic language expression. Communication research should continue to explore the specific conditions that promote language maintenance among dominant discourse so that we can better understand the relationships between individual, intergroup, and social relations (see Harwood & Giles, 2005). By generating comprehensive knowledge about the processes that characterize successful language preservation movements, communication research may assist indigenous group advocates in developing models that address revitalization needs, prepare participants for inherent challenges, and advance methods of overcoming potential difficulties. Our analysis suggests increasing objective vitality (incorporating anecdotal assessments) of the Hawaiian people due to immersion and other revitalization programs. Given that our review has incorporated observations from Hawaiian language experts about students' increasing levels of subjective language vitality, it seems important to initiate quantitative research assessing the subjective vitality experiences of Hawaiian immersion students as they progress through the programs.

Ethnic identification processes often build upon "shared traditions, heritage, and ancestral origin . . . psychologically and historically" (Orbe & Harris, 2001, p. 7). Phinney (1993) contended that cultural identity development progresses through several stages before actualized cultural identity achievement, and Fong (2004) argued that identity construction may be a multifaceted and complex process, subject to modification based on individual or contextual factors.

Considering such issues, we need to determine the ways in which immersion students identify with their language, when they utilize it, for what functions, and why. Exploration could assess how immersion students verbally and nonverbally construct individual, cultural, and ethnic identities toward developing a model with which to understand how marginalized groups reclaim and redefine identity. If long-term research confirms that immersion education builds both subjective and objective vitality of diverse groups, federal, state, nonprofit, and private organizations could be petitioned to encourage greater economic, social, and political support of Hawaiian and other language immersion programs. M. A. Meyer (personal communication, September 11, 2004) suggested that language acquisition is pivotal in shifting an oppressive past and building the previously fragmented identity of Hawaiians:

> There are Hawaiians that need, and must, and want to speak our language. To wake up and understand lovingly that oppression, racism, and bigotry are at the core of our inability to express ourselves in Hawaiian. . . . This is Hawai'i, Hawaiian is our language, we've been oppressed, we oppress ourselves now, and now we're not fearing talking to others to get the help we need to speak our language. In that, we will reclaim a broken identity, and that to me is vital.

It would also be valuable to assess how familial, peer, and broader social interactions may affect the identity development and reclamation of Hawaiians in a complex and rapidly evolving global environment.

As our analysis indicates, because students are obtaining a firm foundation in the Hawaiian language and its allied cultural identity, immersion education increases awareness and appreciation of other ethnic and cultural groups. For instance, K. Kawai'ae'a (personal communication, September 13, 2004) argued that immersion demonstrates to students that:

> The culture you came from is an important culture. It's an honorable one that will raise your own level as a person, to a higher place, because you have a real understanding of all the things that came before you and its application today. The kids have a very receptive ear to learning other languages and cul-

tures . . . and a very accepting nature of other cultures. . . . When you have your own [culture], it's your [opportunity] to . . . being much more global because you have a lens from which to view the world. That's a real advantage for our children.

It may be useful to determine how immersion education affects cognitive and social processing of individuals toward acceptance of others. Drawing from the immersion paradigm and applying similar principles to the dominant education paradigm may promote increased tolerance and harmony among individuals comprising Hawai'i's unique cultural fabric. Future research should also continue to explore communicative interactions among immersion participants in diverse locations globally to determine how media and Internet resources may mediate communication among students from different cultures and to what effect.

Given the ongoing dialogue among educators in the Hawaiian language and cultural revitalization movement regarding oral skills in comparison with written literacy, it would also be interesting to pursue research that explores intergroup communication among Hawaiians who speak the language and those who do not. M. A. Meyer (personal communication, September 11, 2004) contended that some Hawaiian people who are unable to attend immersion education or thoroughly learn the language may feel excluded from reclaiming their Hawaiian culture and language. For this reason, as well as the need to elaborate the rarely invoked concept and processes of *cultural reclamation* further, M. A. Meyer suggested that it may be beneficial to expand valuable philosophies underlining immersion education into the larger community:

Let's be flexible so that more people can enter into the reclamation of Hawaiian identity. . . . The Hawaiian immersion movement has been pivotal, helpful, and joyful for many families. . . . I am forever grateful. . . . I'm just ready for it now to be more effective for more families. . . . We can make it more mainstream and it would be more vital, or revitalized, if we would allow it to seep into mainstream consciousness so that we're not shy about our request to speak. . . . Because we're [people who are not fluent] shy now. . . . I think our language needs to be spoken in the streets and not just in the classroom.

Potentially, increasing Hawaiian language instruction access, assistance, and involvement among the nonacademic community may assist in the alleviation of language skill differences within the community. Further research evaluating language acquisition effectiveness in contexts other than immersion would also be a valuable contribution to the literature on language reclamation and survival.

Globally, tourism comprises a primary industry for many countries, with employment of indigenous and nonindigenous groups in service sectors such as hotels, restaurants, and tour contexts. Hence, it would be advantageous to determine when and how indigenous groups use their native language, in addition to local words and phrases with tourists. For instance, when is authentic language used to socially distance locals from tourists in commercial or interactive contexts, and when is it adopted to enrich and diversify the social climate from a public relations perspective? How is the pronunciation of indigenous languages modified—and even commodified—to accommodate tourists' speech? How, and to what extent, is language use (e.g., words, address forms, phrases) accommodated by tourists, locals, and émigrés, and to what effect? Furthermore, it may be useful to explore whether an increase in local linguistics promotes exotic perceptions and experiences of indigenous life-styles that engenders the communicative climate more attractive for visitors. It may be that state and national identities become salient in different interactions, depending upon tourist cultural sensitivity. Illuminating how language use plays into this communicative matrix would be extremely useful, especially given that intergroup contexts of local-tourist interactions afford their own accommodative dilemmas (see Jaworski, Ylänne-McEwen, Thurlow, & Lawson, 2003).

As many authentic language and cultural groups seek to reclaim or maintain unique communicative modes of expression, global trends of tourism and commodified culture may also significantly influence this process. Indeed, we do not conceive of an inevitable dichotomy between authentic "versus" commodified language revitalization because future research may indicate that they may operate performatively at different levels simultaneously yet be symbiotic, despite their different dialectical pushes and pulls. Hence, do people construe an inherent tension associated with authentic identities in comparison with contexts that foster a commodified identity, and, if so, how do they reconcile them? More concretely, and as an empirical question, do positive outcomes of linguistic commodification bolster subjective vitality for indigenous group members (such as Hawaiians) and, thereby, trigger further revitalizing investments in authenticity?

Considering the widespread impact of mainstream American media depictions, it would also be valuable to examine how language portrayals in visual media, theatre, and new technology influence adults' and students' sense of vitality, ethnic identification, and life satisfaction in diverse immersion movements globally (Abrams et al., 2003; Reid, Giles, & Abrams, 2004). Perhaps theatrical plays, cinema, and other performance contexts depicting an authentic cultural and linguistic identity further increase collective esteem and group identification. Addressing this issue, K. Kawai'ae'a (personal communication, September 13, 2004) observed that "most of them [children] are much more visual . . . visual communication is becoming more popular, especially with the interactivity with the younger kids." Notably, research may find that web technology among immersion students in a variety of locations significantly increases global interactions, language vitality, ethnic identification, and group esteem among indigenous groups.

As reviewed, the continued proliferation of global communication interactions has already profoundly affected the identity formation and experiences of many indigenous groups, including those in Hawai'i. Such insights reinforce the importance of language revitalization movements, and they also encourage communication scholars to recognize the value of empirically addressing how, when, and why global exchange contributes to or detracts from indigenous preservation and how language interactions affect various elements of identity (i.e., cognitive, emotional, and social). As Monge (1998) and Stohl (2005) asserted, communicative interpretations of language, identity, and social interaction are increasing in importance, especially given that "levels of global consciousness derived through processes of reflexivity and communication are also associated with . . . a heightened sense of the importance of community, social movement organizing designed to counter the new world order, and individuals' desperate struggles for identity" (Stohl, 2005, p. 254). Echoing the importance of linguistic and cultural revitalization, Wilson (1998) wrote: "Hawaiian is being revived and is assuring the future existence of a distinct Hawaiian people and a distinct Hawai'i, just as the words of Ke Mele A Pāku'i assured their creation in antiquity. I ka 'ōlelo Hawai'i ke ola 'Life rests in the Hawaiian language'" (p. 135).[2]

The Hawaiian language example that we explore in this chapter already reverberates among many indigenous people still struggling for basic survival in the Americas, the Pacific, and globally. Like the traditional Hawaiian conch shell blare, Hawaiian language revitalization is rapidly becoming a reveille, a signal for inspired gathering and solemn reflection on that which was lost and which may be found again through a rebirth of language. Though only a beginning, it may well be an auspicious one that heralds a prototype of cultural revival for other immersed groups still searching for identity in a world that seems fixed on establishing a universal language system. Indigenous revitalization constitutes an important process worthy of further inquiry and investigation precisely because it explores the foundations of authentic language and questions of how cultural identity flows from the roots to the shoots, as Hawaiians have professed.

ACKNOWLEDGMENTS

The authors express enormous gratitude to the faculty of Ka Haka ÿUla O Keÿelikōlani College of Hawaiian Language of the University of Hawai'i at Hilo for their honesty and assistance with the completion of this project. We especially wish to acknowledge Professors Kalena Silva, William H. Wilson, Theresa Haunani Bernardino, and Keiki Kawaiaÿaeÿa; the Hale Kuamoÿo Hawaiian Language Center, and Professor Manu Aluli Meyer. The first author interviewed respondents for over 10 hours about interlocking issues of the Hawaiian language, communication, education, and culture. We also thank John W. Marlow, Professor of Communication at Hawai'i Community College, for valuable comments on this chapter. Finally, we wish to express our gratitude to the editor and three anonymous reviewers for their insightful and comprehensive comments on earlier versions of this chapter, which was also presented in abridged form at the 3rd Annual Hawai'i International Conference on Arts & Humanities, Honolulu, January 2005.

NOTES

1. Kamehameha Schools is a private educational institution established by Princess Bernice Pauahi Bishop in 1884, the last direct descendent of King Kamehameha I, for the education of children of Hawai'i. The trust's estimated worth is six billion dollars, and revenue from the 300,000 acres of investments in Hawai'i and globally is used to fund and operate Kamehameha Schools.

2. Wilson (personal communication, December 18, 2004) has expressed the opinion that most research in indigenous studies by academics is of primary value in the academic advancement of the researchers themselves. He sees little value in broad-stroke research to language revitalization or to indigenous communities other than publicity. Furthermore, Wilson suggests that such research attention can develop a false sense within universities that they are assisting indigenous communities, thus delaying the development of programs, such as those of Ka Haka ÿUla O Keÿelikölani College, that directly affect the revitalization of indigenous languages. This perspective reflects the history of the Hawaiian Language College, which grew out of a realization about the minimal impact of standard university research on the survival of the Hawaiian language as well as subsequent faculty struggles to have the direct products of language revitalization valued equally with academic research within the University of Hawai'i.

REFERENCES

Abrams, J., Eveland, W. P. Jr., & Giles, H. (2003). The effects of television on group vitality: Can television empower? In P. Kalbfleisch (Ed.), *Communication yearbook 27* (pp. 193–219). Mahwah, NJ: Lawrence Erlbaum Associates.

Allard, R., & Landry, R. (1986). Subjective ethnolinguistic vitality viewed as a belief system. *Journal of Multilingual and Multicultural Development, 7*, 1–12.

Barker, V., & Giles, H. (2003). English-only policies: Perceived support and social limitations. *Language and Communication, 24*, 77–95.

Barker, V., Giles, H., Noels, K. A., Duck, J., Hecht, M. L., & Clément, R. (2001). The English-only movement: A communication perspective. *Journal of Communication, 51*, 3–37.

Berger, J. (2001, May 31). Despite economic challenges faced by the local industry, islanders are optimistic that there's a bright future in store for Hawaiian music. *Billboard, 115*, 63–66.

Bickerton, D. (1983). Creole languages. *Scientific American, 249*, 116–122.

Bishop, H. (2005, August 7). Thousands turn out for protests: 300–400 march in downtown Kailua-Kona. *West Hawai'i Today*, Local Report, A1 & A5.

Bourhis, R. Y., Giles, H., & Rosenthal, D. (1981). Notes on the construction of a "subjective vitality questionnaire" for ethnolinguistic groups. *Journal of Multilingual and Multicultural Development, 2,* 145–155.

Bourhis, R.Y., & Sachdev, I. (1984). Vitality perceptions and language attitudes: Some Canadian data. *Journal of Language and Social Psychology, 3,* 97–126.

Cameron, D. (2000). Styling the worker: Gender and the commodification of language in the globalized service economy. *Journal of Sociolinguistics, 4,* 323–347.

Cargile, A, Giles, H., & Clément, R. (1996). The role of language in ethnic conflict. In J. Gittler (Ed.), *Racial and ethnic conflict: Perspectives from the social disciplines* (pp. 189–208). Greenwich, CT: JAI Press.

Castells, M. (2000). *The information age: Economy, society and culture.* Oxford, England: Blackwell.

Cenoz, J., & Valencia, J. (1993). Ethnolinguistic vitality, social networks and motivation in second language acquisition: Some data from the Basque country. *Language, Culture, and Curriculum, 6,* 113–187.

Chebatoris, J. (2005, February 14). Beyond the hula. *Newsweek, 145,* 64.

Cope, B., & Kalantzis, M. (Eds.). (2000). *Multiliteracies: Literacy learning and the design of social futures.* London: Routledge.

Coupland, N. (Ed.). (2003). Sociolinguistics and globalization [special issue]. *Journal of Sociolinguistics, 7.*

Coupland, N., Bishop, H., & Garrett, P. (2003). Home truths: Globalization and the iconizing of Welsh in a Welsh-American Newspaper. *Journal of Multilingual and Multicultural Development, 24,* 153–177.

Crystal, D. (2005). Why a global language? In K. Walters & M. Brody (Eds.), *What's language got to do with it?* (pp. 504–515). New York: Norton.

Currie, M., & Hogg, M. A. (1994). Subjective ethnolinguistic vitality and social adaptation among Vietnamese refugees in Australia. *International Journal of the Sociology of Language, 108,* 97–115.

Dailey, R. M., Giles, H., & Jansma, L. L. (2004). Language attitudes in an Anglo-Hispanic context: The role of the linguistic landscape. *Language and Communication, 25,* 27–38.

Day, R. R. (1982). Children's attitudes toward language. In E. B. Ryan & H. Giles (Eds.), *Attitudes toward language: Social and applied contexts* (pp. 164–175). London: Edward Arnold.

de Swaan, A. (2001). *Words of the world.* Oxford, England: Polity.

DePledge, D. (2005). Akaka bill backers, foes weigh ruling: Passage may gain greater urgency or it might be moot. *Honolulu Advertiser,* p. A17.

du Gay, P. (1996). *Consumption and identity at work.* London: Sage.

England, N. C. (2003). Mayan language revival and revitalization politics: Linguists and linguistic ideologies. *American Anthropologist, 105,* 733–744.

Evans, C. (1996). Ethnolinguistic vitality, prejudice, and family language transmission. *Bilingual Research Journal, 2,* 177–207.

Fairclough, N. (1992). *Discourse and social change.* Cambridge, England: Polity.

Fishman, J. A. (1972). *The sociology of language.* Rowley, MA: Newbury House.

Fishman, J. A. (2001). *Can threatened languages be saved? Reversing language shift, revisited: A 21st century approach.* Clevedon, England: Multilingual Matters.

Fishman, J. A. (2004). Language maintenance, language shift, and reversing language shift. In T. K. Bhatia & W. C. Ritchie (Eds.), *The handbook of bilingualism* (pp. 406–436). Oxford, England: Blackwell.

Fong, M. (2004). Multiple dimensions of identity. In M. Fong and R. Chuang (Eds.), *Communicating ethnic identity and culture* (pp. 3–18). Lanham, MD: Rowman & Littlefield.

Friedman, T. (1999). *The lexus and the olive tree.* New York: Farrar, Straus, & Giroux.

Gallois, C., Ogay, T., & Giles, H. (2005). Communication accommodation theory: A look back and a look ahead. In W. B. Gudykunst (Ed.), *Theorizing about intercultural communication* (pp. 121–148). Thousand Oaks, CA: Sage.

Garrett, P., Giles, H., & Coupland, N. (1989). The contexts of language learning: Extending the intergroup model of second language acquisition. In S. Ting-Toomey & F. Korzenny (Eds.), *Language, communication and culture* (pp. 201–221). Newbury Park, CA: Sage.

Gee, J. P., Hull, G., & Lankshear, C. (1996). *The new work order: Behind the language of new capitalism.* Boulder, CO: Westview.

Giddens, A. (1990). *The consequences of modernity.* Berkeley: University of California Press.

Giddens, A. (1999). The Reith Lectures. BBC Online Network. Retrieved March 6, 2005, from http://news.bbc.co.uk/hi/english/static/events/reith_99/week1/week1.htm.

Giles, H. (Ed.). (1977). *Language, ethnicity and intergroup relations.* London: Academic.

Giles, H. (2001). Ethnolinguistic vitality. In R. Mesthrie (Ed.), *Concise encyclopedia of sociolinguistics* (pp. 472–473). Oxford, England: Elsevier.

Giles, H., Bourhis, R. Y., & Taylor, D. M. (1977). Towards a theory of language in ethnic group relations. In H. Giles (Ed.), *Language, ethnicity, and intergroup relations* (pp. 307–349). London: Academic.

Giles, H., & Johnson, P. (1981). The role of language in ethnic group relations. In J. C. Turner & H. Giles (Eds.), *Intergroup behavior* (pp. 199–243). Oxford, England: Blackwell.

Giles, H., & Johnson, P. (1987). Ethnolinguistic identity theory: A social psychological approach to language maintenance. *International Journal of the Sociology of Language, 63*, 69–99.

Giles, H., Kutchukhides, M., Yagmur, K., & Noels, K. A. (2003). Age vitality: Perceptions of young Canadian, Turkish, and Georgian urban and rural adults. *Journal of Multilingual & Multicultural Development, 24*, 178–183.

Grimes, M. F. (1992). (Ed.). *Ethnologue: Languages of the world.* Retrieved June 20, 1999, from http://www.sil.org/ethnologue/countries/USA.html.

Harwood, J., & Giles, H. (Eds.) (2005). *Intergroup communication: Multiple perspectives.* New York: Peter Lang.

Harwood, J., Giles, H., & Bourhis, R.Y. (1994). The genesis of vitality theory: Historical patterns and discoursal dimensions. *International Journal of the Sociology of Language, 108*, 167–206.

Hedetoft, U. (1999). The nation-state meets the world: National identities in the context of transnationality and cultural globalization. *European Journal of Social Theory, 2*, 71–94.

Heller, M. (2003). Globalization, the new economy, and the commodification of language and identity. *Journal of Sociolinguistics, 7*, 473–492.

Henningham, J. (1992). Flaws in the melting pot: Hawaiian media. In S. H. Riggins (Ed.), *Ethnic minority media: An international perspective* (pp. 149–161). Newbury Park, CA: Sage.

Hildebrandt, N., & Giles, H. (1983). The Japanese as subordinate group: Ethnolinguistic identity theory in a foreign language context. *Anthropological Linguistics, 25,* 436–466,

Hinton, L., & Hale, K. (Eds), (2001). *The green book of language revitalization in practice.* San Diego, CA: Academic.

Hotz, L. (2000, January 25). The struggle to save dying languages: Global pressures threaten them, but more voices are being raised to keep them alive. *Los Angeles Times,* A1.

House, J. (2003). English as a lingua franca: A threat to multilingualism? *Journal of Sociolinguistics, 7,* 556–578.

Hsiau, A. C. (2000). *Contemporary Taiwanese cultural nationalism.* London: Routledge.

Hung, W. (1992). *Taiwan Yuyan Wenzi* [Language and writing of Taiwan]. Taipei, Taiwan: Avantgarde.

Jaworski, A., Ylänne-McEwen, Thurlow, C., & Lawson, S. (2003). Social roles and negotiation of status in host-tourist interaction: A view from British television holiday programs. *Journal of Sociolinguistics, 7,* 135–164.

Johnson, R. K., & Swain, M. (Eds.). (1997). *Immersion education: International perspectives.* Cambridge, England: Cambridge University Press.

Kamana, K, & Wilson, W. H. (1996). Hawaiian language programs. In G. Cantoni (Ed.), *Stabilizing indigenous languages* (pp.153–156). Flagstaff, AZ: Center for Excellence in Education, Northern Arizona University.

Kashoki, M. E. (2003). Language policy formulation in multilingual Southern Africa. *Journal of Multilingual and Multicultural Development, 24,* 184–194.

Kawaihae, N. (2003). *Ka haka 'ula o Ke'elikolani* (The royal standard of Princess Ke'elikolani). Hilo, HI: Hawaiian Language College, University of Hawai'i Press.

Kobayashi, K, & Pang, G. Y. K. (2005, August 3). School says "we will fight for" right to follow princess's will. *Honolulu Advertiser,* pp. A1, A16.

Landry, R., & Bourhis, R. Y. (1997). Linguistic landscape and ethnolinguistic vitality: An empirical study. *Journal of Language and Social Psychology 16,* 23–49.

Leets, L., & Giles, H. (1995). Intergroup cognitions and communication climates: New dimensions of minority language maintenance. In W. Fase, K. Jaspaert, & S. Kroon (Eds.), *The state of minority languages: International perspectives on survival and decline* (pp. 37–74). Lisse, Holland: Swets & Zeitlinger.

Le Menestrel, S. (1999). *La voie des Cadiens.* Paris: Belin.

Li, D., & Lee, S. (2004). Bilingualism in East Asia. In T. K. Bhatia & W. C. Ritchie (Eds.), *The handbook of bilingualism* (pp. 742–779). Malden, MA: Blackwell.

Liu, H. (2000). *Taiwan de Kejiaren* [The Hakka of Taiwan]. Taipei, Taiwan: Chang Min.

Malone, N. J., & Corry, M. (2004). *Make it count: Native Hawaiian population estimates in Census 2000 and implications for other small racial groups.* Honolulu, HI: Kamehameha Schools, PASE Report.

Mansoor, S. (2004). The status and role of regional languages in higher education in Pakistan. *Journal of Multilingual and Multicultural Development, 4,* 333–353.

Mattern, M. (1998). Cajun music, cultural revival: Theorizing political action in popular music. *Popular Music and Society, 22,* 31–48.

Meyer, M. A. (2003). Ho'oulu: Our time of becoming. Hawaiian epistemology and early
    writings. Honolulu, HI: 'Ai Pohaku Press.
Midori, O. (2001). Language and identity in Okinawa today. In M.G. Noguchi and
    S. Fotos (Eds.), Studies in Japanese bilingualism (pp. 68–97). Clevedon, England:
    Multilingual Matters.
Milroy, J., & Milroy, L. (1998). Authority in language (3rd ed.). Oxford, England:
    Blackwell.
Monastersky, R. (2004, December 10). Talking a language back from the brink. Chron-
    icle of Higher Education, pp. 8–14.
Monge, P. (1998). 1998 ICA presidential address: Communication structures and
    processes in globalization. Journal of Communication, 48, 142–153.
Murphy, D.E. (2005, July 17). Bill giving Native Hawaiians sovereignty is too much for
    some, too little for others. New York Times, National Report, p. B12.
Namuo, C. (2004, May 28). Grammys to add Hawaiian music category. Pacific Busi-
    ness News. Retrieved November 5, 2005, from EPSCO database.
Ng, S. H., & Bradac, J. J. (1993). Power in language: Verbal communication and social
    influence. Thousand Oaks, CA: Sage.
Ohama, M. L. F., Gotay, C. C., Pagano, I. S., Boles, L., & Craven, D. D. (2000). Eval-
    uations of Hawaii Creole English and Standard English. Journal of Language
    and Social Psychology, 19, 357–377.
Orbe, M. P., & Harris, T. M. (2001). Interracial communication: Theory into practice.
    Belmont, CA: Wadsworth/Thomson Learning.
Phinney, J. S. (1993). A three-stage model of ethnic identity development in adoles-
    cence. In M. E. Bernal & G. Knight (Eds.), Ethnic identity (pp. 61–79). Albany:
    State University of New York Press.
Pu, Z. C. (1996).Taiwan yuanzhumin de kouchuan wenxue [Oral literature of Aborigines
    in Taiwan]. Taipei, Taiwan: Chang Min.
Pukui, M. K., Haertig, E., & Lee, C. (1972). Nana I Ke Kumu: Look to the source (Vols.
    1–2). Honolulu, HI: Hui Hanai.
Reid, S., Giles, H., & Abrams, J. (2004). A social identity model of media effects.
    Zeitschrift für Medienpsychologie, 16, 17–25.
Reinecke, J. E. (1969). Language and dialect in Hawai'i. Honolulu: University of
    Hawai'i Press.
Sayahi, L. (2005). Language and identity among speakers of Spanish in northern
    Morocco: Between ethnolinguistic vitality and acculturation. Journal of Soci-
    olinguistics, 9, 95–107.
Schutz, A. J. (1994). The voices of Eden. Honolulu: University of Hawai'i Press.
Siddle, R. (1995). The Ainu construction of an image. In J.C. Maher and G. Mac-
    Donald (Eds.), Diversity in Japanese culture and language (pp. 73–94). London:
    Kegan Paul.
Skutnabb-Kangas, T., & Cummins, J. (1988). Minority education. Clevedon, England:
    Multilingual Matters.
Slaughter, H. (1997). Indigenous language immersion in Hawai'i: A case study of
    Kula Kaiapuni Hawai'i, an effort to save the indigenous language of Hawai'i.

In R. K. Johnson & M. Swain (Eds.), *Immersion education: International perspectives* (pp. 105–129). Cambridge, England: Cambridge University Press.

Staton, R. (2003). Poll shows support for Hawaiian federal recognition. Honolulu, HI. Hawaii Associated Press.

Stohl, C. (2005). Globalization theory. In S. May and D. Mumby (Eds.), *Engaging organizational communication theory and research: Multiple perspectives* (pp. 223–262). Thousand Oaks, CA: Sage.

Sur, P. (2005, August 4). Hawaiians show support: Rally to protest court ruling that school policy is discriminatory. *Hawaii Tribune Herald,* pp. A1, A6.

Tagliabue, J. (2005). In Europe, going global means, alas, English. In K. Walters & M. Brody (Eds.), *What's language got to do with it? (*pp. 531–534). New York: Norton.

Tajfel, H., & Turner, J. C. (1986). The social psychology of intergroup behavior. In S. Worchel & W. G. Austin (Eds.), *Psychology of intergroup relations* (pp. 7–24). Chicago: Nelson-Hall.

Taylor, D. M., & Wright, S. C. (2003). Do Aboriginal students benefit from education in their heritage language? Results from a ten-year program of research in Nunavik. *Canadian Journal of Native Studies, 23,* 1–24.

Thurlow, C., & Jaworski, A. (2003). Communicating a global reach: Inflight magazines as a globalizing genre in tourism. *Journal of Sociolinguistics, 7,* 579–606.

Tracy, K., & Haspel, K. (2004). Language and social interaction: Its institutional identity, intellectual landscape, and discipline-shifting agenda. *Journal of Communication, 54,* 788–816.

United States Census Bureau (2000). *Statistical abstract of the United States* (1st ed.). Washington, DC: U.S. Government Printing Office.

Verhoef, M. (1998). In pursuit of multilingualism in South Africa. *Multilingual, 17,* 181–196.

Wallerstein, I. (1983). *Historical capitalism.* London: Verso.

Wallerstein, I. (2001). *Unthinking social science* (2nd ed.). Philadelphia: Temple University Press.

Wallraff, B. (2005). What global language? In K. Walters & M. Brody (Eds.), *What's language got to do with it?* (pp. 535–553). New York: Norton.

Warschauer, M., & Donaghy, K. (1997). Leoki: A powerful voice of Hawaiian language revitalization. *Computer Assisted Language Learning, 10,* 349–362.

Wilson, W. H. (1998). I ka ʻolelo Hawaiʻi ke ola, "Life is found in the Hawaiian language." *International Journal of the Sociology of Language, 132,* 123–137.

Wilson, W. H., & Kamanā, K. (2001). "*Mai Loko Mai O Ka ʻIini*: Proceeding from a Dream": The ʻAha Pānana Leo connection in Hawaiian language revitalization. In L. Hinton & K. Hale (Eds.), *The green book of language revitalization in practice* (pp. 147–176). San Diego, CA: Academic.

Yagmur, K., & Kroon, S. (2003). Ethnolinguistic vitality perceptions and language revitalization in Bashkortostan. *Journal of Multilingual and Multicultural Development, 24,* 319–336.

CHAPTER CONTENTS

9 The Latina/o Problematic: Categories and Questions in Media Communication Research

ESTEBAN DEL RÍO
University of San Diego

This chapter examines the field of Latina/o media studies as an emergent and highly relevant area of study in communication research. Beginning with the assumption that Latinas/os constitute an imagined community, I argue for a communication approach to the study of Latina/o unity in the United States. I explore some of the politics, purposes, and problematics of Latina/o coherence and chart the negative regimes of representation that define Latinidad in general market cultural expressions by reviewing film criticism and media content analysis literature that paint a picture of consistent marginalization and persistent racist stereotypes. I argue for a consideration of theories of articulation and classification to address the unifying problematic in expressions of Latinidad in mainstream culture and discuss different domains that communication scholars interrogate to study the possibilities and consequences of Latina/o coherence. The transdisciplinary and critical nature of Latina/o media studies makes this fertile ground, not only for those who study media communication, but also for scholars of interaction and institutions who try to enhance understandings of communication dynamics in diverse cultures and problematize the rationality of human categorization.

O n the shelves of neighborhood bookshops and strip-mall superstores, one is likely to find an interesting selection of accessible titles making sense of a people living in the United States who trace a common ancestry to Latin America, individuals known variously as Latinas/os, Hispanics, or Latins. Stavans's (2000) *Latino USA: A Cartoon History* tells a 500-year story with funny illustrations by the popular cartoonist Lalo Alcatraz. J. A. Gutiérrez's (2001) tongue-in-cheek *A Gringo Manual on How to Handle Mexicans* sits alongside the earnest *Complete Idiot's Guide to Latino History*

Correspondence: Esteban del Río, Assistant Professor, Department of Communication Studies, University of San Diego, 5998 Alcala Park, San Diego, CA 92110; email: edelrio@sandiego.edu *and Culture* by Figueredo (2002). After assuring his readers that they are not idiots after all, Figueredo invites his *amigos* to "put on your *sombrero* and let's head out to the *barrio* to find out more about Americans' new *compadres*— about their culture and traditions, where they live and why, their social and economic realities, and even what they really look like" (p. 3). In the same section, one also likely discovers books displaying a different tone, including Ruiz's (1999) *From Out of the Shadows* and Santa Ana's (2002) *Brown Tide Rising*. These books detail the rise of Latinas/os within the historical and contemporary United States. Santa Ana described this rise as inspiring both "anxiety as well as interest about Latinos" (p. 3) during the culture wars of the early 1990s. As culture wars and identity politics become more complex than in decades past, curiosity and anxiety mix with celebration when writers and other cultural producers acknowledge and understand Latinas/os in bookstores and beyond.

In the pages that follow, I map theoretical positions and research examples that illustrate the key questions, concerns, and problematics of Latina/o media studies.[1] I endeavor to cast Latina/o media studies as a deeply relevant project for communication scholarship, and I argue for communication scholars to consider Latina/o representation, subjectivity, and communities in their research. I explore some of the problems that Latinas/os pose for communication scholars and review research that examines how Latinas/os are both excluded from and connected with the U.S. national imaginary. I draw upon theories of articulation and classification to urge communication scholars to address the Latina/o problematic by examining the central questions that constitute Latina/o unity in social life. Finally, I explore some of the domains that scholars interrogate as unifying constructs for the Latina/o category.

OVERVIEW OF LATINA/O STUDIES
AS COMMUNICATION DOMAIN

In many important areas of United States institutional and popular culture, Latinas/os and the mainstream intersect in media texts, museum exhibits, corporate boardrooms, and national politics. The new bronze chic is evident in television, film, pop music, fashion, and celebrity magazines. As the current "It" ethnicity (Guzmán & Valdivia, 2004), Latinas/os inhabit the imaginations of corporate demographers and political strategists who try to identify new markets and constituencies for products and policy. Fueled by 2000 U.S. Census Bureau (2002) reports of a dramatic demographic rise, Latinas/os step to the public stage, and the culture seems ready to embrace them. However, placing Latinas/os at the doorstep of dominant U.S. culture is not new, nor is it a simple endeavor. Ideological and historical complexities circulate through discussions of race, ethnicity, and nation. Latina/o hybridity presents special problems for the creation and application of broad cultural categories employed to mark and organize human difference. Discourses of geographical ancestry connect Latinas/os to each other rather than to a coherent symbolic potency of race or nationalism. Even the Latin American roots of Latina/o solidarity in the United States contain contradictions. As Canclini (1995) commented, "Latin American countries are currently the result of the sedimentation, juxtaposition, and interweaving of indigenous traditions . . . of Catholic colonial hispanism, and of modern political, educational, and communicational actions" (p. 46). Race, language, and citizenship sit among many incongruities within the U.S. "Latina/o" or "Hispanic" designation. Valdivia (1999) noted that even the term "U.S. Latinas/os" is problematic because of Puerto Rico's colonial relationship to the United States and the presence of Chicanas/os in the Southwest that predates the founding of the United States. These complexities call for wider memories and deeper understandings of how different groups are constructed and positioned in relation to each other. However, contemporary expressions of popular and public culture contain few acknowledgments of the historical presence of U.S. Latina/o populations or the ongoing civil rights and political movements that received greater public attention in the 1970s. Instead, general market media texts and mainstream popular culture reconfigure—if not invent—a new Latina/o imaginary for Anglo and capitalist sensibilities and celebrate Latina/o life as an exotic, spicy, and new addition to the multicultural mainstream.

Given the visibility afforded to Latinas/os in contemporary culture, we should now take stock of how media communication research addresses the politics and poetics of Latina/o representation. The term *Latinalo media studies* describes the research reviewed in this essay, but yet, it can be misleading as an all-encompassing category. I use it here to describe conventional communication and cultural studies approaches to the circulation, content, production, and reception of television, film, radio, and print media that represent Latina/o subjects and Latina/o life in the United States. Latina/o media studies also draw upon studies of popular culture, political communication, transnational communication, and philosophy of communication to add depth and breadth to questions and arguments made about Latina/o media processes. Communication scholars who study Latina/o representation must also be in touch with relevant literature from other disciplines in the social studies and humanities, including the important work emanating from ethnic studies and Latina/o studies. The transdisciplinary nature of Latina/o media studies makes it a difficult field to contain, but it also contributes to its vitality as a site of inquiry and opens productive possibilities for collaboration across communication divisions and with scholars from other disciplines.

Latina/o media studies require immediate attention, as new regimes of representation emerge and old ones recur across media texts. Regimes of representation, according to Hall (1997), refer to "the whole repertoire of imagery and visual effects through which 'difference' is represented at any one historical moment" (p. 232). The dominant, historical regime of representation for Latinas/os consists of invisibility, marginalization, and negative stereotypes. For example, Denzin (2002) argued that Hollywood films assign negative stereotypes such as "barbarian, greaser, lustful, treacherous, untrustworthy, lawless, and violent" (p. 29) to characters with Spanish accents and brown skin. Moral panics that construct Latinas/os as a threat to the social fabric of American life draw on such stereotypes in news coverage of public policy (Davis, 2000; Santa Ana, 2002). Although negative stereotypes and moral panics come and go according to political need, they are neither stamped out nor completely replaced. These discourses deserve continuing attention from scholars, critics, and advocacy organizations such as the National Council of La Raza. The new, emerging regime of representation that celebrates Latinas/os in mainstream culture with positive meanings also points to the need for communication scholars to study how, why, and the conditions under which Latinas/os are represented positively and incorporated into the U.S. national imaginary. For-profit culture industries and multiculturalist institutions create the new Latina/o subject for public consumption rather than exclusion or subjugation. Recent positive associations promoted in the media do not necessarily point to the triumph of cultural critics who have long sought just and equitable Latina/o representation. Instead, representations of Latina/o success, sexiness, assimilation, and acceptance by mainstream culture require critics and scholars to pose new questions and problems about the nature and quality of Latina/o representation. Stories and images of successful or acceptable minorities can support the myth of the American Dream, with its ideologies of social ascendancy through capitalism and merit (Jhally & Lewis, 1992), or promote benign multiculturalism that avoids critical discussions of relations of power (Omi & Winant, 1996; Shohat & Stam, 1994).

Some of the most important and innovative debates about transnationalism, gender, class, hybridity, and citizenship occur in Latina/o media studies. The lack of agreement about whether Latinas/os constitute a race, ethnicity, linguistic category, or affinity group opens up compelling opportunities for communication scholars to understand how these constructs are negotiated within the processes of signification and stratification. Latina/o media studies shed light on the complexities of media production, circulation, and reception in multicultural societies. If communication scholarship and pedagogy are intended to "demystify the features of everyday life" (Zelizer, 2001, p. 297), then the politics of difference and the processes of cultural categorization deserve empirical and theoretical attention from communication scholars. Latina/o media studies address the heterogeneity that is palatable as a structure of feeling in contemporary society but that might be difficult to approach as an analytic concept for public and scholarly deliberation.

Until recently, communication research followed the assumptions of popular and institutional culture, which largely ignored Latinas/os in favor of the traditional black/white binary that constitutes the frame of U.S. race relations (Domke, 2000; Entman, 1992; Valle & Torres, 2000). As recently as the late 1980s, Valdivia (2004) wrote, "[T]here was relatively little work on Latinas/os and communications or the mass media, including the mainstream research areas of television, advertising, and journalism and the press" (p. 107). The Chicana/o movement and nation-based social groups, such as Mexican Americans and Puerto Ricans, provided opportunities for communication scholars to study the situated and visible ways in which ethnic difference operates outside the black/white binary (Greenberg, M. Burgoon, J. Burgoon, & Korzenny, 1983; Nicolini, 1986; Noriega, 1992). Scholarship that focused on Latina/o media began to paint a compelling picture of media representation of pan-ethnic groups (Conquergood, 1985; Ramírez Berg, 1990; Subervi-Vélez, 1986; Wilson & F. Gutiérrez, 1985). Over the last five to ten years, as the culture announced and celebrated the coming of a new Latina/o subject, media communication scholarship produced several significant studies of Latina/o representation and the construction of a pan-ethnic cultural category, *Latinidad*. These studies enable scholars, teachers, and students to move beyond the terms and frames of difference that are presented in mainstream popular and institutional culture and to seek new and innovative ways of exploring how difference is constructed in relation to subaltern and/or dominant practices.

Latina/o media studies offer an important opportunity to interrogate the construction of broad cultural categories in mainstream media representations and to examine how subaltern or vernacular texts contest, negotiate, or integrate dominant meanings. Cultural producers, audiences, critics, and scholars might move forward by assuming the static coherence of Latina/o unity. Such assumptions are not without risk; they can reproduce an unproblematic and incomplete understanding of difference by working within mythologies of race and nation that assume the rationality of human categorization. These assumptions might also cultivate a collective memory of division and difference that identity politics cannot completely address and that ongoing culture wars exploit (Gitlin, 1995). As media and popular culture representations change according to shifting demographics and social trends, communication research must adjust, adapt, and recover relevant literature to remain critically engaged not only with the *zeitgeist*, but also with the fast-moving strategies of ideological projects and fickle tastes of commercial culture. Later in this chapter, I detail the relevance of the Latina/o media studies literature to various areas of inquiry in communication research. The positions and debates within Latina/o media studies demonstrate the utility and problems of representational dynamics in popular culture as well as the analytic strategies of scholarly inquiry.

Given the complexities that face Latina/o representation, some readers might begin to regard Latina/o media studies as relevant only for those researchers with transdisciplinary expertise or for scholars with Spanish surnames. The emergent nature of Latina/o media studies might also leave some readers with the impression that the questions and concerns discussed here lie at the periphery of communication studies. However, in this essay, I hope to demonstrate that Latina/o media studies pose some of the most central questions that drive our field and that those questions remain relevant to communication scholars across divisional boundaries and subject positions. The politics of representation, citizenship, race, gender, class, hybridity, and transnationalism unfold in the literature reviewed in this chapter and intersect with the construction of a multicultural U.S. national imaginary. Latina/o media studies directly inform research perspectives in the areas of media, identity, community, language, and social interaction. The dynamics and processes of Latina/o representation are also relevant to individuals who study health communication, business communication, family communication, and political communication. The stakes are high for Latina/o media studies, as attempts to articulate pan-ethnic unity come from Latina/o communities as well as corporations, politicians, and established institutions. As Latinas/os ascend the national stage and garner growing attention from mainstream culture, the need for clear-minded and informed communication research grows increasingly urgent.

PROBLEMS AND ASSUMPTIONS
IN LATINA/O MEDIA STUDIES

Communication scholars interested in familiarizing themselves with Latina/o media studies and who want to incorporate Latina/o representation into their research and teaching confront an array of compelling issues regarding the politics and processes of cultural categorization. Behind assumptions of Latina/o coherence lie questions fundamental to communication studies. What imaginary bonds allow for Latina/o unity? How are unities constructed? What identity terms do group members find salient? How are collective identities politically useful? Such questions lie at the heart of much communication research, and I direct our attention to how communities are imagined in communication processes.

Latinas/os as Imagined Community

When Anderson (1991) argued that nations constitute imagined communities, we could easily proceed with the impression that these communities are whole and agreeable. The fluidity and discursive nature of Anderson's postulation must be held together by some common culture, some shared faith in the bonds of community beyond the village or the town. Yet the national imaginary is perhaps better characterized as something more polyvalent, contentious, and even disagreeable. Critics note the absence of racial inequality, gender dynamics, and transnational forces in Anderson's notion of the imagined community (Ong, 1999; Rosaldo, 1989). Rosaldo and W. Flores (1997) commented that Anderson "does not recognize the contestation and conflict that animate a hegemonic process" (p. 93). We could contend that our different orientations to collective identity unite us more than some exclusive commonality that is often gathered from Anderson's work. The imagined community can be large and inclusive in scope, and it can also function as a smaller, fortified idea agreed upon by elites and policed at the borders. As Anderson asserted, for a nation to exist, people must be brought into the story one way or another. The mechanisms of this process are sometimes delicate and persuasive, other times blunt and coercive.

Any coherent group must be articulated from different, sometimes contradictory elements. Just as a nation is held together in discourse and under the signs of ideological struggle and human agency, racial and ethnic categories must be rendered coherent through communication practices and public rituals. Individuals envision themselves as participants in the concept of collectivity, casting themselves as actors in the national drama of community, solidarity, and identity. This enactment reflects Carey's (1989) argument for a cultural approach to communication, where the rituals of everyday life and collective action, deliberation, and debate become the sites where we create, maintain, and affirm our symbolic reality. Cultural action—including discordant moments of struggle and domination—has a primary role in the constitution of identity categories, suggesting differences between systems of classification and processes of identification. Authority often assigns individuals or groups to categories, whereas identity stems from something below. When conditions are more free than restricted, identity formation should be an affirmative act where individuals inhabit a collective position and cultivate community through the construction of shared meanings and through collective agency. Racial and ethnic classification at the level of the nation is more of an administrative endeavor. As Gandy (1998) contended, "In an important sense the acceptance of administrative labels is a form of submission to an external authority. While the acceptance of a classification as a marker or index of one's identity may be enabling, oft it is not" (p. 48). The hegemonic

dynamic of race and ethnicity lies at the meeting place of identity and classification. The moment of hegemony occurs when individuals claim a collective
identity that matches up with the imagined community cultivated and maintained by elite groups. However, hegemonic processes always include coun-
terarguments from multiple positions, challenging and potentially changing
the balance that hegemonic leadership must sustain. As a result, the nature
of any imagined community constantly fluctuates, subject to shifting conditions and political ruptures.

Latinas/os in the United States constitute an imagined community. No
essential Latina/o subject exists. Instead, a collective is fashioned out of a
multitude of differences through communication. Mato (1998) argued that
Latinidad is not an inherited position, but, instead, something that is produced, reproduced, and struggled over in communication. Any coherent category obscures, erases, or marginalizes some constitutive elements in favor of
others. The process and politics of articulation and classification remain at the
center of any expression of Latina/o unity in popular culture, and they merit
inclusion in the growing field of Latina/o media studies. When undertaken,
this analytic move can reveal the fictional and inventive nature of the Latina/o
imaginary. On the other hand, assumptions of a coherent and unified Latina/o
imaginary might lead scholars and critics away from critical analyses of the
internal diversity of Latinas/os and interrogations of the power relationships
inside and outside of Latinidad.

Media Assumptions of Latina/o Unity

In order to be sustained as a coherent idea, the Latina/o imaginary must
touch some form of collective experience while, at the same time, being negotiated, administered, and policed by the cultural, corporate, and governmen-
tal elite. Among the many ways that collective experience can inform the
meaning of the Latina/o imaginary, two ideas stand out as foundational.
First, a shared Latin American ancestry dominates as the most rudimentary
unifying force. Second, and of greater consequence, is the shared experience
of being read as Latina/o in everyday culture. The denotative markers of
complexion, accent, or surname mark us as Latinas/os, mirroring Fanon's
(1967) discussion of the fact of blackness—the inescapable experience of
being marked as other by Anglo eyes. J. Flores (1997) described the tensions
between conceptions of Latina/o unity that come from outside of the community and an imaginary notion of Latina/o solidarity that "infuses the
clamor for civil rights with a claim to sovereignty on an international scale;
retribution involves reversing the history of conquest and subordination,
including its inherent migratory imperative" (p. 189). Flores internationalized
the Latina/o imaginary as not merely an identity category, but as a construct

of self-determination and as a starting point for the search for "a new *América*" (p. 191).

Although the fluidity, transnationality, and polysemy of Latinidad are clear upon close examination, media texts (e.g., fashion features in *Vogue*, broadcast news stories about the U.S. Census on ABC, entertainment television programs such as *Desperate Housewives*, and billboard advertising featuring *mestizos* sipping *mojitos*) often assume that the Latina/o imaginary stands for a coherent collective experience and prescribed taste culture. People located within the Latina/o imaginary connect through shared tastes in food, music, and dance, particular family structures, migration story, political preference, and language. In other words, mainstream media representations of the Latinas/os assume a necessary correspondence between one's subject position and particular set of ideological, cultural, economic, and social practices. Communication scholarship also assumes Latina/o coherence. Mayer (2004) asserted:

> By ameliorating the divisions between Latinos, the centers of power within Latino communities, and the multiple margins where *panlatinidad* is contested, communication scholarship sits dangerously poised to cooperate in the mythification of a unified, though unique, national, if not global, Latino identity. (p. 116)

Before media communication scholarship embarks on serious interrogations of pan-ethnic cultural processes, as Mayer encouraged, the field must understand how and why Latina/o coherence makes sense. By addressing these questions, media communication research can also provide key insights into how Latinas/os are brought into contact with the U.S. national imaginary—either through the traditional strategies of marginalization or through new, innovative processes of incorporation through multiculturalism and assimilation.

What Do We Call Ourselves?

In the fall of 2004, the *New York Times* described the controversy surrounding racial classification and Latinas/os in the United States. For the 2000 U.S. Census, respondents could identify themselves as "Hispanic" and then proceed to answer a separate question about their race, which included the option "some other race." In the article, Kathia Mendez, a Maryland resident, identified as black, explained, "I'm not black and I'm not white; we don't define ourselves that way" (Swarns, 2004, p. A1). In 2004, the U.S. Census Bureau debated whether to drop the "some other race" category for the 2010 count, forcing people who trace their ancestry to Latin America to either skip the question altogether or choose a race from the prescribed racial categories of white, black, Asian, American Indian, or Pacific Islander. Ultimately, with

pressure from various Latina/o advocacy groups and the Congressional Hispanic Caucus, Congress barred the Census Bureau from eliminating "some
other race." Although this episode makes sense in the context of ongoing
deliberation and debate over how the Census Bureau counts and classifies
Latina/o identities (Martin, 2002; Navarro, 2003), it also reveals the slipperi-
ness of the fit of Latinas/os within a U.S. national imaginary that relies on
coherent categorization.

The questions of whether Latinas/os constitute a race, ethnicity, linguistic
group, or taste culture remain unresolved in popular culture. This confusion encourages news journalists, commentators, writers, television and film
producers, and editors to hurdle difficult questions of difference and categorization and settle comfortably within the confines of a coherent Latina/o
unity. Yet scholarship demonstrates that the Latina/o imaginary is socially
produced according to the politics and assumptions of specific conjunctures.
Over the last 20 years, important work has detailed how the Latina/o imaginary makes sense in specific contexts. Such contributions include Padilla's
(1985) *Latino Ethnic Consciousness*, Oboler's (1995) *Ethnic Labels, Latino
Lives*, C. Rodríguez's (2000) *Changing Race*, and Dávila's (2001) *Latinos,
Inc.* Based on case studies in the late 1970s, Padilla found that Latina/o ethnic identity rang true for Mexican-Americans and Puerto Ricans in Chicago,
who unified around shared language and class position. However, Padilla
concluded that a Latina/o imaginary could not be relied upon to build meaningful coalitions around common goals. The solidarity of "Latinismo" is a
politics without guarantees. Oboler examined the use of the term "Hispanic"
and "Latino" among New York City Latina/o textile workers and learned
that Latinidad organized various immigrant identities. Although the thrust
of her study emphasized identities formed in the home nations of these
immigrant women, Oboler maintained, "to identify oneself with the issues
that Latinos confront in U.S. society today is *also* a conscious choice to
acknowledge one's history and sociocultural background, as well as the need
to struggle for social justice" (p. 163). In more recent studies, C. Rodríguez
and Dávila found that the Latina/o category is fluid; it changes according
to the shifting needs of the U.S. Census Bureau and marketing demographers. C. Rodríguez's history of U.S. Census categorization depicts how
Latinas/os have been classified as foreigners, as a race, and as "other." Dávila
provided a complex reading of marketing discourses that sell a Latina/o
audience that is generic in terms of looks and language. Not surprisingly,
Dávila discovered that Latina/o marketing professionals use the terms "Hispanic" and "Latina/o" interchangeably. Together, these works draw attention
to the changing conditions under which Latina/o unity is created, celebrated,
resisted, or looked upon with ambivalence, and they call for communication scholars to investigate how Latinidad becomes meaningful in a wide

range of contexts—from community health centers to the studios of television networks.

Yet the defining terms of the imaginary remain, and they merit clarification. In her research on the U.S. Census, C. Rodríguez (2000) chronicled how the census placed Mexicans in their own category in 1930 until the 1940 count placed them back into "white," unless they appeared to be Indian by census interviewers. Forty years later, in 1980, "Spanish/Hispanic" became a choice for respondents. *Hispanic* typically refers to "all people with 'ties' to Spanish-speaking countries" (Olivarez, 1998, p. 427). *Hispanic* occurs more frequently in institutional discourse and quite widely in New Mexico and Texas. However, many, especially in California and the Northeast, regard *Hispanic* as state-imposed and politically conservative in its ties to Spain (Ramírez Berg, 2002) and assumption of Spanish language ability. The term *Latinalo* emerged to confront this problem, encompassing linguistic diversity, including English-only Latinas/os, and it connected more to Latin America and solidarity with the global south. Members invoke the gender-inclusive *a/o* less consistently, but it counters the patriarchal forms of Spanish words. Within, or in opposition to the Latina/o imaginary, national and diasporic names range from *Cuban, Salvadorian,* and *Chilean* to the more political and situated *Chicanas/os, Tejanas/os, Nuyoricans,* and *Boricuans.* Aparicio (2003) discussed what many would agree is the most problematic term for Latinas/os, *Latin,* which appears regularly in the popular music and professional sports industries. In a discussion of popular music, Aparicio argued that the term *Latin* "deflects the social, demographic, and cultural realities of everyday life among US Latinos and replaces what is socially real Latino with historically familiar, acceptable, and contained images of Latinos that the US can integrate into its own logic" (pp. 91–92). Although debates over group names sometimes raise the specter of circular debates that characterize identity politics and "thought police" discourses on college campuses, Aparicio's argument illustrates the power of cultural terms that are not derived from situated social action but instead link diverse people, positions, and experiences into an imaginary, apolitical relationship. For example, the media can place both Latin pop stars and Latin baseball players inside a generic, homogeneous notion of difference that largely does not threaten U.S. mainstream sensibilities. These different terms raise an important problem for communication investigations into the Latina/o imaginary—does the solidarity of Latinidad come "from below," or does Anglo culture impose the imaginary "from above"?

Why Do We Call Ourselves?

Recent communication and Latina/o studies scholarship use *Latinidad* as a signifier for the Latina/o imaginary, solidarity, and affinity in scholarly and critical discourses (Guzmán, 2005; Rojas, 2004). The term helps communication scholars to understand how and why Latina/o unity might make sense in community, media, and political contexts. *Latinidad* refers to the political, economic, and cultural activities that produce a pan-ethnic identity in the United States (Mayer, 2004) or in a transnational sense (Dávila, 2001). Many scholars of media and popular culture believe that Latinidad extends from Latina/o agency rather than from the dominant culture. In a study of Jennifer Lopez's mainstream success in the late 1990s and early 2000s, Beltrán (2002) applied Sandoval-Sánchez's (1999) notions of Latinization and Latinidad. In addition to being part of the moral panic about the Brown Peril during the California Proposition 187 debates, the idea of Latinization refers to the commodification and use of Latina/o culture in mainstream cultural expressions, whereas Latinidad comes from community agency and Latina/o sensibilities. Crossover figures such as Jennifer Lopez, whose sexualized behind is often at the center of her persona, fit somewhere in between Latinization and Latinidad. Beltrán argued that Lopez is not just a victim of racist and colonial sexual objectification, but she works "as empowered and empowering through asserting qualities such as intelligence, assertiveness, and power—while also proudly displaying her non-normative body and declaring it beautiful" (p. 82). Although Lopez serves Latinidad as a role model for alternative notions of beauty and sexuality, her community transgressions are limited by Latinization—by the way in which popular culture locates her as a foreign, exotic subject. Aparicio (2003) noted that Latinidad can also serve as a homogenizing force when it emerges from mainstream popular and institutional culture, inscribing all of the diversity of Latinas/os into a construct that serves Hollywood, politicians, and corporations. Aparicio approached "Latinidad as a concept that allows us to explore moments of convergences and divergences in the formation of a Latino/a (post)colonial subjectivities and in hybrid cultural expressions among various Latino groups" (p. 93). Indeed, Latinidad offers promise for communication researchers as an analytic concept related to the construction of Latina/o identity, pan-Latina/o solidarity, and a Latina/o imaginary. Valdivia (2004) described Latinidad as the "state of being or performing a Latina/o identity" (p. 108), from which political demands might be made on the state or on other institutions, organizations, and corporations.

Borderlands, hybridity, and transnationalism complicate the use-value of Latinidad as a site of pan-ethnic solidarity and political resistance. The work of Anzaldúa (1999), Gutiérrez-Jones (1995), Canclini (1995), and Saldívar (1997) locates the concept of radical *mestizaje*, or mixture, at the center of U.S. and hemispheric notions of Latinidad. Borderlands, informed by Chicana/o cultural studies, suggest a "deconstruction of the discourse of boundaries" (Saldívar, p. 25), where hybrid identities challenge the notion of cultural purity. In the context of borderlands, Latina/o communication practices are transnational, cutting through the literal and figurative boundaries separating nations and communities. Valdivia (2003) encouraged us to "move beyond this culture/subculture binary divide to a position wherein there is more flexibility to acknowledge and account for fluidity, hybridity, and collaboration and/or cooptation between substream and the commercialized mainstream" (p. 151). Latinas/os in the U.S. represent, according to Valdivia, a radical hybridity—layer upon layer of mestizaje—that deeply challenges mainstream U.S. culture as well as the theories and perspectives used in communication research. Borderlands and hybridity pose challenges and opportunities for the use-value of a pan-ethnic Latinidad. For communication scholars, mestizaje problematizes our reliance on the static coherence of "Latina/o media" or "Latina/o audiences." Yet, if expressions of radical hybridity can be incorporated into media texts and drawn upon in the decoding activity of Latina/o audiences, mestizaje has the potential to transform communication and cultural practices, not only for Latinas/os, but also for other communities caught in between.

The politics and processes of Latinidad pose important questions for communication scholars interested in understanding how identity construction and media representation create meanings about Latinas/os from subaltern as well as powerful positions. Traditional content analyses map racialized regimes of representation and tell us about Latinas/os' relationship with the broader national imaginary by coding media texts and painting a picture of exclusion and negative stereotypes (Harwood & Anderson, 2002; Mastro & Greenberg, 2000). On the other hand, interpretive and critical studies that interrogate the construction and maintenance of Latinidad, whether it comes from mainstream commercial culture or a more vernacular, subaltern community location, provide innovative arguments and directions for understanding the processes and politics of cultural categorization and the vitality or fissures in U.S. pan-ethnic solidarity (Aparicio, 1998; Olivarez, 1998; A. Rodriguez, 1997). Upon considering the growing field of Latina/o media studies, emergent research interrogating Latinidad demonstrates how media texts invite Latinas/os into the U.S. imagined community as foreign others, criminalized scapegoats, sexualized objects of Anglo desire, celebrated elements of multiculturalism, and resistors to assimilation.

NOT BELONGING IN AMERICA:
TRADITIONAL LATINA/O MEDIA STUDIES

In recent years, serious considerations of the Latina/o experience emerge out of more than 25 years of important scholarly work in Latina/o media studies. With the publication of special issues of *Communication Review*, *Howard Journal of Communications*, and *Cultural Studies* on Latina/o issues, and with studies of Latinidad and Latina/o representation appearing in other major journals, serious considerations of difference beyond the black/white binary are making their way into research and the institutional agenda of the discipline. Along with this trend, scholarly journals such as *Aztlan, Textos*, and *Latino Studies* publish compelling studies of Latina/o representation, demonstrating how the fields of ethnic studies, Latina/o studies, Chicano studies, and Puerto Rican studies take media and popular culture seriously. With these perspectives and interests merging, a great opportunity for interdisciplinary collaboration exists for communication scholars. Traditional Latina/o media studies of advertising, television, film, and news provide a good starting point for understanding how communication scholarship illustrates the relationship between Latinas/os and the U.S. national imaginary. I refer to these studies as "traditional" because they often assume the coherence of Latinidad and the unity of Latina/o identity, and many of the studies employ quantitative methods that operationalize Latinas/os as a variable. Such features impose limits on the use-value of the studies if we focus on ways of articulating Latinidad as a cultural category. Nevertheless, these studies reveal how negative stereotypes, underrepresentation, and racialized regimes of representation continue to inform how Latinas/os are positioned at the margins of U.S. culture. However, we cannot consider anything traditional about studying Latinas/os, who remain underrepresented in communication literature.

Many Latina/o media scholars focus on the quality and nature of Latina/o representation, against the backdrop of a stark absence and underrepresentation that serve to erase the Latina/o experience (Lichter & Amundson, 1994, 1996; Navarrete & Kamasaki, 1994). Among the relatively few images that circulate in the culture, research indicates consistent negative stereotypes and marginalization (R. Chavez, 1996; Harwood & Anderson, 2002; Subervi-Vélez, 1986). Historical studies of media demonstrate how regimes of representation work within racial hierarchies through news discourses (Johnson, 1999; Shah & Thornton, 1994), magazines (Taylor & Bang, 1997), and cinema (Beruman, 1995; Hadley-Garcia, 1990; Keller, 1994; C. Rodríguez, 2004). Ramírez Berg's work on Latina/o imagery in film (2002) illustrates how a few powerful stereotypes historically emerge in Hollywood film: El Bandido, The Harlot, The Male Buffoon, The Female Clown, The Latin Lover, and The Dark Lady. Together, these stereotypes create what Ramírez Berg dubbed Latinism, or the construction of a version of Latinidad that can justify U.S. displacement of Mexican landowners and exploitation of Latinas/os as cheap labor. Ramírez Berg asserted:

> In order to rationalize the expansionist goals laid out by the Monroe Doctrine and Manifest Destiny, Latinos—whether U.S. citizens, newly arrived migrants from the south, or Latin Americans in their own countries—needed to be shown as lesser beings. (p. 4)

Ramírez Berg noted that contemporary cinema continues to marginalize Latinas/os through stereotypes despite their increasing participation in Hollywood as well as a growing oppositional, independent film community of documentarians and activists.

The negative stereotypes and marginalization evident in the past and present of Hollywood film are amplified across texts and over time. Studies of contemporary advertising and television representation continue to detail how Latinas/os are brought into contact with the national imaginary but kept at the borders of mainstream tolerance, even in the context of Latinidad's celebration as the trendy ethnicity. The absence of Latinas/os from television programs and advertising remains a consistent finding. For example, Mastro and Stern (2003) determined that Latinas/os continue to be marginalized and absent from advertising messages in their content analysis of national primetime network television advertising. Mastro and Stern contended that, although Latinas/os made up 12.5% of the U.S. population at the time of their study, they made up only 1% of speaking characters in the advertisements. Along with Native Americans and Asian Americans, Latinas/os are underrepresented and, in some cases, negatively represented. Mastro and Stern noted that, in their sample, Latina/o actors with speaking roles "are highly attractive, younger adults with noticeable accents, who are more suggestively clad" (p. 645) than their counterparts. Their findings suggest that the relative absence of more complex and differentiated characters in English-language television advertising amplifies stereotypical representations. However, Mastro and Atkin (2002) revealed how advertisements that feature Latina/o models might not be completely salient for Latina/o audiences. Latina/o representation in advertising tells a distressing story of stereotypical images and underrepresentation, and Mastro and Atkin suggest that, when we do see greater Latina/o representation, it is due to potentially exploitative target marketing that lacks images that speak to Latina/o audiences.

Recent studies of entertainment television programs point to more positive representation, but prime-time network programming continues to portray very few Latina/o characters. Mastro and Greenberg (2000) conducted a content analysis of prime-time network television programs in 1996 and found only 18 Latina/o characters in major or minor roles out of 64 shows, and half of the 18 appeared in one program. Although they were statistically insignificant for the purposes of the study by Mastro and Greenberg, those characters were positive in general and somewhat stereotypical in terms of accent, talk, and dress. Mastro and Greenberg commented that "some major—earlier dominant stereotypical characteristics—dirty and dumb—were not evident" (p. 700) in the sample. The National Hispanic Media Coalition (NHMC) recently gave ABC a letter grade of B in its 2004 report card on network diversity, lauding the *George Lopez Show* and ABC's efforts to recruit Latina/o writers as indicative of the network's commitment to diverse programming in the future.

If prime-time entertainment television tentatively moves toward more positive representations and slowly embraces the new Latina/o subject, news discourses continue to marginalize Latinas/os as sources and subjects (Poindexter, Smith, & Heider, 2003). In a study sponsored by the National Association of Hispanic Journalists (NAHJ), "Network Brownout 1998: The Portrayal of Latinos on Network Television News," Carveth and Alverio (1998) examined 546 hours of network television news, only to find 4 hours and 40 minutes devoted to Latinas/os, with a majority of the stories covering crime, affirmative action, and immigration. As a testament to the ongoing marginalization of Latinas/os in network news, Subervi-Vélez's (2004) contribution to an annual study, "Network Brownout 2004," surveyed 639 hours of network news and found 4 hours and 2 minutes devoted to Latina/o stories. A majority of those stories did not feature an interview with a Latina/o source. Subervi-Vélez stressed that, "in addition to the lack of news stories, the total amount of air time devoted to Latinos remains dismal and Latinos continue to be covered within a narrow framework" (p. 15) of crime and immigration stories. The report includes a qualitative, critical reading of 45 news stories. Subervi-Vélez noted a general lack of contextualization and complexity and a preference for stories of struggle and success within the discourse of the American Dream, despite stories of Latina/o soldiers fighting in Iraq and the rising influence of Latina/o voters in mainstream politics. Between 1997 and 2004, popular and institutional culture paid renewed attention to Latinas/os, yet the NAHJ studies show how network news coverage changed little, relying on the typical frameworks of crime and immigration, even with a miniscule rise in human-interest stories in the 2004 survey. Most surprisingly, Latina/o representation in 2004 actually decreased in network news when compared with studies done in the 1990s.

Traditional Latina/o media studies also look inside media industries in search of implications for Latina/o representation. In a study of local television news broadcasts in 30 cities, Campbell (1995) determined that journalistic habits reproduce many mythologies about racial difference that "preclude the kind of understanding necessary to attain the tolerance and compassion that must proceed the elimination of racial prejudice and discrimination in the United States" (p. 65). Campbell reported that myths that circulated in local television news include the consistent marginalization of minority life, the use of subtle stereotypes that construct nonwhites as other, and the prevalence of liberal multiculturalism in news frames that reinforce notions of white supremacy by lauding African Americans and Latinas/os who have assimilated into Anglo cultural or economic norms. Part of the problem, as Campbell discussed, involves the glaring lack of diversity in newsrooms that might be implicated in the absence of counter-narratives or alternative representations against the criminalized and/or absent Latina/o subject in local news broadcasting. The 2005 Radio-Television News Directors Association (RTNDA)/Ball State University Annual Survey specified that Latinas/os hold 8.7% of general market broadcast television news positions and 6% of jobs in radio news (Papper, 2005). In an examination of public radio hosts and newscasters in urban centers across the United States, Fairness and Accuracy in Reporting (FAIR) revealed vast underrepresentation of Latinas/os, African Americans, Asian Americans, and Native Americans in cities where those populations are significant and historically established (Rendall & Creely, 2002). For example, at the time of the study, Latinas/os made up 46% of the population in Los Angeles, yet represented 0% of the on-air hosts at KCRW, which is based in Santa Monica and is available nationally through iTunes and internet simulcast. Taken together, 91% of KCRW's hosts were non-Latina/o whites, who made up only 31% of the population of Los Angeles. These findings are especially significant, considering how the founding documents of public broadcasting call for public television and radio outlets to represent the diverse citizens and communities that they serve (Carnegie Commission, 1967).

Studies confirm the worst fears of community leaders and advocacy groups haunted by the Frito Bandito when regular news attention focuses on Latina/o criminals. Dixon and Linz (2000a, 2000b) conducted content analyses of television news stories in Los Angeles and Orange County, finding that stories underrepresented Latinas/os as victims as well as perpetrators of violent crime when compared with overrepresentation of Anglos as victims and African Americans as perpetrators, signaling a comparative absence of Latinas/os from these crime stories. Yet, in a later study of negative pretrial publicity for criminal suspects, Dixon and Linz (2002) asserted that "Latinos are three times as likely as Whites to have prejudicial information aired [before a trial] when they victimize Whites" (p. 133). Content analyses discussed above combine with the efforts of advocacy organizations such as FAIR, the RTNDA, and the NHJA and university-based research programs like the Chicano Studies Research Center at the University of California, Los Angeles, to make forceful arguments about the continuing marginalization of Latinas/os behind the scenes and in news and advertising content.

Traditional Latina/o media studies map a regime of representation where Latinas/os are connected to U.S. culture by way of their exclusion and marginalization from the imagined community. However, assumptions of a unified Latina/o imaginary point to obvious questions raised by recent positive, multicultural versions of Latinidad circulating in the culture—what *is* a Latina/o, and under what conditions is Latinidad rendered meaningful as part of the national imaginary?

THE LATINA/O PROBLEMATIC

As Latina/o media scholars examine the processes and politics of Latina/o cultural activity, they necessarily address what we might call the *Latina/o problematic*. This phrase refers to the fundamental construct from which more specific theoretical and empirical questions about Latina/o representation flow. The problematic determines the shape of any inquiry. Chang (1996) argued that the problematic "grants legitimacy and viability to specific research questions," thus endowing them "with coherence and unity by setting the parameters of theorists' collective explorations" (p. 37). Chang elaborated:

> The problematic can be viewed as the internal mechanism of inclusion and exclusion. As a behind-the-scenes decision maker over what can be problematized and what must remain unquestioned throughout a theory's development, the problematic brings into play the *first* determination a theory must undergo—instituting, without explicitly justifying itself, a structure of di-*vision* that predisposes the theorist's gaze as it opens up the theoretical or ideological field. (p. 38)

As a determining force, the problematic shapes the contours of cultural explorations, limits their scope, and places the theorist within a prescribed set of questions. It provides a pre-understanding of cultural phenomena taken up as areas or topics of research and theory. At the same time, and despite its centrality, the problematic often functions invisibly and without acknowledgment. This absence is clearly evident in popular discussions of cultural and philosophical issues. Interestingly, theorists, empirical researchers, and cultural critics also often render the problematic invisible by assuming the unity of a scholarly area. For Chang, the hidden nature of the problematic can be partly explained by risk: too much specificity can reduce its "vital complexity" (p. 36). This kind of apprehension, especially in serious scholarship, makes some sense. Naming and addressing the problematic can limit the questions that it inspires and ensnarl the theorist in the traps of precision and exclusion. It opens a Pandora's box of questions and concerns that previously sat quietly below the surface of assumed coherence. For the purposes of this chapter, however, an exploration into what might be considered the problematic of Latina/o provides a more fundamental understanding of Latinidad and its constitutive subjects. Such an exploration sheds light on what anchors contemporary articulations of Latina/o culture and subjectivity.

Althusser (1979) described the problematic as the question of questions: "the constitutive unity of the effective thoughts that make up the domain of the existing *ideological field* with which a particular author must settle accounts in his own thought" (p. 66). What, then, constitutes the Latina/o problematic? What comprises the center of expressions, structures of feeling, and scholarly inquiry of Latinidad? Recent Latina/o media studies research attempts to address how Latinidad is articulated according to the politics of specific conjunctures. These studies explicitly or implicitly consider how unities are constructed in meaning and ordered in hierarchies. Any instance of Latina/o representation begins with the logic of cultural classification along the lines of difference. However, media texts and other forms of cultural expression regularly ignore the politics of classification and difference, preferring to assume a coherent Latina/o unity for ideological or representational purposes without diving into the problematics of race, class, or citizenship that operate with potency but relative invisibility beneath the assumption of a coherent Latina/o imaginary. In *Sorting Things Out: Classification and Its Consequences*, Bowker and Star (2002) observed that "good, usable systems disappear almost by definition. The easier they are to use, the harder they are to see" (p. 33). Classification is ubiquitous, material, indeterminate, and political. It is systematic and can be understood as an infrastructure that invisibly organizes social life from the inside. With careful research attentive to these properties, infrastructures can be revealed. As such, the assumptions behind various representations of Latinidad in mainstream cultural expressions become even more important to uncover.

These ideas about classification infrastructures point to the concept of articulation as we strive to understand how unity and coherence of cultural categories and systems of classification emerge. In a summative essay on articulation, Slack (1996) traced the theoretical contours of articulation in cultural studies. Generally, articulation describes the connection of different elements into a social reality. The unity and coherence of a discourse are brought together—or articulated—in ideology so that it might enter hegemonic struggle or serve a dominant social group. Articulation turns attention to the discursive nature of social unities, and it takes into consideration both resistance and the exercise of power in ideological struggle. Slack clearly asserted that articulation is neither a precise theory nor a method in the traditional sense. Instead, it serves as an orientation to cultural inquiry—an orientation that disrupts certainty and undermines scholarly and popular assumptions about the coherence of ideas. The work of Laclau and Hall led communication scholars in quite the opposite direction, toward theoretical rigor and political application.

Laclau (1977) argued that the links between concepts that form a unity do not occur automatically, but intersect in discourse. When formed, a unity serves hegemonic purposes. Drawing on the work of Gramsci (1971), Laclau placed communication—language, discourse, and symbols—at the center of any articulated unity. Within the processes of communication, ideology actively brings different concepts, positions, interests, and goals together into a coherent social force. Hall's (1996) argument for a theory and a political struggle absent of guarantees echoed the contingent nature of articulation. For Hall, articulation really encompasses the assembly of different, sometimes contradictory, elements into a unity. These elements do not necessarily belong together, but they develop coherence through representational work. Just as a unity evolves through communication, it can be disassembled and re-articulated into something new. Hall contended that "a theory of articulation is both a way of understanding how ideological elements come, under certain conditions, to cohere together within a discourse, and a way of asking how they do or do not become articulated" (p. 141). As a theoretical and methodological orientation, articulation maps the conditions under which unities are constructed and charts the ideological forces involved. Hegemonic organize summon different elements into a coherent social reality to serve their own purposes—to suture its interests with those of subordinate groups in careful and purposeful ideological manipulation of how a unity is brought together. The notion of articulation begs the questions of construction and coherence to the Latina/o imaginary. Latinidad functions as a social reality in popular and institutional culture, yet its active construction provokes communication scholars to inquire about the purposeful articulation of different and sometimes contradictory identities, subject positions, histories, and politics into something that makes sense for communities or put to use by powerful agents.

In the following sections, I discuss recent Latina/o media studies that seriously consider the organizing forces of Latina/o coherence and group them according to how the authors address the Latina/o problematic. This research attends to the often overlooked processes of classification and articulation, and it can be clustered around nationalism, citizenship, language, culture, and the politics of race, class, and gender. These areas overlap significantly, but they all pose significant problems and questions for the viability and legitimacy of Latinidad as a subject position, a representational technique, and a politically strategic category. Because research examples that explicitly interrogate the mechanics of Latina/o coherence are still relatively rare in mainstream media studies, I draw upon studies of popular culture to illustrate the vitality of these areas. For communication scholars, investigations into the Latina/o problematic can shed light on the foundational questions and concepts that organize and classify other pan-ethnic identities and communities.

Nationalism

Puerto Ricans, Mexicans, Cubans, Chileans, Costa Ricans, Dominicans, and Salvadorians comprise but a sample of the many national identities that are pulled into the Latina/o imaginary. For many Latinas/os, national heritage remains an important marker of community and identity in the United States.

Some communities, such as Chicanas/os and Puerto Ricans, employ politically informed ethnic nationalism to challenge dominant relations of power through discourses of resistance and spaces of community, such as the *casitas* constructed in upper Manhattan. For example, Chicana/o film scholarship (Fregoso, 1995; List, 1996; Noriega, 2000) examines how the political work of Chicana/o filmmakers in the borderlands directly confronts relations of power in the U.S./Mexico borderlands. Noriega argued that Chicana/o cinema provides more than movies about Mexican Americans; it constitutes an extension of the Chicana/o political movements that make demands on the state for just and equitable status as U.S. citizens. One of the most obvious ways for researchers to address the Latina/o problematic and to interrogate how unities are articulated is to focus on one or more of the national or nationalistic positions that serve as constitutive components of Latinidad.

Studies of Latina/o nationalism tell of situated cultural action that originates in specific geographic locations and becomes meaningful according to the frameworks of interpretive communities. Media research that focuses on Latin American national communities within the United States pursues media processes of producers and audiences that are not easily bundled into pan-ethnic solidarity. Mayer's ethnographic work on Mexican American media in San Antonio, Texas demonstrates the rich findings and arguments that can be made through media studies field work in situated communities. *Producing Dreams, Consuming Youth: Mexican Americans and Mass Media* (Mayer, 2003a) features a two-year study of media production and reception by Mexican American youth that encompasses the political economy of Spanish-language media, subaltern and alternative media production, media influence, and the tension between art and commerce to understand how the Mexican American imaginary was articulated and challenged in San Antonio. In many ways, this grounded study takes up Radway's (1988) call for a location-based ethnography of media production and reception. Mayer found that innovative and hybrid media production and reception create a sense of Mexican American community while, at the same time, helping Mexican Americans to imagine their relationship with other Americans. Mayer's thick description and careful tracking of nomadic audiences and producers testify to the depth and breadth of Mexican American specificity.

Mayer's time in San Antonio yielded an interesting audience analysis of how Mexican American teenage girls comprised an interpretive community as readers of *telenovelas*, the Spanish-language soap operas produced in Latin America and popular on U.S. Spanish-language television. Through their interpretive activity, the girls in Mayer's study (2003b) bonded with Mexico through the programs but also differentiated themselves from the housewives who inhabit the more traditional gender roles in Mexico as well as a large segment of the telenovela audience. The girls "reappropriated the national meanings in the telenovela to fit their own experiences, making the program more pleasurable but also a potential source of alienation" (p. 489). The serial *Maria Isabel* proved to be especially engaging for the girls, as they followed the title character, who overcame poverty through the love of her employer. In interviews, the girls identified with Maria Isabel in her struggle to assimilate into a wealthy Mexican family. This interpretive activity reflected the girls' negotiation of their own hybrid identity as both Americans and Mexicans and their willingness to use the terms *Mexican, American,* and *Mexican American* interchangeably. Mayer (2003b) also noted that the girls' responses acknowledged how they linked the social mobility of Maria Isabel to her whiteness and conventional beauty, which the girls read as a contradiction of meritocracy and a challenge to the American Dream.

Mayer (2004) proposed that we widen the scholarly lens with nationality-based studies that move beyond Mexican Americans, Cuban Americans, and Puerto Ricans, groups that dominate the demographics and symbolic space of Latinidad. She argued for attention to less visible groups that might challenge the essentialism and homogenizing function of Latinidad, such as the Argentinean diaspora (which is complex in terms of both class and racial expectations). Argentineans become Latina/o, and, in the process, they must enter a new form of racialization where, according to mainstream assumptions, they cease to be European or even middle class despite their transnational ties to Argentinean systems of classification. This process challenges the celebratory multiculturalism that is assumed to be part of U.S. pan-ethnic categorization because it is state-directed and Argentineans are nowhere to be found in representations of Latinidad. Mayer contended that, for new Latin American diasporic subjects, Latinidad in the United States "is less an essence or a choice but a requisite—a cooptation into a liberal multiculturalism where they are both spoken for yet invisible" (p. 119). She recommended that scholars concentrate on how these national diasporas connect with the U.S. national imaginary by studying the lived processes of Latina/o identity, the administrative function of the state, and transnational connections in a global economy. Mayer's expanding work demonstrates the richness of situated Latina/o inquiry and the ways in which new national identities within the United States speak to the process or racialization and the construction of Latinidad.

Rhetorical studies of Chicana/o self-representation (Calafell, 2004; Delgado, 1995; L. Flores, 1996; Hammerback & Jensen, 1985) and studies of Puerto Rican popular culture (Aparicio, 1998; J. Flores, 2000; Rivera, 2002) also open interesting discussions about how national and nationalist positions disrupt the celebratory multiculturalism often inscribed within more bland versions of Latinidad. Popular-culture studies of music provide useful examples of how communication scholars might approach Latina/o representation through the oppositional politics of Chicana/o or Puerto Rican nationalism.

Delgado's work on Chicano rap music describes how Chicano ideology, or Chicanismo, is articulated through performance and cultural action. Delgado (1998a) explained that Chicanismo "developed as a social movement's ideology expressed through indigenous and traditional social forms" (p. 97), staying in touch with the contemporary experience of Mexican Americans and indigenous roots through agit/prop theater, novels, and poetry. Delgado described how Chicanos use rap lyrics and musical forms to rearticulate the nationalist and resistant ideology of Chicanismo through self-affirmation, critiques of power, and the resurgence of a Chicano movement "as a means of rectifying past and present ills" (p. 107). Kid Frost, a Chicano rapper, symbolizes the rearticulation of Chicanismo through the performance of a proud brown masculinity that claims the U.S./Mexico borderlands as a homeland. Delgado (2000) noted that the cultural pride and self-awareness performed by Kid Frost represent Chicanismo as an "empowered identity" (p. 398). El Vez, the stage persona of performance artist Robert Lopez, serves a similar function of affirming Chicana/o politics. Yet, instead of using the oppositional form of rap music, El Vez subverts the iconography and music of Elvis Presley. Habell-Pallán (1999) studied El Vez performances as the articulation of oppositional politics, with lyrics that tell the story of Chicana/o ideology through the style of a central U.S. figure. While simultaneously appropriating Elvis for social justice and using Presley's popularity as a vehicle for creating broad interest, El Vez promotes a critical, oppositional identity and alternative form of community to audiences around the world. These studies of Chicana/o popular culture can be linked with international cultural studies (Chabram-Dernersesian, 1999, 2000, J. Flores, 1997) and encourage scholars to seriously consider both power and resistance in the articulation of Latinidad.

Citizenship and Immigration

Citizenship and immigration constitute contentious issues in public culture, and the anxiety, negotiation, and resistance to the legal and cultural realities of citizenship unfold in Latina/o media studies. Historically, citizenship has been used as a tool of legal exclusion and cultural marginalization for many people and communities that are inscribed within Latinidad. Although history texts, memorials, and political campaigns now celebrate immigration narratives of white ethnicities during the late 1800s and early 1900s, contemporary identity politics make immigration a difficult issue, full of tension, passion, opportunity, and fear. Former California Governor Pete Wilson, who became known for his participation in a series of contentious immigration and affirmative action debates, exhibited these contradictions when he announced his candidacy for the U.S. presidency in front of the Statue of Liberty in New York in 1995. This event, which attempted to draw a line between the legitimacy of

European-immigrant citizenship and the illegality of Latina/o migration and subjectivity, revealed a central tension in the articulation of Latinidad. Mainstream representations continue to enforce a foreign status on Latinidad and raise the specter of fear of the invading masses from the south. As L. R. Chavez (2001) points out in his study of news magazine covers, mainstream media representations construct a Latina/o immigrant who threatens the economic and cultural survival of the nation. Summarizing the content of magazine covers of Latina/o immigration from 1994–1999, Chavez remarked:

> Their sheer numbers, both coming across our borders and reproducing once here, threaten the stability of the nation by adding to social discord, increasing the cost of social services, displacing citizens from jobs and lowering wages, and maintaining cultural and linguistic differences. (p. 213)

During the moral panic and racialization of immigration debates in the 1990s, Latinas/os were represented not merely at the margins of U.S. culture but as a threat to the national social fabric.

Davis (2000) identified one specific instance where the politics of Latina/o immigration became a discourse of peril that disrupted the tidy cul-de-sacs and mission-style mansions of Orange County, California in 1993. When a local Anglo boy was accidentally killed one evening at Califia Beach as groups of Anglo and Latina/o youth harassed each other to the point of violence, local news coverage ignored the shared blame of the tragic incident. Instead, newspapers painted the Latina/o immigrant youth as violent gang members who brutally murdered the boy, despite testimony from experts and witnesses who described the killing as an accident. The news coverage brought the event in touch with Anglo anxiety about the "Latinization" of southern California and fueled popular suspicion of Latina/o legitimacy and legality. The boy's mother became a potent symbol of Anglo victimization at Proposition 187 campaigns, and she contributed to the passage of the "Save Our State Initiative" in 1994. Davis explained: "the new 'brown peril' became the moral equivalent of the obsolete red menace" (p. 75).

The identity politics and culture wars informing Latina/o representation in the early and mid-1990s vividly illustrate how the legal and cultural issues of citizenship and migration serve as organizing forces for the meaning of Latinidad and set material conditions of existence for Latinas/os within the national imaginary. Their threat to the imagined community—both regional and national—fits with a historical regime of representation that is likely to recur according to changing economic conditions and political projects.

The brown peril described by Davis (2000) casts Latinas/os as outlaws, regardless of their length of residency in the United States. Historical narratives that speak to the deep-rooted Latina/o nature of the Southwest are often erased as moral panics, and nativist political movements operate largely through amnesia. L. Flores (2003) provided a historical study of how news accounts leading to repatriation drives during the 1930s branded Mexican immigrants as illegal and described their bodies negatively. L. Flores documented the story of the guest worker program during the Great Depression, when journalists, public figures, and business owners created two narratives that would define Mexican immigrants: the need for temporary labor and the Mexican problem. The narrative of need brought in cheap, nonthreatening labor interested in temporary jobs. L. Flores detailed the development of the narrative of the Mexican problem, which "directed public attention to borders and the potential influence of Mexicans on the national body" (p. 372). News stories told of disease and criminality, and civic leaders began to use the rhetoric of borders to separate the United States from Mexico with stricter immigration laws and the creation of a hostile climate, resulting in the articulation of the Mexican as the illegal alien—with an undesirable, unclean body and a criminal status. L. Flores reminded readers that such images are recycled into our media texts and cultural expressions whenever it is politically useful for those in power, and racialization serves as a key representational strategy for exclusion. News coverage and public discourse emphasized crime, economics, and disease; L. Flores noted that "these rhetorical strategies hid the underlying racial arguments that surrounded immigration" (p. 381).

In their respective works, L. R. Chavez (2001), Davis (2000), and L. Flores (2003) documented how citizenship and immigration integrate racist regimes of representation into political and economic policy discussions. This important work reminds scholars, critics, and activists of the power of discourse and ideology, as carefully guided moral panics transformed public policy in a series of popular initiatives across the West. As an organizing force, immigration discourses and policies position Latinidad outside the national imaginary, if not as a threat to the dominant social order. However, when scholars consider citizenship as cultural rather than merely legal, it can be understood as a site of cultural action and contestation. The notion of cultural citizenship opens up the legal definition of national belonging for criticism and inquiry.

Rosaldo and W. Flores (1997) presented cultural citizenship as "the right to be different (in terms of race, ethnicity, or native language) with respect to the norms of the dominant national community, without compromising one's right to belong, in a sense of participating in the nation-state's democratic process" (p. 57). Cultural citizenship reconfigures the state-imposed definition of legal belonging and replaces it with an expanded notion of citizenship in which culture becomes a way to claim the rights of belonging. Citizenship itself has become a terrain of struggle and a point of articulating Latinidad and contesting legal designations of people, as globalization challenges the relevance of nation states, and Latinas/os find little use in a legal system where they have been historically excluded (Rocco, 2004). Citizenship is not a neutral category, as Dávila (2000) observed, but a system of privilege for "white, monolingual, middle-class producers of and contributors to a political body defined in national terms" (p. 77) that even Latina/o and Spanish-language media do not always challenge. Cultural citizenship serves as an emancipatory concept, inverting the traditional function of legal citizenship. Communication scholars who approach Latinidad through the politics of cultural citizenship directly confront the stereotypes historically assigned to Latinas/os as newcomers and illegal burdens to the state and approach Latina/o social movements and cultural action as attempts to create a space for transnational connections and national integration (Mirón & Inda, 2004).

In a study of Mexican immigrants and *banda* music in southern California, Lipsitz (1999) found that musical performance, fandom, and coordinated dance operate as a form of cultural citizenship and a way of coping with the harsh conditions that immigrant laborers must endure in exile and at home. Lipsitz argued that immigration came under intense political pressure in the 1980s and 1990s in the United States, and power and greed in Mexico created a condition where immigrants feel economic hatred in their home country and displacement, exile, and homelessness in the United States. Neoliberal trade policies bring transnational corporate preferences to the farms and villages of Mexico, amplifying the economic subjugation of many Latin American workers. Thus, the market ideology of late capitalism makes migration a logical choice for many people and a fact of life for people in the underdeveloped world who want to participate in a global economy, where unbounded industries meet situated workers. Lipsitz studied how immigrants use banda music as a way to adapt to the harsh realities of migration in southern California. The music itself represents "a complex site where identities adapt to dramatically new political, economic, and social realities" (p. 198). Dancing to banda music rejects assimilation and encourages community and solidarity through synchronized motion. As such, banda music becomes a point of articulation for the construction of Latinidad that positions belonging in the midst of harsh realities of citizenship laws.

Latina/o media scholarship and transdisciplinary studies of popular culture explicate the marginalizing dynamics of citizenship and how Latinas/os resist the harsh conditions of legal citizenship and cultural marginalization. L. Flores (2003) and Lipsitz (1999) historicized and rationalized Latina/o migration in the Americas and encouraged further situated inquiry into cultural citizenship and challenges to racist structures within the politics of belonging. There are problems, of course, in treating citizenship as the organizing question in the construction of Latinidad. The most pressing issue involves the suturing of Latinas/os to the immigration experience through stereotypes that erase their historical presence in U.S. territory. Yet, by approaching citizenship as an organizing construct for the articulation of Latinidad, scholars have uncovered practices of resistance to state-imposed citizenship status and the global capitalist system while also historicizing the racist regimes of representation that operate powerfully against Latinas/os through immigration debates. The cultural turn in articulations in citizenship underscores the centrality of language and culture to the articulation of Latinidad.

Language and Culture

Investigations into Spanish-language media provide an accessible site of cultural production where the Latina/o imaginary unifies around linguistic specificity. The use of language as an organizing principle for Latinidad reaches back several decades, and, consequently, the study of Spanish-language media is well established as an area of interest in communication research (F. Gutiérrez, 1985, 1990; O'Guinn, Faber, & Meyer, 1985). Histories of national (A. Rodríguez, 1999a) and local (Mayer, 2001) Spanish-language media indicate how the construction of a Latina/o audience developed along with a broadcasting industry. In *Making Latino News: Race, Language, Class* (1999b), A. Rodríguez explained how marketing strategists construct a Hispanic audience as "racially non-white, linguistically Spanish speaking, and socio-economically poor" (p. 47). In effect, marketers encourage stereotypes to "reproduce U.S. Latino ethnicity and U.S. nationalism as they create commercially viable Hispanic audience product" (p. 51). A. Rodríguez also detailed how Latina/o journalists in Spanish-language news broadcasts identify their audiences as "culturally distinct, often oppressed, and exploited people" (p. 78). The journalists identify with their audience because many of them testify to facing the same challenges of being marked as different in the United States, despite their whiteness and middle-class position. The journalists construct a pan-ethnic Latina/o imaginary in order to hold this audience together through a limited advocacy of Latina/o issues and coverage of both U.S. and Latin American stories. The inclusion of Latin American news serves the important function of cultivating a collective memory for U.S. Latinas/os that brings them into a pan-ethnic identity. Spanish-language news creates a Latinidad that, in turn, affirms the vitality and legitimacy of the Latina/o market and television networks such as Univision. The work by A. Rodríguez complements Dávila's (2001) ethnographic study of Latina/o marketing that uses the Spanish language and other appeals to Latina/o cultural sensibilities to articulate and sell a coherent market demographic to advertisers. Dávila asserted that "language means money for Hispanic media and marketing agencies, and this equation is likely to continue to affect the correlation of Latinas with Spanish, impairing attempts to broaden the media's definition of Latinas" (p. 180). A. Rodríguez and Dávila described a marketing machine that relies on language to articulate a Latina/o imaginary for the purposes of profit, resulting in a bland, apolitical Latinidad that misses important opportunities to interrogate the power structures of race, gender, and citizenship at work in the United States. An imagined community emerges through the assumed unifying power of Spanish, which we can see from Rodríguez and Dávila is highly limited as an emancipatory, politically strategic unifying force.

The growth of the Latina/o market provides incentives for the burgeoning field of Spanish-language marketing and media programs. New markets and marketing opportunities spark changes to the industry, such as the ownership consolidation of Spanish-language radio stations discussed by Paredes (2003). Paredes argued that, in a deregulatory environment, Spanish-language radio consolidation and conglomeration result in a more homogeneous and predictable commercial programming format that resembles the much-criticized contemporary English radio menu. Paredes depicted Spanish-language media as the primary way for advertisers to reach the Latina/o audience. The narrowcasting in Spanish radio results in decreasing programming diversity for both music and news, and it affords few choices for many Spanish-speaking Latina/o listeners who already face limited options in a radio spectrum still dominated by English-language programming. Paredes's analysis contributes to the field of media political economy and the work of analysts such as McChesney (1997) and Bagdikian (2000), who raised serious questions about the threat posed to diverse, democratic expression by corporate media consolidation. Policy studies of Spanish-language media challenge and complement traditional political economy perspectives. For example, Paredes's study of how increased ownership concentration in Spanish-language radio leads to less content diversity supports and expands many of the key arguments put forth by media critics and scholars about English-language texts. However, Paredes also challenged the dominant approach to political economy by arguing for urgency in the study of Spanish-language media consolidation because of its more concentrated effect through fewer outlets across the broadcast spectrum and a growing Spanish-speaking audience in the United States.

These studies of Spanish-language television and radio paint a picture that is very different from the politically transgressive Chicana/o and Puerto Rican media practices. Although analyses and findings in this research do little to build excitement for the politically liberating possibilities of Latinidad, they do explain how Latinas/os are bound up in the structures of commercial media. Like other groups, Latinas/os are organized into a coherent marketing demographic to be sold to advertisers. Spanish unifies a version of Latinidad whose subjects must do the work of media economics by watching and listening to targeted advertisements (Jhally & Livant, 1986). In this respect, the Latina/o imaginary grows stronger by becoming a reliable unified audience, and language serves as a unifying force. In the economics of commercial media, younger demographic groups with higher disposable incomes are valuable to advertisers who seek consumers who are ready and able to turn their reading, listening, and watching into active consumption. For these and other reasons, bilingual and English-only Latinas/os have become very interesting to media corporations and advertisers. Research suggests that increases in Latina/o-themed texts in English-language media over the last several years, such as *Latina* and *Fuego* magazines, *Latino USA* on National Public Radio, and the Sí-TV satellite network, might have more to do with market forces than with a mainstream acknowledgement of the internal diversity of Latinidad.

Spanish- and English-language texts, industries, and interpretive activities construct and negotiate Latinidad as a unified concept. Media scholars (Martínez, 2004; Olivarez, 1998; Tovares, 2000) tackle the various tensions and divergent consequences of Spanish- and English-language media by comparing and contrasting how outlets treat different news and entertainment events. Olivarez examined coverage of the Tejana pop-star Selena's life and death in 1995 through an analysis of Spanish- and English-language entertainment news media. Olivarez argued that Spanish-language media's desire to create a bland Hispanic category presented difficulties in representing Selena's hybrid Tejana subjectivity. Both Spanish- and English-language media promoted her rags-to-riches story, which supports the ideology of the American Dream, but Selena coverage "was constructed by each media system based on their respective conceptions of the audience" (p. 434). Lacking interpretive frameworks about Tejana identity, English-language media had a difficult time grasping what culture or community Selena represented as a Tejana singer, whereas Spanish-language media needed to create generalizations to support a pan-ethnic Hispanicness that also did little to account for the specificity of her Tejana style. Olivarez argued that these findings indicate the limitations of content analyses that consistently find very few Latina/o characters on television and stereotypical news coverage. She contended that, although such studies remain important, "numbers only provide us with information on the absence or presence of people" (p. 431) while ignoring how the media specifically articulate Latinidad as a pan-ethnic imaginary. Comparative studies of Spanish- and English-language media can show how culture industries construct Latinidad for their own purposes and demonstrate an unwillingness to confront the internal contradictions and complexity of such a broad imaginary.

Investigations into English-language media, such as Martínez's study of *Latina* magazine (2004), specify how Latinidad can be organized around cultural norms and stereotypes. Martínez asserted that *Latina* targets traditional notions of family to articulate Latina unity among readers and to appeal to a modern woman in touch with middle-class notions of social ascendancy. Stories of Latina/o celebrities emphasize their connections with family and national heritage. Martínez explained that "the invocation of the idea of family and the identification of the national heritage of celebrities featured in *Latina*, whether briefly mentioned or discussed in detail, situates the women, and *Latina's* readers, within an imagined panethnic Latino family" (p. 163). Martínez maintained that *Latina* uses language to separate the Latino imaginary into class positions, with their English-speaking demographic worth more to advertisers than Spanish-only Latinas. This study's findings reinforce earlier research into Latina/o-themed magazines, which promote the frames of both assimilation into mainstream English-speaking culture and pluralism within the Latina/o imaginary (Johnson, 2000). Like similar texts, these magazines employ stereotypes about family, food, aesthetics, and taste to promote an upscale pan-ethnic identity while simultaneously attempting to speak to the internal diversity of Latinidad.

Tovares's (2000) study of the National Public Radio program *Latino U.S.A.* supports Martínez's (2004) argument about the use of language as a signifier of class differences. The initial idea for the program was to provide a public radio show devoted to issues and ideas germane to the Mexican American community. In interviews, program producers described how they thought the decision to broadcast in English would expand the audience to incorporate non-Latinas/os as well as bilingual and English-only Latinas/os. By creating a program for all Latinas/os and serving other Americans interested in Latinidad, they justified budgets for the program, and *Latino U.S.A.* obtained a green light in 1993 and began production out of Austin, Texas. Tovares contended that this strategy "increases the crossover potential of the program by making it accessible to bilingual and English monolingual Latinos and non-Latinos who may not speak Spanish but are interested in Latino issues" (p. 480). Public broadcasting economics intersected with ethnic identity to create a broad Latina/o identity that expanded the scope of the program at a lower cost per listener than if the program targeted Mexican Americans or Spanish-only speakers.

The politics of language should continue to be examined as Spanish-language media outlets grow and English-language Latina/o-themed programming increases. Language has become a key site for the negotiation of Latina/o unity (Dávila, 2000). An emerging interest in Latina/o audience research and reception studies provides new insights into how readers make sense of Spanish-language or Latina/o-themed media (Moran, 2003). In discussions with viewers and listeners of Spanish-language television and radio, Dávila (2002) described how her respondents resisted forms of identification offered by the media, especially in regard to nationality and race. However, the respondents continued to identify themselves either in relation to, or as part of, the Latina/o imaginary promoted by outlets like Telemundo, Univisión, and La Mega radio. Studies of encoding and decoding activity represented by Tovares (2000) and Dávila (2002) shed light on how language and culture are accepted, negotiated, or resisted as organizing forces for Latina/o collective identity in the grounded situation of production and reception contexts. More audience and reception studies might detect the erosion of the power of Spanish to serve as the de facto unifier of Latinidad, as the politics of race, class, and gender add complexity to any form of identity classification or imagined community.

Race, Class, and Gender: The Politics of Representation

At the center of articulations of Latinidad and the politics of media representation lie the overlapping social constructs and determining structures of race, class, and gender, which scholars struggle to separate in investigations of Latindad (Darder & Torres, 2003; Lugones & Price, 2003). These issues constitute the big three considerations of social science research and cultural criticism, and their dynamics operate across the politics of difference and identity. Discourses of immigration often hide nativist, racist meanings behind the guise of legal citizenship enforcement or economics. Studies of language and culture easily incorporate an explanation of class difference in Latina/o media because Spanish and English increasingly stand for particular economic positions and proximity to the immigration experience. Scholarly consideration of Latina/o nationalisms cannot be severed from the strict patriarchy of the ancestral countries in Latin America that inform media representation and cultural practices in the United States. Researchers incompletely understand Chicana/o and Puerto Rican political movements by failing to acknowledge feminists' challenge to *machismo*. The overlapping concerns do not negate each other, but they testify to the complex, competing, and contradictory processes at work in media texts. Together, race, gender, and class constitute a politics of difference that a small group of media scholars use as the starting point for approaching the complicated questions of how Latinidad is articulated at different historical and political conjunctures.

Scholars can reconfigure race and racial ideologies to engage in what West (1993) describes as the cultural politics of difference. For West, a politics of difference originates from a postmodern turn from the "monolithic and homogeneous in the name of diversity, multiplicity and heterogeneity" (p. 3) while, at the same time, highlighting historical structures involved in cultivating notions of difference. West invites critics, scholars, and cultural practitioners to enter this new arena where the contingency of race and ethnicity serves as a starting point and where the reliance on normative political uses of coherent cultural categories is rejected. By approaching the construction of

Latinidad through the lens of race and racial ideologies, scholars can effectively address the politics of difference and the other social conflicts that race signifies (Lowe, 1996). Serious considerations of race also indicate how ethnicity and multiculturalism function along the representational spectrum between subaltern media practices and mainstream media texts. Scholarly investigations into the politics of difference suggest how, under certain circumstances, the issues of race, nation, and ethnicity remain unresolved. Delgado (1998b) studied readers' letters to *Low Rider Magazine* and found that letter writers employ various terms to speak of their community, including *Chicanalo, Hispanic, Mexicano, Xicano,* and *Raza.* These different terms for Latinidad demonstrate the flexibility of Latina/o identity when we closely examine vernacular, everyday cultural practices. Delgado remarked that the content and tone of *Low Rider Magazine* are strongly Mexican American, despite its multicultural readership. His analysis of 8 issues and 145 reader letters to the magazine illustrates how Latinas/os' use of general identity terms voice some solidarity with "others who are collectively, and self-referentially, labeled *Hispanic, Latinalo,* or *Raza*" (p. 429). The letter writers expressed both skepticism toward these general racial and ethnic terms and the willingness to use them to communicate common interests with and differences from Anglos and African Americans. One letter writer argued that *Raza* signifies groups that share cultural similarities while maintaining differences, proclaiming, "Not Mexicans, Central and South Americans, Cubans, Puerto Ricans, and Dominicans . . . Latinos!" (as cited in Delgado, 1998b, p. 433). In other places, *Latinalo* and *Hispanic* merely function as synonyms for *Chicanalo* and *Mexicano.* The interchangeability of these identity terms implies the ambiguity of Latina/o as a racial construct and complicates pan-ethnic identity and solidarity. This complexity only grows stronger when we examine race and gender together as organizing and defining forces.

The regime of representation known as *tropicalization* serves as a good example of how race and gender intersect to define the central essence of Latinas/os in mainstream U.S. popular culture. Similar to Said's (1979) notion of orientalism, tropicalization refers to the representational strategies that mainstream culture uses to contain and objectify Latinas/os. To tropicalize is "to trope, to imbue a particular space, geography, groups or nation with a set of traits, images, and values" (Aparicio & Chávez-Silverman, 1997, p. 8). Tropicalization encompasses both the sexualization of Latinas/os and the racialization of Latinidad in the United States and throughout the hemisphere. The hegemonic function of tropicalization assigns a sexualized foreign status to Latinas/os. Whereas Said wrote about the British colonial vision that fetishized Middle East Arabs under orientalism, hegemonic tropicalization projects an Anglo vision of Latina/o otherness, desirable only within the Anglo gaze.

The emphasis on olive skin, voluptuous female bodies, bright colors, rhythmic music, and hypersexualized excess led Guzmán and Valdivia (2004) to contend that tropicalization locates Latina/o cultural activity below the belt. Whereas whiteness connotes intellect and reason, "non-whiteness is associated with nature and the everyday needs of the body to consume food, excrete waste, and reproduce sexually" (p. 211). In order to understand how tropicalization defines Latina women, in particular, Guzmán and Valdivia considered the representational dynamics of three Latina icons: Jennifer Lopez, Salma Hayek, and Frida Kahlo. Media representations of Lopez and Hayek focus on their curvy hips, round butts, and full lips. Kahlo's work and her persona signify political resistance to Anglo notions of beauty, but representations of her are commodified as an icon sold on t-shirts and coffee mugs. The women are fetishized as exotic in mainstream popular culture. However, Guzmán and Valdivia asserted that the women disrupt some of the traditional boundaries in the U.S. culture industries by profiting from their position as sexual objects and signifiers of a broad Latinidad. They are "caught in the dialectic between agency and the objectification of identity that operates within many mediated products" (p. 219).

Debates about Latina/o crossover in general market media texts and mainstream popular culture also hold important clues for understanding the relationship between racialization and sexualization (Beltrán, 2002; Valdivia, 2000). Aparicio (2003) took Jennifer Lopez's portrayal of the Tejana pop star Selena Quintanilla-Perez in the Gregory Nava film *Selena* as a way of arguing for a transgressive Latinidad that originates from affinity between identity positions within the Latina/o imaginary. When *Selena* was initially released in 1997, debates erupted about the appropriateness of a Nuyorican-like Lopez portraying the iconic Tejana singer. This dispute became part of what Aparicio called the interlatino "culture wars" at the turn of the century, where different national identities began to be set against each other in national news stories. Journalists started to cover the tensions and turf wars between Latina/o groups as migration shifted populations from their historical locations. Aparicio positioned Lopez's unapologetic claim to Selena's story as a moment of convergence in the formation of Latinidad. Both Selena and Jennifer Lopez contested hegemonic notions of beauty through the presentation of their Latina bodies. Their dance movements demonstrated how each woman was socialized into a community-specific form of dance performance. The women present critics, scholars, and activists with the opportunity to illustrate the possible specificity and unity for different Latina/o groups within a counter-hegemonic form of Latinidad. Lopez, as Selena, revealed a kind of "Latinidad feminista" (p. 103) that links Puerto Ricans and Tejanas in their collective resistance to normative beauty and the hegemonic objectification of Latina/o bodies. Zimmerman (2003) responded to Aparicio by warning about dangers of Latina/o crossover. For Zimmerman, Jennifer Lopez's portrayal of Selena attests to the privileged position of Puerto Ricans in U.S. media representations and the relative failure of Tejana and Mexican American actors and artists to cross over. Gaspar de Alba (2003) added that an affinity might exist between Puerto Ricans and Tejanas/os, but Chicanas/os, who claim the U.S. Southwest as ancestral land, are not immigrants, a dominant discourse of Latinidad. If Selena served as a bridge between Chicana/o culture and Latinidad, Jennifer Lopez cannot make that leap because she remains outside of Chicana/o specificity. This debate underscores the complexities and overlapping dynamics of race and gender within Latinidad. The conflict about Selena and Jennifer Lopez also points to the limited success of Latinidad as representation practice.

Latina/o crossover in general market media and popular culture often ushers Latina/o producers or performers into the difficult spotlight of identity politics that rage inside and outside of Latinidad (Valdivia, 2000). Yet some media texts aim to cross over into non-Latina/o reception in order to rehabilitate Latinidad and contest persistent racist regimes of representation discussed earlier in this essay. Actor and producer Edward James Olmos initiated one such effort in partnership with Time Warner in 1999. The multimedia project *Americanos: Latino Life in the United States/La vida Latina en los Estados Unidos* uses photographs and epigraphs to convey a positive and affirmative vision of Latina/o life that finds honor in hard work and commonality with Anglo audiences through human universalism. Throughout their rhetorical analysis of the *Americanos* book, Calafell and Delgado (2004) laud the work of Olmos and his colleagues for creating a "remarkably nuanced view of Latina/o personhood, community and experience" (p. 2) by constructing a pan-Latina/o unity through the celebration of hybridity, crossover success, and cultural solidarity. They conclude their piece with a few qualifiers about the *Americanos* book: the absence of politics, the failure to completely come to terms with interethnic difference, and the assumption of a non-Latina/o reader. Calafell and Delgado praised *Americanos'* broad vision of Latinidad; indeed, the project stands in stark contrast and in direct opposition to the racist regimes of representation that define Latinas/os historically and continue to operate in contemporary culture. The project defied stereotypes and offered a transcultural Latina/o imaginary that challenges binary notions of difference. Calafell and Delgado's terse discussion of the book's shortcomings, together with their suggestion that future research should explore the "challenges and barriers or realizing a coherent Latina/o community" (p. 18), are perhaps as important to Latina/o media studies as their affirmative analysis. When devoid of critical politics and constructed under the auspices of corporate and institutional interests, positive imagery creates a new set of problems within the politics of representation. The dynamics and implications of neoliberal multiculturalism and ruling ideologies, such as the American Dream, deserve deeper, more central interrogation by media scholars.

CONCLUSION

Early in this essay, I argue that Latina/o media studies function as a small but emergent research area in communication studies. Indeed, the important and invigorating work in this area is still shared by a relatively small group of scholars who are committed to mapping the nature and scope of Latina/o representation and media practice. Yet this chapter does not chart a niche interest area or small corner of the field; rather, it depicts a dynamic body of work that maintains dialogue with scholarship across communication divisions and academic disciplines.

For those studying interpersonal, intercultural, organizational, health, and/or family communication and/or language and social interaction, the cultural meanings associated with Latinas/os flow directly into the dynamics of Latina/o interaction. For scholars more focused on areas such media studies, political communication, rhetoric, and political economy, the problems and problematics of Latina/o media hold important clues about the industries, audiences, and artists of the future as well as multifaceted and complex communities of individuals—people for whom such mediated representations shape, constrain, and even contradict their enactment of roles and identities in daily life, especially as the Latina/o population grows and becomes a stronger force as doctors and patients, co-workers, clients, business leaders, and public figures.

When considered together with these areas, Latina/o media studies demonstrates tremendous breadth and depth—more so than can be fully accounted for here. Throughout this chapter, I endeavor to cast some order over Latina/o media studies by examining how communication and cultural studies theories illuminate the problematic of Latina/o unity and by charting research that considers how Latinas/os and the U.S. national imaginary are linked in representation and media practice. Overall, I strived to convey the complexity, vitality, and legitimacy of Latina/o media studies and to invite communication scholars to enter this area and participate in productive deliberation about the meaning of Latinidad in the United States.

Assumptions about the coherence of Latinidad make some sense in contemporary culture. Latina/o commonality can serve the project of strategic essentialism in community and national politics. The terms *Latina/o* and *Hispanic* occur commonly in public culture, and we can gather excellent and illuminating data when we operationalize the Latina/o category in media studies and other social science research. In this chapter, I argue for a communication approach to Latina/o representation, identity, and agency. The theory of articulation, gathered from cultural studies, opens up Latina/o unity so that scholars can observe how and under what conditions Latinidad emerges as a coherent and viable unity.

As scholars begin to address how the Latina/o imaginary is articulated in popular and institutional culture, the investigations into the problematic must center on racial hierarchies and powerful classifications such as class, gender, and citizenship. We also must bring in more critical work in Latina/o queer studies and political communication. Although Latinas/os represent many subject positions, social structures in U.S. culture define how other forms of difference are rendered meaningful. By placing powerful social structures at the center of the Latino category, the "bronzing" of America can be contextualized within a national narrative of cultural struggle. Studies of the Latina/o imaginary can bring the problems and processes of race, ethnicity, and multiculturalism into their analyses and embrace what L. Flores and Moon (2002) called the racial paradox, exploring "how the tensions between exposing the social construction of race while living in a world in which race is as real as our physically different bodies" (p. 182). Media communication scholarship is specially equipped to address the fact and fiction—the politics and processes of cultural categorization.

ACKNOWLEDGMENTS

Portions of this chapter appear in my Ph.D. dissertation, "All of Us *Americanos*: The Rise of Latinas/os within a National Imaginary" (University of Massachusetts, 2006). My sincere thanks to colleagues in the Department of Communication Studies and Ethnic Studies Program at the University of San Diego and to the graduate faculty and good friends from the Department of Communication at the University of Massachusetts, Amherst, for their support and encouragement; also to Christina S. Beck and the three anonymous reviewers for their insightful comments, guidance, and careful editorial attention to my work; thanks also to Carolyn Anderson, Mari Castañeda Paredes, Henry Geddes Gonzales, and Marla Miller, who provided early feedback on this subject, and especially to Alicia Kemmitt for her sharp questions, unwavering encouragement, patience, and generosity.

NOTES

1. Although I refer to the literature reviewed here as "Latina/o media studies," I acknowledge that many of the studies cited may not fall inside the traditional boundaries of media studies.

Transdisciplinary work in popular culture, performance, film criticism, and Chicana/o and Latina/o studies lies beyond the scope of print and electronic media, but enlivens and enriches the emergent and dynamic interests in studying the signification of Latinidad.

REFERENCES

Althusser, L. (1979). *For Marx* (B. Brewster, Trans.). London: Verso.

Anderson, B. (1991). *Imagined communities* (Rev. ed.). New York: Verso.

Anzaldúa, G. (1999). *Borderlands/la frontera: The new mestiza* (2nd ed.). San Francisco: Aunt Lute Books.

Aparicio, F. R. (1998). *Listening to salsa: Gender, Latin popular music, and Puerto Rican cultures: Martínez's argument about the use of language as a signifier of class differences*. Hanover, NH: Wesleyan University Press.

Aparicio, F. R. (2003). Jennifer as Selena: Rethinking Latinidad in media and popular culture. *Latino Studies, 1*, 90–105.

Aparicio, F. R., & Chávez-Silverman, S. (Eds.). (1997). *Tropicalizations: Transcultural representations of Latinidad*. Hanover, NH: University Press of New England.

Bagdikian, B. H. (2000). *The media monopoly* (6th ed.). Boston: Beacon.

Beltrán, M. (2002). The Hollywood Latina body as site of social struggle: Media constructions of stardom and Jennifer Lopez's "cross-over butt." *Quarterly Review of Film & Video, 19*, 71–86.

Berumen, F. J. G. (1995). *The Chicano/Hispanic image in American film*. New York: Vantage.

Bowker, G., & Star, S. L. (2002). *Sorting things out: Classification and its consequences*. Cambridge, MA: MIT Press.

Calafell, B. M. (2004). Disrupting the dichotomy: "Yo soy Chicana/o?" in the new Latina/o South. *Communication Review, 7*, 175–204.

Calafell, B. M., & Delgado, F.P. (2004). Reading Latina/o images: Interrogating Americanos. *Critical Studies in Media Communication, 21*, 1- 21.

Campbell, C. P. (1995). What local television tells us about race in America. *Television Quarterly, 27*(4), 65–73.

Canclini, N. G. (1995). *Hybrid cultures: Strategies for entering and leaving modernity*. Minneapolis: University of Minnesota Press.

Carey, J. W. (1989). *Communication as culture*. New York: Routledge.

Carnegie Commission. (1967). *Public television: A program for action*. New York: Bantam.

Carveth, R., & Alverio, D. (1998). *Network brownout 1998: The portrayal of Latinos in network television news*. Washington, DC: National Association of Hispanic Journalists.

Chabram-Dernersesian, A. (1999). Chicana/o Latina/o cultural studies: Transnational and transdisciplinary movements. *Cultural Studies, 13*, 173–194.

Chabram-Dernersesian, A. (2000). Critical dialogues on Chicana/o cultural studies. In P. Gilroy, L. Grossberg, & A. McRobbie (Eds.), *Without guarantees: In honour of Stuart Hall* (pp. 53–66). New York: Verso.

Chang, B. G. (1996). *Deconstructing communication.* Minneapolis: Minnesota University Press.

Chavez, R. (1996). The Mexican Americans. In P. M. Lester (Ed.), *Images that injure: Pictorial stereotypes in the media* (pp. 27–33). Westport, CT: Praeger.

Chavez, L. R. (2001). *Covering immigration: Popular images and the politics of the nation.* Berkeley: University of California Press.

Conquergood, D. (1985). Performing as a moral act: Ethical dimensions of the ethnography of performance. *Literature in Performance, 5,* 1–13.

Darder, A., & Torres, R. (2003). Mapping Latino studies: Critical reflections on class and social theory. *Latino Studies, 1,* 303–324.

Dávila, A. (2000). Mapping Latinidad: Language and culture in the Spanish TV battlefront. *Television & New Media, 1,* 75–94.

Dávila, A. (2001). *Latinos, Inc.: The marketing and making of a people.* Berkeley: University of California Press.

Dávila, A. (2002). Talking back: Spanish media and U.S. Latinidad. In M. Habell-Pallán & M. Romero (Eds.), *Latino/a popular culture* (pp. 25–37). New York: New York University Press.

Davis, M. (2000). *Magical urbanism: Latinos reinvent the U.S. city.* New York: Verso.

Delgado, F. P. (1995). Chicano movement rhetoric: An ideographic interpretation. *Communication Quarterly, 43,* 446–455.

Delgado, F. P. (1998a). Chicano ideology revisited: Rap music and the (re)articulation of Chicanismo. *Western Journal of Communication, 62,* 95–114.

Delgado, F. P. (1998b). When the silenced speak: The textualization and complications of Latina/o identity. *Western Journal of Communication, 62,* 420–438.

Delgado, F. P. (2000). All along the border: Kid Frost and the performance of brown masculinity. *Text and Performance Quarterly, 20,* 388–401.

Denzin, N. (2002). *Reading race: Hollywood and the cinema of racial violence.* London: Sage.

Dixon, T. L., & Linz, D. (2000a). Overrepresentation and underrepresentation of African Americans and Latinos as lawbreakers on television news. *Journal of Communication, 50,* 131–155.

Dixon, T. L., & Linz, D. (2000b). Race and the misrepresentation of victimization on local television news. *Communication Research, 27,* 547–573.

Dixon, T. L., & Linz, D. (2002). Television news, prejudicial pretrial publicity, and the depiction of race. *Journal of Broadcasting and Electronic Media, 46,* 112–136.

Domke, D. (2000). Strategic elites, the press, and race relations. *Journal of Communication, 50,* 115–140.

Entman, R. (1992). Blacks in the news: Television, modern racism, and cultural change. *Journalism Quarterly, 69,* 101–113.

Fanon, F. (1967). *Black skin, white masks.* New York: Grove.

Figueredo, D.H. (2002). *The complete idiot's guide to Latino history and culture.* New York: Alpha.

Flores, J. (1997). The Latino imaginary: Dimensions of community and identity. In F. R. Aparicio & S. Chávez Silverman (Eds.), *Tropicalizations: Transcultural representations of Latinidad* (pp. 183–193). Hanover, NH: Dartmouth College Press.

Flores, J. (2000). *From bomba to hip-hop: Puerto Rican culture and Latino identity.* New York: Columbia University Press.

Flores, L. A. (1996). Creating discursive space through a rhetoric of difference: Chicana feminists craft a homeland. *Quarterly Journal of Speech, 82,* 142–156.

Flores, L. A. (2003). Constructing rhetorical borders: Peons, illegal aliens, and competing narratives of immigration. *Critical Studies in Media Communication 20,* 362–387.

Flores, L. A., & Moon, D. G. (2002). Rethinking race, revealing dilemmas: Imagining a new racial subject in Race Traitor. *Western Journal of Communication, 66,* 181–207.

Fregoso, R. L. (1995). *The bronze screen: Chicana and Chicano film culture.* Minneapolis: University of Minnesota Press.

Gandy, O. (1998) *Communication and race: A structural perspective.* New York: Arnold.

Gaspar de Alba, A. (2003). The Chicana/Latina dyad, or identity and perception. *Latino Studies, 1,* 106–114.

Gitlin, T. (1995). *The twilight of common dreams: Why America is wracked by culture wars.* New York: Metropolitan.

Gramsci, A. (1971). *Selections from the prison notebooks of Antonio Gramsci.* (Q. Hoare & G. N. Smith, Trans.). New York: International.

Greenberg, B., Burgoon, M., Burgoon, J., & Korzenny, F. (1983). *Mexican Americans and the mass media.* Norwood, NJ: Ablex.

Gutiérrez, F. F. (1985). The increase in Spanish-language media in California from 1970 to 1975: An index of the growing use of Spanish. *International Journal of the Sociology of Language, 53,* 115–125.

Gutiérrez, F. F. (1990). Advertising and the growth of minority markets and media. *Journal of Communication Inquiry, 14,* 6–16.

Gutiérrez, J. A. (2001). *A gringo manual on how to handle Mexicans* (Rev. ed.). Houston, TX: Arte Publico Press.

Gutiérrez-Jones, C. S. (1995). *Rethinking the borderlands: Between Chicano culture and legal discourse.* Berkeley: University of California Press.

Guzmán, I. M. (2005). Genderizing Latinidad through the Elián news discourse about Cuban women. *Latino Studies, 3,* 179–204.

Guzmán, I. M., & Valdivia, A. N. (2004). Brain, brow, and booty: Latina iconicity in U.S. popular culture. *The Communication Review, 7,* 205–221.

Habell-Pallán, M. (1999). El Vez is "taking care of business": The inter/national appeal of Chicano popular music. *Cultural Studies, 13,* 195–210.

Hadley-Garcia, G. (1990). *Hispanic Hollywood: The Latins in motion pictures.* New York: Citadel.

Hall, S. (1996). On postmodernism and articulation: An interview with Stuart Hall. In D. Morley & K. Chen (Eds.), *Stuart Hall: Critical dialogues in cultural studies* (pp. 131–150). New York: Routledge.

Hall, S. (1997). The spectacle of the "other." In S. Hall (Ed.), *Representation: Cultural representations and signifying practices* (pp. 223–290). Thousand Oaks, CA: Open University Press.

Hammerback, J. C., & Jensen, R. C. (1985). No revolution without poets: The rhetoric of Rodolfo "Corky" Gonzales. In J. C. Hammerback, R. C. Jensen, and J. A. Gutiérrez (Eds.), *A war of words: Chicano protest in the 1960s and 1970s* (pp. 53–80). Westport, CT: Greenwood.

Harwood, J., & Anderson, K. (2002). The presence and portrayal of social groups on prime-time television. *Communication Reports, 15*(2), 81–98.

Jhally, S., & Lewis, J. (1992). *Enlightened racism: The Cosby Show, audiences, and the myth of the American dream.* Boulder, CO: Westview.

Jhally, S., & Livant, B. (1986). Watching as working: The valorization of audience consciousness. *Journal of Communication, 36*, 134–144.

Johnson, M. A. (1999). Pre-television stereotypes: Mexicans in U.S. newsreels, 1919–1932. *Critical Studies in Mass Communication 16*, 417–435.

Johnson, M. A. (2000). How ethnic are U.S. ethnic media: The case of Latina magazines. *Mass Communication and Society 3*, 229–249.

Keller, G. D. (1994). *Hispanics and United States film: An overview and handbook.* Tempe, AZ: Bilingual.

Laclau, E. (1977). *Politics and ideology in Marxist theory.* London: New Left Books.

Lichter, S. R., & Amundson, D. A. (1994). *Distorted reality: Hispanic characters in TV entertainment.* Washington, DC: Center for Media and Public Affairs.

Lichter, S. R., & Amundson, D. A. (1996). *Don't blink: Hispanics in television entertainment.* Washington, DC: National Council of La Raza.

Lipsitz, G. (1999). "Home is where the hatred is": Work, music, and the transnational economy. In H. Naficy (Ed.), *Home, exile, homeland: Film, media, and the politics of place* (pp. 193–212). New York: Routledge.

List, C. (1996). *Chicano images: Refiguring ethnicity in mainstream film.* New York: Garland.

Lowe, L. (1996). *Immigrant acts: On Asian American cultural politics.* Durham, NC: Duke University Press.

Lugones, M., & Price, J. (2003). The inseparability of race, class, and gender in Latino studies. *Latino Studies, 1*, 329–332.

Martin, E. (2002). The effects of questionnaire design on reporting of detailed Hispanic origin in Census 2000 mail questionnaires. *Public Opinion Quarterly, 66*, 582–593.

Martínez, K. Z. (2004). *Latina* magazine and the invocation of panethnic family: Latino identity as it is informed by celebrities and *papis chulos. Communication Review, 7*, 155–174.

Mastro, D. E., & Atkin, C. (2002). Exposure to alcohol billboards and beliefs and attitudes toward drinking among Mexican American high school students. *Howard Journal of Communications, 13*, 129–151.

Mastro, D., & Greenberg, B. S. (2000). The portrayal of racial minorities on prime time television. *Journal of Broadcasting and Electronic Media, 44*, 690–703.

Mastro, D. E., & Stern, S. (2003). Representations of race in television commercials: A content analysis of prime-time advertising. *Journal of Broadcasting and Electronic Media, 47*, 638–647.

Mato, D. (1998). On the making of transnational identities in the age of globalization: The U.S. Latina/o-"Latin" American case. *Cultural Studies, 12*, 598–620.

Mayer, V. (2001). From segmented to fragmented: Latino media in San Antonio, Texas. *Journalism & Mass Communication Quarterly 78*, 291–306.

Mayer, V. (2003a). *Producing dreams, consuming youth: Mexican Americans and mass media*. New Brunswick, NJ: Rutgers University Press.

Mayer, V. (2003b). Living telenovelas/telenovelizing life: Mexican American girls' identities and transnational telenovelas. *Journal of Communication, 53*, 479–495.

Mayer, V. (2004). Please pass the pan: Retheorizing the map of panlatinidad in communication research. *Communication Review 7*, 113–124.

McChesney, R. W. (1997). *Corporate media and the threat to democracy*. New York: Seven Stories.

Mirón, L. F., & Inda, J. X. (2004). Constructing cultural citizenship: Latino immigrant students and learning English. *Latino Studies, 2*, 237–245.

Moran, K. (2003). A reception analysis: Latina teenagers talk about telenovelas. *Global Media Journal, 1*(2) Retrieved October 12, 2004, from http://calumet.purdueedu/caa/gmj/submitted/Documents/archivedpapers/Spring2003/moran.htm

National Hispanic Media Coalition. (2004). *National Latino Media Council reports limited progress on network television*. Retrieved July 15, 2005, from http://www.nhmc.org/Reportcards/Reportcards2004.htm

Navarrete, L. & Kamasaki, C. (1994). *Out of the picture: Hispanics and the media*. Washington, DC: National Council of La Raza.

Navarro, M. (2003, November 9). Going beyond black and white, Hispanics choose "other." *New York Times*, p. A1.

Nicolini, P. (1986). Philadelphia Puerto Rican community leaders' perceptions of Spanish-languaged media. *Mass Communication Review, 13*, 11–17.

Noriega, C. (Ed.). (1992). *Chicanos and film: Representation and resistance*. Minneapolis: University of Minnesota Press.

Noriega, C. (2000). *Shot in America: Television, the state, and the rise of Chicano cinema*. Minneapolis: University of Minnesota Press.

Oboler, S. (1995). *Ethnic labels, Latino lives: Identity and the politics of (re)presentation in the United States*. Minneapolis: University of Minnesota Press.

O'Guinn, T. C., Faber, R. J., & Meyer, T. P. (1985). Ethnic segmentation and Spanish-language television. *Journal of Advertising, 14*(3), 63–66.

Olivarez, A. (1998). Studying representations of U.S. Latino culture. *Journal of Communication Inquiry, 22*, 426–437.

Omi, M., & Winant, H. (1996). *Racial formation in the United States: From the 1960s to the 1990s* (2nd ed.). New York: Routledge.

Ong, A. (1999). *Flexible citizenship: The cultural logics of transnationality*. Chapel Hill, NC: Duke University Press.

Padilla, F. (1985). *Latino ethnic consciousness: The case of Mexican Americans and Puerto Ricans in Chicago*. South Bend, IN: University of Notre Dame Press.

Papper, B. (2005, July/August). Running in place: Minorities and women in television see little change, while minorities fare worse in radio. *Communicator, 59*, 26–32.

Paredes, M. C. (2003). The transformation of Spanish-language radio in the U.S. *Journal of Radio Studies, 10*, 5–17.

Poindexter, P. M., Smith, L., & Heider, D. (2003). Race and ethnicity in local television news: Framing, story assignments, and source selections. *Journal of Broadcasting and Electronic Media, 47*, 524–536.

Radway, J. (1988). Reception study: Ethnography and the problems of dispersed audiences and nomadic subjects. *Cultural Studies, 2*, 359–376.

Ramírez Berg, C. (1990). Stereotyping in films in general and of the Hispanic in particular. *Howard Journal of Communications, 2*, 286–301.

Ramírez Berg, C. R. (2002). *Latino images in film: Stereotypes, subversion, and resistance*. Austin: University of Texas Press.

Rendall, S., & Creely, W. (2002). White noise: Voices of color scarce on urban public radio [electronic version]. *Extra!* September/October. Retrieved May 4, 2003, from http://www.fair.org/index.php?page=1122

Rivera, R. (2002). Hip hop and New York Puerto Ricans. In M. Habell-Pallán & M. Romero (Eds.), *Latino/a popular culture* (pp. 127–143). New York: New York University Press.

Rocco, R. (2004). Transforming citizenship: Membership, strategies of containment, and the public sphere in Latino communities. *Latino Studies, 2*, 4–25.

Rodríguez, A. (1997). Commercial ethnicity: Language, class, and race in the marketing of the Hispanic audience. *Communication Review 2* (3), 283–310.

Rodríguez, A. (1999a). Creating an audience and remapping a nation: A brief history of US Spanish language broadcasting 1930–1980. *Quarterly Review of Film & Video, 16*, 357–374.

Rodríguez, A. (1999b). *Making Latino news: Race, language, class*. Thousand Oaks, CA: Sage.

Rodríguez, C. (2000). *Changing race: Latinos, the census, and the history of ethnicity in the United States*. New York: New York University Press.

Rodríguez, C. (2004). *Heroes, lovers, and others: The story of Latinos in Hollywood*. Washington, DC: Smithsonian Books.

Rojas, V. (2004). The gender of Latinidad: Latinas speak about Hispanic television. *Communication Review, 7*, 125–153.

Rosaldo, R. (1989). *Culture and truth: The remaking of social analysis*. Boston: Beacon.

Rosaldo, R., & Flores, W. V. (1997). Identity, conflict, and evolving Latino communities. In W. V. Flores & R. Benmayor (Eds.), *Latino cultural citizenship: Claiming identity, space, and rights* (pp. 57–96). Boston: Beacon.

Ruiz, V. (1999). *From out of the shadows: Mexican women in the twentieth-century America*. New York: Oxford University Press.

Said, E. (1979). *Orientalism* (Rev. ed.). New York: Vintage Books.

Saldívar, J. D. (1997). *Border matters: Remapping American cultural studies*. Berkeley: University of California Press.

Sandoval-Sánchez, A. (1999). *José can you see? Latinos on and off Broadway*. Madison: University of Wisconsin Press.

Santa Ana, O. (2002). *Brown tide rising: Metaphors of Latinos in contemporary American public discourse*. Austin: University of Texas Press.

Shah, H., & Thornton, M.C. (1994). Racial ideology in U.S. mainstream news magazine coverage of Black-Latino interaction, 1980–1992. *Critical Studies in Mass Communication, 11*, 141–161.

Shohat, E., & Stam, R. (1994). *Unthinking Eurocentrism: Multiculturalism and the media*. New York: Routledge.

Slack, J. D. (1996). The theory and method of articulation in cultural studies. In D. Morley & K. Chen (Eds.), *Stuart Hall: Critical dialogues in cultural studies* (pp. 112–130). New York: Routledge.

Stavans, I. (2000). *Latino U.S.A.: A cartoon history*. New York: Basic Books.

Subervi-Vélez, F.A. (1986). The mass media and ethnic assimilation and pluralism: A review and research proposal with special focus on Hispanics. *Communication Research, 13*, 71–96.

Subervi-Velez, F. A. (2004). *Network brownout 2004: The portrayal of Latinos & Latino issues in network television news, 2003*. Washington, DC: National Association of Hispanic Journalists.

Swarns, R. L. (2004, October 24). Hispanics resist racial grouping by census. *New York Times*, pp. A1, 21.

Taylor, C. R., & Bang, H. (1997). Portrayals of Latinos in magazine advertising. *Journalism & Mass Communication Quarterly, 74*, 285–303.

Tovares, R. (2000). Latino U.S.A: Constructing a news and public affairs radio program. *Journal of Broadcasting & Electronic Media, 44*, 471–486.

U.S. Census Bureau. (2002). *U.S. Summary: 2000*. Washington, DC: U.S. Department of Commerce.

Valdivia, A. N. (1999). La vida es loca Latina/o/Live is crazy Latina/o. *Critical Studies in Mass Communication 16*, 482–485.

Valdivia, A. N. (2000) *A Latina in the land of Hollywood and other essays in media culture*. Tucson: University of Arizona Press.

Valdivia, A. N. (2003). Radical hybridity: Latinas/os as the paradigmatic transnational post-subculture. In D. Muggleton & R. Weinzierl (Eds.), *The post-subcultures reader* (pp. 151–166). New York: Berg.

Valdivia, A. N. (2004). Latina/o communication and media studies today: An introduction. *Communication Review, 7*, 107–112.

Valle, V. M., & Torres, R. D. (2000). *Latino metropolis*. Minneapolis: University of Minnesota Press.

West, C. (1993). *Keeping faith: Philosophy and race in America*. New York: Routledge.

Wilson, C. C., & Gutiérrez, F. (1985). *Minorities and media: Diversity and the end of mass communication*. Beverly Hills, CA: Sage.

Zelizer, B. (2001). Popular communication in the contemporary age. In W.B. Gudykunst, (Ed.), *Communication yearbook 24* (pp. 297–317). Thousand Oaks, CA: Sage.

Zimmerman, M. (2003). Erasure, imposition and crossover of Puerto Ricans and Chicanos in U.S. film and music culture. *Latino Studies, 1*, 115–122.

CHAPTER CONTENTS

10 Older Adults' Television Viewing from a Life-Span Perspective: Past Research and Future Challenges

MARGOT VAN DER GOOT
JOHANNES W. J. BEENTJES
MARTINE VAN SELM
Radboud University Nijmegen

This chapter overviews research on older adults' television viewing and discusses the assumptions and empirical findings in terms of a life-span perspective. The life-span perspective emphasizes that gains and losses jointly occur in later life. Selection and compensation constitute two central strategies in gerontological models of how people adapt to gains and losses. With regard to television viewing, selection means that people can choose television viewing over other activities for reaching goals in high-priority domains because television viewing is appropriate given environmental demands and individual motivations, skills, and capacities. Compensation means that people can use television viewing as a substitute for diminished abilities or activities. This chapter reviews available literature in three sections: time use, social functions, and content preferences. A large share of previous research on older adults' television viewing appears to be biased toward compensation, whereas research in this field insufficiently considered selection strategies.

T he purpose of this chapter is twofold. First, we provide an overview of research on older adults' television viewing. Second, we discuss the assumptions and empirical findings included in our overview in terms of selection and compensation strategies.

We focus our overview on the relations that authors assumed and studied between older adults' television viewing and characteristics of old age. Interestingly, research on older people's television viewing includes assumptions

---

Correspondence: Margot van der Goot, Radboud University Nijmegen, Department of Communication, P.O. Box 9104, 6500 HE Nijmegen, the Netherlands; email: m.vandergoot@maw.ru.nl

and findings about the relationships between television viewing and other forms of communication, such as interpersonal communication and intergenerational communication. In the discussion section, we argue that intersections between the functions of mediated and nonmediated communication, including communication through newer communication technologies, such as internet and e-mail, should be pursued by communication scholars.

Our emphasis on older people corresponds with the growing scholarly interest in the health, socioeconomic, psychological, and communicative aspects of aging (Barker, Giles, & Harwood, 2004). This growing interest stems partly from the increasing longevity across societies (Giles, 1999). In the second half of the twentieth century, the average life span increased by 20 years (Annan, 1999). Moreover, older people comprise an increasing percentage of the world population. The proportion of older persons (aged 60 years and over) was 8% in 1950 and 10% in 2005, and it will grow to about 21% by 2050. In the more developed countries, one fifth of the population was aged 60 years and older in 2005; experts project that proportion to reach one third in 2050. The fastest-growing age group in the world is the oldest, those aged 80 years and older. By 2050, one fifth of older persons will be aged 80 years and older (United Nations, 2004).

Our reason for focusing on television viewing instead of other communication activities is that it seems to have a special importance for older adults: older people spend more time watching television than younger people do. Previous literature reviews, largely based on American research, consistently concluded that older adults spent more time watching television than any other age group (Davis & Kubey, 1982; Gunter, 1998; Kubey, 1980; Robinson, Skill, & Turner, 2004; A. M. Rubin, 1982; Schulze, 1998; Young, 1979). This finding was confirmed by a recent analysis that included several cohorts (Mares & Woodard, in press) and by recent large-scale European research. Mares and Woodard analyzed data from the General Social Survey. The General Social Survey is an almost annual, personal interview survey of U.S. households. With regard to television viewing, respondents were asked: "On the average day, about how many hours do you personally watch television?" Mares and Woodard used six measurement times: 1978, 1982, 1986, 1990, 1994, and 1998. They found that older viewers (60 years and older) indeed watched more television than younger age groups, even after controlling for cohort, period, sex, and education levels.

The European Social Survey (2002/2003) asked respondents ($N = 40,856$) how many hours per weekday they spent watching television. Of the people aged 65 years and older ($N = 7796$), 36% watched television more than three hours a day versus 20% of the whole sample. Eurostat (2003) listed the results of time budget studies in 12 European countries. These studies showed that, in all of the countries studied, with the exception of Rumania, people aged

65 years and older spent more time watching television than the whole sample. For example, in the United Kingdom, people aged 65 years and older watched television daily for three hours and two minutes, whereas the whole sample aged eight years and older daily watched for 2 hours and 27 minutes.

Notably, in the Mares and Woodard (in press) study, mean differences masked the fact that variability within groups was substantial. Standard error terms indicated that levels of overall viewing were relatively homogeneous among middle-aged adults but were more variable among older viewers. Thus, although we emphasize viewing trends of older adults in this chapter, we do acknowledge the diversity of those viewers, and we revisit older audience heterogeneity as we conclude this chapter.

We base our review on empirical research regarding older adults and television viewing. To identify relevant literature, we searched the databases Sociological Abstracts, PsycINFO, and Web of Science with combinations of the following key words: *elderly, old, television, media use, media, mass media*. We used the same key words in Current Contents to keep track of the emergent literature. In addition, we found literature in the reference lists of relevant articles and books. We selected empirical studies on television viewing that authors specified as being about older people. These studies differed in terms of the precise age group studied. The minimum age of older respondents varied from about 50 to 70 years.

As part of our overview of this field of research, we also include assumptions and empirical studies on television and old age that were published decades ago (e.g., Bliese, 1986; Graney, 1974; Meyersohn, 1961; Schramm, 1969). These perspectives remain relevant because of their significant influence in this field of research. These assumptions also underscore the observation that attributions to older adults and aging (and to other life stages) are not fixed but change over time (Hareven, 1995).

We begin by detailing the benefits of a life-span approach as a theoretical framework for exploring television viewing. We then present our literature review on older adults' television viewing in three sections: time use, social functions, and content preferences. In each section, we summarize assumptions and empirical research around this theme; subsequently, we discuss this literature in terms of selection and compensation.

A LIFE-SPAN APPROACH TO TELEVISION VIEWING

This chapter is intended to show what the life-span perspective can contribute to communication scholars' approach to older adults' television use. Nussbaum, Pecchioni, Baringer, and Kundrat (2002) applied the life-span perspective to the field of communication. The life-span perspective, as advanced by P. B. Baltes (1987), involves the study of constancy and change through-out the life span. According to Nussbaum et al., this perspective, applied to the field of communication, frames change across the life span as an essential element in any attempt to examine the nature and functions of communication processes.

In addition to this general orientation on change across the life span, P. B. Baltes (1987) identified seven propositions that underlie life-span research. First, development is a life-long process. Development extends over the entire life span, and life-long development may involve processes of change that do not originate in birth but emerge in later periods of the life span. Second, there is considerable diversity in the directionality of changes that constitute development, even within the same domain. The direction of change varies by categories of behavior. During the same developmental periods, some systems of behavior show increases, whereas others exhibit decreases in level of functioning. Third, throughout life, development always consists of the joint occurrence of gain (growth) and loss (decline). Fourth, much intra-individual plasticity (within-person modifiability) occurs in psychological development. Fifth, individual development can also differ substantially in accordance with historical-cultural conditions. Sixth, for the purpose of organizing the multitude and complexity of developmental influences, scholars have assumed that individuals need to deal with three types of influences: age-graded influences that correspond to chronological age, similar in direction among individuals for the most part; history-graded influences that relate to historical time, and nonnormative influences that do not follow a general and predictable course. Seventh, development needs to be studied interdisciplinarily.

Viewing development as a gain-loss dynamic holds particular importance for research on older adults because this proposition criticizes the focus on losses, a common orientation among social science researchers of old age, including media researchers. This focus on losses leads to an underestimation of the potential for development in later life. In order to conceptualize how people adapt to gains and losses, P. B. Baltes and M. B. Baltes (1990) developed the Selective Optimization with Compensation (SOC) model. This model describes a general process of adaptation. According to P. B. Baltes and M. B. Baltes, individuals likely engage in this process throughout life. In the SOC model and elaborations hereof (Heckhausen & Schulz, 1993), two strategies are central: selection and compensation. P. B. Baltes and M. B. Baltes explained that selection means that persons concentrate on high-priority domains that are appropriate, given environmental demands and individual motivations, skills, and biological capacity. Although selection connotes a reduction in the number of high-efficacy domains, it can also involve new or transformed domains and goals of life. P. B. Baltes and M. B. Baltes contended that compensation becomes operative when specific behavioral capacities are lost or reduced below a standard required for adequate functioning. Compensation involves using alternative means of reaching a goal to keep performance at desired levels. This strategy reflects the need for adults to react to constraints or losses by taking countersteps (O'Hanlon & Coleman, 2004). As P. B. Baltes and M. B. Baltes detailed, examples of this mechanism include the use of new mnemonic strategies (including external memory aids) and the use of a hearing aid.

We can study communication from a life-span perspective by focusing on selection and compensation strategies. These strategies show how people adapt to gains and losses throughout the life span (P. B. Baltes & M. B. Baltes, 1990), and we argue that communication is part of these strategies. In this chapter, we concentrate on mediated communication and on television viewing in particular. Hence, with regard to television viewing, selection means that people can choose television viewing over other activities for reaching goals in high-priority domains because television viewing is appropriate given environmental demands and individual motivations, skills, and capacities. Compensation means that people can use television viewing as a substitute for diminished abilities or activities.

Looking at the available research in terms of selection and compensation strategies makes visible that a large share of previous research on older adults' television viewing was biased toward compensation, thus neglecting the possible role of television viewing in selection strategies. That is to say, an important perspective in research on older adults' television viewing holds that older adults value television viewing because it substitutes for diminished activities, such as interpersonal communication. However, this vista leads to an underestimation of the possibility that television viewing can be part of older adults' selection strategies. Older adults can choose to watch television over doing some other activity because television viewing relates to goals in high-priority domains (such as interest in current events and political issues or intellectual stimulation). Therefore, discussing research in terms of selection and compensation illustrates that the life-span perspective can help us to identify biases and weaknesses in previous communication research and that this perspective can give an impetus (both theoretically and methodologically) to future communication research.

SELECTION AND COMPENSATION IN OLDER
ADULT TELEVISION VIEWING

We review the literature with respect to three themes: time use, social functions, and content preferences. We focus on time use and social functions because the main perspectives on the role of television viewing in old age center on these themes. In short, scholars have assumed that older adults watch more television than younger people because they have more time on their hands (e.g., Robinson et al., 2004), and scholars have supposed that television has a specific social function for older people because their social networks diminish (e.g., Doolittle, 1979; Schramm, 1969). In addition, we detail older adults' content preferences because we think that, in order to understand the role of television in older adults' lives, we have to pay attention to which television contents older people select and the reasons for these selections. Within each subsection (time use, social functions, and content preferences), we first summarize the perspectives and empirical research on the theme, whereas subsequently we discuss the literature in terms of selection and compensation.

Time Use

The literature on older adults and television viewing makes the important assumption that older people spend more time watching television than younger people do because they experience an increase in leisure time. Traditionally, scholars have proposed that three changes result in this increase: older people retire from work; activities decline because of physical aging, and older adults experience losses in social contacts (Comstock, Chaffee, Katzman, McCombs, & Roberts, 1978; Doolittle, 1979; Meyersohn, 1961).

Some authors suggested that television viewing can be a substitute for decreased activities (e.g., Graney, 1974, 1975; Schramm, 1969). Bliese (1986) labeled this supposition the *substitution hypothesis*, in which we can distinguish two main ideas. First, television viewing can be a substitute in terms of time use. When activities decrease, television viewing can be used to fill the available time; it can offer a pastime when people are feeling bored, and it can help to structure the days. Second, television viewing can replace social functions that were previously fulfilled by interpersonal communication. These social functions will be discussed in the next section, whereas, in the present section, we focus on substitution in terms of time use.

Television as a substitute for decreased activities

Two qualitative studies support the idea that television viewing can replace diminished activities (Gauntlett & Hill, 1999; Vandebosch & Eggermont, 2002). Gauntlett and Hill analyzed diaries in which approximately 140 respondents of 60 years and older answered questions about their television use. Respondents filled in 15 diaries between 1991 and 1996. On the basis of these diaries, Gauntlett and Hill argued that the importance of television viewing in older people's lives was influenced by several changes. Respondents who grew older and became more used to their retirement experienced an increase in the amount of time spent on watching television. Furthermore, watching television gained importance among diarists who had an insufficient or low income, moderate or bad health, or intermittent contact with friends or family. For this group, television replaced other activities to become a primary source of entertainment and information. On the basis of in-depth interviews in Belgium with persons between 60 and 85 years of age ($N = 101$), Vandebosch and Eggermont reported that respondents with mobility problems spent more time at home and indicated that media, especially television, gained importance for them. Most respondents were in good health, however. Mobility problems also contributed to the larger dependence of widows and widowers on television; for example, several female respondents became immobile after their husbands' death because they lacked a driver's license. Because of these mobility problems, some people listened to church services on television or on the radio.

In addition to these qualitative studies, correlational research (longitudinal and cross-sectional) sheds light on the substitution hypothesis. Several studies examined the relationship between the amount of television viewing and the amount of other activities (Doolittle, 1979; Graney, 1974, 1975; Kent & Rush, 1976; Mayer, Maas, & Wagner, 1999; A. M. Rubin, 1986). The substitution hypothesis predicts negative correlations between television viewing and other activities (Graney, 1974), but most studies revealed no correlations or positive ones.

Only Graney (1974, 1975) and A. M. Rubin (1986) found negative correlations. Graney (1974) interviewed 60 women between 62 and 89 years of age about their media use (television, radio, books, newspapers, magazines) and other activities (contact with neighbors within walking distance, visiting people outside walking distance, making phone calls, membership of organizations, and attending meetings of voluntary organizations and the church). When the women were first interviewed, it appeared that the older respondents made fewer visits outside walking distance than younger respondents, as was expected, but no correlations emerged between amount of visits outside walking distance and media use (Graney, 1974). After four years, Graney (1975) spoke with 46 of 60 respondents again to determine whether changes in media use in these four years were related to changes in other activities. This study concluded that watching television was negatively related to two activities: attending religious services and reading. A. M. Rubin conducted a secondary analysis on data from two empirical studies (A. M. Rubin & R. B. Rubin, 1982a; R. B. Rubin & A. M. Rubin, 1982c). The first study involved a written questionnaire completed by 340 nonconfined people, aged 55 to 92 years (A. M.

Rubin & R. B. Rubin, 1982a, 1982b); the second study consisted of interviews held in two Wisconsin counties with 300 people aged 17 to 83 years (R.B. Rubin & A. M. Rubin, 1982c). The secondary analysis of the data of the respondents aged 65 years and older ($N = 346$) indicated that people watched more television when they were less mobile, healthy, active, and satisfied.

In the other correlational studies, no correlations (Kent & Rush, 1976) or positive correlations (Doolittle, 1979; Mayer et al., 1999) were found. In a sample of 150 persons contacted through three projects for older adults, Kent and Rush discovered no substantial relations between watching television, on the one hand, and, on the other hand, participation in local groups, making phone calls, meeting friends outside the home and living alone or with someone. Doolittle interviewed people between 48 and 93 years of age ($N = 108$) about their interpersonal communication and their news consumption in newspapers, news magazines, and television and radio news. News use appeared to correlate positively with interpersonal communication. Therefore, the author suggested that older adults do not use news media to fill an interpersonal void, but rather, as preparation for social situations. Mayer et al. analyzed data from the Berlin Aging Study that consisted of a stratified sample of people aged 70 years and older in West Berlin, Germany ($N = 516$). The study showed that people who were more active outside the home also used the media more. According to the authors, this result showed that media were not used to compensate for a lower activity level.

A specification of the substitution hypothesis is the idea that religious services on television or radio can substitute for church attendance when older people's church attendance diminishes because of deteriorating health. Hays et al. (1998) and Benjamins, Musick, Gold, and George (2003) analyzed interviews that were conducted in the "Bible Belt" in North Carolina at a three-year interval (1986 and 1989) with people aged 65 years and older ($N = 2971$ and $N = 2958$, respectively). Hays et al. used "functional ability" as an indicator for health, whereas Benjamins et al. operationalized health by asking respondents if they had chronic conditions such as a broken hip, cancer, diabetes, heart attack, or stroke. However, neither study supported the hypothesis. Declining health did lead to a decline in church attendance, but it did not lead to an increase in the use of religious television (or radio).

In sum, two qualitative studies revealed that television viewing gained importance for some older adults who experienced a decrease in activities. However, correlational studies did not lead to uniform results about the relation between television viewing and other activities. The inconsistent findings are difficult to interpret because only bivariate relations were analyzed and because the kind of activities that were related to television use differed between the studies. Moreover, cross-sectional research is not really suitable for the study of changes over time.

Television viewing to pass time and to structure the days

Television can be a substitute for diminished activities by offering a way to pass the increased amount of leisure time; in this way, television viewing can relieve boredom. In addition, television viewing can help to structure the days (Davis, 1971; Meyersohn, 1961). A first type of empirical support comes from qualitative research among older people. Haddon (2000) held interviews with older adults between 60 and 75 years of age in 20 households. The respondents also completed time-use diaries. The study indicated that older adults who felt a bit bored and not at ease with their retirement turned on the television by default because it helped them pass the time. For many older persons, the extra leisure time originating from retirement or the children leaving home meant that they could turn on the television a bit more every now and then to fill the gaps between activities. In addition, Haddon argued that the television program scheme offered temporal orientation when few other time markers occurred during the days, particularly with less active and more homebound respondents.

Uses and gratifications (U&G) research among older adults (Eggermont & Vandebosch, 2002; Korzenny & Neuendorf, 1980; A. M. Rubin & R. B. Rubin, 1982a, 1982b) did not address television as a means for structuring the days, but it did include items about television as a means to pass time. In these U&G studies, respondents could designate agreement with items such as "I watch television because it helps me pass the time" on a scale. In this chapter, we report percentages of older people who said that a particular motive applied to them. When no percentages were reported, we give the mean score on the item and report whether the mean was above or below the midpoint of the scale.

The U&G studies among older adults showed that part of the older audience watched television to pass time (Eggermont & Vandebosch, 2002; Korzenny & Neuendorf, 1980; A. M. Rubin & R. B. Rubin, 1982a, 1982b). Korzenny and Neuendorf interviewed 112 people 60 years of age and older, and they reported that the mean scores of the items "I watch television because it helps me pass time" (3.7) and "I watch television because it alleviates boredom" (3.3) were above the midpoint. However, the mean score on the item "I watch television because I have nothing else to do" was below the midpoint (2.5). A. M. Rubin and R. B. Rubin (1982a, 1982b) interviewed 340 people between 55 and 92 years of age, and they concluded that the item "I watch television because it helps me to pass the time of day, particularly when I feel bored" achieved a mean score above the midpoint (3.1). Eggermont and Vandebosch discovered that 38% of 284 respondents, aged 60 years and older, watched television because they were bored.

U&G studies in which older adults were compared with younger people are also available (Gunter, Sancho-Aldridge, & Winstone, 1994; Mundorf &

Brownell, 1990; Ostman & Jeffers, 1983; A. M. Rubin & R. B. Rubin, 1981). When we discuss these studies, we report percentages of older and younger respondents who indicated that particular motives for watching television applied to them. Most of these studies did not report on statistical significance in differences between older and younger people. Only Ostman and Jeffers reported on statistical significance of correlations between age and motives for viewing.

The results of these U&G studies were ambiguous: A. M. Rubin and R. B. Rubin (1981) and Gunter et al. (1994) concluded that, for older people, passing time comprised a more important motive than for younger people and the general population, but Ostman and Jeffers (1983) reported a negative correlation between age and the motive "television viewing to relieve boredom." A. M. Rubin and R. B. Rubin interviewed older ($N = 79$; between 62 and 93 years old) and younger ($N = 73$; between 23 and 60 years old) hospital patients about their television use at home and in the hospital. A. M. Rubin and R. B. Rubin speculated that chronological age did not influence older adults' television use, but their living situations did. According to these authors, older people may live in more confined situations, perhaps comparable to hospitalization. Therefore, the authors expected more differences between older and younger people regarding their television use in the home situation than in the hospital situation. In agreement with this expectation, older people mentioned "television to pass time" twice as much as the younger group (22% and 6%) with regard to the home situation, whereas, in the hospital situation, "television to pass time" constituted the most important reason to watch television for both groups (older group: 50% and younger group: 69%). This result supported the notion that television viewing is important for older adults because older people have much leisure time and television viewing offers a way to pass the time.

Gunter et al. (1994) conducted a survey in the United Kingdom; on the basis of this survey, Gunter (1998) reported that 20% of the people aged 65 years and older ($N = 164$) responded that they often watched television because they had nothing better to do at that time, whereas this response applied to 16% of the complete sample aged 16 years and older ($N = 1421$).

Ostman and Jeffers (1983) held telephone interviews with 140 persons aged 18 years and older to determine the extent to which motives for watching television correlated with age. In contradiction to author expectations, "television viewing to pass the time when one is bored" correlated negatively with age ($-.19$).

In sum, the qualitative study conducted by Haddon (2000) showed that some older adults used television to pass time and to structure days, and U&G studies among older people also demonstrated that part of the older audience watched television to pass the time. However, U&G studies did not reveal consistently whether this reason was more or less important for older people than for younger age groups.

Time use in terms of selection and compensation

Researchers seem to imply that television viewing functions as compensation when they argue that older people watch more television because they retire, experience physical aging, and experience a diminishing social network (e.g., Doolittle, 1979; Meyersohn, 1961). However, that older people have more time on their hands and watch more television than younger people does not necessarily mean that television viewing compensates for lost activities (substitution hypothesis). Possibly, people prefer television viewing to other activities, but earlier in their lives, they are prevented from watching television as much as they would like (Robinson et al., 2004).

Empirical findings regarding the substitution hypothesis are inconclusive: negative, positive, and zero correlations were found between television viewing and other activities (Doolittle, 1979; Graney, 1974, 1975; Kent & Rush, 1976; Mayer et al., 1999; A. M. Rubin, 1986). In addition, two studies found that "television viewing to pass the time and because there was nothing better to do at the time" was a more important motive for older people than for younger people (A. M. Rubin & R. B. Rubin, 1981; Gunter et al., 1994), whereas another study found a negative correlation between age and "television viewing to pass the time when one is bored" (Ostman & Jeffers, 1983). As mentioned earlier in this section, these inconsistent results may be due to methodological problems. In addition, the substitution hypothesis itself can be criticized from a theoretical point of view, with the use of the concepts of assimilation and accommodation as presented in the gerontological literature (Brandtstädter, Rothermund, & Schmitz, 1998; Brandtstädter, Wentura, & Greve, 1993).

Assimilative coping refers to strategies that aim at actively adjusting circumstances so that personal goals and activities can still be realized despite barriers (Brandtstädter et al., 1993, 1998). We argue that the substitution hypothesis (e.g., Graney, 1974, 1975) assumes behavior that is an example of assimilative coping. In his work on the substitution hypothesis, Graney (1975) argues that an *activity constant* is maintained throughout an individual's life as the result of exchanges between behaviors that decline and other behaviors that increase in aging. This contention implies that, when older adults experience a decrease in activities, they have to find other activities, such as media use, to reach the same goals as they had before.

However, besides assimilative coping strategies, people apply accommodative coping strategies, especially when obstacles or losses become too predominant (Brandtstädter et al., 1993, 1998). Accommodation means adjusting one's goals and aspiration levels in correspondence with personal limitations and obstacles in the environment. One may, for instance, start to appreciate smaller goals, judge particular experiences more positively, and use downward comparisons (Brandtstädter et al., 1993, 1998). Brandtstädter et al. (1993) found that elderly participants address negative consequences of particular age-related changes (such as physical aging) by employing accommodative coping strategies.

We argue that, when older adults enact accommodative coping strategies, they feel less need to achieve the same activity level as before. Thus, they do not experience a decrease in activities as problematic; they feel less need to fill their time with activities, and they will be satisfied with fewer activities. This approach may explain why not all correlational studies found negative relations between television viewing and other activities and why some older adults are less inclined to mention television viewing as a way to fill their time or as a way to alleviate boredom. When researchers wish to know what role television viewing plays in substituting for diminished activities, they need to gain insight regarding the strategies (assimilative or accommodative) that their older respondents use.

Social Functions

Television viewing can fulfill social functions. In the literature on older adults and television viewing, scholars argue that these functions become particularly important for older people because older adults experience a decrease in the amount of social contacts (e.g., Doolittle, 1979; Meyersohn, 1961). In this context, many authors (e.g., Atkin, 1976; Doolittle, 1979; Fouts, 1989; A. M. Rubin, 1982; Vandebosch & Eggermont, 2002) referred to Schramm (1969), who used the concept *disengagement* to explain the special (social) function that the mass media have for older people. Cumming and Henry (1961) introduced the concept of disengagement and described it as a process of mutual withdrawal between aging people and the social systems to which they belong. Schramm emphasized that, for older adults, feelings such as loneliness, uselessness, and alienation accompany the process of disengagement. He supposed that older persons can keep in touch with their environment through television viewing. Thus, they can maintain the feeling of belonging to society. In this way, television viewing can help to combat feelings such as loneliness, boredom, uselessness, and alienation.

However, gerontologists criticize the disengagement concept. Although they generally agree that rates of social interaction decrease in old age, empirical research did not support the main propositions of disengagement theory about the nature of this decline (Carstensen, 1992). For example, according to Carstensen, the idea of emotional withdrawal during old age remains unsubstantiated, and emotional relationships in old age positively predict happiness and adjustment. Although the concept of disengagement is not very useful for understanding the social changes in old age, the decrease in rates of social interaction in old age still raises the question of which social functions television viewing fulfills for older adults.

Television viewing as a substitute for social contacts: combating loneliness and offering company

Several authors contended that television viewing can be a substitute for diminished social activities (e.g., Bliese, 1986). Hess (1974), for example, wrote that television personalities can substitute for individuals who are not available anymore. In this way, television may ensure that older adults, especially those living alone, maintain the illusion of being in a populated world. Bliese offered support for the idea that television viewing can be a substitute for personal contact, drawing from research in which respondents addressed the issue of television as a replacement for interpersonal communication. In addition, qualitative research and U&G research indicated that, at least for part of the older audience, television viewing played a role in combating loneliness by offering company (Bliese, 1986; Davis, 1971; Davis & Westbrook, 1985; Eggermont & Vandebosch, 2002; Gauntlett & Hill, 1999; Haddon, 2000; Korzenny & Neuendorf, 1980; A. M. Rubin & R. B. Rubin, 1982a, 1982b; Schultz & Moore, 1984; Vandebosch & Eggermont, 2002; Willis, 1995).

Bliese (1986) held interviews with people aged 70 years and older ($N = 214$) and group interviews with people aged 65 years and older (12 groups of 8 to 13 participants). Bliese asked open-ended questions about television and other media. A large majority of the respondents (89%) said that they more or less frequently used media instead of unavailable or difficult interpersonal communication. Forty percent of the respondents sometimes used the media in this manner when they were ill or when friends or family were away. A smaller share of the respondents (32%) revealed that the media regularly compensate for loneliness that they experienced because friends and family members had died or moved away. For 17% of the respondents, media use substituted for interpersonal contact almost completely; most of these respondents were homebound. Another indication that television can be an alternative to personal contact came from a study in the United Kingdom (Randall, 1995), in which the author conducted in-depth interviews with 10 people aged 60 years and older and concluded that television compensated for lack of social participation.

In several diary and interview studies (Bliese, 1986; Gauntlett & Hill, 1999; Haddon, 2000; Vandebosch & Eggermont, 2002; Willis, 1995), older adults mentioned that television served as an important form of company for them. Bliese found that respondents turned on the television (or the radio or a phonograph) to have the feeling that they were not alone in their homes. Half of them (54%) said they used media for company at least part of the time. Willis analyzed diaries from a longitudinal study in which questions were answered by people aged 70 years and older ($N = 58$). Willis reported that older people who were still active with several interests gave television a complementary or secondary role, whereas others assigned a greater role to television. For many respondents, television offered company in the evening or a relief from being alone. Gauntlett and Hill based their analysis on more diaries from the same longitudinal study ($N =$ approximately 140; 60 years and older). They asserted that television functioned as a friend for some people, something that filled the gap in their social lives. Some of the respondents listened to the television when they were alone in their homes. For older people who experienced the loss of loved ones, television could be a welcome friend. Haddon discovered that television broke the silence in the evenings, and it offered some company for older persons who were homebound because of increasing physical immobility or who had lost their partners. On the basis of semistructured in-depth interviews with people aged 60 years and older ($N = 101$), Vandebosch and Eggermont came to a similar conclusion. Widows and widowers often were lonely, and they watched television because it provided company.

Although interview studies concluded that television viewing substituted for social contacts and offered company for part of the older audience, Bliese (1986) reported that media use as a substitute for interpersonal contact was far from satisfying. A large majority (93%) of the respondents who used media as a substitute for interpersonal contact were moderately to extremely dissatisfied with this alternative. Gauntlett and Hill (1999) reported that television fits into older people's mourning processes in complex ways. Television could be a welcome friend, but it also reminded them of what once was and thus became a marker of loneliness. In this manner, television constitutes a "double-edged sword" in relation to the mourning process.

Like the interview studies, U&G research among older adults indicated that television viewing offered company to part of the older audience (Davis, 1971; Davis & Westbrook, 1985; Eggermont & Vandebosch, 2002; Korzenny & Neuendorf, 1980; A. M. Rubin & R. B. Rubin, 1982a, 1982b; Schultz & Moore, 1984). Nevertheless, the percentages reported vary widely, so we lack a consensus on how many older people turn to television viewing as a means of fulfilling this function.

In a written questionnaire administered to 174 people aged between 55 and 80 years, 63% of the respondents confided that television offered them company (Davis, 1971). In a sequel to this research, 92% of the 274 respondents aged 55 years and over affirmed this function (Davis & Westbrook, 1985). Korzenny and Neuendorf (1980) reported that the mean score of "I watch television because it provides companionship" was below the midpoint (2.9)

(N = 112; 60 years and older). However, A. M. Rubin and R. B. Rubin (1982a, 1982b) reported that the mean score of company was above the midpoint (3.38) (N = 340; between 55 and 92 years old). Schultz and Moore (1984) asked respondents to complete the statement, "When I am alone, I usually . . . ." Of the respondents (N = 57; between 55 and 92 years old), 37% filled in "watch television or listen music." In comparison, 26% chose "talking to or corresponding with someone." Eggermont and Vandebosch (2002) noted that 40% of the respondents (N = 284; 60 years and older) said that they watched television because of parasocial contact. The mean score was below the midpoint (2.3 on a scale from 1 to 4).

Four U&G studies that compared older people with younger age groups did not uniformly support the idea that television viewing for company would be more important for older people than for younger people (Gunter et al., 1994; Mundorf & Brownell, 1990; Ostman & Jeffers, 1983; A. M. Rubin & R. B. Rubin, 1981). A. M. Rubin and R. B. Rubin showed that only small parts of both the older group (N = 79; 62 to 93 years old) and the younger group (N = 73; 23 to 60 years old) mentioned company (4% and 3%, respectively). Ostman and Jeffers asked respondents (N = 140; 18 to 87 years) about their motives for watching television. In correspondence with the authors' expectation, they discovered a positive correlation between age and "television viewing to combat loneliness" (.18). However, the reason "I watch television when there is nobody to be with or to talk to" did not show a correlation with age. Mundorf and Brownell measured the viewing preferences of older adults (N = 74; between 65 and 93 years old) and compared them with those of younger adults (N = 149; between 19 and 23 years old). They reported that older adults mentioned company as the most important motive more often than younger people did (10% and 7%, respectively). Even so, the differences between men and women were larger than the differences between the older and the younger group with regard to this motive. Gunter (1998) compared a subgroup of people aged 65 years and older (N = 164) with the complete sample of people aged 16 years and older (N = 1421). Gunter reported that older people mentioned the motive "company" more often than the whole sample (21% and 14%, respectively). However, older people did not differ from the whole sample with regard to the reason, "I watch television just for background whilst doing something else."

In sum, the findings that media substitute for unavailable or difficult interpersonal communication (Bliese, 1986) and that television offers company support the assumption that television can serve as an alternative for diminishing social contacts. How many and which older adults watch television for these reasons remains unclear because the percentages reported differ substantially between studies. A possible explanation for these differences involves the wording of items. Two U&G studies employed two items about social functions, and, in both studies, the two largely comparable items led to different results (Gunter, 1998; Ostman & Jeffers, 1983).

Contribution of television to the feeling of belonging to society

Schramm (1969) suggested that television viewing gives older adults the feeling that they belong to society. Research supported this idea in that older people said that television viewing helped them to understand modern life (Gauntlett & Hill, 1999; Haddon, 2000; Randall, 1995; Willis, 1995).

Willis (1995) reported, on the basis of a diary study ($N = 58$), that many respondents had the feeling that television had opened their lives. Moreover, for some respondents, television was useful for understanding modern life. Willis argued that there is little support for the idea that older persons disengage themselves from the working society; television seemed to play a supporting role in enabling older people to have an outward-looking perspective. Gauntlett and Hill (1999) concluded, on the basis of a larger sample from the same longitudinal diary study ($N = $ approximately 140), that older people kept contact with the world through television. Television created "virtual mobility" for those who had lost mobility because of physical or financial reasons. On the basis of 10 interviews, Randall (1995) concluded that older adults kept in touch with the world outside their homes through television, particularly with regard to news about their own region. Randall asserted that television strengthened the connection between older viewers and the rest of society by keeping them up to date about news, fashion and trends. Interviews in 20 households in the study conducted by Haddon (2000) revealed that most respondents between 60 and 75 years old felt that television provided a window on the world and that it had positive educational value. Some respondents shared that television "offered them a different level at which to engage," enabling many of them to feel part of the social world. According to Haddon, these findings indicate that older people do not become disengaged when they are no longer involved in the social world of work.

In sum, qualitative diary and interview studies attest that television gives some older adults the feeling that they belong to society. Future qualitative research should address the question of what parts of television content contribute to this feeling, whereas future quantitative research should answer the question about the extent of this reaction among older adults.

Television as part of interpersonal communication

Meyersohn (1961) suggested that an important function of television viewing is that it offers universal topics for conversation. Three qualitative studies showed that some older adults, indeed, watched television because it offered topics for conversation (Bliese, 1986; Riggs, 1996, 1998; Willis, 1995). In the study conducted by Bliese, 43% of the respondents said they used television (and radio and newspapers) in this way. Respondents turned to television for gathering specific as well as general information. Part of the respondents (29%) mentioned that they watched particular programs that friends viewed as well so that they could use the program as a topic for conversation. Gathering general information was mentioned by 40%. For example, some claimed that "I watch the news so that I do not look stupid." Willis asserted that television as a topic for conversation comprised a recurring theme in the diaries that she analyzed. Finally, in her article and subsequent book, Riggs specified topics that television contributed to social interactions among residents of a retirement community. The population of this community was homogeneous: white, upper middle class, and well educated. The sample consisted of 26 out of 290 residents; Riggs conducted interviews, focus groups, and observations over a period of two years. Residents relied on high culture content, such as broadcasts of government proceedings and opera productions, to afford them material for meaningful conversation. Residents who said they might not seek out such content on their own confided that they felt some pressure to watch it in order to succeed socially.

U&G studies among older adults also showed that part of the older audience watched television because it offered topics for conversation. Korzenny and Neuendorf (1980) reported that the mean score on the item "television gives me ideas to talk about with others" was above the midpoint (3.4). On the other hand, A. M. Rubin and R. B. Rubin (1982a, 1982b) noted that the mean score on "television viewing as a topic for conversation" was below the midpoint (2.8). Eggermont and Vandebosch (2002) concluded that 40% watched television to have something to talk about. Finally, Ostman and Jeffers (1983) found a positive correlation (.24) between age and "watching television to find something to talk about with others."

In addition to offering topics for conversation, television viewing has a function in interpersonal communication because it can be a shared activity. A few qualitative studies showed that older people watched television together with grandchildren (Fouts, 1989; Gauntlett & Hill, 1999; Vandebosch & Eggermont, 2002). According to Fouts, older people indicated that they enjoyed watching television with their children, grandchildren, and great-grandchildren when they had the opportunity. For older adults, it was important to be with family; watching television together marked only one of several activities shared. Television offered a possibility for cross-generational communication. On the basis of a diary study, Gauntlett and Hill concluded that some grandparents experienced pleasure from watching children's programs with their grandchildren and participating in related activities. As Vandebosch and Eggermont discovered, grandparents often mentioned that they watched children's programs together with their grandchildren.

Some U&G studies included items about watching together (Gunter et al., 1994; A. M. Rubin & R. B. Rubin, 1981, 1982a, 1982b). Although some older adults enjoyed watching television together (Fouts, 1989; Gauntlett & Hill, 1999), quantitative U&G studies indicated that social interaction was not an important reason to watch television. A. M. Rubin and R. B. Rubin (1981) reported that no one in the older group ($N = 79$; 62 to 93 years) said that they watched television as part of social interaction, whereas only 1% of the younger group mentioned this reason. A. M. Rubin and R. B. Rubin (1982a, 1982b) indicated that the mean score of "watching television to facilitate interaction when there are visitors" was far below the midpoint (1.73). Gunter (1998) asserted, on the basis of the survey conducted by Gunter et al., that respondents aged 65 years and older ($N = 164$) mentioned that they watched television "to be sociable when others are watching" a bit more often than the complete sample (13% and 10%, respectively). Nine percent of the people aged 65 years and older noted that they watch television "because somebody else is watching and seems interested," in the whole sample, only 1% more acknowledged this reason.

In sum, for part of the older audience, television appears to contribute to interpersonal communication by providing topics for conversation and by providing the opportunity to do something together. Not much is known, however, regarding the topics that television contributes to conversations between older people and their peers and between older people and people from other generations, both family members and non-family members. Future research about watching television together can be designed analogously to questionnaire studies on parental guidance of children's television viewing (e.g., Warren, Gerke, & Kelly, 2002) or to ethnographic studies of the role of television in everyday life (e.g., Riggs, 1998).

Social functions in terms of selection and compensation

The idea of television as compensation for lost interpersonal communication clearly resounds in the literature. Researchers assumed that, when interpersonal contact diminishes, television can combat loneliness and provide company and a feeling of belonging to society. Empirical research provides evidence that television viewing can have these social functions for some older adults, but we cannot determine how many or which older people utilize television in this manner. However, some previous research findings lend themselves to interpretation in terms of selection. Specifically, television appears to function as a source for conversation topics and as an activity that people can share with other persons, for example, with spouses or grandchildren. As such, television use can be said to contribute to a high-priority domain, namely interpersonal communication, including intergenerational communication.

With regard to television and compensation, one study indicated that many older adults are dissatisfied with media use as a substitute for interpersonal contact (Bliese, 1986). To interpret this finding, Carstensen's (1992, 1998) socioemotional selectivity theory can be useful. This theory addresses the functions of social interaction across the life span. These functions include, among others, information acquisition, identity construction, identity maintenance, and emotion regulation. Social interaction also has costs, such as energy and the risk of negative emotions and threats to the self-concept. Therefore, people make choices among social partners to optimize the gains from social contact (Carstensen, 1992). Socioemotional selectivity theory states that the relative importance of the functions of social interaction changes across the life span. An important factor involves "perceived time." Future-oriented goals (such as information acquisition) become more important when people treat time as open-ended. Yet present-oriented goals such as emotional goals take priority when people experience time as limited (Carstensen, 1998). Early in the life span, people strive to attain much information through social interactions, whereas, later on in the life span, social interactions give less new information and, thus, offer less profit in that respect. Therefore, older adults tend to prefer emotionally satisfying contacts with a limited group of close relations over a larger network that may be more beneficial in terms of information gathering (Carstensen, 1992). This supposition seems relevant for the finding that, on the one hand, television offers company and helps to combat loneliness, whereas on the other hand, older people do not seem completely satisfied with these social functions of television viewing. Because the emotional side of social interaction is of particular importance to older adults (Carstensen, 1992), it is understandable that the use of television as compensation for diminished social contact is unsatisfactory.

Content Preferences

In this section, we describe the parts of television content that are watched more by older adults than by younger adults. In terms of genres, older people view more news than younger people (Bower, 1973; Doolittle, 1979; Durand, Klemmack, Roff, & Taylor, 1980; European Social Survey, 2002/2003; Hopf & Bedwell, 1970; Mares & Woodard, in press; Pew Biennial Media Consumption Survey, 2000; Steiner, 1963); they also prefer quiz shows more (Gunter et al., 1994; Hopf & Bedwell, 1970; Steiner, 1963). With regard to fiction, we struggled to determine which genres are watched more by older people because studies differed in terms of program categories, or they used individual program titles. Instead, we discuss the suggestion advanced by Gauntlett and Hill (1999) and Willis (1995) that older people favor nostalgic and gentle fiction. Finally, we examine the proposition that older viewers prefer older television characters to younger characters.

News

Older adults prefer news more than younger age groups. Three kinds of research about the differences between older people and other age groups supported this claim: research that measured frequency of news use (Doolittle, 1979; Hopf & Bedwell, 1970; Mares & Woodard, in press; Steiner, 1963), research that used viewing diaries (Bower, 1973; Durand et al., 1980; Steiner, 1963), and research that measured preference for genres (Hopf & Bedwell, 1970; Gunter et al., 1994; A. M. Rubin & R. B. Rubin, 1981).

In 1959, in Columbus, Ohio, Hopf and Bedwell (1970) asked a sample aged 10 years and older ($N = 3218$) in a written questionnaire whether they watched television news fairly regularly (at least three times a week). More respondents between 56 and 70 years of age than respondents between 19 and 70 years of age answered in the affirmative. The percentage of fairly regular viewers increased with the age of the respondents. Steiner (1963) posed the following question to people aged 18 and older in personal interviews: "What are some of your favorite programs—those you watch regularly or whenever you get a chance?" The percentage of people aged 55 years and older who mentioned news as their first answer was larger than this percentage in younger age groups. Doolittle (1979) conducted a third study of the frequency of news use. In this study, frequency of watching television news was combined with news use through newspapers, magazines, and radio, so we cannot draw a conclusion about television news per se. Doolittle measured the frequency of news use through personal interviews with people between 48 and 93 years of age ($N = 108$). The study showed that the age groups older than 67 years (between 67 and 74 years old, and between 75 and 93 years old) consumed more news than the group between 48 and 66 years of age. Mares and Woodard (in press) analyzed the General Social Survey. This survey only included a question on television news in 1993. This question was: "Would you tell me how often you watch world or national news programs? Would you say every day, several times a week, several times a month, rarely, or never?" The analysis indicated that the positive relationship between age and news viewing was much stronger than the relationship between age and overall viewing, and it was only slightly affected by controls for, among other things, gender, education, health, and levels of social involvement.

In viewing diaries completed by people in New York ($N = 237$), Steiner (1963) found that people aged 55 years and older watched more news programs than people from two younger age groups. Older viewers observed more news programs in total, and they viewed more news programs relative to the amount of programs watched. On the basis of viewing diaries filled in by people aged 18 years and older ($N = 344$), Bower (1973) concluded that people aged 55 and older spent a larger part of their time watching news (19%) than the two younger age groups. On the basis of viewing diaries ($N = 6056$), Durand et al. (1980) noted that an average news program reached a larger share of the audience aged 65 years and older than of the general audience.

In a written questionnaire, Hopf and Bedwell (1970) gave the respondents ($N = 3218$; 10 years and older) a list with 22 program types from which the respondents selected their favorite six types. The percentage of respondents indicating news as one of their top six was about the same in the following age groups: between 41 and 55 years old, between 56 and 70 years old, and older than 71 years. However, these three groups mentioned news more often than the four age groups younger than 40 years. A. M. Rubin and R. B. Rubin (1981) asked respondents ($N = 128$) to specify their favorite programs. The study found that more respondents in the older group (62 to 93 years old) than in the younger group (23 to 60 years old) mentioned news/talk. Gunter et al. (1994) provided respondents aged 16 years and older ($N = 1421$) in interviews with a list of 35 program types and invited the respondents to indicate their degree of interest. This study reported that more people in the oldest age group than in the younger groups were very interested in several news categories (the oldest age group reported with regard to international and national news was 45 years and older; the oldest age group reported with regard to local and regional news was 55 years and older).

Recent, large-scale research (European Social Survey and Pew Biennial Media Consumption Survey) also supported the impression that older people watch more news and information than the rest of the population. The European Social Survey (2002/2003) asked respondents what part of their television viewing time that they spent on watching news or programs about politics and current affairs. The survey showed that 78% of the people aged 65 years and older watched news and current affairs at least half an hour per day, compared with 64% of the whole sample. With regard to the American situation, the Pew Biennial Media Consumption Survey (2000) is useful. This survey consisted of telephone interviews held in April and May 2000 with a nationwide sample of people aged 18 years and older ($N = 3142$). In response to being asked whether they had watched the news or a news program on television yesterday, 74% of the people aged 65 years and older ($N = 970$) offered confirmation, as opposed to 56% of the whole sample. When asked whether they watched news programs regularly, 86% of the people aged 65 years and older answered affirmatively, compared with 75% of the whole sample.

Current affairs and information

In earlier literature reviews on older people and television, the relatively strong preference of older viewers for news was reported together with their relatively strong preference for current affairs (Davis & Kubey, 1982; Young, 1979) and information programs (Kubey, 1980; A. M. Rubin, 1982; Schulze, 1998). However, the supposition that older viewers have a stronger preference for current affairs and information than younger age groups received less empirical support than the stronger preference for news described above.

Steiner (1963) found support for the supposition that older people watch more current affairs and information than younger people. Viewing diaries ($N = 237$) indicated that people aged 55 and older watched more information and current affairs than younger age groups. They watched more of those programs in total, and they viewed more of them relative to the total amount of programs watched. Viewing diaries ($N = 344$) analyzed by Bower (1973) revealed that people aged 55 years and older spent 1% more of their television viewing time on information and public affairs than the two younger age groups.

Questionnaires ($N = 3218$) analyzed by Hopf and Bedwell (1970) did not support the supposition. Respondents aged 55 years and older did not list public affairs more often as one of their six favorite programs than younger groups. Program preference measured by Gunter et al. (1994) did affirm the expectation. People aged 55 and older were very interested in current affairs more often than younger age groups.

Explanation of preference for news and information

Several authors have sought to explain older viewers' preference for news and information programs. Some authors suggested that older people have a greater need for information than younger people because they miss the information that they had received through their work or on the streets before they retired (Kubey, 1980) and because their interpersonal networks often disintegrate (Nussbaum, Pecchioni, Robinson, & Thompson, 2000). These explanations correspond with the substitution hypothesis discussed earlier. When activities decrease, television viewing can take over functions previously fulfilled by other activities.

U&G studies (Gunter et al., 1994; Mundorf & Brownell, 1990; Ostman & Jeffers, 1983; A. M. Rubin & R. B. Rubin, 1981) upheld the supposition that older people seek information through television more than younger people. A. M. Rubin and R. B. Rubin reported that 23% of the older group versus 19% of the younger group identified "learning/information" as a reason. Ostman and Jeffers found a positive correlation between "television viewing because it teaches me things I do not learn elsewhere" and age (.20). Mundorf and Brownell specified that 20% of the older group versus 15% of the younger group said they watched television because of information. Finally, Gunter (1998) asserted that 23% of the people aged 65 years and older watched television because they think they can learn something, whereas 20% of the sample aged 16 years and older gave this reason.

In addition to the idea that older people feel more need for information than younger people, researchers have also argued that, compared with younger people, older adults feel less need for relaxation and escape. Most of them no longer work, so they do not need relaxation after a working day (Kubey, 1980), and they experience less pressure, so they do not need television to forget (Ostman & Jeffers, 1983).

However, U&G studies have not clearly supported the supposition that older people feel less need for relaxation. This idea was affirmed by A. M. Rubin and R. B. Rubin (1981) and Mundorf and Brownell (1990), but not by Ostman and Jeffers (1983). A. M. Rubin and R. B. Rubin reported that 6% of the older group specified "relaxation," versus 19% of the younger group; Mundorf and Brownell observed that 69% of the older group noted "entertainment," versus 74% of the younger group; however, Ostman and Jeffers did not find a correlation between relaxation and age.

U&G studies have also not clearly affirmed the idea that older people watch less because of escape. Only one study (Ostman & Jeffers, 1983) supported this supposition, in contrast to two other studies (Gunter et al., 1994; A. M. Rubin & R. B. Rubin, 1981). Ostman and Jeffers found a negative correlation between "television to forget" and age (−.17); A. M. Rubin and R. B. Rubin determined that 1.3% of the older group mentioned "escape/forget" versus 0% in the younger group, and Gunter (1998) reported that "escape" was a reason for 13% of the people aged 65 years and older, compared with 11% of the whole sample.

Quiz shows

Older people prefer quiz shows more than younger people (Gunter et al., 1994; Hopf & Bedwell, 1970; Steiner, 1963). With regard to quiz shows, studies employed a variety of terms, for example, *audience quiz programs* and *quiz and panel game shows*. By *quiz shows*, we mean programs in which contestants have to answer questions. Only three studies reported results on quiz shows; these studies measured either viewing frequency or preference.

As detailed earlier, Hopf and Bedwell (1970) invited respondents to choose their favorite six program types from a list of 22 types. People aged 55 years and older clearly chose "audience quiz programs" and "panel quiz programs" more often than younger age groups did. Steiner (1963) asked the question,

"What are some of your favorite programs—those you watch regularly or whenever you get a chance?" He reported that people aged 55 years and older picked a program from the categories "panel, games and light quiz" or "quiz shows" as the first answer more often than the two younger age groups. Gunter et al. (1994) analyzed a survey in which respondents could indicate degree of interest in 35 program types. The authors reported that, compared with the younger age groups, a larger share of the people aged 45 years and older expressed significant interest in "quiz and panel game shows." On the basis of this survey, Gunter (1998) concluded that quiz and panel game shows were among the most interesting program types for people aged 65 years and older.

Explanation of preference for quiz shows

Older people explained that watching quiz shows helped them to test and sharpen their cognitive abilities (Bliese, 1986; Vandebosch & Eggermont, 2002; Willis, 1995). Bliese reported that, in order to challenge themselves, 76% of the respondents watched game shows that demanded skill or memory. They preferred difficult games to games in which luck played the main role. They believed that participating in difficult game shows helped them to preserve intellectual functions. Willis noted that respondents referred to their memory capacity in viewing diaries. They watched quiz shows to exercise and maintain their memory. The author speculated that this kind of stimulation would not be available to older people without television. On the basis of in-depth interviews, Vandebosch and Eggermont concluded that some older people employed media to avoid mental deterioration, for example, when they tested their general knowledge by participating in quiz shows (at home).

Watching television to test and maintain cognitive abilities does not apply to quiz programs only. On the basis of diaries, Gauntlett and Hill (1999) observed that older viewers tested critical skills by dealing with current affairs in an informed and critical manner. On the basis of their interviews, Vandebosch and Eggermont (2002) argued that avoiding mental deterioration also related to watching foreign television programs to learn languages. A U&G study that included an item on "television viewing to keep the mind in shape" revealed that 65% of the respondents ($N = 284$; aged 60 years and older) watched television for this reason (Eggermont & Vandebosch, 2002).

Nostalgia

Gauntlett and Hill (1999) and Willis (1995) contended that older people feel attracted to fiction related to the past. So far, no research has been conducted on nostalgia in younger people's media use so we lack information about preferences for nostalgic programs according to chronological age. It is very well possible that young people appreciate nostalgia too. According to Willis, many diary respondents (aged 70 years and older) wrote about the pleasure they derived from programs that related to their pasts. Programs shed light on aspects from their pasts and evoked memories. Gauntlett and Hill interpreted the top 10 programs that attracted the largest share of viewers aged 55 years and older in the United Kingdom in 1996. These authors asserted that such programs often had nostalgic themes. Among others, the programs in this top 10 were the *Antiques Roadshow*; the sitcom *Only Fools and Horses*; the light, nostalgic police drama *Heartbeat*, and three episodes of the least gritty British soap opera, *Coronation Street*. In addition, Gauntlett and Hill analyzed diaries from the same longitudinal research as Willis (N = approximately 140; aged 60 years and older). These authors indicated that a feeling of nostalgia was reported in many diaries. The desire of the respondents not only related to the actual programs, but it seemed to extend to the period that was represented in the programs. Respondents felt that the world used to be far nicer.

A few other studies also supported the idea that older people like watching nostalgic television programs (Riggs, 1998; Vandebosch & Eggermont, 2002). Riggs conducted a study among older female fans of the television series *Murder She Wrote*, and she reported that, for these women, the program corresponded with nostalgia for an ideal past. On the basis of in-depth interviews, Vandebosch and Eggermont asserted that older people in Belgium were interested in fiction about the country life in the first half of the twentieth century and in programs with traditional German folk music.

Empirical results with regard to music programs on television also corresponded with the supposition that older people like nostalgic programs. Older people expressed preference for programs featuring light music more often than younger people (Bower, 1973; Hopf & Bedwell, 1970; A. M. Rubin & R. B. Rubin, 1981; Steiner, 1963), whereas they expressed less preference than other groups for programs with modern music (Hopf & Bedwell, 1970), teen music or dance (Steiner, 1963), and pop or rock music (Gunter et al., 1994).

Gentleness

The term *gentleness* was used by Gauntlett and Hill (1999) when they characterized the top 10 programs that attracted that largest share of the audience aged 55 years and older. The authors noted that the programs shared some kind of gentleness. The programs did not contain much violence, sex, or bad language; they often had light, pleasant, nostalgic and middle-class themes, and the main characters often were not very young.

Other empirical studies affirmed the supposition that older people do not like sex and violence on television (Bliese, 1986; Davis, 1971; Riggs, 1998; Tulloch, 1989). Davis detailed findings based on a written questionnaire administered to people between 55 and 80 years old ($N = 174$). In answer to an open-ended question about what the respondents found objectionable on television, they mentioned violence and sex. Bliese reported that the respondents preferred programs with little sex and violence and with mild humor, such as *Little House on the Prairie* and *The Waltons*. Many older viewers watched soap operas, but they said that the soaps had gone downhill since they had started to get dirty. According to Bliese, older viewers were more conservative with regard to sex and violence than the younger generation. Tulloch also upheld the supposition by observing that older viewers' letters to the production company of the soap opera *A Country Practice* underlined the clean and nice aspects of the show, as opposed to the constant obscenities, cruelty, and violence that they saw on television in general. On the basis of her study among older female fans of the program *Murder, She Wrote*, Riggs also emphasized that these respondents opposed sex and violence on television.

Explanation of preference for nostalgic and gentle programs

Willis (1995) and Gauntlett and Hill (1999) explained that older people like to remember the period in which they were young. In this context, Gauntlett and Hill referred to Coleman (1991), who wrote that reminiscence about the past contributes to maintaining the self-concept and self-esteem during old age. Gauntlett and Hill argued that people watched nostalgic programs to maintain a picture of the world as they would like to remember it: polite, civilized, and good-humored. Viewing certain programs, such as light sitcoms and dramas, may help to maintain an idealistic, traditional view of the world. In addition, costume dramas and programs like the *Antiques Roadshow* may give reassurance that the past is relevant for the future. For most older people, watching such programs played a role in negating depressive feelings that would result from the impression that all good things that people enjoyed in the past had disappeared. In line with this reasoning, Vandebosch and Eggermont (2002) explained the preference of their respondents for German music programs with traditional folk music by suggesting that some respondents romanticized the rural community they once lived in as opposed to the industrial society they were part of later.

Gauntlett and Hill (1999) went a step further when they contended that older adults like to be reminded of their younger years because of the attainment of *ego integrity* (Erikson, 1950). Erikson wrote that ego integrity comprises the eighth and last life stage, in which people come to terms with the lives that they have lived. People who attain integrity know that an individual life is the accidental co-occurrence of just one life cycle with only one segment of history, and they accept their lives as they have lived them.

Older television characters

Three types of studies lend some support to the idea that older viewers prefer older television characters over younger television characters. First, research attended to the age of characters in older adults' favorite fiction programs (Bell, 1992) and compared this finding with the age of characters in younger age groups' favorite programs (Harwood, 1997; Mundorf & Brownell, 1990; Robinson et al., 2004). Second, Mundorf and Brownell requested both older and younger respondents to name their favorite television characters, and third, research examined which programs older adults would like to view (Mares & Cantor, 1992).

The first type of research supports the idea that older viewers' favorite fiction programs feature more older characters than younger viewers' favorite programs. Mundorf and Brownell (1990) asked respondents to rank their seven favorite programs out of Nielsen's top 25 entertainment programs. On the basis of the responses, Mundorf and Brownell reported the top five for younger adults ($N = 149$; between 19 and 23 years old) and for older adults ($N = 74$, between 65 and 93 years old). The two favorite programs for older adults were *Murder, She Wrote* and *Golden Girls*, whereas these programs did not appear in the top five for younger adults. Both programs showcased female leading characters in their fifties through seventies. Bell (1992) reported the top 10 prime-time television programs, according to adults aged 55 years and older for the seasons 1989–1990 and 1990–1991 (Nielsen Media Research). These top ten lists included *Murder, She Wrote; Golden Girls; Jake and the Fatman*, and *In the Heat of the Night*, which all featured older characters portrayed by older actors. Harwood (1997) explored the television ratings of the first 10 weeks of the 1994–1995 season for three different age groups: children (age 2–11), younger adults (18–54 years old), and older adults (65+). For each age group, the four shows that were rated highest and that did not appear in any other age group's top ten were selected for further analysis. Two independent coders assessed the ages of all characters with speaking roles in four episodes of each show. In agreement with Harwood's expectations, the three age groups watched a television population of lead characters that was skewed in favor of their own age. Robinson et al. (2004) examined the viewing patterns from 1991 and 1997. In 1991, *Golden Girls* and *Murder, She Wrote* were the fictional programs most often watched by the older audience, and both contained older characters. These programs were also popular with other age groups, but they were much more beloved by the older age groups (Robinson & Skill, 1995). Similarly, in the 1997 data, the highest rated programs for older viewers (55 to 64 years, and 65+) contained actors and characters that were similar in age. For example, *Walker, Texas Ranger* star Chuck Norris was 57 at the time; *Diagnosis Murder* star Dick van Dyke was 72, and *Cosby Show* star

Bill Cosby was 60, clearly different from the ages of central characters in the shows most often watched by younger adults (such as *Seinfeld* and *Friends*).

Mundorf and Brownell (1990) invited older and younger viewers to list their five favorite television characters. In this study, older women preferred television characters of their own gender and age. Three out of older women's five favorite characters were females, and three were over 60 years of age. However, according to Mundorf and Brownell, for the older males, only one out of the five actors was over 60 years of age.

Mares and Cantor (1992) asked respondents ($N = 94$, 70 years and older) to indicate interest in programs, based on 12 brief scenarios. Respondents rated each scenario on a scale from 1 (no!) to 7 (yes!). Six scenarios described documentaries in which the chief protagonist was an older person: three featured a happy, successful person, and three depicted an unhappy, lonely person. In two other scenarios, a young person was the main character: one was positively portrayed, the other negatively. Results showed that lonely respondents preferred negative portrayals to positive portrayals, whereas nonlonely respondents favored positive portrayals. Within their favorite (positive or negative) category, however, both lonely and nonlonely respondents preferred the scenarios about the older characters to the scenario about the young character. However, the finding in this study with regard to the age of characters is suggestive rather than conclusive because the scenarios differed in more respects than in their portrayal of older or younger characters.

Explanation of preference for older characters

Two explanations were provided in the literature for the finding that older viewers prefer older television characters. First, Mares and Cantor (1992) asserted that this result coincided with social comparison theory's postulate that information about similar people is most relevant in making comparisons. Second, Harwood (1999) referred to social identity theory in order to suggest that the finding that older viewers prefer older television characters can be understood as an attempt to seek support for an important part of their self-concept: *social identity*. The rewards from such viewing choices can be described as *social identity gratifications*. According to Harwood, viewing members of one's own age group on television may serve to reinforce notions that one's age group is powerful in society, that an important societal institution (i.e., the media) values this group, and that this group is demographically strong.

In sum, research revealed that older people prefer news and quiz shows more than younger people. In addition, research suggests that older people like nostalgic and gentle fiction. There is also some empirical support for the notion that older viewers prefer older characters over younger characters.

However, this research does not make clear how these preferences are related to each other. It would be interesting to analyze television ratings of older viewers and younger viewers in terms of genres as well as themes (particularly nostalgia and gentleness) and characters (particularly age) in order to gain insight into the factors that determine older adults' content preferences.

Content preferences in terms of selection and compensation

Explanations with regard to preference for nostalgic and gentle fiction and older characters can be categorized as indicative of selection strategies. Willis (1995) and Gauntlett and Hill (1999) asserted that nostalgic and gentle programs fit with older adults' need to remember the period in which they were young and that this preference possibly relates to the attainment of ego integrity. Harwood (1997, 1999) argued that older viewers select programs with older characters because they strive for a positive social identity.

In the explanations that authors offered for older viewers' preference for news and quiz shows, the idea of television as compensation is prominent. Older people's preference for news and information has been explained by the suggestion that older adults miss the information that they previously received through work (Kubey, 1980) or social contacts (Nussbaum et al., 2000). In addition, Willis (1995) suggested that that older adults watch quiz shows because they lack other ways of obtaining intellectual stimulation.

The research findings regarding news and quiz shows can also be interpreted in terms of selection instead of compensation, resulting in other explanations. An alternative explanation for older people's larger preference for news is that older people take their citizenship more seriously than younger people. Support for this explanation comes from research on political participation showing that older adults vote more often, are more interested in politics, and know more about politics than younger generations (Holladay & Coombs, 2004). Hence, politics constitutes a domain that has priority for older adults, and television viewing may be useful in satisfying this interest. An alternative explanation for older people's interest in quiz shows is that older adults regard practicing their cognitive capacities as a high priority because they expect that their memory and cognitive flexibility may diminish.

DISCUSSION

The purpose of this chapter is twofold: to give an overview of research on older adults' television viewing and to discuss the assumptions and findings included in our overview from a life-span perspective. In this section, first, we summarize our findings in the light of a life-span approach. Second, we advance a research agenda that situates television viewing within a larger life context, and third, we note the need for more complex descriptions that can capture and appreciate the rich diversity of older adults.

Summary of Findings

We have discussed the literature on older adults' television viewing in terms of selection and compensation strategies as defined by P. B. Baltes and M. B. Baltes (1990). Gerontological models present both compensation and selection as strategies that people use to cope with gains and losses in later life. Applied to television viewing, selection means that people can choose television viewing over other activities for reaching goals in high-priority domains. Compensation means that people use television as a substitute for abilities or activities that have diminished in later life.

Discussing the available research on older adults and television viewing in terms of selection and compensation makes clear that a large share of this field of research is biased toward compensation. Specifically, research tends to treat old age as a life stage characterized by losses, in which television viewing presumably functions as a substitute for decreased activities (e.g., Doolittle, 1979; Graney, 1974, 1975; Schramm, 1969). This substitution hypothesis asserts that television viewing can be a substitute in terms of time use (e.g., Graney, 1974, 1975) and that television viewing can replace social functions that were previously fulfilled by interpersonal communication (e.g., Bliese, 1986; Schramm, 1969).

Empirical support for these two ideas remains far from conclusive. Notably, studies do not consistently affirm that older people use television to fill the time when other activities decrease (e.g., Doolittle, 1979; Mayer et al., 1999; Ostman & Jeffers, 1983). The ambiguity of these findings stems at least partly from methodological problems, specifically the use of cross-sectional designs that failed to include third variables. The notion that television replaces social functions has received more empirical support. Qualitative (e.g., Gauntlett & Hill, 1999; Haddon, 2000) and quantitative (e.g., A. M. Rubin & R. B. Rubin, 1982a, 1982b; Schulz & Moore, 1984) studies indicate that some older people watch television because it offers them company. In addition, qualitative interview and diary studies show that television can contribute to a feeling of belonging to society (e.g., Gauntlett & Hill, 1999; Haddon, 2000). However, it is unclear what types of television content fulfill these social functions, and which subgroups of older people these functions apply to.

The idea of television as compensation is also prominent in the explanations that authors offered for older adults' content preferences. Older people's preference for news and information has been explained by suggesting that older people miss the information that they previously received through work (Kubey, 1980) or social contacts (Nussbaum et al., 2000). In accordance with this assumption, studies have demonstrated that viewing television as a means of obtaining information is more important for older viewers than for younger people (e.g, Gunter et al., 1994; Mundorf & Brownell, 1990). Notably, although the preference for other types of informational programs has often been reported in combination with the preference for news, we lack conclusive support for the assumption that older viewers hold a stronger preference for current affairs and information than younger age groups. Furthermore, scholars have suggested that older adults watch quiz shows because they lack other ways of getting intellectual stimulation (Willis, 1995). Qualitative interview research affirms that older people watch quiz shows because it helps them to test and sharpen their cognitive abilities (e.g., Bliese, 1986; Vandebosch & Eggermont, 2002). Yet, because the available studies involve relatively small groups of respondents, we do not know the extent to which this finding can be generalized.

Although our discussion of the literature on older television viewers in terms of selection and compensation makes clear that this field of research is biased toward compensation, some ideas and findings lend themselves to interpretation in terms of selection. With regard to time use, scholars generally assume that older adults watch more than younger people do because older adults have the time and opportunity (Robinson et al., 2004). However, this perspective does not necessarily mean that television use compensates for lost activities. Possibly, as Robinson et al. discussed, people prefer television viewing to other activities, but earlier in their lives, they lacked the opportunity to follow their preference. Research on social functions indicates that television viewing can play a role in interpersonal communication. Television viewing can provide topics for conversation (e.g., Riggs, 1996, 1998; A. M. Rubin & R. B. Rubin, 1982a, 1982b), and it can be a shared activity (e.g., Fouts, 1989; Gauntlett & Hill, 1999). These findings suggest that some older people select television to play a role in a domain that is important to them, namely interpersonal communication, including intergenerational communication. Finally, authors offered explanations for older adults' preference for nostalgic and gentle fiction and their preference for older characters in terms of selection. Older adults may select nostalgic and gentle programs because these programs fit with older adults' desire to remember the period in which they were young (Gauntlett & Hill, 1999; Willis, 1995), and older adults might prefer older characters because people strive for positive social identities (Harwood, 1999).

Consideration of selection strategies can help us to find explanations for older people's television use other than those that have been traditionally provided in this field of research. For example, an alternative explanation for older adults' preference for news is that older people take their citizenship more seriously than younger people do. Indeed, research on political participation suggests that politics is a domain that has priority for older adults (see Holladay & Coombs, 2004). In addition, another explanation for older adults' preference for quiz shows is that older adults regard practicing their cognitive capacities as a high-priority domain because they expect that their memory and cognitive flexibility may diminish.

As argued in this chapter, in order to gain insight in older people's television use, gerontological insights seem particularly valuable. In addition to selection and compensation strategies, we have discussed another conceptual pair (accommodation and assimilation, in Brandtstädter et al., 1993, 1998) in order to understand the inconsistent findings that were found in studies related to the substitution hypothesis (e.g., Doolittle, 1979; Graney, 1974, 1975; Mayer et al., 1999). If people use assimilative strategies, they experience a decrease in activities as a problem, and they seek other activities, such as media use, to reach the same goals as they had before. If, however, people employ accommodative strategies, they adjust their goals and aspiration levels. Consequently, they do not experience a decrease in activities as problematic, and they do not use television as a means to fill their time or as a way to alleviate boredom. Therefore, if researchers want to know the extent to which television viewing replaces decreased activities, they need to investigate the strategies (assimilative or accommodative) that older respondents use.

Need to Explore Intersections of Television Viewing with Other Aspects of Later Life

The main theme of our review is that research on older adults' television viewing appears to be biased toward compensation, whereas research in this field insufficiently considered selection. Therefore, future research should formulate questions on how television viewing is part of selection strategies. This orientation on selection (in addition to compensation) leads to a focus on the function of television in older adults' high-priority domains. The following high-priority domains appeared in our review: interpersonal communication, remembering the past, social identity, political citizenship, and cognitive abilities. In addition, health constitutes a high priority for older adults (e.g., Thompson, Robinson, & Beisecker, 2004) that may be related to their television use. Research should ask about the extent to which older adults employ television to reach goals in the above-mentioned domains. For example, how do older people use television in intergenerational communication?

In order to answer this type of question, knowledge of older adults' high-priority domains is essential. For example, in our review, we argued that the socioemotional selectivity theory (Carstensen, 1992) can contribute to our understanding of television viewing. This theory relates to interpersonal communication and analyzes how the functions of social interactions change across the life span. This knowledge contributes to our understanding of why some social functions of television viewing are unsatisfactory for older adults.

Our review not only suggests that media researchers should consider findings from other research areas, but also that research in other domains can benefit from the incorporation of knowledge of older adults' television viewing. Television viewing appears to have diverse functions in older people's lives and can hence contribute to various areas. Therefore, research on, for instance, older adults' interpersonal communication, political communication, and health communication should include older adults' television viewing.

Computer-mediated communication constitutes another domain that should be studied in relation to older adults' television viewing. Older adults' selection of media is influenced by the media that are available to them, and cohorts of older adults differ in the media they grew up and live with. Baby boomers, the generation who will retire in the next decade (Holladay & Coombs, 2004), were not only acquainted with television at an early age, they also live in a different media situation characterized by an increasing choice of television channels and an increasing integration of television with other, more interactive media (Riggs, 1998). It has been suggested that new, more interactive media may widen older adults' horizons because limitations of the aging body (with regard to, for example, mobility and appearance) may be irrelevant in cyberspace (Featherstone, 1995).

Interestingly, analogous to older people's television use, older people's internet use has been met with the assumption that the internet may replace social contacts when older adults can no longer maintain their interpersonal contacts (White et al., 2002; Wright, 2000). The perspective that both television viewing and internet use can compensate for interpersonal communication suggests that the functions of these forms of communication should be studied in relation to each other. Although previous research has shed light on the different functions that television use has had and still can have for older people, we should also be aware that changing circumstances can lead to new functions of mass communication. The changing media situation seems to call for ethnographic research designs in order to trace perhaps unprecedented types of media use.

Need for Explorations of Diversity among Older Viewers

In this review, we discuss the category of older viewers as opposed to younger categories. However, scholars in the field agree that older people form a heterogeneous group (e.g., Bliese, 1986; Robinson et al., 2004; A. M. Rubin, 1982). Because of the accumulation of life experiences, the group of older adults is even more heterogeneous than younger age groups (Mares & Woodard, in press).

The concepts of selection and compensation underline the diversity in the older audience. Selection means that people choose television in correspondence with their high-priority domains, and older adults differ in what domains are important to them. This choice probably depends, for example, on marital status, social network, gender, health, and socioeconomic status. Qualitative research is needed to reveal the ways in which television viewing is related to high-priority domains. In addition, quantitative research should assess the extent of these television uses among older populations and the extent to which these uses are related to older adults' characteristics.

Diversity between cohorts of older adults is also apparent. Cohorts differ in terms of societal structures, and these societal structures influence people's lives (Riley, Kahn, & Foner, 1994). Indeed, one of the propositions within the life-span perspective emphasizes that historical circumstances influence individual development (P. B. Baltes, 1987). From the life-span perspective, cross-sectional research that compares older adults with younger people is defective because it cannot show whether differences in television use between these age groups are caused by age-related influences or by cohort-related influences (Meyersohn, 1961). Specifically, communication researchers should consider that different cohorts (generations) grow up in different media landscapes, possibly yielding specific patterns of media use that people remain faithful to across the life span (Mares & Woodard, in press).

Final Reflections

Older adults constitute a growing part of our society. They spend more time on television viewing than any other age group, which raises the question of what functions television viewing has for them. In our review, we discuss the available research in terms of selection and compensation. Generally, older adults' television viewing has been framed as compensation. We have argued that research can be enriched by taking a selection perspective that regards television viewing as an activity that helps people to reach goals in high-priority domains. In this context, we underlined the relations between television viewing and other aspects of later life. We hope that our approach will inspire future research on older adults' television viewing that acknowledges that older adults not only watch television to compensate for losses, but that they also watch because television viewing relates to domains that are important to them.

ACKNOWLEDGMENTS

The authors thank three anonymous reviewers and the editor for their valuable comments on earlier versions of this chapter.

REFERENCES

Annan, K. (1999). Address at ceremony launching the international year of older persons. *Journals of Gerontology Series B-Psychological Sciences and Social Sciences, 54*, P5–P6.

Atkin, C. K. (1976). Mass media and the aging. In H. J. Oyer & E. J. Oyer (Eds.), *Aging and communication* (pp. 99–118). Baltimore, MD: University Park Press.

Baltes, P. B. (1987). Theoretical propositions of life-span developmental psychology: On the dynamics between growth and decline. *Developmental Psychology, 23*, 611–626.

Baltes, P. B., & Baltes, M. B. (1990). Psychological perspectives on successful aging: The model of selective optimization with compensation. In P. B. Baltes & M. B. Baltes (Eds.), *Successful aging: Perspectives from the behavioral sciences* (pp. 1–34). Cambridge, England: Cambridge University Press.

Barker, V., Giles, H., & Harwood, J. (2004). Inter- and intragroup perspectives on intergenerational communication. In J. F. Nussbaum & J. Coupland (Eds.), *Handbook of communication and aging research* (2nd ed., pp. 139–165). Mahwah, NJ: Lawrence Erlbaum Associates.

Bell, J. (1992). In search of a discourse on aging: The elderly on television. *Gerontologist, 32*, 305–311.

Benjamins, M. R., Musick, M. A., Gold, D. T., & George, L. K. (2003). Age-related declines in activity level: The relationship between chronic illness and religious activities. *Journals of Gerontology Series B—Psychological Sciences and Social Sciences, 58*, S377–S385.

Bliese, N. W. (1986). Media in the rocking chair: Media uses and functions among the elderly. In G. Gumpert & R. Cathcart (Eds.), *Intermedia: Interpersonal communication in a media world* (pp. 573–582). New York: Oxford University Press.

Bower, R. T. (1973). *Television and the public.* New York: Holt, Rinehart, & Winston.

Brandtstädter, J., Rothermund, K., & Schmitz, U. (1998). Maintaining self-integrity and efficacy through adulthood and later life: The adaptive functions of assimilative persistence and accommodative flexibility. In J. Heckhausen & C. S. Dweck (Eds.), *Motivation and self-regulation across the life-span* (pp. 365–421). Cambridge, England: Cambridge University Press.

Brandtstädter, J., Wentura, D., & Greve, W. (1993). Adaptive resources of the aging self: Outlines of an emergent perspective. *International Journal of Behavioral Development, 16*, 323–349.

Carstensen, L. L. (1992). Social and emotional patterns in adulthood: Support for socioemotional selectivity theory. *Psychology and Aging, 7*, 331–338.

Carstensen, L. L. (1998). A life-span approach to social motivation. In J. Heckhausen & C. S. Dweck (Eds.), *Motivation and self-regulation across the life-span* (pp. 341–364). Cambridge, England: Cambridge University Press.

Coleman, P. (1991). Ageing and life history: The meaning of reminiscence in late life. In S. Dex (Ed.), *Life and work history analyses: Qualitative and quantitative developments* (pp. 120–143). London: Routledge.

Comstock, G., Chaffee, S., Katzman, N., McCombs, M., & Roberts, D. (1978). *Television and human behavior.* New York: Columbia University Press.

Cumming, E., & Henry, W. E. (1961). *Growing old: The process of disengagement*. New York: Basic.

Davis, R. H. (1971). Television and the older adult. *Journal of Broadcasting, 15*, 153–159.

Davis, R. H., & Kubey, R. W. (1982). Growing old on television and with television. In D. Pearl, L. Bouthilet, & J. Lazar (Eds.), *Television and behavior: Ten years of scientific progress and implications for the eighties* (Vol. 2, pp. 201–208). Rockville, MD: National Institute of Mental Health.

Davis, R. H., & Westbrook, G. J. (1985). Television in the lives of the elderly: Attitudes and opinions. *Journal of Broadcasting & Electronic Media, 29*, 209–214.

Doolittle, J. C. (1979). News media use by older adults. *Journalism Quarterly, 56*, 311–317, 345.

Durand, R. M., Klemmack, D. L., Roff, L. L., & Taylor, J. L. (1980). Communicating with the elderly: Reach of television and magazines. *Psychological Reports, 46*, 1235–1242.

Eggermont, S., & Vandebosch, H. (2002). Leven voor het scherm: Het belang van televisiekijken voor ouderen in een maatschappelijk en persoonlijk ontwikkelingsperspectief [Living in front of the screen: The importance of television viewing for older adults in a societal and personal developmental perspective]. *Tijdschrift voor Sociologie, 23*, 483–508.

Erikson, E. H. (1950). *Childhood and society*. New York: W. W. Norton.

European Social Survey (2002/2003) [Data file]. Retrieved June 9, 2004, from http://ess.nsd.uib.no/

Eurostat (2003). *Time use at different stages of life: Results from 13 European countries*. Luxembourg: Office for Official Publications of the European Communities.

Featherstone, M. (1995). Post-bodies, aging and virtual reality. In M. Featherstone & A. Wernick (Eds.), *Images of aging: Cultural representations of later life* (pp. 227–244). London: Routledge.

Fouts, G. T. (1989). Television use by the elderly. *Canadian Psychology–Psychologie Canadienne, 30*, 568–577.

Gauntlett, D., & Hill, A. (1999). *TV living: Television, culture and everyday life*. London: Routledge, in association with the British Film Institute.

Giles, H. (1999). Managing dilemmas in the "silent revolution": A call to arms! *Journal of Communication, 49*, 170–182.

Graney, M. J. (1974). Media use as a substitute activity in old age. *Journal of Gerontology, 29*, 322–324.

Graney, M. J. (1975). Communication uses and the social activity constant. *Communication Research, 2*, 347–366.

Gunter, B. (1998). *Understanding the older consumer: The grey market*. London: Routledge.

Gunter, B., Sancho-Aldridge, J., & Winstone, P. (1994). *Television: The public's view 1993*. London: John Libbey.

Haddon, L. (2000). Social exclusion and information and communication technologies: Lessons from studies of single parents and the young elderly. *New Media and Society, 2*, 387–406.

Hareven, T. K. (1995). Changing images of aging and the social construction of the life course. In M. Featherstone & A. Wernick (Eds.), *Images of aging: Cultural representations of later life* (pp. 119–134). London: Routledge.

Harwood, J. (1997). Viewing age: Lifespan identity and television viewing choices. *Journal of Broadcasting & Electronic Media, 41*, 203–213.

Harwood, J. (1999). Age identification, social identity gratifications, and television viewing. *Journal of Broadcasting & Electronic Media, 43*, 123–136.

Hays, J. C., Landerman, L. R., Blazer, D. G., Koenig, H. G., Carroll, J. W., & Musick, M. A. (1998). Aging, health, and the "electronic church." *Journal of Aging and Health, 10*, 458–482.

Heckhausen, J., & Schulz, R. (1993). Optimization by selection and compensation: Balancing primary and secondary control in life-span development. *International Journal of Behavioral Development, 16*, 287–303.

Hess, B. B. (1974). Stereotypes of the aged. *Journal of Communication, 24*, 76–85.

Holladay, S. J., & Coombs, W. T. (2004). The political power of seniors. In J. F. Nussbaum & J. Coupland (Eds.), *Handbook of communication and aging research* (2nd ed., pp. 383–405). Mahwah, NJ: Lawrence Erlbaum Associates.

Hopf, H. L., & Bedwell, R. T. J. (1970). Characteristics and program preferences of television listeners in Columbus, Ohio—April 1959. In L. W. Lichty & J. M. Ripley (Eds.), *American broadcasting: Introduction and analysis: Readings* (2nd ed., pp. V-102–V-111). Madison, WI: College Printing and Publishing.

Kent, K. E. M., & Rush, R. R. (1976). How communication behavior of older persons affects their public affairs knowledge. *Journalism Quarterly, 53*, 40–46.

Korzenny, F., & Neuendorf, K. (1980). Television viewing and self-concept of the elderly. *Journal of Communication, 30*, 71–80.

Kubey, R. W. (1980). Television and aging: Past, present, and future. *Gerontologist, 20*, 16–35.

Mares, M. L., & Cantor, J. (1992). Elderly viewers responses to televised portrayals of old-age: Empathy and mood management versus social-comparison. *Communication Research, 19*, 459–478.

Mares, M. L., & Woodard, E. (in press). Desperately seeking the elderly audience: Adult age differences in television viewing. *Journal of Broadcasting & Electronic Media.*

Mayer, K. U., Maas, I., & Wagner, M. (1999). Socioeconomic conditions and social inequalities in old age. In P. B. Baltes & K. U. Mayer (Eds.), *The Berlin aging study: Aging from 70 to 100* (pp. 227–255). Cambridge, England: Cambridge University Press.

Meyersohn, R. (1961). A critical examination of commercial entertainment. In R. W. Kleemeier (Ed.), *Aging and leisure* (pp. 258–279). New York: Oxford University Press.

Mundorf, N., & Brownell, W. (1990). Media preferences of older and younger adults. *Gerontologist, 30*, 685–691.

Nussbaum, J. F., Pecchioni, L. L., Baringer, D. K., & Kundrat, A. L. (2002). Lifespan communication. In W. B. Gudykunst (Ed.), *Communication yearbook 26* (pp. 366–389). Mahwah, NJ: Lawrence Erlbaum Associates.

Nussbaum, J. F., Pecchioni, L. L., Robinson, J. D., & Thompson, T. L. (2000). *Communication and aging* (2nd ed.). Mahwah, NJ: Lawrence Erlbaum Associates.

O'Hanlon, A., & Coleman, P. (2004). Attitudes towards aging: Adaptation, development and growth into later years. In J. F. Nussbaum & J. Coupland (Eds.), *Handbook of communication and aging research* (2nd ed., pp. 31–63). Mahwah, NJ: Lawrence Erlbaum Associates.

Ostman, R. E., & Jeffers, D. W. (1983). Life stage and motives for television use. *International Journal of Aging and Human Development, 17*, 315–322.

Pew Biennial Media Consumption Survey (2000) [Data file]. Retrieved June 10, 2004, from http://www.webuse.umd.edu/

Randall, E. (1995). Switching on at 60-plus. In D. Petrie & J. Willis (Eds.), *Television and the household. Reports from the BFI's audience tracking study* (pp. 49–62). London: BFI.

Riggs, K. E. (1996). Television use in a retirement community. *Journal of Communication, 46*, 144–158.

Riggs, K. E. (1998). *Mature audiences: Television in the lives of elders.* New Brunswick, NJ: Rutgers University Press.

Riley, M. W., Kahn, R. L., & Foner, A. (with Mack, K.A.) (1994). Introduction: The mismatch between people and structures. In M. W. Riley, R. L. Kahn & A. Foner (Eds.), *Age and structural lag: Society's failure to provide meaningful opportunities in work, family, and leisure* (pp. 1–12). New York: John Wiley & Sons.

Robinson, J. D., & Skill, T. (1995). Media usage patterns and portrayals of the elderly. In J. F. Nussbaum & J. Coupland (Eds.), *Handbook of communication and aging research* (pp. 359–391). Hillsdale, NJ: Lawrence Erlbaum Associates.

Robinson, J. D., Skill, T., & Turner, J. W. (2004). Media usage patterns and portrayals of seniors. In J. F. Nussbaum & J. Coupland (Eds.), *Handbook of communication and aging research* (2nd ed., pp. 423–446). Mahwah, NJ: Lawrence Erlbaum Associates.

Rubin, A. M. (1982). Directions in television and aging research. *Journal of Broadcasting, 26*, 537–551.

Rubin, A. M. (1986). Television, aging and information seeking. *Language & Communication, 6*, 125–137.

Rubin, A. M., & Rubin, R. B. (1981). Age, context and television use. *Journal of Broadcasting, 25*, 1–13.

Rubin, A. M., & Rubin, R. B. (1982a). Contextual age and television use. *Human Communication Research, 8*, 228–244.

Rubin, A. M., & Rubin, R. B. (1982b). Older persons' TV viewing patterns and motivations. *Communication Research, 9*, 287–313.

Rubin, R. B., & Rubin, A. M. (1982c). Contextual age and television use: Reexamining a life-position indicator. In M. Burgoon (Ed.), *Communication yearbook 6* (pp. 583–604). Beverly Hills, CA: Sage.

Schramm, W. (1969). Aging and mass communication. In M. W. Riley, J. W. Riley, & M. E. Johnson (Eds.), *Aging and society. Volume 2: Aging and the professions* (pp. 352–375). New York: Russell Sage.

Schultz, N. R., & Moore, D. (1984). Loneliness: Correlates, attributions, and coping among older adults. *Personality and Social Psychology Bulletin, 10*, 67–77.

Schulze, B. (1998). *Kommunikation im alter: Theorien—studien—forschungsperspektiven [Communication in old age: Theories—studies—research perspectives]*. Opladen/ Wiesbaden, Germany: Westdeutscher Verlag.

Steiner, G. A. (1963). *The people look at television: A study of audience attitudes*. New York: Alfred A. Knopf.

Thompson, T. L., Robinson, J. D., & Beisecker, A. E. (2004). The older patient-physician interaction. In J. F. Nussbaum & J. Coupland (Eds.), *Handbook of communication and aging research* (2nd ed., pp. 451–477). Mahwah, NJ: Lawrence Erlbaum Associates.

Tulloch, J. (1989). Approaching the audience: The elderly. In E. Seiter, H. Borchers, G. Kreutzner & E. M. Warth (Eds.), *Remote control: Television, audiences, and cultural power* (pp. 180–203). London: Routledge.

United Nations: Economic and Social Council. (2004). *World demographic trends. Report of the secretary-general*. Retrieved March 3, 2005, from http://www.un.org

Vandebosch, H., & Eggermont, S. (2002). Elderly people's media use: At the crossroads of personal and societal developments. *Communications: The European Journal of Communication Research, 27*, 437–455.

Warren, R., Gerke, P., & Kelly, M. A. (2002). Is there enough time on the clock? Parental involvement and mediation of children's television viewing. *Journal of Broadcasting & Electronic Media, 46*, 87–111.

White, H., McConnell, E., Clipp, E., Branch, L. G., Sloane, R., Pieper, C., et al. (2002). A randomized controlled trial of the psychosocial impact of providing internet training and access to older adults. *Aging & Mental Health, 6*, 213–221.

Willis, J. (1995). Staying in touch: Television and the over-seventies. In D. Petrie & J. Willis (Eds.), *Television and the household. Reports from the BFI's audience tracking study.* (pp. 32–48). London: BFI.

Wright, K. (2000). Computer-mediated social support, older adults, and coping. *Journal of Communication, 50*, 100–118.

Young, T. J. (1979). Use of the media by older adults. *American Behavioral Scientist, 23*, 119–136.

Author Index

Subject Index

ABOUT THE EDITOR

CHRISTINA S. BECK (Ph.D., University of Oklahoma, 1992) is a professor in the School of Communication Studies at Ohio University. In addition to editing *Communication Yearbook*, she also contributes to *Journal of Health Communication: International Perspectives* as book review editor and serves on the editorial boards of five communication journals. She has authored/ co-authored two award-winning books on health communication, *Communicating for Better Health: A Guide Through the Medical Mazes* (2001) and *Partnership for Health: Building Relationships Between Women and Health Caregivers* (1997) (with Sandra Ragan and Athena duPre), as well as numerous journal articles and invited book chapters. She also co-edited *Narratives, Health, and Healing: Communication Theory, Research, and Practice* (2005) and *The Lynching of Language: Gender, Politics, and Power in the Hill-Thomas Hearings* (1996). Her research interests span the areas of health communication, language and social interaction, and mass communication.

ABOUT THE CONTRIBUTORS

JOHANNES W. J. BEENTJES (Ph.D., Leiden University, 1990) is a professor of communication science at the Radboud University Nijmegen in the Netherlands. He graduated in psychology and wrote a dissertation on children's television viewing and reading. He is a member of the advisory board of *Sesamstraat*, the Dutch version of *Sesame Street*. In addition to children and media, his current interests include the production, nature, and effects of persuasive communication.

JAMES J. BRADAC (Ph.D., Northwestern University) was a professor in the Department of Communication at the University of California, Santa Barbara, before his unfortunate death in May 2004. He wrote *Language and Social Knowledge* (with Charles Berger) and *Power in Language* (with Sik Hung Ng). He edited *Message Effects in Communication Science*. He was past editor of *Human Communication Research* and co-editor of the *Journal of Language and Social Psychology*. His main interests were language attitudes, message effects, and, generally, interpersonal communication. He was a Fellow of the ICA and received the Outstanding Scholar Award from the Language and Social Interaction Division of the ICA. He received the Academic Senate Distinguished Teaching Award at UCSB in 1996 and in 2002 the ICA Fellows Book Award for *Language and Social Knowledge*. Some of Professor Bradac's last projects are the chapter he co-authored in this volume and a theory for the gender-linked language effect.

ESTEBAN DEL RÍO (Ph.D., University of Massachusetts, Amherst) is an assistant professor in the Department of Communication Studies and affiliated faculty in the Ethnic Studies Program at the University of San Diego. His research focuses on the construction of difference and unity in U.S. national and transnational contexts, especially in regard to Latina/o representation. His teaching and research interests also include visual and acoustic cultures, political economy, journalism criticism, and audience research.

HOWARD GILES (Ph.D., DSc, University of Bristol, 1971 and 1996) is assistant dean of undergraduate studies and professor (and previous chair) of communication (with affiliated positions in psychology and linguistics) at the University of California, Santa Barbara (UCSB). Previously, he was professor of social psychology as well as head of psychology at the University of Bristol, England. His research explores different areas of applied intergroup communication research and theory, with a focus on intergenerational communication across cultures and, more recently, police-civilian relations. With respect to the latter, he is executive director of the new interdisciplinary Research Center on Police Practices and Community at UCSB and a reserve lieutenant with the Santa Barbara Police Department.

ANNIS G. GOLDEN (Ph.D., Rensselaer Polytechnic Institute, 1998) is an assistant professor in the Communication Department at the University at Albany, State University of New York. Her research focuses on individuals' communicative management of their relationships to collectivities in organizational and health-care contexts, including the ways in which these relationships are mediated by new information and communication technologies. Her work has appeared in *Southern Communication Journal,* the *Journal of Family Communication, Communication Yearbook,* and *The Electronic Journal of Communication/La Revue Electronique de Communication.* She is currently at work on a study examining employees' management of organizational inclusion in a global high-tech corporation.

JAKOB D. JENSEN (M.A., University of Illinois at Urbana-Champaign) is a doctoral candidate in the Department of Speech Communication at the University of Illinois at Urbana-Champaign. His research focuses on social influence, mass communication, and the effective dissemination of health information to the public. He has received top paper awards from several divisions of the National Communication Association, and his work has appeared in the *Journal of Communication.*

JANE JORGENSON (Ph.D., University of Pennsylvania, 1986) is an associate professor in the Department of Communication at the University of South Florida. Her research interests focus on the social construction of work identities and work-life issues, particularly the experiences of home-based workers. She is currently studying the effects of parents' flexible work arrangements on children's life worlds. Recent publications include "Engineering Selves: Negotiating Gender and Identity in Technical Work" in *Management Communication Quarterly* (2002), "Interpreting the Intersections of Work and Family: Frame Conflicts in Women's Work" in *The Electronic Journal of Communication/La Revue Electronique de Communication* (2000), and, with Arthur Bochner, "Imagining Families through Stories and Rituals" in *The Handbook of Family Communication* (2003).

SANNA KARHUNEN (M.A., University of Jyväskylä, Finland, 2004) is a doctoral student working in the research project "Mental Violence in Communication Relationships at School and in the Workplace," directed by Maili Pörhölä in the Department of Communication at the University of Jyväskylä. Her research explores various communication processes related to bullying at school.

KATHY KELLERMANN (Ph.D., Northwestern University) is a senior consultant with Trial Behavior Consulting in Los Angeles, California. Her interest areas include interpersonal communication, language, persuasion, and trial advocacy.

DOUGLAS L. KELLEY (Ph.D., University of Arizona, 1988) is an associate professor of communication studies at Arizona State University. Professor Kelley studies communication in personal relationships, with a specific emphasis on marital interaction and forgiveness processes. His recent work has appeared in such publications as the *Journal of Social and Personal Relationships*, *Journal of Applied Gerontology*, and *Communication Quarterly*.

ERIKA L. KIRBY (Ph.D., University of Nebraska–Lincoln, 2000) is an associate professor and chair of communication studies and director of women's and gender studies at Creighton University. Her teaching and research interests include organizational, applied, and work-family/life communication and discourses as well as their intersections with gender and feminism. She has published articles in such publications as the *Journal of Applied Communication Research, Management Communication Quarterly,* and *Communication Yearbook* and serves on the editorial boards of the *Journal of Applied Communication Research, Communication Studies,* and *Communication Teacher.* She lives in Omaha, Nebraska, with her husband Bob and her daughters Meredith and Samantha.

LAURIE K. LEWIS (Ph.D., University of California, Santa Barbara, 1994) is an associate professor in the Department of Communication Studies at the University of Texas at Austin. She has research interests in the areas of organizational planned change, communication in nonprofit organizations, community collaboration, and interorganizational communication. In the area of community collaboration, her research is focused on describing and explaining the communicative processes involved in creatiing, maintaining, and dissolving interorganizational collaborations, especially in the domain of health and human service. She has published her work in *Human Communication Research, Communication Monographs, Management Communication Quarterly, Journal of Applied Communication Research,* and *Academy of Management Review* and presented at numerous scholarly conferences. She is a member of the International Communication Association, the National Communication Association, ARNOVA, the National Association of Planning Councils, and the Academy of Management.

MIKAELA L. MARLOW (M.A., DePaul University, 2003) is a doctoral student of communication at the University of California, Santa Barbara. Her research explores how intergroup communication is affected by cognitive and societal representations of groups that are defined by language, ethnicity, and differing ability.

JILL J. McMILLAN (Ph.D., University of Texas at Austin, 1982) is a professor of communication at Wake Forest University. Her research has focused on numerous aspects of communication and rhetoric in and around organizations and institutions: corporate identity, the strategies and impact of corporate discourse, communicative dysfunction in organizations, organizational decision-making, and communication pedagogy. Recently she has been involved in a longitudinal study that assesses the role of higher education in civic education and, in particular, gauges the impact of deliberation and deliberative training on the political socialization of college students.

REBECCA J. MEISENBACH (Ph.D., Purdue University) is an assistant professor at University of Missouri-Columbia. Her research focuses on intersections among identity, rhetoric, and ethics, with particular attention to nonprofit and gendered organizing. Her recent work has appeared in *Management Communication Quarterly* and *Communication Studies*.

DANIEL J. O'KEEFE (Ph.D., University of Illinois at Urbana-Champaign) is a professor of communication studies at Northwestern University. His research focuses on persuasion and argumentation. He has received the National Communication Association's Charles Woolbert Research Award, its Golden Anniversary Monograph Award, and its Rhetorical and Communication Theory Division's Distinguished Scholar Award; the American Forensic Association's Daniel Rohrer Memorial Research Award; the International Communication Association's Best Article Award and its Division 1 John E. Hunter Meta-Analysis Award; and the International Society for the Study of Argumentation's Distinguished Scholar Award.

NICHOLAS A. PALOMARES (Ph.D., University of California, Santa Barbara) is an assistant professor in the Department of Communication at the University of California, Davis. He is interested in language use and conversational behavior in face-to-face and mediated social interactions. He is concerned with how individuals detect others' goals during interaction and what factors lead interactants to infer certain goals (in)accurately. His research also focuses on the antecedents for and consequences of gender-based language use. For example, he has examined when, how, and why men and women use language differently and similarly in e-mail messages. His work has appeared in *Human Communication Research, Communication Monographs,* and the *Journal of Language and Social Psychology*.

MAILI PÖRHÖLÄ (Ph.D., University of Jyväskylä, Finland, 1995) is the director of a five-year research project, "Mental Violence in Communication Relationships at School and in the Workplace," which is funded by the Academy of Finland. For several years, Dr. Pörhölä has served as professor in speech communication at the University of Jyväskylä, in the Department of Communication. Her research interests include the areas of bullying and harassment, communication-induced physiological arousal, and public speaking anxiety. She has published a monograph and a number of journal articles and invited book chapters on these areas, both in Finland and internationally. Her work has appeared, for example, in *Communication Education* and *Communication Research Reports*.

SINI RAINIVAARA (M.A., University of Jyväskylä, Finland, 2004) is a doctoral student working in the research project "Mental Violence in Communication Relationships at School and in the Workplace," directed by Maili Pörhölä in the Department of Communication at the University of Jyväskylä. Her research focuses on bullying in the workplace, and her special interest is on the development of bullying relationships.

MARGOT VAN DER GOOT (M.A., Radboud University Nijmegen, 2001) is a doctoral candidate in the Department of Communication at the Radboud University Nijmegen in the Netherlands. Her research focuses on older adults and media use. She also teaches a research seminar on these topics.

MARTINE VAN SELM (Ph.D. Department of Psychogerontology, Radboud University Nijmegen, 1998) is an associate professor in the Department of Social Science Research Methodology at the Radboud University Nijmegen in the Netherlands. She combines her gerontological expertise on personal meaning systems in later life with researching media content and media use. She has published on portrayals of elderly people in television commercials, older adults' use of (new) media, and research on new media.

VINCENT R. WALDRON (Ph.D., Ohio State University, 1989) is a professor of communication studies at Arizona State University, where he also serves as faculty director of the Osher Lifelong Learning Institute. Dr. Waldron studies communication in personal and work relationships, with a recent emphasis on the relationships of older persons. His recent work has appeared in such publications as the *Journal of Social and Personal Relationships*, *Journal of Applied Gerontology*, and *Communication Quarterly*.